CRIMINAL BEHAVIOR

Readings in Criminology

CRIMINAL BEHAVIOR

Readings in Criminology

DELOS H. KELLY
California State University, Los Angeles

ST. MARTIN'S PRESS
New York

Acknowledgments

Acknowledgments and copyrights continue at the back of the book on page 581 and following pages, which constitute an extension of the copyright page.

Gwynn Nettler, "Definition of Crime." Reprinted with permission from *Explaining Crime*, second edition, by Gwynn Nettler. Copyright © 1978, 1974 by McGraw-Hill, Inc.

Howard S. Becker, "Moral Entrepreneurs: The Creation and Enforcement of Deviant Categories." Reprinted with permission of Macmillan Publishing Co., Inc., from *Outsiders* by Howard S. Becker. Copyright © 1963 by The Free Press of Glencoe, a Division of the Macmillan Company.

James M. Graham, "Amphetamine Politics on Capitol Hill." Published by permission of Transaction, Inc., from *Transaction*, Vol. 9., No. 3. Copyright © 1972 by Transaction, Inc.

James A. Inciardi, "Problems in the Measurement of Criminal Behavior." Excerpted and reprinted with permission from James A. Inciardi and Kenneth C. Haas, eds.: *Crime and the Criminal Justice Process*. Copyright © 1978 by Kendall/Hunt Publishing Company.

Donald Black, "Production of Crime Rates." Excerpted and reprinted with permission of The American Sociological Association from *American Sociological Review*, Vol. 35, No. 4.

Wesley G. Skogan, "Dimensions of the Dark Figure of Unreported Crime." Excerpted and reprinted with permission of the National Council on Crime and Delinquency, from *Crime & Delinquency*, January 1977, pp. 41–50.

Michael J. Hindelang, Michael R. Gottfredson, & James Garofalo, "Victims of Personal Crime: An Overview." Excerpted and reprinted with permission from *Victims of Personal Crime: An Empirical Foundation for a Theory of Personal Victimization*. Copyright 1978, Ballinger Publishing Company.

To Erin Lynn

Preface

The study of criminal behavior is in many respects the study of the society that defines it and attempts to control it. Criminologists have always been interested in why people violate laws. Recently, more attention has been given to how the interactions between individuals and institutions affect crime and influence society's methods of identifying and dealing with criminals. *Criminal Behavior: Readings in Criminology* integrates classic and current approaches to criminology into a framework that clarifies these complex interactions.

Laws are not constant; they evolve and are changed over time. It is therefore essential to understand how and why these changes occur, for the content of laws is often closely related to why they are broken. Part one of this book describes the evolution of laws and how various historical forces—primarily legislative and political—influence their creation. The selections show how those with power and resources affect the prevailing definitions of crime, decide who the supposed criminals are, and determine how they should be treated.

Part two examines the measurement of crime. It begins with a description of the various strategies used to assess the nature and extent of criminal activity. A major theme in this section is that measurement techniques are significant because of the role statistics play in the definition, control, and prevention of crime.

Important explanations of why crime exists and why people violate laws are dealt with in part three. The selections present the major sociological and social-psychological theories that have been advanced to explain criminal motivation.

Part four explores how people become exposed to crime and learn criminal values and traditions. The selections discuss the formal and informal socializing experiences that give rise to criminal activities and careers. The effect of criminal involvement on the individual's personal and public identity is also discussed.

Part five describes how those individuals who act in the name of institutions attempt to control lawbreakers. The readings show how institutional representatives, influenced by the official positions they occupy, go about identifying, processing, and sentencing criminals. The effect of this processing on the accused person's personal and public identity is also considered.

Finally, part six looks at methods that might be used to reduce crime and reform the criminal. The selections describe the personal and social obstacles confronting career criminals who attempt to change their behavior and identity as criminals. Rehabilitative programs and their effectiveness are also reviewed, and recommendations are made concerning how laws might be changed to deal more effectively with the problem of serious crime.

Many people have helped in the preparation of this book, and I would like to acknowledge their efforts. First and foremost, I thank my editor, Bob Woodbury, for his encouragement and understanding. I would also like to thank my reviewers, especially Edward Sagarin, for helpful comments and suggestions.

Delos H. Kelly

Contents

CRIMINAL BEHAVIOR

Readings in Criminology

GENERAL INTRODUCTION

Definitions of crime and the criminal are not absolute but emerge out of interactions taking place among people. Understanding these interactional processes requires an awareness of how individual attributes interact with social control institutions vested with the authority to apply criminal labels to lawbreakers. Ultimately a person may be officially judged criminal by the court. In this event, an evolving or precriminal career may become solidified, and the person may be thereafter cast into the role of criminal.

The study of crime, then, entails an understanding of the society that defines it. Other concerns also fall into the purview of criminology. For the purposes of this volume, six major topics are addressed: (1) defining and creating crime, (2) measuring crime, (3) explaining crime, (4) becoming criminal, (5) controlling crime and the criminal, and (6) changing crime and the criminal. All these topics are interrelated.

DEFINING AND CREATING CRIME

How one conceptualizes crime has a direct bearing on all the major topics covered in this book. If, for example, crime is defined according to the legalistic model—that is, the criminal is one who violates a law and is thereafter judged guilty by a court—then lawbreakers become the major object of scrutiny and the basis for the collection of official data. From the analysis of such data, certain factors will emerge as "causes" or correlates of crime. These correlates are, in turn, used not only to explain crime but to justify various types of control, treatment, and prevention strategies. If the official crime data indicate that social class and race are important factors in crime,

1

then certain groups will probably be singled out for special treatment—a strategy that, as we shall see, is frequently unfounded or ill-conceived. Suffice it to say here that reliance on the legalistic model of crime—and especially the data it generates—is associated with serious difficulties.

Criminologists have generally accepted laws as givens and have then proceeded to examine their violation and enforcement. Such an approach masks the fact that new laws are evolving, old laws are changing, and as laws change, so too must the picture of crime and the criminal. Thus it is necessary to examine those processes by which *acts* become defined as criminal; how historical, legislative, and political factors affect the content of the law; and how the powerful endeavor to influence the definitions of crime as well as how criminals are to be processed, sanctioned, and treated.

It is equally important to analyze how *actors* become defined as criminals—that is, how the police, the courts, and the correctional institutions perceive and respond to different offenders (hence the *interactional-organizational* perspective of this book). However, for a criminal to come into being, three conditions must be met: (1) a law must exist, (2) a person must violate the law, and (3) someone must demand enforcement of the law.

MEASURING CRIME

Efforts to assess the nature and extent of crime use two sources of data: official and unofficial. Official data are those collected by some law enforcement agency. However, each of the various agencies of the criminal justice system produces its own data. We are thus confronted with a variety of police, court, and correctional statistics. The best-known data are contained in the FBI's *Uniform Crime Reports*, a summary of national crime statistics released at the end of each year. Although heavily relied upon, official statistics are deficient in many ways. First, much criminal activity is unreported and unrecorded. Second, official crime data are best viewed as an *indication of enforcement activity.* Therefore, not only must official statistics be approached with caution, but an effort must be made to analyze how law enforcement agents go about producing their statistics—especially how stereotypes and preconceptions may affect the labels they apply to people.

Dissatisfaction with official data has led to the development of other, unofficial, techniques of crime measurement. Most notable is the

hod, which examines statements of those who have
es, and the victimization survey, which asks people
es committed against them. Regardless of the strate-
base generated will have a bearing on other crimi-
as. For example, if race and poverty emerge as
es of crime, then attempts to explain motivation
ledge these factors. Unfortunately, many of the well-
ents advanced to explain crime lack grounding in em-
or the real world; this situation no doubt partially ac-
low level of theorizing that plagues the study of crime.

ING CRIME

e choose to violate the law has long been a subject of de-
e investigators have been concerned with how actors become exposed to and learn criminal values and traditions. Some have
stressed biological or psychological factors, while others have concentrated on societal conditions. Still others have invoked a combination
of individual and structural variables. Few, however, have analyzed
how individual traits articulate with organizational structures and
processes to produce crime. Part three presents a sampling of sociological and social-psychological perspectives on crime.

BECOMING CRIMINAL

Most people are not only aware of what the law is, but they have, in
many cases, also made a conscious decision to violate it. This suggests
that people *learn* to become criminals.

The process of becoming a criminal is not necessarily straightforward. Various influences are involved. Most of us, at some time, have
committed illegal acts. Yet few of us would consider ourselves as
criminals. But there are those who do view themselves as criminals
and who act in accordance with their profession and its associated label. The professional fence, the street hustler, the prostitute, the
check forger, the con artist, and the hit man are examples.

Becoming a career criminal involves a socializing process, and
some individuals become successes while others do not. To succeed in
crime, a person must gain exposure and entry to criminal activities
and careers. The novice must become familiar with the content of
the profession's culture and traditions; failure to live up to its dictates
can result in penalization or outright expulsion. Throughout the

training period, would-be criminals also learn the appropriate techniques and rationalizations associated with their chosen activity. These rationalizations help them to legitimate their involvement in crime and shield them from threats to their identity and self-image. A classic case of such training is contained in *Oliver Twist* in the description of how Fagin recruited and trained young boys in the art of becoming successful street hustlers and criminals.

At some time in the socialization process, a person may decide to pursue the chosen profession as a career. Such a decision is often associated with significant *identity* and *behavior* changes. The person, for example, may not only come to view himself as a professional fence but may change his behavior, mannerisms, dress, and acquaintances to accord with his new identity. Ultimately, the criminal may become entangled with the criminal justice system and even be sentenced to a correctional facility. If this occurs, the criminal is often cast into a passive role—a role with limited choices. (There are of course some notable exceptions to this generalization. The Watergate criminals were, predictably, treated and often allowed to respond much differently than common street criminals.)

On the other hand, one might question whether young runaways, male or female, who become prostitutes consciously decide to pursue such a profession or are coerced, however subtly, into it. Selections in part four document those interactional processes and related decisions that may give rise to the early stages of a criminal career.

While some people systematically pursue criminal activities as the source of their livelihood and accept a criminal identity, others who commit illegal acts do not accept the label. They may commit crimes sporadically, such as stealing office supplies or assaulting someone. Or, on a far larger scale, they may be government officials or corporation executives who engage in a pattern of sustained illegal activities. What this suggests is that not only do criminal activities take various forms, but that in terms of identity states and behavioral manifestations, participants respond differently to their involvement. Readings in part four explore contingencies such as these.

Involvement in criminal activities is frequently not without its personal and social costs. Publicly a person may be viewed as a law-abiding citizen; privately, however, he may view himself as a hit man or con artist. To maintain his public image and, of course, to avoid detection by the police, he must conceal his private identity and act according to accepted behavior norms. Some people can accomplish this feat, while others, for various reasons (e.g., a lack of significant contact with others) cannot. In some cases the constant need for monitoring one's behavior, as well as the concomitant lack of genuine interaction, can lead to an identity crisis. The affected person may attempt to resolve the crisis, but this is not an easy matter. The hit man can "come clean," but the cost of his admission would most assuredly be prosecution for murder and a criminal label affixed to him.

CONTROLLING CRIME AND THE CRIMINAL

Being publicly branded as a criminal can serve as a precursor to a criminal career. Whether or not this happens, if a person is formally branded, such as through court processing, and if a specific label, such as that of convicted murderer, is attached to a person, we can speak of the social construction of the criminal. It is in this sense, then, that crime and the criminal can be viewed as social constructs.

The major catalyst in the *status-conferring ceremony* (i.e., the movement of a person from a noncriminal to a criminal status) is *audience reaction* to violations of the law. Observers may ignore the lawbreaker, or they may demand that the law be enforced. Thus predicting audience response is often problematic. If, however, we know something about the audience's values, the actor's attributes, and the nature of the act, we are in a better position to predict the reaction. Elsewhere (Kelly, 1979) I have offered two paradigms that can be used to illuminate interactional-organizational processes that may lead to labeling as a social deviant; these same tools can be applied to the study of crime.

The Interactional Paradigm

A prostitute (the social *actor*) is observed soliciting males (the *act*, a violation of the law in most places) by a police officer (a social *audience*, an enforcer of the laws against prostitution) and is arrested and booked. The prostitute's behavior thus becomes a matter of official record, and, if not released, she may be officially tagged as a criminal. A similar incident is witnessed by another officer who, because he has different values or enforcement priorities, ignores the prostitute's activities. In the first instance, an official, or *institutional*, career may be initiated, while in the second it is not. On the other hand, both officers would probably respond to a liquor store holdup or a case of physical assault. Audience response, then, is in part a function of the type of criminal act being observed. Obviously, not all police officers—or judges or attorneys—will respond to the same event in the same way. They have different opinions about what constitutes "crime" and how the "criminal" should be treated. Thus audience response provides meaning to the actions of others. In short, crime lies in the eye of the beholder.

The beholders of an act may also include *third parties,* or witnesses—the final element in the interactional model. One citizen seeing a prostitute soliciting customers may be offended and attempt to have her arrested; another may be indifferent and ignore the matter. The offended citizen may, moreover, bring still other parties into the picture in an attempt to develop consensus on the seriousness of the offense. As a result, public pressure may be brought to bear to effect a crackdown on prostitution, and the prostitutes caught up in the sweep become, once again, subject to social control and criminal processing.

Although social control agents operate in part on the basis of their own volition and values, they are subject to various constraints. These controls are embedded in the *theory of the office* that an agent occupies. Analyzing how the institution impinges on an agent is critical to an understanding of why a police officer or judge acts the way he or she does. The "organizational paradigm" can help us make such an analysis.

The Organizational Paradigm

Any institution set up to process and change people has a working ideology based on its function and how it carries out its mission. The police exist for the enforcement of the law, and they must have ways of going about their business. Associated with their mandate and enforcement strategies are what Scheff (1966) terms "diagnostic stereotypes"; these are the criteria used to identify and select clients for processing or changing. Through formal and informal socializing experiences, such as in police academies and at social gatherings, the police become familiar with their agency's diagnostic stereotypes. They learn, for example, how to recognize the "typical" street hustler or criminal (Sudnow, 1965). Once identified, the clients are placed into one of the institution's existing slots, or *career lines,* and are thereafter processed in accordance with the expectations associated with the specific career. Similarly, in a correctional facility, sex offenders, "minor" offenders, and "hard core" offenders are each differently typed, processed, and treated.

An institution's diagnostic stereotypes are basic to the *rate production process,* or the application of labels and their subsequent aggregation to form a body of statistics. If, for example, a police officer conveys to others the idea that minorities constitute the "real" crime problem, these groups will become more susceptible to processing as criminal. The statistics generated will, in turn, exhibit a heavy concentration of minority offenders. The statistics can (and frequently do) become a self-fulfilling prophecy. The police may concentrate their efforts in minority communities, and minority groups may come to expect such treatment. This sort of activity breeds disrespect and hostility on both sides.

In the study of crime, then, we must not only dissect the ideology of social control agencies, but we must also examine how they process clients and produce crime data. Like laws, statistics and institutional functioning should not be accepted as givens. The selections in part five offer further insight into how various types of "criminals" are identified, processed, and sentenced.

Legal processing, like the process of becoming a professional criminal, can necessitate changes in a person's identity and behavior. The accused may not only be officially stamped as a criminal but, if sent to prison, is perceived as a convict and is expected to act according to the behavior patterns associated with his or her crime. The inmate, on the other hand, may not accept the identity of criminal. Once again the two competing definitions—this time the institution's and the inmate's—can cause serious identity problems for the person in question.

CHANGING CRIME AND THE CRIMINAL

At some point, a convicted criminal may decide to go straight, or a known street hustler may attempt to curtail his illegal activities. Each can expect to encounter significant individual and structural barriers that often mitigate against the successful transformation of a criminal identity. Such a transformation entails not only desisting from illegal activities but changing one's view of self from criminal to noncriminal. The process is often hardest for the officially stamped criminal. Ex-cons and ex-delinquents are effectively discriminated against in the world of work. Their rejection by society at large drives home the fact that even though they have presumably atoned for their crimes, they must still bear the stigma of criminal. This realization may send them back into a life of crime.

The American corrections system needs to recognize two important principles. First, the desire to reform must come from *within* the individual. Second, efforts to help the individual reform must be meshed with efforts to change the social conditions that encourage criminal activities. Failure to alter such factors as discrimination, injustice, and inequity will only guarantee the continued production of criminals. The burden of reducing crime must be shared by the individual and society alike.

One step that needs to be taken arises from the fact that while institutions are adept at bestowing stigmatizing labels on people, they make no effort to remove such labels. There are no "status-return ceremonies" (Trice and Roman, 1970) that delabel the criminal and return him or her to a noncriminal status in society. The selections in part six deal with this concern and other theoretical issues in corrections, as well as treatment, or rehabilitative, programs that have been mounted to change the criminal's behavior.

In addition to manipulating conditions responsible for crime and finding ways to delabel criminals, other strategies have been advanced to change the picture of crime. One is to change the laws. For example, decriminalizing "victimless crimes"—activities like prostitution and gambling in which people willingly participate—would give crime and its statistics a different appearance. The last two selections in this work recommend specific changes in the law.

SUMMARY

This book aims to help students understand the dynamic and ongoing manner in which crime and the criminal are constructed socially. A main concern is how criminal careers and identities evolve, are perpetuated, and may be transformed. Two other underlying themes are how institutional components and processes interact with individual attributes (the interactional-organizational perspective) and how the powerful and powerless perceive and relate to each other. In the latter sense, it is hoped this collection makes a partial contribution to the sociology of power or conflict.

References

Kelly, Delos H., ed. *Deviant Behavior.* New York: St. Martin's Press, 1979.
Scheff, Thomas J. "Typification in the Diagnostic Practices of Rehabilitation Agencies." In Marvin B. Sussman, ed., *Sociology and Rehabilitation.* Washington, D.C.: American Sociological Association, 1966.
Sudnow, David. "Normal Crimes: Sociological Features of the Penal Code." *Social Problems,* 12 (Winter 1965), 255-270.
Trice, Harrison M. and Paul Michael Roman. "Delabeling, Relabeling, and Alcoholics Anonymous." *Social Problems,* 17 (Spring 1970), 538-546.

PART 1

DEFINING AND CREATING CRIME

As discussed in the introduction, several conditions must be satisfied before a person becomes publicly typed as a criminal: (1) a law must exist, (2) the person must violate the law, and (3) someone must enforce the law. If the enforcement is successful, the wrongdoer takes on the identity of criminal in the eyes of society. The selections in this part deal primarily with the laws themselves. The first reading considers the definitional components of crime, particularly those based on a *legal* conception of crime. This is followed by selections that introduce some of the major concepts and processes involved in the making of laws and provide accounts of how specific laws came into being.

In "Definition of Crime," Gwynn Nettler points out that "crime" derives its meaning from the interpretation of others. If, for example, crime is defined by moral or personal beliefs, then definitions will vary from one person to another. Such personalized conceptions, however, make it difficult to identify criminal acts with any degree of certainty. Thus we rely on the law for needed specificity. Nettler elaborates upon the various notions underpinning this legal conception of crime. Crime, he says, does not exist (1) without law, (2) where an act is justified by law, (3) without intention, and (4) without capacity. He concludes by discussing the justifications or ends served by criminal law, for example, the idea that law has a deterrent effect.

Although the law is at the heart of the study of crime, most criminologists have traditionally skipped over the subject of how laws develop and change. They have taken existing laws as givens and concentrated their attention on the lawbreakers. But it is important to understand how laws evolve, how people and processes interact to determine what constitutes a criminal offense.

One way in which laws come into being is at the instigation of crusaders who seek to reform society. Howard S. Becker considers their roles in "Moral Entrepreneurs," a term he applies to two groups of people: those who see an evil in society and believe that it can only be corrected by legislation; and those who are charged with enforcing the law. To illustrate his analysis, Becker describes how specific legislation—such as the prohibition and sexual psychopath laws—originated and how both the reformers and special interest groups influenced their preparation and final form. Turning to the enforcers, particularly the police, Becker suggests that they typically see the law not as a means of stamping out evil but as a justification for the existence of their jobs. Their attitude is professional and entails winning the respect of the public. Hence they enforce the law selectively, thereby incurring the indignation of the reformers at whose behest the law was made.

The final article by James M. Graham, "Amphetamine Politics on Capitol Hill," provides an example of how powerful business interests and their lobbies can influence legislation. Starting with the first witness before the Senate Subcommittee to Investigate Juvenile Delinquency, Graham describes the hearings and the debates; the testimonies from government officials, representatives of the pharmaceutical industry, and health and medical experts; the moves and countermoves by legislators and lobbyists; and the behind-the-scenes activities that eventually led to the formulation and passage of the Comprehensive Drug Abuse Prevention and Control Act of 1970.

1. Definition of Crime

GWYNN NETTLER

"Crime" is a word, not a deed. It is a word that describes deeds, of course, but as long as it is used only to express moral condemnation, no one will be able to identify a criminal act with certainty. The meaning of the word varies with the morality of the user. Thus people use "crime" variously, as when they say, "It's a crime the way he treats her," "Private property is a crime," or "It's a crime to have to live like that."

Attempts to define crime more rigorously look to the law for help. Crimes, we have seen, are wrongs judged to be deserving of public attention through application of state power. It has been felt, therefore, that crimes are best defined as acts which are harmful to social welfare and which carry the possibility of a penalty imposed by the state. This definition helps a little, but not enough. It does not mark a clear boundary between criminal acts and other wrongs, since the state attends legally to many attacks on public welfare that are not considered criminal. Thus there is no clear line between those wrongs which are regarded as crimes, those personal injuries which are treated as civil actions (torts), and those numerous violations of regulatory laws to which penalties are attached, even though these violations are not called "crimes."

In short, *there is no essence of criminality.* No quality can be found in acts called "criminal" that distinguishes them from noncriminal injuries, breaches of contract, violations of regulations, and other disappointments (G. Williams, 1955).

The question, then, is why we should bother trying to define crime. There are, of course, different reasons for clarifying our terms.

Functions of Definition. Defining words serves several purposes. One purpose is to gain our audience's attention. When we define a term in a particular way, we are saying, "Look here. Attend to what I'm talking about."

Definition also has a personal function. Defining terms for ourselves helps us ascertain whether we know what we're talking about. We use many words automatically, and we often think we know what they mean until we are asked to define them. Defining a word tells us whether we are using it emotionally—to arouse a particular feeling—or denotatively—to refer to something. A third function of definition is that of aiding communication. It derives from the second function, but here definition is an attempt to assure that two or more people attribute the same meaning to a word. If we are interested in communicating our ideas accurately, we need clear definitions. If, on the other hand, we wish to use words merely persuasively, we need be less clear about their definitions.

Legal Definition of Crime. The closest *approximation* to a clear definition is that given by law. As defined by law, *a crime is an intentional violation of the criminal law, committed without defense or excuse and penalized by the state* (Tappan, 1947).

Without further interpretation, this definition draws a circle. It says that a crime is a certain kind of breach of those laws called "criminal laws." However, we can use this unsatisfactory definition for the purposes of gaining attention and aiding communication if our questions are clear. We should keep at least the following questions separate so that we can think more calmly about their answers:

1. Why does this society treat certain acts, but not others, as crimes? This is a question for the sociology of law; it is beyond the scope of this book.

2. Why does a certain society have more or less of those wrongs universally regarded as crimes—those more serious wrongs such as treason, murder, forcible rape, assault, and theft? This is a question for theories of criminogenesis. It is the kind of question raised by *public concern* with crime; the attempts to answer it are the subject of this book.

Wrongs universally regarded as serious violations have been called *mala in se* (wrong in themselves). Public concern with such offenses narrows our attention. Such concern means that we need not ask why people commit those minor infractions which are crimes only because a local jurisdiction has prohibited them—crimes called *mala prohibita*. Social concern about crime is not with such sometime "delinquencies as that of a housewife who shakes her doormat in the street after 8 A.M., or a shopkeeper who fails to stamp a cash receipt, or a guest who fails to enter his name, nationality, and date of arrival in the hotel register, or the proprietor of a milk bar who allows his customers to play a gramophone . . . without an entertainment license from the justices" (G. Williams, 1955, p. 112). Few people want to spend time explaining why such ordinances are violated.

The context of the question asked about crime causation is that of public anxiety about the serious offenses as these have been widely regarded. In this context, it seems most reasonable to employ a legal definition of crime such as that cited by Tappan. This definition regards a "crime" as an intentional act that violates the prescriptions or proscriptions of the criminal law under conditions in which no legal excuse applies and where there is a state with the power to codify such laws and to enforce penalties in response to their breach. This definition says several things that require amplification. It holds that (1) there is no crime without law and without a state to punish the breach of law; (2) there is no crime where an act that would otherwise be offensive is justified by law; (3) there is no crime without intention; and (4) there is no crime where the offender is deemed "incompetent," that is, without "capacity." Each of these elements has its own history, its peculiar difficulties, and a range of implications.

NO CRIME WITHOUT LAW

The legal idea of a crime restricts its meaning to those breaches of custom that a society has recognized in either its common or its statutory law. As it is applied in Western countries, this restriction carries with it four characteristics that define "good" criminal law: politicality, penal sanction, specificity, and uniformity.

"Politicality" refers to the idea that there can be no crime without a *state* to define it. "Penal sanction" refers to the power of a state to punish violations of its law. This definition says that the legal meaning of crime requires a state, an organization with a monopoly of power, to enforce the law and to attach penalties to its breach. Laws that are not backed by force are less than law and more like agreements or aspirations. Laws without penalties are hollow. By this token, the term "war crimes" is a figure of speech, since such crimes are not legally constituted.

Law and Liberty

The conception of crime that places it within the boundaries of *law* has strong implications for civil liberties. The maxim that there can be "no crime without a law" means that people cannot be charged with offenses unless these have been defined. The protection of citizens against vague charges depends upon this ideal—that there must be a clear statement setting the limits of one's conduct in relation to others and defining the limits of the state's power to interfere in our lives.

This ideal has promoted other considerations having to do with the formulation of "good law" as opposed to "poor law," particularly as good and poor laws are conceived in the Anglo-American tradition.

These additional ideals are that the criminal law must be *specific* and that it must be *applied uniformly.*

Good laws *specify actions* that are criminal and *specify penalties* for each breach. Poor laws are omnibus condemnations, such as one from a dead German code which prohibited "behaving in a manner contrary to the common standards of right conduct." This kind of phrasing lacks the specificity that is an ideal of Western criminal jurisprudence.

Similarly, it is an objective of modern jurisprudence that laws be framed and enforced so as to guarantee their *uniform application.* The ideal of uniform application does *not* require that each person and each crime be dealt the same sanction. People, and their crimes and circumstances, vary. Our law therefore allows consideration of individual cases and discretion in judicial response. The ideal of uniform application does require that *extralegal* characteristics of the offender not affect arrest, conviction, or sentence. Extralegal characteristics are those features of the offender that are *not* related to the purposes of the law—characteristics such as race and religion. . . . This ideal is easier to express in general terms than it is to assess in particular instances. It is easier to express than to assess because some extralegal factors are entangled with legally relevant considerations, as is the case when ethnic differences are associated with differences in patterns of criminal activity.

Not All Wrongs Are Crimes

The legal conception of crime as a breach of the criminal law has an additional implication. It narrows the definition of wrongs. Not all the injuries we give each other are recognized by law, nor are all the injuries recognized by law called "crimes."

For example, United States, Canadian, and European law recognizes *breaches of contract or trust,* so that people who feel themselves thus harmed may seek a remedy from the law. Similarly, the law acknowledges other injuries to person, reputation, and property, called "torts," which, while not breaches of contract, may entitle one person to compensation from another. There is an overlap between the ideas of crime and tort. The same act can be both a crime and a tort, as in murder or assault. However, we can distinguish between the wrongs defined by contract and tort law and the wrongs defined by criminal law in terms of the procedures employed in response to these different categories of wrong. The procedural difference lies in "who pursues the offense." A crime is deemed an offense against the public, even though it may have a particular victim and a particular complainant. It is the state that prosecutes crime, but it is individuals who "pursue" offenders against tort and contractual laws.

NO CRIME WHERE AN ACT IS JUSTIFIED BY LAW

A second category of "defense or excuse" against the application of the criminal law consists of legally recognized justifications for committing what otherwise would be called a crime. Both literate and preliterate societies recognize the right of individuals to defend themselves and their loved ones against mortal attack. The injury or death that may be inflicted against one's assailant in self-defense is thereby excused.

Similarly, all states accord themselves the right of self-defense. With the French philosopher Sorel (1908), states distinguish between *force*, the legitimate use of physical coercion constrained by law, and *violence*, its illegitimate use. The damage that occurs through the state's application of force is excused from the criminal sanction. Thus homicide committed in the police officer's line of duty may be deemed "justifiable," and the injury defined as noncriminal.

NO CRIME WITHOUT INTENTION

As a result of our moral and legal history, the criminal law tries to limit its definition of criminal conduct to intentional action. "Accidents" supposedly do not count as crimes. As the American jurist Oliver Wendell Homes, Jr. put it, the law attempts to distinguish between "stumbling over a dog and kicking it." If "a dog can tell the difference between being kicked and being stumbled over," as Justice Holmes believed, so too can judges and juries.

This assumption seems plausible, but it gets sorely tried in practice. It gets tested and disputed because, in real life, some "accidents" are still defined as the actor's fault. "Negligence" may be criminal.

All criminal laws operate with some psychological model of man. According to the model prevalent in Western criminal law, the "reasonable person" ought to use judgment in controlling his behavior in order that some classes of "accidents" will not occur. For example, the reckless driver may not have intended to kill a pedestrian, but the "accident" is judged to have been the probable consequence of his or her erratic driving. Persons licensed to manipulate an automobile are assumed to know the likely results of their actions. They are assumed, further, to be able to control their actions, and they are held accountable, therefore, regardless of lack of homicidal intent.

Western criminal law is based upon this changing, and challenged, set of assumptions. It therefore qualifies its desire to restrict "crime" to intentional breaches of the criminal code. This qualification is accomplished by distinguishing between classes of crime—impulsive rather than premeditated, accidental rather than intentional. Since the law wishes to hold able, but negligent, people to account, it includes the concept of "constructive intent," a term that stretches "intent" to cover the unintended injurious consequences of some of our behavior. The penalties for doing damage through negligence are usually lighter than those for being deliberately criminal; yet the term "crime" covers both classes of conduct.

Intention and Motivation

Motivation is sometimes used by lawyers to prove intention. The two concepts are not the same, however.

An intention is that which we "have in mind" when we act. It is our purpose, the result we wish to effect. The criminal law is particularly concerned to penalize illegal intent when it is acted upon.

A *motive* is, strictly speaking, that which moves a person to act. The word may apply to an intention, but it need not. Intentions are but one of the many motors of action.

Intention is narrow and specific; motivation is broad and general. A jewel thief may *intend* to steal jewels; the *motive* is to become richer. The motive is widespread and does not distinguish one thief from many others. His intention, to steal jewels, is more specific, and it is only one possible way of satisfying his motivation.

An intention may or may not move a person. It may remain a wish, a plot, a dream. *A criminal intention, without the action, is not a crime.*

Motives, on the other hand, may move us haphazardly, purposelessly, without the focus of intent. A motive may be purely physiological and variously gratified. It may even be "unconscious," if we believe the psychoanalysts. *An intention, however, is only something cognitive.* The word "intention" is reserved for thoughts, for verbalizable plans. It does not refer to those subterranean urges or those physiological fires that may have kindled the ideas.

Since "intent" is part of the definition of crime, prosecutors in Western countries must establish such purpose in the actor, and they sometimes try to do this by constructing "the motive." The strategy of demonstrating intention from motivation calls for showing the "good reasons" why a person might act as the accused is alleged to have done. The good reasons, the alleged motives, may all have been there, however, without the actor's having formed the criminal intent which the prosecutor is attempting to establish. This is simply because "good reasons" are not always the real ones.

The distinction between the movers of action and intentions becomes important as criminal law takes heed of another qualification in its definition of crime, the qualification that people shall be held responsible for their actions, and hence liable to the criminal law, *only if* they are mentally competent. The legal meaning of "intention" is embedded in the concept of competence.

NO CRIME WITHOUT CAPACITY

The condemnation that is implicit in calling actions "criminal" is based on moral premises. It is part of our morality to believe that a person ought not to be blamed for actions that are beyond his or her control. The notion that behavior is within or beyond one's control rests upon conceptions of "capacity" or "competence." These conceptions, in turn, are cultural. They vary in time and with place, and they remain disputed today. The dispute concerns the criteria of competence, but it does not challenge the legal and moral principle that people must be somehow "able" before they can be judged culpable.

Among modern states, the tests of competence are cognitive. They look to *mens rea*, the "thing in the mind," as definitive of the ability to form a criminal intent and as the regulator of one's actions. *Until* "the mind"[1] is sufficiently well formed to control the actor's behavior, and *unless* it operates in normal fashion, Anglo-American criminal law *excludes* the agent from criminal liability. Actors are considered "not responsible" or "less responsible" for their offenses if the offense has been produced by someone who is (1) acting under duress, (2) under age, or (3) "insane."

Crime under Duress

The first exclusion consists of criminal deeds performed "against one's will." The law recognizes circumstances in which a person may be forced into a criminal action under threat. Since intent and the capacity to act freely are diminished when this is the case, so too is legal responsibility.

Age and Capacity

A second application of the moral principle that people must have some minimal mental capacity before they ought to be held legally accountable has to do with limitations of age. Laws of modern nations agree that persons below a certain age must be excluded from criminal liability. The number of years required to attain legal responsibility varies by jurisdiction, but the legal principle persists in declaring individuals who are "under age" to be "incompetent" or "legal infants." They may be protected by laws, but they are not subject to the criminal law. In most Anglo-American jurisdictions a child under the age of seven years cannot be held responsible for a crime. . . .

Insanity as a Defense

A third excuse by which one may reduce or escape the application of the criminal law is the claim that the offender's capacity to control his or her behavior has been damaged. The locus of the damage, the "place" in which one looks for this incapacity, is, again, the mind.

Defects of the mind seem clear in the extremities of senility, idiocy, and the incapacitating psychoses. They are clear, too, as one is able to link abnormal performance to lesions of the central nervous system. However, it is in the gray area between these extremities and more normal behavior that citizens, lawyers, and their psychiatric advisers dispute the capacity of offenders.

It bears repeating that this dispute rests upon moral considerations. The quarrel is stimulated by the belief that only people who "choose" their conduct deserve punishment for their crimes, that "accidents" and "irresistible impulses" do not count, and that other classes of behavior beyond one's control should not be penalized. The philosophical questions opened by this debate range beyond our present concern. These questions include, at a minimum, the ancient issues of free will and determinism, of the justice and the value of praise and blame, and of the proper ends of the criminal law.

These questions intrude upon the law and ensure that attempts to define mental competence are all imperfect. They are less than perfect because moral conceptions of the "causes" of behavior color the assignment of responsibility to actors. They are less than perfect, also, because the boundaries of the defense of insanity move with the justifications of the criminal law. That is, who we believe to be "incompetent" before the law varies with what we want the law to do. . . .

CAPACITY AND JUSTIFICATIONS OF THE CRIMINAL LAW

The guidelines for judging the capacity of offenders are imperfect. They continue to be debated because our moral beliefs find the causes of human behavior in different locations. These beliefs move responsibility between the actor and his or her environment so that "who is to blame" and who deserves punishment are points endlessly disputed. Dispute is fostered, too, by the fact that *justifications* of the criminal law are supported by assumptions about the conditions under which human beings can control their own behavior. What we want the law to do and what we believe it does have bearing upon whom we are willing to excuse from criminal liability.

The criminal law is justified by what it supposedly does. If the law is to be respected for what it does, it must be applied in ways that achieve specific ends—or, more accurately, it must be applied in ways that are *believed* to achieve these ends.

The law serves a changing mixture of objectives, however, and this instability of its objectives encourages the continuing quarrel about which people should and which people should not be held responsible for their conduct.

The criminal law is commonly considered to be useful in achieving six ends, some of which are in conflict. These objectives have been described in various ways, but we can classify them as efforts to (1) restrain offenders, (2) deter criminals and others, (3) reform offenders, (4) revive communion symbolically, (5) achieve justice through retribution, and (6) achieve justice through restitution. All these functions are relevant to the issue of who should and who should not be excused for "incompetence."

1   Restraint

The word "arrest" is derived from the Latin word meaning "to stop." A principal function of the criminal law is to stop a person from injuring others. An arrest may involve restraining the miscreant for some time.

The need to restrain a bad actor does not rest upon a desire to punish or correct. Restraint attends only to controlling an offender. Whether the law should also punish or treat the person being restrained is another issue.

Definitions of capacity enter into the problem of achieving restraint principally in terms of determining *how* the lawbreaker is to be repressed. In recent years it has been our practice to restrain sane criminals in prisons and insane ones in mental hospitals. The growing emphasis upon the rehabilitative function of "correctional institutions" has meant, however, that some prisons now have as many psychotherapeutic facilities as mental hospitals (A. S. Goldstein, 1967). It is an open question whether incarceration in prison is more or less painful than incarceration in hospital (A. S. Goldstein, 1967; Kesey, 1964).

2 Deterrence

The criminal law is commonly justified as having a deterrent effect. The notion of deterrence is not a simple one, however, and it is possible to discern many meanings in the concept (Cousineau, 1976). Most criminologists, but not all of them (Zimring and Hawkins, 1973, pp. 224ff.), distinguish between *specific deterrence* and *general deterrence*.

The idea behind specific (or individual) deterrence is that the arrested person is less likely to commit a similar offense in the future as a result of the legal penalty suffered. This concept is similar to that of reforming the offender, although, as we shall see, some people who wish to reform convicts think that their criminal ways ought to be changed by some means other than the threat of punishment.

The assumption underlying the idea of general deterrence is that application of the criminal law to others will reduce the probability that you and I will commit the crimes for which they have been punished. This justification assumes that we are sufficiently normal to get the message. It is further assumed, with some good evidence, that the more closely you and I identify with the miscreant, the more clearly we will get the message. It is believed that the more we resemble the punished person, the more forcefully his or her penalty threatens us and deters us. It is assumed that, if we have felt the same desires as the punished person and have come close to committing similar crimes, the punishment provides us with a deterrent example. If, however, we healthy people observe "sick minds" being punished, then, presumably, the law's lesson is lost on us; in such cases the deterrent example is diluted because we perceive the offender as different from ourselves.

The determination of capacity is considered to be important, therefore, as a means of increasing the efficacy of the law as a deterrent. It is not *known* how effective this determination is in increasing deterrence, but some jurists *believe* it to be very important.

Morals seem more important here than *consequences*. Our moral beliefs find it cruel and unjust to punish persons who are "not responsible for their actions," regardless of the societal ends that such punishment might serve. The test of capacity tries, in a fumbling manner, to define persons who are sufficiently different from us that they may be excused from accountability under the criminal law.

3 Rehabilitation

It is popularly assumed that the criminal law is applied, or ought to be applied, to correct the offender. If the law is employed to improve the criminal's conduct, then it is believed that the candidate for rehabilitation must be capable of recovery with the attention the law provides. This means, to the conventional way of thinking, that the offender must have a mind capable of guiding behavior and amenable to education. The idea implicit in this justification of the law is that just as one does not pummel hydrocephalic idiots for failing at mathematics, so one does not penalize criminals who "can't help themselves."

Does Rehabilitation Work? It may be humane to refrain from punishing people who seem mentally defective. It may also be humane to refrain from punishing people—period. The ethics of this issue aside, however, some facts ought to inform conceptions of rehabilitation.

A first fact is that arrest "reforms" some offenders, in the sense that their behavior is "corrected." The offensive behavior stops. This change in conduct is seen most notably among some more intelligent criminals, such as embezzlers, and some impassioned offenders, such as murderous spouses. . . .

Despite this fact, many observers do not regard a change of conduct after arrest and upon the threat of additional penalty as "rehabilitation." What they seek is not just a change in behavior, but a change of heart that leads to the change in behavior.

Whether or not one requires that a change of character accompany a change in conduct before a person can be deemed to have been "rehabilitated," a second fact deserves reporting: *Efforts to rehabilitate offenders do not work well.*

There is no science of personality change which has yet been verified or which, in its experimental phases, has proved successful. There is counseling, of course, and some people are helped by advice. In particular, *self-selected* groups—those that people join voluntarily, like Alcoholics Anonymous and Synanon—have a better record of successful counseling. *But there is no science of corrections.*

The demonstration of this fact can be found in many places. Martinson (1974) and Lipton et al. (1975) have summarized the evidence on this point.

4 Symbolism

A neglected, but important, function of the criminal law is symbolic. Exercise of the criminal law reaffirms what we are for and what we are against. Thus the courtroom becomes one of the various educational theaters every society uses.

Capacity is part of this legal drama because, again, the drama depends upon identification. One must be able to identify with the roles portrayed if the dramatic lesson is to be learned. The symbolic and the deterrent functions of the law use capacity in the same way: it is, presumably, the "normal mind," not the defective one, that can appreciate the threats and the symbolism of the law.

5   Retribution

"Retribution" means "to give in return." It may refer to recompense for merit or for evil, although in criminology only the return of harm to the evildoer is implied.

Retribution is the oldest conception of justice. It is the moral demand that evil not go unpunished, that the harm a person does be returned to him or to her in equal degree, if not in kind. Retribution assumes that justice requires a *balance* between the wrong that was done and the penalty the wrongdoer is made to suffer.

Today retribution is not popular as a stated objective of the criminal law, partly because it has become confused with the idea of revenge.

Retribution Is Not Revenge.   Revenge is the emotional impulse to wreak havoc on a person who has injured us. Revenge knows no balance.

It may seem difficult to disentangle revenge and retribution in any particular demand that a wrong be punished. However, the balancing principle of retribution distinguishes it from revenge (Atkinson, 1974; Gerstein, 1974). Retribution sets limits to punishment. It seeks a punishment *proportional* to the wrong done. Its standard of punishment is the law of talion *(lex talionis),* the law of "like for like" (Kant, 1965, p. 101). This principle is to be found in the laws of many cultures, notably in Mosaic and Roman law. It is expressed in the code of the Babylonian King Hammurabi (1760 B.C.), which recommended "an eye for an eye, a tooth for a tooth."

Justice and Retribution.   Although the idea of retribution runs counter to some facets of the Christian ethic and is opposed by "enlightened" opinion (Long, 1973), the demand for a balancing of wrongs remains a major component of our sense of justice. This conception of justice has been defended on practical grounds (Gerstein, 1974; Kant, 1965; J. G. Murphy, 1971). However, whether or not one agrees with these appeals to the concrete effects of retribution, satisfaction of this motive remains a justice-dealing function of the criminal law.

For example, the moral requirement that evil not go unpunished is well put by the philosopher Hannah Arendt in her study of the trial of the Nazi Eichmann by the Israelis. Arendt justifies the trial and the hanging of Eichmann by saying, "To the question most commonly asked about the Eichmann trial: What good does it do?, there is but one possible answer: It will do justice" (1964, p. 254).

It bears repeating that the criminal law is not merely practical; it is also symbolic. *It expresses morals as well as it intends results.*

Competence and Retribution. It is part of the morality being expressed by the law that people should be held accountable only for what they have "chosen" to do. If Eichmann had been defined as an idiot or a lunatic, justice would not have required his execution. The same sense of justice that calls for retribution also demands some quality of capacity in the offender.

6 Restitution

Restitution is restoration—righting a wrong by returning things to their original state. The idea of restitution is more readily understandable in connection with property offenses, where we can calculate the cost of the damage. However, even in the case of attacks against persons, we often arrive at a price to be paid that may compensate for the injury. In fact, the anthropologist Lowie reports a case in the last century of a North American Indian woman who asked that the murderer of her son be "given" to her as a substitute for her lost boy.

Restitution is recognized in the criminal law of some lands as a proper penalty against the offender and also as a possible means of rehabilitation. The Canadian Criminal Code, for example, recognizes restitution as a form of sentence, but it is a sentence that has rarely been applied. The Law Reform Commission of Canada (1974) found that in 4,294 criminal convictions handed down between 1967 and 1972, the sentence of restitution was given in only six cases.

It is now being urged that restitution be more frequently used as a sentence and that property offenders in particular be given the option of working out their debt to their victims instead of going to prison. This has been recommended in Britain by K. J. Smith (1965), in the United States by Laura Nader (1975), and in Canada by A. J. Katz et al. (1976), directors of the Alberta Restitution Project.

Relevance. The idea of justice through restitution is related to conceptions of competence in several ways. First, it is assumed that only offenders who can understand the restitutive contract and who are able to fulfill it are properly eligible for this sentence. Second, it is assumed that a contract between a thief and his or her victim will restore some sense of the humanity of both. This objective depends, too, on the emotional and intellectual capacities of the contracting parties.

The restitutive contract is an interesting experiment in the uses of the criminal law—one that may save citizens the expense of imprisonment, help in the rehabilitation of wrongdoers, and, at the same time, satisfy a sense of justice. The results are yet to be tallied.

Notes

1. Placing the word "mind" in quotation marks indicates its vagueness. Like many other useful terms, "mind" has many meanings. It may be interesting to consider how you use the word.

References

Arendt, H. 1964. *Eichmann in Jerusalem: A Report on the Banality of Evil.* New York: Viking.

Atkinson, M. 1974. "Interpreting retributive claims," *Ethics,* 85:80–86.

Cousineau, D. F. 1976. *General Deterrence of Crime: An Analysis.* Edmonton: University of Alberta, Department of Sociology, Ph.D. dissertation.

Gerstein, R. S. 1974. "Capital punishment: 'Cruel and unusual'?: A retributivist response," *Ethics,* 85:75–79.

Goldstein, A. S. 1967. *The Insanity Defense.* New Haven, Conn.: Yale University Press.

Kant, I. 1965. *The Metaphysical Elements of Justice.* Trans. by J. Ladd. Indianapolis: Bobbs-Merrill.

Katz, A. J., et al. 1976. *Progress Report: The Pilot Alberta Restitution Centre.* Calgary: The Centre.

Kesey, K. 1964. *One Flew over the Cuckoo's Nest.* New York: Compass Books.

Law Reform Commission of Canada. 1974. *Restitution and Compensation.* Working Paper No. 5. Ottawa: Information Canada.

Lipton, D., et al. 1975. *The Effectiveness of Correctional Treatment: A Survey of Treatment Evaluation Studies.* New York: Praeger.

Long, T. A. 1973. "Capital punishment: 'Cruel and unusual'?" *Ethics,* 83:214–223.

Martinson, R. 1974. "What works?: Questions and answers about prison reform," *The Public Interest,* 35:22–54.

Murphy, J. G. 1971. "Three mistakes about retributivism," *Analysis,* 31:166–169.

Nader, L. 1975. Address at the First International Symposium on Restitution, Minneapolis (November 10–11).

Smith, K. J. 1965. *A Cure for Crime.* London: Duckworth.

Sorel, G. 1908. *Reflections on Violence.* Reprinted 1950. Glencoe, Ill: Free Press.

Tappan, P. W. 1947. "Who is the criminal?" *American Sociological Review,* 12:96–102.

Williams, G. 1955. "The definition of crime." *Current Legal Problems,* 8:107–130.

Zimring, F. E., and G. J. Hawkins. 1973. *Deterrence: The Legal Threat in Crime Control.* Chicago: University of Chicago Press.

2. Moral Entrepreneurs: The Creation and Enforcement of Deviant Categories

HOWARD S. BECKER

RULE CREATORS

The prototype of the rule creator, but not the only variety as we shall see, is the crusading reformer. He is interested in the content of rules. The existing rules do not satisfy him because there is some evil which profoundly disturbs him. He feels that nothing can be right in the world until rules are made to correct it. He operates with an absolute ethic; what he sees is truly and totally evil with no qualification. Any means is justified to do away with it. The crusader is fervent and righteous, often self-righteous.

It is appropriate to think of reformers as crusaders because they typically believe that their mission is a holy one. The prohibitionist serves as an excellent example, as does the person who wants to suppress vice and sexual delinquency or the person who wants to do away with gambling.

These examples suggest that the moral crusader is a meddling busybody, interested in forcing his own morals on others. But this is a one-sided view. Many moral crusades have strong humanitarian overtones. The crusader is not only interested in seeing to it that other people do what he thinks right. He believes that if they do what is right it will be good for them. Or he may feel that his reform will prevent certain kinds of exploitation of one person by another. Prohibitionists felt that they were not simply forcing their morals on others, but attempting to provide the conditions for a better way of life for people prevented by drink from realizing a truly good life. Abolitionists were not simply trying to prevent slave owners from doing the wrong thing; they were trying to help slaves to achieve a better life. Because of the importance of the humanitarian motive, moral crusaders (despite their relatively single-minded devotion to their particular cause) often lend their support to other humanitarian crusades. Joseph Gusfield has pointed out that:

> The American temperance movement during the 19th century was a part of a general effort toward the improvement of the worth of the human being through improved morality as well as economic conditions. The mixture of the religious, the equalitarian, and the humanitarian was an outstanding facet of the moral reformism of many movements. Temperance supporters formed a large segment of movements such as sabbatarianism, abolition, woman's rights, agrarianism, and humanitarian attempts to improve the lot of the poor. . . .
>
> In its auxiliary interests the WCTU [Woman's Christian Temperance Union] revealed a great concern for the improvement of the welfare of the lower classes. It was active in campaigns to secure penal reform, to shorten working hours and raise wages for workers, and to abolish child labor and in a number of other humanitarian and equalitarian activities. In the 1880s the WCTU worked to bring about legislation for the protection of working girls against the exploitation by men.[1]

As Gusfield says,[2] "Moral reformism of this type suggests the approach of a dominant class toward those less favorably situated in the economic and social structure." Moral crusaders typically want to help those beneath them to achieve a better status. That those beneath them do not always like the means proposed for their salvation is another matter. But this fact—that moral crusades are typically dominated by those in the upper levels of the social structure—means that they add to the power they derive from the legitimacy of their moral position, the power they derive from their superior position in society.

Naturally, many moral crusades draw support from people whose motives are less pure than those of the crusader. Thus, some industrialists supported Prohibition because they felt it would provide them with a more manageable labor force.[3] Similarly, it is sometimes rumored that Nevada gambling interests support the opposition to attempts to legalize gambling in California because it would cut so heavily into their business, which depends in substantial measure on the population of Southern California.[4]

The moral crusader, however, is more concerned with ends than with means. When it comes to drawing up specific rules (typically in the form of legislation to be proposed to a state legislature or the federal Congress), he frequently relies on the advice of experts. Lawyers, expert in the drawing of acceptable legislation, often play this role. Government bureaus in whose jurisdiction the problem falls may also have the necessary expertise, as did the Federal Bureau of Narcotics in the case of the marihuana problem.

As psychiatric ideology, however, becomes increasingly acceptable, a new expert has appeared—the psychiatrist. Sutherland, in his discussion of the natural history of sexual psychopath laws, pointed to the psychiatrist's influence.[5] He suggests the following as the conditions under which the sexual psychopath law, which provides that a person "who is diagnosed as a sexual psychopath may be confined for an indefinite period in a state hospital for the insane,"[6] will be passed.

First, these laws are customarily enacted after a state of fear has been aroused in a community by a few serious sex crimes committed in quick succession. This is illustrated in Indiana, where a law was passed following three or four sexual attacks in Indianapolis, with murder in two. Heads of families bought guns and watch dogs, and the supply of locks and chains in the hardware stores of the city was completely exhausted. . . .

A second element in the process of developing sexual psychopath laws is the agitated activity of the community in connection with the fear. The attention of the community is focused on sex crimes, and people in the most varied situations envisage dangers and see the need of and possibility for their control. . . .

The third phase in the development of those sexual psychopath laws has been the appointment of a committee. The committee gathers the many conflicting recommendations of persons and groups of persons, attempts to determine "facts," studies procedures in other states, and makes recommendations, which generally include bills for the legislature. Although the general fear usually subsides within a few days, a committee has the formal duty of following through until positive action is taken. Terror which does not result in a committee is much less likely to result in a law.[7]

In the case of sexual psychopath laws, there usually is no government agency charged with dealing in a specialized way with sexual deviations. Therefore, when the need for expert advice in drawing up legislation arises, people frequently turn to the professional group most closely associated with such problems:

In some states, at the committee stage of the development of a sexual psychopath law, psychiatrists have played an important part. The psychiatrists, more than any others, have been the interest group back of the laws. A committee of psychiatrists and neurologists in Chicago wrote the bill which became the sexual psychopath law of Illinois; the bill was sponsored by the Chicago Bar Association and by the state's attorney of Cook County and was enacted with little opposition in the next session of the State Legislature. In Minnesota all the members of the governor's committee except one were psychiatrists. In Wisconsin the Milwaukee Neuropsychiatric Society shared in pressing the Milwaukee Crime Commission for the enactment of a law. In Indiana the attorney-general's committee received from the American Psychiatric Association copies of all the sexual psychopath laws which had been enacted in other states.[8]

The influence of psychiatrists in other realms of the criminal law has increased in recent years.

In any case, what is important about this example is not that psychiatrists are becoming increasingly influential, but that the moral crusader, at some point in the development of his crusade, often requires the services of a professional who can draw up the appropriate rules in an appropriate form. The crusader himself is often not concerned with such details. Enough for him that the main point has been won; he leaves its implementation to others.

By leaving the drafting of the specific rule in the hands of others, the crusader opens the door for many unforeseen influences. For those who draft legislation for crusaders have their own interests, which may affect the legislation they prepare. It is likely that the sexual psychopath laws drawn by psychiatrists contain many features never intended by the citizens who spearheaded the drives to "do something about sex crimes," features which do however reflect the professional interests of organized psychiatry.

RULE ENFORCERS

The most obvious consequence of a successful crusade is the creation of a new set of rules. With the creation of a new set of rules we often find that a new set of enforcement agencies and officials is established. Sometimes, of course, existing agencies take over the administration of the new rule, but more frequently a new set of rule enforcers is created. The passage of the Harrison Act presaged the creation of the Federal Narcotics Bureau, just as the passage of the Eighteenth Amendment led to the creation of police agencies charged with enforcing the Prohibition Laws.

With the establishment of organizations of rule enforcers, the crusade becomes institutionalized. What started out as a drive to convince the world of the moral necessity of a new rule finally becomes an organization devoted to the enforcement of the rule. Just as radical political movements turn into organized political parties and lusty evangelical sects become staid religious denominations, the final outcome of the moral crusade is a police force. To understand, therefore, how the rules creating a new class of outsiders are applied to particular people we must understand the motives and interests of police, the rule enforcers.

Although some policemen undoubtedly have a kind of crusading interest in stamping out evil, it is probably much more typical for the policeman to have a certain detached and objective view of his job. He is not so much concerned with the content of any particular rule as he is with the fact that it is his job to enforce the rule. When the rules are changed, he punishes what was once acceptable behavior just as he ceases to punish behavior that has been made legitimate by a change in the rules. The enforcer, then, may not be interested in the content of the rule as such, but only in the fact that the existence of the rule provides him with a job, a profession, and a *raison d'être.*

Since the enforcement of certain rules provides justification for his way of life, the enforcer has two interests which condition his enforcement activity: first, he must justify the existence of his position and, second, he must win the respect of those he deals with.

These interests are not peculiar to rule enforcers. Members of all occupations feel the need to justify their work and win the respect of others. Musicians . . . would like to do this but have difficulty finding ways of successfully impressing their worth on customers. Janitors fail to win their tenants' respect, but develop an ideology which stresses the quasi-professional responsibility they have to keep confidential the intimate knowledge of tenants they acquire in the course of their work.[9] Physicians, lawyers, and other professionals, more successful in winning the respect of clients, develop elaborate mechanisms for maintaining a properly respectful relationship.

In justifying the existence of his position, the rule enforcer faces a double problem. On the one hand, he must demonstrate to others that the problem still exists: the rules he is supposed to enforce have some point, because infractions occur. On the other hand, he must show that his attempts at enforcement are effective and worthwhile, that the evil he is supposed to deal with is in fact being dealt with adequately. Therefore, enforcement organizations, particularly when they are seeking funds, typically oscillate between two kinds of claims. First, they say that by reason of their efforts the problem they deal with is approaching solution. But, in the same breath, they say the problem is perhaps worse than ever (though through no fault of their own) and requires renewed and increased effort to keep it under control. Enforcement officials can be more vehement than anyone else in their insistence that the problem they are supposed to deal with is still with us, in fact is more with us than ever before. In making these claims, enforcement officials provide good reason for continuing the existence of the position they occupy.

We may also note that enforcement officials and agencies are inclined to take a pessimistic view of human nature. If they do not actually believe in original sin, they at least like to dwell on the difficulties in getting people to abide by rules, on the characteristics of human nature that lead people toward evil. They are skeptical of attempts to reform rule-breakers.

The skeptical and pessimistic outlook of the rule enforcer, of course, is reinforced by his daily experience. He sees, as he goes about his work, the evidence that the problem is still with us. He sees the people who continually repeat offenses, thus definitely branding themselves in his eyes as outsiders. Yet it is not too great a stretch of the imagination to suppose that one of the underlying reasons for the enforcer's pessimism about human nature and the possibilities of reform is that fact that if human nature were perfectible and people could be permanently reformed, his job would come to an end.

In the same way, a rule enforcer is likely to believe that it is necessary for the people he deals with to respect him. If they do not, it will be very difficult to do his job; his feeling of security in his work will be lost. Therefore, a good deal of enforcement activity is devoted not to the actual enforcement of rules, but to coercing respect from the people the enforcer deals with. This means that one may be labeled as deviant not because he has actually broken a rule, but because he has shown disrespect to the enforcer of the rule.

Westley's study of policemen in a small industrial city furnishes a good example of this phenomenon. In his interview, he asked policemen, "When do you think a policeman is justified in roughing a man up?" He found that "at least 37 percent of the men believed that it was legitimate to use violence to coerce respect."[10] He gives some illuminating quotations from his interviews:

> Well, there are cases. For example, when you stop a fellow for a routine questioning, say a wise guy, and he starts talking back to you and telling you you are no good and that sort of thing. You know you can take a man in on a disorderly conduct charge, but you can practically never make it stick. So what you do in a case like that is to egg the guy on until he makes a remark where you can justifiably slap him and, then, if he fights back, you can call it resisting arrest.
>
> Well, a prisoner deserves to be hit when he goes to the point where he tries to put you below him.
>
> You've gotta get rough when a man's language becomes very bad, when he is trying to make a fool of you in front of everybody else. I think most policemen try to treat people in a nice way, but usually you have to talk pretty rough. That's the only way to set a man down, to make him show a little respect.[11]

What Westley describes is the use of an illegal means of coercing respect from others. Clearly, when a rule enforcer has the option of enforcing a rule or not, the difference in what he does may be caused by the attitude of the offender toward him. If the offender is properly respectful, the enforcer may smooth the situation over. If the offender is disrespectful, then sanctions may be visited on him. Westley has shown that this differential tends to operate in the case of traffic offenses, where the policeman's discretion is perhaps at a maximum.[12] But it probably operates in other areas as well.

Ordinarily, the rule enforcer has a great deal of discretion in many areas, if only because his resources are not sufficient to cope with the volume of rule-breaking he is supposed to deal with. This means that he cannot tackle everything at once and to this extent must temporize with evil. He cannot do the whole job and knows it. He takes his time, on the assumption that the problems he deals with will be around for a long while. He establishes priorities, dealing with things in their turn, handling the most pressing problems immediately and leaving others for later. His attitude toward his work, in short, is professional. He lacks the naive moral fervor characteristic of the rule creator.

If the enforcer is not going to tackle every case he knows of at once, he must have a basis for deciding when to enforce the rule, which persons committing which acts to label as deviant. One criterion for selecting people is the "fix." Some people have sufficient political influence or know-how to be able to ward off attempts at enforcement, if not at the time of apprehension then at a later stage in the process. Very often, this function is professionalized; someone performs the job on a full-time basis, available to anyone who wants to hire him. A professional thief described fixers this way:

> There is in every large city a regular fixer for professional thieves. He has no agents and does not solicit and seldom takes any case except that of a professional thief, just as they seldom go to anyone except him. This centralized and monopolistic system of fixing for professional thieves is found in practically all of the large cities and many of the small ones.[13]

Since it is mainly professional thieves who know about the fixer and his operations, the consequence of this criterion for selecting people to apply the rules to is that amateurs tend to be caught, convicted, and labeled deviant much more frequently than professionals. As the professional thief notes:

> You can tell by the way the case is handled in court when the fix is in. When the copper is not very certain he has the right man, or the testimony of the copper and the complainant does not agree, or the prosecutor goes easy on the defendant, or the judge is arrogant in his decisions, you can always be sure that someone has got the work in. This does not happen in many cases of theft, for there is one case of a professional to twenty-five or thirty amateurs who know nothing about the fix. These amateurs get the hard end of the deal every time. The coppers bawl out about the thieves, no one holds up his testimony, the judge delivers an oration, and all of them get credit for stopping a crime wave. When the professional hears the case immediately preceding his own, he will think, "He should have got ninety years. It's the damn amateurs who cause all the heat in the stores." Or else he thinks, "Isn't it a damn shame for that copper to send that kid away for a pair of hose, and in a few minutes he will agree to a

small fine for me for stealing a fur coat?" But if the coppers did not send the amateurs away to strengthen their records of convictions, they could not sandwich in the professionals whom they turn loose.[14]

Enforcers of rules, since they have no stake in the content of particular rules themselves, often develop their own private evaluation of the importance of various kinds of rules and infractions of them. This set of priorities may differ considerably from those held by the general public. For instance, drug users typically believe (and a few policemen have personally confirmed it to me) that police do not consider the use of marihuana to be as important a problem or as dangerous a practice as the use of opiate drugs. Police base this conclusion on the fact that, in their experience, opiate users commit other crimes (such as theft or prostitution) in order to get drugs, while marihuana users do not.

Enforcers, then, responding to the pressures of their own work situation, enforce rules and create outsiders in a selective way. Whether a person who commits a deviant act is in fact labeled a deviant depends on many things extraneous to his actual behavior: whether the enforcement official feels that at this time he must make some show of doing his job in order to justify his position, whether the misbehaver shows proper deference to the enforcer, whether the "fix" has been put in, and where the kind of act he has committed stands on the enforcer's list of priorities.

The professional enforcer's lack of fervor and routine approach to dealing with evil may get him into trouble with the rule creator. The rule creator, as we have said, is concerned with the content of the rules that interest him. He sees them as the means by which evil can be stamped out. He does not understand the enforcer's long-range approach to the same problems and cannot see why all the evil that is apparent cannot be stamped out at once.

When the person interested in the content of a rule realizes or has called to his attention the fact that enforcers are dealing selectively with the evil that concerns him, his righteous wrath may be aroused. The professional is denounced for viewing the evil too lightly, for failing to do his duty. The moral entrepreneur, at whose instance the rule was made, arises again to say that the outcome of the last crusade has not been satisfactory or that the gains once made have been whittled away and lost.

Notes

1. Joseph R. Gusfield, "Social Structure and Moral Reform: A Study of the Woman's Christian Temperance Union," *American Journal of Sociology*, LXI (November, 1955), 223.

2. *Ibid.*

3. See Raymond G. McCarthy, editor, *Drinking and Intoxication* (New Haven and New York: Yale Center of Alcohol Studies and The Free Press of Glencoe, 1959), pp. 395–396.

4. This is suggested in Oscar Lewis, *Sagebrush Casinos: The Story of Legal Gambling in Nevada* (New York: Doubleday and Co., 1953), pp. 233–234.

5. Edwin H. Sutherland, "The Diffusion of Sexual Psychopath Laws," *American Journal of Sociology*, LVI (September, 1950), 142–148.

6. *Ibid.*, p. 142.

7. *Ibid.*, pp. 143–145.

8. *Ibid.*, pp. 145–146.

9. See Ray Gold, "Janitors Versus Tenants: A Status-Income Dilemma," *American Journal of Sociology*, LVII (March, 1952), 486–493.

10. William A. Westley, "Violence and the Police," *American Journal of Sociology*, LIX (July, 1953), 39.

11. *Ibid.*

12. See William A. Westley, "The Police: A Sociological Study of Law, Custom, and Morality" (unpublished Ph.D. dissertation, University of Chicago, Department of Sociology, 1951).

13. Edwin H. Sutherland, editor, *The Professional Thief* (Chicago: University of Chicago Press, 1937), pp. 87–88.

14. *Ibid.*, pp. 91–92.

3. Amphetamine Politics on Capitol Hill

JAMES M. GRAHAM

The American pharmaceutical industry annually manufactures enough amphetamines to provide a month's supply to every man, woman, and child in the country. Eight, perhaps ten, billion pills are lawfully produced, packaged, retailed, and consumed each year. Precise figures are unavailable. We must be content with estimates because until 1970, no law required an exact accounting of total amphetamine production.

Amphetamines are the drug of the white American with money to spend. Street use, contrary to the popular myths, accounts for a small percentage of the total consumption. Most of the pills are eaten by housewives, businessmen, students, physicians, truck drivers, and athletes. Those who inject large doses of "speed" intravenously are but a tiny fragment of the total. Aside from the needle and the dose, the "speed freak" is distinguishable because his use has been branded as illegal. A doctor's signature supplies the ordinary user with lawful pills.

All regular amphetamine users expose themselves to varying degrees of potential harm. Speed doesn't kill, but high sustained dosages can and do result in serious mental and physical injury, depending on how the drug is taken. The weight-conscious housewife, misled by the opinion-makers into believing that amphetamines can control weight, eventually may rely on the drug to alter her mood in order to face her monotonous tasks. Too frequently an amphetamine prescription amounts to a synthetic substitute for attention to emotional and institutional problems.

Despite their differences, all amphetamine users, whether on the street or in the kitchen, share one important thing in common—the initial source of supply. For both, it is largely the American pharmaceutical industry. That industry has skillfully managed to convert a chemical, with meager medical justification and considerable potential for harm, into multihundred-million-dollar profits in less than 40 years. High profits, reaped from such vulnerable products, require extensive, sustained political efforts for their continued existence. The lawmakers who have declared that possession of marijuana is a serious crime have simultaneously defended and protected the profits of the amphetamine pill-makers. The Comprehensive Drug Abuse Prevention and Control Act of 1970 in its final form constitutes a victory for that alliance over compelling contrary evidence on the issue of amphetamines. The victory could not have been secured without the firm support of the Nixon administration. The end result is a national policy which declares an all-out war on drugs which are *not* a source of corporate income. Meanwhile, under the protection of the law, billions of amphetamines are overproduced without medical justification.

HEARINGS IN THE SENATE

The Senate was the first house to hold hearings on the administration's bill to curb drug abuse, The Controlled Dangerous Substances Act (S-3246). Beginning on September 15, 1969 and consuming most of that month, the hearings before Senator Thomas Dodd's Subcommittee to Investigate Juvenile Delinquency of the Committee on the Judiciary would finally conclude on October 20, 1969.

The first witness was John Mitchell, attorney general of the United States, who recalled President Nixon's ten-point program to combat drug abuse announced on July 14, 1969. Although that program advocated tighter controls on imports and exports of dangerous drugs and promised new efforts to encourage foreign governments to crack down on production of illicit drugs, there was not a single reference to the control of domestic manufacture of dangerous drugs. The president's bill when it first reached the Senate placed the entire "amphetamine family" in Schedule III, where they were exempt from any quotas and had the benefit of lesser penalties and controls. Hoffman-LaRoche, Inc. had already been at work; their depressants, Librium and Valium, were completely exempt from any control whatsoever.

In his opening statement, Attorney General Mitchell set the tone of administrative policy related to amphetamines. Certainly, these drugs were "subject to increasing abuse"; however, they have "widespread medical uses" and therefore are appropriately classed under the administration guidelines in Schedule III. Tight-mouthed John Ingersoll, director of the Bureau of Narcotics and Dangerous Drugs (BNDD), reaffirmed the policy, even though a Bureau study over the last year (which showed that 92 percent of the amphetamines and barbiturates in the illicit market were legitimately manufactured) led him to conclude that drug companies have "lax security and record-keeping."

Senator Dodd was no novice at dealing with the pharmaceutical interests. In 1965 he had steered a drug abuse bill through the Senate with the drug industry fighting every step of the way. Early in the hearings he recalled that the industry "vigorously opposed the passage of (the 1965) act. I know very well because I lived with it, and they gave me fits and they gave all of us fits in trying to get it through."

The medical position on amphetamine use was first presented by the National Institute of Mental Health's Dr. Sidney Cohen, a widely recognized authority on drug use and abuse. He advised the subcommittee that 50 percent of the lawfully manufactured pep pills were diverted at some point to illicit channels. Some of the pills, though, were the result of unlawful manufacture as evidenced by the fact that 33 clandestine laboratories had been seized in the last 18 months.

Dr. Cohen recognized three categories of amphetamine abuse, all of which deserved the attention of the government. First was their "infrequent ingestion" by students, businessmen, truck drivers, and athletes. Second were those people who swallowed 50–75 milligrams daily without medical supervision. Finally, there were the speed freaks who injected the drug intravenously over long periods of time. Physical addiction truly occurs, said Dr. Cohen, when there is prolonged use in high doses. Such use, he continued, may result in malnutrition, prolonged psychotic states, heart irregularities, convulsions, hepatitis and with an even chance of sustained brain damage.

As the hearings progressed, the first two classes of abusers described by Dr. Cohen would receive less and less attention, while the third category—the speed freaks—would receive increasing emphasis. The amphetamine industry was not at all unhappy with this emphasis. In fact, they would encourage it.

Ingersoll had already said that BNDD statistics indicated that only 8 percent of illicit speed was illegally manufactured. Thomas Lynch, attorney general of California, testified that his agents had in 1967 successfully negotiated a deal for one-half million amphetamine tablets with a "Tijuana café man." Actual delivery was taken from a California warehouse. All of the tablets seized originated with a Chicago company which had not bothered to question the authenticity of the retailer or the pharmacy. Prior to the 1965 hearings, the Food and Drug Administration completed a ten-year study involving 1,658 criminal cases for the illegal sale of amphetamines and barbiturates. Seventy-eight percent of all convictions involved pharmacists, and of these convictions 60 percent were for illicit traffic in amphetamines.

The pharmacists were not the source of illicit diversion, according to the National Association of Retail Druggists (NARD) and the National Association of Chain Drug Stores. Indeed, NARD had conducted an extensive educational program combating drug abuse for years, and as proof of it, introduced its booklet, "Never Abuse—Respect Drugs," into the record. Annual inventories were acceptable for Schedule I and II drugs, NARD continued, but were unwarranted for the remaining two schedules which coincidently included most of their wares—unwarranted because diversion resulted from forged prescriptions, theft and placebo (false) inventories.

The amphetamine wholesalers were not questioned in any detail about diversion. Brief statements by the National Wholesale Druggists Association and McKesson Robbins Drug Co. opposed separate inventories for dangerous drugs because they were currently comingled with other drugs. Finally, the massive volume of the drugs involved—primarily in Schedule III—was just too great for records to be filed with the attorney general.

DODGING THE DIVERSION ISSUE

The representative of the prescription drug developers was also not pressed on the question of illicit diversion. Instead, the Pharmaceutical Manufacturers' Association requested clarifications on the definitional sections, argued for formal administrative hearings on control decisions and on any action revoking or suspending registration, and endorsed a complete exemption for over-the-counter nonnarcotic drugs.

With some misgivings, Carter-Wallace Inc. endorsed the administration bill providing, of course, the Senate would accept the president's recommendation that meprobamate not be subjected to any control pending a decision of the Fourth Circuit as to whether the drug had a dangerously depressant effect on the central nervous system. On a similar special mission, Hoffman-LaRoche Inc. sent two of its vice-presidents to urge the committee to agree with the president's recommendation that their "minor tranquilizers" (Librium and Valium) remain uncontrolled. Senator Dodd was convinced that both required inclusion in one of the schedules. The Senator referred to a BNDD investigation which had shown that from January 1968 to February 1969, three drugstores were on the average over 30,000 dosage units short. In addition, five inspected New York City pharmacies had unexplained shortages ranging from 12 to 50 percent of their total stock in Librium and Valium. Not only were the drugs being diverted, but Bureau of Narcotics information revealed that Librium and Valium, alone or in combination with other drugs, were involved in 36 suicides and 750 attempted suicides.

The drug company representatives persisted in dodging or contradicting Dodd's inquiries. Angry and impatient, Senator Dodd squarely asked the vice-presidents, "Why do you worry about putting this drug under control?" The response was as evasive as the question was direct: There are hearings pending in HEW, and Congress should await the outcome when the two drugs might be placed in Schedule III. (The hearings had begun in 1966; no final administrative decision had been reached and Hoffman-LaRoche had yet to exercise its right to judicial review.)

In the middle of the hearings, BNDD Director Ingersoll returned to the subcommittee to discuss issues raised chiefly by drug industry spokesmen. He provided the industry with several comforting administrative interpretations. The fact that he did not even mention amphetamines is indicative of the low level of controversy that the hearings had aroused on the issue. Ingersoll did frankly admit that his staff had met informally with industry representatives in the interim. Of course, this had been true from the very beginning.

The president of the American Pharmaceutical Association, the professional society for pharmacists, confirmed this fact: His staff participated in "several" Justice Department conferences when the bill was being drafted. (Subsequent testimony in the House would reveal that industry participation was extensive and widespread.) All the same, the inventory, registration, and inspection (primarily "no-knock") provisions were still "unreasonable, unnecessary, and costly administrative burden(s)" which would result in an even greater "paper work explosion."

For the most part, however, the administration bill had industry support. It was acceptable for the simple reason that, to an unknown degree, the "administration bill" was a "drug company bill" and was doubtless the final product of considerable compromise. Illustrative of that give-and-take process is the comparative absence of industry opposition to the transfer of drug-classification decision and research from HEW to Justice. The industry had already swallowed this and other provisions in exchange for the many things the bill could have but did not cover. Moreover, the subsequent windy opposition of the pill-makers allowed the administration to boast of a bill the companies objected to.

When the bill was reported out of the Committee on the Judiciary, the amphetamine family, some 6,000 strong, remained in Schedule III. Senator Dodd apparently had done some strong convincing because Librium, Valium and meprobamate were now controlled in Schedule III. A commission on marijuana and a declining penalty structure (based on what schedule the drug is in and whether or not the offense concerned trafficking or possession) were added.

DEBATE IN THE SENATE—ROUND I

The Senate began consideration of the bill on January 23, 1970. This time around, the amphetamine issue would inspire neither debate nor amendment. The energies of the Senate liberals were consumed instead by unsuccessful attempts to alter the declared law enforcement nature of the administration bill.

Senator Dodd's opening remarks, however, were squarely directed at the prescription pill industry. Dodd declared that the present federal laws had failed to control the illicit diversion of lawfully manufactured dangerous drugs. The senator also recognized the ways in which all Americans had become increasingly involved in drug use and that the people's fascination with pills was by no means an "accidental development": "Multihundred-million-dollar advertising budgets, frequently the most costly ingredient in the price of a pill, have, pill by pill, led, coaxed, and seduced post-World War II generations into the 'freaked-out' drug culture. . . . Detail men employed by drug companies propagandize harried and harassed doctors into pushing their special brand of palliative. Free samples in the doctor's office are as common nowadays as inflated fees." In the version adopted by the Senate, Valium, Librium and meprobamate joined the amphetamines in Schedule III.

HEARINGS IN THE HOUSE

On February 3, 1970, within a week of the Senate's passage of S-3246, the House began its hearings. The testimony would continue for a month. Although the Senate would prove in the end to be less vulnerable to the drug lobby, the issue of amphetamines—their danger and medical justification—would be aired primarily in the hearings of the Subcommittee on Public Health of the Committee on Interstate and Foreign Commerce. The administration bill (HR 13743), introduced by the chairman of the parent committee, made no mention of Librium or Valium and classified amphetamines in Schedule III.

As in the Senate, the attorney general was scheduled to be the first witness, but instead John Ingersoll of the BNDD was the administration's representative. On the question of amphetamine diversion, Ingersoll gave the administration's response: "Registration is . . . the most effective and least cumbersome way" to prevent the unlawful traffic. This coupled with biennial inventories of all stocks of controlled dangerous drugs and the attorney general's authority to suspend, revoke, or deny registration would go a long way in solving the problem. In addition, the administration was proposing stronger controls on imports and exports. For Schedules I and II, but not III or IV, a permit from the attorney general would be required for exportation. Quotas for Schedules I and II, but not III or IV, would "maximize" government control. For Schedules III and IV, no approval is required, but a supplier must send an advance notice on triple invoice to the attorney general in order to export drugs such as amphetamines. A prescription could be filled only five times in a six-month period and thereafter a new prescription would be required, whereas previously such prescriptions could be refilled as long as a pharmacist would honor them.

The deputy chief counsel for the BNDD, Michael R. Sonnenreich, was asked on what basis the attorney general would decide to control a particular drug. Sonnenreich replied that the bill provides one of two ways: Either the attorney general "finds *actual street abuse* or an interested party (such as HEW) feels that a drug should be controlled." (Speed-freaks out on the street are the trigger, according to Sonnenreich; lawful abuse is not an apparent criterion.)

The registration fee schedule would be reasonable ($10.00—physician or pharmacist; $25.00—wholesalers; $50.00—manufacturers). However, the administration did not want a formal administrative hearing on questions of registration and classification, and a less formal rule-making procedure was provided for in the bill.

Returning to the matter of diversion, Sonnenreich disclosed that from July 1, 1968 to June 30, 1969 the BNDD had conducted full-scale compliance investigations of 908 "establishments." Of this total, 329 (or about 36 percent) required further action, which included surrender of order forms (162), admonition letters (38), seizures (36), and hearings (31). In addition to these full-scale investigations, the Bureau made 930 "visits." (It later came to light that when the BNDD had information that a large supply of drugs was unlawfully being sold, the Bureau's policy was to warn those involved and "90 percent of them do take care of this matter.") Furthermore, 574 robberies involving dangerous drugs had been reported to the Bureau.

Eight billion amphetamine tablets are produced annually, according to Dr. Stanley Yolles, director of the National Institute of Mental Health, and although the worst abuse is by intravenous injection, an NIMH study found that 21 percent of all college students had taken amphetamines with the family medicine cabinet acting as the primary source—not surprising in light of the estimate that 1.1 billion prescriptions were issued in 1967 at a consumer cost of $3.9 billion. Of this total, 178 million prescriptions for amphetamines were filled at a retail cost of $692 million. No one knew the statistics better than the drug industry.

Representing the prescription-writers, the American Medical Association also recognized that amphetamines were among those drugs "used daily in practically every physician's armamentarium." This casual admission of massive lawful distribution was immediately followed by a flat denial that physicians were the source of "any significant diversion."

The next witness was Donald Fletcher, manager of distribution protection, Smith Kline & French Laboratories, one of the leading producers of amphetamines. Fletcher, who was formerly with the Texas state police, said his company favored "comprehensive controls" to fight diversion and stressed the company's "educational effort." Smith Kline & French favored federal registration and tighter controls over exports (by licensing the exporter, *not* the shipment). However, no change in present record-keeping requirements on distribution, production, or inventory should be made, and full hearings on the decisions by the attorney general should be guaranteed.

The committee did not ask the leading producer of amphetamines a single question about illicit diversion. Upon conclusion of the testimony, Subcommittee Chairman John Jarman of Oklahoma commented, "Certainly, Smith Kline & French is to be commended for the constructive and vigorous and hard-hitting role that you have played in the fight against drug abuse."

Dr. William Apple, executive director of the American Pharmaceutical Association (APhA), was the subject of lengthy questioning and his responses were largely typical. Like the entire industry, the APhA was engaged in a massive public education program. Apple opposed the inventory provisions, warning that the cost would be ultimately passed to the consumer. He was worried about the attorney general's power to revoke registrations ("without advance notice") because it could result in cutting off necessary drugs to patients.

Apple admitted organizational involvement "in the draft stage of the bill" but all the same, the APhA had a "very good and constructive working relationship" with HEW. Apple argued that if the functions are transferred to Justice, "We have a whole new ball game in terms of people. While some of the experienced people were transferred from HEW to Justice, there are many new people, and they are law-enforcement oriented. We are health-care oriented." Surely the entire industry shared this sentiment, but few opposed the transfer as strongly as did the APhA.

Apple reasoned that since the pharmacists were not the source of diversion, why should they be "penalized by costly overburdensome administrative requirements." The source of the drugs, Apple said, were either clandestine laboratories or burglaries. The 1965 Act, which required only those "records maintained in the ordinary course of business" be kept, was sufficient. Anyway, diversion at the pharmacy level was the responsibility of the pharmacists—a responsibility which the APhA takes "seriously and (is) going to do a better job (with) in the future."

Congress should instead ban the 60 mail-order houses which are not presently included in the bill. (One subcommittee member said this was a "loophole big enough to drive a truck through.") The corner druggist simply was not involved in "large-scale diversionary efforts."

The Pharmaceutical Manufacturers' Association (PMA) was questioned a bit more carefully in the House than in the Senate. PMA talked at length about its "long and honorable history" in fighting drug abuse. Its representative echoed the concern of the membership over the lack of formal hearings and requested that a representative of the manufacturing interests be appointed to the Scientific Advisory Committee. Significantly, the PMA declined to take a position on the issue of transfer from HEW to Justice. The PMA endorsed the administration bill. PMA Vice-President Brennan was asked whether the federal government should initiate a campaign, similar to the one against cigarettes, "to warn people that perhaps they should be careful not to use drugs excessively." Brennan's response to this cautious suggestion is worth quoting in full:

> I think this is probably not warranted because it would have the additional effect of giving concern to people over very useful commodities. . . . There is a very useful side to any medicant and to give people pause as to whether or not they should take that medication, particularly those we are talking about which are only given by prescription, I think the negative effect would outweigh any sociological benefit on keeping people from using drugs.

"LIMITED MEDICAL USE"

There was universal agreement that amphetamines are medically justified for the treatment of two very rare diseases, hyperkinesis and narcolepsy. Dr. John D. Griffith of the Vanderbilt University School of Medicine testified that amphetamine production should be limited to the needs created by those conditions: "A few thousand tablets (of amphetamines) would supply the whole medical needs of the country. In fact, it would be possible for the government to make and distribute the tablets at very little cost. This way there would be no outside commercial interests involved." Like a previous suggestion that Congress impose a one cent per tablet tax on drugs subject to abuse, no action was taken on the proposal.

The very next day, Dr. John Jennings, acting director of the Food and Drug Administration (FDA), testified that amphetamines had a "limited medical use" and their usefulness in control of obesity was of "doubtful value." Dr. Dorothy Dobbs, director of the Marketed Drug Division of the FDA further stated that there was now no warning on the prescriptions to patients, but that the FDA was proposing that amphetamines be labeled indicating among other things that a user subjects himself to "extreme psychological dependence" and the possibility of "extreme personality changes . . . (and) the most severe manifestation of amphetamine intoxication is a psychosis." Dr. Dobbs thought that psychological dependence even under a physician's prescription was "quite possible."

Congressman Claude Pepper of Florida, who from this point on would be the recognized leader of the anti-amphetamine forces, testified concerning a series of hearings which his Select Committee on Crime had held in the fall of 1969 on the question of stimulant use.

Pepper's committee had surveyed medical deans and health organizations on the medical use of amphetamines. Of 53 responses, only one suggested that the drug was useful "for *early* stages of a diet program." (Dr. Sidney Cohen of NIMH estimated that 99 percent of the total legal prescriptions for amphetamines were ostensibly for dietary control.) Pepper's investigation also confirmed a high degree of laxness by the drug companies. A special agent for the BNDD testified that by impersonating a physician, he was able to get large quantities of amphetamines from two mail-order houses in New York. One company, upon receiving an order for 25,000 units, asked for further verification of medical practice. Two days after the agent declined to reply, the units arrived. Before Pepper's committee, Dr. Cohen of NIMH testified that amphetamines were a factor in trucking accidents due to their hallucinatory effects.

Dr. John D. Griffith from Vanderbilt Medical School, in his carefully documented statement on the toxicity of amphetamines, concluded "amphetamine addiction is more widespread, more incapacitating, more dangerous and socially disrupting than narcotic addiction." Considering that 8 percent of all prescriptions are for amphetamines and that the drug companies make only one-tenth of one cent a tablet, Dr. Griffith was not surprised that there was so little scrutiny by manufacturers. Only a large output would produce a large profit.

Treatment for stimulant abuse was no easier than for heroin addiction and was limited to mild tranquilization, total abstinence, and psychiatric therapy. But heroin has not been the subject of years of positive public "education" programs nor has it been widely prescribed by physicians or lawfully produced. A health specialist from the University of Utah pointed out that the industry's propaganda had made amphetamines "one of the major ironies of the whole field of drug abuse. We continue to insist that they are good drugs when used under medical supervision, but their greatest use turns out to be frivolous, illegal, and highly destructive to the user. People who are working in the field of drug abuse are finding it most difficult to control the problem, partly because they have the reputation of being legal and good drugs."

The thrust of Pepper's presentation was not obvious from the questioning that followed, because the subcommittee discussions skirted the issue. Pepper's impact could be felt in the subsequent testimony of the executive director of the National Association of Boards of Pharmacy. The NABP objected to the use of the word "dangerous" in the bill's title because it "does little to enhance the legal acts of the physician and pharmacist in diagnosing and dispensing this type of medication." (The Controlled Dangerous Substances Act would later become the Comprehensive Drug Abuse Prevention and Control Act of 1970.)

As in the Senate hearings, Ingersoll of the BNDD returned for a second appearance and, this time, he was the last witness. Ingersoll stated that he wished "to place . . . in their proper perspective" some "of the apparent controversies" which arose in the course of testimony. A substantial controversy had arisen over amphetamines, but there was not a single word on that subject in Ingersoll's prepared statement. Later, he did admit that there was an "overproduction" of amphetamines and estimated that 75 percent to 90 percent of the amphetamines found in illicit traffic came from the American drug companies.

Several drug companies chose to append written statements rather than testifying.

Abbott Laboratories stated that it "basically" supported the administration bills and argued that because fat people had higher mortality rates than others, amphetimines were important to the public welfare, ignoring the charge that amphetamines were not useful in controlling weight. Abbott then argued that because their products were in a sustained-release tablet, they were "of little interest to abusers," suggesting that "meth" tablets per se cannot be abused and ignoring the fact that they can be easily diluted.

Eli Lilly & Co. also endorsed "many of the concepts" in the president's proposals. They as well had "participated in a number of conferences sponsored by the (BNDD) and . . . joined in both formal and informal discussions with the Bureau personnel regarding" the bill. Hoffman-LaRoche had surely watched, with alarm, the Senate's inclusion of Librium and Valium in Schedule III. They were now willing to accept all the controls applying to Schedule III drugs, including the requirements of record-keeping, inventory, prescription limits, and registration as long as their "minor tranquilizers" were not grouped with amphetamines. Perhaps, the company suggested, a separate schedule between III and IV was the answer. The crucial point was that they did not want the negative association with speed, and they quoted a physician to clarify this: "If in the minds of my patients a drug which I prescribe for them has been listed or branded by the government in the same category as 'goofballs' and 'pep pills' it would interfere with my ability to prescribe . . . and could create a mental obstacle to their . . . taking the drug at all."

When the bill was reported out of committee to the House, the amphetamine family was in Schedule III, and Hoffman-LaRoche's "minor tranquilizers" remained free from control.

DEBATE IN THE HOUSE—ROUND I

On September 23, 1970, the House moved into Committee of the Whole for opening speeches on the administration bill now known as HR 18583. The following day, the anti-amphetamine forces led by Congressman Pepper carried their arguments onto the floor of the House by way of an amendment transfering the amphetamine family from Schedule III into Schedule II. If successful, amphetamines would be subject to stricter import and export controls, higher penalties for illegal sale and possession, and the possibility that the attorney general could impose quotas on production and distribution. (In Schedule III, amphetamines were exempt from quotas entirely.) Also, if placed in Schedule II, the prescriptions could be filled only once. Pepper was convinced from previous experience that until quotas were established by law the drug industry would not voluntarily restrict production.

Now the lines were clearly drawn. The House hearings had provided considerable testimony to the effect that massive amphetamine production coupled with illegal diversion posed a major threat to the public health. No congressman would argue that this was not the case. The House would instead divide between those who faithfully served the administration and the drug industry and those who argued that Congress must act or no action could be expected. The industry representatives dodged the merits of the opposition's arguments, contending that a floor amendment was inappropriate for such "far reaching" decisions.

"Legislating on the floor . . . concerning very technical and scientific matters," said subcommittee member Tim Lee Carter of Kentucky, "can cause a great deal of trouble. It can open a Pandora's box" and the amendment which affected 6,100 drugs "would be disastrous to many companies throughout the land."

Paul G. Rogers of Florida (another subcommittee member) stated that the bill's provisions were based on expert scientific and law enforcement advice and that the "whole process of manufacture and distribution had been tightened up." Robert McClory of Illinois, though not a member of the subcommittee, revealed the source of his opposition to the amendment:

> Frankly . . . there are large pharmaceutical manufacturing interests centered in my congressional district. . . . I am proud to say that the well-known firms of Abbott Laboratories and Baxter Laboratories have large plants in my (district). It is my expectation that C.D. Searl & Co. may soon establish a large part of its organization (there). Last Saturday, the American Hospital Supply Co. dedicated its new building complex in Lake County . . . where its principal research and related operations will be conducted.

Control of drug abuse, continued McClory, should not be accomplished at the cost of imposing "undue burdens or (by taking) punitive or economically unfair steps adversely affecting the highly successful and extremely valuable pharmaceutical industries which contribute so much to the health and welfare of mankind."

Not everyone was as honest as McClory. A parent committee member, William L. Springer of Illinois, thought the dispute was basically between Pepper's special committee on crime and the subcommittee on health and medicine chaired by John Jarman of Oklahoma. Thus phrased, the latter was simply more credible than the former. "There is no problem here of economics having to do with any drug industry."

But economics had everything to do with the issue according to Representative Jerome R. Waldie of California: "The only opposition to this amendment that has come across my desk has come from the manufacturers of amphetamines." He reasoned that since the House was always ready to combat crime in the streets, a "crime that involved a corporation and its profits" logically merits equal attention. Waldie concluded that the administration's decision "to favor the profits (of the industry) over the children is a cruel decision, the consequences of which will be suffered by thousands of our young people." Pepper and his supporters had compiled and introduced considerable evidence on scientific and medical opinions on the use and abuse of amphetamines. It was now fully apparent that the evidence would be ignored because of purely economic and political considerations. In the closing minutes of debate, Congressman Robert Giaimo of Connecticut, who sat on neither committee, recognized the real issue: "Why should we allow the legitimate drug manufacturers to indirectly supply the (sic) organized crime and pushers by producing more drugs than are necessary? When profits are made while people suffer, what difference does it make where the profits go?"

Pepper's amendment was then defeated by a voice vote. The bill passed by a vote of 341 to 6. The amphetamine industry had won in the House. In two days of debate, Librium and Valium went unmentioned and remained uncontrolled.

DEBATE IN THE SENATE—ROUND II

Two weeks after the House passed HR 18583, the Senate began consideration of the House bill. (The Senate bill, passed eight months before, continued to languish in a House committee.) On October 7, 1970, Senator Thomas Eagleton of Missouri moved to amend HR 18583 to place amphetamines in Schedule II. Although he reiterated the arguments used by Pepper in the House, Eagleton stated that his interest in the amendment was not solely motivated by the abuse by speed freaks. If the amendment carried, it would "also cut back on abuse by the weight-conscious housewife, the weary long-haul truck driver, and the young student trying to study all night for his exams."

The industry strategy from the beginning was to center congressional outrage on the small minority of persons who injected large doses of diluted amphetamines into their veins. By encouraging this emphasis, the drug companies had to face questioning about illicit diversion to the "speed community," but they were able to successfully avoid any rigorous scrutiny of the much larger problem of lawful abuse. The effort had its success. Senator Thomas J. McIntyre of New Hampshire, while noting the general abuse of the drugs, stated that the real abuse resulted from large doses either being swallowed, snorted, or injected.

Senator Roman Hruska of Nebraska was not surprisingly the administration and industry spokesman. He echoed the arguments that had been used successfully in the House: The amendment seeks to transfer between 4,000 and 6,000 products of the amphetamine family; "some of them are very dangerous" but the bill provides a mechanism for administrative reclassification; administration and "HEW experts" support the present classification and oppose the amendment; and, finally, the Senate should defer to the executive where a complete study is promised.

It would take three to five years to move a drug into Schedule II by administrative action, responded Eagleton. Meanwhile amphetamines would continue to be "sold with reckless abandon to the public detriment." Rather than placing the burden on the government, Eagleton argued that amphetamines should be classed in Schedule II and those who "are making money out of the misery of many individuals" should carry the burden to downgrade the classification.

Following Eagleton's statement, an unexpected endorsement came from the man who had steered two drug control bills through the Senate in five years. Senator Dodd stated that Eagleton had made "a good case for the amendment." Senator John Pastore was sufficiently astonished to ask Dodd pointedly whether he favored the amendment. Dodd unequivocally affirmed his support. Dodd's endorsement was clearly a turning point in the Senate debate. Hruska's plea that the Senate should defer to the "superior knowledge" of the attorney general, HEW, and BNDD was met with Dodd's response that, if amphetamines were found not to be harmful, the attorney general could easily move them back into Schedule III. In Schedule II, Dodd continued, "only the big powerful manufacturers of these pills may find a reduction in their profits. The people will not be harmed." With that, the debate was over and the amendment carried by a vote of 40 in favor, 16 against and 44 not voting.

Dodd may have been roused by the House's failure, without debate, to subject Librium and Valium to controls which he had supported from the beginning. Prior to Eagleton's amendment, Dodd had moved to place these depressants in Schedule IV. In that dispute, Dodd knew that economics was the source of the opposition: "It is clearly evident ... that (the industry) objections to the inclusion of Librium and Valium are not so much based on sound medical practice as they are on the slippery surface of unethical profits." Hoffman-LaRoche annually reaped 40 million dollars in profits—"a tidy sum which (they have) done a great deal to protect." Senator Dodd went on to say that Hoffman-LaRoche reportedly paid a Washington law firm three times the annual budget of the Senate subcommittee staff to assure that their drugs would remain uncontrolled. "No wonder," exclaimed Dodd, "that the Senate first, and then the House, was overrun by Hoffman-LaRoche lobbyists," despite convincing evidence that they were connected with suicides and attempted suicides and were diverted in large amounts into illicit channels.

By voice vote Hoffman-LaRoche's "minor tranquilizers" were

brought within the control provisions of Schedule IV. Even Senator Hruska stated that he did not oppose this amendment, and that it was "very appropriate" that it be adopted so that a "discussion of it and decision upon it (be) made in the conference."

The fate of the minor tranquilizers and the amphetamine family would now be decided by the conferees of the two houses.

IN CONFERENCE

The conferees from the Senate were fairly equally divided on the issue of amphetamine classification. Of the eleven Senate managers, at least six were in favor of the transfer to Schedule II. The remaining five supported the administration position. Although Eagleton was not appointed, Dodd and Harold Hughes would represent his position. Hruska and Strom Thurmond, both of whom had spoken against the amendment, would act as administration spokesmen.

On October 8, 1970, before the House appointed its conferees, Pepper rose to remind his colleagues that the Senate had reclassified amphetamines. Although he stated that he favored an instruction to the conferees to support the amendment, he inexplicably declined to so move. Instead, Pepper asked the conferees "to view this matter as sympathetically as they think the facts and the evidence they have before them will permit." Congressman Rogers, an outspoken opponent of the Pepper amendment, promised "sympathetic understanding" for the position of the minority.

Indeed, the minority would have to be content with that and little else. All seven House managers were members of the parent committee, and four were members of the originating subcommittee. Of the seven, only one would match support with "sympathetic understanding." The other six were not only against Schedule II classification, but they had led the opposition to it in floor debate: Jarman, Rogers, Carter, Staggers, and Nelsen. Congressman Springer, who had declared in debate that economics had nothing to do with this issue, completed the House representation. Not a single member of Pepper's Select Committee on Crime was appointed as a conferee. On the question of reclassification, the pharmaceutical industry would be well represented.

Hoffman-LaRoche, as well, was undoubtedly comforted by the presence of the four House subcommittee conferees: The subcommittee had never made any attempt to include Valium and Librium in the bill. On that question, it is fair to say that the Senate managers were divided. The administration continued to support no controls for these depressants.

At dispute were six substantive Senate amendments to the House bill: Three concerned amphetamines, Librium, and Valium; one required an annual report to Congress on advisory councils; the fifth lessened the penalty for persons who gratuitously distributed a small amount of marijuana; and the sixth, introduced by Senator Hughes, altered the thrust of the bill and placed greater emphasis on drug education, research, rehabilitation, and training. To support these new programs, the Senate had appropriated $26 million more than the House.

The House, officially, opposed all of the Senate amendments.

From the final compromises, it is apparent that the Senate liberals expended much of their energy on behalf of the Hughes amendment. Although the Senate's proposed educational effort was largely gutted in favor of the original House version, an additional $25 million was appropriated. The bill would also now require the inclusion in state public health plans of "comprehensive programs" to combat drug abuse, and the scope of grants for addicts and drug-dependent persons was increased. The House then accepted the amendments on annual reports and the possession charge for gratuitous marijuana distributors.

The administration and industry representative gave but an inch on the amphetamine amendment: Only the liquid injectible methamphetamines, speed, would be transferred to Schedule II. All the pills would remain in Schedule III. In the end, amphetamine abuse was restricted to the mainlining speed freak. The conference report reiterated the notion that further administrative action on amphetamines by the attorney general would be initiated. Finally, Librium and Valium would not be included in the bill. The report noted that "final administrative action" (begun in 1966) was expected "in a matter of weeks." Congress was contented to await the outcome of those proceedings.

ADOPTION OF THE CONFERENCE REPORT

Pepper and his supporters were on their feet when the agreement on amphetamines was reported to the House on October 14, 1970. Conferee Springer, faithful to the industry's tactical line, declared that the compromise is a good one because it "singles out the worst of these substances, which are the liquid injectible methamphetamines and puts them in Schedule II." If amphetamine injection warranted such attention, why, asked Congressman Charles Wiggins, were the easily diluted amphetamine and methamphetamine pills left in Schedule III? Springer responded that there had been "much discussion," yes and "some argument" over that issue, but the conferees felt it was best to leave the rest of the amphetamine family to administrative action.

Few could have been fooled by the conference agreement. The managers claimed to have taken the most dangerous and abused member of the family and subjected it to the more rigorous controls. In fact, as the minority pointed out, the compromise affected the least abused amphetamine: Lawfully manufactured "liquid meth" was sold strictly to hospitals, not in the streets, and there was no evidence of any illicit diversion. More importantly, from the perspective of the drug manufacturers, only five of the 6,000-member amphetamine family fell into this category. Indeed, liquid meth was but an insignificant part of the total methamphetamine, not to mention amphetamine, production. Pepper characterized the new provision as "virtually meaningless." It was an easy pill for the industry to swallow. The Senate accepted the report on the same day as the House.

Only Eagleton, the sponsor of the successful Senate reclassification amendment, would address the amphetamine issue. To him, the new amendment "accomplish(ed) next to nothing." The reason for the timid, limpid compromise was also obvious to Eagleton: "When the chips were down, the power of the drug companies was simply more compelling" than any appeal to the public welfare.

A week before, when Dodd had successfully classified Librium and Valium in the bill, he had remarked (in reference to the House's inaction): "Hoffman-LaRoche, at least for the moment, have reason to celebrate a singular triumph, the triumph of money over conscience. It is a triumph . . . which I hope will be shortlived."

THE BILL BECOMES LAW

Richard Nixon appropriately chose the Bureau of Narcotics and Dangerous Drugs offices for the signing of the bill on November 2, 1970. Flanked by Mitchell and Ingersoll, the president had before him substantially the same measure that had been introduced 15 months earlier. Nixon declared that America faced a major crisis of drug abuse, reaching even into the junior high schools, which constituted a "major cause of street crime." To combat this alarming rise, the president now had 300 new agents. Also, the federal government's jurisdiction was expanded: "The jurisdiction of the attorney general will go far beyond, for example, heroin. It will cover the new types of drugs, the barbiturates and amphetamines that have become so common *and are even more dangerous because of their use*" (author emphasis).

The president recognized amphetamines were "even more dangerous" than heroin, although he carefully attached the qualifier that this was a result "of their use." The implication is clear: The president viewed only the large dosage user of amphetamines as an abuser. The fact that his full statement refers only to abuse by "young people" (and not physicians, truck drivers, housewives, or businessmen) affirms the implication. The president's remarks contained no mention of the pharmaceutical industry, nor did they refer to any future review of amphetamine classification. After a final reference to the destruction that drug abuse was causing, the president signed the bill into law.

PART 2

MEASURING CRIME

In part one we saw how legislative and political processes affect the creation of definitions of crime. Obviously, how crime is defined will have a bearing on how criminal involvement is measured. If, for example, a researcher takes an *official*, or legalistic, approach to the study of crime, then the emphasis will be on the violators of the law, particularly those who have come into contact with the criminal justice system. Traditionally, statements and generalizations about the nature and extent of crime have been based on two categories of official data: (1) crimes known to the police and (2) arrests.

Official data, however, are incomplete and hence often misleading. This occurs in part because of differential law enforcement policies. If, for example, the police believe minorities to be a major crime problem, they will maintain heavy surveillance in the minority community. This, in turn, may mean that members of minority groups are overrepresented in the crime statistics. In this way, official data can promote and perpetuate myths about crime and the criminal.

Enforcement policies are not the only problems that plague crime statistics. Another is that the police do not report and record events uniformly. Still another is that victims frequently fail to report criminal acts to the police.

Because of the inadequacies of official data, other ways have been devised to measure crime. Chief among these are the *self-report* methods and the *victimization* survey.

Researchers have primarily used the self-report strategy to measure delinquency. A sample group of juveniles is given a questionnaire and asked to check, in confidence, those illegal acts they have committed and the number of times they have committed them; this information is then used to make inferences about the nature and extent of delinquent involvement. The weaknesses of the technique are that respondents are not always able to recall offenses they have com-

53

mitted; they may exaggerate their involvement; and many of the questionnaires itemize only minor offenses. Still self-reports do provide useful information on the volume of crime and delinquency. When self-report data are compared with official statistics, it becomes clear that a substantial amount of criminal and delinquent activity goes unreported.

Victimization surveys attempt to measure the extent of unrecorded crime by asking people what offenses were committed against them and whether the offenses were reported. The data collected are then compared with official statistics. Although widely used, victimization surveys also suffer from problems, such as people's inability to remember events or their reluctance to report them.

The initial selections in this part describe and evaluate these three measurement strategies, that is, official crime statistics, self-report studies, and victimization surveys. These are followed by studies that examine some of the traditional correlates of crime—such as sex and race—that have been used in explanations of crime.

MEASUREMENT AND COSTS OF CRIME

In "Problems in the Measurement of Criminal Behavior," James A. Inciardi describes how official crime statistics came into being. He also discusses some of the specific limitations that characterize crime data. A major deficiency he points to is that many areas of criminal behavior do not become a part of official statistics; this is especially true of offenses that occur within sexual, family, and business relationships. Using the example of a study made in Pueblo, Colorado, Inciardi concludes by suggesting that a reasonable estimate of criminal activity can be drawn up for a given community by using official statistics to verify data gathered in victimization surveys.

Explicit in the Inciardi piece is the idea that differential law enforcement and reporting lead to inaccuracies in official data; this too is a contention of Donald Black's "Production of Crime Rates." In particular, Black takes up the role played by the complainants of crimes. On the basis of a study of precincts in Boston, Chicago, and Washington, D.C., the author considers the effect of five conditions on a police officer's decision to file a formal report: (1) the seriousness of the crime; (2) how the complainant wishes to have the crime treated; (3) the nature of the relationship between the complainant and the offender; (4) the degree of deference shown the officer by the complainant; and (5) the race and social class of the complainant. Black concludes that all but the race of the complainant have a significant effect on whether a crime is officially recognized.

Wesley G. Skogan, in "Dimensions of the Dark Figure of Unreported Crime," examines the volume, distribution, and social consequences—on the victims and on society—of unreported crime. In the process, he discredits several popular hypotheses: that nonreporting works to the disadvantage of racial minorities; that much serious crime goes unreported; and that increases in reporting rates would necessitate the reorganization of police work. Skogan's data, based on a national survey conducted by the Census Bureau, indicate that 72 out of every 100 crimes were not recorded in official statistics. Overall, however, "the pool of unreported crime consists mainly of minor property offenses." Hence it appears that unreported crimes are less significant socially than reported ones.

"Victims of Personal Crime: An Overview," by Michael J. Hindelang, Michael R. Gottfredson, and James Garofalo, offers a closer look at patterns of victimization. These researchers summarize patterns based on Bureau of Census data gathered in Atlanta, Baltimore, Cleveland, Dallas, Denver, Newark, Portland, and St. Louis. The results indicate that personal victimization is linked to the age, sex, marital status, family income, and race of the victims. For example, the probability of victimization increases with age and decreases as income rises; males are more likely to be victimized than females; those who are married or widowed are less likely to be victimized than single, divorced, or separated people. The second part of the analysis examines the rates of victimization for each group in light of the seriousness of the event.

CORRELATES OF CRIME

In the attempt to understand why people become criminals, a host of variables has been studied. Some researchers study poverty and urbanization, while others explore the effects of racial, familial, and educational factors. The pieces in this section introduce a few of the more common themes.

"Race, Culture, and Crime" by Charles E. Silberman introduces a correlate that has traditionally been given much attention: race. Silberman contends that "race and racism continue to shape American life," whether one looks at the welfare situation, labor problems, school busing problems—or crime. He notes that blacks, compared with other low-income minority groups such as Mexican-Americans and Puerto Ricans, are much more likely to be involved in violent crimes. Thus poverty and social class, Silberman maintains, are not the culprits. Rather, the overinvolvement of blacks in violent crimes is an outgrowth of how they have been treated by American society.

Although other ethnic groups have suffered problems of acculturation, blacks must operate under the brunt of two additional burdens: "their color and their heritage of slavery." Consequently, it is hard to accept the view of some scholars that, just like other migrants from rural areas, blacks will, given time, become part of the mainstream of American life.

Sex is another variable that has been emphasized. According to Stephen A. Cernkovich and Peggy C. Giordano in "A Comparative Analysis of Male and Female Delinquency," males have traditionally occupied the theoretical and research interests of investigators. Recently, however, female crime has received greater scrutiny; this interest is due in part to the rise of the women's liberation movement. Some criminologists believe that patterns of female crime have changed significantly in recent years. Others disagree, questioning the validity of data that support claims for increased female delinquency and crime. Cernkovich and Giordano explore the issue of female crime through use of self-report data obtained from a sample of 822 students attending two midwestern urban high schools. Their results challenge many of the traditional notions about female crime. For example, and contrary to expectations, their data exhibit "considerable uniformity between males and females" in mean frequency of involvement in delinquent acts. Also, the overall male-female ratio for percent reporting involvement is much smaller than the ratio shown by official statistics. Cernkovich and Giordano conclude by arguing that solid theory must be grounded on empirical reality. Such has not been the case in the explanations of female crime. Rather, scholars, they contend, have been too eager to promote various causes of crime without actually knowing "what it is they should be explaining."

In the search for correlates of crime that can help explain it, some researchers have looked to institutional components and processes. And rather frequently attention has been directed on the family and the schools. In "The Family as Cradle of Violence," Suzanne K. Steinmetz and Murray A. Straus paint a grim portrait of intrafamily violence. They then discuss various myths and theories that have been used to explain family violence, such as the idea that violence emerges as a result of sexual repression. Implicit in their view is the notion of what can be termed *careers in violence*. Steinmetz and Straus suggest that people who have been subjected to violence are likely to resort to violence themselves.

The notion of careers or *career flows* is the focus of Kenneth Polk's "Delinquency and Adult Criminal Careers." Polk examines how various types of institutional labels may affect individuals, particularly those labels bestowed upon adolescents by *socializing* (the school) and *social control* (the juvenile court) institutions. Polk argues that failure in school, when coupled with delinquency status, may be predictive of adult crime. He offers some preliminary data on this possibility. For example, among those individuals who had both delinquent standing and low grade point averages as adolescents, 83 percent had criminal records, contrasted to 18 percent of those who had been academically successful and nondelinquent as adolescents. Polk also provides some data on the impact of social class, another familiar correlate of crime. His data offer little support for the primacy of the class variable—a finding that has recently been replicated on many fronts.

4. Problems in the Measurement of Criminal Behavior

JAMES A. INCIARDI

There have been varying conceptions on the part of legal scholars and both social and behavioral scientists as to the explicit nature and definition of crime, with the majority of approaches occupying legalistic or social orientations. Yet, since the collection of statistical data on crime has traditionally been the responsibility of alternative segments of the criminal justice system, the measurement of crime necessarily has been grounded in terms of rigid legal definitions. Within this perspective, crime would include any intentional act or omission in violation of the criminal law, and its occurrence would be reflected by the legal adjudication of given categories of behavior. Furthermore, while "arrests" and "convictions" relate to legally defined categories, individual perceptions of "crime" are similarly based on legalistic parameters.

The measurement of criminal behavior descends from three sources of data—official criminal statistics, self-reports, and victimization surveys—all of which typically reflect standardized definitional categories of crime. It is intended here to review the development, reliability, and utility of each of these as they relate to estimating the incidence of crime.

OFFICIAL CRIMINAL STATISTICS

Historically, criminal statistics in the United States have been limited to two independent sets of data—enumerations of crimes known to the police compiled at local levels, and characteristics of offenders based on arrest, judicial, and prison records. The statistical enumerations of crimes, which have typically had the strongest influence on crime control and legislative policy, have had perhaps the longest history, dating back to the earliest days of the colonies.

The first rudimentary "criminal statistics" in this country were generally of a local nature, drawn from the records of city and town jails and district or county courts. These compilations were, at best, little more than head-counting exercises, but history does suggest that these data did influence the planning of social control mechanisms in pre-Revolutionary America. The daily reports of tavern brawls and burglaries by seamen on shore leave, accumulated by the municipal night watch in New Amsterdam, for example, were utilized to initiate legislation in 1638 which forbade the crews of vessels riding in harbor to remain on shore leave during the night time hours.[1] During the eighteenth century, a notable portion of crime data were compiled by designates of the local press, and such records clearly documented the growth and trends of crime in the towns of Boston, Newport, New York, and Charlestown.[2] The fragmentary evidence from these early periods does not allow any sophisticated analysis of crime in early America, but a review of what has endured indeed suggests that some degree of sensitivity to the need for compiling data on crime was evolving.

The organization of a formal police department in New York City on July 15, 1845 initiated one of the earliest uniform bases for the collection of criminal statistics on a regular basis. Although these data were limited to arrests, they nevertheless provided the chief of police, the Common Council, and the New York City Board of Aldermen with the relative indices of crime in the city which were necessary for police budgetary appropriations and manpower deployment. New York was only one of many American cities that had developed a program of criminal statistics during the nineteenth century. The city of Boston, for example, has issued arrest reports annually since 1849.[3] And while municipal jurisdictions such as these were compiling hard data on crime, attempts at gathering state and national crime data also had begun.

The first states to becomes involved with statistics on crime and criminals were New York, Massachusetts, and Maine, and it is probable that the stimulus for their initiative came from European scholars. These states had turned their attention to statistics almost simultaneously with the publication of Lambert-Adolphe-Jacques Quetelet's *Cherches statistiques sur le Royaume de Pays-Bas* in 1829, his *Physique sociale, ou essai sur le developpement des faculies de l'homme* in 1835, and Andre-Michel Guerry's *Essai sur la statistique morale de la France* in 1833. France was the first country in the world to give birth to criminal statistics in the modern sense, with the first volume of the *Compte general de l'administration de la justice criminelle en France* (General account of the administration of criminal justice in France) issued in 1827.[4] Both Quetelet and Guerry were quick to seize upon the records of crime newly available in their country as the raw material for an analytical exploration into the distribution of crime in society and an assessment of its significance. Quetelet's "social physics" and Guerry's "moral statistical analysis" explored the incidence of crime in relation to age, sex, profession, education, economic conditions, climate, and ethnicity. It became rapidly apparent from their calculations that the annual totals of recorded crimes and the main classes of crime remained essentially the same from year to year, and from this they suggested that the budget of crime could be calculated in advance:

> We can count in advance how many individuals will soil their hands with the blood of their fellows, how many will be swindlers, how many poisoners, almost as we can number in advance the births and deaths that will take place.... Here is a budget which we meet with a frightful regularity—it is that of prisons, chains, and the scaffold.[5]

Generally, the *state* criminal statistics were those derived from reports forwarded by states' attorneys or clerks of criminal courts to a governor, attorney general, or secretary of state. They were for a specific time period, a year or two years, and were typically incomplete.[6] In New York, the *Revised Statutes of 1829* made it the duty of the court clerks of records to enter judgment of any conviction in the transcript of the minutes they forwarded to the secretary of state.[7] The sole purpose of filing these transcripts was that they might furnish evidence of previous convictions when an old offender was committed for trial on a new charge. Similar compilations were initiated in Massachusetts in 1832, when it became the duty of the attorney general to present a report to the legislature concerning the prosecutions attended by himself and the district attorneys.[8] In 1839, the Maine legislature put into law the requirement that county attorneys report each year to the attorney general the number of persons prosecuted, the offenses involved, the results of the prosecutions, and the resulting punishments.[9]

The state *judicial* statistics, as first collected by New York, Massachusetts, and Maine, and later by other states, were generally incomplete, and as a result, of little value. A later development in state statistics were those collected on *prisoners,* beginning in 1834 with the state of Massachusetts.[10] As with the judicial statistics, these too were incomplete, intermittently collected, and of little value for planning purposes.

Although *federal* criminal statistics historically began with the census of 1880, enumerations of criminals referred to as "statistics of crime" appeared in the census volumes for the years 1850, 1860, and 1870. With few exceptions, the figures reported from 1850 through the turn of the century were prison statistics, relating to individuals found in prison on a certain day of the year or to those committed during the year preceding the census inquiries. The statistics were first collected by United States marshals, and later by the regular Bureau of Census enumerators.[11]

The uniform collection of criminal statistics on a national basis received its initial stimulus by the International Association of Chiefs of Police. At the 1927 annual meeting of the association, a "Committee on Uniform Crime Records" was appointed and commissioned to prepare a manual on "Uniform Crime Reporting" for use by police departments. Based on the efforts of the committee, on June 11, 1930 Congress authorized the Federal Bureau of Investigation (FBI) to collect and compile nationwide data on crime. Pursuant to the congressional order, the FBI assumed responsibility for directing the voluntary recording of data by police departments on standardized forms provided by the FBI and for receiving, compiling, and publishing the data received. Known as the *Uniform Crime Reports* (UCR), these figures were issued monthly at first, quarterly until 1951, semiannually through 1957, and annually since 1958.[12]

The *Uniform Crime Reports* are based on the compilations of local law enforcement agencies throughout the nation, and hence, this local activity rests at the foundation of our current national crime statistics program. Both the local and UCR reports, however, fail to reflect the full spectrum of crime in any given community. The data are typically dichotomized into "crimes known to the police" and "arrests." By definition, "crimes known to the police" include only officially reported offenses, and the unreliability of these statistics as measures of the prevalence and incidence of offense behavior has been well documented. Crime, by its very nature, is not easily measurable. It is subject to both concealment and nonreporting—concealment by victims and nonreporting by authorities—and, as a result, "crimes known to the police" are generally far short of the full volume and range of offenses.

More specifically, there are wide areas of criminal behavior that fail to become a part of official statistics. In sex and family relationships there are numerous instances in which the criminal law is often in conflict with social norms and human emotions, resulting in the concealment of homosexual relations, statutory rape, adultery, sodomy, illegal abortion, desertion, and nonsupport. In the independent professions there are unreported violations by clients and practitioners, predominantly in the area of illegal abortions and child adoption practices, fee-splitting, illegal prescription practices, falsification of claims, perjury, and conflicts of interest. Among business professionals there occur consumer fraud, fencing of stolen merchandise, concealment of income, and numerous white-collar offenses. Employees are responsible for a myriad of unreported cases of embezzlement and pilferage while customers account for untold instances of shoplifting and petty check forgery. Among public officials, businessmen, and employers there are acts of omission and commission in the form of bribes and other corruption. In addition, the so-called victimless crimes and syndicate rackets involving prostitution, drugs, gambling, and loan-sharking reflect another level of nonreporting clientele. Most importantly, these areas of nonreporting are compounded by the millions of victims of conventional crimes who do not report offenses as a result of a fear of publicity or reprisals, a lack of confidence in the police, or a desire to avoid involvement with crime control and criminal justice procedures.[13]

The other category of official data—"arrests"—is affected by an alternate set of problems. Arrests, first of all, reflect only a portion of the criminal activity in any given community. Furthermore, differential law enforcement with respect to various crimes, communities, and population groups impinges on the utility of arrest data even as gross indicators of crime density and distribution.

Finally, when "crimes known to the police" and "arrests" from local communities are nationally compiled for the UCR system, both data categories are plagued by the fact that not all law enforcement agencies report to the FBI, and among those that do, the standardized definitions of crime categories set up by the FBI are not always followed. An even more serious problem affecting the validity and reliability of the UCR data revolves around the erroneous way in which some local agencies may be compiling and distributing their data.[14]

SELF-REPORTS

Self-reported data on deviant activity have generally been confined to the area of juvenile delinquency, and a vast body of literature has emerged during the past few decades which has commented on the problems with these type of data.[15] In general, these criticisms have focused on the difficulties of sample bias and other methodological issues which might impinge on the reliability of particular findings. In spite of the difficulties which have reportedly existed in a number of these efforts, it has been concluded that self-reported data can be used to estimate the nature and extent of offense behavior of specific groups of individuals.

VICTIM SURVEY RESEARCH

In an effort to discover the extent to which crimes in all legal categories go unreported in official statistics, the President's Commission on Law Enforcement and Administration of Justice initiated the first national survey of crime victimization.[16] In 1956, the University of Chicago's National Opinion Research Center (NORC) questioned ten thousand households, asking whether any member of the household had been a victim of crime during the previous year and whether the crime had been reported. More detailed surveys of high and medium crime-rate precincts were made in Boston, Washington, and Chicago. The surveys suggested that the amount of crime in the United States was several times that reported in the *Uniform Crime Reports.* The NORC survey suggested, for example, that forcible rapes were three-and-a-half times the reported rate, burglaries three times greater, aggravated assaults and larcenies of $50 and over more than double, and robbery 50 percent greater than the reported rate. The overall number of personal injury crimes reported to NORC was almost twice the *UCR* rate and the amount of property crimes more than twice as much. For certain specific offenses the Washington survey showed from three to ten times as many crimes as the number indicated by police statistics. Even these rates were believed to understate the actual amounts of crime, partly because, as Biderman pointed out, "most incidents of victimization, even many that are 'serious' legally, are not highly salient experiences in a person's life."[17]

During January 1971, surveys were conducted in a representative sample of homes and businesses in Montgomery County, Ohio (Dayton) and Santa Clara County, California (San Jose).[18] The subject of these surveys was the extent to which citizens and businesses in the two counties had been the victims of crime in the preceding year. These surveys again suggested that the incidence of crime was significantly higher in both cities than had been apparent in official statistics. For example, when comparing these survey findings with 1970 *UCR* data for Dayton, the following selected disparities could be seen:

	Survey Data	*UCR Data*
Robbery	3,638	1,752
Burglary	34,292	6,813
Aggravated Assault	1,440	972

More recently, the preliminary results of the Law Enforcement Assistance Administration's (LEAA) survey of the incidence and characteristics of crime pointed out that unreported crime was twice as high as reported crime in eleven of thirteen cities studied.[19] The survey was conducted for LEAA by the Bureau of Census from July–October, 1972, and was based on victimization data from the previous twelve months. A portion of the findings, based on victimization rates for rape, robbery, assault, household larceny, burglary, and auto theft, indicated the following:

	Ratio of Unreported Crime to Reported Crime
Philadelphia	5.1 to 1
Denver	2.9 to 1
Los Angeles	2.9 to 1
Chicago	2.8 to 1
Detroit	2.7 to 1
Dallas	2.6 to 1
Portland	2.6 to 1
Cleveland	2.4 to 1
Atlanta	2.3 to 1
Baltimore	2.2 to 1
New York	2.1 to 1
St. Louis	1.5 to 1
Newark	1.4 to 1

In addition to providing more complete information on the extent of crime, these surveys also offered significant data on the characteristics of victims and offenders, victim-offender relationships, and the circumstances under which the offenses occurred. Furthermore, since much of this research was undertaken on an in-depth basis, reliable data were obtained on citizen attitudes and perceptions relative to the fear of crime, personal safety, police effectiveness, and the quality and functions of the criminal justice system. However, although victimization studies have consistently pointed to the nature and extent of unreported crime, little has been done in terms of testing this research technique as to its reliability for estimating the "actual" incidence of crime in any given area.

ESTIMATING THE NATURE AND EXTENT OF CRIME

Reasonable estimates of the nature and extent of crime could conceivably be compiled for a given community through the combined use of victimization data and official statistics.

• Victimization data could be collected for estimating the extent of reported and unreported crime; and
• Official statistics could be used for verifying victimization estimates.

The technique for using these two data services has been suggested by a recent victimization study undertaken in Pueblo, Colorado, and by the findings of the self-reported criminal activity studies. Traditional victimization surveys generally have addressed the extent to which crimes went unreported, but rarely have used these data to estimate the actual incidence of crime in a given community. The study of criminal victimization in Pueblo went beyond the traditional methods to accomplish this specific task.[20]

The survey was accomplished by means of a strategy designed uniquely for Pueblo. A total of 1,800 households were drawn for study (17.2 percent of all Pueblo households), and these were selected in a manner that would insure the statistical reliability of the findings when projected to the total population of the city. All persons in each of these 1,800 households who had been victims of crime during the preceding twelve months (May 1973–April 1974) were personally interviewed. . . .

In an effort to determine the reliability of these projections, Pueblo Department of Police statistics on reported crimes were examined for the corresponding period of time (May 1973–April 1974). An interpretation of the victimization data and the official statistics suggested that the projections reflected a high degree of accuracy. There were, for example, 1,715 burglaries (residential) projected to have occurred in Pueblo during the May 1973–April 1974 study period. The survey data also projected that only 58 percent (995) of these 1,715 burglaries were reported to the police, suggesting, therefore, that some 995 residential burglary reports should have appeared in police files. An analysis of the police files yielded 1,043 residential burglary cases reported during the survey period—a variation of less than 5 percent from the projected number of reports. In the case of robbery, 360 of these offenses were projected to have occurred in Pueblo during the May 1973–April 1974 study period. The survey also projected that some 58 percent of these robberies were reported to the police, suggesting that approximately 209 robberies ought to have been in the Pueblo police files. An examination of the files yielded 212 cases—a variation of only three cases. And in most other offense categories where comparable data were available, the differences between the projected reports and actual reports were only minimal.

This analysis suggests that mechanisms for the more accurate measurement of crime are within the realm of the possible, but the probability of such a technique being employed on a widespread basis seems unlikely. The costs of victim survey research are exceedingly high and far beyond the budgets of most jurisdictions. As such, it seems reasonable to assume that official criminal statistics will remain in their unreliable state until technology and social science can develop more cost-efficient methods. Furthermore, since victimization studies, regardless of their possible greater efficiency in the future, only examine the more traditional property and person offenses while neglecting white-collar criminality and other obscure crimes, the exact magnitude undoubtedly will never be known.

Notes

1. *Laws of New Netherland*, 10, 15; Recs. N. Am., I, 31.
2. *N.Y. Journal*, Nov. 8, 1737; *R.I. Gaz.*, Oct. 11, 1732; *Eve. Post*, Sept. 6, 1736; Nov. 7, 1737; *S.C. Gaz.*, Mar. 26, 1741.
3. Theodore N. Ferdinand, "The Criminal Patterns of Boston Since 1849," *American Journal of Sociology*, 73 (July 1967), pp. 84–99.
4. Leon Radzinowicz, *Ideology and Crime* (New York: Columbia University Press, 1966), p. 31.
5. L. A. J. Quetelet, "Recherches sur le Penchant au Crime aux differens Ages," report presented to the Royal Belgian Academy of Sciences (9 July 1831). It might be noted here that Quetelet and Guerry were not the first to grasp the significance of statistical data on crime. As early as 1778 Jeremy Bentham had proposed in his "A View of the Hard-Labour Bill" that periodical returns on criminals would represent "a measure of most excellent use in furnishing *data* for the legislator to work upon."
6. Louis Newton Robinson, *History and Organization of Criminal Statistics in the United States* (New York: Hart, Schaffner & Marx, 1911), p. 40.
7. *Revised Statutes of 1829*, part iv, title 6, secs, 5, 6, 7, 8.
8. *Law of 1832*, ch. 130, secs, 8 and 9.
9. *Law of 1839*, ch. 408.
10. Louis Newton Robinson, *op. cit.*, p. 90.
11. Social Science Research Council, *The Statistical History of the United States from Colonial Times to the Present* (Stanford: Fairfield Publishers, 1965), p. 215.
12. Albert Morris, *What Are the Sources of Knowledge about Crime in the U.S.A.?* Bulletin No. 15, United Prison Association of Massachusetts, November 1965.
13. See Harry Manuel Shulman, "The Measurement of Crime in the United States," *Journal of Criminal Law, Criminology and Police Science*, 57 (1966), pp. 483–492; Donald R. Cressey, "The State of Criminal Statistics," *National Probation and Parole Association Journal*, 3 (July 1957), pp. 230–241; Ronald H. Beattie, "Criminal Statistics in the United States—1960," *Journal of Criminal Law, Criminology and Police Science*, 51 (1960), pp. 49–65.
14. In the city of St. Petersburg, Florida, for example, data compiled by the local police are transmitted to the FBI for inclusion in the *Uniform Crime Reports*, and to the Florida State Department of Law Enforcement for inclusion in *Crime in Florida*, a publication similar to the *UCR*. An inspection of the *UCR* data and the *Crime in Florida* data for 1973 reflects a high degree of consistency in the two reports. However, an overview of local data compiled by the St. Petersburg police reflects numerous significant differences.
15. For discussions of self-reported data problems, see F. J. Murphy, M. M. Shirley and H. L. Wilmer. "The Incidence of Hidden Delinquency," *Ameri-*

can Journal of Orthopsychiatry, 16(1946), pp. 686–696; James F. Short and F. I. Nye, "Extent of Unrecorded Juvenile Delinquency: Tentative Conclusions," *Journal of Criminal Law, Criminology and Police Science*, 49 (1958), pp. 296–312; Eugene Doleschal, "Hidden Crime," *Crime and Delinquency Literature*, 2 (October 1970), pp. 546–572; F. H. McClintock, "The Dark Figure," in European Committee on Crime Problems, *Collected Studies in Criminological Research*, Vol. 5. (Strasbourg: Council of Europe, 1970), pp. 2–34.

16. Philip H. Ennis, *Criminal Victimization in the United States: A Report of a National Survey* (Washington, D.C.: U.S. Government Printing Office, 1967).

17. Albert D. Biderman, "An Overview of Victim Survey Research." Paper presented at the annual meeting of the American Sociological Association, Washington, D.C., 1967.

18. U.S. Department of Justice, Law Enforcement Assistance Administration, *Crimes and Victims: A Report on the Dayton–San Jose Pilot Survey of Victimization* (Washington, D.C.: U.S. Government Printing Office, 1974).

19. *LEAA News Release*, April 1974.

20. The research in Pueblo, Colorado was supported by the Law Enforcement Assistance Administration, undertaken by Resource Planning Corporation of Washington, D.C., with project direction by the author of this essay.

5. Production of Crime Rates

DONALD BLACK

SOCIAL ORGANIZATION OF CRIME DETECTION

Detection of deviance involves (1) the discovery of deviant *acts* or behavior and (2) the linking of *persons* or groups to those acts. Types of deviance vary widely according to the extent to which either or both of these aspects of detection are probable. Some deviant acts are unlikely to be discovered, although discovery generally is equivalent to the detection of the deviant person as well. Examples are homosexual conduct and various other forms of consensual sexual deviance. Acts of burglary and auto theft, by contrast, are readily detected, but the offending persons often are not apprehended. These differential detection probabilities stem in part from the empirical patterns by which various forms of violative behavior occur in time and social space. In part they stem as well from the uneven climate of social control.

The organization of police control lodges the primary responsibility for crime detection in the citizenry rather than in the police. The uniformed patrol division, the major line unit of modern police departments, is geared to respond to citizen calls for help via a centralized radio-communications system. Apart from traffic violations, patrol officers detect comparatively little crime through their own initiative. This is all the more true of legally serious crime. Thus crime detection may be understood as a largely *reactive* process from the standpoint of the police as a control system. Far less is it a *proactive* process. Proactive operations aimed at the discovery of criminal behavior predominate in the smaller specialized units of the large police department, particularly in the vice or morals division, including the narcotics squad, and in the traffic division. Most crimes, unlike vice offenses, are not susceptible to detection by means of undercover work or the enlistment of quasi-employed informers (see Skolnick, 1966). Unlike traffic offenses, furthermore, most crimes cannot be discovered through the surveillance of public places. Since the typical criminal act occurs at a specifically unpredictable time and place, the police must rely upon citizens to involve them in the average case.

The law of privacy is another factor that presses the police toward a reactive detection system (Stinchcombe, 1963). Even without legal limitations on police detective work, however, the unpredictability of crime itself would usually render the police ignorant in the absence of citizens. Most often the citizen who calls the police is a victim of a crime who seeks justice in the role of *complainant*.

Vice control and traffic enforcement generally operate without the assistance of complainants. It appears that most proactive police work arises when there is community pressure for police action but where, routinely, there are no complainants involved as victims in the situations of violative behavior in question. In the average case proactive detection involves a simultaneous detection of the violative act and of the violative person. Proactively produced crime rates, therefore, are nearly always rates of arrest rather than rates of known criminal acts. In effect the proactive clearance rate is 100 percent. Crime rates that are produced in proactive police operations, such as rates of arrest for prostitution, gambling, homosexual behavior, and narcotics violation, directly correlate with police manpower allocation. Until a point of total detection is reached and holding all else constant, these vice rates increase as the number of policemen assigned to vice control is increased. On the other hand, the more important variable in rates of "crimes known to the police" is the volume of complaints from citizens.

Nevertheless, rates of known crimes do not perfectly reflect the volume of citizen complaints. A complaint must be given official status in a formal written report before it can enter police statistics, and the report by no means automatically follows receipt of the complaint by the police. In the present investigation patrol officers wrote official reports in only 64 percent of the 554 crime situations where a complainant, but no suspect, was present in the field setting. The decision to give official status to a crime ordinarily is an outcome of face-to-face interaction between the police and the complainant rather than a programmed police response to a bureaucratic or legal formula. The content and contours of this interaction differentially condition the probability that an official report will be written, much as they condition, in situations where a suspect is present, the probability that an arrest will be made (Black, 1968; Black and Reiss, 1970).

Whether or not an official report is written affects not only the profile of official crime rates; it also determines whether subsequent police investigation of the crime will be undertaken at a later date. Subsequent investigation can occur only when an official report is forwarded to the detective division for further processing, which includes the possibility of an arrest of the suspect. Hence the rate of detection and sanctioning of deviant *persons* is in part contingent upon whether the detection of deviant *acts* is made official. In this respect justice demands formality in the processing of crimes. This paper considers the following conditions as they relate to the probability of an official crime report in police-complainant encounters: the legal seriousness of the alleged crime, the preference of the complainant, the relational distance between the complainant and the absentee suspect, the degree of deference the complainant extends to the police, and the race and social-class status of the complainant.

FIELD METHOD

Systematic observation of police-citizen transactions was conducted in Boston, Chicago, and Washington, D.C., during the summer of 1966. Thirty-six observers—persons with law, social science, and police administration backgrounds—recorded observations of routine encounters between uniformed patrolmen and citizens. Observers accompanied patrolmen on all work-shifts on all days of the week for seven weeks in each city. However, the times when police activity is comparatively high (evening shifts, particularly weekend evenings) were given added weight in the sample.

Police precincts were chosen as observation sites in each city. The precincts were selected so as to maximize observation in lower socioeconomic, high crime rate, racially homogeneous residential areas. This was accomplished through the selection of two precincts in Boston and Chicago and four precincts in Washington, D.C.

The data were recorded in "incident booklets," forms structurally similar to interview schedules. One booklet was used for each incident that the police were requested to handle or that they themselves noticed while on patrol. These booklets were not filled out in the presence of policemen. In fact the officers were told that our research was not concerned with police behavior but only with citizen behavior toward the police and the kinds of problems citizens make for the police. Thus the study partially utilized systematic deception.

A total of 5,713 incidents were observed and recorded. In what follows, however, the statistical base is only 554 cases, roughly one-in-ten of the total sample. These cases comprise nearly all of the police encounters with complainants in crime situations where no suspect was present in the field situation. They are drawn from the cases that originated with a citizen telephone call to the police, 76 percent of the total. Excluded are, first, encounters initiated by policemen on their own initiative (13 percent). Police-initiated encounters almost always involve a suspect or offender rather than a complainant; complainants usually must take the initiative to make themselves known to the police. Also excluded are encounters initiated by citizens who walk into a police [station] to ask for help (6 percent) or who personally flag down the police on the street (5 percent). Both of these kinds of police work have peculiar situational features and should be treated separately. The great majority of citizen calls by telephone are likewise inappropriate for the present sample. In almost one-third of the cases no citizen is present when the police arrive to handle the complaint. When a citizen is present, furthermore, the incident at issue pertains to a noncriminal matter in well over one half of the cases. Even when there is a criminal matter a suspect not infrequently is present. When a suspect is present the major official outcome possible is arrest rather than a crime report. Finally, the sample excludes cases in which two or more complainants of mixed race or social-class composition participated. It may appear that, in all, much has been eliminated. Still, perhaps surprisingly, what remains is the *majority of crime situations* that the police handle in response to citizen telephone calls for service. There is no suspect available in 77 percent of the felonies and in 51 percent of the misdemeanors that the police handle on account of a complaint by telephone. There is only a complainant. These proportions alone justify a study of police encounters with complainants. In routine police work the handling of crime is in large part the handling of complainants. Policemen see more victims than criminals.

LEGAL SERIOUSNESS OF THE CRIME

Police encounters with complainants where no suspect is present involve a disproportionately large number of felonies, the legally serious category of crime. This was true of 53 percent of the cases in the sample of 554. When a suspect is present, with or without a citizen complainant, the great majority of police encounters pertain only to misdemeanors (Black, 1968). In other words, the police arrive at the scene too late to apprehend a suspect more often in serious crime situations than in those of a relatively minor nature.[1] In police language, felonies more often are "cold." A moment's reflection upon the empirical patterns by which various crimes are committed reveals why this is so. Some of the more common felonies, such as burglary and auto theft, generally involve stealth and occur when the victim is absent; by the time the crime is discovered, the offender has departed. Other felonies such as robbery and rape have a hit-and-run character, such that the police rarely can be notified in time to make an arrest at the crime setting. Misdemeanors, by contrast, more often involve some form of "disturbance of the peace," such as disorderly conduct and drunkenness, crimes that are readily audible or visible to potential complainants and that proceed in time with comparative continuity. In short, properties of the social organization of crime make detection of felony offenders relatively difficult and detection of misdemeanor offenders relatively simple, given detection of the act.[2]

When the offender has left the scene in either felony or misdemeanor situations, however, detection and sanctioning of the offender is precluded unless an official report is written by the police. Not surprisingly, the police are more likely to write these reports in felony than in misdemeanor situations.[3] Reports were written in 72 percent of the 312 felonies, but in only 53 percent of the 242 misdemeanors. It is clear that official recognition of crimes becomes more likely as the legally defined seriousness of the crime increases. Even so, it remains noteworthy that the police officially disregard one-fourth of the felonies they handle in encounters with complainants. These are not referred to the detective division for investigation; offenders in these cases thus unknowingly receive a pardon of sorts.

Now the reader might protest an analysis that treats as crimes some incidents that the police themselves do not handle as crimes. How can we call an event a law violation when a legal official ignores that very event? This is a definitional problem that plagues a sociology of law as well as a sociology of deviance and social control. How is a violation of the "law on the books" properly classified if "in practice" it is not labeled as such? It is easy enough to argue that either of these criteria, the written law or the law-in-action, should alone define the violative behavior in question. No answer to this dilemma is true or false. It is of course all a matter of the usefulness of one definition or another. Here a major aim is to learn something about the process by which the police select for official attention certain technically illegal acts while they bypass others. If we classify as crimes only those acts the police officially recognize as crimes, then what shall we call the remainder? Surely that remainder should be conceptually distinguished from acts that are technically legal and which carry no sanctions. For that reason, the present analysis operates with two working categories, crimes and officially recognized crimes, along with an implicit residual category of non-crimes. Crime differs from other behavior by dint of a probability, the probability that it will be sanctioned in a particular administrative system if it is detected. The written law usually—though not always—is a good index of whether that probability exists. "Dead letter" illegal acts, i.e., those virtually never sanctioned, are not classified as crimes in this analysis. Crime as a *general category* consists in a probability of sanction; official recognition in the form of a crime report is one factor that escalates that probability for a *specific instance* of crime. It is worthwhile to have a vocabulary that distinguishes *between crimes* on the basis of how the police relate to them. Without a vocabulary of this kind police invocation of the law in the face of a law violation cannot be treated as empirically or theoretically problematic. Rather, invocation of the law would *define* a law violation and would thereby deprive sociology of an intriguing problem for analysis. Indeed, if we define a law violation *with* invocation of the law, we are left with the peculiar analytical premise that enforcement of the law is total or universal. We would definitionally destroy the possibility of police leniency or even of police discretion in law enforcement.

THE COMPLAINANT'S PREFERENCE

Upon arriving at a field setting, the police typically have very little information about what they are going to find. At best they have the crude label assigned to the incident by a dispatcher at the communications center. Over the police radio they hear such descriptions as "a B and E" (breaking and/or entering), "family trouble," "somebody screaming," "a theft report," "a man down" (person lying in a public place, cause unknown), "outside ringer" (burglar-alarm ringing), "the boys" (trouble with juveniles), and suchlike. Not infrequently these labels prove to be inaccurate. In any case policemen find themselves highly dependent upon citizens to assist them in structuring situational reality. Complainants, biased though they may be, serve the police as primary agents of situational intelligence.

What is more, complainants not infrequently go beyond the role of providing information by seeking to influence the direction of police action. When a suspect is present the complainant may pressure the police to make an arrest or to be lenient. When there is no available suspect, it becomes a matter of whether the complainant prefers that the crime be handled as an official matter or whether he wants it handled informally. Of course many complainants are quite passive and remain behaviorally neutral. During the observation period the complainant's preference was unclear in 40 percent of the encounters involving a "cold" felony or misdemeanor. There were 184 felony situations in which the complainant expressed a clear preference; 78 percent lobbied for official action. Of the 145 misdemeanor situations where the complainant expressed a clear preference, the proportion favoring official action was 75 percent, roughly the same proportion as that in felony situations. It seems that complainants are, behaviorally, insensitive to the legal seriousness of crimes when they seek to direct police action.

Police action displays a striking pattern of conformity with the preferences of complainants. Indeed, in not one case did the police write an official crime report when the complainant manifested a preference for informal action. This pattern seen in legal perspective is particularly interesting given that felony complainants prefer informal action nearly as frequently as misdemeanor complainants. Police conformity with those complainants who do prefer official action, however, is not so symmetrical. In felony situations the police comply by writing an official report in 84 percent of the cases, whereas when the complaint involves a misdemeanor their rate of compliance drops to 64 percent. Thus the police follow the wishes of officially-oriented complainants in the majority of encounters, but the majority is somewhat heavier when the occasion is a legally more serious matter. In the field setting proper the citizen complainant has much to say about the official recognition of crimes, though the law seemingly screens his influence.[4]

Recall that the raw inputs for the official detection rate are generated by the citizenry who call the police. At two levels, then, the operational influence of citizens gives crime rates a peculiarly democratic character. Here the servant role of the police predominates; the guardian role recedes. Since an official report is a prerequisite for further police investigation of the crime, this pattern also implies that complainants are operationally endowed with an adjudicatory power. Their observable preferences can ultimately affect probabilities of arrest and conviction. While the structure of the process is democratic in this sense, it most certainly is not universalistic. The moral standards of complainants vary to some extent across the citizen population, thereby injecting particularism into the production of outcomes. There appears a trade-off between democratic process and universalistic enforcement in police work. This is an organizational dilemma not only of the police but of the legal system at large. When the citizenry has the power to direct the invocation of law, it has the power to discriminate among law-violators. Moral diversity in the citizen population by itself assures that some discrimination of this kind will occur. This is true regardless of the intentions of individual citizens. When a legal system organizes to follow the demands of the citizenry, it must sacrifice uniformity, since the system responds only to those who call upon it while it ignores illegality that citizens choose to ignore. A legal system that strives for universalistic application of the law, by contrast, must refuse to follow the diverse whims of its atomized citizenry. Only a society of citizens homogeneous in their legal behavior could avoid this dilemma.

RELATIONAL DISTANCE

Like any other kind of behavior, criminal behavior is located within networks of social organization. One aspect of that social organization consists in the relationship existing between the criminal offender and the complainant prior to a criminal event. They may be related by blood, marriage, friendship, neighborhood, membership in the same community, or whatever. In other words, the adversarial relation that is created by a crime may itself be viewed as it is structured within a wider social frame. The findings in this section permit the conclusion that the probability of official recognition of a crime varies with the relational network in which the crime occurs.[5] The greater the relational distance between citizen adversaries, the greater is the likelihood of official recognition.

Citizen adversaries may be classified according to three levels in relational distance: (1) fellow family members, (2) friends, neighbors, or acquaintances, and (3) strangers. The vast majority of the cases fall into the "stranger" category, though some of these probably would be reclassified into one of the other relational categories if the criminal offender were detected. The complainant's first speculation generally is that a stranger committed the offense in question.

. . . When a complainant expresses a preference for official action the police comply most readily when the adversaries are strangers to one another. They are less likely to comply by writing an official crime report when the adversaries are friends, neighbors, or acquaintances, and they are least likely to give official recognition to the crime when the complainant and suspect are members of the same family. The small number of cases in the "fellow family members" category prohibits comparison between felony and misdemeanor situations. In the other relational categories this comparison reveals that the police follow the same pattern in the handling of both felonies and misdemeanors. With the relational distance between the adversaries held constant, however, the probability of an official report is higher for felony than for misdemeanor situations. The highest probability of an official response occurs when the crime is a felony and the adversaries are strangers to one another (91 percent); the lowest calculable probability is that for misdemeanors when the adversaries are related by friendship, neighborhood, or acquaintanceship (42 percent). On the other hand, it appears that relational distance can override the legal seriousness of crimes in conditioning police action, since the police are more likely to give official recognition to a misdemeanor involving strangers as adversaries (74 percent) than to a felony involving friends, neighbors, or acquaintances (62 percent). Here again, therefore, the law screens but does not direct the impact of an extra-legal element in the production of crime rates.

Beyond the importance of relational distance for an understanding of crime rates as such is another implication of these findings. Because a follow-up investigation of the crime report by the detective division may result in apprehension of the criminal offender, it is apparent that the probability of an official sanction for the offender lessens as the degree of social intimacy with his adversary—usually his victim—increases. When an offender victimizes a social intimate the police are most apt to let the event remain a private matter, regardless of the complainant's preference. A more general consequence of this pattern of police behavior is that the criminal law gives priority to the protection of strangers from strangers while it leaves vulnerable intimates to intimates. Indeed, victimizations of strangers by strangers may be comparatively more damaging to social order and hence, from a functional standpoint, require more attention from the forces of control. A victimization between intimates is capsulated by intimacy itself. Furthermore, as social networks are more intimate, it surely is more likely that informal systems of social control operate. Other forms of legal control also may become available in the more intimate social relationships. In contrast there is hardly anyone but the police to oversee relations among strangers. Seemingly the criminal law is most likely to be invoked where it is the only operable control system. The same may be said of legal control in general (see Pound, 1942; Schwartz, 1954; Nader and Metzger, 1963). Legal control melds with other aspects of social organization.

THE COMPLAINANT'S DEFERENCE

Evidence accumulates from studies of police sanctioning that the fate of suspects sometimes hangs upon the degree of deference or respect they extend to policemen in field encounters (Westley, 1953; Piliavin and Briar, 1964; Black, 1968; Black and Reiss, 1970). As a rule, the police are especially likely to sanction suspects who fail to defer to police authority whether legal grounds exist or not. Situational etiquette can weigh heavily on broader processes of social life (see Goffman,

1956 and 1963). This section offers findings showing that the complainant's deference toward the police conditions the official recognition of crime complaints.

The deference of complainants toward the police can be classified into three categories: (1) very deferential or very respectful, (2) civil, and (3) antagonistic or disrespectful. As might be expected, complainants are not often antagonistic toward policemen; it is the suspect who is more likely to be disrespectful (Black and Reiss, 1967:63–65). The number of cases of police encounters with antagonistic complainants is too few for separate analysis of felony and misdemeanor situations. When felonies and misdemeanors are combined into one statistical base, however, it becomes clear that by a large margin the probability of an official crime report is lowest when the complainant is antagonistic in the face-to-face encounter.... Less than one-third of the disrespectful complainants who prefer official action see their wishes actualized in a crime report. Because of the small number of cases this finding nevertheless should be taken as tentative. The comparison between the very deferential and the civil complainants, which is more firmly grounded, is equally striking. The police are somewhat more likely to comply with very deferential complainants than with those who are merely civil. In sum, then, the less deferential the complainant, the less likely are the police to comply with his manifest preference for official action in the form of an official crime report.[6]

... The complainant's degree of deference conditions crime-reporting in both felony and misdemeanor situations. In fact, it seems that the complainant's deference can predict official recognition as well, or even slightly better than the legal seriousness of the crime. The probability of a crime report in misdemeanor situations where the complainant is very deferential (85 percent) is as high as it is in felony situations where he is only civil toward the police (80 percent). Still, when we hold constant the complainant's deference, the legal seriousness of the incident looms to importance. In felony situations where the complainant is very respectful, the police satisfy his preference for official action in no less than 100 percent of the cases.

The findings in this section reveal that the level of citizen respect for the police in field encounters has consequences beyond those known to operate in the sanctioning of suspects. Here we see that the fate of citizens who are nominally served, as well as those who are controlled by the police, rides in part upon their etiquette. The official response to an avowed victimization in part depends upon the situational *style* in which the citizen presents his complaint to the control system. Official crime rates and the justice done through police detection of criminal offenders, therefore, reflect the politeness of victims. That sanctions are sometimes more severe for alleged offenders who are disrespectful toward the police can be understood in many ways as a possible contribution to the control function. Perhaps, for example, disrespectful offenders pose a greater threat to society, since they refuse to extend legitimacy to its legal system. Perhaps deterrence is undermined by leniency toward disrespectful suspects. Perhaps not. The point is that rationales are available for understanding this pattern as it relates to the police control function. It should be apparent that such rationales do not apply as readily to the tendency of the police to underreport the victimizations of disrespectful complainants. Surely this pattern could have only the remotest connection to deterrence of illegal behavior. Etiquette, it would seem, can belittle the criminal law.

THE COMPLAINANT'S STATUS

The literature on police work abounds in speculation but provides little observational evidence concerning the relation of social status to police outcomes. The routine policing of Negroes differs somewhat from that of whites, and the policing of blue-collar citizens differs quite massively from that of white-collar citizens. Nevertheless, there is a dearth of evidence that these differences arise from discriminatory behavior by policemen. It appears that more consequential in determining these outcomes are aggregative differences between the races and classes in the kinds of incidents the police handle along with situational factors such as those the present analysis examines (e.g., Skolnick, 1966; Black, 1968; Black and Reiss, 1970). Nevertheless, the research literature remains far too scanty to permit confident generalization on these questions.

Studies in the discretionary aspects of police work focus almost solely upon police encounters with suspects. The present sample provides an opportunity to investigate the relation between a complainant's race and social-class status and the probability that the police will give official recognition to his complaint. The tabulation limits the cases to those where the complainant expresses a preference for official action and to those where he is civil toward the police. This section concludes that the race of complainants does not independently relate to the production of official crime rates, but there is some evidence that the police give preferential treatment to white-collar complainants in felony situations.

For all crimes and social-class statuses taken together, the difference between Negroes and whites in the probability of an official crime report is slight and negligible; ... it is a bit higher for whites. . . . this probability is the same for blue-collar Negroes and blue-collar whites in felony situations, though it is comparatively higher for blue-collar Negroes in misdemeanor situations. Evidence of racial discrimination thus appears weak and inconsistent. It should nonetheless be noted that if there were consistent evidence of a race differential it is not readily clear to whom a disadvantage could be attributed. Considered from the complainant's standpoint, a higher frequency of police failure to comply with complainants of one race could be viewed as discrimination *against* that race. But police failure to write a crime report also lowers the likelihood that the offender will be subjected to the criminal process. Since we may assume that complainants more commonly are victims of offenses committed by members of their own race than by members of another race (Reiss, 1967), then disproportionate police failure to comply with complainants could be viewed as discrimination *in favor* of that race, considered from the offender's standpoint. Race differentials in arrest rates for crimes where there is an identifiable victim necessarily pose a similar dilemma of interpretation. Definitionally, there always is a conflict of legal interests between offenders and victims. Offender-victim relationships tend to be racially homogeneous. The social organization of crime therefore complicates questions of racial discrimination in law enforcement.[7]

Along social-class lines there is some evidence of discrimination against complainants and offenders. . . . in felony situations the police are somewhat more likely to comply with white-collar complainants than with those of blue-collar status. In fact an official crime report resulted from every encounter between the police and a white-collar felony complainant of either race. The probability of official recognition drops to about three-fourths for blue-collar felony complainants. There does not appear to be a clear social-class differential in misdemeanor situations, however.

Only in felony situations, then, does an inference of discrimination offer itself. In these encounters the police seem to discriminate against blue-collar complainants. Moreover, when both white-collar and blue-collar complainants report felonious offenses, we should be able to assume that the offenders characteristically are of blue-collar status. There is every reason to believe, after all, that white-collar citizens rarely commit the common felonies such as burglary, robbery, and aggravated assault. A possible exception is auto theft, a crime in which youths from white-collar families occasionally indulge. Since this study was conducted in predominantly blue-collar residential areas the assumption should be all the more warranted. It would follow that the police discriminate against blue-collar citizens who feloniously offend white-collar citizens by being comparatively lenient in the investigation of felonies committed by one blue-collar citizen against another. In this instance the legal system listens more attentively to the claims of higher-status citizens. The pattern is recorded in the crime rate.

OVERVIEW

The foregoing analysis yields a number of empirical generalizations about the production of crime rates. For the sake of convenience they may be listed as follows:

I. The police officially recognize proportionately more legally serious crimes than legally minor crimes.

II. The complainant's manifest preference for police action has a significant effect upon official crime-reporting.

III. The greater the relational distance between the complainant and the suspect, the greater is the likelihood of official recognition.

IV. The more deferential the complainant toward the police, the greater is the likelihood of official recognition of the complaint.

V. There is no evidence of racial discrimination in crime-reporting.

VI. There is some evidence that the police discriminate in favor of white-collar complainants, but this is true only in the official recognition of legally serious crime situations.

On the surface these findings have direct methodological relevance for those who would put official statistics to use as empirical data, whether to index actual crime in the population or to index actual police practices. Crime rates, as data, systematically underrepresent much crime and much police work. To learn some of the patterns by which this selection process occurs is to acquire a means of improving the utility of crime rates as data.

It should again be emphasized that these patterns of police behavior have consequences not only for official rates of detection as such; they also result in differential investigation of crimes and hence differential probabilities of arrest and conviction of criminal offenders. Thus the life chances of a criminal violator may depend upon who his victim is and how his victim presents his claim to the police. The complainant's role is appreciable in the criminal process. Surely the complainant has a central place in other legal and nonlegal control contexts as well, though there is as yet little research on the topic. Complainants are the consumers of justice. They are the prime movers of every known legal system, the human mechanisms by which legal services are routed into situations where there is a felt need for law. Complainants are the most invisible and they may be the most important social force binding the law to other aspects of social organization.

Notes

1. It is interesting to note that in ancient Roman law the offender caught in the act of theft was subject to a more serious punishment than the offender apprehended some time after detection of his theft. In the *Laws of the Twelve Tables* these were called "manifest" and "non-manifest" thefts. The same legal principle is found in the early Anglo-Saxon and other Germanic codes (Maine, 1963:366–367). It could well be that a similar pattern is found in present-day law-in-action. What is formal in one legal system may be informal in another.

2. The heavier penalties that the law provides for felonies may compensate for a loss in deterrence that could result from the relatively low rate at which felons are apprehended. Likewise, the law of arrest seemingly compensates for the social organization of crime that gives felons a head start on the police. In most jurisdictions the police need less evidence in felony than in misdemeanor situations to make a legal arrest without warrant. By a second technique, then, the legal system increases the jeopardy of felony offenders. The power of substantive law increases as procedural restrictions on legal officials are weakened. By both penalty and procedure, the law pursues the felon with a special vengeance.

3. Crime situations were classified as felonies or misdemeanors according to legal criteria. These criteria were applied to the version of the crime that prevailed in the police-citizen transaction. The observation reports required the observer to classify the incident in a detailed list of categories as well as to write a long-hand description of the incident. The felony-misdemeanor breakdown was made during the coding stage of the investigation.

The major shortcoming of this strategy is that the tabulation allows no gradations of legal seriousness within the felony and misdemeanor categories. This shortcoming was accepted in order to facilitate more elaborate statistical analysis with a minimum of attrition in the number of cases.

It should also be noted that the tabulations do not provide information pertaining to the kind of official report the police wrote for a given kind of crime situation. Occasionally, the police officially characterize the crime with a category that seems incorrect to a legally sophisticated observer. Most commonly this involves reducing the legal seriousness of the crime. However, there are cases where the officer, sometimes through sheer ignorance of the law or inattention, increases the legal seriousness of the crime. In one case, for example, a woman complained about two young men in an automobile who had made obscene remarks to her as she walked along the street near her residence. She claimed she was prepared to press charges. After leaving the scene the officer filled out an official report, classifying the incident as an "aggravated assault," the felonious level of assault. Before doing so he asked the observer for his opinion as to the proper category. The observer feigned ignorance.

4. Here two general remarks about analytical strategy seem appropriate. One is that the present approach abdicates the problematics of psychological analysis. The observational study does not provide data on the motives or

cognitions of the police or the citizens whose behavior is described. Still, findings on patterns of behavior make prediction of police behavior possible. They also offer opportunities for drawing inferences about the impact or implications of police work for social organization. Much can be learned about man's behavior in a social matrix without knowing how he experiences his behavior. The consequences of behavior, moreover, are indifferent to their mental origins.

Secondly, the strategy pursued in this analysis is not sensitive, except in the broadest terms, to the temporal dimension of police-citizen transactions. Thus, simply because the complainant's preference is treated prior to other variables does not mean that it is temporally prior to other aspects of police-citizen interaction. Like the other variables treated in this investigation, the complainant's preference is prior in time only to the final police response to the encounter.

5. Hall (1952:318) suggests that the relational distance between the victim and offender may influence the probability of *prosecution*. The present investigation, following Hall, seeks to predict social control responses from variations in relational distance. A different strategy is to predict community organization from the relationships between adversaries who enter the legal system, under the assumption that legal disputes bespeak a relative absence of informal control in the relational contexts where they arise (see Nader, 1964).

6. The findings in this section present a problem of interpretation, since no information about the police officer's behavior toward the citizen is provided apart from whether or not he wrote an official report. Therefore, nothing is known from the tabulation about whether the officer behaved in such a way as to *provoke* the citizen into one or another degree of deference. Nothing is known about the subtle exchange of cues that takes place in any instance of face-to-face interaction. Other studies of the role of deference in police work are subject to the same criticism. Here, again, no inquiry is made into the motivational dimensions of the pattern. It nevertheless should be emphasized that whatever the motivation of the complainant behavior, the motivation was not the failure of the police to write an official report. In the cities studied the complainant ordinarily did not even know whether or not an official report was written, since the police ordinarily wrote the report in the police car or at the police station after leaving the encounter with the complainant. During the encounter they recorded the relevant facts about the incident in a notebook, whether or not they intended to write an official report. As some officers say, they do this "for show" in order to lead the complainant to believe they are "doing something." Thus, in the average case, it can be assumed that the complainant's deference is not a consequence of the situational outcome. Furthermore, the observers were instructed to record only the level of citizen deference that appeared prior to the situational outcome. A separate item was provided in the observation booklet for recording the citizen's manifest level of satisfaction at the close of the encounter. It therefore remains reasonable to hold that the complainant's deference can aid in calculating the probability of an official crime report.

7. It may seem that in criminal matters the costs are slight for the complainant when the police fail to comply with his preference for official action. However, it should be remembered that crimes frequently involve an economic loss for the victim, a loss that can sometimes be recouped if and when the offender is discovered. In other cases, discovery and punishment of the

offender may net the victim nothing more than a sense of revenge or security or a sense that justice has been done—concerns that have received little attention in social science. For that matter, social scientists generally examine questions of discriminatory law enforcement *only* from the offender's standpoint. Ordinary citizens in high crime rate areas probably are more interested in questions of discrimination in police allocation of manpower for community protection.

References

Biderman, Albert D. 1967. "Surveys of population samples for estimating crime incidence." The Annals of the American Academy of Political and Social Science 374 (1967):16–33.

Black, Donald J. 1968. Police Encounters and Social Organization: An Observation Study. Unpublished Ph.D. Dissertation, Department of Sociology, University of Michigan.

Black, Donald J. and Albert J. Reiss, Jr. 1967. "Patterns of behavior in police and citizen transactions." Pp. 1–139 in President's Commission on Law Enforcement and Administration of Justice, Studies in Crime and Law Enforcement in Major Metropolitan Areas, Field Surveys III, Volume 2. Washington, D.C.: U.S. Government Printing Office.

———. 1970. "Police control of juveniles." American Sociological Review 35 (February):63–77.

Goffman, Erving. 1956. "The nature of deference and demeanor." American Anthropologist 58 (1956):473–502.

———. 1963. Behavior in Public Places: Notes on the Social Organization of Gatherings. New York: The Free Press.

Hall, Jerome. 1952. Theft, Law and Society. Indianapolis, Ind.: The Bobbs-Merrill Company. (2nd Ed.)

Maine, Henry Sumner. 1963. Ancient Law: Its Connection with the Early History of Society and Its Relation to Modern Ideas. Boston: Beacon Press. (orig. pub. 1861)

Nader, Laura. 1964. "An analysis of Zapotec Law cases." Ethnology 3 (1964):404–419.

Nader, Laura and Duane Metzger. 1963. "Conflict resolution in two Mexican communities." American Anthropologist 65 (1963):584–592.

Piliavin, Irving and Scott Briar. 1964. "Police encounters with juveniles." American Journal of Sociology 70 (1964):206–214.

Pound, Roscoe. 1942. Social Control through Law. New Haven: Yale University Press.

Reiss, Albert J., Jr. 1967. "Measurement of the nature and amount of crime." Pp. 1–183 in President's Commission on Law Enforcement and Administration of Justice, Studies in Crime and Law Enforcement in Major Metropolitan Areas, Field Surveys III, Volume 1. Washington, D.C.: U.S. Government Printing Office.

Schwartz, Barry. 1968. "The social psychology of privacy." American Journal of Sociology 73 (1968):741–752.

Schwartz, Richard D. 1954. "Social factors in the development of legal control: A case study of two Israeli settlements." Yale Law Journal 63 (1954):471–491.

Skolnick, Jerome H. 1966. Justice without Trial: Law Enforcement in Democratic Society. New York: John Wiley and Sons.

Stinchcombe, Arthur L. 1963. "Institutions of Privacy in the determination of police administrative practice." American Journal of Sociology 69 (1963):150–160.

Westley, William A. 1953. "Violence and the police." American Journal of Sociology 59 (1955):34–41.

6. Dimensions of the Dark Figure of Unreported Crime

WESLEY G. SKOGAN

A great deal of the criminal activity that goes on in the United States evades the attention of monitoring systems devised to measure its volume and distribution and to record the identity of its victims. The existence of this reservoir of unrecorded crime has a number of vexatious consequences. It limits the deterrent capability of the criminal justice system, for it shields offenders from police action. In the increasingly large number of cities which distribute police manpower and equipment in response to demands for service, it contributes to the misallocation of resources and leads to the understatement of protection due certain victims under "equal crime coverage" policies. It may help shape the police role: the selective nonrecognition of certain classes of activity in their environment may enable the police to avoid the organizational and individual innovations that would be demanded by serious confrontation of these problems. The victims of crimes who do not become "officially known" to the criminal justice system thereby also become ineligible for many of the supportive and ameliorative benefits supplied by public and private agencies. Finally, the pool of unrecorded criminal incidents shapes the "socialized" costs of crime: private insurance premiums and the ·public cost of victim compensation programs are affected by the number and character of events that remain hidden from view.

The development of new techniques for measuring crime may shed some additional light on the magnitude of problems associated with the "dark figure" of unrecorded crime. Population surveys can provide new information on one portion of the dark figure, those incidents that were not brought to the attention of the police but are later recalled in an interview. Our knowledge of criminal events is obscured by other sources of error, to be sure, but there is some reason to believe that citizen nonreporting is more important than most police nonrecording practices in determining the magnitude of official crime statistics.[1] This essay explores some of the characteristics of unreported incidents, using data from a national survey of the victims of crime. It examines the social consequences, for victims and for society, of the entry or nonentry of events into the crime-recording process. To the extent that the operation of the criminal justice system and related institutions is shaped by demands for service, the volume and character of reported and unreported crime are powerful determinants of the consequences of and responses to criminal victimization.

KNOWING ABOUT CRIME

The problem is well known: an activity which is by some criterion a crime may occur without being registered in the systems devised to count it, thus reducing the accuracy of inferences from the data. This elusive subtotal was dubbed "the dark figure of crime" by European criminologists.[2] The recognition of the threat to valid inference posed by this pool of unmeasured events has stimulated the development of new procedures for probing its dimensions and greater care by users of official crime data. It is now always necessary to refute systematically all plausible, error-based, rival interpretations of research findings based on reported crime data.

The dark figure of criminality has been examined by the use of techniques that elicit anonymous confessions of delinquency directly from offenders. These self-reporting studies generally suggest that inferences based on arrest data unduly skew the distribution of criminality in the direction of minorities and the poor.[3] While European scholars long insisted that court statistics (which "correct" police errors in construing events and making arrests) were the best measure of the true distribution of crime, observational studies of charging decisions, preliminary hearings, and plea bargaining have laid that argument to rest.[4] Field studies of patrol performance indicate the enormous impact of police organization and tactics upon arrest totals and even on the decision that a crime has occurred.[5] Finally, both proactive and reactive procedures have been developed to provide ways for the victims or witnesses of crime to register their experiences. "Heroin Hot Lines" and consumer fraud complaint offices are data-collection devices that open channels for citizen-initiated information, while victimization surveys require only the passive participation of those respondents chosen to represent their fellow citizens.

These efforts are important, for errors in the measurement of crime-related phenomena may have serious consequences: they create and conceal major social problems, and they complicate the interpretation of crime statistics and the validity of statistical inferences made from them. Errors in our knowledge of the volume and distribution of criminal incidents may considerably disguise human misery and limit our ability to understand even the most basic facts about society.

The social consequences of the failure of citizens to record their experiences may be considerable. First, failing to register criminal acts with the authorities virtually assures their perpetrators immunity from the attention of the police. While they may be harassed on general grounds or in response to other suspicions, those who prey upon individuals who will not or cannot relate their experiences to the police enjoy considerable advantages. This is well understood by criminals who victimize youths, homosexuals, minorities, or their fellow felons, and it redoubles the burden of the social and economic disadvantages that those victims already bear. While the empirical evidence on deterrence processes is mixed, it is too early to write off the pursuit of a great number (in fact, probably a numerical majority) of offenders.[6]

Those whose victimizations do not enter the system may also receive less routine protection in return. Increasingly, big-city police departments allocate manpower and equipment in response to the distribution of demands for their services. These are measured primarily by crimes known to the police, usually weighted to reflect their "seriousness" or the probability that a swift response will produce an arrest. Victimizations which are not reported to the police can attract neither future deterrent effort in the neighborhood nor event-specific responses from the criminal justice system.

Reporting practices may also shape the police mandate. The self-image of the policeman is that of a "crime fighter"; police officers see themselves as strong, masculine protectors of the weak against criminal predators.[7] In reality, a great deal of their time is spent resolving or suppressing conflicts which have little to do with this role model: assaults in bars, husbands beating their wives (and wives killing their husbands), and disputes between neighbors over land or property. In fact, a large number of behaviorally "illegal" activities take place between persons who know, live with, or are related to each other. There is growing recognition in police circles that traditional forms of police intervention into these relationships may be unproductive and that new styles of police operation may be required.[8] Police officers and police unions, on the other hand, usually resist the grafting of "social work" onto their role and struggle to define their mission in ways more congruent with their preferred self-image.

A problematic aspect of this role conflict is the extent to which differences in reporting rates reinforce one task definition or another. Reporting practices in part set the agenda for police work. If problems brought to the police reflect the universe of problems only selectively, this will have some impact upon police operations. In this case, if the pool of reported crimes is more likely to contain victimizations perpetrated by anonymous assailants, the workload facing the police will favor the perpetuation of the traditional police role; on the other hand, changes in reporting practices might divert from the pool of unreported events those calling for different kinds of skills, making new demands upon police departments.

Nonreporting may also affect the distribution of ameliorative programs designed to confer financial benefits, psychological support, or special protection for the victims of crime. For example, public and private rape crisis intervention units cannot fulfill their intended functions in the absence of information about incidents; special tactical units cannot provide protection for unknown victims or apprehend offenders who prey upon frequently victimized, nonreporting establishments. Funds for the rebuilding of public and private space to render them more "defensible," high-intensity street lighting, and other efforts to physically structure neighborhood safety may be allocated in response to measured needs.[9]

Finally, several states are implementing programs for compensation of victims of physical attacks.[10] Like private insurance programs, public victim compensation schemes (which socialize the cost of our inability to protect individuals from violence) depend upon the assertion of claims by those who suffered injury. Variations in victim-reporting practices will affect insurance premium rates and the cost to the taxpayer of public claims, as well as the distribution of individual benefits.

In short, information about the volume and distribution of criminal incidents plays an important role in shaping the response of private agencies and the state to crime. Events which do not register on social indicators—events which are not "officially known"—will evade attempts to redress their dysfunctional consequences.

THE DATA

The data employed here to probe the dimensions of unreported victimization were gathered through a national sample survey designed to measure the incidence of crimes against households and individuals in the United States. Conducted by the Bureau of the Census, the program involves continuing interviews with all residents twelve years of age and older in a rotating national panel of 60,000 households.[11] The large sample is necessary to uncover a workable number of such events as robbery and rape and to make reasonable inferences from the sample to the population. The interview schedule is designed to elicit self-reports from victims of some of the crimes which the FBI has placed on it Part I list: rape, robbery, assault, larceny, burglary, and auto theft. Homicide, a well-understood and infrequent event (and one which leaves no victim capable of reporting it), was not considered. The survey items have been subjected to an extensive series of methodological tests.[12]

Estimates of the magnitude of unreported crime are based upon respondents' recollections of their actions. After eliciting details of the incidents from their victims, interviewers inquired whether they were brought to the attention of the police. Each incident may thus be treated as "reported" or "unreported," giving us an empirical handle on events that did not become official statistics.

This measure of unreported crime is itself subject to error. In some circles it may be socially desirable to recall that one reported an event to the authorities, and this will inflate survey estimates of "crimes which should be known to the police." More important is the problem of nonrecall. Methodological tests of the victimization survey instrument indicate that certain classes of events, notably rape and assaults between friends or relatives, sometimes are not recalled even in anonymous, face-to-face interviews.[13] This survey's practice of "bounding" the visit of the interviewer with a previous visit to encourage victims to remember their experiences, asking respondents to recall only serious crimes, and requiring brief periods of recall (in the national survey, only six months) alleviates many of the methodological shortcomings of earlier victimization surveys.[14] But the "doubly dark" figure of crime which is reported neither to the police nor to an interviewer remains elusive.

VOLUME AND DISTRIBUTION OF CRIME

According to estimates projected from a national sample of victims of crime in the United States in 1973, there were more than 34 million incidents of auto theft, robbery, burglary, rape, assault, and larceny.... Most of them went unreported, the victims recollecting that less than one-third of these incidents—28 percent—were reported to the police. Even if the police did not err in classifying and processing incidents which were brought to their attention, it appears that, of every 100 crimes that actually occurred, 72 were not recorded in official statistics.

... Nonreporting varies considerably by offense type, ranging from 32 percent in incidents of auto theft to 82 percent for larceny.* Robberies and burglaries were not reported to the police in a little

---

* Limited by definition in this survey to thefts from households and individuals.

more than half the instances. Rape was not reported in 56 percent of the cases; assault, not reported in 60 percent. Larceny shows the widest gap between actual incidence and official reporting. In 1973, thefts from individuals and households constituted about 64 percent of all crime, but only about 18 percent of them found their way into police reports. How significant is this discrepancy?

SOCIAL CONSEQUENCES OF NONREPORTING

Contrary to considerable speculation about the portentous implications of unreported crime, these data indicate that the vast pool of incidents which do not come to the attention of the police does not conceal a large amount of serious crime with immediate social significance and does not further disadvantage groups in the population already burdened with other disabilities.

The first popular hypothesis is that nonreporting works to the disadvantage of racial minorities. It is often argued that the victimization experiences of blacks are less likely to be reported to the police. Traditional police-ghetto hostility, the unwillingness of many police officers to take complaints by blacks seriously, simple nonresponse by the police to calls for assistance, and outright citizen fear of any encounters with these representatives of the dominant society have all been cited as reasons for the presumed undercounting of the crime experiences of black citizens. While these data cannot speak to the organizational effectiveness of the police once complaints have been entered, they indicate clearly that race is not related in any simple way to patterns of crime reporting.

[With regard to] the distribution of reported and unreported household offenses (burglary, larceny, auto theft) across racial categories . . . nonreporting in fact is more commonly found among white victims; unreported crime is fractionally more likely to involve whites than blacks. The extremely low correlation between reporting and race (contingency coefficient = .03) indicates that this cleavage is not substantially related to the burdens and benefits attendant on crime reporting: the effect is similar across many subdivisions of crime (including personal crimes of passion and profit) and across major UCR categories; rarely does nonreporting vary by more than 2 percent across racial lines.

This lack of co-variation suggests that nonreporting does not play a major role in shaping the distribution by race of goods and services made available by governments in response to the crime problem. *Nonreporting* does not deflate the apparent need of blacks for increased police protection, and it does not guarantee greater immunity from apprehension for predators in the black community. Crime remains hidden from the authorities and thus cannot be employed to allocate squad cars or justify foot patrols, but the burden of this misallocation does not fall along racial lines. Likewise, the data suggest that victim compensation programs are unlikely to reinforce existing disparities between blacks and whites; the "eligiblity" of victims from both groups is unaffected by the distribution of officially known events.

... The pool of unreported events does not harbor a great deal of serious crime, incidents which cause substantial social harm but which remain hidden. First, unreported property crime tends to involve relatively small amounts of money.... The vast majority of unreported larcenies of this type involve small financial loss: in 84 percent of the incidents the lost merchandise was worth less than $50. Less than 7 percent of these thefts involved more than $100. It should not be surprising that in this survey, as in other victim surveys, "it wasn't worth the effort," "it was inconvenient," or "it was unimportant" are frequently volunteered excuses for nonreporting. It also should be noted that $50 is usually the lower limit for insurance claims, which may explain why the relative volume of unreported theft drops at that point.

The bulk of unreported personal crime also appears to be less serious than incidents which were brought to the attention of the police. The victims of these events are less likely to be injured, they lose less if there is a robbery or theft (and those incidents are more likely to be unsuccessful attempts), and unreported incidents are less likely than reported ones to breach the security of the victim's home.... Crimes involving weapons are much more likely to result in injury or death and to undermine the morale of the community. These effects are recognized in many states by statutes which impose harsher penalties upon felons who employ guns.... a substantial number of unreported robberies do involve the use of a weapon (about 30 percent), but that many more (by 22 percent) reported events can be counted as serious by this measure. While a significant amount of crime involving weapons continues to remain unknown to the police, incidents which come to the attention of the authorities are much more likely to be serious.

To the extent that the police role is shaped by the nature of their task, reporting practices may shape police work by determining the distribution of problems facing officers. If nonreporting reduces the proportion of domestic disturbances or other nonstranger crimes entering the criminal justice system, pressure for the adoption of crisis-intervention or dispute-settlement roles for police officers may be reduced. [The survey data] report the distribution of unreported and reported crime across the relationship between victims and their assailants. The category "stranger," in this case, includes unknown attackers and those known only "by sight." ... Differences in the distribution of reported and unreported crime were slight: 69 percent of all personal crimes which were reported to the police involved strangers, while 66 percent of unreported incidents were of the anonymous variety. Within the personal crime category, only simple rape (not involving theft) differed markedly by offender: unreported rapes were 14 percent more likely to involve nonstrangers than reported rapes. The comparable difference for personal larceny (picked pockets, purse snatchings) was only 0.8 percent. It does not appear that general increases in reporting rates would greatly affect the *distribution* of demands for radically different forms of police service, although it certainly would affect their volume.

SUMMARY AND CONCLUSIONS

It has long been argued that official statistics fail to reflect the volume of events which are by some definition a crime. A major source of this error has been attributed to the nonreporting of events to the police. While some types of criminal events are relatively fully reported (homicide, successful auto theft), for others the modal event is not brought to the attention of the authorities. In a 1973 national survey of crime victims, the reporting rate for simple larceny was only 18 percent.

There has been considerable speculation about nonreporting and its consequences for crime victims and the operation of the criminal justice system. The vast pool of unreported crime (estimated by this survey to approach 24 million incidents in 1973) could conceal a great deal of human misery, isolate deserving victims from the ameliorative activities of the state, shield dangerous criminals from official attention, and shape the operation of the criminal justice system by defining the nature of its day-to-day workload. All the pernicious consequences of nonreporting could overlay existing social cleavages, redoubling the burdens of those who already suffer disproportionately from other social evils.

While it is not possible to speak to all of these issues in detail through the analysis of survey data, figures from the 1973 victimization survey conducted by the Census Bureau suggest that general shifts in reporting rates would not greatly affect the present distribution of known crime across many social and behavioral categories. The pool of unreported crime consists mainly of minor property offenses. Unreported crimes against persons appear to be of less social significance than those which are brought to the attention of the police. The victims of unreported personal crime are much less likely to have been injured, their financial losses are small, and weapons are less likely to have been employed by the offenders. The pool of unreported incidents does not appear to conceal a disproportionate array of intra-acquaintance offenses, and changes in reporting habits may not dramatically affect the relative mix of crime-fighting and social-working demanded of the police. (However, some serious methodological problems cloud the interpretation of this aspect of the data.) Finally, across a number of crime categories, there were virtually no racial differences in the distribution of known and officially unknown incidents. Whatever the burdens of nonreporting, they do not appear to reinforce racial cleavages.

A great deal of research remains to be done on the social and individual *consequences* of nonreporting. Those who report crimes become enmeshed in stressful social and organizational processes. They must confront the police and they may face prosecutors, courts, and the hostile glares of their assailants. Given the debilitating round of appearances and continuances facing victims or witnesses in many criminal courts and the fear that threats of reprisal may generate along the way, it is important to discover whether the ultimate adjustment to their new status arrived at by the victims of crime is any happier than among those whose problems never come to the attention of the state. There is good reason to suspect that it often is not. There also have been no experimental or *post hoc* analyses of the effects of programs aimed at increasing the rate at which citizens report crimes to the police, except for the impact that fluctuation in reporting has on official crime statistics.[15] It is important that we discover the effects of media campaigns, police-community relations programs, and the implementation of victim-compensation schemes upon the rate at which the problems of particular subgroups in the population come to the attention of the police. There simply are no data upon which to estimate the temporal stability of even the simple relationships reported here.

Notes

1. Wesley G. Skogan, "Measurement Problems in Official and Survey Crime Rates," *Journal of Criminal Justice*, Spring 1975, pp. 17–31.

2. Albert D. Biderman and Albert J. Reiss, Jr., "On Exploring the 'Dark Figure' of Crime," *Annals*, November 1967, pp.1–15.

3. Richard Quinney, *The Social Reality of Crime* (Boston: Little, Brown, 1970).

4. F. H. McClintock, "The Dark Figure," in *Collected Studies in Criminological Research*, vol. 4 (Strasbourg, France: Council of Europe, 1970). pp. 7–34.

5. Donald M. McIntyre, "A Study of Judicial Dominance of the Charging Process," *Journal of Criminal Law, Criminology and Police Science*, December 1968, pp. 463–90; Abraham Blumberg, *Criminal Justice* (Chicago: Quadrangle Books, 1967); Albert J. Reiss, Jr., *The Police and the Public* (New Haven: Yale University Press, 1971); Donald J. Black, "Production of Crime Rates," *American Sociological Review*, August 1970, pp. 733–48.

6. George E. Antunes and A. Lee Hunt, "The Impact of Certainty and Severity on Levels of Crime in American States: An Extended Analysis," *Journal of Criminal Law and Criminology*, December 1973, pp. 486–93; Harold Votey and Llad Phillips, "An Economic Analysis of the Deterrent Effect of Law Enforcement on Criminal Activity," *Journal of Criminal Law, Criminology and Police Science*, September 1972, pp. 335–42.

7. Arthur Niederhoffer, *Behind the Shield: The Police in Urban Society* (New York: Doubleday, 1967).

8. Raymond Parnas, "Police Discretion and Diversion of Incidents of Intra-Family Violence," *Law and Contemporary Problems*, Autumn 1971, pp. 539–65.

9. Oscar Newman, *Defensible Space: Crime Prevention through Urban Design* (New York: Praeger, 1974).

10. Herbert Edelhertz and Gilbert Geis, *Public Compensation to Victims of Crime* (New York: Praeger, 1974).

11. Official findings from the National Survey are reported in *Criminal Victimization in the United States: 1973 Advance Report* (Washington, D.C.: National Criminal Justice Information and Statistics Service, Law Enforcement Assistance Administration, May 1975).

12. U.S. Dept. of Justice, Law Enforcement Assistance Administration, National Institute of Law Enforcement and Criminal Justice, Statistics Division, *San Jose Methods Test of Known Crime Victims*, Statistics Technical Report No. 1, 1971.

13. *Ibid.*

14. Philip H. Ennis, *Criminal Victimization in the United States: A Report on a National Survey* (Washington, D.C.: U.S. Govt. Printing Office, 1967); Albert D. Biderman *et al.*, *Report on a Pilot Study in the District of Columbia on Victimization and Attitudes toward Law Enforcement* (Washington, D.C.: U.S. Govt. Printing Office, 1967).

15. Anne L. Schneider, "The Portland Evaluation Studies: Uses of Victimization Surveys for Evaluation and Planning," paper presented at the National Conference on Patterns of Criminal Victimization, Washington, D.C., June 1975.

7. Victims of Personal Crime: An Overview

MICHAEL J. HINDELANG
MICHAEL R. GOTTFREDSON
JAMES GAROFALO

The survey* results indicate that rates of victimization are closely linked to the characteristics of victims—especially to age, sex, marital status, family income, and race. Personal victimizations are those suffered by individual victims who, at least in some sense, come into contact with the offender. Personal victimizations include crimes that threaten or actually result in personal injury to the victim[1] (such as assault), crimes in which an offender confronts the victim and takes or attempts to take property from the victim's possession by force or threat of force, and crimes in which property is taken (including attempts) from the victim's person by stealth (such as pocket picking).

In the earlier work,* personal victimizations were analyzed using a threefold classification scheme for personal victimization. The first category, "assaultive violence without theft," includes assaults and rapes in which property theft was not attempted or completed. "Personal theft without injury" includes robberies without injury to the victim and larcenies from the person, such as pocket picking and purse snatching without force. "Assaultive violence with theft" includes robberies with injury and rape with theft or attempted theft.[2]

FAMILY INCOME AND RACE

In general, it was found that for both whites and black/others,[3] rates of personal victimization decreased as family income increased. Among whites, the rate of total personal victimization decreased from a high of 83 in the under-$3,000 category to 51 in the $7,500-to-$9,999 category but then *increased* to 59 in the $10,000-to-$14,999 category, finally decreasing gradually to 51 in the $25,000-or-more

* Michael J. Hindelang, *Criminal Victimization in Eight American Cities: A Descriptive Analysis of Common Theft and Assault* (Cambridge, Mass.: Ballinger, 1976).

category. Among black/others, the rate of total personal victimization decreased steadily from 72 in the under-$3,000 category to 49 in the $15,000-to-$24,999 category, before rising sharply to 64 in the $25,000-or-more category (Hindelang, 1976: Table 5–6).[4] Despite this up-swing in the total personal victimization rate at the highest income level of the black/others, the generally decreasing pattern in the total personal victimization rate for black/others is more consistent than is the pattern for whites.

The rate of assaultive violence without theft for whites was about one and one-half times greater than for black/others, while for personal theft without injury the rate for black/others was about one and one-half times greater than the rate for whites. These differences maintained with about the same strength even when income was controlled.[5] Furthermore, rates of assaultive violence with theft were higher for black/others than for whites, a relationship that generally held across income categories (Hindelang, 1976: Table 5–6).

In sum, within each racial group, the rate of personal victimization involving theft generally decreased as income increased—except that the rate for black/others in the highest income group showed an up-turn. For personal theft without injury in particular, black/others had higher rates than whites in each income group; in fact, black/others in the higher income groups endured personal theft without injury at rates comparable to those endured by whites in the lower income groups. On the other hand, rates of assaultive victimization not involving theft were higher for whites than black/others in each income category, and for both whites and black/others, rates of assaultive violence without theft showed a U-shaped pattern: the rate in the $7,500-to-$9,999 income group was the lowest and the rates at the income extremes were higher.

AGE

Age was strongly associated with personal victimization. . . . total personal victimization peaked in the sixteen-to-nineteen-year-old age group and declined monotonically as age increased beyond that point. . . . However, the pattern for total personal victimizations is determined almost wholly by the pattern for assaultive violence without theft; although the rate of assaultive violence without theft for those in the sixteen-to-nineteen-year-old group was 76 per 1,000, the rate in the sixty-five-or-older group was only 6 per 1,000. It might be argued that this gulf between victimization rates for the age extremes reflects, in part, the relatively minor altercations that are common among adolescents. However, because the assaultive violence without theft victimization rate in the twenty-five-to-thirty-four-year-old group, an age group well beyond adolescence, was *three* times greater than that in the fifty-to-sixty-four-year-old group and *six* times greater than that in the sixty-five-or-older group, more than simple "schoolyard" fights account for the generally decreasing rates of assaultive violence without theft as age increased.

For those under thirty-five years of age, theft without injury showed a pattern similar to, though much less exaggerated than, that of assaultive violence without theft. The rate of victimization for theft without injury increased slightly from the twelve-to-fifteen-year-old to the sixteen-to-nineteen-year-old groups and then decreased gradually with age for the next two age groups before leveling off. Assaultive violence with theft shows a similar general pattern; the rate of assaultive violence with theft victimization was about one and one-half times as great in the twenty to twenty-four age group as in the sixty-five-or-older group.

. . . Not only . . . *rates* but also . . . the *patterns* of personal victimization are strongly related to age. For the four age groups made up by those less than thirty-five years old, assaultive violence without theft was the model personal victimization suffered; about six out of ten victimizations involved assaultive violence without theft. For those in the thirty-five-to-forty-nine, fifty-to-sixty-four, and sixty-five-or-older age groups the respective percentages of total personal victimizations that involved assaultive violence without theft were 40 percent, 30 percent, and 20 percent. Although assaultive violence with theft made up a slightly greater percentage of total personal victimizations in the older age groups than in the younger age groups, theft without assault constituted a *markedly* higher proportion of total victimizations in the three older age groups (from about one-half to two-thirds) than in the four younger age groups (from about one-quarter to one-third). These data suggest, then, that for persons thirty-five years or older, personal victimization tends to be directed against the victim's property rather than the victim's person. In personal victimizations involving persons under thirty-five years of age, assaultive violence was much more likely to be an element of the victimization than it was for the personal victimization of older persons.

SEX AND MARITAL STATUS

Males in both racial groups had rates of personal victimization that were substantially greater than those of their female counterparts. Among whites, for example, the rate for males was 77 compared with a rate of 45 for females; among black/others the respective rates were 74 and 51. In general, these race-specific sex differences held for each age group except that the magnitude of the sex difference decreased with age (Hindelang, 1976: Table 5–5).

Marital status was strongly related to rates of personal victimization. Persons who were never married (90) or who were divorced or separated (90) had total personal victimization rates that were more than twice the rates found for those who were married (39) or widowed (42). These differences persisted across subcategories of total personal victimization with varying degrees of intensity. Under assaultive violence without theft, for example, those who were never married had a rate that was more than two and one-half times that found for those who were married (54 versus 20), whereas for personal theft without injury the rate for those who were never married was slightly less than twice as great as the rate for those who were married (28 versus 15). Further, when the age of the victim was controlled, these differences in victimization rates among the various categories of marital status continued to hold (Hindelang, 1976: Table 5–7).

SERIOUSNESS-WEIGHTED RATES

One limitation of examining rates of victimization in this fashion is that each victimization reported to survey interviewers is given equal weight; a minor assault and a serious assault both contribute equally to the total personal victimization rate. In order to avoid this shortcoming of using raw rates of total personal victimization, the Sellin-Wolfgang (1964) seriousness-weighting scheme was used to calculate seriousness-weighted rates of total personal victimization. Sellin and Wolfgang have developed a scaling technique designed to provide a composite seriousness score for delinquency incidents. Their seriousness scoring system takes into account: (1) the number of victims of bodily harm and the extent to which they are injured; (2) the number of victims of forcible sexual intercourse; (3) the number of victims intimidated verbally or with a weapon; (4) the number of premises unlawfully entered; (5) the number of motor vehicles stolen; and (6) the value of property stolen, damaged, or destroyed (1964: Appendix F). Each of these elements is weighted according to the nature and the extent of the injury or loss involved. For example, if a victim receives minor injuries requiring no professional medical attention, the seriousness score is one. If the victim is treated and discharged, the seriousness weight is four, and if the victim is hospitalized, the weight is seven. In the event that the victim dies, the seriousness weight is twenty-six. Similarly, seriousness weights are attached to the value of property lost; these weights range from one for losses of less than $10, to three for losses of $251–$2,000, to seven for losses in excess of $80,000.

Under the Sellin-Wolfgang scheme, each element is scored; therefore, if a rape also involves injuries requiring hospitalization and a theft of property, the seriousness score of each element is cumulated. Further, because the Sellin-Wolfgang procedure is designed to gauge the seriousness of *incidents*, the injuries and losses suffered by each victim in a given incident are summed to yield an incident score. In our application of their method, only the consequences suffered by the victim interviewed were scored, and that score was not dependent on the number of co-victims (if any). Thus, the seriousness-weighted rates (per 1,000 persons twelve years old or older) of total personal victimization were computed by summing (across victims) the seriousness score for each victimization reported, times 1,000, divided by the number of persons at risk. A comparable procedure has been illustrated by Sellin and Wolfgang (1964: Table 70) and used by Wolfgang, Figlio, and Sellin (1972: Table 5–5). The result of using this procedure is that victimizations are differentially weighted according to their estimated seriousness. . . .

As earlier results foreshadowed, the seriousness-weighted rates of total personal victimization are closely linked to age. Within each of the four race-sex groups, the rate increased from the youngest to the sixteen-to-nineteen age group and then declined monotonically for each age group thereafter.[6] . . . males had a higher seriousness-weighted rate than females; for most age groups the ratio of the male to the female rates was about 2:1 for whites and about 3:2 for black/others. Finally, . . . for both males and females under twenty years of age the rate for whites exceeded that for black/others; however, for those twenty years of age or older this pattern is reversed. . . .

The data . . . indicate that the seriousness-weighted rates of total personal victimization for black/others exceeded those for whites in each income group. Overall, the rate for the former was about one-quarter again as great as that for the latter. Within each racial group, the trend was for the seriousness-weighted rate of total personal victimization to decrease as income increased. One notable finding . . . is that the rate for black/others in the $25,000-or-more income category showed a marked upturn to 209 after having declined monotonically from 268 in the lowest income category to 165 in the second highest income category. As noted earlier, however, only 1 percent of the black/others are found in the highest income group.

What happens to the race and income findings when age is controlled? . . . For each of the three groups, within both races, there was a generally decreasing seriousness-weighted rate of victimization as income increased, except that the highest income group tended to show an upswing in the rate. One exception to the inverse relationship between income and seriousness-weighted rates of personal victimization is that black/others in the youngest age group showed a U-shaped pattern of victimization such that those in the extreme income groups had the highest seriousness-weighted rates of personal victimization. Once again, the small number of black/others in the highest income group should be noted.

The familiar inverse relationship between age and victimization held when income and race were controlled. . . . when income is controlled, whether whites or black/others had higher seriousness-weighted rates of total personal victimization is dependent on age. Among twelve-to-nineteen-year-old respondents, whites in each income category except the $25,000 or more had higher rates than black/others. For respondents who were twenty to thirty-four years of age, the racial differences were small; only for those with incomes between $7,500 and $9,999, where the rate for black/others was higher, was there a large difference. Finally, for respondents who were thirty-five years of age or older, black/others in each income category had seriousness-weighted rates of victimization that were greater than those of whites. . . . even when income is controlled, racial differences are age-contingent.

The seriousness-weighted rates of total personal victimization by marital status and age . . . are striking for their consistency. Almost without exception, there was a substantial decline in the seriousness-weighted rate of total personal victimization as age increased for each of the marital status groups. Further, generally in each age group except the youngest, those who were divorced or separated had the highest seriousness-weighted rate, followed in turn by those who were never married, those who were widowed, and finally, by those who were married.

Notes

1. Specifically excluded is murder.

2. See Hindelang (1976: ch. 4) for further details.

3. Black/others is a designation used to encompass blacks and persons of other races. About 90 percent of the persons in this group are black, and hence persons of "other" races are too few to analyze separately. According to Bureau of the Census conventions, persons of Spanish heritage are counted as white.

4. It should be noted that a relatively small proportion (1 percent) of black/others had incomes in excess of $25,000; the reliability of the estimated rate for this group is less than that of other rates reported.

5. The only reversal was for personal theft without injury in the under-$3,000 category, in which the rate for black/others was only slightly larger than the rate for whites (35 versus 31).

6. For the black/other females, the peak is in the twenty-to-twenty-four-year-old group.

References

Hindelang, Michael J. *Criminal Victimization in Eight American Cities: A Descriptive Analysis of Common Theft and Assault.* Cambridge, Mass.: Ballinger Publishing Co., 1976.

Sellin, Thorsten and Wolfgang, Marvin. *The Measurement of Delinquency.* New York: John Wiley & Sons, 1964.

Wolfgang, Marvin; Figlio, Robert; and Sellin, Thorsten. *Delinquency in a Birth Cohort.* Chicago: University of Chicago Press, 1972.

8. Race, Culture, and Crime

CHARLES E. SILBERMAN

In the end, there is no escaping the question of race and crime. To say this is to risk, almost to guarantee, giving offense; it is impossible to talk honestly about the role of race in American life without offending and angering both whites and blacks—and Hispanic browns and native American reds as well. The truth is too terrible, on all sides; and we are all too accustomed to the soothing euphemisms and inflammatory rhetoric with which the subject is cloaked.

But race and racism continue to shape American life, as they have for three and a half centuries. At its core, the urban problem is a problem of race; so is the welfare problem, the migrant and farm labor problem, the school busing problem—and, to a degree that few have been willing to acknowledge openly, the crime problem. The uncomfortable fact is that black offenders account for a disproportionate number of the crimes that evoke the most fear. Whites of good will have shied away from acknowledging this fact for fear of hurting black sensibilities, and both they and blacks have avoided talking about the problem lest they provide ammunition to bigots.

To the extent to which they do talk about black crime, liberals of both races generally attribute it to the wrenching poverty in which so many black Americans live. In 1976, blacks comprised 11.5 percent of the American population, but 31.3 percent of those officially classified as poor.* Since most street criminals are drawn from the ranks of the poor, it would be surprising if blacks did not turn to theft more often than do whites. In fact, the rate of property crime is just about what one would expect from the poverty statistics: in 1976, blacks comprised 31 percent of the people arrested for the three property crimes (burglary, larceny-theft, and auto theft) in the FBI's Crime Index.

It is violent crime, however, that evokes the most fear—and blacks commit more violent crimes than one would expect from the income statistics alone. As we have seen, robbery is the prototypical street

---

* Each year, the U.S. Bureau of the Census estimates the cash income needed to provide a minimally decent standard of living for unattached individuals and for families of various sizes; all those with incomes below this level are classified as poor. In 1976, the poverty threshold for a non-farm family of four people was $5,815.

crime, involving both violence (or the threat of violence) and theft. Injury is frequent—one robbery victim in three is injured nowadays—and robbery always has been a crime committed predominantly by strangers. It is also preeminently a black offense: in 1976, 59 percent of those arrested for robbery were black, and black offenders account for nearly three-quarters of the increase in robbery arrests since 1960. Black offenders are disproportionately involved in other violent crimes as well; in 1976, more than half those arrested for murder, nearly half those arrested for rape, and two-fifths of those arrested for aggravated assault were black.*

It is essential that we understand why black offenders are responsible for so much violent crime. The explanation does not lie in the genes; as Mark Twain once observed, "there is no distinctly native American criminal class except Congress," which has few black members. Black crime is rooted in the nature of the black experience in this country—an experience that differs from that of other ethnic groups. To be poor and black is different from being poor and Puerto Rican, or poor and Chicano, or poor and a member of any other ethnic group.

Not the least of these differences involves ethnically distinctive patterns of crime. New York City, with its large numbers of poor black and Hispanic residents, provides an interesting case in point. The two minority groups are roughly comparable in size: blacks comprise a little more than 20 percent of the city's population; Hispanics (mostly Puerto Ricans, but with a growing number of immigrants from Cuba, the Dominican Republic, Colombia, Ecuador, and other Latin-American countries), between 15 and 20 percent. (Since no one knows how many illegal immigrants from Latin America there are in New York, the exact size of the city's Hispanic population is a matter of considerable dispute; some estimates run as high as 30 percent.)

As a group, New York's Puerto Ricans are poorer than its blacks. The median family income among Puerto Ricans is 20 percent below the black median, and the proportion of families officially classified as poor is half again as high. Puerto Rican New Yorkers have less education than blacks, and a larger proportion hold menial jobs.[1] To the degree to which it exists as a distinctive entity, lower-class culture encompasses Puerto Ricans and other Hispanics, as well as blacks; the anthropologist Oscar Lewis coined the term "culture of poverty" to

* It is quite possible, even probable, that because of race prejudice police are more likely to arrest blacks than whites for minor offenses such as drunkenness, shoplifting, or disturbing the peace. It is highly unlikely, however, that discriminatory behavior on the part of police can account for much of the disparity between black and white arrest rates for homicide and robbery.

describe the lower-class Mexican and Puerto Rican families he had studied.

If violence were a simple function of poverty and social class, therefore, one would expect as much violent crime among Puerto Rican and other Hispanic residents of New York as among black residents. In fact, the rates are strikingly different. According to an analysis of police statistics by David Burnham of *The New York Times,* 63 percent of the people arrested for violent crimes in the period 1970–72 were black, and only 15.3 percent were Hispanic.* Relative to population, blacks were arrested for a violent crime more than three times as often as were Hispanics, and for robbery, nearly four and one half times as often. Although the disparities vary from crime to crime, they remain consistently large:

Crime	% Black	% Hispanic	Disparity between Black and Hispanic Crime, Relative to Population
Homicide	59	25	1.8 to 1
Robbery	69	12	4.4 to 1
Felonious assault	56	14	3 to 1
Forcible rape	58.5	16.6	2.7 to 1

The same picture emerges from a profile of the New York State prison population. Of a random sample of felons sentenced to a state prison in 1973, two-thirds of them for a violent crime, 58.3 percent were black and 15.3 percent Puerto Rican; relative to population, three times as many blacks are incarcerated.[2]

There are similar, and equally striking, differences between the criminal activity of blacks and of Mexican-Americans, the second-largest minority group in the country. In 1976, according to Census Bureau estimates, there were 6,590,000 people of Mexican origin in the United States, nearly 85 percent of them living in the five southwestern states of Arizona, California, Colorado, New Mexico, and

---

* Most of the usual objections to the use of arrest statistics as an index of criminal activity disappear when we compare black and Hispanic arrest rates, since members of both groups are the objects of prejudice and discrimination. It would be hard to convince a Puerto Rican New Yorker that the police treat Puerto Ricans more deferentially than they treat blacks. It would be even harder to persuade Mexican-Americans in the Southwest that they receive preferential treatment from the police; as a bitter joke among Chicanos in southern Texas has it, members of the feared and hated Texas Rangers all have Mexican blood—"on their boots."

Texas; the Census estimate almost certainly is on the low side.* As a group, Mexican-Americans are only marginally better off than black Americans; nationwide, 28.6 percent of the former were living below the official poverty threshold in 1975, compared to 31.1 percent of the latter.

In Texas, Mexican-Americans (18.4 percent of the population) are about as poor as blacks (12.5 percent of the population); yet 40 percent of the felons committed to state prison in 1973 were black, and 14.2 percent were Chicano. Relative to population, four times as many blacks as Chicanos were committed to prison for a felony. In San Antonio, a south Texas city that is 52.1 percent Mexican-American and 7.6 percent black, blacks account for 44 percent of the robbery convictions, Mexican-Americans for 40 percent; blacks account for 20 percent and Chicanos for 62 percent of the burglary convictions. Relative to population, blacks are convicted 7.5 times as often as Chicanos for robbery, and more than twice as often for burglary.

More detailed information is available for San Diego, a large city that is 7.6 percent black and 12.7 percent Mexican-American. (San Diego was one of the few cities whose police departments willingly supplied arrest data broken down by ethnicity, as well as by race. The FBI does not ask for such data, and most departments pretended that they do not collect it—hence I had to supplement arrest statistics with data on prison admissions.) Below are the arrest rates for the years 1971 to 1973; the last column shows the disparity between black and Chicano arrest rates, relative to population.

The same pattern shows up in statewide data on first admissions to the California Youth Authority, to which offenders under the age of twenty-one are committed for incarceration. The table below shows

---

* There is uncertainty, and heated controversy, over just how many Mexican-Americans and other Hispanic Americans there are in the United States; it is only in the last several years, in response to pressure from Mexican-American organizations, that the Census Bureau and other federal agencies began to view Hispanic Americans as ethnic groups worth studying with care. Illegal immigration makes it difficult to get a precise count of the number of Mexican-Americans. The enumeration problem has been compounded by the fact that there is no single term to describe Americans of Mexican ancestry that is acceptable to all segments of that community—no term that does not evoke pride in some and anger in others. The divisions are partly (but not wholly) generational: younger people tend to prefer "Chicano," which older people often consider demeaning. There are regional differences as well. In New Mexico and Colorado, and to a lesser degree in Arizona, many Hispanic Americans dislike "Mexican-American" almost as much as "Chicano"; they consider themselves descendants of the Conquistadors and call themselves "Hispanic," "Hispanos," or "Spanish-American"—a practice that those who call themselves Chicanos consider an affectation at best, evidence of self-hatred at worst. (To confuse the matter still more, some people prefer "Mexican" or "Mexicano.") Because there is no universally accepted term, I will alternate among Mexican-American, Chicano, and Hispanic, where possible using the term that is most appropriate for the particular subgroup being described.

San Diego Arrests, 1971–73

Offense	% Black	% Mexican-American	Disparity, Relative to Population
Homicide	46.9	11.6	7 to 1
Forcible rape	39.9	14.3	4.6 to 1
Robbery	53.4	11.4	7.8 to 1
Felonious assault	38.5	15.0	4.2 to 1
Burglary	29.2	13.8	3.5 to 1
Theft (grand and petty)	18.6	12.1	2.6 to 1

the proportions of Mexican-Americans and blacks committed to the Youth Authority for various crimes in the fiscal year 1973–74; as in the San Diego table, the last column shows the ratio of black to Mexican-American offenses, relative to population.

Offense	% Black	% Mexican-American	Disparity, Relative to Population
Homicide	55.3	18.4	4.9 to 1
Sex offenses	39	32	2 to 1
Robbery	49.9	12.3	6.6 to 1
Assault	35.4	30.1	1.9 to 1
Burglary	35.9	14.4	4.1 to 1
Auto theft	21.4	20.4	1.7 to 1
Narcotics	11.6	23.7	.8 to 1

Much the same picture obtains for commitments to the Department of Corrections, which receives offenders twenty-one years of age and older; relative to population, three times as many black felons as Mexican-Americans were committed to the Department in 1973.

The pattern cuts across states as well as age groups.

• In Arizona, the number of blacks in prison at the end of 1973 was five times as large, relative to population, as the number of Mexican-Americans.

• Relative to population, 3.4 times as many blacks as Chicanos were in the Utah state prison for the first time in 1972, and more than five times as many were in prison for the second time.

• In Colorado, in 1972, nearly five times as many blacks as Mexican-Americans were committed to prison for robbery; for burglary, the disparity was 1.25 to 1.

• In New Mexico, in 1973, the number of black prison inmates was nearly three times as large as the number of Mexican-American inmates, relative to population.

The pattern has also been stable over time; analysis of data assembled by the 1931 Wickersham Commission suggests that there were large disparities between black and Mexican-American arrest and conviction rates for violent crimes in the 1920s as well.[3]

II

A propensity to violence was not part of the cultural baggage black Americans carried with them from Africa; the homicide rate in black Africa is about the same as in western Europe, and well below the rate in either white or black America. Indeed, the black American homicide rate is three to five times the black African rate. Violence is something black Americans learned in this country.[4]

They had many teachers; violence has been an intrinsic part of the black American experience from the start. Every other immigrant group came here voluntarily, often illegally; Africans came in chains, having been uprooted from their homes and transported across the sea, at a ghastly cost in human life. (Two Africans in three died en route.) Moreover, slavery was maintained by violence; so was the racial caste system that was erected after Emancipation and that still endures, in diminished form, in parts of the rural South.

For most of their history in this country, in fact, blacks were victims, not initiators, of violence. In the Old South, violence against blacks was omnipresent—sanctioned both by custom and by law. Whites were free to use any methods, up to and including murder, to control "their Negroes." As Raymond Fosdick learned when he studied American police methods shortly before the country's entry into World War I, southern police departments had three classes of homicide. "If a nigger kills a white man, that's murder," one official told Fosdick. "If a white man kills a nigger, that's justifiable homicide. If a nigger kills another nigger, that's one less nigger." A quarter of a century later, Gunnar Myrdal found little change: "Any white man can strike or beat a Negro, steal or destroy his property, cheat him in a transaction and even take his life without fear of legal reprisal."[5]

There was little blacks could do to protect themselves. To strike back at whites, or merely to display anger or insufficient deference, was not just to risk one's own neck, but to place the whole community in danger. It was equally dangerous, or at best pointless, to appeal to the law; two lines from an old blues song describe the "justice" blacks received in court: "White folks and nigger in great Co't house/

Like Cat down Cellar wit' no-hole mouse." Or, as Nate Shaw, the extraordinary black farmer and farm-union organizer, whose life story has been recorded by Theodore Rosengarten, remarked, "Nigger had anything a white man wanted, the white man took it. . . ." It was, Shaw observed, "a time of brutish acts, brutish acts."[6]

Life has been brutish for other minority groups. During the nineteenth century, Irish immigrants were objects of scorn and derision, as well as intense discrimination; a generation weaned on "Polish jokes" may be surprised to learn that "Irish jokes" were a staple of American humor until the 1930s or '40s. Prejudice against Jews, Italians, and Poles became intense in the late nineteenth century and reached a peak in the 1920s, when nativist sentiment led Congress to cut immigration from southern and eastern Europe to a trickle; for those in their fifties, or older, the prejudice of those days remains a vivid memory.

And the treatment accorded Chinese, Japanese, Mexican, and native Americans makes the discrimination suffered by European immigrant groups seem like a royal reception. Hysteria over "the yellow peril" waxed and waned (but mainly waxed) for a century; it was not until after World War II that prejudice against Chinese- and Japanese-Americans began to lose some of its sting. The record of perfidy and violence in white people's dealings with native Americans remains a national disgrace; so is the exploitation, brutality, and outright chicanery with which Mexican-Americans have been treated. Both groups continue to suffer from prejudice and discrimination, mingled with indifference.[7]

If I emphasize the violence and oppression visited upon black people, therefore, it is not to gloss over the discrimination from which other minority groups have suffered. It is to argue that other groups' scars notwithstanding, the black experience has been different—in kind, not just degree—from that of any other American group. It is to argue, too, that we cannot understand the contemporary crime problem, let alone do anything about it, without understanding that difference and the ways in which it contributes to criminal violence.

Some distinguished scholars claim the reverse. In their view, poverty, crime, family breakdown, welfare dependency—all the problems we associate with race—are simply manifestations of the difficulty every rural group has had adjusting to city life. Like the European peasants who flocked to American cities in the nineteenth and early twentieth centuries, these scholars argue, black city dwellers today come from backward rural areas. These black migrants—the "last of the immigrants"—turn to crime and other forms of deviance because they are not yet "acculturated" into American society; they have not yet acquired the education, attitudes, values, and skills needed to hold decent jobs or to function effectively in contemporary urban, industrial life. Because black migration is of such recent origin, the argument continues, the problems that always have been associated with migration and urbanization have not had time to run their course, as they inevitably will. Patience is required. Just as European ethnics ultimately "made it" into the mainstream of American life, so too will blacks—given enough time.[8]

It would be hard to imagine a more profound misreading of American history. Rural black migrants to metropolitan areas face all the problems of acculturation that other rural migrants have faced, but they carry two additional burdens: their color and their heritage of slavery. Prejudice against black people is more virulent and intractable than is prejudice against Orientals, Chicanos, native Americans, Catholics, or Jews. Negative symbolism about blackness is built into our language: "black" connotes death, mourning, evil, corruption, and sin, while "white" implies purity, goodness, and rebirth. . . .

Notes

1. See *A Socio-Economic Profile of Puerto Rican New Yorkers* (New York: U.S. Department of Labor, Bureau of Labor Statistics, Middle Atlantic Regional Office Report 46, 1975), pp. 106–13.

2. David Burnham, "3 of 5 Slain by Police Here Are Black, Same as Arrest Rate," New York *Times* (August 25, 1973), p. 1; New York State Senate Standing Committee on Crime and Correction and Select Committee on Crime, mimeo. (Prison records are likely to record offenders' ethnic background accurately, since black, Puerto Rican, and non-Hispanic white inmates segregate themselves almost completely. There is no reason to believe that New York State judges are more likely to send black offenders to prison for any given offense than they are Puerto Rican offenders.)

3. National Commission on Law Observance and Enforcement, *Crime and the Foreign Born* (Wickersham Commission Reports, No. 10) (Montclair, N.J.: Patterson Smith Reprint Series, 1968), esp. Parts II, III, IV. (Originally published in 1931.)

4. Paul Bohannan, "Patterns of Murder and Suicide," in Bohannan, ed., *African Homicide and Suicide* (Princeton, N.J.: Princeton University Press, 1960). Ch. 9, esp. pp. 236–38.

5. Raymond Fosdick, *American Police Systems* (Montclair, N.J.: Patterson Smith Reprint Series, 1972), p. 45. (Fosdick's book was originally published in 1920.) Gunnar Myrdal, *An American Dilemma* (New York: Harper & Row, 1944), p. 559.

6. Lawrence W. Levine, *Black Culture and Black Consciousness* (New York: Oxford University Press, 1977), p. 251; Theodore Rosengarten, *All God's Dangers: The Life of Nate Shaw* (New York: Alfred A. Knopf, 1974), pp. 308, 302.

7. See for example Stanford M. Lyman, *Chinese Americans* (New York: Random House, Inc., 1974); Victor G. and Brett deBary Nee, *Longtime Californ': A Documentary Study of an American Chinatown* (New York: Panthe-

on Books, 1973); William Petersen, *Japanese Americans* (New York: Random House, Inc., 1971); Vine Deloria, *Custer Died for Your Sins* (New York: Macmillan Co. 1969); Wilcomb E. Washburn, ed., *The Indian and the White Man* (Garden City, N.Y.: Anchor Books, 1964); John R. Howard, ed., *Awakening Minorities* (New Brunswick, N.J.: Transaction Books, 1970); Stan Steiner, *La Raza* (New York: Harper & Row, 1970); Matt S. Meier and Feliciano Rivera, *The Chicanos* (New York: Hill & Wang, 1972); Julian Samora and Patricia Vandel Simon, *A History of the Mexican-American People* (Notre Dame, Ind.: University of Notre Dame Press, 1977); Ellwyn R. Stoddard, *Mexican Americans* (New York: Random House, Inc., 1973); Robert Coles, *Eskimos, Chicanos, Indians*, Vol. IV, *Children of Crisis* (Boston: Atlantic–Little, Brown, 1977), Parts II, IV.

8. The most recent (and, in some ways, most thoughtful) statement of this view is in Thomas Sowell, *Race and Economics* (New York: David McKay Co., Inc., 1975). See also Oscar Handlin, *The Newcomers: Negroes and Puerto Ricans in a Changing Metropolis* (Cambridge, Mass.: Harvard University Press, 1969); Philip M. Hauser, "Demographic Factors in the Integration of the Negro," *Daedalus*, Vol. 94, No. 4 (Fall, 1965), pp. 847–77, and Hauser, *Rapid Growth: Key to Understanding Metropolitan Problems* (Washington, D.C.: Washington Center for Metropolitan Studies, 1961); Irving Kristol, "The Negro Today Is Like the Immigrant of Yesterday," *New York Times Magazine* (September 11, 1966).

9. A Comparative Analysis of Male and Female Delinquency

STEPHEN A. CERNKOVICH
PEGGY C. GIORDANO

Criminological theory and research have focused predominantly on males, virtually excluding any systematic examination of females.[1] Undoubtedly, this was due largely to the historically persistent orientation that female deviation is so infrequent and innocuous compared to that of males, that to study it was unproductive at best and useless at worst. The assumption has been that patterns of sex-role socialization and restrictions placed upon females limits their involvement in delinquency or at least in serious persistent misconduct.

Only recently has the study of female crime and delinquency begun to be taken seriously. This sudden interest is partly a function of the belief, still unsubstantiated, that the women's liberation movement has had a significant impact on female involvement in deviant activities (Adler, 1975; Simon, 1975). As a result of this reorientation, many criminologists now assume that patterns of female delinquency have changed significantly over the past few years, both in terms of increased frequency and versatility of involvement (Adler, 1975; Noblit and Burcart, 1976). Some others have not been willing to make such an assumption, however, and are skeptical about the validity of data used to support claims of increasing female delinquency rates (Steffensmeier, 1978; Steffensmeier and Jordan, 1978). Thus, there are two views which can be identified: (1) that, as reflected in the official statistics, female participation in delinquency has increased significantly, especially in areas that have been considered "masculine" crimes; and (2) that not much has changed. This view suggests that any increase in female delinquency reflected in official statistics is merely an artifact of data collection methodologies, or of changes in the behavior of official agents of control rather than changes in the behavior of females.

Unfortunately this debate has remained at a rhetorical level, with little recent data brought to bear on it. This is not to say that data are unavailable or that proponents of the two perspectives do not refer to many studies as support for their positions. Generally, impressionistic evidence (cf. Adler, 1975), official sources of data (cf. Simon, 1975), or resurrected self-report studies from the mid-1960s and early 1970s (cf. Datesman, et al., 1975) are the basis for these arguments. The use of such data, however, has resulted in an incomplete and sometimes misleading profile of female delinquency. We will not review all previous studies, or engage in a detailed examination of the relative usefulness of the data sources, but we shall review the major conclusions drawn from these studies because often they are the only bases for current understandings about female delinquency.

Most studies show that males commit more delinquent acts than do females, especially serious crimes. While male delinquency includes a wide variety of offenses, female delinquency often is shown to be limited to a much narrower range of activities (Vedder, 1954; Wattenberg and Saunders, 1954; Shaclay, 1965; Doleschal, 1970; Gold, 1970; Jongman and Smale, 1972; Strouse, 1972; Haggart, 1973). Researchers argue that overt-aggressive delinquency and property crimes are more characteristic of male offenders, while female misbehavior is largely limited to incorrigibility (Barker and Adams, 1962; Forer, 1970; Vedder and Somerville, 1970), various sex offenses (Vedder, 1954; Barker and Adams, 1962; O'Reilly et al., 1968; Vedder and Somerville, 1970; Chesney-Lind,1973; Datesman et al., 1975), running away from home (Barker and Adams, 1962; Forer, 1970; Vedder and Somerville, 1970; Chesney-Lind, 1973), truancy (Forer, 1970; Vedder and Somerville, 1970; Miller, 1973), and shoplifting (Adler, 1975).

Official statistics are frequently used to make or support such arguments. For example, the 1975 FBI *Uniform Crime Reports* indicates that the male/female arrest ratio (for those under 18 years of age) is 3.72 for all crimes, 8.39 for violent crimes, and 4.05 for property crimes. The ratios are significantly smaller for such offenses as prostitution (0.32), offenses against the family (1.70), and larceny-theft (2.37), all of which are considered traditional "female offenses." Even though these recent official statistics are used to indicate considerably greater percentage increases for females than for males in almost every offense category (Adler, 1975), the male/female ratio continues to show significantly more male involvement, particularly in the serious offense categories.

Such data notwithstanding, some researchers argue that females may be more versatile in their delinquent involvement than official records and early self-report studies suggest. For example, Hindelang (1971) found, consistent with official data, a greater *frequency* of self-reported acts by males, but surprisingly, that the *patterns* of delinquent involvement were virtually identical for males and females. Males and females commit roughly the same types of offenses, the only difference between the sexes is that males commit them more often.

As a result of such studies and the large percentage increase in female arrests reflected in the official statistics, some criminologists have suggested that the behavior of males and females is converging, at least in terms of the versatility of delinquency involvement and in some cases even the frequency. Such contentions are often made, however, without the benefit of *comprehensive* or *recent* supporting evidence. The use of official records, impressionistic evidence, or the resurrection of pre-1970 data to substantiate (or to invalidate) assumptions of increasing levels of female delinquency is incomplete at best, and tells us little about present-day patterns.

As a result, an up-to-date profile is essential so that a reasonable estimation of the frequency, nature, and versatility of female delinquency can be established. While Hindelang's (1971) research is an excellent foundation, it has become dated (the study was done in 1968). Nonetheless, it remains a valuable example of the type of basic information needed to conduct informed research. We will use his work as a model from which to proceed in the presentation, analysis, and discussion of our data. The reader is cautioned, however, that although there is similarity with Hindelang's earlier research, methodological and sampling differences in the two studies prohibit any systematic comparison.

The remainder of this paper will focus on a comparative analysis of male and female self-reported delinquency involvement. The goals of the analysis are threefold: (1) to examine the frequency of adolescent self-reported involvement in a wide variety of delinquent offenses, (2) to determine the degree of specialization or versatility of involvement in these offenses, and (3) to compare males and females, in general and by race, along these dimensions in order to isolate similarities and differences in their delinquent involvement. To the extent that basic data which specify the nature, extent, and patterning of delinquency are (or should be) the point of departure for researchers, both in identifying research questions and in guiding theory construction, it is essential that these data be as representative as possible. Many of the data currently used do not meet this criterion. In addition to providing a comparative assessment of male and female delinquency involvement, our analysis seeks to augment the existing data to allow for a more comprehensive understanding of female delinquency.

SAMPLE CHARACTERISTICS AND
OPERATIONALIZATION OF VARIABLES

Our data were obtained from anonymous self-report questionnaires which were administered to a 1977 sample of 822 students in two midwestern urban high schools. The questionnaires were administered during regularly scheduled, small-sized classes. Participation was voluntary, and the students were given the options of refusing to participate in the study, or of omitting those sections of the schedule which they found to be threatening or objectionable. All students agreed to participate.

While the sample is not random, it was selected to maximize variation along important demographic dimensions. One of the high schools selected is a lower-status inner-city school, the other a higher-status suburban school. The mean age of the subjects is 16.68 years. Females constitute 56.5 percent of the sample. Forty-eight percent of the subjects are white, the remaining non-whites being predominantly black (43 percent of the total sample). Warner's et al. (1949) seven-point Revised Occupational Scale (recoded so that "1" represents the lowest status category, "7" the highest) yielded the following socioeconomic distributuion: 1 = 11.8 percent, 2 = 17.9 percent, 3 = 15.3 percent, 4 = 14.9 percent, 5 = 12.4 percent, 6 = 17.6 percent, and 7 = 10.1 percent, with a mean of 3.92 and a standard deviation of 1.92.

These demographic characteristics remain virtually the same for males and females. For the male sub-sample, 46.8 percent are white, the remaining non-whites being predominantly black (45.4 percent of the total male sub-sample). For the females, 49.1 percent are white, the remaining non-whites again being predominantly black (41.1 percent of the total female sub-sample). The mean age is 16.72 for males, 16.65 for females. The Warner et al. socioeconomic distribution for the two sub-samples differ slightly. Males: 1 = 11.6 percent, 2 = 17.5 percent, 3 = 11.9 percent, 4 = 16.5 percent, 5 = 10.9 percent, 6 = 21.1 percent, and 7 = 10.5 percent, with a mean of 4.03 and a standard deviation of 1.94. Females: 1 = 11.7 percent, 2 = 18.3 percent, 3 = 18.0 percent, 4 = 13.7 percent, 5 = 13.7 percent, 6 = 14.9 percent, and 7 = 9.7 percent, with a mean of 3.83 and a standard deviation of 1.90.

In evaluating the analysis to follow, the reader is cautioned about a possible race-class bias in the data. The socioeconomic distribution is skewed toward the higher statuses for whites (mean = 4.82) and toward the lower statuses for non-whites (mean = 2.84). The problem is minimized somewhat, however, by the fact that neither race nor class are significantly related to delinquency at the zero-order. The same holds true for the relationship between class and delinquency, controlling for race. The relationship between race and delinquency, controlling for class (as a trichotomy), produces one small although significant relationship, with middle-class whites tending to be slightly more delinquent than middle-class non-whites.

Delinquency involvement is measured by a combination of items selected from the Short-Nye (1957) and Sellin-Wolfgang (1964) self-report inventories. Individual items were selected to maximize the seriousness range of the behaviors. A total of thirty-six personal, property, and victimless/status offense items are included in the scale. The coding scheme for self-reported involvement in each of these acts is as follows: "very often" = 3, "several times" = 2, "once or twice" = 1, and "never" = 0.

Two observations regarding the use of self-report data in this study are appropriate. First, while measurement of a wide variety of delinquent acts is important in any self-report analysis, it is crucial in the present investigation. Traditionally, it has been assumed that males and females differ greatly in the *type* and *seriousness* of the delinquent acts they commit. While many of the minor forms of misbehavior included in the questionnaire (e.g., disobeying parents, running away from home, being placed on school probation, defying parents' authority to their face) would be considered only marginally delinquent by many researchers, the fact remains that it is these types of activities which are argued to be the most characteristic forms of delinquency among females. Any analysis which seeks to determine the scope and nature of female delinquency involvement must consider these relatively innocuous, benign acts, as well as the more serious, clearly delinquent acts. This becomes even more essential because many of these less serious forms of misbehavior are often combined in a residual "all other offenses except traffic" category in most official records, prohibiting specific offense analysis. An accurate and complete assessment of female delinquency demands information on a broad range of delinquent acts. The scale items included here reflect this necessity to specify the full range of female delinquency involvement.

The second observation concerns the general utility and validity of self-report data. While we recognize the limitations of such data, we would argue that a self-report profile is essential for broadening existing baseline data on female delinquency. There has been an overreliance on official statistics in the study of female delinquency and in drawing distinctions between males and females. Although official data are not without merit, they are confounded by untold biases, and to establish a valid female profile is extremely problematic. It is impossible, for example, to separate the biasing effects of differential processing, an acute problem in the case of female offenders. Official statistics simply give no indication of the extent to which arrest or court referral rates are influenced by such factors as the over- and under-processing of females depending on the offense committed, fluctuations in the orientation of criminal justice personnel regarding the extent to which they desire to equalize the treatment of male and female offenders, and various other legal and extra-legal considerations (Chesney-Lind, 1973, 1974, 1977; Anderson, 1976; Armstrong, 1977; Conway and Bogdan, 1977). If race is introduced as a variable, the reliability and validity of official data are further confounded (cf. Piliavin and Briar, 1964; Black and Reiss, 1970). We suggest that both official and self-report data are necessary for an informed and comprehensive understanding of female delinquency. While self-report data also have actual and potential sources of bias (cf. Nettler, 1978:97–117), we contend that they add new and valuable information about delinquency involvement not evident from official sources. In this sense, we use self-reports for the purpose they were originally intended, as both an alternative and a supplement to official statistics.

ANALYSIS AND FINDINGS

Dimensions of male and female involvement in all thirty-six delinquent acts included on the questionnaire are in Table 1. It is clear, and not surprising, from an examination of the "Percent Engaging in Act One or More Times" columns of Table 1, that more males than females report engaging in the various delinquent acts. Exceptions include disobeying parents, running away from home, defying parents' authority, and, surprisingly, using hard drugs. Over half of both the males and females report participation in truancy, disobeying parents, petty theft, sexual intercourse, drinking alcohol, smoking marijuana, gambling, and disturbing the peace, all relatively minor offenses from a legal standpoint. The relatively benign nature of these acts notwithstanding, there is a good deal of similarity in the kinds of acts both sexes report.

The male/female ratios of those reporting involvement in the thirty-six acts are also reported in Table 1, and these data address more directly the issue of degree of uniformity in patterns of delinquency involvement. The largest ratios (indicating a greater percentage of males than of females reporting involvement) include theft of car parts, robbery, car theft, sex for money, burglary-unoccupied, and burglary-occupied. (It is surprising of course that more males than fe-

Table 1. Male and Female Self-Reported Delinquency Involvement

| Delinquent Act | Percent Engaging in Act One or More Times | | | Frequency of Delinquency Involvement | | | | t-VALUE[a] |
| | | | | Male | | Female | | |
	MALE	FEMALE	RATIO	MEAN	SD	MEAN	SD	
1. Drive car without permission	41.7	25.4	1.64	.64	.89	.35	.68	4.89*
2. Skip school	81.7	80.8	1.01	1.54	1.01	1.55	1.00	−.11
3. Disobey parents	89.6	93.6	0.96	1.66	.87	1.79	.83	−2.12***
4. Attack someone with fists	47.8	25.1	1.90	.68	.83	.34	.66	6.30*
5. Run away from home	16.0	16.1	0.99	.21	.54	.20	.51	.25
6. School probation/ suspension/ expulsion	31.8	26.6	1.19	.43	.70	.37	.68	1.18
7. Defy parents' authority	40.7	42.1	0.97	.52	.71	.60	.82	−1.54
8. Theft (less than $2.00)	66.5	58.2	1.14	.95	.86	.79	.80	2.61*
9. Use weapon to attack someone	11.6	6.6	1.76	.16	.49	.09	.35	2.48*
10. Use fake ID	34.8	26.5	1.31	.53	.83	.44	.83	1.58
11. Sex with opposite sex	77.7	62.0	1.25	1.72	1.14	1.23	1.13	6.00*
12. Gang fight	38.9	14.5	2.68	.50	.70	.19	.50	6.86*
13. Drink alcohol	82.8	72.6	1.14	1.77	1.08	1.48	1.10	3.75*
14. Smoke marijuana	67.2	58.7	1.14	1.46	1.24	1.33	1.25	1.51
15. Theft ($2.00–$50.00)	33.9	26.0	1.30	.47	.76	.36	.70	2.10#
16. Use hard drugs	14.8	19.3	0.77	.25	.65	.32	.74	−1.50
17. Sell marijuana	35.2	19.5	1.80	.67	1.01	.32	.71	5.44*
18. Car theft	5.5	1.1	5.00	.09	.43	.02	.18	2.97*

19. Driving while under influence of liquor	38.1	21.8	1.75	.70	1.01	.34	.73	5.41*
20. Property destruction of under $10.00	36.6	16.1	2.27	.44	.65	.19	.47	5.95*
21. Driving while under influence of marijuana	40.4	21.8	1.85	.78	1.08	.41	.86	5.04*
22. Gamble	85.3	60.8	1.40	1.70	1.03	.96	.97	10.02*
23. Burglary-occupied	9.7	2.3	4.22	.15	.51	.03	.24	3.89*
24. Sell hard drugs	11.6	9.5	1.22	.18	.53	.15	.52	.69
25. Robbery	5.0	0.9	5.55	.08	.37	.01	.15	2.80*
26. Theft (over $50.00)	12.7	4.6	2.76	.16	.47	.06	.32	3.31*
27. Disturb the peace	71.6	68.9	1.04	1.11	.91	.98	.82	1.96##
28. Property destruction of over $10.00	20.3	5.9	3.44	.26	.58	.08	.37	4.78*
29. Sex with same sex	4.2	3.3	1.27	.09	.45	.06	.33	1.01
30. Burglary-unoccupied	16.5	3.7	4.46	.20	.51	.05	.27	4.94*
31. Driving while under influence of hard drugs	11.7	7.2	1.62	.18	.54	.12	.47	1.71
32. Extortion	13.6	8.3	1.64	.22	.62	.11	.41	2.84*
33. Theft of car parts	20.4	3.2	6.37	.27	.60	.04	.22	6.66*
34. Joyride	18.1	6.1	2.97	.25	.59	.08	.32	4.81*
35. Sex for money	5.3	1.1	4.82	.08	.36	.02	.22	2.54*
36. Carry weapon	34.3	17.1	2.01	.53	.86	.27	.67	4.59*

[a] Significance levels are meaningless for these data because they are based on a non-random sample. They are reported here for heuristic and descriptive rather than inferential purposes. The symbols for level of probability are: * = .01, ** = .02, *** = .03, # = .04, ## = .05.

males report involvement in "sex for money." In accounting for a similar finding, Hindelang (1971:527) notes that ". . . Gold (1970) has found that females of high school age tend to underreport having had sexual intercourse while Clark and Tifft (1966) have found that male college students tend to overreport heterosexual adventures." We suspect that this argument is valid in interpreting the meaning of male/female self-reported participation in the "sex for money" behavioral item.) The ratios are smallest (indicating a comparable percentage of males and females reporting involvement) for using hard drugs, disobeying parents, defying parents' authority, running away from home, truancy, and disturbing the peace. The overall ratio for all thirty-six acts is 2.18, compared to Hindelang's (1971) ratio of 2.56, and the 1975 *Uniform Crime Reports* overall ratio of 3.72. Although comparison with the Hindelang and official figures indicates a greater male-female similarity in our sample, a large portion of this similarity is due to a high percentage of both sexes' involvement in relatively innocuous, benign behaviors. When many of the more serious offenses are examined, the male-female gap begins to widen.

But most of the ratios obtained are considerably smaller than those revealed in arrest rates for males and females under 18 years of age. For example, the 1975 *Uniform Crime Reports* indicates male/female arrest ratios of 12.24 for robbery, 4.94 for aggravated assault, 18.98 for burglary, 2.37 for larceny-theft, 12.53 for auto theft, 13.92 for carrying weapons, 19.28 for gambling, and 11.54 for driving while under the influence of alcohol. Comparison of those ratios with ours suggest that official statistics may be useful indicators of the *legal processing* of juveniles but they are not accurate indices of the *real* extent and nature of delinquency involvement. They nevertheless continue to be used for this purpose (cf. Simon, 1975; Noblit and Burcart, 1976; Steffensmeier and Jordan, 1978). While the official data give the impression of significantly different patterns of delinquency involvement by males and females, our self-report data suggest quite the opposite. A comparison of the rank-ordering of the percent of males and females reporting involvement in each of the thirty-six acts yields a Spearman coefficient (Blalock, 1972:416–18) of 0.90, suggesting high correspondence between the misbehavior of males and females.

This aspect of the analysis, however, deals only with the percentage of males and females who report involvement in each act. It reveals nothing about the *extent* of that involvement. Because the frequency of delinquent behavior is an important variable in the determination of arrest rates, it is instructive to know something about levels of involvement for males and females. The higher arrest rate for males may reflect the fact that they are more persistent offenders than females. The extent of delinquency involvement is presented in the second half of Table 1 which shows the mean frequency of male/female participation in each of the thirty-six delinquent acts.

These data indicate that almost 28 percent (10/36) of the male-female differences in extent of involvement are statistically nonsignificant. Ths is an important departure from everyday thinking and from the official statistics which suggest significant male-female differences in virtually every offense category. We find no significant sex difference for truancy, running away from home, school probation/suspension/expulsion, defying parents' authority, using a fake ID, smoking marijuana, using hard drugs, selling hard drugs, sex with the same sex, and driving while under the influence of hard drugs. Especially interesting is the comparison of truancy and running away from home. Males and females are thought to differ considerably in their involvement in these offenses. Our data do not support this view. These offenses clearly are neither restricted to females nor are they the dominant areas of specialization for female offenders.

Small but statistically significant male-female differences characterize the remaining twenty-six acts. Only one of the reported t-values, however, is impressive (gambling). The large sample size no doubt contributes to the statistical significance of what are otherwise substantially small differences in the frequency of male and female delinquency involvement. Both males and females have high rates of involvement (whether there are significant sex differences or not) in truancy, disobeying parents, intercourse, drinking alcohol, and smoking marijuana (males also have a comparatively high rate for gambling). Similarly, both groups evidence low rates of involvement in car theft, burglary-occupied, robbery, sex with the same sex, and sex for money (males have comparatively low rates for use of weapons and theft greater than $50.00, while females also infrequently are involved in theft of car parts and burglary-unoccupied).

These data reveal a striking male-female uniformity in delinquency involvement. A rank-order comparison of mean involvement rates yields a coefficient of 0.91, indicating, as was the case for percent reporting involvement, considerable similarity between males and females. As was the case in Hindelang's (1971) data, what seems to differentiate male and female delinquents is their *frequency of involvement*, not the *type of acts* in which they engage. The acts most frequently committed are virtually identical for males and females, tending to be the less serious, victimless/status offenses. Similarly, the acts least frequently engaged in by both males and females are the more serious personal and property offenses, although males tend to engage in these more often than females do.

Because of the significance of this overall similarity it is important

Table 2. Frequency of Delinquency Involvement by Sex and Race

| | Male | | | | Female | | | | T-VALUE[a] | | | |
| | A WHITE | | B NON-WHITE | | C WHITE | | D NON-WHITE | | | | | |
Delinquent Act	Mean	SD	Mean	SD	Mean	SD	Mean	SD	AB	CD	AC	BD
1. Drive car without permission	.61	.84	.66	.94	.38	.66	.32	.69	−.49	.91	2.98*	3.96*
2. Skip school	1.48	1.06	1.61	.95	1.56	1.06	1.55	.95	−1.11	.14	−.69	.62
3. Disobey parents	1.95	.75	1.38	.90	1.94	.79	1.63	.84	6.28*	4.01*	.05	−2.84*
4. Attack someone with fists	.65	.79	.71	.88	.26	.58	.41	.73	−.60	−2.35**	5.44**	3.69*
5. Run away from home	.21	.55	.21	.54	.23	.51	.16	.48	.05	1.67	−.41	1.00
6. School probation/ suspension/ expulsion	.32	.65	.52	.74	.31	.68	.42	.69	−2.53*	−1.64	.16	1.35
7. Defy parents' authority	.73	.76	.32	.59	.88	.86	.32	.65	5.44*	7.78*	−1.82	.04
8. Theft (less than $2.00)	1.03	.84	.87	.87	.79	.79	.80	.82	1.72	−.14	2.89*	.83
9. Use weapon to attack someone	.12	.46	.21	.52	.03	.21	.14	.44	−1.54	−3.54*	2.51*	1.30
10. Use fake ID	.62	.89	.45	.76	.46	.86	.40	.80	1.83	.76	1.68	.54
11. Sex with opposite sex	1.44	1.13	2.01	1.07	1.10	1.14	1.36	1.10	−4.59*	−2.46*	2.93*	5.66*
12. Gang fight	.44	.68	.56	.71	.11	.35	.26	.60	−1.62	−3.24*	5.54*	4.41*
13. Drink alcohol	1.90	1.06	1.65	1.08	1.77	1.10	1.19	1.02	2.06#	5.74*	1.17	4.28*
14. Smoke marijuana	1.41	1.27	1.52	1.20	1.40	1.31	1.26	1.18	−.80	1.17	.07	2.09#
15. Theft ($2.00–$50.00)	.44	.73	.51	.79	.38	.70	.34	.70	−.80	.62	.78	2.15***
16. Use hard drugs	.38	.78	.12	.45	.48	.88	.17	.53	3.74*	4.58*	−1.15	−1.00
17. Sell marijuana	.65	1.02	.70	.99	.42	.81	.20	.56	−.42	3.39*	2.31**	5.74*

122

Offense												
18. Car theft	.09	.44	.09	.41	.01	.07	.03	.24	.04	−1.61	2.51*	1.68
19. Driving while under influence of liquor	.80	1.08	.60	.94	.53	.88	.16	.50	1.81	5.60*	2.64*	5.55*
20. Property destruction of under $10.00	.57	.72	.31	.54	.28	.55	.08	.31	3.65*	4.71*	4.24*	4.65*
21. Driving while under influence of marijuana	.87	1.14	.69	1.02	.58	1.00	.23	.64	1.53	4.45*	2.59*	4.96*
22. Gamble	1.78	.98	1.62	1.07	.93	.90	.98	1.03	1.39	−.51	8.68*	5.73*
23. Burglary-occupied	.14	.46	.17	.56	.03	.22	.03	.22	−.66	.14	2.65*	3.08*
24. Sell hard drugs	.26	.63	.09	.40	.21	.58	.08	.44	2.99*	2.59*	.85	.10
25. Robbery	.04	.28	.11	.45	.01	.07	.02	.20	−1.55	−1.29	1.72	2.22***
26. Theft (over $50.00)	.14	.44	.19	.50	.04	.19	.09	.41	−.96	−1.76	2.75*	2.01#
27. Disturb the peace	1.27	.93	.94	.87	1.07	.79	.89	.84	3.21*	2.31**	2.17***	.55
28. Property destruction of over $10.00	.20	.48	.32	.68	.07	.35	.10	.40	−1.79	−.79	3.00*	3.62*
29. Sex with same sex	.07	.38	.10	.52	.04	.30	.07	.37	−.49	−.74	.82	.63
30. Burglary-unoccupied	.18	.46	.22	.55	.05	.29	.04	.25	−.67	.24	3.31*	3.76*
31. Driving while under influence of hard drugs	.25	.63	.11	.42	.21	.62	.02	.18	2.33**	4.34*	.61	2.52*
32. Extortion	.12	.49	.33	.72	.04	.26	.18	.51	−3.01*	−3.39*	1.83	2.30**
33. Theft of car parts	.26	.54	.28	.66	.06	.29	.01	.12	−.31	2.29**	4.29*	5.10*
34. Joyride	.23	.55	.27	.64	.08	.30	.06	.31	−.59	.68	3.18*	3.80*
35. Sex for money	.07	.34	.09	.38	.02	.22	.02	.22	−.54	.17	1.49	2.07#
36. Carry weapon	.53	.84	.54	.87	.19	.57	.34	.74	−.07	−2.38*	4.45*	2.30**

[a] The symbols for level of probability are: * = .01, ** = .02, *** = .03, # = .04.

to determine the degree to which the uniformities persist in separate examinations by race. The rationale for this stage of the analysis is two-fold: (1) the composition of our sample creates the possibility that the findings reported in Table 1 may be confounded by race, and (2) previous work on female delinquency has revealed interesting racial variations (cf. Adler, 1969; Katzenelson, 1975; Giordano, 1976). The data for this analysis are presented in Table 2, which reveals uniformities even more pronounced than the data in Table 1. Looking first at sex differences within racial categories, these data show that for white males and females, 16 of the 36 (44 percent) frequency of involvement differences are not significant statistically. With the exception of theft ($2.00–$50.00), robbery, and extortion, this reflects comparable rates of male and female involvement in victimless, drug-related, or relatively minor offenses. Significant sex differences tend to be for offenses which are more serious personal and property offenses. In every case, males report higher levels of involvement in these acts than females report. The overall mean level of involvement across all thirty-six offenses is 22.36 for the white males and 16.94 for the white females. This reflects the fact that while there is an overall uniformity, males commit more offenses, particularly the more serious ones, than females commit.

The same pattern characterizes non-whites. Non-white males report an average of 21.19 delinquent acts, while non-white females report 14.46. Twelve of the thirty-six (33 percent) differences are nonsignificant, and tend again to be isolated to relatively minor offenses (exceptions are using a weapon to attack someone and car theft). The offenses for which there are significant male-female differences, while including some minor, victimless/status offenses, tend to be offenses of a more serious variety. With the single exception of disobeying parents, non-white males report significantly greater levels of involvement than do non-white females. As was the case with the white sub-sample, the males in the non-white group tend to be more persistent than females in their delinquency, particularly in misbehavior of a serious nature.

Turning to racial differences within sex categories, these data show a remarkable uniformity in the delinquency of white and non-white males. There are no significant differences between the two groups for twenty-five of the thirty-six (69 percent) acts. Of the few differences that are significant, whites report greater levels of involvement in disobeying parents, defying parents' authority, drinking alcohol, using hard drugs, property destruction of under $10.00, selling hard drugs, disturbing the peace, and driving while under the influence of hard drugs. Non-white males report higher rates of participation in school probation/suspension/expulsion, sex with the opposite sex, and extortion. In spite of these differences, white and non-white males show almost identical patterns of delinquent involvement. The mean rate of delinquency across all thirty-six acts is 22.36 for the white males, 21.19 for the non-white males.

Similarly, the data in Table 2 reveal that among females, whites engage in slightly more delinquency than do non-whites. The overall mean frequency for white females is 16.94, while for non-whites it is 14.46. Closer inspection of specific delinquent acts, however, suggests that such a comparison is somewhat misleading. Mean frequency of involvement differences between white and non-white females are nonsignificant for eighteen of the thirty-six (50 percent) acts. Most of these are relatively minor, victimless/status offenses. Exceptions include theft ($2.00–$50.00), car theft, burglary-occupied, robbery, theft (over $50.00), property destruction over $10.00, and burglary-unoccupied.

This uniformity notwithstanding, a distinctive pattern emerges for the eighteen acts in which there are statistically significant differences. Non-white females report higher levels of involvement in fist fighting, using a weapon to attack someone, sex with the opposite sex, gang fighting, extortion and carrying weapons. The common characteristic of these offenses, with the exception of sexual intercourse, is that they are all personal, potentially violent offenses. White females report greater rates of participation in disobeying parents, defying parents' authority, drinking alcohol, using hard drugs, selling marijuana, driving while under the influence of alcohol, property destruction of under $10.00, driving while under the influence of marijuana, selling hard drugs, disturbing the peace, driving while under the influence of hard drugs, and theft of car parts. While white females report a greater overall mean level of involvement in delinquency, this is largely a function of their higher rates of participation in relatively minor or drug-related offenses. Non-white females, while reporting less overall delinquency than whites, have higher involvement rates in the more serious, personal offenses.

In order to examine these patterns further a series of rank order correlations (based on mean frequency of involvement in the thirty-six delinquent acts) were computed. The average correlation of 0.87 indicates that there is a great deal of similarity among all four subgroups, and does not support many of the racial and sex differences suggested by official data. Interestingly, these rank orders also show *that there are more similarities within racial groups than within sex groups* (see Katzenelson, 1975, for similar findings). White females are more similar in their delinquency involvement to white males (0.96) than to non-whites, female (0.84) or male (0.81). Non-white females' delinquency more closely approximates that of non-white males (0.88) than that of whites, female (0.84) or male (0.84). While important, these differences should not be allowed to obscure the overall similarity among the sub-groups. The *pattern* of delinquency is almost identical for all four groups. Significant differences appear primarily on the basis of *frequency* of involvement.

SUMMARY AND CONCLUSION

As if to compensate for an historical omission, criminologists have initiated an intense study of the female offender. Aside from the effect of the women's liberation movement, the most hotly debated issue, and one important reason for the increased focus on female deviance, centers around answering a number of related questions: What are the basic similarities and differences between male and female delinquency? Has there been a real increase in female involvement in delinquent activities? If so, what is the nature of this increase? Have females moved beyond involvement in relatively specific, less serious offenses, to participation in what traditionally have been considered "masculine crimes?" For the most part, answers to questions such as these have been based on impressionistic, resurrected pre-1970 self-report data, or official sources of data. There is an increased awareness, however, that the problems and limitations inherent in these data have retarded our basic understanding of female deviance, and that we need valid, more comprehensive baseline data from which research and theory construction can proceed.

Our major findings are that (1) with the exception of a few minor offenses, more males than females report engaging in each of the thirty-six delinquent acts; (2) the overall male-female ratio for percent reporting involvement in each of the delinquent offenses is 2.18, considerably smaller than both Hindelang's (1971) self-report ratio of 2.56, and the official arrest ratio of 3.72; (3) when mean frequency of involvement in each of the delinquent acts is examined, almost 28 percent of the male/female differences are shown to be nonsignificant, and there is considerable uniformity between males and females; (4) while there are virtually no important differences between white and non-white males, a distinctive pattern emerges for the females in that white more than non-white females report participation in more delinquent acts overall and in relatively minor and drug-related offenses, while non-white more than white females report significantly more involvement in the more serious personal offenses; and (5) rank order correlations indicate more uniformities in frequency and type of delinquency involvement within racial groups than within sex groups.

The focus of this research has been largely descriptive but the findings have several etiological implications. Much criticism has been directed at the stereotypic and oversimplified explanations which have dominated theoretical thinking on female crime and delinquency. A particular model's stress on "personal maladjustments," "women's liberation," or some other factor as the dominant causal ingredient, however, is not as critical as the fact that many of these explanations are based on incomplete and often biased data. A *priori* assumptions are made about the nature of female deviance which often extend far beyond the validity and generalizability of available data.

It is clear from the findings presented here that many of these assumptions are inaccurate. It is equally clear that subsequent research and theory-construction must first establish an up-to-date profile of female delinquency and must consider fully the entire range and complexity of females' involvement. Accurate theory must be based on empirical reality, but the development of accurate theory continues to suffer because some scholars rush to print with the causes of delinquency before they know what it is they should be explaining.

Note

1. Revision of a paper presented at the 1977 meetings of the International Sociological Association Research Committee for the Sociology of Deviance and Social Control (August 9–11), Dublin. This study was supported by PHS Research Grant No. MN 29095-01, NIMH (Center for Studies of Crime and Delinquency) and a Faculty Research Grant from Bowling Green State University.

References

Adler, Freda. 1969. The Female Offender in Philadelphia. Unpublished Ph.D. Dissertation. University Park: University of Pennsylvania.

———. 1975. Sisters in Crime. New York: McGraw-Hill.

Anderson, Etta A. 1976. "The 'chivalrous' treatment of the female offender in the arms of the criminal justice system: A review of the literature." Social Problems 23:350–57.

Armstrong, Gail. 1977. "Females under the law—'protected' but unequal." Crime and Delinquency 23:109–20.

Barker, Gordon H. and William T. Adams. 1962, "Comparison of the delinquencies of boys and girls." Journal of Criminal Law, Criminology and Police Science 53:470–75.

Black, Donald J. and Albert J. Reiss, Jr. 1970. "Police control of juveniles." American Sociological Review 35:63–77.

Blalock, Hubert M., Jr. 1972. Social Statistics, 2d Ed. New York: McGraw-Hill.

Chesney-Lind, Meda. 1973. "Judicial enforcement of the female sex role: The family court and the female delinquent." Issues in Criminology 8:51–69.

_____. 1974. "Juvenile delinquency: The sexualization of female crime." Psychology Today 8:43–46.

_____. 1977. "Judicial paternalism and the female status offender: Training women to know their place." Crime and Delinquency 23:121–30.

Clark, John P. and Larry L. Tifft. 1966. "Polygraph and interview validation of self-reported deviant behavior." American Sociological Review 31:516–23.

Conway, Allan and Carol Bogdan. 1977. "Sexual delinquency: The persistence of a double standard." Crime and Delinquency 23:132–35.

Datesman, Susan K., Frank R. Scarpitti and Richard M. Stephenson. 1975. "Female delinquency: An application of self and opportunity theories." Journal of Research in Crime and Delinquency 12:107–23.

Doleschal, Eugene. 1970. "Review: Hidden crime." Crime and Delinquency Literature 2:546–72.

Forer, Lois G. 1970. No One Will Listen: How Our Legal System Brutalizes the Poor. New York: John Day.

Giordano, Peggy C. 1976. "Changing sex roles and females' involvement in delinquency." Paper read at the meeting of the Midwest Sociological Society, St. Louis, April 21–24.

Gold, Martin. 1970. Delinquent Behavior in an American City. Belmont, California: Brooks/Cole.

Haggart, Joy Reeve. 1973. "Women and crime." Humboldt Journal of Social Relations 1:42–47.

Hindelang, Michael J. 1971. "Age, sex, and the versatility of delinquent involvements." Social Problems 18:522–35.

Jongman, R. W. and G. J. A. Smale. 1972. "Unrecorded delinquency among female students." Tijdschrift Voor Criminologie 14:1–11.

Katzenelson, Susan. 1975. "The female offender in Washington, D.C." Paper read at the meeting of the American Society of Criminology, Toronto, October 30–November 2.

Miller, Walter B. 1973. "The Molls." Society 11:32–35.

Nettler, Gwynn. 1978. Explaining Crime. 2d Ed. New York: McGraw-Hill.

Noblit, George W. and Janie M. Burcart. 1976. "Women and crime: 1960–1970." Social Science Quarterly 56:650–57.

O'Reilly, Charles, Frank Cizon, John Flanagan and Steven Pflanczer. 1968. "Sentenced women in a county jail." American Journal of Corrections 30:23–25.

Piliavin, Irving and Scott Briar. 1964. "Police encounters with juveniles." American Journal of Sociology 70:206–14.

Sellin, Thorsten and Marvin E. Wolfgang. 1964. The Measurement of Delinquency. New York: John Wiley.

Shaclay, Cockbern E. 1965. "Sex differentials in juvenile delinquency." British Journal of Criminality 5:289–308.

Short, James F., Jr. and F. Ivan Nye. 1957. "Reported behavior as a criterion of deviant behavior." Social Problems 5:207–13.

Simon, Rita James. 1975. The Contemporary Woman and Crime. Rockville, Maryland: National Institute of Mental Health: Crime and Delinquency Issues.

Steffensmeier, Darrell. 1978. "Crime and the contemporary woman: An analysis of changing levels of female property crime, 1960–75." Social Forces 57:566–84.

Steffensmeier, Darrell J. and Charlene Jordan. 1978. "Changing patterns of female crime in rural America, 1962–75." Rural Sociology 43:87–102.

Strouse, Jean. 1972. "To be minor and female." Ms. (August): 70–75, 116.

Uniform Crime Reports for the United States. 1975. Clarence M. Kelley, Director, Federal Bureau of Investigation, U.S. Department of Justice. Washington, D.C.: U.S. Government Printing Office.

Vedder, Clyde B. 1954. The Juvenile Offender. New York: Doubleday.

Vedder, Clyde B. and Dora B. Somerville. 1970. The Delinquent Girl. Springfield, Illinois: Charles C. Thomas.

Warner, W. Lloyd, Marchia Meeker and Kenneth Eells. 1949. Social Class in America. Chicago: Science Research Associates.

Wattenberg, William and Frank Saunders. 1954. "Sex differences among juvenile offenders." Sociology and Social Research 39:24–31.

10.   The Family as Cradle of Violence

SUZANNE K. STEINMETZ
MURRAY A. STRAUS

Lizzie Borden took an ax
And gave her father 40 whacks.
When the job was neatly done
She gave her mother 41.

Although intrafamily violence like that attributed to Lizzie Borden is occasionally reported, such behavior is considered totally out of the ordinary—families are supposed to be oases of serenity where love and good feeling flow from each parent and child.

Unfortunately, that lovely picture is not accurate. In fact, the grisly tale of Lizzie Borden may not be unique. Violence seems as typical of family relationships as love; and it would be hard to find a group or institution in American society in which violence is more of an everyday occurrence than it is within the family. Family members physically abuse each other far more often than do nonrelated individuals. Starting with slaps and going on to torture and murder, the family provides a prime setting for every degree of physical violence. So universal is the phenomenon that it is probable that some form of violence will occur in almost every family.

The most universal type of physical violence is corporal punishment by parents. Studies in England and the United States show that between 84 and 97 percent of all parents use physical punishment at some point in their child's life. Moreover, such use of physical force to maintain parental authority is not confined to early childhood. Data on students in three different regions of the United States show that half of the parents sampled either used or threatened their high school seniors with physical punishment.

Of course, physical punishment differs significantly from other violence. But it is violence, nonetheless. Despite its good intentions, it has some of the same consequences as other forms of violence. Research shows that parents who use physical punishment to control the aggressiveness of their children probably increase rather than decrease their child's aggressive tendencies. Violence begets violence, however peaceful and altruistic the motivation.

The violent tendencies thus reinforced may well be turned against the parents, as in the case of Lizzie Borden. Although most intrafamily violence is less bloody than that attributed to Lizzie, some family abuse does go as far as ax murder. Examination of relationships between murderer and victim proves that the largest single category of victim is that of family member or relative.

HOMICIDE AT HOME

The magnitude of family violence became particularly obvious during the summer heat wave of 1972. Page 1 of the July 22, 1972 *New York Times* carried an article describing the increase in murders during the previous few days of extreme heat in New York City and summarizing the statistics for murder in New York during the previous six months. Page 2 held an article totalling deaths in Northern Ireland during three and a half years of disturbances. About as many people were murdered by their relatives in one six-month period in New York City as had been killed in three and a half years of political upheaval in Northern Ireland.

Murder, though relatively rare, gets far more attention than less violent abuse. Even though more murders are committed on family members than any other type of person, and even though the United States has a high degree of homicide, the rate is still only four or five per 100,000 population. What about nonlethal physical volence between husband and wife? While accurate statistics are hard to find, one way of estimating the magnitude of the phenomenon is through the eyes of the police.

Just as relatives are the largest single category of murder victim, so family fights are the largest single category of police calls. One legal researcher estimates that more police calls involve family conflict than do calls for all criminal incidents, including murders, rapes, nonfamily assaults, robberies and muggings. "Violence in the home" deserves at least as much public concern as "crime in the streets." The police hate and fear family conflict calls for several reasons. First, a family disturbance call lacks the glamour, prestige, and public appreciation of a robbery or an accident summons. More important, such calls are extremely dangerous. Many a policeman coming to the aid of a wife who is being beaten has had a chair or a bottle thrown at him or has been stabbed or shot by a wife who suddenly becomes fearful of what is going to happen to her husband, or who abruptly turns her rage from her husband to the police. Twenty-two percent of all police fatalities come from investigating problems between husband and wife or parent and child.

One cannot tell from these data on police calls just what proportion of all husbands and wives have had physical fights, since it takes an unusual combination of events to have the police summoned. The closest published estimate is found in the research of George Levinger and John O'Brien. In studying applicants for divorce, O'Brien found that 17 percent of his cases spontaneously mentioned overt violent behavior, and Levinger found that 23 percent of the middle-class couples and 40 percent of the working-class couples gave "physical abuse" as a major complaint.

Both of these figures probably underestimate the amount of physical violence between husbands and wives because there may well have been violent incidents which were not mentioned or which were not listed as a main cause of divorce. Even doubling the figure, however, leaves us far from knowing the extent of husband-wife violence. First, there is a discrepancy between the O'Brien and the Levinger figures. Second, these figures apply only to couples who have applied for divorce. It may be that there is a lower incidence of physical violence among a cross-section of couples; or it may be, as we suspect, that the difference is not very great.

A survey conducted for the National Commission of the Causes and Prevention of Violence deals with what violence people would approve. These data show that one out of four men and one out of six women approve of slapping a wife under certain conditions. As for a wife slapping a husband, 26 percent of the men and 19 percent of the women approve. Of course, some people who approve of slapping will never do it and some who disapprove *will* slap—or worse. Probably the latter group is larger. If that is true, we know that husband-wife violence at the minimal level of slapping occurs in at least one quarter of American families.

Our own pilot studies also give some indication of the high rate of violence in the family. Richard Gelles of the University of New Hampshire, who has done a series of in-depth case studies of a sample of eighty families, found that about 56 percent of the couples have used physical force on each other at some time.

In a second study, freshman college students responded to a series of questions about conflicts which occurred in their senior year in high school, and to further questions about how these conflicts were handled. Included in the conflict resolution section were questions on whether or not the parties to the disputes had ever hit, pushed, shoved, thrown things, or kicked each other in the course of a quarrel.

The results show that during that one year 62 percent of the high school seniors had used physical force on a brother or sister and 16 percent of their parents had used physical force on each other. Since these figures are for a single year, the percentage who had *ever* used violence is probably much greater. How much greater is difficult to estimate because we cannot simply accumulate the 16 percent for one year over the total number of years married. Some couples will never have used violence and others will have used it repeatedly. Nevertheless, it seems safe to assume that it will not always be the same 16 percent. So, it is probably best to fall back on the 56 percent estimate from the eighty earlier interviews.

Since a vast amount of family violence can be documented, what accounts for the myth of family nonviolence? At least one basis for the rosy, if false, view is that the family is a tremendously important social institution, which must be perserved. In Western countries one supportive device is the ideology of familial love and gentleness, an ideology which helps encourage people to marry and to stay married. It tends to maintain satisfaction with the family system despite the stresses and strains of family life. From the viewpont of preserving the integrity of a critical social institution, such a mythology is highly useful.

Other simplifications and generalizations also block knowledge and understanding of the nature of violence in the family. The psycho-pathology myth, the class myth, the sex myth and the catharsis myth must be exposed and examined if the true nature of intrafamily abuse is to emerge.

A growing number of sociologists and psychologists have suggested that a focus on conflict and violence may be a more revealing way of understanding the family than a focus on consensus and solidarity. Most members of this group, however, recognize that family conflict is legitimate, but still consider physical violence only as an abnormal-ity—something which involves sick families. The facts do not support this *psychopathology myth*. According to Richard J. Gelles, only a tiny proportion of those using violence—even child abusers—can be considered mentally ill. Our own studies reveal that physically abu-sive husbands, wives, and children are of overwhelmingly sound mind and body.

The fact that almost all family violence, including everyday beat-ing, slapping, kicking, and throwing things, is carried out by normal everyday Americans rather than deranged persons should not lead us to think of violence as being desirable or even acceptable. The im-portant question is, Why is physical violence so common between members of the closest and most intimate of all human groups?

Although social scientists are still far from a full understanding of the causes of violence between family members, evidence is accumulating that family violence is learned—and learned in childhood in the home. This fact does not deny the importance of the human biological heritage. If the capacity for violence were not present in the human organism, learning and social patterning could not produce it.

If a child actually observes and experiences the effects of violence, he will learn to be violent. Husbands, wives and parents play out models of behavior which they learned in childhood from *their* parents and from friends and relatives. Rather than being deviant, they are conforming to patterns learned in childhood. Of course, in most cases they also learned the opposite message—that family violence is wrong. However, a message learned by experience and observation, rather than the message learned Sunday-school-style, has more force, especially when social stresses become great—and family stresses are often very great. The high level of interaction and commitment which is part of the pleasure of family life also produces great tensions.

Another widespread but hard-to-prove belief is the *class myth,* the idea that intrafamily violence occurs mainly in lower- and working-class families. Studying divorce applicants, George Levinger found that 40 percent of the working-class wives and 23 percent of the middle-class wives indicated "physical abuse" as a reason for seeking divorce. If almost one out of four middle-class women can report physical abuse, violence hardly seems absent from middle-class families. The nationwide sample survey conducted for the United States Commission on Violence reveals that over one-fifth of the respondents approve of slapping a spouse under certain conditions. There were no social-class differences in this *approval* of slapping, nor in reports of having ever spanked a child. At the same time, almost twice as many less educated respondents spank *frequently* (42 percent) as more educated respondents (22 percent).

CLASS DIFFERENCES

Other research on physical punishment is also contradictory. Most studies report more use of physical punishment by working-class parents, but some find no difference. Howard S. Erlanger undertook a comprehensive review of studies of social-class differences in the use of physical punishment and concluded that, although the weight of the evidence supports the view of less use of this technique among the middle class, the differences are small. Sizeable differences between social classes show up only when the analysis takes into account differences within social classes of such things as race, the sex of the child and of the parent, parental ambition for the child, and the specific nature of the father's occupation. Differences *within* social classes are at least as important as differences *between* classes.

Despite the mixed evidence, and despite the fact that there is a great deal of violence in middle-class families, we believe that research will eventually show that intrafamily violence is more common as one goes down the socioeconomic status ladder. Many social scientists attribute this to a lower-class "culture of violence" which encourages violent acts, and to an opposite middle-class culture which condemns violence. Although these cultural elements are well documented, we see them not as a cause, but as a response to fundamental social structural forces which affect families at all social levels but press harder and more frequently on the lower and working classes.

COMPENSATORY VIOLENCE

Willingness and ability to use physical violence may compensate for lack of other resources such as money, knowledge, and respect. If the social system does not provide an individual with the resources needed to maintain his or her family position, that individual will use violence if he is capable of it. John E. O'Brien asserts that ". . . there is considerable evidence that . . . husbands who . . . displayed violent behavior were severely inadequate in work, earner, or family support roles." While lack of the occupational and economic resources needed to fulfill the position of husband in our society is more characteristic of lower-class families than others, it is by no means confined to that stratum. The 1970–72 recession, with its high rates of unemployment among middle-class occupational groups (such as aerospace engineers), provides an opportunity to test this theory. The *resource theory* of violence would predict that unemployed husbands would engage in more intrafamily violence than comparable middle-class husbands who have not lost their jobs.

Some indication that the predicted results might be found is suggested by statistics for Birmingham, England, which showed a sharp rise in wife-beating during a six-month period when unemployment also rose sharply. A 1971 *Parade* report characterized these men as "frustrated, bored, unable to find a satisfying outlet for their energy. Britishers who are reduced to life on the dole meet adversity like men: they blame it on their wives. Then, pow!!!"

In a society such as ours, in which aggression is defined as a normal response to frustration, we can expect that the more frustrating the familial and occupational roles, the greater the amount of violence. Donald McKinley found that the lower the degree of self-direction a man has in his work, the greater the degree of aggressiveness in his relationship with his son. McKinley's data also show that the lower the job satisfaction, the higher the percentage using harsh punishment of children. The same relationship was found within each social class.

Both husbands and wives suffer from frustration, but since the main avenue of achievement for women has been in the family rather than in occupational roles, we must look within the family for the circumstances that are frustrating to women. Both residential crowding and too many children have been found to be related to the use of physical punishment. As with men, frustrations of this type are more common in the lower class, since lower-class wives are unlikely to have sufficient equipment and money for efficient, convenient housekeeping.

Although intrafamily violence probably is more common among lower-class families, it is incorrect to see it as only a lower-class or working-class phenomenon. What we have called the class myth overlooks the basic structural conditions (such as lack of adequate resources and frustrating life experiences) which are major causes of intrafamily violence and are present at all social levels, though to varying degrees. Some kinds of intrafamily violence are typical of all social classes—such as hitting children—even though the rate may be lower for the middle class—while other kinds of intrafamily violence are typical of *neither* class—like severe wife-beating—even though the rate is probably greater for the working class and especially the lower class.

The *sex myth* is the idea that sexual drives are linked to violence by basic biological mechanisms developed in the course of human evolution. Violence in sex is directly related to violence in the family because the family is the main way in which sex is made legitimate. To the extent that there is an inherent connection between sex and violence, it would be part of the biological basis for violence within the family.

There is abundant evidence that sex and violence go together, at least in our society and in a number of others. At the extreme, sex and warfaɪe have been associated in many ways, ranging from societies which view sex before a battle as a source of strength (or in some tribes, as a weakness) to the almost universally high frequency of ɪape by soldiers, often accompanied by subsequent genital mutilation and murder. In the fighting following the independence of the Congo in the early 1960s, rape was so common that the Catholic church is said to have given a special dispensation so that nuns could take contraceptive pills. More recently, in the Pakistan civil war, rape and mutilation were everyday occurrences. In Vietnam, scattered reports suggest that rapes and sexual tortures have been widespread. Closer to home, we have the romantic view of the aggressive he-man who "takes his woman" as portrayed in westerns and James Bond-type novels. In both cases, sex and gunfights are liberally intertwined.

SEXUAL REPRESSION

Then there are the sadists and masochists—individuals who can obtain sexual pleasure only by inflicting or receiving violent acts. We could dismiss such people as pathological exceptions, but it seems better to consider sadism and masochism as simply extreme forms of widespread behavior. The sex act itself typically is accompanied at least by mild violence and often by biting and scratching.

Nevertheless, despite all of this and much other evidence which could be cited, we feel that there is little biological linkage between sex and violence. It is true that in our society and in many other societies, sex and violence are linked. But there are enough instances of societies in which this is not the case to raise doubts about the biological linkage. What social conditions produce the association between violence and sex?

The most commonly offered explanation attributes the linkage between sex and violence to rules of the culture which limit or prevent sex. Empirical evidence supporting this sexual repression theory is difficult to establish. Societies which are high in restriction of extra-marital intercourse are also societies which tend to be violent—particularly in emphasizing military glory, killing, torture and mutilation of an enemy. But just how this carries over to violence in the sex act is not clear. Our interpretation hinges on the fact that sexual restriction tends to be associated with a definition of sex as intrinsically evil. This combination sets in motion two powerful forces making sex violent in societies having such a sexual code. First, since sex is normally prohibited or restricted, engaging in sexual intercourse may imply license to disregard other normally prohibited or restricted aspects of interpersonal relations. Consequently, aggressively inclined persons will tend to express their aggressiveness when they express their sexuality. Second, since sex is defined as evil and base, this cultural definition of sex may create a label or an expectancy which tends to be acted out.

By contrast, in societies such as Mangaia, which impose minimal sex restrictions and in which sex is defined as something to be enjoyed by all from the time they are first capable until death, sex is nonviolent. In Mangaia, exactly the opposite of the two violence-producing mechanisms just listed seem to operate. First, since sex is a normal everyday activity, the normal standards for control of aggression apply. Second, since sex is defined as an act expressing the best in man, it is an occasion for altruistic behavior. Thus, Donald S. Marshall says of the Mangaia: "My several informants generally agreed that the really important thing in sexual intercourse—for the married man or for his unwed fellow—was to give pleasure to his partner; that her pleasure in orgasm was what gave the male partner a special thrill, separate from his own orgasm."

Socially patterned antagonism between men and women is at the heart of a related theory which can also account for the association of sex and violence. The sex antagonism and segregation theory suggests that the higher the level of antagonism between men and women, the greater the tendency to use violence in sexual acts. Since, by itself, this statement is open to a charge of circular reasoning, the theory must be backed up by related propositions which account for the sex role antagonism.

In societies such as ours, part of the explanation for antagonism between the sexes is probably traceable to the sexual restrictions and sexual denigration mentioned above. The curse God placed on all women when Eve sinned is the earliest example in our culture of the sexually restrictive ethic, the placing of the "blame" for sex on women, and the resulting negative definition of women—all of which tend to make women culturally legitimate objects of antagonism and aggression. The New Testament reveals much more antipathy to sex than the Old and contains many derogatory (and implicitly hostile) statements about women.

The present level of antagonism between the sexes is probably at least as great as that in biblical times. In novels, biographies and everyday speech, words indicating femaleness, especially in its sexual aspect (such as "bitch"), are used by men as terms of disparagement, and terms for sexual intercourse, such as "screw" and "fuck," are used to indicate an aggressive or harmful act. On the female side, women tend to see men as exploiters and to teach their daughters that man are out to take advantage of them.

It would be a colossal example of ethnocentrism, however, to attribute antagonism between the sexes to the Western Judeo-Christian tradition. Cultural definitions of women as evil are found in many societies. Obviously, more fundamental processes are at work, of which the Christian tradition is only one manifestation.

CATHARSIS MYTH

A clue to a possibly universal process giving rise to antagonism between the sexes may be found in the cross-cultural studies which trace this hostility back to the division of labor between the sexes and other differences in the roles of men and women. This sex-role segregation gives rise to differences in child-rearing practices for boys and girls and to problems in establishing sexual identity. Beatrice Whiting, for example, concludes: "It would seem as if there were a never-ending circle. The separation of the sexes leads to a conflict of identity in the boy children, to unconscious fear of being feminine, which leads to protest masculinity, exaggeration of the differences between men and women, antagonism against and fear of women, male solidarity, and hence back to isolation of women and very young children." This process can also be observed in the matrifocal family of the urban slum and the Caribbean. The relationships between the sexes have been labeled by Jackson Toby as "compulsive masculinity" and vividly depicted in Eldridge Cleaver's "Allegory of the Black Eunuchs." Slightly more genteel forms of the same sexual antagonism are to be found among middle-class men, as illustrated by the character of Jonathan in the movie *Carnal Knowledge.*

Obviously, the linkages between sex and violence are extremely complex, and many other factors probably operate besides the degree of restrictiveness, the cultural definition of sexuality, and antagonism between the sexes. But even these indicate sufficiently that it is incorrect to assume a direct connection between sexual drives and violence, since such an assumption disregards the sociocultural framework within which sexual relations take place. These social and cultural factors, rather than sex drives *per se,* give rise to the violent aspects of sexuality in so many societies.

The *catharsis myth* asserts that the expression of "normal" aggression between family members should not be bottled up: if normal aggression is allowed to be expressed, tension is released, and the likelihood of severe violence is therefore reduced. This view has a long and distinguished intellectual history. Aristotle used the term "catharsis" to refer to the purging of the passions or sufferings of spectators through vicarious participation in the suffering of a tragic hero. Both Freud's idea of "the liberation of affect" to enable reexperiencing blocked or inhibited emotions and the view of John Dollard and his associates that "the occurrence of any act of aggression is assumed to reduce the instigation of aggression" are modern versions of this tradition.

Applying this approach to the family, Bettelheim urges that children should learn about violence in order to learn how to handle it. Under the present rules (at least for the middle class), we forbid a child to hit, yell, or swear at us or his playmates. The child must also refrain from destroying property or even his own toys. In teaching this type of self-control, however, Bruno Bettelheim holds that we have denied the child outlets for the instinct of human violence and have failed to teach him how to deal with his violent feelings.

Proof of the catharsis theory is overwhelmingly negative. Exposure to vicariously experienced violence has been shown to increase rather than decrease both aggressive fantasy and aggressive acts. Similarly, experiments in which children are given the opportunity to express violence and aggression show that they express more aggression after the purported cathartic experience than do controls.

Theoretical arguments against the catharsis view are equally cogent. The instinct-theory assumptions which underlie the idea of catharsis have long been discarded in social science. Modern social psychological theories—including social learning theory, symbolic interaction theory, and labeling theory—all predict the opposite of the catharsis theory: the more frequently an act is performed, the greater the likelihood that it will become a standard part of the behavior repertory of the individual and of the expectations of others for that individual.

CULTURAL BELIEFS

In light of largely negative evidence and cogent theoretical criticism, the sheer persistence of the catharsis theory becomes an interesting phenomenon. There seem to be several factors underlying the persistence of the catharsis myth:

1. *Prestige and influence of psychoanalytic theory.* Albert Bandura and Richard Walters suggest that the persistence of the catharsis view is partly the result of the extent to which psychoanalytic ideas have become part of both social science and popular culture. Granting this, one must also ask why this particular part of Freud's vast writing is unquestioned. After all, much of what Freud wrote has been ignored, and other parts have been dropped on the basis of contrary evidence.

Whenever an element of cultural belief persists in spite of seemingly sound reasons for discarding it, one should look for ways in which the belief may be woven into a system of social behavior. Certain behavior may be at least partially congruent with the "false" belief: various social patterns may be justified by such beliefs.

2. *Justification of existing patterns.* Intrafamily violence is a recurring feature of our society, despite the cultural commitment to nonviolence. It is not far-fetched to assume that, under the circumstances, the catharsis theory which in effect justifies sporadic violence will be attractive to a population engaged in occasional violence.

3. *Congruence with the positive value of violence in nonfamily spheres of life.* Although *familial* norms deprecate or forbid intra-

family violence, the larger value system of American society is hardly nonviolent. In fact, the overwhelming proportion of American parents consider it part of their role to train sons to be tough. The violence commission survey reveals that 70 percent of the respondents believed it is good for boys to have a few fist-fights. Thus, a social theory which justifies violence as being psychologically beneficial to the aggressor is likely to be well received.

4. *Congruence with the way familial violence often occurs.* Given the antiviolence norms, intrafamily physical abuse typically occurs as a climax to a repressed conflict. As Louis Coser points out:

> Closely knit groups in which there exists a high frequency of interaction and high personality involvement of the members have a tendency to suppress conflict. While they provide frequent occasions for hostility (since both sentiments of love and hatred are intensified through frequency of interaction), the acting out of such feelings is sensed as a danger to such intimate relationships, and hence there is a tendency to suppress rather than to allow expression of hostile feelings. In close-knit groups, feelings of hostility tend, therefore, to accumulate and hence to intensify.

At some point the repressed conflict has to be resolved. Frequently, the mechanism which forces the conflict into the open is a violent outburst. This is one of the social functions of violence listed by Coser. In this sense, intrafamily violence does have a cathartic effect. But the catharsis which takes place comes from getting the conflict into the open and resolving it—not the releasing effects of violent incidents *per se,* but on the ability to recognize these as warning signals and to deal with the underlying conflict honestly and with empathy.

5. *Confusion of immediate with long-term effects.* There can be little doubt that a sequence of violent activity is often followed by a sharp reduction of tension, an emotional release, and even a feeling of quiescence. To the extent that tension release *is* produced by violence, this immediate cathartic effect is likely to powerfully reinforce the violence which preceded it. Having reduced tension in one instance, it becomes a mode of behavior likely to be repeated later in similar instances. An analogy with sexual orgasm seems plausible. Following orgasm, there is typically a sharp reduction in sexual drive, most obvious in the male's loss of erection. At the same time, however, the experience of orgasm is powerfully reinforcing and has the long-term effect of increasing the sex drive. We believe that violence and sex are similar in this respect. The short-term effect of violence is, in one sense, cathartic; but the long-term effect is a powerful force toward including violence as a standard mode of social interaction.

While the assumptions outlined in this article in some ways contribute to preserving the institution of family, they also keep us from taking a hard and realistic look at the family and taking steps to change it in ways which might correct the underlying problems. Such stereotypes contain a kernel of truth but are dangerous oversimplifications. Although there are differences between social classes in intrafamily violence, the class myth ignores the high level of family violence present in other social strata. The sex myth, although based on historically accurate observation of the link between sex and violence, tends to assume that this link is biologically determined and fails to take into account the social and cultural factors which associate sex and violence in many societies. The catharsis myth seems to have the smallest kernel of truth at its core, and its persistence, in the face of devastating evidence to the contrary, may be due to the subtle justification it gives to the violent nature of American society and to the fact that violent episodes in a family can have the positive function of forcing a repressed conflict into the open for nonviolent resolution.

11. Delinquency and Adult Criminal Careers

KENNETH POLK

EARLY ADULT LIFE: ACHIEVEMENT AND DEVIANCE

The argument here is that these promissory [educational] experiences are in fact connected with experiences in early adulthood. Functioning as institutional systems, there evolve over time patterns of institutional career "flows," the consequences of which are clearly observable (or at least these should be) in what happens as young persons move into early adulthood. The "straight" students, who have maintained institutional careers as exemplary students and who have avoided the definition of deviant, should show high levels of access to adult success and low levels of adult criminality. On the other hand, the unsuccessful students, especially those who accumulate over time public definitions as deviants, can be expected to show both high levels of official adult deviance and low levels of access to adult success.

THE PROMISSORY AND INSTITUTIONAL CHARACTER OF THE ARGUMENT

What should be clear by now about this formulation is first, that it is based on notions of probabilistic promise. The two sets of institutions, socialization and social control, are both seen as being fundamentally based on notions of youthful promise. This is perhaps clearest in the case of the educational work linkage since the process is so clearly based on notions of recruitment, selection, and preparation. But this logic of the status future operates in the social control institutions as well. The contemporary concern about the negative effects of labeling and stigma, and the consequent emphasis on diversion, provides an obvious demonstration of this point. The argument to eliminate these negative processes contains the premise that the alternative need is to protect the interests of the child, especially with respect to the future. In fact, the whole range of status offenses (ungovernable behavior, endangering one's welfare, out of control, being in manifest danger of engaging in lewd or immoral conduct) can be viewed explicitly within this future-oriented, promissory framework. The reason why these statutes are provided is to protect the future interests of the child, to redirect her or him during these youthful years so that "worse problems don't develop later." The concern for the protection of the future of children is so strong, in fact, that the legal system is willing to promulgate unconstitutionally vague conditions for the imposition of the coercive power of the state in order to accomplish the task. Not only is the *intent* of the juvenile justice system to protect (however one may question the effectiveness of such procedures) the futures of children, it also in its *processes* uses as a basic criterion for decision-making the perceived future potential of the child. The child most likely to be either ignored or diverted is the individual who exhibits a multitude of symptoms of success, i.e., if the individual who is doing well in school, who is involved in a lot of legitimate school activities, who is part of the inner circle, and so on happens to be arrested, it is highly likely that the justice system will extend to the limit its capacity to nonintervene. The cases where intervention is likely to be viewed as necessary are instances where there are, instead of indicators of success, symptoms of failure and illegitimacy. It is in such cases that there is likely to be a perceived need for the social control institutions to enter into the scene, quite likely *with the intent of protecting the interests of the child,* i.e., to engage in action to try to improve the status future prospects of the child, at least in terms of the control aspects of status.

A further feature of this status future argument is that the system operates *bureaucratically,* such that *organizational careers* evolve out of the institutional organization of status. In the contemporary world, terms such as "college prep" or "delinquent" derive their basic meaning in bureaucratic process. Interlocking sets of *institutional labels* are generated which derive their logic and meaning in organizational process, and one must sort out issues at the institutional level before discourse about individual issues around labeling can make much sense. Thus, it is important to know how the label exists in the first place, and the role it plays within the institutional context, before it is possible to make sense of the question of how one kind of actor, e.g., the teacher, is able to impose upon another kind of actor, e.g., the student, one or another type of label, e.g., bright or dumb.

Finally, this perspective argues that critical intersections exist between institutional labels in the "socializing" and in the "social control" bureaucracies. The process of building a career definition of a deviant, to give a specific example, is likely to be a slow and cumulative process, involving the building up over time of failure labels in the socializing institutions and "need for control" labels in the social control institutions. The importance of this assumption is that, first, it avoids the mistake of viewing a single negative label event as a catastrophic and transforming experience without reference to the context of other labels. Certainly some experiences which produce labels can lead to basic transformation of identity, e.g., murderer, narc, or spy. It seems likely, however, that a single experience with delinquency, when that experience is contradicted by powerful institutional definitions of success, may have limited impact. The exact same offense, at the exact same time, for another young person with a history of unsuccessful and problematic behavior labels, may have quite different institutional and personal consequences. Second, as illustrated in this last instance, it calls attention to the hypothesis that much of the basis for the imposition of control labels may lie well outside the social control system. If success and nonsuccess have their definition in the institutional intersections of work, school, and family experiences, and if the definition of nonsuccess is a fundamental feature of individuals who ultimately occupy the most persistent and problematic categories of career delinquents, then attempts to alter basic behavior patterns within the context of the social control institutions may be of little consequence. This includes attempts to "radically nonintervene," since the basic features of social vulnerability remain. Putting it another way, for those persons caught most firmly in the intersection of institutional processes that lead to social vulnerability, the presence of the justice system is merely one of a gamut of problematic roles that must be negotiated, however unsuccessfully. However important it may be for social policy to urge and support the limitation of the power of the juvenile justice system, for those young persons who are most vulnerable the critical features of the vulnerability remain: they will possess few educational credentials and have virtually no chance to enter the job market in a satisfying and legitimate role, to give but two features of such vulnerability.

SOME SUPPORTIVE EVIDENCE

The nature of this exercise creates a unique set of demands for a discussion of data. What will be done here will be to examine the key set of institutional intersections and to generate either data drawn from previously published research or new data, depending on the nature of the question and what data are available. The new data will be drawn from an ongoing longitudinal investigation of adolescents in a medium-sized county (1960 population: 120,888) in the Pacific Northwest. A 25 percent random sample was drawn from a sample frame consisting of all male sophomores enrolled in the schools of the coun-

ty in 1964. From a total of 309 subjects selected, 284 usable interviews were obtained, giving a response rate of 92 percent. The one-
hour interviews conducted by the project staff members covered a
range of demographic, school, family, work, and peer variables. To
these data were added grade point average from school transcripts
and delinquency reports from juvenile court records. Further description of this study can be found in Polk and Schafer (1972).

The discussion of evidence will be organized by asking a series of
questions:

1. Is there evidence of a connection between school performance
and adult success? The question is seen as one of the most critical to
the argument, since most of the premises are based on the notion of
the institutional connection between school and work. Here a variety
of supporting evidence can be cited. Census results persistently report that the highest paying occupations are professional and technical positions, i.e., those requiring the most education (Bureau of the
Census, 1973a: 1 and 1973b: 213), and, furthermore, these are the occupations with the highest prestige ranking (Miller, 1967: 201). Using
as a criterion the amount of lifetime earnings, males with four or
more years of college will earn over the course of their lifetime approximately twice the income of persons who do not finish high
school, and recent research suggests that this gap is widening over
time (U.S. National Center for Educational Statistics, 1975: 22). A
strong connection does seem to exist, then, between the educational
and work institutions.

2. Is there evidence of a connection between indicators of family
power/vulnerability and school performance? Here again, there
seems to be wide and general support for the proposition from the literature. Certainly, countless studies have been conducted which
show the relationship between class and performance, i.e., to use the
language of this argument, that a working-class background, one
measure of family vulnerability, renders it more likely that the child
will come to be defined as academically unsuccessful (a review, summary, and annotation of a great number of such studies can be found
in Squibb, 1973). Using less abstract and less neutral language, Pearl
(1965: 92) argues: " 'special ability classes,' 'basic track,' or 'slow learn-
er classes' are various names for another means of systematically denying the poor adequate access to education."

3. Is there evidence of a connection between school performance
and deviance? As before, so much evidence exists for this basic premise from earlier research that there is little need for extensive discussion. Considerable data have been gathered showing the
relationship between such academic performance variables as
grades, tracking or streaming, dropping out, and deviance/delin-

quency (for examples, see Polk and Schafer, 1972; Stinchcombe, 1964; Hargreaves, 1967; and Elliott and Voss, 1974).

4. Is there evidence of significant independent connections between family background, school performance, and deviance? Now the argument begins to grow more complex. Perhaps it is time to draw upon some actual data, especially to make sense of the earlier distinction between delinquency and the troublesome life style. Extracting part of a table from a previously published study, it can be seen that when the simultaneous effects of class background and academic performance on deviant behavior are examined, both contribute some independent effect, but the strongest effects are a result of academic performance (see Table 1). Persistently, the percentage differences are greater in the contrasts between academic performance categories than is true for the social-class categories. Note here that the pattern is the same for the measure of official delinquency as it is for the wider measures of troublesome behavior. We will use this consistency to argue in the tables which follow that there

Table 1. Percentage of Troublesome and Delinquent Responses by Social Class Background and Grade Point Average

	Grade Point Average			
	HIGH		LOW	
	(1)	(2)	(3)	(4)
	White Collar	Blue Collar	White Collar	Blue Collar
Troublesome Item	(N = 111)	(N = 77)	(N = 28)	(N = 44)
"Friends in trouble"	30	43	75	64
"Drink with friends"	46	52	75	61
"Enjoy cruising"	57	61	82	84
"Peers vs. principal"	52	48	83	70
"Peers vs. parents"	28	31	65	46
"Peers vs. police"	59	57	82	79
"Drink beer"	35	44	64	72
"Like to fight"	18	20	43	48
"Official delinquency"	14	21	36	41

Mean Percentage Difference by:
    a. Social Class, indicated by comparing columns
      1) 1 vs. 2 = 4.2%
      2) 3 vs. 4 = 4.2%

    b. G.P.A., indicated by comparing columns
      1) 1 vs. 3 = 29.6%
      2) 2 vs. 4 = 20.9%

Source: Polk, 1969.

is at least some reason to presume that it may be legitimate to link the specific behavior of official delinquency to a wider troublesome life style. (Making this assumption is necessary both because in some studies to be cited the only measure of deviance available is delinquency and because in other cases the tables would be too complex if a great number of deviance outcome measures were included. Nonetheless, while the empirical measure is based on delinquency, the theoretical conception of delinquency that is being suggested nests such behavior in the context of a wider troublesome life style.)

5. Is there evidence that when academic failure occurs, the nature of the involvement with adolescent peers mediates between the deviant and nondeviant experiences? At this point we can draw on some original data. Among those young persons in the Pacific Northwest study who were academically unsuccessful, the level of delinquency involvement varies considerably by involvement in the teenage culture. Using a composite measure of teenage culture suggested by Galvin (1975), students with low grades who had little involvement with teenage culture had low levels of delinquency (14 percent), while among failing students with high involvement with teenage culture, close to half (46 percent) became labeled as juvenile delinquents.

6. Is there evidence that the connection between educational performance and deviance extends into early adult life? At this point we begin to explore virtually virgin territory, since few previous research findings exist on the link between adolescent or adult school careers and adult criminality. Data from the Pacific Northwest cohort indicate that such a link can be traced. Looking first at high school performance, slightly over half (54 percent) of individuals with low grade point averages (low meaning in this case below 2.00) had been charged with an adult offense, in contrast with 23 percent so charged among individuals with higher grade point averages. A similar pattern exists in the case of adult educational attainment. Drawing the line at three years or more of college completed (since some of the successful elements of the cohort are at the time this research is being done still in college), we find low levels of adult criminality (15 percent) among those with high adult educational attainment, and high levels of criminality (39 percent) among those with less educational attainment.

7. Is there evidence of a connection between the labels attached by the socializing (school) and the social control (juvenile court) institutions to *adolescent* and *adult* criminality? To get at this question, it is helpful to generate a table (see Table 2); the resultant data indicate strong links between these institutional experiences. Among the small group of individuals who had both delinquent and academically unsuccessful labels, the level of adult criminality was quite high (83

Table 2.   Percentage of Individuals with Adult Criminal Records by Delinquency Status as Adolescent and by High School Grade Point Average

| | Percentage Criminal | |
	DELINQUENT	NONDELINQUENT
High G.P.A.	50	18
	(N = 32)	(N = 164)
Low G.P.A.	83	40
	(N = 18)	(N = 38)

percent). At the opposite extreme, relatively low levels of adult criminality (18 percent) were observed among individuals who were both academically successful and nondelinquent as adolescents. Interestingly, if the young person had earned a label of delinquent, in half the cases (50 percent) even the experience of academic success was not powerful enough to protect against the eventual experience with adult criminal behavior, while 40 percent of the nondelinquent youth who were academically unsuccessful were pulled toward adult criminality.

8. Is there evidence of a link between the labels attached by the socializing (school) and the social control (juvenile court) institutions to adolescents and adult success? We unfortunately cannot obtain a good test of this question from the Pacific Northwest data, since as of this writing some of the potentially successful elements of the cohort are still in college. Nonetheless, if we use as a temporary measure of potential adult success significant levels of higher education involvement, we can draw upon some previous research to look tentatively at the issue (Noblit, 1973). The findings of that study (see Table 3) indicate that, as might be expected from the earlier discussion, the highest levels of adult success (75 percent with high educational attainment) are found among young persons with high levels of aca-

Table 3.   Percentage of Young Persons with High Access to Adult Success (Defined by College Attendance) by Academic Performance and Delinquency

| | Percentage with High Access to Adult Success | |
	DELINQUENT	NONDELINQUENT
High G.P.A.	60	75
Low G.P.A.	26	20

Source: Noblit, 1973.

demic success as adolescents who were not involved with the juvenile justice system. An interesting facet of these findings is that these data are somewhat interactive. What is observed is that the basic factor operating among the most vulnerable is simply academic failure, i.e., among those with low grade point averages the level of success attainment is low, regardless of delinquency involvement (26 percent of the low g.p.a. delinquents and 20 percent of the low g.p.a. nondelinquents being considered as successful adults, the difference between these two categories appearing to be nonsignificant). The barrier to adult success is, apparently, first and foremost academic. Once you have failed, you have little chance to succeed, and the experience of delinquency does not make your chances any worse. Among the academically successful, on the other hand, the experience of delinquency does appear to suppress the level of success (60 percent achieving high levels of educational attainment, contrasted with the earlier mentioned 75 percent among the high g.p.a. nondelinquents).

References

Elliott, D. S. and H. L. Voss (1974) *Delinquency and Dropout.* Lexington, Mass.: D. C. Heath.

Galvin, J. L. (1975) "Youth culture and adult success." Ph.D. dissertation. University of Oregon, Department of Curriculum and Instruction. September. (unpublished)

Hargreaves, D. H. (1967) *Social Relations in a Secondary School.* London: Routledge & Kegan Paul.

Miller, H. P. (1967) *Rich Man, Poor Man.* New York: Thomas Y. Crowell.

Noblit, G. (1973) "Delinquency and access to success: a study of the consequences of the delinquency label." Ph.D. dissertation. University of Oregon, Department of Sociology. (unpublished)

Pearl, A. (1965) "Youth in lower class settings," in Muzafer Sherif and Carolyn W. Sherif (eds.) Problems of Youth. Chicago: Aldine.

Polk, K. (1969) "Class, strain, and rebellion among adolescents." Social Problems 17(Fall):214–224.

_____ and W. E. Schafer (1972) Schools and Delinquency. Englewood Cliffs, N.J.: Prentice-Hall.

Squibb, P. G. (1973) "Education and class." Educational Research 15 (June):194–209.

Stinchcombe, A. (1964) *Rebellion in a High School.* Chicago: Quadrangle.

U.S. Bureau of the Census (1973a) Census of the Population: 1970. Subject Reports, Final Report PC (2)-8B, Earnings by Occupation and Education. Washington, D.C.: Government Printing Office.

_____ (1973b) Census of the Population: 1970, Subject Reports, Final Report PC (2)-5B Educational Attainment. Washington, D.C.: Government Printing Office.

U.S. National Center for Educational Statistics (1975) Digest of Educational Statistics—1974. Washington, D.C.: Government Printing Office.

PART 3

EXPLAINING CRIME

In parts one and two selections were presented on how laws evolve and change over time and how crime is measured. This part deals with the question of *why* people violate the law. Attempts to provide answers to this question have taken many forms.

Biologists, psychologists, and psychiatrists tend to favor an individual, or *clinical*, model, which attempts to identify the pathological or crime-producing factors *within* the individual, such as defective genetic combinations or arrested personality adjustments. Sociologists are more likely to follow a *structural* model, which looks to societal conditions—poverty, urbanization, blocked opportunity, racism—for their explanations. Still others, including some social psychologists, analyze how individual and structural elements interact with each other to produce pressures for crime. Regardless of the approach taken, it is generally recognized that various conditions must be present before "criminal" behavior can occur. Selected factors or combinations of factors may stand out in the backgrounds of people labeled as criminals.

In this part an overview of the various types of explanations is followed by some of the better-known sociological and social-psychological explanations. They fall into six major categories: (1) the Marxian, or conflict, perspective, (2) the subculture of violence perspective, (3) anomie theory, (4) the cultural transmission perspective, (5) control theory, and (6) the societal reactions, or labeling, perspective. While each approach focuses on certain processes, there frequently exists an overlap among the statements, apparent in the following discussion.

TYPES OF EXPLANATIONS

Even though major attention is being given today to sociological and social-psychological viewpoints, other types of explanations continue to receive serious consideration. The lead article, by C. Ronald Huff, "Historical Explanations of Crime: From Demons to Politics," underscores this point. Huff presents a chronology of the major explanations of crime. Many of the schools of thought reviewed, such as the supernatural, the physical-biological, and the psychopathological, are clinical, that is, they look to individual traits for an understanding of crime. In his discussion of sociological explanations, the author provides an excellent outline of Sutherland and Cressey's "differential association theory," a statement often invoked to explain how individuals learn criminal values and traditions. Huff's review concludes with a brief introduction to the labeling, conflict, and radical perspectives; these developing views, Huff maintains, have shifted the focus from an examination of the individual criminal to an analysis of social and political systems.

THE MARXIAN, OR CONFLICT, PERSPECTIVE

The Marxian, or conflict, view of crime causation argues that it is the powerful who decide what behavior is criminal and how criminals are to be treated by the state. Steven Spitzer, in "Toward a Marxian Theory of Deviance," presents this position. He points out that most traditional theories of deviance (or crime) are preoccupied with dramatic and predatory forms of social behavior and have neglected the problems of how deviance comes to be defined. Instead of accepting the prevailing definitions as givens, one must become aware of the process by which deviance is "subjectively constructed" and the way in which deviants are "objectively handled," as well as "the structural bases of behavior and characteristics which come to official attention." Spitzer provides an insightful account of deviance production and control in capitalist societies. Several of his statements have relevance for the selections on government and corporate crime in part four.

THE SUBCULTURE-OF-VIOLENCE PERSPECTIVE

Howard S. Erlanger, in "The Empirical Status of the Subculture of Violence Thesis," provides a critical assessment of the cultural conflict, or subculture-of-violence, perspective. In this view, members of some groups, by adhering to values that encourage and support violence, find themselves at odds with the values of the dominant culture. Behavior viewed as criminal by the larger society may be considered acceptable or even expected within the subculture. Noting that this thesis has been used to explain various types of gang activities, Erlanger presents data that challenge the subculture of violence perspectives. He concludes that, as the evidence now stands, black and low-income white communities do not appear to differ significantly from the dominant society in their approval of violence.

ANOMIE THEORY

Proponents of the anomie framework are concerned with analyzing how the class structure affects the channels of social mobility that are open to different groups in society. "Differential Opportunity and Delinquent Subcultures" by Richard A. Cloward and Lloyd E. Ohlin offers a representative statement of this position. They argue that, just as there are differentials in access to legitimate means of becoming successful, there are also differentials in access to illegitimate means. In other words, illegitimate avenues to goal achievement are not necessarily open or freely available to those who might aspire to pursue them. These contentions become apparent in Cloward and Ohlin's discussion of the varieties of delinquent subcultures. The type of subculture that emerges is a function of the relative accessibility of illegitimate opportunities in a given neighborhood. For example, a criminal subculture is likely to develop among adolescents in a community where illegal activities are an accepted means of achieving material gain and power. Such a subculture enables status-deprived, lower-class males to learn values and techniques from the adult criminal world.

THE CULTURAL-TRANSMISSION PERSPECTIVE

As is apparent from Cloward and Ohlin's view, one often learns criminal behavior systems through interaction with others. Gresham M. Sykes and David Matza, in "Techniques of Neutralization: A Theory of Delinquency," provide further content to this notion. They are concerned specifically with how delinquents learn to justify the deviance of their acts and thus avoid self-blame and the blame of others. For example, they may deny responsibility for the act, claiming that bad companions, unloving parents, or slum conditions are at fault. Sykes and Matza stress the point that rationalizations are operative before, during, and after the act has been committed.

The statement by Sykes and Matza puts the focus on the actor. He or she has to weigh the relative costs and advantages associated with committing a crime. Obviously, if one can legitimate one's action, then the probability of crime occurring is much greater. The career criminal frequently possesses a rather sophisticated system of rationalization. The remaining two selections also focus on the actor.

CONTROL THEORY

In "A Control Theory of Delinquency," Travis Hirschi outlines some of the basic tenets underlying control theory. A major assumption of control theorists is that when an individual's *bond* to society is weak or broken, criminal or delinquent acts are likely to result. Hirschi discusses various elements of the bond to society. For example, the "commitment" element refers to the fact that many people invest a great deal of time and energy in certain pursuits, such as obtaining an education or a job. Thus, when criminal activity is considered, they must assess the risks they run of losing their investment. Many of the elements of the bond to society can provide further insight into various selections in part four, particularly those that describe evolving criminal careers.

THE SOCIETAL REACTIONS PERSPECTIVE

Advocates of the labeling, or societal reactions, perspective are primarily concerned with how social control agents react to violators of the law and how interactional processes affect one's personal and public identity. Thus definitional processes and products, as well as their effects, are given prominence. The article by Charles Wellford, "Labeling Theory and Criminology: An Assessment," outlines some of the basic notions of this perspective and assesses its usefulness in explaining crime. His review of the existing evidence leads him to conclude that the labeling model, as it is often conceptualized and constructed, lacks any significant explanatory power. Wellford contends that criminologists should explore other ways to explain crime, most specifically through an analysis of *situational determinants.* He thus anticipates several readings in part four, such as those of Luckenbill, Blum and Fisher, and Henn.

12. Historical Explanations of Crime: From Demons to Politics

C. RONALD HUFF

Man's historical concern with the existence of crime has been reflected in his diverse attempts to explain how and why crime occurs. Long before there was a scientific approach to the crime problem, there were speculative "explanations" of criminal behavior. Some of these earlier views concerning the nature of crime may seem absurd according to contemporary standards, but they must be viewed as symbolic expressions of the prevailing ideas and concerns of their own era. Similarly, it would be surprising if our currently fashionable theories of crime are not viewed as naive and unsophisticated in the next century.

Before discussing the major historical explanations of crime, it seems appropriate to ask what, if any, relevance such a discussion can have for students of criminology and criminal justice. While intellectual inquiry is justifiable for its own sake, the current discussion has contemporary relevance in at least two ways: (1) It presents an overview of the development of criminological theory, which should permit a greater understanding of contemporary explanations and their place in the continuity of thought on the subject of crime. (2) Since society's responses to crime depend, to a large extent, on its theories and its assumptions about the nature of crime, an understanding of those views is useful in attempting to analyze the numerous attempts to "prevent," "control," "deter," "cure," or otherwise contain criminal behavior. The operations of the various components of the criminal justice system (such as the police, the courts, and the prisons) can perhaps best be viewed by understanding the various assumptions which underlie their policies and procedures. Every major theory, explanation, or assumption about the nature and causes of crime may be viewed as having important implications for the strategies of social control which society elects to implement. The following discussion examines the existence of such connections between theory and practice.

SUPERNATURAL EXPLANATIONS

Primitive man's basic explanation of "criminal" behavior was that of diabolical possession. Criminal behavior was viewed as evidence that the culprit was under the control of evil spirits, or demons.[1] This view of deviant behavior was simply an extension of the prevailing view of nature—i.e., that every object or being was controlled by spiritual forces.[2] Obviously, such an explanation requires *belief* or *faith*, since it does not lend itself to scientific verification. Nevertheless, demonology had important implications for man's responses to crime.

Given such an explanation of crime, the only sensible solution was to try to exorcise the demons which were responsible for the behavior or, failing that, to do away with the criminal, either by exile or by execution. In a society where the gods were perceived as omnipotent and omnipresent, it was clearly a matter of the highest priority to appease them, no matter what the costs. Thus, the fate of the criminal was less related to the protection of society than to compliance with the will of the gods. The failure of the group to punish the wrongdoer was believed to leave the tribe open to the wrath and vengeance of the gods.

One who violated the norms dealing with endogamy, witchcraft, or treason was likely to receive the harshest punishment in primitive society. The offender might be hacked to pieces, exiled, or even eaten. All three of these sanctions accomplished the same goal—the removal of the offender from the group. Offenses of a private, rather than public, nature were generally dealt with by the victim's clan through the process known as "blood feud." Essentially, it was the duty of each member of a clan to avenge a fellow clan member. The principle which guided this pursuit of retaliation was the well-known *lex talionis*[3] ("an eye for an eye and a tooth for a tooth"). The idea of *lex talionis*, roughly, was that the punishment should fit the crime. Primitive obsession with making the retaliation exact was in some cases so fanatical that inanimate objects which had been instrumental in accidental deaths were actually "punished."[4]

There was very little use of any form of incarceration in primitive society, except for periods of detention while awaiting disposition and the incarceration related to cannibalistic practices. The only other major type of punishment did not appear until the late stages of primitive society. It was a form of compensation or restitution. This practice developed in response to the failure of blood feud as a method of criminal justice. Blood feuds all too often resulted in prolonged vendettas which exacted heavy tolls on both sides. The practice of paying a fixed monetary penalty therefore evolved as an alternative to the potentially genocidal blood feuds. Later, in the feudal period, the extended families or clans established a system of "wergeld" (man-money) by which the victim's status determined the amount assessed against the offender. This concept was gradually broadened to include differences in degree of responsibility, the individualization of responsibility, and even a distinction between "intent" and "accident." Eventually a specified value was set for each *type* of offense, and the system of restitutive fines paid by the offender to the victim came to be preferred over the blood feud. With the subsequent development of an appeal procedure whereby either party could protest an injustice, the roots of the modern-day court system emerged in embryonic form. Finally, through the absolute authority which accompanied kingships, especially in early *historic* society and during feudalism, all crimes became "crimes against the king's peace"; in other words, crimes came to be regarded as offenses against the *public* welfare. At that point man had, in a sense, come "full circle" in his efforts to rationalize law and punishment:

> The heavy fines imposed on places and people became an important source of revenue to the crown and to the barons and the lords of manors. . . .
> The State was growing strong enough to take vengeance; the common man was no longer feared as had been the well-armed Saxon citizen of old, and to the "common" criminal was extended the ruthless severity once reserved for the slaves . . . and the idea of compensation began to wane before the revenge instinct now backed by power.[5]

RATIONALISM AND FREE WILL

Just as demonological explanations dominated the thinking of early man, the so-called "classical period" of criminology (roughly 1700–1800) was characterized by its own conceptions of the nature of man. Man was seen as being rational, having free will, and seeking that which would be most productive of pleasure or happiness. Such views, of course, represented a significant departure from the idea that man was under the control of supernatural forces and that criminal behavior was a function of demons. For an understanding of the magnitude of this shift in thinking during the eighteenth century, it is best to examine the ideas of the two most influential contributors to classical criminology—Cesare Beccaria and Jeremy Bentham.

Beccaria, who was influenced by French rationalism and humanitarianism, strongly attacked the arbitrary and inconsistent "criminal justice" practices of the mid-eighteenth century. In his major work,[6]

Beccaria reacted against the secret accusations, inhumane punishments, and lack of concern for the defendant's rights that characterized criminal justice. He articulated the framework of what came to be known as the classical school of criminology, i.e.: (1) that the motivation underlying all social action must be the utilitarian value of that action (the greatest happiness for the greatest number); (2) that crime is an injury to *society* and can only be measured by assessing the extent of that injury (focus on the act and the extent of damage, not intent); (3) that the prevention of crime is more important than its punishment; (4) that secret accusations and torture should be eliminated, while the trial process ought to be speedy and the accused treated fairly and humanely throughout the process; (5) that the only valid purpose of punishment is deterrence, *not* social revenge; and (6) that incarceration should be utilized more widely, but, at the same time, conditions for those confined must be vastly upgraded and systems of classification developed to prevent haphazardly mixing all types of inmates.

Beccaria had enormous influence on the reformation of criminal justice. For example, he proposed that the courts should mete out punishments to the offender in direct proportion to the harm caused by his crime. To accomplish this, it was necessary that all crimes be classified according to some assessment of their social harm and, further, that the penal codes must prescribe for each crime exact penalties that would be useful deterrents to crime:

> A scale of crimes may be formed of which the first degree should consist of those which immediately tend to the dissolution of society; and the last, of the smallest possible injustice done to a private member of society. Between those extremes will be comprehended all actions contrary to the public good, which are called criminal. . . . Any action which is not comprehended in the above mentioned scale, will not be called a crime, or punished as such.[7]

One need only observe the deliberations of state legislatures today during the process of revising a state's criminal code to understand and appreciate the lasting effect which Beccaria has had on our criminal laws. The arguments and considerations of lawmakers today are, for the most part, still influenced by this concept of the criminal as a rational person who acts as a result of free will on a pleasure-seeking basis. Contemporary punishments prescribed by the law are generally well-defined, even though they are administered in a very inexact manner. And the widespread belief that the enactment of laws is the best method of social control clearly has at least some of its intellectual roots in the work of Beccaria.

Several of Beccaria's other ideas have contemporary significance.

Perhaps the most notable of these is his assertion that the speed and certainty of punishment, rather than its severity, are the most critical factors in deterrence. The modern criminal justice system, characterized by broad discretion on the part of the police, prosecutors, judges, guards, and parole boards; discrimination against the poor and minorities; court delays and months of pretrial detainment; and the use of plea-bargaining, offers neither swiftness nor certainty. Furthermore, Beccaria's advocacy of the humane treatment of incarcerated offenders has certainly never been fully realized. Indeed, many contemporary reformers claim that we have largely replaced corporal punishment with psychological and social persecution.[8]

Jeremy Bentham, a contemporary of Beccaria, was also a major figure in utilitarian social philosophy, and he proposed that all acts must be evaluated so that "the greatest happiness for the greatest number" results. To make such assessments, one would obviously need some method of calculation; Bentham happened to have just such a method. His "felicity calculus" was a superficial, quasi-mathematical attempt to quantify the utility of all conceivable acts. Humorous in retrospect, his attempt to catalogue the almost infinite varieties of behavior was nevertheless understandable, given the uncertainties of the criminal justice system he was attempting to reform.

Bentham's theory of human motivation—that man pursues pleasure and tries to avoid pain—led him to argue that criminal penalties should prescribe a degree of punishment (pain) just sufficient to offset the potential gains (pleasure) of criminal behavior, so that the net result (negative utility) would be deterrence. Bentham further believed that the punishment should "fit the crime," and generally seemed to favor restitution over physical punishment. Given Bentham's concept of deterrence, punishment in general was regarded as a necessary evil intended to prevent greater harm or evil.[9]

The social control philosophy which characterized classical criminology, then, was based on the assumption that the would-be criminal could be deterred by the threat of punishment if that punishment were swift, certain, appropriate for the offense, and sufficiently unpleasant to offset any potential gains to be realized by committing the act. These principles were advocated by classicists across the entire range of available punishments, whether they involved the loss of money, the loss of freedom, or the loss of life. The impact of classical criminology on the penal codes remains clear, even though in actual practice much of the vagueness and arbitrary abuse of discretion remains problematic.

Despite the anticipated ability to administer the principles of the classical school, the fact was that enforcement and implementation were quite problematic. Especially controversial was the classical position that individual differences and particular situations were irrelevant in assigning responsibility. The focus on the act committed, rather than on any characteristics or qualities of the person, came to be regarded as imprudent as did the practice of treating persons who clearly were incompetent, for various reasons, as competent solely because of commission of a given act. These principles were criticized strongly because they did not promote justice anywhere except on paper, in an abstract sort of way.

The idealized concept of justice held by the classicists, perhaps best symbolized by the familiar image of a blindfolded Lady Justice holding scales in her hands, was regarded by neo-classical revisionists (1800–1876) as too impersonal and rigid. The classical theorists, in their indignation over the inconsistencies and other inadequacies of the criminal justice system, had overreacted. They had designed a system which was so dispassionate and "objective" that it could not deliver justice to a society of human beings not identical to one another.

The neo-classicists were successful in introducing some modifications of the free will doctrine. Criminological thought was revised to re-admit some determinism—not the magical, supernatural determinism of demonology, but rather an awareness that certain factors could operate to impair one's reason and thereby mitigate personal responsibility to an extent. While retaining the essential positions articulated by the classicists, considerations involving individual differences began to appear during the neo-classical period. Age, mental status, physical condition, and other factors which could alter one's ability to discern right from wrong were acknowledged grounds for a decision of partial responsibility.

Far from regarding their views as a general theory of human behavior, the neo-classicists were actually focusing on what they viewed as a small minority of the population. There was no attempt to assert that all persons (not even all criminals) are partially shaped and controlled by deterministic forces. On the contrary, neo-classicists continued to view man as a rational, pleasure-seeking being who was personally responsible for his behavior except in abnormal circumstances or in the case of children who were not old enough to know right from wrong.

The neo-classical revisions outlined above meant that criminology had developed a dominant theoretical perspective which viewed man as essentially rational and behavior as volitional, but allowed for some mitigation of responsibility under certain circumstances. This theoretical framework provided the foundation for many legal systems, including that of the United States. The implications for sentencing and for the criminal justice system included the recognition that a particular sentence could have different effects on different offenders and an awareness that the prison environment could affect the *future* criminality of the offender. This allowed for much more flexibility than did the classical school in determining the appropriate punishment. Many recent "reforms" in penology, such as probation, parole, suspended sentences, and many programs designed for certain "types" of offenders, would be inconsistent with the classical emphases on uniformity and certainty of punishment.[10]

DETERMINISM

A book written in 1876 by an Italian psychiatrist was to provide the impetus necessary to shift the focus of criminology from the crime to the criminal. The book was called *The Criminal Man*[11] and its author was Cesare Lombroso; the result was the development of the "positive school" in criminology. Lacking the moralistic tones of the earliest positivist, Auguste Comte,[12] Lombroso's approach was clearly Darwinian, focusing on biological determinism.

As the title of his classic book implies, Lombroso believed that there was indeed a criminal *type*, or "born criminal," who was discernibly different from non-criminals in physical ways. In short, he was convinced that criminals bore bodily stigmata which marked them as a separate class of people. Following Darwin's monumental work by less than two decades, Lombrosian theory postulated that criminals had not fully evolved but were, instead, inferior organisms reminiscent of apelike, pre-primitive man, incapable of adapting to modern civilization. Specifically, Lombroso described the criminal as "atavistic" (a concept used earlier by Darwin) in that he was physically characteristic of a lower phylogenetic level. From his extensive physical measurements, autopsy findings, and other observations, Lombroso concluded that criminals disproportionately possessed an asymmetrical cranium; prognathism (excessive jaw); eye defects; oversized ears; prominent cheekbones; abnormal palate; receding forehead; sparse beard; wooly hair, long arms; abnormal dentition; twisted nose; fleshy and swollen lips; and inverted sex organs. He also noted such non-physical anomalies as a lack of morality, excessive vanity, cruelty, and tatooing.[13]

It would be misleading to imply that Lombroso held firmly to the idea that his was the sole explanation for crime. While continuing to believe that his theory explained part of the difference between criminals and non-criminals, Lombroso ultimately accepted environmental and other factors as equally valid contributing causes of crime.

While positivism, since Lombroso's day, has taken in a lot of intellectual territory, there remains a unifying framework which is visible in the work of his successors. That general framework consists of the following:

1. A general rejection of metaphysical and speculative approaches.
2. Denial of the "free-will" conception of man and substitution of a "deterministic" model.
3. A clear distinction between science and law, on one hand, and morals, on the other.
4. The application, as far as practicable, of the scientific method.[14]

These principles of positivism have been applied to the study of the criminal from various and diverse theoretical perspectives. Although these perspectives differ in significant ways, they retain the essence of positivism as described above. The theories to be discussed range from purely individualistic approaches to more macrolevel sociological theories.

The "Italian School"

The origins of positivism in criminology have a decidedly Italian character. Besides Lombroso, the other Italian pioneers in this school of thought were Enrico Ferri and Raffaele Garofalo. Although emphasizing different points as critical in the study of the criminal, both Ferri and Garofalo were adamant in their espousal of, and adherence to, the positivist approach.

Enrico Ferri, a pupil of Lombroso, is perhaps best known for his classification of criminals as insane, born, occasional, habitual, and drawn to criminality as a result of passion.[15] This typology of offenders represented an attempt by Ferri to conceptualize in anthropological categories the continuum of criminality. He believed that the differences between categories were differences of degree and of the danger represented for society.

The third member of the "Italian school," Raffaele Garofalo, attempted to construct a universal definition of crime—one which would be based on the concept of "natural crime," or acts which offend the basic moral sentiments of pity (a revulsion against the voluntary infliction of suffering on others) and probity (respect for the property rights of others). Garofalo's approach to the crime problem was primarily psychological and legal. He perceived some criminals as psychological degenerates who were morally unfit. His background as a jurist led him to advocate reforms in the criminal justice system so that the criminal could be dealt with in a manner more in line with his theory. Garofalo believed that the criminal must be eliminated, citing Darwin's observations on the functions of biological adaptation as a rationale for this "remedy." Since, according to this bio-organismic analogy, the criminal was one who had not adapted to civilized life, Garofalo saw only three alternatives—all of which involved some type of elimination: (1) death, where there is a permanent psychological defect; (2) partial elimination for those suitable to live only in a more primitive environment, including long-term or life imprisonment, transportation, and relatively mild isolation; and (3) enforced reparation, for those whose crimes were committed as a result of the press of circumstances.[16]

Physical-Biological Theories

The prototype for all physical-biological theories of crime were the early (and non-positivist) craniologists-phrenologists, who believed that the "faculties of the mind" were revealed by the external shape of the skull.[17] This vastly oversimplified and pseudo-scientific approach nevertheless pre-dates all other theories of a physical-biological nature.

Such theories have grown increasingly sophisticated and scientific since those earliest attempts to explain man's function by analyzing his cranial structure. In addition to the "Italian school," there have been a number of other intellectual contributions to this physical-biological tradition.

Charles Goring has been widely credited with refuting Lombroso's contention that there is a criminal "physical type." However, Goring's critique was aimed at Lombroso's methodology, not necessarily his theory or his conclusions, for which Goring had a certain affinity.[18] In Goring's famous book, *The English Convict*,[19] he presented an analysis of 3,000 English convicts and, as a matter of fact, he did find what he regarded as a positive association between certain physical differences and the offender's crime and social class. As Mannheim noted:

> In the controversy "heredity or enviroment" . . . he was on Lombroso's side, and perhaps even more than the latter he was inclined to underrate environmental influences: "Crime is only to a trifling extent (if to any) the product of social inequalities, of adverse environment or of other manifestations of . . . the force of circumstances."[20]

Goring's general interpretation of the height and weight deficiencies of the criminal population he studied was that the criminal suffered from hereditary inferiority. He also believed that criminals were most different from non-criminals with respect to their intelligence, which he found to be defective. Finally, Goring added a third category—that of moral defectiveness—to account for those whose criminality could not be explained by either of the first two factors. But the main thrust of Goring's theoretical position was a physiological one, thus placing him within this tradition of thought.

Not everyone agreed that Goring's criticisms of Lombroso's methodology were valid. The leading skeptic was Earnest Hooton, an anthropologist at Harvard University. In *The American Criminal*,[21] Hooton presented data and interpretations based on a twelve-year study of 13,873 criminals and 3,203 non-criminals. After analyzing 107 physical characteristics, Hooton concluded that criminals, when compared with the control group, were "organically inferior." Describing their distinctive characteristics, he included low foreheads, high pinched nasal roots, compressed faces, and narrow jaws. These he cited as evidence for his assertion of organic inferiority, and he attributed crime to "the impact of environment upon low grade human organisms."[22]

Hooton also constructed a typology of criminals based on physical constitution. He argued that murderers and robbers tended to be tall and thin; tall heavy men were most likely to be killers and to commit forgery and fraud as well; undersized men were disposed to commit assault, rape, and other sex crimes; and men lacking any notable physical characteristics had no criminal specialty. The primary problem with all of this is that Hooton had considered only the offender's *current* crime, while in fact half or more of Hooton's prisoners had previously been imprisoned for an offense *other than* that noted by Hooton.[23]

Studies by Ernst Kretschmer[24] and William Sheldon[25] are typical of the work of more recent proponents of the constitutional inferiority-body type theorists. Although differing in the details of their approaches, both men advocated the idea that body type and temperament are closely related. Both developed typologies relating body types to certain forms of behavior, including crime.

Some investigators have focused specifically on the effects of heredity, especially genetic deficiencies, in producing criminality. In this regard, the studies of "criminal families" were quite interesting. Perhaps the most well-known efforts along these genealogical lines were those of Richard Dugdale[26] and Henry Goddard,[27] both of whom attempted to analyze the apparently excessive criminality of entire families by relating it to feeble-mindedness. The term "mental testers" has often been applied to this method of inquiry.

More recently, another line of inquiry has focused on the criminality of twins. Lange,[28] Rosanoff,[29] Christiansen,[30] and others have studied twins in an attempt to determine the effect of heredity in producing criminality. The basic idea has been that if a greater percentage of monozygotic ("identical") twins than of dizygotic ("fraternal") twins are concordant in being criminal (both criminal), then the effect of heredity would, theoretically at least, have to be given greater weight than other factors. Although the methodological criticisms aimed at Rosanoff have been less damaging than those directed at Lange, the fact remains that neither study can be regarded as conclusive in finding that identical twins are far more likely to be concordant in terms of criminality.

Finally, some of the most sophisticated research employing a physical-biological model has been focused on the neuroendocrine system. The essential proposition of these theories has been that criminal behavior is often due to emotional disturbances produced by glandular imbalance. Often utilizing the electroencephalogram (EEG) as a diagnostic aid, this biochemical approach to crime thus far offers more promise than clear-cut and unequivocal findings.[31]

Psychopathology

A number of positivist theories of crime have utilized the paradigm based on individual psychopathology. The father of this approach was, of course, Sigmund Freud. His work, along with that of his intellectual successors, has focused on man's unconscious. The explanation for criminal behavior which grew out of this approach was that such behavior is largely the result of drives which are uncontrolled because of a defective personality structure. There are a seemingly endless number of applications of psychoanalytic theory to crime. Conditions such as psychosis and neurosis have been related to criminal behavior by psychoanalysts, as have most forms of deviant behavior. The essential contention of the psychoanalytic approach is that *all* behavior is purposive and meaningful. Such behavior is viewed as the symbolic release of repressed mental conflict. From this perspective, the criminal is one who acts not out of free will, as the classicists believed, but as an expression of deterministic forces of a subconscious nature. Such a view, of course, leads to a theory of social control based upon a clinical model of therapeutic rehabilitation.

A derivation of the psychoanalytic approach and the "mental testers" has been the emphasis on personality deviation as an explanation for crime. Relying on theoretical constructs of the "healthy" personality and the "abnormal" personality, the personality deviation approach has become increasingly popular, though not well validated. Using psychological tests such as the Rorschach, the Wechsler

Adult Intelligence Scale, the Minnesota Multiphasic Personality Inventory, the Thematic Apperception Test, and many others, psychologists have led in this attempt to construct causal theory. Advocates of this approach generally attempt to diagnose the psychopathological features of one's personality and then focus on these "target areas" using a variety of interventions.

Economic Factors

The effects of economic inequality are undeniably instrumental in producing great variability in one's "life chances." The pervasive day-to-day realities of poverty limit the chances of millions of people in securing adequate health care, housing, education, jobs, and opportunities. The crippling effects of poverty can hardly be comprehended by those not confronted with them on a daily basis. For these and related reasons, some theorists have attempted to relate at least some crimes to economic inequality. Such a theoretical position has had a special attraction for Marxists.

Historically, the most extensive application of Marxist theory to criminology was provided by Willem Bonger.[32] The central argument Bonger made is that capitalism, more than any other system of economic exchange, is characterized by the control of the means of production by relatively few people, with the vast majority of the population totally deprived of these means. The economic subjugation of the masses, he argues, stifles men's "social instincts" and leads to unlimited egoism, insensitivity, and a spirit of domination on the part of the powerful, while the poor are subjected to all sorts of pathogenic conditions: bad housing, constant association with "undesirables," uncertain physical security, terrible poverty, frequent sickness, and unemployment. Bonger maintained that the historical condition of this class of people was severely damaged by these conditions of economic subjugation. He attempted to demonstrate connections between certain types of crime (e.g., prostitution, alcoholism, and theft) and economic inequality. This explanation of crime suggests that the socioeconomic system is causally related to crime and would have to be restructured in order to reduce crime.

Although Bonger did not deny the influence of hereditary traits, he attributed no causal power to them in the absence of criminogenic environmental conditions. Throughout most of his writings, he stressed a socioeconomic view of crime and attacked the views of Lombroso and others of a physical-biological persuasion. His deterministic approach, along with his application of quantitiative methods and his rejection of metaphysical, speculative "explanations" for crime, place Bonger in the positivist school, even though his primary focus was on the social structure, rather than the individual. Bonger's theory, which illustrates the economic approach to criminal etiology, is quite near the sociological approach in many ways, especially in its macrolevel focus on the structure of society.

Sociological Explanations

The economic depression of the 1930s and the social problems which accompanied it helped further an interest in socioeconomic factors related to crime. Not only the economic condition of the nation but also the seemingly disorganized condition of many areas of major American cities were causes for great concern on the part of those seeking explanations for crime. The so-called "Chicago school" dominated criminological thought for a number of years, focusing on a social disorganization model. Specifically, this school of thought held that the interstitial areas of our major cities (heavily populated at the time by immigrants) reflected a high degree of sociocultural heterogeneity. This, they believed, resulted in a breakdown in social organization and norms, which made deviant behavior much more commonplace. Utilizing analogies based on plant ecology, the Chicago school believed that rapid social change in "natural areas" of the city was undermining the basic social controls of a stable cultural heritage.

The theoretical successor to the Chicago school and its social disorganization approach was the culture conflict perspective, best articulated by Thorsten Sellin.[33] This theory was based on the assertion that crime should be viewed as the result of conduct norms, which might occur in any of three ways:

1. when these codes clash on the border of contiguous culture areas;
2. when, as may be the case with legal norms, the law of one cultural group is extended to cover the territory of another; or
3. when members of one cultural group migrate to another.

The essential contention of culture conflict theory is that crime results from the absence of one clear-cut consensual model of normative behavior. The increasing conflict in norms which came with immigration and the rapid pluralization of our society provided the most fertile ground for culture conflict theory. Although still applicable in nations with significant levels of immigration (such as Israel), it has largely been replaced in the United States by other perspectives.

There have been several sociological theories of cultural transmission, each of which has stressed different dynamics. One, known generally as "subcultural theory," had its general intellectual origins in the work of Emile Durkheim, but was initially applied in the U.S. by Robert Merton. For Merton, the explanation for crime rested in the disjunction existing for many between culturally-defined success goals and the institutionalized means available to meet those goals. For some, this discrepancy results in criminal behavior, according to Merton.[34]

Elaborations of this same general statement were made later by Albert Cohen,[35] who saw the subculture which developed from this disjunction as a negative one which attempted to invert society's success goals and create its own, more realistic goals; and by Richard Cloward and Lloyd Ohlin,[36] who added the idea that illegitimate, as well as legitimate, opportunity structures were differentially accessible to individuals and that one could become either a criminal or a respected citizen, depending on which means were available.

Walter Miller[37] offered an alternative view of the lower-class subculture. He saw it as essentially characterized by its own value system and goals, not perpetually seeking to emulate the higher strata in order to gain status. Crime, for Miller, was a function of the normal socialization occurring in the subculture.

Another type of cultural transmission theory is that of Edwin Sutherland. Known as "differential association theory," it is essentially a learning theory suggestive of the earlier work of Gabriel Tarde,[38] a French social psychologist. Differential association theory posits that criminal behavior occurs via the following processes:

1. Criminal behavior is learned.

2. Criminal behavior is learned in interaction with other persons in a process of communication.

3. The principal part of the learning of criminal behavior occurs within intimate personal groups.

4. When criminal behavior is learned, the learning includes (a) techniques of committing the crime, which are sometimes very simple; (b) the specific direction of motives, drives, rationalizations, and attitudes.

5. The specific direction of motives and drives is learned from definitions of the legal codes as favorable or unfavorable.

6. A person becomes delinquent because of an excess of definitions favorable to violation of law over definitions unfavorable to violation of law.

7. Differential associations may vary in frequency, duration, priority, and intensity.

8. The process of learning criminal behavior by association with criminal and anticriminal patterns involves all of the mechanisms that are involved in any other learning.

9. While criminal behavior is an expression of general needs and values, it is not explained by those general needs and values, since noncriminal behavior is an expression of the same needs and values.[39]

Sutherland's theory was later modified by Daniel Glaser to take into account the perceived effect of the mass media and other methods of transmitting culture. Glaser's "differential identification theory" substituted for Sutherland's required personal interaction the following definition of the dynamics:

> A person pursues criminal behavior to the extent that he identifies himself with real or imaginary persons from whose perspective his criminal behavior seems acceptable.[40]

The foregoing presentation of positivism has been intended to provide an overview of the various types of theories comprising this "school." No attempt has been made to be exhaustive, but merely illustrative. Numerous other theoretical and empirical contributions could have been discussed; however, the above provide a representative sampling of positivist thought. Unlike either the demonologists of the pre-classical period or the classical advocates of a free-will, rational view of man, the positivists' concepts of causation were deterministic and anti-metaphysical. Therefore, their theories of social control have also been vastly different. They have advocated change—change of the personality, of the economic system, of the social system. Each of the positivist perspectives on crime developed its own ideas of how to deal with the crime problem, and these "solutions" were, of course, of a physical-biological, psychiatric-psychological, or social-economic nature. Their effect on penal policy is perhaps best symbolized in the name changes of our prisons—from "penitentiaries" to "correctional institutions."

But positivism is not the final chapter of this story. More recent theoretical developments have tended to concentrate on crime as a phenomenon which is determined by factors such as societal reaction (labeling), a system of laws which disproportionately reflect the interests of the wealthy and the powerful, and/or a corrupt and corrupting political system which is itself viewed as producing crime and criminals.

THE NEW EMPHASIS: "THE SYSTEM"

If positivism shifted society's focus from the crime to the criminal, then clearly that focus has shifted again with the development of the labeling and conflict perspectives, and especially with the emergence of a "radical" criminology perspective in the U.S. While these theories differ substantially in their interpretation of crime, one central feature which they have in common is their emphasis on the social and political systems as factors which help to generate the crime problem. Frequently, "the system" is identified as the "cause" of crime because of its unequal distribution of social and political power. Increasingly, the criminal is viewed as a victim—a victim of class struggle, racial discrimination, and other manifestations of inequality.

While there is, to be certain, some continuity between these relatively recent theories and some earlier sociological and economic perspectives, the general thrust of these new explanations is quite different. Most importantly, there is a much more pervasive political emphasis in current theoretical perspectives.

Labeling, Conflict, and Radical Perspectives

The labeling or "social reaction" approach to crime is reflected in the works of Becker,[41] Lemert,[42] Erikson,[43] Kitsuse,[44] and Schur.[45] This approach represents a significant departure from the absolute determinism of the positivists. The essence of labeling theory is its assertion that crime is relative and is defined (and thus *created*) socially. The oft-quoted statement of Howard Becker perhaps best sums up the approach:

> (S)ocial groups create deviance by making the rules whose infraction constitutes deviance, and by applying those rules to particular people and labeling them as outsiders. From this point of view, deviance is not a quality of the act the person commits, but rather a consequence of the application by others of rules and sanctions to an "offender." The deviant is one to whom that label has successfully been applied; deviant behavior is behavior that people so label.[46]

The labeling approach clearly shifts the focus of inquiry from the individual being labeled and processed to the group and the system doing the labeling and processing.

Finally, recent contributions to what has been called "radical" or "critical" or "Marxist" criminology include Richard Quinney,[47] Ian Taylor, Paul Walton, and Jock Young,[48] Anthony Platt,[49] Barry Krisberg,[50] and Herman and Julia Schwendinger.[51] While there are some theoretical differences among these writers, they occupy common intellectual ground within this overview of the development of criminology theory. Their analysis of crime and social control, essentially Marxist in nature, is to be distinguished from the applications of conflict theory to criminology made by Austin Turk[52] and other non-Marxian conflict theorists, as well as the positivist approach taken by the formal Marxist Willem Bonger.

The "radical Marxist" criminologists focus their analysis on the state as a political system controlled by the interests of the "ruling capitalist class," especially through the use of law as a tool to preserve existing inequalities. Much of the work of these theorists deals with the historical conditions of classes which they link, theoretically, with the development and differential enforcement of criminal law. They reject the traditional (functionalist) view that law reflects society's consensus on the norms and values which should control behavior; instead, they argue that law emerges from a conflict of competing interests and serves the interests of the elite "ruling class."

Turk, on the other hand, essentially continues the intellectual tradition of Ralf Dahrendorf[53] and other non-Marxist conflict theorists who have analyzed crime as a result of conflict concerning the distribution of power and authority within society. Rather than isolating the economic system and the class structure related to it, this perspective takes a broader view of the structural factors which produce conflict.

The implications of these perspectives for a philosophy of social control and for the criminal justice system are dramatically different from those suggested by earlier theorists. Again, the centrality of the political dimension is inescapable, whether one is discussing labeling theory, conflict theory, or "radical Marxist" theory. The labeling perspective, which emphasizes the discrepancy between actual criminal behavior and officially detected crime, is a societal reaction theory. It is not the deviance itself that is so important, but the way in which society reacts. This perspective generally is interpreted as advocating *less* intervention and less labeling of people as "criminal."[54] The criminal justice system is viewed as one which exacerbates the problem of crime; therefore, that system should be reduced and made less powerful.

Conflict and radical Marxist theory also would suggest that there is a need for societal restructuring. However, from these perspectives the criminal justice system merely reflects broader structural arrangements (i.e., the economy, the class system, and/or the distribution of power and authority). Radical Marxists advocate the abolition of capitalism and the development of a socialist society. They tend to view anything less than that as piecemeal "liberal tinkering" with a fatally flawed system. The alternative conflict view would argue that the particular economic system (e.g., capitalism) is not the basic problem and that crime exists in noncapitalist states as well. Crime is viewed as a structural problem resulting from the distribution of power and authority and as a reflection of unstable relationships between legal authorities and subjects.

In conclusion, it should be apparent that while man's attempts to explain crime have covered a tremendous range of ideas, there are parallels among these ideas. The idea that crime is a result of demonic possession is perhaps not a great deal different than the "mental illness" explanation advanced at a much later point in history. Both are largely deterministic, even though one is "magical" and the other "scientific."

Similarly, the rationales cited by the state for the use of imprisonment have varied from "moral reform" to "deterrence" to "rehabilitation," "public protection," and "punishment." Meanwhile, the perceptions of those imprisoned by the state have also changed, from passive acceptance of society's reaction to the increasing tendency to view themselves as "political prisoners" of an unjust legal and political system. It is apparent, therefore, that the linkage between theories of crime and social control philosophies must be evaluated on two levels: (1) the connections between theoretical explanations and formal policies, and (2) the changing rationales for employing essentially similar social control practices (e.g., "punitive" imprisonment vs. "therapeutic" correctional rehabilitation).

Notes

1. This is not to suggest that such views of man's nature were confined to primitive times. There are numerous contemporary examples of similar beliefs. However, the intent here is to present a chronology of the major explanations of crime.
2. George B. Vold, *Theoretical Criminology*. New York: Oxford University Press, 1958, pp. 5–6.
3. Harry Elmer Barnes and Negley K. Teeters, *New Horizons in Criminology*. New York: Prentice-Hall, 1945 (revised edition), p. 399.
4. E. P. Evans, *The Criminal Prosecution and Capital Punishment of Animals*. London: Heinemann, 1906.
5. George Ives. *A History of Penal Methods* (1914). Montclair, N.J.: Patterson Smith, 1970 (reprinted), pp. 9–10.
6. Cesare Beccaria, *An Essay on Crimes and Punishments* (originally published as *Trattato dei delitti e delle pene*, 1764). Albany, N.Y.: W. C. Little, 1872.
7. Vold, *op. cit.*, p. 21.
8. See, for example, Thomas S. Szasz, "Crime, Punishment, and Psychiatry." Pp. 262–285 in Abraham S. Blumberg (Ed.), *Current Perspectives on Criminal Behavior*. New York: Alfred A. Knopf, 1974.
9. Gilbert Geis, "Jeremy Bentham." Pp. 51–68 in Hermann Mannheim (Ed.), *Pioneers in Criminology* (1955). Montclair, N.J.: Patterson Smith, 1972 (revised).
10. Leon Radzinowicz, *Ideology and Crime: A Study of Crime in Its Social and Historical Context*. New York: Columbia University Press, 1966, p. 123.
11. Cesare Lombroso, *L'Uomo Delinquente*. Milan, Italy: Hoepli, 1876.
12. Lewis A. Coser, "Auguste Comte," *Masters of Sociological Thought*. New York: Harcourt Brace Jovanovich, 1971, pp. 2–41. Also see Norman Birnbaum, *Toward a Critical Sociology*. New York: Oxford University Press, 1971, p. 205.

13. Marvin E. Wolfgang, "Cesare Lombroso." Pp. 232–291 in Mannheim, *op. cit.*

14. Hermann Mannheim (Ed.), *Pioneers in Criminology* (1955). Montclair, N.J.: Patterson Smith, 1972 (revised), pp. 10–11.

15. See Enrico Ferri, *Criminal Sociology*. Boston: Little, Brown, 1917.

16. Vold, *op. cit.*, p. 38.

17. Barnes and Teeters, *op. cit.*, p. 160.

18. Edwin D. Driver, "Charles Buckman Goring." Pp. 429–442 in Mannheim, *op. cit.*

19. Charles Buckman Goring, *The English Convict*. London: Her Majesty's Stationery Office, 1913.

20. Hermann Mannheim (Ed.), *Comparative Criminology*. Boston: Houghton Mifflin, 1965, p. 22B.

21. Earnest A. Hooton, *The American Criminal: An Anthropological Study*. Cambridge, Mass.: Harvard University Press, 1939.

22. Stephen Schafer, *Theories in Criminology*. New York: Random House, 1969, p. 187.

23. Vold, *op. cit.*, pp. 62–63.

24. Ernst Kretschmer, *Physique and Character*, trans. W. J. H. Sprott. New York: Harcourt, Brace, 1926.

25. William H. Sheldon, *The Varieties of Human Physique: An Introduction to Constitutional Psychology*. New York: Harper and Row, 1940.

26. Richard Dugdale, *The Jukes*. New York: Putnam's, 1877.

27. Henry H. Goddard, *The Kallikaks*. New York: Macmillan, 1914.

28. Johannes Lange, *Crime as Destiny*, trans. Charlotte Haldane. New York: C. Boni, 1930.

29. Aron J. Rosanoff, Leva M. Handy, and Isabel Rosanoff, "Criminality and Delinquency in Twins," *Journal of Criminal Law and Criminology*, 24 (Jan.-Feb.), 1934, pp. 923–924.

30. Karl O. Christiansen, "Threshold of Tolerance in Various Population Groups Illustrated by Results from the Danish Criminologic Twin Study." In A. V. S. de Reuck and R. Porter (Eds.), *The Mentally Abnormal Offender*. Boston: Little, Brown, 1968.

31. For an excellent summary and assessment of this research, see Saleem A. Shah and Loren H. Roth, "Biological and Psychophysiological Factors in Criminality." Pp. 144–147 in Daniel Glaser (Ed.), *Handbook of Criminology*. Chicago: Rand McNally, 1974.

32. Willem Bonger, *Criminality and Economic Conditions*, trans. Henry P. Horton. Boston: Little, Brown, 1916.

33. Thorsten Sellin, *Culture Conflict and Crime*. New York: Social Science Research Council, 1938.

34. See, for example, Robert K. Merton, "Anomie, Anomia and Social Interaction." Pp. 213–242 in Marshall B. Clinard (Ed.), *Anomie and Deviant Behavior*. New York: Free Press, 1964.

35. Albert K. Cohen, *Delinquent Boys: The Culture of the Gang*. New York: Free Press, 1955.

36. Richard A. Cloward and Lloyd E. Ohlin, *Delinquency and Opportunity: A Theory of Delinquent Gangs*. New York: Free Press, 1960.

37. Walter B. Miller, "Lower-class Culture as a Generating Milieu of Gang Delinquency." Pp. 351–363 in Marvin E. Wolfgang, Leonard Savitz, and Norman Johnston (Eds.), *The Sociology of Crime and Delinquency*. New York: Wiley, 1970.

38. Gabriel Tarde, *Penal Philosophy*. Boston: Little, Brown, 1912.

39. Edwin H. Sutherland and Donald R. Cressey, *Criminology.* Philadelphia: J. B. Lippincott, 1974 (9th edit.), pp. 75–76.

40. Daniel Glaser, "Criminality Theories and Behavior Images," *American Journal of Sociology,* 61 (March), 1956, p. 440.

41. Howard S. Becker, *Outsiders: Studies in the Sociology of Deviance.* New York: Free Press, 1963.

42. Edwin M. Lemert, *Human Deviance, Social Problems and Social Control.* Englewood Cliffs, N.J.: Prentice-Hall, 1972 (2nd edit.).

43. Kai T. Erikson, "Notes on the Sociology of Deviance," *Social Problems,* 9 (Spring), 1962, pp. 307–314.

44. John I. Kitsuse, "Societal Reaction to Deviant Behavior: Problems of Theory and Method," *Social Problems,* 9 (Winter), 1962, pp. 847–856.

45. Edwin M. Schur, *Labeling Deviant Behavior: Its Sociological Implications.* New York: Harper and Row, 1971.

46. Becker, *op. cit.,* p. 9.

47. Richard Quinney, *Critique of Legal Order: Crime Control in Capitalist Society.* Boston: Little, Brown, 1974.

48. Ian Taylor, Paul Walton, and Jock Young, *The New Criminology: For a Social Theory of Deviance.* London: Routledge & Kegan Paul, 1973.

49. Anthony Platt, "Prospects for a Radical Criminology in the United States," *Crime and Social Justice: A Journal of Radical Criminology,* I (Spring-Summer), 1974, pp. 2–10.

50. Barry Krisberg, *Crime and Privilege: Toward a New Criminology.* Englewood Cliffs, N.J.: Prentice-Hall, 1975.

51. Herman Schwendinger and Julia Schwendinger, "Defenders of Order or Guardians of Human Rights?" *Issues in Criminology,* 5 (Summer), 1970, pp. 123–157.

52. Austin T. Turk, *Criminality and the Legal Order.* Chicago: Rand McNally, 1969; also "Conflict and Criminality," *American Sociological Review,* 31 (June), 1966, pp. 338–352.

53. Ralf Dahrendorf, *Class and Class Conflict in Industrial Society.* London: Routledge & Kegan Paul, 1959.

54. See, for example, Edwin Schur, *Radical Non-intervention: Rethinking the Delinquency Problem.* Englewood Cliffs, N.J.: Prentice-Hall, 1973.

13. Toward a Marxian Theory of Deviance

STEVEN SPITZER

Within the last decade American sociologists have become increasingly reflective in their approach to deviance and social problems. They have come to recognize that interpretations of deviance are often ideological in their assumptions and implications, and that sociologists are frequently guilty of "providing the facts which make oppression more efficient and the theory which makes it legitimate to a larger constituency" (Becker and Horowitz, 1972:48). To combat this tendency students of deviance have invested more and more energy in the search for a critical theory. This search has focused on three major problems: (1) the definition of deviance, (2) the etiology of deviance, and (3) the etiology of control.

TRADITIONAL THEORIES AND THEIR PROBLEMS

Traditional theories approached the explanation of deviance with little equivocation about the phenomenon to be explained. Prior to the 1960s the subject matter of deviance theory was taken for granted, and few were disturbed by its preoccupation with "dramatic and predatory" forms of social behavior (Liazos, 1972). Only in recent years have sociologists started to question the consequences of singling out "nuts," "sluts," "perverts," "lames," "crooks," "junkies," and "juicers" for special attention. Instead of adopting conventional wisdom about *who* and *what* is deviant, investigators have gradually made the definitional problem central to the sociological enterprise. They have begun to appreciate the consequences of studying the powerless (rather than the powerful)—both in terms of the relationship between *knowledge of* and *control over* a group, and the support for the "hierarchy of credibility" (Becker, 1967) that such a focus provides. Sociologists have discovered the significance of the definitional process in their own, as well as society's response to deviance, and this discovery has raised doubts about the direction and purpose of the field.

Even when the definitional issue can be resolved, critics are faced with a second and equally troublesome problem. Traditional theories of deviance are essentially *non-structural* and *ahistorical* in their mode of analysis. By restricting investigation to factors which are manipulable within existing structural arrangements, these theories embrace a "correctional perspective" (Matza, 1969) and divert attention from the impact of the political economy as a whole. From this point of view deviance is *in* but not *of* our contemporary social order. Theories that locate the source of deviance in factors as .diverse as personality structure, family systems, cultural transmission, social disorganization, and differential opportunity share a common flaw— they attempt to understand deviance apart from historically specific forms of political and economic organization. Because traditional theories proceed without any sense of historical development, deviance is normally viewed as an episodic and transitory phenomenon rather than an outgrowth of long-term structural change. Sensitive sociologists have come to realize that critical theory must establish, rather than obscure, the relationship between deviance, social structure, and social change.

A final problem in the search for a critical theory of deviance is the absence of a coherent theory of control. More than ever before, critics have come to argue that deviance cannot be understood apart from the dynamics of control. Earlier theories devoted scant attention to the control process precisely because control was interpreted as a natural response to behavior generally assumed to be problematic. Since theories of deviance viewed control as a desideratum, no theory of control was required. But as sociologists began to question conventional images of deviance, they revised their impressions of social control. Rather than assuming that societal reaction was necessarily defensive and benign, skeptics announced that controls could actually cause deviance. The problem was no longer simply to explain the independent sources of deviance and control, but to understand the reciprocal relationship between the two.

In elevating control to the position of an independent variable, a more critical orientation has evolved. Yet this orientation has created a number of problems of its own. If deviance is simply a *status*, representing the outcome of a series of control procedures, should our theory of deviance be reduced to a theory of control? In what sense, if any, is deviance an achieved rather than an ascribed status? How do we account for the historical and structural sources of deviance apart from those shaping the development of formal controls?

TOWARD A THEORY OF DEVIANCE PRODUCTION

A critical theory must be able to account for both *deviance* and *deviants*. It must be sensitive to the process through which deviance is subjectively constructed and deviants are objectively handled, as well as the structural bases of the behavior and characteristics which come to official attention. It should neither beg the explanation of deviant behavior and characteristics by depicting the deviant as a helpless victim of oppression, nor fail to realize that his identification as deviant, the dimensions of his threat, and the priorities of the control system are part of a broader social conflict. While acknowledging the fact that deviance is a *status* imputed to groups who share certain structural characteristics (e.g. powerlessness) we must not forget that these groups are defined by more than these characteristics alone.[1] We must not only ask why specific members of the underclass are selected for official processing but also why they behave as they do. Deviant statuses, no matter how coercively applied, are in some sense achieved, and we must understand this achievement in the context of political-economic conflict. We need to understand why capitalism produces both patterns of activity and types of people that are defined and managed as deviant.

In order to construct a general theory of deviance and control it is useful to conceive of a process of deviance production which can be understood in relationship to the development of class society. *Deviance production involves all aspects of the process through which populations are structurally generated, as well as shaped, channeled into, and manipulated within social categories defined as deviant.* This process includes the development of and changes in: (1) deviant definitions, (2) problem populations, and (3) control systems.

Most fundamentally, deviance production involves the development of and changes in deviant categories and images. A critical theory must examine where these images and definitions come from, what they reflect about the structure of and priorities in specific class societies, and how they are related to class conflict. If we are to explain, for example, how mental retardation becomes deviance and the feebleminded deviant, we need to examine the structural characteristics, economic and political dimensions of the society in which these definitions and images emerged. In the case of American society we must understand how certain correlates of capitalist development (proletarianization and nuclearization of the family) weakened traditional methods of assimilating these groups, how others (the emergence of scientific and meritocratic ideologies) sanctioned intellectual stratification and differential handling, and how still others (the attraction of unskilled labor and population concentrations) heightened concern over the "threat" that these groups were assumed to represent. In other words, the form and content of deviance definition must be assessed in terms of its relationship to both structural and ideological change.

A second aspect of deviance production is the development of and changes in problem behaviors and problem populations. If we assume that class societies are based on fundamental conflicts between groups, and that harmony is achieved through the dominance of a specific class, it makes sense to argue that deviants are culled from groups who create specific problems for those who rule. Although these groups may victimize or burden those outside of the dominant class, their problematic quality ultimately resides in their challenge to the basis and form of class rule. Because problem populations are not always "handled," they provide candidates for, but are in no sense equivalent to, official deviants. A sophisticated critical theory must investigate where these groups come from, why their behaviors and characteristics are problematic, and how they are transformed in a developing political economy. We must consider, for instance, why Chinese laborers in nineteenth-century California and Chicanos in the Southwest during the 1930s became the object of official concern, and why drug laws evolved to address the "problems" that these groups came to represent (Helmer and Vietorisz, 1973; Musto, 1973).

The changing character of problem populations is related to deviance production in much the same way that variations in material resources affect manufacturing. Changes in the quantity and quality of raw materials influence the scope and priorities of production, but the characteristics of the final product depend as much on the methods of production as the source material. These methods comprise the third element in deviance production—the development and operation of the control system. The theory must explain why a system of control emerges under specific conditions and account for its size, focus, and working assumptions. The effectiveness of the system in confronting problem populations and its internal structure must be understood in order to interpret changes in the form and content of control. Thus, in studying the production of the "mentally ill" we must not only consider why deviance has been "therapeutized," but also how this development reflects the subtleties of class control. Under capitalism, for example, formal control of the mad and the birth of the asylum may be examined as a response to the growing demands for order, responsibility, and restraint (cf. Foucault, 1965).

THE PRODUCTION OF DEVIANCE IN CAPITALIST SOCIETY

The concept of deviance production offers a starting point for the analysis of both deviance and control. But for such a construct to serve as a critical tool it must be grounded in an historical and structural investigation of society. For Marx, the crucial unit of analysis is the mode of production that dominates a given historical period. If we are to have a Marxian theory of deviance, therefore, deviance production must be understood in relationship to specific forms of socio-economic organization. In our society, productive activity is organized capitalistically, and it is ultimately defined by "the process that transforms on the one hand, the social means of subsistence and of production into capital, on the other hand the immediate producers into wage labourers" (Marx, 1967:714).

There are two features of the capitalist mode of production important for purposes of this discussion. First, as a mode of production it forms the foundation or infrastructure of our society. This means that the starting point of our analysis must be an understanding of the economic organization of capitalist societies and the impact of that organization on all aspects of social life. But the capitalist mode of production is an important starting point in another sense. It contains contradictions which reflect the internal tendencies of capitalism. These contradictions are important because they explain the changing character of the capitalist system and the nature of its impact on social, political, and intellectual activity. The formulation of a Marxist perspective on deviance requires the interpretation of the process through which the contradictions of capitalism are expressed. In particular, the theory must illustrate the relationship between specific contradictions, the problems of capitalist development, and the production of a deviant class.

The superstructure of society emerges from and reflects the ongoing development of economic forces (the infrastructure). In class societies this superstructure preserves the hegemony of the ruling class through a system of class controls. These controls, which are institutionalized in the family, church, private associations, media, schools, and the state, provide a mechanism for coping with the contradictions and achieving the aims of capitalist development.

Among the most important functions served by the superstructure in capitalist societies is the regulation and management of problem populations. Because deviance processing is only one of the methods available for social control, these groups supply raw material for deviance production, but are by no means synonymous with deviant populations. Problem populations tend to share a number of social characteristics, but most important among these is the fact that their behavior, personal qualities, and/or position threaten the *social relations of production* in capitalist societies. In other words, populations become generally eligible for management as deviant when they disturb, hinder or call into question any of the following:

1) capitalist modes of appropriating the product of human labor (e.g. when the poor "steal" from the rich)

2) the social conditions under which capitalist production takes place (e.g. those who refuse or are unable to perform wage labor)

3) patterns of distribution and consumption in capitalist society (e.g. those who use drugs for escape and transcendence rather than sociability and adjustment)

4) the process of socialization for productive and non-productive roles (e.g. youth who refuse to be schooled or those who deny the validity of "family life")[2]

5) the ideology which supports the functioning of capitalist society (e.g. proponents of alternative forms of social organization)

Although problem populations are defined in terms of the threat and costs that they present to the social relations of production in capitalist societies, these populations are far from isomorphic with a revolutionary class. It is certainly true that some members of the problem population may under specific circumstances possess revolutionary potential. But this potential can only be realized if the problematic group is located in a position of functional indispensability within the capitalist system. Historically, capitalist societies have been quite successful in transforming those who are problematic and indispensable (the protorevolutionary class) into groups who are either problematic and dispensable (candidates for deviance processing), or indispensable but not problematic (supporters of the capitalist order). On the other hand, simply because a group is manageable does not mean that it ceases to be a problem for the capitalist class. Even though dispensable problem populations cannot overturn the capitalist system, they can represent a significant impediment to its maintenance and growth. It is in this sense that they become eligible for management as deviants.

Problem populations are created in two ways—either directly through the expression of fundamental contradictions in the capitalist mode of production or indirectly through disturbances in the system of class rule. An example of the first process is found in Marx's analysis of the "relative surplus-population."

Writing on the "General Law of Capitalist Accumulation" Marx explains how increased social redundance is inherent in the development of the capitalist mode of production:

> With the extension of the scale of production, and the mass of the labourers set in motion, with the greater breadth and fullness of all sources of wealth, there is also an extension of the scale on which greater attraction of labourers by capital is accompanied by their greater repulsion. . . . The labouring population therefore produces, along with the accumulation of capital produced by it, the means by which itself is made relatively superfluous, . . . and it does this to an always increasing extent (Marx, 1967: 631).

In its most limited sense the production of a relative surplus-population involves the creation of a class which is economically redundant. But insofar as the conditions of economic existence determine social existence, this process helps explain the emergence of groups who become both threatening and vulnerable at the same time. The marginal status of these populations reduces their stake in the maintenance of the system while their powerlessness and dispensability renders them increasingly susceptible to the mechanisms of official control.

The paradox surrounding the production of the relative surplus-population is that this population is both useful and menacing to the accumulation of capital. Marx describes how the relative surplus-population "forms a disposable industrial army, that belongs to capital quite as absolutely as if the latter had bred it at its own cost," and how this army "creates, for the changing needs of the self-expansion of capital, a mass of human material always ready for exploitation" (Marx, 1967:632).

On the other hand, it is apparent that an excessive increase in what Marx called the "lowest sediment" of the relative surplus-population might seriously impair the growth of capital. The social expenses and threat to social harmony created by a large and economically stagnant surplus-population could jeopardize the preconditions for accumulation by undermining the ideology of equality so essential to the legitimation of production relations in bourgeois democracies, diverting revenues away from capital investment toward control and support operations, and providing a basis for political organization of the dispossessed.[3] To the extent that the relative surplus-population confronts the capitalist class as a threat to the social relations of production, it reflects an important contradiction in modern capitalist societies: a surplus-population is a necessary product of and condition for the accumulation of wealth on a capitalist basis, but it also creates a form of social expense which must be neutralized or controlled if production relations and conditions for increased accumulation are to remain unimpaired.

Problem populations are also generated through contradictions which develop in the system of class rule. The institutions which make up the superstructure of capitalist society originate and are maintained to guarantee the interests of the capitalist class. Yet these institutions necessarily reproduce, rather than resolve, the contradictions of the capitalist order. In a dialectical fashion, arrangements which arise in order to buttress capitalism are transformed into their opposite—structures for the cultivation of internal threats. An instructive example of this process is found in the emergence and transformation of educational institutions in the United States.

The introduction of mass education in the United States can be traced to the developing needs of corporate capitalism (cf. Karier, 1973; Cohen and Lazerson, 1972; Bowles and Gintis, 1972; Spring, 1972). Compulsory education provided a means of training, testing and sorting, and assimilating wage-laborers, as well as withholding certain populations from the labor market. The system was also intended to preserve the values of bourgeois society and operate as an "inexpensive form of police" (Spring, 1973:31). However, as Gintis (1973) and Bowles (1973) have suggested, the internal contradictions of schooling can lead to effects opposite of those intended. For the poor, early schooling can make explicit the oppressiveness and alienating character of capitalist institutions, while higher education can instill critical abilities which lead students to "bite the hand that feeds them." In both cases educational institutions create troublesome populations (i.e. dropouts and student radicals) and contribute to the very problems they were designed to solve.

After understanding how and why specific groups become generally bothersome in capitalist society, it is necessary to investigate the conditions under which these groups are transformed into proper objects for social control. In other words, we must ask what distinguishes the generally problematic from the specifically deviant. The rate at which problem populations are converted into deviants will reflect the relationship between these populations and the control system. This rate is likely to be influenced by the:

(1) *Extensiveness and Intensity of State Controls.* Deviance processing (as opposed to other control measures) is more likely to occur when problem management is monopolized by the state. As state controls are applied more generally, the proportion of official deviants will increase.

(2) *Size and Level of Threat Presented by the Problem Population.* The larger and more threatening the problem population, the great-

er the likelihood that this population will have to be controlled through deviance processing rather than other methods. As the threat created by these populations exceeds the capacities of informal restraints, their management requires a broadening of the reaction system and an increasing centralization and coordination of control activities.

(3) *Level of Organization of the Problem Population.* When and if problem populations are able to organize and develop limited amounts of political power, deviance processing becomes increasingly less effective as a tool for social control. The attribution of deviant status is most likely to occur when a group is relatively impotent and atomized.

(4) *Effectiveness of Control Structures Organized through Civil Society.* The greater the effectiveness of the organs of civil society (i.e. the family, church, media, schools, sports) in solving the problems of class control, the less the likelihood that deviance processing (a more explicitly political process) will be employed.

(5) *Availability and Effectiveness of Alternative Types of Official Processing.* In some cases the state will be able effectively to incorporate certain segments of the problem population into specially created "pro-social" roles. In the modern era, for example, conscription and public works projects (Piven and Cloward, 1971) helped neutralize the problems posed by troublesome populations without creating new or expanding old deviant categories.

(6) *Availability and Effectiveness of Parallel Control Structures.* In many instances the state can transfer its costs of deviance production by supporting or at least tolerating the activities of independent control networks which operate in its interests. For example, when the state is denied or is reluctant to assert a monopoly over the use of force, it is frequently willing to encourage vigilante organizations and private police in the suppression of problem populations. Similarly, the state is often benefited by the policies and practices of organized crime, insofar as these activities help pacify, contain, and enforce order among potentially disruptive groups (Schelling, 1967).

(7) *Utility of Problem Populations.* While problem populations are defined in terms of their threat and costs to capitalist relations of production, they are not threatening in every respect. They can be supportive economically (as part of a surplus labor pool or dual labor market), politically (as evidence of the need for state intervention), and ideologically (as scapegoats for rising discontent). In other words, under certain conditions capitalist societies derive benefits from maintaining a number of visible and uncontrolled "troublemakers" in their midst. Such populations are distinguished by the fact that while

they remain generally bothersome, the costs that they inflict are most immediately absorbed by other members of the problem population. Policies evolve, not so much to eliminate or actively suppress these groups, but to deflect their threat away from targets which are sacred to the capitalist class. Victimization is permitted and even encouraged, as long as the victims are members of an expendable class.

Two more or less discrete groupings are established through the operations of official control. These groups are a product of different operating assumptions and administrative orientations toward the deviant population. On the one hand, there is *social junk* which, from the point of view of the dominant class, is a costly yet relatively harmless burden to society. The discreditability of social junk resides in the failure, inability, or refusal of this group to participate in the roles supportive of capitalist society. Social junk is most likely to come to official attention when informal resources have been exhausted or when the magnitude of the problem becomes significant enough to create a basis for "public concern." Since the threat presented by social junk is passive, growing out of its inability to compete and its withdrawal from the prevailing social order, controls are usually designed to regulate and contain rather than eliminate and suppress the problem. Clear-cut examples of social junk in modern capitalist societies might include the officially administered aged, handicapped, mentally ill, and mentally retarded.

In contrast to social junk, there is a category that can be roughly described as *social dynamite*. The essential quality of deviance managed as social dynamite is its potential actively to call into question established relationships, especially relations of production and domination. Generally, therefore, social dynamite tends to be more youthful, alienated, and politically volatile than social junk. The control of social dynamite is usually premised on an assumption that the problem is acute in nature, requiring a rapid and focused expenditure of control resources. This is in contrast to the handling of social junk frequently based on a belief that the problem is chronic and best controlled through broad reactive rather than intensive and selective measures. Correspondingly, social dynamite is normally processed through the legal system with its capacity for active intervention, while social junk is frequently (but not always)[4] administered by the agencies and agents of the therapeutic and welfare state.

Many varieties of deviant populations are alternatively or simultaneously dealt with as either social junk and/or social dynamite. The welfare poor, homosexuals, alcoholics, and "problem children" are among the categories reflecting the equivocal nature of the control process and its dependence on the political, economic, and ideological priorities of deviance production. The changing nature of these

priorities and their implications for the future may be best understood by examining some of the tendencies of modern capitalist systems.

MONOPOLY CAPITAL AND DEVIANCE PRODUCTION

Marx viewed capitalism as a system constantly transforming itself. He
explained these changes in terms of certain tendencies and contradictions immanent within the capitalist mode of production. One of
the most important processes identified by Marx was the tendency
for the organic composition of capital to rise. Simply stated, capitalism requires increased productivity to survive, and increased productivity is only made possible by raising the ratio of machines (dead
labor) to men (living labor). This tendency is self-reinforcing since
"the further machine production advances, the higher becomes the
organic composition of capital needed for an entrepreneur to secure
the average profit" (Mandel, 1968:163). This phenomenon helps us
explain the course of capitalist development over the last century
and the rise of monopoly capital (Baran and Sweezy, 1966).

For the purposes of this analysis there are at least two important
consequences of this process. First, the growth of constant capital
(machines and raw material) in the production process leads to an expansion in the overall size of the relative surplus-population. The reasons for this are obvious. The increasingly technological character of
production removes more and more laborers from productive activity for longer periods of time. Thus, modern capitalist societies have
been required progressively to reduce the number of productive
years in a worker's life, defining both young and old as economically
superfluous. Especially affected are the unskilled, who become more
and more expendable as capital expands.

In addition to affecting the general size of the relative surplus-population, the rise of the organic composition of capital leads to an increase in the relative stagnancy of that population. In Marx's original
analysis he distinguished between forms of superfluous population
that were floating and stagnant. The floating population consists of
workers who are "sometimes repelled, sometimes attracted again in
greater masses, the number of those employed increasing on the
whole, although in a constantly decreasing proportion to the scale of
production" (1967:641). From the point of view of capitalist accumulation the floating population offers the greatest economic flexibility
and the fewest problems of social control because they are most effectively tied to capital by the "natural laws of production." Unfortunately (for the capitalists at least), these groups come to comprise a

smaller and smaller proportion of the relative surplus-population. The increasing specialization of productive activity raises the cost of reproducing labor and heightens the demand for highly skilled and "internally controlled" forms of wage labor (Gorz, 1970). The process through which unskilled workers are alternatively absorbed and expelled from the labor force is thereby impaired, and the relative surplus-population comes to be made up of increasing numbers of persons who are more or less permanently redundant. The boundaries between the "useful" and the "useless" are more clearly delineated, while standards for social disqualification are more liberally defined.

With the growth of monopoly capital, therefore, the relative surplus-population begins to take on the character of a population which is more and more absolute. At the same time, the market becomes a less reliable means of disciplining these populations and the "invisible hand" is more frequently replaced by the "visible fist." The implications for deviance production are twofold: (1) problem populations become gradually more problematic—both in terms of their size and their insensitivity to economic controls, and (2) the resources of the state need to be applied in greater proportion to protect capitalist relations of production and insure the accumulation of capital.

STATE CAPITALISM AND NEW FORMS OF CONTROL

The major problems faced by monopoly capitalism are surplus population and surplus production. Attempts to solve these problems have led to the creation of the welfare/warfare state (Baran and Sweezy, 1966; Marcuse, 1964; O'Connor, 1973; Gross, 1970). The warfare state attacks the problem of overconsumption by providing "wasteful" consumption and protection for the expansion of foreign markets. The welfare state helps absorb and deflect social expenses engendered by a redundant domestic population. Accordingly, the economic development of capitalist societies has come to depend increasingly on the support of the state.

The emergence of state capitalism and the growing interpenetration of the political and economic spheres have had a number of implications for the organization and administration of class rule. The most important effect of these trends is that control functions are increasingly transferred from the organs of civil society to the organs of political society (the state). As the maintenance of social harmony becomes more difficult and the contradictions of civil society intensify, the state is forced to take a more direct and extensive role in the management of problem populations. This is especially true to the extent that the primary socializing institutions in capitalist societies (e.g. the family and the church) can no longer be counted on to produce obedient and "productive" citizens.

Growing state intervention, especially intervention in the process of socialization, is likely to produce an emphasis on general-preventive (integrative) rather than selective-reactive (segregative) controls. Instead of waiting for troublemakers to surface and managing them through segregative techniques, the state is likely to focus more and more on generally applied incentives and assimilative controls. This shift is consistent with the growth of state capitalism because, on the one hand, it provides mechanisms and policies to nip disruptive influences "in the bud," and, on the other, it paves the way toward a more rational exploitation of human capital. Regarding the latter point, it is clear that effective social engineering depends more on social investment and anticipatory planning than coercive control, and societies may more profitably manage populations by viewing them as human capital than as human waste. An investment orientation has long been popular in state socialist societies (Rimlinger, 1961, 1966), and its value, not surprisingly, has been increasingly acknowledged by many capitalist states.[5]

In addition to the advantages of integrative controls, segregative measures are likely to fall into disfavor for a more immediate reason—they are relatively costly to formulate and apply. Because of its fiscal problems the state must search for means of economizing control operations without jeopardizing capitalist expansion. Segregative handling, especially institutionalization, has been useful in manipulating and providing a receptacle for social junk and social dynamite. Nonetheless, the per capita cost of this type of management is typically quite high. Because of its continuing reliance on segregative controls the state is faced with a growing crisis—the overproduction of deviance. The magnitude of the problem and the inherent weaknesses of available approaches tend to limit the alternatives, but among those which are likely to be favored in the future are:

(1) *Normalization.* Perhaps the most expedient response to the overproduction of deviance is the normalization of populations traditionally managed as deviant. Normalization occurs when deviance processing is reduced in scope without supplying specific alternatives, and certain segments of the problem population are "swept under the rug." To be successful this strategy requires the creation of invisible deviants who can be easily absorbed into society and disappear from view.

A current example of this approach is found in the decarceration movement which has reduced the number of inmates in prisons (Bureau of Prisons, 1972) and mental hospitals (National Institute of Mental Health, 1970) over the last fifteen years. By curtailing commitments and increasing turnover rates the state is able to limit the scale and increase the efficiency of institutionalization. If, however, direct release is likely to focus too much attention on the shortcomings of the state, a number of intermediate solutions can be adopted. These include subsidies for private control arrangements (e.g. foster homes, old-age homes) and decentralized control facilities (e.g. community treatment centers, halfway houses). In both cases, the fiscal burden of the state is reduced while the dangers of complete normalization are avoided.

(2) *Conversion.* To a certain extent the expenses generated by problem and deviant populations can be offset by encouraging their direct participation in the process of control. Potential troublemakers can be recruited as policemen, social workers, and attendants, while confirmed deviants can be "rehabilitated" by becoming counselors, psychiatric aides, and parole officers. In other words, if a large number of the controlled can be converted into a first line of defense, threats to the system of class rule can be transformed into resources for its support.[6]

(3) *Containment.* One means of responding to threatening populations without individualized manipulation is through a policy of containment or compartmentalization. This policy involves the geographic segregation of large populations and the use of formal and informal sanctions to circumscribe the challenges that they present. Instead of classifying and handling problem populations in terms of the specific expenses that they create, these groups are loosely administered as a homogeneous class who can be ignored or managed passively as long as they remain in their place.

Strategies of containment have always flourished where social segregation exists, but they have become especially favored in modern capitalist societies. One reason for this is their compatibility with patterns of residential segregation, ghettoization, and internal colonialism (Blauner, 1969).

(4) *Support of Criminal Enterprise.* Another way the overproduction of deviance may be eased is by granting greater power and influence to organized crime. Although predatory criminal enterprise is assumed to stand in opposition to the goals of the state and the capitalist class, it performs valuable and unique functions in the service of class rule (McIntosh, 1973). By creating a parallel opportunity structure, organized crime provides a means of support for groups who might otherwise become a burden on the state. The activities of organized crime are also important in the pacification of problem populations. Organized crime provides goods and services which ease the hardships and deflect the energies of the underclass. In this

role the "crime industry" performs a cooling-out function and offers a control resource which might otherwise not exist. Moreover, insofar as criminal enterprise attempts to reduce uncertainty and risk in its operations, it aids the state in the maintenance of public order. This is particularly true to the extent that the rationalization of criminal activity reduces the collateral costs (i.e. violence) associated with predatory crime (Schelling, 1967).

CONCLUSION

A Marxian theory of deviance and control must overcome the weaknesses of both conventional interpretations and narrow critical models. It must offer a means of studying deviance which fully exploits the critical potential of Marxist scholarship. More that "demystifying" the analysis of deviance, such a theory must suggest directions and offer insights which can be utilized in the direct construction of critical theory. Although the discussion has been informed by concepts and evidence drawn from a range of Marxist studies, it has been more of a sensitizing essay than a substantive analysis. The further development of the theory must await the accumulation of evidence to refine our understanding of the relationships and tendencies explored. When this evidence is developed, the contributions of Marxist thought can be more meaningfully applied to an understanding of deviance, class conflict, and social control.

Notes

1. For example, Turk (1969) defines deviance primarily in terms of the social position and relative power of various social groups.

2. To the extent that a group (e.g. homosexuals) blatantly and systematically challenges the validity of the bourgeois family it is likely to become part of the problem population. The family is essential to capitalist society as a unit for consumption, socialization, and the reproduction of the socially necessary labor force (cf. Frankford and Snitow, 1972; Secombe, 1973; Zaretsky, 1973).

3. O'Connor (1973) discusses this problem in terms of the crisis faced by the capitalist state in maintaining conditions for profitable accumulation and social harmony.

4. It has been estimated, for instance, that one-third of all arrests in America are for the offense of public drunkenness. Most of these apparently involve "sick" and destitute "skid row alcoholics" (Morris and Hawkins, 1969).

5. Despite the general tendencies of state capitalism, its internal ideological contradictions may actually frustrate the adoption of an investment approach. For example, in discussing social welfare policy Rimlinger (1966:571) concludes that "in a country like the United States, which has a strong individualistic heritage, the idea is still alive that any kind of social protection has adverse productivity effects. A country like the Soviet Union, with a centrally

planned economy and a collectivist ideology, is likely to make an earlier and more deliberate use of health and welfare programs for purposes of influencing productivity and developing manpower."

6. In his analysis of the lumpenproletariat Marx (1964) clearly recognized how the underclass could be manipulated as a "bribed tool of reactionary intrigue."

References

Baran, Paul, and Paul M. Sweezy. 1966. Monopoly Capital. New York: Monthly Review Press.

Becker, Howard S. 1967. "Whose side are we on?" Social Problems 14(Winter): 239–247.

Becker, Howard S., and Irving Louis Horowitz. 1972. "Radical politics and sociological research: Observations on methodology and ideology." American Journal of Sociology 78(July): 48–66.

Blauner, Robert. 1969. "Internal colonialism and ghetto revolt." Social Problems 16(Spring): 393–408.

Bowles, Samuel. 1973. "Contradictions in United States higher education." Pp. 165–199 in James H. Weaver (ed.), Modern Political Economy: Radical versus Orthodox Approaches. Boston: Allyn and Bacon.

Bowles, Samuel, and Herbert Gintis. 1972. "I.Q. in the U.S. class structure." Social Policy 3(November/December): 65–96.

Bureau of Prisons. 1972. National Prisoner Statistics. Prisoners in State and Federal Institutions for Adult Felons. Washington, D.C.: Bureau of Prisons.

Cohen, David K., and Marvin Lazerson. 1972. "Education and the corporate order." Socialist Revolution (March/April): 48–72.

Foucault, Michel. 1965. Madness and Civilization. New York: Random House.

Frankford, Evelyn, and Ann Snitow. 1972. "The trap of domesticity: Notes on the family." Socialist Revolution (July/August): 83–94.

Gintis, Herbert. 1973. "Alienation and power." Pp. 431–465 in James H. Weaver (ed.), Modern Political Economy: Radical versus Orthodox Approaches. Boston: Allyn and Bacon.

Gorz, Andre. 1970. "Capitalist relations of production and the socially necessary labor force." Pp. 155–171 in Arthur Lothstein (ed.), All We Are Saying . . . . New York: G. P. Putnam.

Gross, Bertram M. 1970. "Friendly fascism: A model for America." Social Policy (November/December): 44–52.

Helmer, John, and Thomas Vietorisz. 1973. "Drug use, the labor market and class conflict." Paper presented at Annual Meeting of the American Sociological Association.

Karier, Clarence J. 1973. "Business values and the educational state." Pp. 6–29 in Clarence J. Karier, Paul Violas, and Joel Spring (eds.), Roots of Crisis: American Education in the Twentieth Century. Chicago: Rand McNally.

Liazos, Alexander. 1972. "The poverty of the sociology of deviance: Nuts, sluts and preverts." Social Problems 20(Summer): 103–120.

Mandel, Ernest. 1968. Marxist Economic Theory (Volume I). New York: Monthly Review Press.

Marcuse, Herbert. 1964. One-Dimensional Man. Boston: Beacon Press.

Marx, Karl. 1964. Class Struggles in France, 1848–1850. New York: International Publishers; 1967. Capital (Volume I). New York: International Publishers.

Matza, David. 1969. Becoming Deviant. Englewood Cliffs, N.J.: Prentice-Hall.

McIntosh, Mary. 1973. "The growth of racketeering." Economy and Society (February): 35–69.

Morris, Norval, and Gordon Hawkins. 1969. The Honest Politician's Guide to Crime Control. Chicago: University of Chicago Press.

Musto, David F. 1973. The American Disease: Origins of Narcotic Control. New Haven: Yale University Press.

National Institute of Mental Health. 1970. Trends in Resident Patients—State and County Mental Hospitals 1950–1968. Biometry Branch, Office of Program Planning and Evaluation. Rockville, Maryland: National Institute of Mental Health.

O'Connor, James. 1973. The Fiscal Crisis of the State. New York: St. Martin's Press.

Piven, Frances, and Richard A. Cloward. 1971. Regulating the Poor: The Functions of Public Welfare. New York: Random House.

Rimlinger, Gaston V. 1961. "Social security, incentives, and controls in the U.S. and U.S.S.R." Comparative Studies in Society and History 4(November): 104–124; 1966. "Welfare policy and economic development: A comparative historical perspective." Journal of Economic History (December): 556–571.

Schelling, Thomas. 1967. "Economics and criminal enterprise." Public Interest (Spring): 61–78.

Secombe, Wally. 1973. "The housewife and her labour under capitalism." New Left Review (January–February): 3–24.

Spring, Joel. 1972. Education and the Rise of the Corporate State. Boston: Beacon Press; 1973. "Education as a form of social control." Pp. 30–39 in Clarence J. Karier, Paul Violas, and Joel Spring (eds.), Roots of Crisis: American Education in the Twentieth Century. Chicago: Rand McNally.

Turk, Austin T. 1969. Criminality and Legal Order. Chicago: Rand McNally.

Zaretsky, Eli. 1973. "Capitalism, the family and personal life: Parts 1 & 2." Socialist Revolution (January–April/May–June): 69–126, 19–70.

14. The Empirical Status of the Subculture of Violence Thesis

HOWARD S. ERLANGER

In the study of adult interpersonal violence (which may be defined as acts of physical aggression directed at persons, excluding acts under the aegis of, or directed against, political, parental, or other authority), one of the most important and most often cited theoretical statements has been the "subculture of violence" thesis (Wolfgang, 1958; Wolfgang and Ferracuti, 1967). According to Wolfgang and Ferracuti, violence results from adherence to a set of values which supports and encourages its expression. These values are seen as being in conflict with, but not totally in opposition to, those of the dominant culture. It is said that within the subculture, various stimuli such as a jostle, a slightly derogatory remark, or the appearance of a weapon in the hands of an adversary are perceived differently than in the dominant culture; in the subculture they evoke a combative reaction.

Although violence obviously is not and cannot be used continuously, Wolfgang and Ferracuti see the requirement to be violent as a norm governing a wide variety of situations. They judge the subcultural theme to be "penetrating and diffuse" and argue that violations of the subcultural norm are punished within the subculture. Adherence to the norm is not necessarily viewed as illicit conduct, and "a carrier and user of violence will [generally] not be burdened by conscious guilt ... [and] even law-abiding members of the local subcultural area may not view various expressions of violence as menacing or immoral" (Wolfgang and Ferracuti, 1967:161).

When preparing the 1967 volume, Wolfgang and Ferracuti could locate no data on the distribution of values regarding violence, so they were forced to rely on inferences from available data on criminal acts of interpersonal violence. Since criminal statistics indicate that the groups with the highest rates of homicide are males, nonwhites, lower- and working-class whites, and young adults, it is, therefore, among these groups that "we should find in most intense degree a subculture of violence" (Wolfgang and Ferracuti, 1967:153). They

192

acknowledge that their reasoning here is circular, and they agree that individual data on values are necessary for an adequate test of the theory.

In the years since the subculture of violence thesis was first introduced, there have been a variety of studies which directly or indirectly bring data to bear on the thesis. In the study of juvenile delinquency, for example, there has been a related controversy over the value system of adolescent gangs. W. Miller (1958) has argued that these gangs reflect the "focal concerns" of lower-class culture, which he sees as including "toughness" and "excitement." However, the analysis of gang values by Short and Strodtbeck (1965) failed to confirm the existence of these focal concerns, and a study by Lerman (1968) has questioned the existence of a distinctive lower-class culture reflected in gangs. In addition, various studies (e.g., Short and Strodtbeck, 1965; Jansyn, 1966) have concluded that gang activity is related more to group processes than to a violence-oriented subculture,[1] and later work by Miller and his colleagues does not indicate that physical aggression is an important part of lower-class gang life (Miller et al., 1961; Miller, 1966).

Some studies, such as those of Kobrin et al. (1967) and Yablonsky (1962), have found that status within the gang is at least in part based on the criteria outlined by Wolfgang and Ferracuti, but Yablonsky has also emphasized the fluid nature of group membership and the limited ability of leaders to sanction members who do not conform (see also Matza, 1964; Short and Strodtbeck, 1965). Moreover, it is important to remember that the existence of violence as a criterion of status in gangs in low-income neighborhoods is insufficient to establish the existence of such norms among nongang juveniles in those neighborhoods, especially since it is generally the most extreme gangs that have been studied. When the whole juvenile population is studied, the patterns can be quite different (Hirschi, 1969).

In the study of adult interpersonal violence, research has been much more limited. Various studies and texts in sociology (e.g., Amir, 1971; Clinard, 1973; Schur, 1969) and social psychology (e.g., Akers, 1973; Toch, 1969) have stressed the subcultural view, but they have not used individual data to support their arguments. The idea of a subculture of violence is conspicuous by its *absence* in various well-known ethnographic studies of adult lower-class communities (e.g., Liebow, 1967; Suttles, 1968; Whyte, 1955). Since these writers are not explicitly concerned with the issue, the absence of discussion is not definitive evidence against the thesis. It does, however, suggest that violence is not a major theme in the groups studied.[2]

Few systematic studies of class differences in values or attitudes among adults have been reported in the literature, and some of the most often cited are quite dated. Most studies that do exist do not specifically deal with low-income groups; the lower class is either omitted or combined with the working class for analysis.[3] Insofar as the present author can determine, until the late 1960s no survey data on the values or attitudes of adults toward violence were available.

In a recent paper, Ball-Rokeach (1973) analyzes responses to the Rokeach Value Survey given by males with various degrees of participation in violence. She finds no important differences in the ranking of eighteen "terminal values" or of eighteen "instrumental values" by men classified as having no, a "moderate," or a "high" degree of participation in violence at any time in their life. She reports that controls for education and income, which are crucial for the examination of a subculture which is said to be class-based, do not affect the findings. A comparison of prisoners convicted of violent crimes and persons convicted of nonviolent crimes also found no important differences in the ranking of values. Although there are some difficulties with the data used in these studies,[4] they are the only recent materials which attempt to measure directly value hierarchies; and they yield findings incompatible with the subculture of violence thesis.

Attitudinal data collected for the President's Commission on the Causes and Prevention of Violence in 1968 also call the subcultural thesis into question. In a national survey, for which questionnaire construction was supervised by Ball-Rokeach, respondents were asked about their general approval of the use of physical aggression in certain kinds of interpersonal interactions; those who gave this general approval were then asked about four or five more specific situations. The general approval questions asked whether there were "any situations that you can imagine" in which the respondent would approve of such acts as a husband slapping his wife's face; a husband shooting his wife; a man punching (or choking) an adult male stranger; one teenage boy punching (or knifing) another. Because these items and their follow-ups are so general, acceptance of them does not imply membership in a subculture of violence. But conversely, it seems reasonable to assume that persons who are in such a subculture would find it quite easy to support many of the items, especially those dealing with relatively minor forms of violence. If levels of support in low-status groups are relatively low, then the finding can be taken as suggestive evidence contrary to the thesis.[5]

Preliminary analysis of these data has been reported elsewhere (Baker and Ball, 1969; Stark and McEvoy, 1970). The present author has undertaken a detailed analysis of these data, using cross tabulation and multiple regression. My analysis does not alter the basic preliminary findings, which showed an absence of major differences by race or class[6] in approval of interpersonal violence, and in general a low rate of approval. For example, marital fighting is often thought to be a characteristic of the "subculture of violence," but when approval of a husband slapping his wife's face is examined, only 25 percent of white and 37 percent of black married men aged eighteen to sixty say that they can imagine *any* situation in which they would approve, with no systematic variation by income or education. (There is an age effect, with men over forty being sharply lower in approval, but it is independent of race, education, or income.) Moreover, both the level of support and the variation by race decrease markedly when follow-up items are examined. A similar pattern is found for items relating to approval of a man choking an adult male stranger; while on items relating to punching an adult male stranger, approval by whites is higher than that by blacks.

Attitudes toward machismo can be gauged by an index made up of items relating to approval of teenage fighting. The items on this index seem to be very easy to support—"Are there any situations you can imagine in which you would approve of a teenage boy punching another teenage boy?" If yes, or not sure, "would you approve if he didn't like the other boy?" . . . "if he had been ridiculed and picked on by the other boy?" . . . "if he had been challenged by the other boy to a fist fight?" . . . "if he had been hit by the other boy?" The index was constructed by scoring a yes response to each of the five items as 2, a not sure as 1, and a no as 0. The range is thus 0–10.

Whites tend to score higher than blacks on this index; and when parents with at least one teenage child are analyzed separately, only 12 percent of black parents, compared to 38 percent of white parents, score above six on the ten-point index. Among whites, parents with low income score lower than those with high income.

If a subculture of violence existed among low-status adults, or if low-status adults valued the expression of violence among their children, the general trend on this index would be expected to be the reverse of that found, and the rate of support at the high end of the index would have been much higher. The data and conclusions say nothing about the extent of fighting among lower-class or black teenagers; and the questions of unintentional socialization through the latent effects of parental behavior, or of socialization to violence by teenage peers, remain open. It may well be that lower-class or black teenagers are involved in a disproportionate number of fights, and the lower rate of approval by their parents could be a result of the frequency or seriousness of these fights. But such a situation would only support the conclusion that lower-class parents in general, and black parents in particular, do not especially like the idea of their children fighting and that teenage fighting is probably not a product of an adult value system emphasizing violence.

Some New Data: Peer Esteem and Psychological Correlates of Fighting

In addition to the investigation of verbal support for a "subculture of violence," support and sanction in peer interactions can be examined. Wolfgang and Ferracuti (1967:160) argue that nonviolent members of a subcultural group are subject to great pressure to conform, that sanction is an integral part of the existence of a norm, and that "alienation of some kind ... seems to be a form of punitive action most feasible to this subculture." It seems to follow that, conversely, persons who adhere to the values would be more likely than those who do not to be liked, respected, and accorded high status in the group. Data from a 1969 survey of black and white males aged twenty-one to sixty-four in Milwaukee, Wisconsin, give some evidence on this point.[7] Physical aggression is indicated by the item "How often do you get in angry fist fights with other men?" (never, almost never, sometimes, often); perceived esteem accorded by others is indicated by two items, "How do you compare with most men you know on being respected and listened to by other people?" (five point code, from much worse to much better) and "How do you compare with most men you know on being well liked by other people and having lots of friends?" (same code). Since the esteem items are double-barreled, they are less precise than desirable. However, they are useful for exploratory purposes.

Because the subcultural hypothesis posits statistical interaction, separate analyses were made for the "lower class" (income less than $5,000) and "nonpoor" (income over $5,000), and for blacks and whites. As a result, low-income whites have a small sample size and detailed analysis cannot be carried out for this subsample.

[The data collected] show that the pattern of fighting by race and income group is consistent with the subcultural thesis; blacks are more likely to fight than whites, and the poor are more likely to fight than the nonpoor.[8] (Contrary to expectations, poor whites are more likely to fight than poor blacks, but the percentage for whites is unreliable because of the [small sample]). However, this pattern is also consistent with several other non-subcultural theories, such as those of Henry and Short (1954), Coser (1963), Gold (1958), or Cloward and Ohlin (1960). The important question here is whether men who fight are accorded (or at least see themselves as being accorded) more esteem by others.

Although the subculture of violence thesis does not make a prediction about the overall association between race or economic status and peer respect or high status among peers, it predicts that the basis of the respect of status will be different in different groups. Subcultural theory would seem to predict a relatively strong positive correlation between the peer esteem item and fighting for low-income blacks, a somewhat smaller (but at least statistically significant) positive correlation for low-income whites and nonpoor blacks,[9] and a relatively strong negative correlation for nonpoor whites.

[The data] show the relationship between fighting and perceiving "respect by others," in terms of zero order correlations and as the net effect (beta) of fighting on perceived esteem by others, controlling first for social desirability bias[10] and then for social desirability bias, occupation, and age.[11] The findings are inconsistent with the predictions outlined, with the betas and zero order correlations being either very close to zero or having a sign opposite that predicted.[12] [The data also] show the relationship between fighting and perceptions of being "liked by others," in terms of zero order correlations and the net effect of fighting on perceived esteem. Here the findings are somewhat as predicted by subcultural theory, with low-income blacks and low-income whites showing a positive net effect of fighting on perceived esteem. But the former beta is rather small; and although the latter is larger, neither of them is statistically significant. Moreover, for nonpoor white men, the predicted strong negative correlation does not appear.

Although the findings here do not refute the subculture of violence thesis, taken as a whole they cast doubt on it. To the extent that violence is important to low-income or black men, and to the extent that a subcultural norm is being enforced through ostracism or peer rebuke, we would expect to find a relatively strong positive relationship between fighting and perceived general esteem. Similarly, if a counternorm of nonviolence is important in the white middle class, a strong negative relationship should have been found. Overall the data here are not consistent with this predicted pattern; and if we take statistical significance as a minimal criterion of support, none of the predictions of subcultural theory is supported. It is possible, of course, that the available indicators mask the relationships predicted. For example, perhaps responses to fighting draw approval or rebuke as predicted, but these reponses do not affect the overall evaluation perceived by the violent person. In this case, however, we would have to conclude that violence is not as important to the subculture as hypothesized, for as the sanction gets stronger—e.g., ostracism—consequences for general esteem should follow.

As a corollary to the analysis of violence and esteem, the relationship between violence and feeling of well-being can be examined. The subcultural thesis holds that violence is normal behavior and is the product of normal group processes. Similarly, it posits that violent people do not feel guilty about their actions. An empirical inquiry could examine psychiatric records or administer various personality tests (see, e.g., Ferracuti, Lazzari, and Wolfgang, 1970); alternatively, various measures of psychological adjustment can be included in an interview schedule or questionnaire. One such measure is an index of happiness which can be constructed from items in the Milwaukee survey.[13] It would seem that outside the subculture men who are violent would be less likely to be happy than would nonviolent men, both because they were receiving negative sanctions for their violence and because in this group it would be the more marginal men who would be violent. By contrast, within the subculture, happiness would be positively correlated with violence, since violence is posited as not being a pathological condition and since nonviolent men are hypothesized to be negatively sanctioned. [The findings] show that fighting is negatively correlated with happiness for all four subgroups, and (statistically) significantly so for blacks. Except for nonpoor whites, these findings run directly counter to the predictions of the subcultural thesis. And even for nonpoor whites, the finding of a correlation even less negative than for blacks can also be considered evidence contrary to the thesis.[14]

DISCUSSION

Although much suggestive evidence on the subculture of violence exists, there is a clear need for further research in this area. Methodologically, this research should be designed so that there is adequate representation of minorities and of poor whites for analysis; and it should make some attempt to cover both "streetcorner men" and more traditional householders (cf. Hannerz, 1969). A major limitation of existing survey data is that they are based only on persons in households (cf. Parsons, 1972). Another is that the surveys do not have concentrated samples in a given neighborhood. These difficulties are alleviated, but not erased, by the data from the field studies.

Substantively, work needs to be done on establishing the pervasiveness of a subculture. At least three quite different degrees of pervasiveness may exist. In the most extreme case, a large majority of the demographic group presumed to have the subcultural trait would exhibit it in some way, as opposed to a minority of members of other demographic groups. In this case, one could characterize the demographic group as subcultural. A more limited pervasiveness exists when the trait is exhibited by a minority of a particular demographic group, as compared to a virtual absence in other groups; this would constitute a subculture *within* a demographic group. Finally, some analysts would consider a small but statistically significant difference between demographic groups as evidence of a subculture. However, it seems incorrect to characterize such a subculture as being located in the demographic group with greater support for the value, or to characterize that demographic group as a subculture. Rather, the subculture would have to be defined as the group of people who hold the value, irrespective of their demographic group.[15]

These differences in the pervasiveness of subcultures have important implications for the public imagery of social groups. In the case of the subculture of violence, if class or racial groups can in fact be characterized as being different (or if findings are presented as though they could), popular conceptions of widespread pathology among nonwhites and low-income whites would be supported. By contrast the existence of a subculture within a class or racial group, or of value differences that are statistically significant but not large, would be more consonant with the view that there is wide variation in the values, needs, and problems of the poor and of nonwhites.

Future research should also focus more closely on the precise content of supposed subcultural differences.[16] It is possible, for example, that rather than a "subculture of violence," something like a "subculture of masculinity" exists, with violence being only one of many possible outlets, and not necessarily the preferred one. In this case, violence may result from the blocking of alternative opportunities to exhibit "machismo" (cf. Miller, 1966). Another possibility is that the use of liquor may be part of a broader social configuration which generates situations conducive to violence. A value system which sanctions or even encourages either drunken brawls or wild behavior on certain special occasions would not necessarily be the same as one which requires "quick resort to physical combat as a measure of daring, courage, or defense of status" in everyday interaction.[17]

Finally, the origins, permanence, and relationship to social structure must also be given careful consideration in future research. These considerations are especially important in the formation of social policy (cf. Banfield, 1968; Lewis *et al.*, 1969; Liebow, 1971; Valentine, 1968).

CONCLUSION

Although the subculture of violence thesis has received a certain measure of acceptance in the field, a wide variety of evidence suggests that it is questionable. All of the data available have limitations of various sorts, and the thesis cannot be said to have been definitively tested. On balance, however, more of available evidence is inconsistent with the thesis than consistent with it.

At this time we do not know how important a deviant value system is in explaining violence in the United States;[18] and, if it exists, we do not know whether such a value system can be said to be found predominantly within the black or low-income white communities or whether it can be said to be relatively independent of social structure. But there is enough evidence to conclude that these groups are not *characteristically* different from the dominant society in their rate of approval of the use of physical aggression. This conclusion, along with a growing empirical literature on other aspects of the lives of poor and black (and other minority) persons in the United States, is compatible with the view that the social and economic deprivations experienced by members of these groups are primarily the result of social structural factors, rather than the product of group pathology (cf. Goodwin, 1972; Institute for Social Research, 1974; Kriesberg, 1970; Shiller, 1973).

Notes

1. Some critics of this manuscript have held that the group process material in the Short and Strodtbeck work supports the subculture of violence thesis. Although the material may be open to varying interpretations, Short reports that he "never felt that our data were supportive of the subculture of violence thesis" (personal communication). Short feels that the group process mechanisms are related to subcultural variations, but that the subculture of violence thesis is not particularly helpful in explaining the outcomes they observed.

2. One anthropological study that does recount many violent incidents is Lewis's biography of the Rios family in Puerto Rico and New York. But although a degree of machismo is clearly present, violence is often criticized by the family. Most of the family members feel hurt by the violence and deprivation they experienced as children, and many resolve to do better with their children. In an earlier discussion of poverty in Mexico, Lewis (1961) lists "frequent resort to violence" as an element of the culture of poverty, while in *La Vida* (1966) he talks more generally of lack of impulse control. In neither case does he say that the culture requires acts of violence.

3. One relevant study which combines class data in this way is Schneider and Lysgaard's (1953) work on the "deferred gratification pattern." Although the findings of class differences are open to criticism (see Miller, 1965), note that at any rate the differences in the use of physical violence were small and were considered unimpressive by the authors.

4. On the dependent variable, there are weaknesses in the indicators of the values supporting violence. "An Exciting Life," "Pleasure," "Social Recognition," and being "Courageous" are examples of the indicators of the machismo concept; yet the phrases accompanying these and each of the other value choices suggest a very broad interpretation, e.g., "a stimulating and ac-

tive life;" "an enjoyable, leisurely life;" "respect, admiration;" "standing up for your beliefs." On the independent variable, in the national study, the "degree of participation in violence" includes both aggression and victimization, is based on the variety rather than the extent of experience, and weighs childhood incidents equally with any recent ones. Even if a respondent's aggression were being estimated with some accuracy, the violence may have occurred long before the contemporary value patterns were established. Also the studies apparently do not control for age or race.

5. Of course, this does not mean that a person's response to the general item directly indicates his attitude or action in some actual instance in which he may become (or have been) involved.

6. Social class is indicated by income and education. Occupational data were not coded.

7. The data are from an ongoing study of correlates of self-esteem directed by Russell Middleton (sponsored by the National Science Foundation); I am grateful to him for permission to analyze and report the relationships presented here. The interviews were conducted by the Wisconsin Survey Research Laboratory and respondents and interviewers were matched by race. An area probability sample for the Milwaukee city limits was used.

8. The differences by class and race reported for the samples here are larger than those found on items in the Violence Commission survey, which asked retrospectively about acts of physical aggression. See Baker and Ball (1969) or Stark and McEvoy (1970).

9. An alternative prediction would be that, because of strong norms against violence among the "black bourgeoisie," the correlation between violence and esteem would be negative at least for those nonpoor blacks in white-collar jobs.

10. "Social desirability bias" is indicated by a five-item adaptation of Crowne and Marlow's (1964) scale, which includes items which are either socially desirable but probably untrue or probably true but socially undesirable. (For example, True or False: "I never hesitate to go out of my way to help someone in trouble.") Of the five items, three were worded such that agreement was socially desirable, and two worded such that disagreement was socially desirable. Respondents scoring high on this scale are somewhat more likely to report that they do not get in fights and that they are held in high esteem by others.

11. Both occupation and age were indicated by sets of dummy variables. For occupation, the categories were white collar, blue collar, farm; for age they were 21–25, 26–30, 31–35, 36–45, 46–55, 56–64.

12. A competing interpretation of the zero and near zero relationships in [the data] is that they mask a strong reciprocal causality. The possibility of such reciprocal causality, which would be consistent with the subcultural thesis, has been explored for blacks using two stage least squares analysis. The results of that analysis support the conclusion in the text.

13. The items were these: "On the whole, how happy would you say you are now?" "On the whole, how happy would you say you are now compared with other men you know?" "How often do you feel very discouraged and depressed?" "How often do you get the feeling that life is not worth living?" Each item had four possible responses.

14. Because of the uncertain direction of causation, partial correlation coefficients may be a more appropriate measure of association here than regression coefficients. However, use of partial r's would not have changed the findings.

15. Also, as Rodman (1963) suggests, this case might be better understood as one of a variation on a common cultural theme, not as a tension between the values of a dominant culture and a subculture. Of course, even if such a difference is not considered subcultural, it may still be descriptively interesting and important in the explanation of violence.

16. This can probably best be done by beginning with relatively unstructured in-depth interviews with informants. A move in this direction is made by Toch (1969), who conducted intensive interviews with both convicts and policemen who had frequently engaged in assault. But even here the subcultural thesis is drawn from the literature rather than grounded in the accounts of those interviewed.

17. Similar considerations hold for the question of the existence of a subculture of violence in the American South. Many writers have noted the quite disproportionately high rate of homicide in the South, and recently Gastil (1971), Hackney (1969), and Reed (1972) have argued that this divergence can be explained by regional differences in the acceptability of violence. But again, the exact content of the hypothesized subculture is generally unclear, and data do not support the application of the subculture of violence thesis to the South.

18. This analysis does not address Wolfgang and Ferracuti's contention that a subculture of violence exists in Colombia, Sardinia, Mexico, Albania, and Albanova, Italy. The case of Sardinia is explored in more detail in Ferracuti *et al.* (1970), who find some evidence in support of the hypothesis but conclude that "the subculture of violence in Sardinia is limited to violent offenders" (1970:110). This suggests that although it may be that violent offenders in Sardinia receive support for their actions from a limited group, Sardinia itself cannot be characterized as embracing a subculture of violence.

References

Akers, Ronald L. 1973. Deviant Behavior: A Social Learning Approach. Belmont: Wadsworth Publishing.

Amir, Menachem. 1971. Patterns in Forcible Rape. Chicago: University of Chicago Press.

Baker, Robert K. and Sandra J. Ball. 1969. Mass Media and Violence; Report to the National Commission on Causes and Prevention of Violence. Washington, D.C.: U.S. Government Printing Office.

Ball-Rokeach, Sandra J. 1973. Values and Violence: A Test of the Subculture of Violence Thesis. American Sociological Review 38:6 (December) pp. 736–49.

Banfield, Edward C. 1968. The Unheavenly City. Boston: Little, Brown.

Clinard, Marshall B. 1973. Sociology of Deviant Behavior. New York: Holt, Rinehart and Winston.

Cloward, Richard A. and Lloyd Ohlin. 1960. Delinquency and Opportunity. New York: The Free Press.

Coser, Lewis A. 1963. "Violence and the social structure." Science and Psychoanalysis 6:30–42. Reprinted in Shalom Endleman (ed.), Violence in the Streets. Chicago: Quadrangle (1968).

Crain, Robert L. and Carol Sachs Weisman. 1972. Discrimination, Personality, and Achievement. New York: Seminar Press.

Crowne, Douglas P. and David Marlowe. 1964. The Approval Motive. New York: John Wiley.

Ferracuti, Franco, Renato Lazzari, and Marvin E. Wolfgang. 1970. "A Study of the Subculture of Violence Thesis," in Ferracuti *et al.*, Violence in Sardinia. Rome: Mario Bulzoni, editor.

Gastil, Raymond D. 1971. "Homicide and a regional culture of violence." American Sociological Review 36(June): 412–27.

Gold, Martin. 1958. "Suicide, homicide, and socialization of aggression." American Journal of Sociology 63(May): 651–61.

Goodwin, Leonard. 1972. Do the Poor Want to Work? Washington, D.C.: Brookings Institution.

Hackney, Sheldon. 1969. "Southern Violence," in Hugh Davis Graham and Ted Robert Gurr (eds.), History of Violence in America. Report of the Task Force of the President's Commission on Causes and Prevention of Violence. New York: Bantam Books, 505–28.

Hannerz, Ulf. 1969. Soulside: Inquiries into Ghetto Culture and Community. New York: Columbia University Press.

Henry, Andrew and James F. Short. 1954. Suicide and Homicide. New York: The Free Press.

Hirschi, Travis. 1969. Causes of Delinquency. Berkeley and Los Angeles: The University of California Press.

Institute for Social Research. 1974. The Changing Status of Five Thousand American Families: Highlights from the Panel Study of Income Dynamics. Mimeo. Ann Arbor: The University of Michigan.

Jansyn, Leon R., Jr. 1966. "Solidarity and delinquency in a street corner group." American Sociological Review 31(October): 600–14.

Kobrin, Solomon, Joseph Puntil, and Emil Peluso. 1967. "Criteria of status among street groups." Journal of Research in Crime and Delinquency 4(January).

Kriesberg, Louis. 1970. Mothers in Poverty: A Study of Fatherless Families. Chicago: Aldine.

Lerman, Paul. 1968. "Individual values, peer values, and subcultural delinquency." American Sociological Review 33(April): 219–35.

Lewis, Oscar. 1961. Children of Sanchez. New York: Vintage; 1966. La Vida: A Puerto Rican Family in the Culture of Poverty. San Juan and New York: Random House; 1969. *et al.*, Review Symposium: Culture and Poverty (Charles A. Valentine). Current Anthropology 10(April, June): 189–201.

Liebow, Elliot. 1967. Talley's Corner. Boston: Little, Brown; 1971. "Comment on Miller's Paper," pp. 131–36 in J. Alan Winter (ed.), The Poor. Grand Rapids, Michigan: W. B. Eerdmans.

Matza, David. 1964. Delinquency and Drift. New York: John Wiley.

Miller, S. M., Arthur Seagull, and Frank Riessman. 1965. "The Deferred Gratification Pattern: A Critical Appraisal," in Louis Ferman *et al.*, Poverty in America. Ann Arbor: University of Michigan Press.

Miller, Walter B. 1958. "Lower class culture as a generating milieu of gang delinquency." Journal of Social Issues 14(Summer): 5–19; 1961; *et al.* "Aggression in a boy's street-corner group." Psychiatry 24(November): 283–98; 1966. "Violent crimes in city gangs." Annals of American Academy of Political and Social Science 364(March): 96–112.

Mulvihill, Donald J. and Melvin Tumin. 1969. Crimes of Violence. Staff Report to the National Commission on Causes and Prevention of Violence. Vols. 11, 12, and 13. Washington, D.C.: U.S. Government Printing Office.

Parsons, Carole W. (ed.). 1972. America's Uncounted People. Washington, D.C.: National Academy of Sciences.

Reed, John S. 1972. The Enduring South: Subcultural Persistence in Mass Society. Lexington, Massachusetts: D. C. Heath.

Rodman, Hyman. 1963. "The lower class value stretch." Social Forces 42(December): 205–15.

Schneider, Louis and Sverre Lysgaard. 1953. "The deferred gratification pattern: A preliminary study." American Sociological Review 18(April): 142–49.

Schur, Edwin. 1969. Our Criminal Society. Englewood Cliffs, New Jersey: Prentice-Hall.

Schiller, Bradley R. 1973. "Empirical studies of welfare dependency: A survey." Journal of Human Resources 8(Supplement): 19–32.

Short, James F. and Fred L. Strodtbeck. 1965. Group Process and Gang Delinquency. Chicago: University of Chicago Press.

Stark, Rodney and James McEvoy III. 1970. "Middle class violence." Psychology Today 4(November): 52–4, 110–12.

Suttles, Gerald D. 1968. The Social Order of the Slum. Chicago: University of Chicago Press.

Toch, Hans H. 1969. Violent Men. Chicago: Aldine.

Valentine, Charles A. 1968. Culture and Poverty—Critique and Counter-Proposals. Chicago: University of Chicago Press.

Whyte, William F. 1955. Street Corner Society. Chicago: University of Chicago Press.

Wolfgang, Marvin E. 1958. Patterns of Criminal Homicide. Philadelphia: University of Pennsylvania Press; 1967. And Franco Ferracuti. The Subculture of Violence, Towards an Integrated Theory in Criminology. London: Tavistock-Social Science Paperbacks.

Yablonsky, Lewis. 1962. The Violent Gang. New York: Macmillan.

15. Differential Opportunity and Delinquent Subcultures

RICHARD A. CLOWARD
LLOYD E. OHLIN

THE AVAILABILITY OF ILLEGITIMATE MEANS

Social norms are two-sided. A prescription implies the existence of a prohibition, and *vice versa*. To advocate honesty is to demarcate and condemn a set of actions which are dishonest. In other words, norms that define legitimate practices also implicitly define illegitimate practices. One purpose of norms, in fact, is to delineate the boundary between legitimate and illegitimate practices. In setting this boundary, in segregating and classifying various types of behavior, they make us aware not only of behavior that is regarded as right and proper but also of behavior that is said to be wrong and improper. Thus the criminal who engages in theft or fraud does not invent a new way of life; the possibility of employing alternative means is acknowledged, tacitly at least, by the norms of the culture.

This tendency for proscribed alternatives to be implicit in every prescription, and *vice versa*, although widely recognized, is nevertheless a reef upon which many a theory of delinquency has foundered. Much of the criminological literature assumes, for example, that one may explain a criminal act simply by accounting for the individual's readiness to employ illegal alternatives of which his culture, through its norms, has already made him generally aware. Such explanations are quite unsatisfactory, however, for they ignore a host of questions regarding the *relative availability* of illegal alternatives to various potential criminals. The aspiration to be a physician is hardly enough to explain the fact of becoming a physician; there is much that transpires between the aspiration and the achievement. This is no less true of the person who wants to be a successful criminal. Having decided that he "can't make it legitimately," he cannot simply choose among an array of illegitimate means, all equally available to him. . . . it is assumed in the theory of anomie that access to conventional means is differentially distributed, that some individuals, because of their social class, enjoy certain advantages that are denied to those elsewhere in the class structure. For example, there are variations in the degree to which members of various classes are fully exposed to and thus acquire the values, knowledge, and skills that facilitate upward mobility. It should not be startling, therefore, to suggest that there are socially structured variations in the availability of illegitimate means as well. In connection with delinquent subcultures, we shall be concerned principally with differentials in access to illegitimate means within the lower class.

Many sociologists have alluded to differentials in access to illegitimate means without explicitly incorporating this variable into a theory of deviant behavior. This is particularly true of scholars in the "Chicago tradition" of criminology. Two closely related theoretical perspectives emerged from this school. The theory of "cultural transmission," advanced by Clifford R. Shaw and Henry D. McKay, focuses on the development in some urban neighborhoods of a criminal tradition that persists from one generation to another despite constant changes in population.[1] In the theory of "differential association," Edwin H. Sutherland described the processes by which criminal values are taken over by the individual.[2] He asserted that criminal behavior is learned, and that it is learned in interaction with others who have already incorporated criminal values. Thus the first theory stresses the value systems of different areas; the second, the systems of social relationships that facilitate or impede the acquisition of these values.

Scholars in the Chicago tradition, who emphasized the processes involved in learning to be criminal, were actually pointing to differentials in the availability of illegal means—although they did not explicitly recognize this variable in their analysis. This can perhaps best be seen by examining Sutherland's classic work, *The Professional Thief*. "An inclination to steal," according to Sutherland, "is not a sufficient explanation of the genesis of the professional thief."[3] The "self-made" thief, lacking knowledge of the ways of securing immunity from prosecution and similar techniques of defense, "would quickly land in prison; . . . a person can be a professional thief only if he is recognized and received as such by other professional thieves." But recognition is not freely accorded: "Selection and tutelage are the two necessary elements in the process of acquiring recognition as a professional thief. . . . A person cannot acquire recognition as a professional thief until he has had tutelage in professional theft, *and tutelage is given only to a few persons selected from the total population*." For one thing, "the person must be appreciated by the professional thieves. He must be appraised as having an adequate equipment of wits, front, talking-ability, honesty, reliability, nerve and determination." Furthermore, the aspirant is judged by high standards of performance, for only "a very small percentage of those who start on this process ever reach the stage of professional thief. . . ." Thus motivation and pressures toward deviance do not fully account for deviant behavior any more than motivation and pressures toward conformity account for conforming behavior. The individual must have access to a learning environment and, once having been trained, must be allowed to perform his role. Roles, whether conforming or deviant in content, are not necessarily freely available; access to them depends upon a variety of factors, such as one's socio-economic position, age, sex, ethnic affiliation, personality characteristics, and the like. The potential thief, like the potential physician, finds that access to his goal is governed by many criteria other than merit and motivation.

What we are asserting is that access to illegitimate roles is not freely available to all, as is commonly assumed. Only those neighborhoods in which crime flourishes as a stable, indigenous institution are fertile criminal learning environments for the young. Because these environments afford integration of different age-levels of offender, selected young people are exposed to "differential association" through which tutelage is provided and criminal values and skills are acquired. To be prepared for the role may not, however, ensure that the individual will ever discharge it. One important limitation is that more youngsters are recruited into these patterns of differential associations than the adult criminal structure can possibly absorb. Since there is a surplus of contenders for these elite positions, criteria and mechanisms of selection must be evolved. Hence a certain proportion of those who aspire may not be permitted to engage in the behavior for which they have prepared themselves.

Thus we conclude that access to illegitimate roles, no less than access to legitimate roles, is limited by both social and psychological factors. We shall here be concerned primarily with socially structured differentials in illegitimate opportunities. Such differentials, we contend, have much to do with the type of delinquent subculture that develops.

LEARNING AND PERFORMANCE STRUCTURES

Our use of the term "opportunities," legitimate or illegitimate, implies access to both learning and performance structures. That is, the individual must have access to appropriate environments for the acquisition of the values and skills associated with the performance of a particular role, and he must be supported in the performance of the role once he has learned it.

Tannenbaum, several decades ago, vividly expressed the point that criminal role performance, no less than conventional role performance, presupposes a patterned set of relationships through which the requisite values and skills are transmitted by established practitioners to aspiring youth:

> It takes a long time to make a good criminal, many years of specialized training and much preparation. But training is something that is given to people. People learn in a community where the materials and the knowledge are to be had. A craft needs an atmosphere saturated with purpose and promise. The community provides the attitudes, the point of view, the philosophy of life, the example, the motive, the contacts, the friendships, the incentives. No child brings those into the world. He finds them here and available for use and elaboration. The community gives the criminal his materials and habits, just as it gives the doctor, the lawyer, the teacher, and the candlestick-maker theirs.[4]

Sutherland systematized this general point of view, asserting that opportunity consists, at least in part, of learning structures. Thus "criminal behavior is learned" and, furthermore, it is learned "in interaction with other persons in a process of communication." However, he conceded that the differential-association theory does not constitute a full explanation of criminal behavior. In a paper circulated in 1944, he noted that "criminal behavior is partially a function of opportunities to commit [i.e., to perform] specific classes of crime, such as embezzlement, bank burglary, or illicit heterosexual intercourse." Therefore, "while opportunity may be partially a function of association with criminal patterns and of the specialized techniques thus acquired, it is not determined entirely in that manner, and consequently differential association is not the sufficient cause of criminal behavior."[5]

To Sutherland, then, illegitimate opportunity included conditions favorable to the performance of a criminal role as well as conditions favorable to the learning of such a role (differential associations). These conditions, we suggest, depend upon certain features of the social structure of the community in which delinquency arises.

We believe that each individual occupies a position in both legitimate and illegitimate opportunity structures. This is a new way of defining the situation. The theory of anomie views the individual primarily in terms of the legitimate opportunity structure. It poses questions regarding differentials in access to legitimate routes to success-goals; at the same time it assumes either that illegitimate avenues to success-goals are freely available or that differentials in their availability are of little significance. This tendency may be seen in the following statement by Merton:

> Several researches have shown that specialized areas of vice and crime constitute a "normal" response to a situation where the cultural emphasis upon pecuniary success has been absorbed, but where there is little access to conventional and legitimate means for becoming successful. The occu-

pational opportunities of people in these areas are largely confined to manual labor and the lesser white-collar jobs. Given the American stigmatization of manual labor *which has been found to hold rather uniformly for all social classes,* and the absence of realistic opportunities for advancement beyond this level, the result is a marked tendency toward deviant behavior. The status of unskilled labor and the consequent low income cannot readily compete *in terms of established standards of worth* with the promises of power and high income from organized vice, rackets and crime. . . . [Such a situation] leads toward the gradual attenuation of legitimate, but by and large ineffectual, strivings and the increasing use of illegitimate, but more or less effective, expedients.[6]

The cultural-transmission and differential-association tradition, on the other hand, assumes that access to illegitimate means is variable, but it does not recognize the significance of comparable differentials in access to legitimate means. Sutherland's "ninth proposition" in the theory of differential association states:

Though criminal behavior is an expression of general needs and values, it is not explained by those general needs and values since non-criminal behavior is an expression of the same needs and values. Thieves generally steal in order to secure money, but likewise honest laborers work in order to secure money. The attempts by many scholars to explain criminal behavior by general drives and values, such as the happiness principle, striving for social status, the money motive, or frustration, have been and must continue to be futile since they explain lawful behavior as completely as they explain criminal behavior.[7]

In this statement, Sutherland appears to assume that people have equal and free access to legitimate means regardless of their social position. At the very least, he does not treat access to legitimate means as variable. It is, of course, perfectly true that "striving for social status," "the money motive," and other socially approved drives do not fully account for either deviant or conforming behavior. But if goal-oriented behavior occurs under conditions in which there are socially structured obstacles to the satisfaction of these drives by legitimate means, the resulting pressures, we contend, might lead to deviance.

The concept of differential opportunity structures permits us to unite the theory of anomie, which recognizes the concept of differentials in access to legitimate means, and the "Chicago tradition," in which the concept of differentials in access to illegitimate means is implicit. We can now look at the individual, not simply in relation to one or the other system of means, but in relation to both legitimate and illegitimate systems. This approach permits us to ask, for example, how the relative availability of illegitimate opportunities affects the resolution of adjustment problems leading to deviant behavior.

We believe that the way in which these problems are resolved may depend upon the kind of support for one or another type of illegitimate activity that is given at different points in the social structure. If, in a given social location, illegal or criminal means are not readily available, then we should not expect a criminal subculture to develop among adolescents. By the same logic, we should expect the manipulation of violence to become a primary avenue to higher status only in areas where the means of violence are not denied to the young. To give a third example, drug addiction and participation in subcultures organized around the consumption of drugs presuppose that persons can secure access to drugs and knowledge about how to use them. In some parts of the social structure, this would be very difficult; in others, very easy. In short, there are marked differences from one part of the social structure to another in the types of illegitimate adaptation that are available to persons in search of solutions to problems of adjustment arising from the restricted availability of legitimate means.[8] In this sense, then, we can think of individuals as being located in two opportunity structures—one legitimate, the other illegitimate. Given limited access to success-goals by legitimate means, the nature of the delinquent response that may result will vary according to the availability of various illegitimate means.[9]

VARIETIES OF DELINQUENT SUBCULTURE

As we have noted, there appear to be three major types of delinquent subculture typically encountered among adolescent males in lower-class areas of large urban centers. One is based principally upon criminal values; its members are organized primarily for the pursuit of material gain by such illegal means as extortion, fraud, and theft. In the second, violence is the keynote; its members pursue status ("rep") through the manipulation of force or threat of force. These are the "warrior" groups that attract so much attention in the press. Finally, there are subcultures which emphasize the consumption of drugs. The participants in these drug subcultures have become alienated from conventional roles, such as those required in the family or the occupational world. They have withdrawn into a restricted world in which the ultimate value consists in the "kick." We call these three subcultural forms "criminal," "conflict," and "retreatist," respectively.[10]

These shorthand terms simply denote the *principal* orientation of each form of adaptation from the perspective of the dominant social order; although one can find many examples of subcultures that fit accurately into one of these three categories, subcultures frequently appear in somewhat mixed form. Thus members of a predominantly conflict subculture may also on occasion engage in systematic theft; members of a criminal subculture may sometimes do combat in the streets with rival gangs. But this should not obscure the fact that these subcultures tend to exhibit essentially different orientations.

The extent to which the delinquent subculture organizes and controls a participant's allegiance varies from one member to another. Some members of the gang are almost totally immersed in all the perspectives of the subculture and bring them into play in all their contacts; others segregate this aspect of their lives and maintain other roles in the family, school, and church. The chances are relatively slight, however, that an adolescent can successfully segregate delinquent and conforming roles for a long period of time. Pressures emanate from the subculture leading its members to adopt unfavorable attitudes toward parents, school teachers, policemen, and other adults in the conventional world. When he is apprehended for delinquent acts, the possibility of the delinquent's maintaining distinctly separate role involvements breaks down, and he is confronted with the necessity of choosing between law-abiding and delinquent styles of life. Since family, welfare, religious, educational, law-enforcement, and correctional institutions are arrayed against the appeal of his delinquent associates, the decision is a difficult one, frequently requiring either complete acceptance or complete rejection of one or the other system of obligations.[11]

At any one point in time, however, the extent to which the norms of the delinquent subculture control behavior will vary from one member to another. Accordingly, descriptions of these subcultures must be stated in terms of the fully indoctrinated member rather than the average member. Only in this way can the distinctiveness of delinquent styles of life be made clear. It is with this understanding that we offer the following brief empirical characterizations of the three main types of delinquent subculture.

The Criminal Pattern

The most extensive documentation in the sociological literature of delinquent behavior patterns in lower-class culture describes a tradition which integrates youthful delinquency with adult criminality.[12] In the central value orientation of youths participating in this tradition, delinquent and criminal behavior is accepted as a means of achieving success-goals. The dominant criteria of in-group evaluation stress achievement, the use of skill and knowledge to get results. In this culture, prestige is allocated to those who achieve material gain and power through avenues defined as illegitimate by the larger soci-

ety. From the very young to the very old, the successful "haul"—
which quickly transforms the penniless into a man of means—is an
ever-present vision of the possible and desirable. Although one may
also achieve material success through the routine practice of theft or
fraud, the "big score" remains the symbolic image of quick success.

The means by which a member of a criminal subculture achieves
success are clearly defined for the aspirant. At a young age, he learns
to admire and respect older criminals and to adopt the "right guy" as
his role-model. Delinquent episodes help him to acquire mastery of
the techniques and orientation of the criminal world and to learn
how to cooperate successfully with others in criminal enterprises. He
exhibits hostility and distrust toward representatives of the larger society. He regards members of the conventional world as "suckers,"
his natural victims, to be exploited when possible. He sees successful
people in the conventional world as having a "racket"—e.g., big businessmen have huge expense accounts, politicians get graft, etc. This
attitude successfully neutralizes the controlling effect of conventional
norms. Toward the in-group the "right guy" maintains relationships
of loyalty, honesty, and trustworthiness. He must prove himself reliable and dependable in his contacts with his criminal associates although he has no such obligations toward the out-group of
noncriminals.

One of the best ways of assuring success in the criminal world is to
cultivate appropriate "connections." As a youngster, this means running with a clique composed of other "right guys" and promoting an
apprenticeship or some other favored relationship with older and
successful offenders. Close and dependable ties with income-producing outlets for stolen goods, such as the wagon peddler, the junkman,
and the fence, are especially useful. Furthermore, these intermediaries encourage and protect the young delinquent in a criminal way of
life by giving him a jaundiced perspective on the private morality of
many functionaries in conventional society. As he matures, the young
delinquent becomes acquainted with a new world made up of predatory bondsmen, shady lawyers, crooked policemen, grafting politicians, dishonest businessmen, and corrupt jailers. Through
"connections" with occupants of these half-legitimate, half-illegiti-
mate roles and with "big shots" in the underworld, the aspiring
criminal validates and assures his freedom of movement in a world
made safe for crime.

The Conflict Pattern[13]

The role-model in the conflict pattern of lower-class culture is the
"bopper" who swaggers with his gang, fights with weapons to win a
wary respect from other gangs, and compels a fearful deference from

the conventional adult world by his unpredictable and destructive assaults on persons and property. To other gang members, however, the key qualities of the bopper are those of the successful warrior. His performance must reveal a willingness to defend his personal integrity and the honor of the gang. He must do this with great courage and displays of fearlessness in the face of personal danger.

The immediate aim in the world of fighting gangs is to acquire a reputation for toughness and destructive violence. A "rep" assures not only respectful behavior from peers and threatened adults but also admiration for the physical strength and masculinity which it symbolizes. It represents a way of securing access to the scarce resources for adolescent pleasure and opportunity in underprivileged areas.

Above all things, the bopper is valued for his "heart." He does not "chicken out," even when confronted by superior force. He never defaults in the face of a personal insult or a challenge to the integrity of his gang. The code of the bopper is that of the warrior who places great stress on courage, the defense of his group, and the maintenance of honor.

Relationships between bopping gang members and the adult world are severely attenuated. The term that the bopper uses most frequently to characterize his relationships with adults is "weak." He is unable to find appropriate role-models that can designate for him a structure of opportunities leading to adult success. He views himself as isolated and the adult world as indifferent. The commitments of adults are to their own interests and not to his. Their explanations of why he should behave differently are "weak," as are their efforts to help him.

Confronted by the apparent indifference and insincerity of the adult world, the ideal bopper seeks to win by coercion the attention and opportunities he lacks and cannot otherwise attract. In recent years the street-gang worker who deals with the fighting gang on its own "turf" has come to symbolize not only a recognition by conventional adult society of the gang's toughness but also a concession of opportunities formerly denied. Through the alchemy of competition between gangs, this gesture of attention by the adult world to the "worst" gangs is transformed into a mark of prestige. Thus does the manipulation of violence convert indifference into accommodation and attention into status.

The Retreatist Pattern

Retreatism may include a variety of expressive, sensual, or consummatory experiences, alone or in a group. In this analysis, we are interested only in those experiences that involve the use of drugs and that are supported by a subculture. We have adopted these limitations in order to maintain our focus on subcultural formations which are clearly recognized as delinquent, as drug use by adolescents is. The retreatist preoccupation with expressive experiences creates many varieties of "hipster" cult among lower-class adolescents which foster patterns of deviant but not necessarily delinquent conduct.

Subcultural drug-users in lower-class areas perceive themselves as culturally and socially detached from the life-style and everyday preoccupations of members of the conventional world. The following characterization of the "cat" culture, observed by Finestone in a lower-class Negro area in Chicago, describes drug use in the more general context of "hipsterism."[14] Thus it should not be assumed that this description in every respect fits drug cultures found elsewhere. We have drawn heavily on Finestone's observations, however, because they provide the best descriptions available of the social world in which lower-class adolescent drug cultures typically arise.

The dominant feature of the retreatist subculture of the "cat" lies in the continuous pursuit of the "kick." Every cat has a kick—alcohol, marijuana, addicting drugs, unusual sexual experiences, hot jazz, cool jazz, or any combination of these. Whatever its content, the kick is a search for ecstatic experiences. The retreatist strives for an intense awareness of living and a sense of pleasure that is "out of this world." In extreme form, he seeks an almost spiritual and mystical knowledge that is experienced when one comes to know "it" at the height of one's kick. The past and the future recede in the time perspective of the cat, since complete awareness in present experience is the essence of the kick.

The successful cat has a lucrative "hustle" which contrasts sharply with the routine and discipline required in the ordinary occupational tasks of conventional society. The many varieties of the hustle are characterized by a rejection of violence or force and a preference for manipulating, persuading, outwitting, or "conning" others to obtain resources for experiencing the kick. The cat begs, borrows, steals, or engages in some petty con-game. He caters to the illegitimate cravings of others by peddling drugs or working as a pimp. A highly exploitative attitude toward women permits the cat to view pimping as a prestigeful source of income. Through the labor of "chicks" engaged in prostitution or shoplifting, he can live in idleness and concentrate his entire attention on organizing, scheduling, and experiencing the esthetic pleasure of the kick. The hustle of the cat is secondary to his interest in the kick. In this respect the cat differs from his fellow delinquents in the criminal subculture, for whom income-producing activity is a primary concern.

The ideal cat's appearance, demeanor, and taste can best be characterized as "cool." The cat seeks to exhibit a highly developed and sophisticated taste for clothes. In his demeanor, he struggles to reveal a self-assured and unruffled manner, thereby emphasizing his aloofness and "superiority" to the "squares." He develops a colorful, discriminating vocabulary and ritualized gestures which express his sense of difference from the conventional world and his solidarity with the retreatist subculture.

The word "cool" also best describes the sense of apartness and detachment which the retreatist experiences in his relationships with the conventional world. His reference group is the "society of cats," an "elite" group in which he becomes isolated from conventional society. Within this group, a new order of goals and criteria of achievement is created. The cat does not seek to impose this system of values on the world of the squares. Instead, he strives for status and deference within the society of cats by cultivating the kick and the hustle. Thus the retreatist subculture provides avenues to success-goals, to the social admiration and the sense of well-being or oneness with the world which the members feel are otherwise beyond their reach.

Notes

1. See esp. C. R. Shaw, *The Jack-Roller* (Chicago: University of Chicago Press, 1930); Shaw, *The Natural History of a Delinquent Career* (Chicago: University of Chicago Press, 1931); Shaw et al., *Delinquency Areas* (Chicago: University of Chicago Press, 1940); and Shaw and H. D. McKay, *Juvenile Delinquency and Urban Areas* (Chicago: University of Chicago Press, 1942).

2. E. H. Sutherland, ed., *The Professional Thief* (Chicago: University of Chicago Press, 1937); and Sutherland, *Principles of Criminology*, 4th Ed. (Philadelphia: Lippincott, 1947).

3. All quotations on this page are from *The Professional Thief*, pp. 211–13. Emphasis added.

4. Frank Tannenbaum, "The Professional Criminal," *The Century*, Vol. 110 (May-Oct. 1925), p. 577.

5. See A. K. Cohen, Alfred Lindesmith, and Kark Schuessler, eds., *The Sutherland Papers* (Bloomington, Ind.: Indiana University Press, 1956), pp. 31–35.

6. R. K. Merton, *Social Theory and Social Structure*, Rev. and Enl. Ed. (Glencoe, Ill.: Free Press, 1957), pp. 145–46.

7. *Principles of Criminology, op. cit.*, pp. 7–8.

8. For an example of restrictions on access to illegitimate roles, note the impact of racial definitions in the following case: "I was greeted by two prisoners who were to be my cell buddies. Ernest was a first offender, charged with being a 'hold-up' man. Bill, the other buddy, was an older offender, going through the machinery of becoming a habitual criminal, in and out of jail. . . . The first thing they asked me was, 'What are you in for?' I said, 'Jack-rolling.' The hardened one (Bill) looked at me with a superior air and said, 'A hoodlum, eh? An ordinary sneak thief. Not willing to leave jack-rolling to the niggers, eh? That's all they're good for. Kid, jack-rolling's not a white man's

job.' I could see that he was disgusted with me, and I was too scared to say anything" (Shaw, *The Jack-Roller, op. cit.*, p. 101).

9. For a discussion of the way in which the availability of illegitimate means influences the adaptations of inmates to prison life, see R. A. Cloward, "Social Control in the Prison," *Theoretical Studies of the Social Organization of the Prison*, Bulletin No. 15 (New York: Social Science Research Council, March 1960), pp. 20–48.

10. It should be understood that these terms characterize these delinquent modes of adaptation from the reference position of conventional society; they do not necessarily reflect the attitudes of members of the subcultures. Thus the term "retreatist" does not necessarily reflect the attitude of the "cat." Far from thinking of himself as being in retreat, he defines himself as among the elect.

11. Tannenbaum summarizes the community's role in this process of alienation by the phrase "dramatization of evil" (Frank Tannenbaum, *Crime and the Community* [New York: Columbia University Press, 1938], pp. 19–21). For a more detailed account of this process, see Chap. 5, *infra*.

12. See esp. C. R. Shaw, *The Jack-Roller* (Chicago: University of Chicago Press, 1930); Shaw, *The Natural History of a Delinquent Career* (Chicago: University of Chicago Press, 1940); Shaw and H. D. McKay, *Juvenile Delinquency and Urban Areas* (Chicago: University of Chicago Press, 1942); E. H. Sutherland, ed., *The Professional Thief* (Chicago: University of Chicago Press, 1937); Sutherland, *Principles of Criminology*, 4th ed. (Philadelphia: J. P. Lippincott Co., 1947); and Sutherland, *White Collar Crime* (New York: Dryden Press, 1949).

13. For descriptions of conflict groups, see Harrison Salisbury, *The Shook-up Generation* (New York: Harper & Bros., 1958); *Reaching the Unreached*, a Publication of the New York City Youth Board, 1952; C. K. Myers, *Light the Dark Streets* (Greenwich, Conn.: Seabury Press, 1957); Walter Bernstein, "The Cherubs Are Rumbling," *The New Yorker*, Sept. 21, 1957; Sam Glane, "Juvenile Gangs in East Side Los Angeles," *Focus*, Vol. 29 (Sept. 1959), pp. 136–41; Dale Kramer and Madeline Karr, *Teen-Age Gangs* (New York: Henry Holt, 1953); S. V. Jones, "The Cougars—Life with a Brooklyn Gang," *Harper's*, Vol. 209 (Nov. 1954), pp. 35–43; P. C. Crawford, D. I. Malamud, and J. R. Dumpson, *Working with Teen-Age Gangs* (New York Welfare Council, 1950); Dan Wakefield, "The Gang That Went Good," *Harper's*, Vol. 216 (June 1958), pp. 36–43.

14. Harold Finestone, "Cats, Kicks and Color," *Social Problems*, Vol. 5 (July 1957), pp. 3–13.

16. Techniques of Neutralization: A Theory of Delinquency

GRESHAM M. SYKES
DAVID MATZA

As Morris Cohen once said, one of the most fascinating problems about human behavior is why men violate the laws in which they believe. This is the problem that confronts us when we attempt to explain why delinquency occurs despite a greater or lesser commitment to the usages of conformity. A basic clue is offered by the fact that social rules or norms calling for valued behavior seldom if ever take the form of categorical imperatives. Rather, values or norms appear as *qualified* guides for action, limited in their applicability in terms of time, place, persons, and social circumstances. The moral injunction against killing, for example, does not apply to the enemy during combat in time of war, although a captured enemy comes once again under the prohibition. Similarly, the taking and distributing of scarce goods in a time of acute social need is felt by many to be right, although under other circumstances private property is held inviolable. The normative system of a society, then, is marked by what Williams has termed *flexibility;* it does not consist of a body of rules held to be binding under all conditions.[1]

This flexibility is, in fact, an integral part of the criminal law in that measures for "defenses to crimes" are provided in pleas such as nonage, necessity, insanity, drunkenness, compulsion, self-defense, and so on. The individual can avoid moral culpability for his criminal action—and thus avoid the negative sanctions of society—if he can prove that criminal intent was lacking. *It is our argument that much delinquency is based on what is essentially an unrecognized extension of defenses to crimes, in the form of justifications for deviance that are seen as valid by the delinquent but not by the legal system or society at large.*

These justifications are commonly described as rationalizations. They are viewed as following deviant behavior and as protecting the individual from self-blame and the blame of others after the act. But there is also reason to believe that they precede deviant behavior and make deviant behavior possible. It is this possibility that Sutherland mentioned only in passing and that other writers have failed to exploit from the viewpoint of sociological theory. Disapproval flowing from internalized norms and conforming others in the social environment is neutralized, turned back, or deflected in advance. Social controls that serve to check or inhibit deviant motivational patterns are rendered inoperative, and the individual is freed to engage in delinquency without serious damage to his self-image. In this sense, the delinquent both has his cake and eats it too, for he remains committed to the dominant normative system and yet so qualifies its imperatives that violations are "acceptable" if not "right." Thus the delinquent represents not a radical opposition to law-abiding society but something more like an apologetic failure, often more sinned against than sinning in his own eyes. We call these justifications of deviant behavior techniques of neutralization; and we believe these techniques make up a crucial component of Sutherland's "definitions favorable to the violation of law." It is by learning these techniques that the juvenile becomes delinquent, rather than by learning moral imperatives, values, or attitudes standing in direct contradiction to those of the dominant society. In analyzing these techniques, we have found it convenient to divide them into five major types.

THE DENIAL OF RESPONSIBILITY

Insofar as the delinquent can define himself as lacking responsibility for his deviant actions, the disapproval of self or others is sharply reduced in effectiveness as a restraining influence. As Justice Holmes has said, even a dog distinguishes between being stumbled over and being kicked, and modern society is no less careful to draw a line between injuries that are unintentional, i.e., where responsibility is lacking, and those that are intentional. As a technique of neutralization, however, the denial of responsibility extends much further than the claim that deviant acts are an "accident" or some similar negation of personal accountability. It may also be asserted that delinquent acts are due to forces outside of the individual and beyond his control such as unloving parents, bad companions, or a slum neighborhood. In effect, the delinquent approaches a "billiard ball" conception of himself in which he sees himself as helplessly propelled into new situations. From a psychodynamic viewpoint, this orientation toward one's own actions may represent a profound alienation from self, but it is important to stress the fact that interpretations of responsibility are cultural constructs and not merely idiosyncratic beliefs. The similarity between this mode of justifying illegal behavior assumed by the delinquent and the implications of a "sociological" frame of reference or a "humane" jurisprudence is readily apparent.[2]

It is not the validity of this orientation that concerns us here, but its function of deflecting blame attached to violations of social norms and its relative independence of a particular personality structure.[3] By learning to view himself as more acted upon than acting, the delinquent prepares the way for deviance from the dominant normative system without the necessity of a frontal assault on the norms themselves.

THE DENIAL OF INJURY

A second major technique of neutralization centers on the injury or harm involved in the delinquent act. The criminal law has long made a distinction between crimes which are *mala in se* and *mala prohibita*—that is, between acts that are wrong in themselves and acts that are illegal but not immoral—and the delinquent can make the same kind of distinction in evaluating the wrongfulness of his behavior. For the delinquent, however, wrongfulness may turn on the question of whether or not anyone has clearly been hurt by his deviance, and this matter is open to a variety of interpretations. Vandalism, for example, may be defined by the delinquent simply as "mischief"—after all, it may be claimed, the persons whose property has been destroyed can well afford it. Similarly, auto theft may be viewed as "borrowing," and gang fighting may be seen as a private quarrel, an agreed upon duel between two willing parties, and thus of no concern to the community at large. We are not suggesting that this technique of neutralization, labeled the denial of injury, involves an explicit dialectic. Rather, we are arguing that the delinquent frequently, and in a hazy fashion, feels that his behavior does not really cause any great harm despite the fact that it runs counter to law. Just as the link between the individual and his acts may be broken by the denial of responsibility, so may the link between acts and their consequences be broken by the denial of injury. Since society sometimes agrees with the delinquent, e.g., in matters such as truancy, "pranks," and so on, it merely reaffirms the idea that the delinquent's neutralization of social controls by means of qualifying the norms is an extension of common practice rather than a gesture of complete opposition.

THE DENIAL OF THE VICTIM

Even if the delinquent accepts the responsibility for his deviant actions and is willing to admit that his deviant actions involve an injury or hurt, the moral indignation of self and others may be neutralized by an insistence that the injury is not wrong in light of the circumstances. The injury, it may be claimed, is not really an injury; rather, it is a form of rightful retaliation or punishment. By a subtle alchemy the delinquent moves himself into the position of an avenger and the victim is transformed into a wrong-doer. Assaults on homosexuals or suspected homosexuals, attacks on members of minority groups who are said to have gotten "out of place," vandalism as revenge on an unfair teacher or school official, thefts from a "crooked" store owner— all may be hurts inflicted on a transgressor, in the eyes of the delinquent. As Orwell has pointed out, the type of criminal admired by the general public has probably changed over the course of years and Raffles no longer serves as a hero;[4] but Robin Hood, and his latter-day derivatives such as the tough detective seeking justice outside the law, still capture the popular imagination, and the delinquent may view his acts as part of a similar role.

To deny the existence of the victim, then, by transforming him into a person deserving injury is an extreme form of a phenomenon we have mentioned before, namely, the delinquent's recognition of appropriate and inappropriate targets for his delinquent acts. In addition, however, the existence of the victim may be denied for the delinquent, in a somewhat different sense, by the circumstances of the delinquent act itself. Insofar as the victim is physically absent, unknown, or a vague abstraction (as is often the case in delinquent acts committed against property), the awareness of the victim's existence is weakened. Internalized norms and anticipations of the reactions of others must somehow be activated if they are to serve as guides for behavior; and it is possible that a diminished awareness of the victim plays an important part in determining whether or not this process is set in motion.

THE CONDEMNATION OF THE CONDEMNERS

A fourth technique of neutralization would appear to involve a condemnation of the condemners or, as McCorkle and Korn have phrased it, a rejection of the rejectors.[5] The delinquent shifts the focus of attention from his own deviant acts to the motives and behavior of those who disapprove of his violations. His condemners, he may claim, are hypocrites, deviants in disguise, or impelled by personal spite. This orientation toward the conforming world may be of particular importance when it hardens into a bitter cynicism directed against those assigned the task of enforcing or expressing the norms of the dominant society. Police, it may be said, are corrupt, stupid, and brutal. Teachers always show favoritism and parents always "take it out" on their children. By a slight extension, the rewards of conformity—such as material success—become a matter of pull or luck, thus decreasing still further the stature of those who stand on the side of the law-abiding. The validity of this jaundiced viewpoint is not so important as its function in turning back or deflecting the negative sanctions attached to violations of the norms. The delinquent, in effect, has changed the subject of the conversation in the dialogue between his own deviant impulses and the reactions of others; and by attacking others, the wrongfulness of his own behavior is more easily repressed or lost to view.

THE APPEAL TO HIGHER LOYALTIES

Fifth, and last, internal and external social controls may be neutralized by sacrificing the demands of the larger society for the demands of the smaller social groups to which the delinquent belongs, such as the sibling pair, the gang, or the friendship clique. It is important to note that the delinquent does not necessarily repudiate the imperatives of the dominant normative system, despite his failure to follow them. Rather, the delinquent may see himself as caught up in a dilemma that must be resolved, unfortunately, at the cost of violating the law. One aspect of this situation has been studied by Stouffer and Toby in their research on the conflict between particularistic and universalistic demands, between the claims of friendship and general social obligations, and their results suggest that "it is possible to classify people according to a predisposition to select one or the other horn of a dilemma in role conflict."[6] For our purposes, however, the most important point is that deviation from certain norms may occur not because the norms are rejected but because other norms, held to be more pressing or involving a higher loyalty, are accorded precedence. Indeed, it is the fact that both sets of norms are believed in that gives meaning to our concepts of dilemma and role conflict.

   The conflict between the claims of friendship and the claims of law, or a similar dilemma, has of course long been recognized by the social scientist (and the novelist) as a common human problem. If the juvenile delinquent frequently resolves his dilemma by insisting that he must "always help a buddy" or "never squeal on a friend," even when it throws him into serious difficulties with the dominant social order, his choice remains familiar to the supposedly law-abiding. The delinquent is unusual, perhaps, in the extent to which he is able to see the fact that he acts in behalf of the smaller social groups to which he belongs as a justification for violations of society's norms, but it is a matter of degree rather than of kind.

   "I didn't mean it." "I didn't really hurt anybody." "They had it coming to them." "Everybody's picking on me." "I didn't do it for myself." These slogans or their variants, we hypothesize, prepare the juvenile for delinquent acts. These "definitions of the situation" represent tangential or glancing blows at the dominant normative system rather than the creation of an opposing ideology; and they are extensions of patterns of thought prevalent in society rather than something created *de novo.*

Techniques of neutralization may not be powerful enough to fully shield the individual from the force of his own internalized values and the reactions of conforming others, for as we have pointed out, juvenile delinquents often appear to suffer from feelings of guilt and shame when called into account for their deviant behavior. And some delinquents may be so isolated from the world of conformity that techniques of neutralization need not be called into play. Nonetheless, we would argue that techniques of neutralization are critical in lessening the effectiveness of social controls and that they lie behind a large share of delinquent behavior. Empirical research in this area is scattered and fragmentary at the present time, but the work of Redl,[7] Cressey,[8] and others has supplied a body of significant data that has done much to clarify the theoretical issues and enlarge the fund of supporting evidence. Two lines of investigation seem to be critical at this stage. First, there is need for more knowledge concerning the differential distribution of techniques of neutralization, as operative patterns of thought, by age, sex, social class, ethnic group, etc. On a priori grounds it might be assumed that these justifications for deviance will be more readily seized by segments of society for whom a discrepancy between common social ideals and social practice is most apparent. It is also possible, however, that the habit of "bending" the dominant normative system—if not "breaking" it— cuts across our cruder social categories and is to be traced primarily to patterns of social interaction within the familial circle. Second, there is need for a greater understanding of the internal structure of techniques of neutralization, as a system of beliefs and attitudes, and its relationship to various types of delinquent behavior. Certain techniques of neutralization would appear to be better adapted to particular deviant acts than to others, as we have suggested, for example, in the case of offenses against property and the denial of the victim. But the issue remains far from clear and stands in need of more information.

In any case, techniques of neutralization appear to offer a promising line of research in enlarging and systematizing the theoretical grasp of juvenile delinquency. As more information is uncovered concerning techniques of neutralization, their origins, and their consequences, both juvenile delinquency in particular and deviation from normative systems in general may be illuminated.

Notes

1. Cf. Robin Williams, Jr., *American Society*, New York: Knopf, 1951, p. 28.
2. A number of observers have wryly noted that many delinquents seem to show a surprising awareness of sociological and psychological explanations for their behavior and are quick to point out the causal role of their poor environment.
3. It is possible, of course, that certain personality structures can accept some techniques of neutralization more readily than others, but this question remains largely unexplored.
4. George Orwell, *Dickens, Dali, and Others*, New York: Reynal, 1946.
5. Lloyd W. McCorkle and Richard Korn, "Resocialization within Walls," *The Annals of the American Academy of Political and Social Science*, 293 (May, 1954), pp. 88–98.
6. See Samuel A. Stouffer and Jackson Toby, "Role Conflict and Personality," in *Toward a General Theory of Action*, edited by Talcott Parsons and Edward A. Shils, Cambridge, Mass.: Harvard University Press, 1951, p. 494.
7. See Fritz Redl and David Wineman, *Children Who Hate*, Glencoe, Ill.: The Free Press, 1956.
8. See D. R. Cressey, *Other People's Money*, Glencoe, Ill.: The Free Press, 1953.

17. A Control Theory of Delinquency

TRAVIS HIRSCHI

Control theories assume that delinquent acts result when an individual's bond to society is weak or broken. Since these theories embrace two highly complex concepts, the *bond* of the individual to *society*, it is not surprising that they have at one time or another formed the basis of explanations of most forms of aberrant or unusual behavior. It is also not surprising that control theories have described the elements of the bond to society in many ways, and that they have focused on a variety of units as the point of control. . . .

ELEMENTS OF THE BOND

Attachment

In explaining conforming behavior, sociologists justly emphasize sensitivity to the opinion of others.[1] Unfortunately, . . . they tend to suggest that man *is* sensitive to the opinion of others and thus exclude sensitivity from their explanations of deviant behavior. In explaining deviant behavior, psychologists, in contrast, emphasize insensitivity to the opinion of others.[2] Unfortunately, they too tend to ignore variation, and, in addition, they tend to tie sensitivity inextricably to other variables, to make it part of a syndrome or "type," and thus seriously to reduce its value as an explanatory concept. The psychopath is characterized only in part by "deficient attachment to or affection for others, a failure to respond to the ordinary motivations founded in respect or regard for one's fellows";[3] he is also characterized by such things as "excessive aggressiveness," "lack of superego control," and "an infantile level of response."[4] Unfortunately, too, the behavior that psychopathy is used to explain often becomes part of the *definition* of psychopathy. As a result, in Barbara Wootton's words: "[The psychopath] is . . . *par excellence*, and without shame or qualification, the model of the circular process by which mental abnormality is inferred from anti-social behavior while anti-social behavior is explained by mental abnormality."[5]

The problems of diagnosis, tautology, and name-calling are avoided if the dimensions of psychopathy are treated as causally and therefore problematically interrelated, rather than as logically and therefore necessarily bound to each other. In fact, it can be argued that all of the characteristics attributed to the psychopath follow from, are effects of, his lack of attachment to others. To say that to lack attachment to others is to be free from moral restraints is to use lack of attachment to explain the guiltlessness of the psychopath, the fact that he apparently has no conscience or superego. In this view, lack of attachment to others is not merely a symptom of psychopathy, it *is* psychopathy; lack of conscience is just another way of saying the same thing; and the violation of norms is (or may be) a consequence.

For that matter, given that man is an animal, "impulsivity" and "aggressiveness" can also be seen as natural consequences of freedom from moral restraints. However, since the view of man as endowed with natural propensities and capacities like other animals is peculiarly unpalatable to sociologists, we need not fall back on such a view to explain the amoral man's aggressiveness.[6] The process of becoming alienated from others often involves or is based on active interpersonal conflict. Such conflict could easily supply a reservoir of *socially derived* hostility sufficient to account for the aggressiveness of those whose attachments to others have been weakened.

Durkheim said it many years ago: "We are moral beings to the extent that we are social beings."[7] This may be interpreted to mean that we are moral beings to the extent that we have "internalized the norms" of society. But what does it mean to say that a person has internalized the norms of society? The norms of society are by definition shared by the members of society. To violate a norm is, therefore, to act contrary to the wishes and expectations of other people. If a person does not care about the wishes and expectations of other people—that is, if he is insensitive to the opinion of others—then he is to that extent not bound by the norms. He is free to deviate.

The essence of internalization of norms, conscience, or superego thus lies in the attachment of the individual to others.[8] This view has several advantages over the concept of internalization. For one, explanations of deviant behavior based on attachment do not beg the question, since the extent to which a person is attached to others can be measured independently of his deviant behavior. Furthermore, change or variation in behavior is explainable in a way that it is not when notions of internalization or superego are used. For example, the divorced man is more likely after divorce to commit a number of deviant acts, such as suicide or forgery. If we explain these acts by reference to the superego (or internal control), we are forced to say that the man "lost his conscience" when he got a divorce; and, of course, if he remarries, we have to conclude that he gets his conscience back.

This dimension of the bond to conventional society is encountered in most social control-oriented research and theory. F. Ivan Nye's "internal control" and "indirect control" refer to the same element, although we avoid the problem of explaining changes over time by locating the "conscience" in the bond to others rather than making it part of the personality.[9] Attachment to others is just one aspect of Albert J. Reiss's "personal controls"; we avoid his problems of tautological empirical *observations* by making the relationship between attachment and delinquency problematic rather than definitional.[10] Finally, Scott Briar and Irving Piliavin's "commitment" or "stake in conformity" subsumes attachment, as their discussion illustrates, although the terms they use are more closely associated with the next element to be discussed.[11]

Commitment

"Of all passions, that which inclineth men least to break the laws, is fear. Nay, excepting some generous natures, it is the only thing, when there is the appearance of profit or pleasure by breaking the laws, that makes men keep them."[12] Few would deny that men on occasion obey the rules simply from fear of the consequences. This rational component in conformity we label commitment. What does it mean to say that a person is committed to conformity? In Howard S. Becker's formulation it means the following:

First, the individual is in a position in which his decision with regard to some particular line of action has consequences for other interests and activities not necessarily [directly] related to it. Second, he has placed himself in that position by his own prior actions. A third element is present though so obvious as not to be apparent: the committed person must be aware [of these other interests] and must recognize that his decision in this case will have ramifications beyond it.[13]

The idea, then, is that the person invests time, energy, himself, in a certain line of activity—say, getting an education, building up a business, acquiring a reputation for virtue. When or whenever he considers deviant behavior, he must consider the costs of this deviant behavior, the risk he runs of losing the investment he has made in conventional behavior.

If attachment to others is the sociological counterpart of the superego or conscience, commitment is the counterpart of the ego or common sense. To the person committed to conventional lines of action, risking one to ten years in prison for a ten-dollar holdup is stupidity, because to the committed person the costs and risks obviously exceed ten dollars in value. (To the psychoanalyst, such an act exhibits failure to be governed by the "reality-principle.") In the sociological control theory, it can be and is generally assumed that the decision to commit a criminal act may well be rationally determined—that the actor's decision was not irrational given the risks and costs he faces. Of course, as Becker points out, if the actor is capable of in some sense calculating the costs of a line of action, he is also capable of calculational errors: ignorance and error return, in the control theory, as possible explanations of deviant behavior.

The concept of commitment assumes that the organization of society is such that the interest of most persons would be endangered if they were to engage in criminal acts. Most people, simply by the process of living in an organized society, acquire goods, reputations, prospects that they do not want to risk losing. These accumulations are society's insurance that they will abide by the rules. Many hypotheses about the antecedents of delinquent behavior are based on this premise. For example, Arthur L. Stinchcombe's hypothesis that "high school rebellion . . . occurs when future status is not clearly related to present performance"[14] suggests that one is committed to conformity not only by what one has but also by what one hopes to obtain. Thus "ambition" and/or "aspiration" play an important role in producing conformity. The person becomes committed to a conventional line of action, and he is therefore committed to conformity.

Most lines of action in a society are of course conventional. The clearest examples are educational and occupational careers. Actions thought to jeopardize one's chances in these areas are presumably avoided. Interestingly enough, even nonconventional commitments may operate to produce conventional conformity. We are told, at least, that boys aspiring to careers in the rackets or professional thievery are judged by their "honesty" and "reliability"—traits traditionally in demand among seekers of office boys.[15]

Involvement

Many persons undoubtedly owe a life of virtue to a lack of opportunity to do otherwise. Time and energy are inherently limited: "Not that I would not, if I could, be both handsome and fat and well dressed, and a great athlete, and make a million a year, be a wit, a bon vivant, and a lady killer, as well as a philosopher, a philanthropist, a statesman, warrior, and African explorer, as well as a 'tone-poet' and saint. But the thing is simply impossible."[16] The things that William James here says he would like to be or do are all, I suppose, within the realm of conventionality, but if he were to include illicit actions he would still have to eliminate some of them as simply impossible.

Involvement or engrossment in conventional activities is thus often part of a control theory. The assumption, widely shared, is that a person may be simply too busy doing conventional things to find time to engage in deviant behavior. The person involved in conventional activities is tied to appointments, deadlines, working hours, plans, and the like, so the opportunity to commit deviant acts rarely arises. To the extent that he is engrossed in conventional activities, he cannot even think about deviant acts, let alone act out his inclinations.[17]

This line of reasoning is responsible for the stress placed on recreational facilities in many programs to reduce delinquency, for much of the concern with the high school dropout, and for the idea that boys should be drafted into the army to keep them out of trouble. So obvious and persuasive is the idea that involvement in conventional activities is a major deterrent to delinquency that it was accepted even by Sutherland: "In the general area of juvenile delinquency it is probable that the most significant difference between juveniles who engage in delinquency and those who do not is that the latter are provided abundant opportunities of a conventional type for satisfying their recreational interests, while the former lack those opportunities or facilities."[18]

The view that "idle hands are the devil's workshop" has received more sophisticated treatment in recent sociological writings on delinquency. David Matza and Gresham M. Sykes, for example, suggest that delinquents have the values of a leisure class, the same values ascribed by Veblen to *the* leisure class: a search for kicks, disdain of work, a desire for the big score, and acceptance of aggressive toughness as proof of masculinity.[19] Matza and Sykes explain delinquency by reference to this system of values, but they note that adolescents at all class levels are "to some extent" members of a leisure class, that they "move in a limbo between earlier parental domination and future integration with the social structure through the bonds of work and marriage."[20] In the end, then, the leisure of the adolescent produces a set of values, which, in turn, leads to delinquency.

Belief

Unlike the cultural deviance theory, the control theory assumes the existence of a common value system within the society or group whose norms are being violated. If the deviant is committed to a value system different from that of conventional society, there is, within the context of the theory, nothing to explain. The question is, "Why does a man violate the rules in which he believes?" It is not, "Why do men differ in their beliefs about what constitutes good and desirable conduct?" The person is assumed to have been socialized (perhaps imperfectly) into the group whose rules he is violating; deviance is not a question of one group imposing its rules on the members of another group. In other words, we not only assume the deviant *has* believed the rules, we assume he believes the rules even as he violates them.

How can a person believe it is wrong to steal at the same time he is stealing? In the strain theory, this is not a difficult problem. (In fact, . . . the strain theory was devised specifically to deal with this question.) The motivation to deviance adduced by the strain theorist is so strong that we can well understand the deviant act even assuming the deviator believes strongly that it is wrong.[21] However, given the control theory's assumptions about motivation, if both the deviant and the nondeviant believe the deviant act is wrong, how do we account for the fact that one commits it and the other does not?

Control theories have taken two approaches to this problem. In one approach, beliefs are treated as mere words that mean little or nothing if the other forms of control are missing. "Semantic dementia," the dissociation between rational faculties and emotional control which is said to be characteristic of the psychopath, illustrates this way of handling the problem.[22] In short, beliefs, at least insofar as they are expressed in words, drop out of the picture; since they do not differentiate between deviants and nondeviants, they are in the same class as "language" or any other characteristic common to all members of the group. Since they represent no real obstacle to the commission of delinquent acts, nothing need be said about how they are handled by those committing such acts. The control theories that do not mention beliefs (or values), and many do not, may be assumed to take this approach to the problem.

The second approach argues that the deviant rationalizes his behavior so that he can at once violate the rule and maintain his belief in it. Donald R. Cressey has advanced this argument with respect to embezzlement,[23] and Sykes and Matza have advanced it with respect to delinquency.[24] In both Cressey's and Sykes and Matza's treatments, these rationalizations (Cressey calls them "verbalizations," Sykes and Matza term them "techniques of neutralization") occur prior to the commission of the deviant act. If the neutralization is successful, the person is free to commit the act(s) in question. Both in Cressey and in Sykes and Matza, the strain that prompts the effort at neutralization also provides the motive force that results in the subsequent deviant act. Their theories are thus, in this sense, strain theories. Neutralization is difficult to handle within the context of a theory that adheres closely to control theory assumptions, because in the control theory there is no special motivational force to account for the neutralization. This difficulty is especially noticeable in Matza's later treatment of this topic, where the motivational component, the "will to delinquency," appears *after* the moral vacuum has been created by the techniques of neutralization.[25] The question thus becomes: Why neutralize?

In attempting to solve a strain-theory problem with control-theory tools, the control theorist is thus led into a trap. He cannot answer the crucial question. The concept of neutralization assumes the existence of moral obstacles to the commission of deviant acts. In order plausibly to account for a deviant act, it is necessary to generate motivation to deviance that is at least equivalent in force to the resistance provided by these moral obstacles. However, if the moral obstacles are removed, neutralization and special motivation are no longer required. We therefore follow the implicit logic of control theory and remove these moral obstacles by hypothesis. Many persons do not have an attitude of respect toward the rules of society; many persons feel no moral obligation to conform regardless of personal advantage. Insofar as the values and beliefs of these persons are consistent with their feelings, and there should be a tendency toward consistency, neutralization is unnecessary; it has already occurred.

Does this merely push the question back a step and at the same time produce conflict with the assumption of a common value system? I think not. In the first place, we do not assume, as does Cressey, that neutralization occurs in order to make a specific criminal act possible.[26] We do not assume, as do Sykes and Matza, that neutralization occurs to make many delinquent acts possible. We do not assume, in other words, that the person constructs a system of rationalizations in order to justify commission of acts he *wants* to commit. We assume, in contrast, that the beliefs that free a man to commit deviant acts are *unmotivated* in the sense that he does not construct or adopt them in order to facilitate the attainment of illicit ends. In the second place, we do not assume, as does Matza, that "delinquents concur in the conventional assessment of delinquency."[27] We assume, in contrast, that there is *variation* in the extent to which people believe they should obey the rules of society, and, furthermore, that the less a person believes he should obey the rules, the more likely he is to violate them.[28]

In chronological order, then, a person's beliefs in the moral validity of norms are, for no teleological reason, weakened. The probability that he will commit delinquent acts is therefore increased. When and if he commits a delinquent act, we may justifiably use the weakness of his beliefs in explaining it, but no special motivation is required to explain either the weakness of his beliefs or, perhaps, his delinquent act.

The keystone of this argument is of course the assumption that there is variation in belief in the moral validity of social rules. This assumption is amenable to direct empirical test and can thus survive at least until its first confrontation with data. For the present, we must return to the idea of a common value system with which this section was begun.

The idea of a common (or, perhaps better, a single) value system is consistent with the fact, or presumption, of variation in the strength of moral beliefs. We have not suggested that delinquency is based on beliefs counter to conventional morality; we have not suggested that delinquents do not believe delinquent acts are wrong. They may well believe these acts are wrong, but the meaning and efficacy of such beliefs are contingent upon other beliefs and, indeed, on the strength of other ties to the conventional order.[29]

Notes

1. Books have been written on the increasing importance of interpersonal sensitivity in modern life. According to this view, controls from within have become less important than controls from without in *producing* conformity. Whether or not this observation is true as a description of historical trends, it is true that interpersonal sensitivity has become more important in *explaining* conformity. Although logically it should also have become more important in explaining nonconformity, the opposite has been the case, once again showing that Cohen's observation that an explanation of conformity should be an explanation of deviance cannot be translated as "an explanation of conformity has to be an explanation of deviance." For the view that interpersonal sensitivity currently plays a greater role than formerly in producing conformity, see William J. Goode, "Norm Commitment and Conformity to Role-Status Obligations," *American Journal of Sociology*, LXVI (1960), 246–258. And, of course, also see David Riesman, Nathan Glazer, and Reuel Denney, *The Lonely Crowd* (Garden City, New York: Doubleday, 1950), especially Part I.

2. The literature on psychopathy is voluminous. See William McCord and Joan McCord, *The Psychopath* (Princeton: D. Van Nostrand, 1964).

3. John M. Martin and Joseph P. Fitzpatrick, *Delinquent Behavior* (New York: Random House, 1964), p. 130.

4. *Ibid.* For additional properties of the psychopath, see McCord and McCord, *The Psychopath*, pp. 1–22.

5. Barbara Wootton, *Social Science and Social Pathology* (New York: Macmillan, 1959), p. 250.

6. "The logical untenability [of the position that there are forces in man 'resistant to socialization'] was ably demonstrated by Parsons over 30 years ago, and it is widely recognized that the position is empirically unsound because it assumes [!] some universal biological drive system distinctly separate from socialization and social context—a basic and intransigent human nature" (Judith Blake and Kingsley Davis, "Norms, Values, and Sanctions," *Handbook of Modern Sociology*, ed. Robert E. L. Faris [Chicago: Rand McNally, 1964], p. 471).

7. Emile Durkheim, *Moral Education*, trans. Everett K. Wilson and Herman Schnurer (New York: The Free Press, 1961), p. 64.

8. Although attachment alone does not exhaust the meaning of internal-

ization, attachments and beliefs combined would appear to leave only a small residue of "internal control" not susceptible in principle to direct measurement.

9. F. Ivan Nye, *Family Relationships and Delinquent Behavior* (New York: Wiley, 1958), pp. 5–7.

10. Albert J. Reiss, Jr., "Delinquency as the Failure of Personal and Social Controls," *American Sociological Review*, XVI (1951), 196–207. For example, "Our observations show . . . that delinquent recidivists are less often persons with mature ego ideals or nondelinquent social roles" (p. 204).

11. Scott Briar and Irving Piliavin, "Delinquency, Situational Inducements, and Commitment to Conformity," *Social Problems*, XIII (1965), 41–42. The concept "stake in conformity" was introduced by Jackson Toby in his "Social Disorganization and Stake in Conformity: Complementary Factors in the Predatory Behavior of Hoodlums," *Journal of Criminal Law, Criminology and Police Science*, XLVIII (1957), 12–17. See also his "Hoodlum or Business Man: An American Dilemma," *The Jews*, ed. Marshall Sklare (New York: The Free Press, 1958), pp. 542–550. Throughout the text, I occasionally use "stake in conformity" in speaking in general of the strength of the bond to conventional society. So used, the concept is somewhat broader than is true for either Toby or Briar and Piliavin, where the concept is roughly equivalent to what is here called "commitment."

12. Thomas Hobbes, *Leviathan* (Oxford: Basil Blackwell, 1957), p. 195.

13. Howard S. Becker, "Notes on the Concept of Commitment," *American Journal of Sociology*, LXVI (1960), 35–36.

14. Arthur L. Stinchcombe, *Rebellion in a High School* (Chicago: Quadrangle, 1964), p. 5.

15. Richard A. Cloward and Lloyd E. Ohlin, *Delinquency and Opportunity* (New York: The Free Press, 1960), p. 147, quoting Edwin H. Sutherland, ed., *The Professional Thief* (Chicago: University of Chicago Press, 1937), pp. 211–213.

16. William James, *Psychology* (Cleveland: World Publishing Co., 1948), p. 186.

17. Few activities appear to be so engrossing that they rule out contemplation of alternative lines of behavior, at least if estimates of the amount of time men spend plotting sexual deviations have any validity.

18. *The Sutherland Papers*, ed. Albert K. Cohen et al. (Bloomington: Indiana University Press, 1956), p. 37.

19. David Matza and Gresham M. Sykes, "Juvenile Delinquency and Subterranean Values," *American Sociological Review*, XXVI (1961), 712–719.

20. *Ibid.*, p. 718.

21. The starving man stealing the loaf of bread is the image evoked by most strain theories. In this image, the starving man's belief in the wrongness of his act is clearly not something that must be explained away. It can be assumed to be present without causing embarrassment to the explanation.

22. McCord and McCord, *The Psychopath*, pp. 12–15.

23. Donald R. Cressey, *Other People's Money* (New York: The Free Press, 1953).

24. Gresham M. Sykes and David Matza, "Techniques of Neutralization: A Theory of Delinquency," *American Sociologial Review*, XXII (1957), 664–670.

25. David Matza, *Delinquency and Drift* (New York: Wiley, 1964), pp. 181–191.

26. In asserting that Cressey's assumption is invalid with respect to delinquency, I do not wish to suggest that it is invalid for the question of embezzlement, where the problem faced by the deviator is fairly specific and he can reasonably be assumed to be an upstanding citizen. (Although even here the fact that the embezzler's nonshareable financial problem often results from some sort of hanky-panky suggests that "verbalizations" may be less necessary than might otherwise be assumed.)

27. *Delinquency and Drift*, p. 43.

28. This assumption is not, I think, contradicted by the evidence presented by Matza against the existence of a delinquent subculture. In comparing the attitudes and actions of delinquents with the picture painted by delinquent subculture theorists, Matza emphasizes—and perhaps exaggerates— the extent to which delinquents are tied to the conventional order. In implicitly comparing delinquents with a supermoral man, I emphasize—and perhaps exaggerate—the extent to which they are not tied to the conventional order.

29. The position taken here is therefore somewhere between the "semantic dementia" and the "neutralization" positions. Assuming variation, the delinquent is, at the extremes, freer than the neutralization argument assumes. Although the possibility of wide discrepancy between what the delinquent professes and what he practices still exists, it is presumably much rarer than is suggested by studies of articulate "psychopaths."

18. Labeling Theory and Criminology: An Assessment

CHARLES WELLFORD

INTRODUCTION

In recent years criminologists have begun to emphasize the importance of society's reaction to crime, as an important ingredient in the
perpetuation and intensification of criminal and delinquent careers.
Basically, this perspective has provided a theoretical model by which
criminologists could reassert their interest in the study of the criminal justice system, after decades of focusing on the characteristics of
the offender. In this respect, the reemergence of the sociology of law
and the theoretical and empirical analysis of the police, courts, and
corrections (an important reemergence in the field of criminology)
has been significantly advanced by labeling theorists. While there has
yet to emerge the "crucial experiment" to evaluate the adequacy of
labeling theory for criminology, it is suggested here that we are able
to consider basic characteristics of this perspective and offer an evaluation of those characteristics as a guide for further development in
theoretical criminology. While some have rejected the perspective
without a convincing demonstration of the inadequacy of the theory,
and others have suggested it is not testable, I suggest that one can estimate the validity of the theory for criminology by assessing the assumptions on which the theory is based.*

Before beginning the analysis, it is important to note that labeling
theory itself has been modified by some of the early contributors to
this perspective, in particular, by a move to what is generally described as the conflict perspective.[1] Some have suggested that labeling theory was only a necessary stage in the development of a radical
criminological theory (e.g., Quinney, 1973). However, this analysis
will be restricted to a consideration of labeling theory and not conflict
theory; but since these cannot be completely separated, the most relevant implications for the conflict perspective will be noted.

* Thanks to Marvin Krohn for numerous criticisms and suggested modifications of all
drafts, and to Ronald Akers, Theodore Chiricos, and Gordon Waldo for their comments
and suggestions.

LABELING THEORY ASSUMPTIONS

The present analysis of labeling theory is drawn from the recent discussion of this perspective by Schrag (1971). Following a consideration of the works of Tannenbaum (1938), Lemert (1951), Becker
(1963), Turk (1969), and Quinney (1970), Schrag identifies what he
considers the basic assumptions that distinguish labeling theory from
other theoretical perspectives. The assumptions identified are: (1) no
act is intrinsically criminal; (2) criminal definitions are enforced in the
interest of the powerful; (3) a person does not become a criminal by
violation of the law but only by the designation of criminality by authorities; (4) due to the fact that everyone conforms and deviates,
people should not be dichotomized into criminal and non-criminal
categories; (5) the act of "getting caught" begins the labeling process;
(6) "getting caught" and the decision-making in the criminal justice
system are a function of offender as opposed to offense characteristics; (7) age, socioeconomic class, and race are the major offender
characteristics that establish patterns of differential criminal justice
decision-making; (8) the criminal justice system is established on a
free-will perspective that allows for the condemnation and rejection
of the identified offender; and (9) labeling is a process that produces,
eventually, identification with a deviant image and subculture, and a
resulting "rejection of the rejectors" (Schrag, 1971: 89–91). While one
might extend or modify these assumptions, it is suggested that they
represent a comprehensive analysis of the theory as it is generally
presented and used in criminological theory, research, and policy. In
the remainder of this analysis these assumptions will be considered,
and the literature pertinent to each will be reviewed.

It is clear that in a formal sense the above do not all qualify as assumptions, but rather they are hypotheses which we would suggest
labeling theorists would contend have been demonstrated to be true
(i.e., "facts"). Elements one, three, and eight of Schrag's analysis
should be considered assumptions, while the others represent statements assumed to be established by empirical observations. Thus, although I shall consider each of the points raised by Schrag, nominally
accepting his identification of each as an assumption, I would suggest
that elements one, six, and nine represent the basis of the labeling
perspective.

THE EVALUATION OF THE ASSUMPTIONS

Assumption 1: No act is intrinsically criminal. Basic to the labeling perspective is the assumption that legally proscribed behavior varies considerably from culture to culture, thus demonstrating the relative character of deviance (Schur, 1971:14). This notion of relativism is applied to all forms of deviant behavior and establishes the assumption that crime is a form of behavior defined by the powerful to control the less powerful and to direct the benefits of society to those controlling economic and political power (Assumption 2)—an issue to be discussed in the next section with regard to the benefit of insulation from control by the criminal justice system. While this position may have some validity in the analysis of acts of deviant behavior such as stuttering, certain sexual behaviors, etc., I contend that the assumption has little import for criminology as it attempts to explain those acts that have traditionally occupied criminologists.

Murder, forcible rape, aggravated assault, robbery, burglary, larceny, and auto theft represent one operationalization of crime characteristically considered important by citizens and criminologists (i.e., violations of the criminal law that involve elements of injury, theft, or damage). Serious violations of the criminal law represent the behavioral units that criminologists have attempted to explain. Addressing this notion of crime, it is important to note the similarity and consistency with which these acts are proscribed crossculturally and through time. Lemert (1972: 22), for example, notes that:

> the extreme relevance in some statements of labeling theory leaves the unfortunate impression that almost any meaning can be assigned to human attributes in action. To the contrary, human interaction always occurs within limits: biological, psychological, ecological, technological, and organizational. These explain why certain general kinds of behavior are more likely to be deemed as undesirable than others. Practically all societies in varying degrees and ways disapprove of incest, adultery, promiscuity, cruelty to children, laziness, disrespect for parents and elders, murder, rape, theft, lying, and cheating. Perhaps the point to make is that certain kinds of actions are likely to be judged deleterious in any context—willfully causing the death of others, consuming large amounts of alcohol for long periods of time, spreading infectious disease, or losing one's eyesight. It is not so much that these violate rules, it is that they destroy, downgrade, or jeopardize values universal in nature.

Similarly, Linton (1952: 660) observes, following a review of anthropological literature on ethical norms, that "the resemblances in ethical concepts so far outweigh the differences that a sound basis for mutual understanding between groups and different cultures is already in existence." Hoebel's (1954: 286–287) analysis of primitive law led him to identify certain "legal universals" including homicide, rape, and the right to private property. Finally, Matza (1964: 155–156) observes that "one need not succumb to rampant relativism—the frivolous view that law is completely arbitrary."

Major crosscultural differences can be observed with regard to the procedures by which society enforces its norms; however, this should not lead to the conclusion that criminal behaviors of the type described are not uniformly proscribed. This position need not be interpreted, in fact should not be interpreted, as one that emphasizes the existence or importance of "natural law." The evidence is that all societies have found it functional to control certain kinds of behavior. The fact that the acts described above are proscribed in all societies clearly indicates the weakness of Assumption 1 for criminology. Serious violations of the law are universally understood and *are*, therefore, *in that sense*, intrinsically criminal. The acceptance of this assumption in labeling theory by supporters and critics has been without reference to any data relevant to serious crime. Juvenile status offenses, crimes without victims, etc., may exhibit crosscultural variations but not those criminal behaviors of primary concern to criminologists.

This fact is recognized by Schur (1971: 14), when he observes:

> Some forms of deviation may, it is true, lend themselves less readily to labeling analysis than do others. . . . The value of labeling analysis in explaining a particular form of deviance may be related to the degree of consensus on its social definition . . . borderline forms of deviance seem to be especially good candidates for labeling analysis and those deviations on which widespread consensus exists less promising candidates.

As noted earlier, criminology has long recognized the undesirability of over-legalization and the necessity for criminology to address serious criminal law violations. To the degree that the acceptance of this designation of the unit of analysis for criminologists prevails in the discipline, the labeling theory "holds less promise" of providing a viable model on which to build a theory of criminal behavior.

The issue of consensus on the serious criminal violations can be observed not only with regard to the uniformity of proscriptions but also in the recent research on perception of offense seriousness. The scale of seriousness observed by Sellin and Wolfgang (1964) for the United States has been found to be highly correlated with scales generated from samples in Canada (Akman and Normandeau, 1968), Taiwan (Hsu, 1969), the Belgian Congo (DeBoeck and Houchou, 1968), Puerto Rico (Valez-Diaz and Megargee, 1971), and among United

States prisoners (Figlio, 1972). Consequently, similar behaviors are ranked and weighted in very similar ways by vastly different national and subnational samples.

In sum, if intrinsic is taken to mean nonrelative and consensual, then the presence of "intrinsically criminal acts" is clearly demonstrated. Similar behaviors are proscribed crossculturally and are assessed in terms of seriousness by different national samples. On those criminal behaviors that have been the focus of criminology, there is social consensus. Whether that consensus is determined by value consensus, false consciousness, or some other set of explanatory concepts is not our concern at this time. Our observation is simply that the labeling model may not be useful to criminology when it addresses such consensually (intrinsically) defined deviant acts.

Assumption 1 has also been challenged by Gibbs (1966, 1972) on logical-definitional grounds. He observes that the notion that deviant acts are only known by the reaction they receive raises the issue of defining the reaction—what type of reaction is necessary to define an act as deviant. Can it be a self-reaction or an informal reaction? If not, why not? How are these logically different from "public" or "outsider" reactions? If self- or informal reactions are possible "definers" of deviance, what is their source? Gibbs suggests that the defining of deviance must involve a normative commitment and acceptance of *behavior* as deviant. The consideration of the source and cause of the reaction takes, Gibbs suggests, the labeling theorist towards normative theories, and thus the implicit acceptance of the intrinsic (for that social system) nature of the deviance.

In summary, both empirically (for serious criminal behavior) and logically (for all instances of deviance), the assumption of extreme relativism is seriously questioned. To the degree this assumption is crucial, criminologists should be reluctant to accept the labeling perspective.

Assumptions 2, 3, 5, 6, and 7. All of these assumptions relate to the operation of the criminal justice system. They propose that the person does not become criminal by violating the law (Assumption 3) but by being labeled as a violator of the law (an acceptable but trivial issue in the operationalization of the concept criminal); that the labeling of violations of the law is done in the interest of the powerful at the expense of the less powerful (Assumption 2); that the condition of power relates mainly to the conditions of sex, race, social class, and age (Assumptions 5 and 6); that the applications of criminal sanction by the criminal justice system are similarly dependent on sex, race, age, and social class (Assumption 7).

While it is true, as some contend in reviewing the literature on criminal justice decision-making, that differences can be observed in decision-making with regard to certain basic characteristics of the offender as they affect police and court disposition, I contend that the overwhelming evidence is in the direction of minimal differential law enforcement, determination of guilt, and application of sanction. In the area of law enforcement it now seems clear that for juvenile offenses the variables of complainant behavior and offense type are considerably more important than class, race, demeanor, etc., as variables affecting the decision to arrest (Hohenstein, 1969; Black and Reiss, 1970; Terry, 1967; Ferdinand and Luchterhand, 1970; Williams and Gold, 1972). This is not to imply that offender characteristics are of no consequence, but that in terms of the explanation of variance in criminal justice disposition, offense-related variables are far more important. The primary examples to the contrary (Piliavin and Briar, 1964; Cicourel, 1968; Goldman, 1963) represent studies of questionable rigor which do not control for offense seriousness and focus on non-citizen initiated police behavior, a minor portion of formal sanctioning.[2]

The recent work of Thornberry (1973) presents evidence from a large-scale longitudinal study of juveniles that purports to indicate a class and race effect on arrest, disposition, and sanctions for juveniles. Acknowledging that research reported to date does not support the contention that blacks and those from lower socioeconomic statuses are more severely treated by the juvenile justice system, the author proposes to re-examine this finding with data from a cohort originally studied by Wolfgang *et al.* (1972). Using percentage analysis, he observes that when seriousness of offense and number of previous offenses are controlled, the relationship between race and disposition and the relationship between SES [socioeconomic status] and dispositions remains for police, intake, and court decision-making (1973: 96–97). While recognizing the need for the consideration of other variables, Thornberry (1973: 97–98) concludes:

> We have noted that a number of earlier studies found that racial and social class disparities in dispositions could generally be explained by legal variables such as the seriousness of the offense and the number of previous offenses committed.... An analysis of comparable data for the Philadelphia birth cohort, however, yields findings that are quite different. With the earlier studies, we found that both the legal and nonlegal variables are related to dispositions. But unlike the previous studies, the present study shows that when the two legal variables were held constant, the racial and SES differences did not disappear.... The most important finding, however, in relation to the previous research done in this area, is that the nonlegal variables are still related to the severity of the disposition received, even when the legal variables are held constant.

Since this represents the only rigorous study to reach this conclusion, I will consider it in some detail.

First, it should be noted that the measurement procedures used in this study do not consider, as Thornberry observes, relevant control variables. There is no consideration of complainant behavior, victim-offender relations, or most importantly, offense seriousness, or type. The latter is most crucial because Thornberry *purports* to control for this by use of the Sellin-Wolfgang (1964) seriousness score. However, the control is in terms of only two categories, high or low seriousness, where "low" equals a seriousness score on the Sellin-Wolfgang scale of one (essentially all juvenile status offenses) and "high" equals a seriousness score of greater than one (i.e., the remainder of the range of the seriousness scale—the entire scale as described in the original publication (Sellin and Wolfgang, 1964)). Furthermore, socioeconomic status is measured by the median income of the area in which the subject resided, an obvious example of the ecological fallacy. Thus, one would not expect, on the basis of their measurement, seriousness and SES to affect relationships to the degree suggested by research using more appropriate measurement techniques.

Even if one accepts the measures presented by Thornberry, the data can be analyzed to assess the specific impact of race on disposition. By demonstrating that percentage differences remain between blacks and whites or low and high socioeconomic status groups after controlling for offense-related characteristics, Thornberry concludes that his results are different from previous empirical research and, therefore, must be weighed on the side of confirming the assumption under consideration. If, however, one measures the extent of the relationships, the data come closer to supporting rather than challenging previous rigorous research. . . .

The measures of association (or a careful reading of the percentage differences) indicate a substantial reduction in the association between race and severity of disposition. Furthermore, where seriousness is in fact controlled (i.e., the condition of low seriousness), the relationship is almost reduced to zero for police intake and court disposition; conversely, where seriousness is not controlled (i.e., the highly variable category of high seriousness), the relationships are not uniformly changed for police. The importance of the inadequate control for seriousness is reflected in these data. Similar results were obtained for the analysis of socioeconomic status.

In sum, due to problems of variables that were not included in the study and the measurement of the key control variable of seriousness and the type of analysis, Thornberry reached conclusions not justified. In fact, the data reflect the minimal contribution of race and SES to criminal justice decision-making—the consistent finding of empirical research on this issue.

Despite the above data the issue of differential court decision-making cannot be as conclusively answered. Hood and Sparks (1970) conclude, following an exhaustive review of the literature, that the definitive studies of sentencing demonstrate the importance of offense characteristics and criminal histories and the relative unimportance of "personal factors" (sex, age, and race). There are, however, areas where offender characteristics are considered significant. The application of the death penalty (Bedau, 1964) and the length of the penalties for minor offenses have been suggested as more significantly associated with race and socioeconomic status. Williams and Gold (1972) (although acknowledging the inadequacy of their sample of court cases) also suggest a severe racial effect on juvenile court disposition. Again, however, the weight of evidence would support a conclusion that non-crime-related offender characteristics should be relegated to a low position in the hierarchy of variables explaining the variance in court decision-making for juveniles, as is reflected in the above analysis of Thornberry's data.

In summary, one would conclude that the evaluation of this assumption leads to a generally negative conclusion with regards to the effectiveness of labeling theory to account for the data reflecting an absence of differential criminal justice decision-making based predominantly on offender characteristics. However, it should be observed that if criminal laws are enforced in the interest of the powerful, the powerful must be relatively evenly distributed throughout the racial and social composition of the population; or the powerful have selected laws for uniform enforcement that are only committed by the less powerful and are only considered law violations by the more powerful. . . . neither of these possible defenses of Assumption 2 seem plausible for serious crime.

Assumption 4. This assumption, based on self-report data, deals with the universality of deviant behavior. The assumption is that since deviant behavior is distributed evenly throughout the population and is, therefore, behavior engaged in by both those designated as criminals and non-criminals, the differentials with regard to the proportion of the population arrested and incarcerated cannot reflect variation in behavioral distributions. The evidence on this is from the self-report studies which indicate a general absence of association between social class and delinquency and a rather widespread involvement in delinquent behavior. However, it must be remembered, the extensiveness or universality of delinquency is primarily a function of the items included in self-report studies. For example, in Clark and Wenninger's (1962) study of delinquency those items in which 50 percent or more of the sample indicated involvement were: did things my parents told me not to do; minor theft; told lies to my family, principal, or friends; used swear words or dirty words out loud in school, in church, or on the streets so other people could hear me;

showed or gave someone a dirty picture, a dirty story, or something like that; been out at night just fooling around after I was supposed to be home; hung around other people who I knew had broken the law a lot of times or who were known as bad people; and threw rocks, cans, sticks, and other things at passing cars, bicycles, or persons. On more serious delinquency items (i.e., attack someone with the idea of killing them; beat up on kids who had not done anything to me; carried a razor, switchblade, or gun to be used against other people), the percentage of respondents indicating their involvement in these behaviors was less than 10 percent (Clark and Wenninger, 1962: 829–830). Thus, again as in the case of Assumption 1, the consideration of minor delinquencies (those that would least likely develop into a situation where labels would be applied) lends support to the assumption of labeling theory concerning the universality or predominant distribution of delinquent behavior. However, when one considered behavioral measures of more serious kinds of delinquency, the restricted nature of those behaviors becomes perhaps more evident.

This should not be taken to imply that the deviant or delinquent is to be understood as one entirely different from the general population; for in fact he does engage, in most instances, in conforming behavior. It should, however, raise some questions about the assumption underlying labeling theory concerning the universality of the behavior and allow us to recognize that with regard to serious crime, as previously defined, there is a relatively minor portion of the population that becomes engaged in these behaviors with varying degrees of frequency and commitment, even though this proportion may be generally constant across social class levels for juvenile populations. Again, I would suggest that one would have to conclude that the validity of this assumption for criminology is questionable in terms of the existing data and that, therefore, the strength of the perspective on which this assumption is based is similarly weakened.

Assumption 8. The assumption that behavior is willed as the underlying dimension of the criminal justice system seems neither testable nor of crucial significance for labeling theory. The assumption may well be true as frequent analyses of the historical emergence of the criminal justice system would attest; however, it is difficult to see its importance for the perspective in question. The labeling perspective could equally (and perhaps more forcefully) apply to a system that denied will, emphasized causation, recognized the need for rehabilitation, and stressed diversion, decriminalization, and deinstitutionalization. Unless the system ignored in all significant ways instances of deviant behavior, there would be the potential for labeling. As Schur (1969) has observed, perhaps our system is more unworkable than others; however, it would not appear that any system would avoid problems of labeling and social disapproval. In that sense the assumption is not an important one to the theory, although it may in fact be correct.

Assumption 9. It is contended that being labeled and the subsequent social disapproval contingent upon that label will produce a condition of "rejecting one's rejectors." It is in this assumption that one understands the dynamic aspect of labeling theory; where labels produce hostility, which produce behavior, which produce labels, which produce more hostility, which produce more intensive behavior, etc., etc. The process of creating secondary deviance becomes the focal concern of labeling theory. In this respect, one might wish to modify the assumption to reflect the secondary nature of the labeling effect. That is, the impact of labeling by the criminal justice system is mediated through, in most expositions of labeling theory, the effects this labeling has on areas such as employment, education, community acceptance, etc., and not the direct effect on the subject. This is particularly important in the consideration of the area of delinquency, since juveniles would be most responsive to the impact of primary socializing agencies. The issue then in assessing this assumption is the impact of criminal justice labeling on other segments of one's social environment and the subsequent impact on the actor. The studies of the effects of legal stigma by Schwartz and Skolnick (1964) are frequently cited to support this area, as are the reviews of the legal consequences of conviction for felonies. It is in this area that one can consider the central elements of labeling theory.

Labeling theory represents in its consideration of the relationships between self-concept, attitudes, etc. and behavior that Warner and DeFleur (1968) have described as the postulate of consistency. This postulate assumes that attitudes directly cause behavior, and that one can understand behavioral dimensions simply by understanding the subject's attitudes. Therefore, in labeling theory one assumes that degradation affects self-concept (a logical but not empirically demonstrated assumption), and that the change in self-concept produces a necessary change in behavior (a not logical and not empirically demonstrated occurrence). In the social psychological literature Warner and DeFleur observe that the postulate of consistency was challenged early in the work on racial relations by the postulate of independent variation, i.e., that attitudes and behavior vary independently and need not, and in fact should not, be considered as causally related. The work of Merton (1949) is recognized as a significant statement of the need to consider those factors other than attitudes that might account for discriminatory behavior. This led to the postulate of contingent consistency, a postulate which suggests that attitudes and behavior will be isomorphic only under certain kinds of social and environmental conditions and that for most behaviors the social or situational determinants can alter the intensity and direction of the relationship between attitudes and behavior.

Similarly the assumption in labeling theory that implies a consistent relationship between such entities as self-concept, attitude, and behavior may well represent a gross oversimplification of the determinants of behavior and draws one's attention again to the subject as opposed to the situation in which behavior occurs. While again the assumption may be deemed to be correct to the degree to which it is addressing only attitudinal change, the evidence from other areas of analysis suggest that it would need to be significantly modified before one could use this as a way of understanding the effect of the labeling process on behavior. Behavior would still be understood as situationally determined with labeling effects being primarily related to attitudinal changes which then would have to be studied to determine if in fact they are involved in the proportion of subsequent behavior changes. In this sense, then, the theoretical position of labeling theory is challenged by the notion that it has presented a simplistic view of behavior causation, one that stresses the explanation of intellectual as opposed to the behavioral characteristics of the subject.

The work of Lofland (1969) is frequently cited as an effort to enlarge the conceptual structure of labeling theory. He identifies four primary sources of deviance facilitants: place, hardware, other, and actor. The social (pivotally) deviant is most likely when others are united in imputing deviance, normal hardware is removed, deviant hardware is provided, place rounds are integrated, and actor becomes disoriented and attached to the deviant identity. The apparent complexity of Lofland's theory would suggest that the above criticism of the simpler labeling model could not be applied to his analysis. Unfortunately, it is not clear that Lofland intended to or in fact produced a theory of deviance. Rather he generated an analysis of the impact of uncorrelated, independent variables (i.e., place, hardware, actor, and other) and has not systematically considered their interaction. His work is less a theory of deviance than it is a listing of elements to be considered in a theory. As he notes:

> Although Tannenbaum noted the components of others, places, hardware and actor and alluded to the more specific operation of more specific elements, he did not, as others have not, bring them to specific and *separate* (emphasis added) consideration. If it is now even remotely more possible directly to address the analytic task posed by him and others before and after him, then my aim has been accomplished (1969: 203–204).

Despite the richness of his examples, Lofland does not address the task identified above of establishing the relative importance and strength of these explanatory sets. Again, our suggestion, following the more general social psychological research, would be that while the research suggested by Lofland's conceptual development must be done, the results will most likely demonstrate the importance of place *vis-à-vis* actor and other. Labeling *theory* is not advanced by Lofland's analysis—rather, as he observes, the analytical tools are developed from which a theory could emerge. Thus, labeling theory remains at the less complex level reflected in Assumption 9—an assumption that is easily rejected.

LABELING THEORY ASSUMPTIONS: A SUMMARY

The assumptions of labeling theory as presented by Schrag have been submitted to a review based upon existing empirical evidence in criminology and related disciplines. In each instance my conclusion is that the assumptions underlying the theory are at significant variance with the data as we now understand it, or are not crucial to the labeling perspective. Labels are distributed and labels may affect attitudes. The assumption that labels are differentially distributed, and that differential labeling affects behavior is not supported by the existing criminological research. In sum, one should conclude that to the degree that these assumptions can be taken to be basic to the labeling perspective, the perspective must be seriously questioned; and criminologists should be encouraged to explore other ways to conceptualize the causal process of the creation, perpetuation, and intensification of criminal and delinquent behavior—most obviously the analysis of situational determinants. At the same time we can recognize the potential value of labeling theory for other forms of deviant behavior, and as a component of a more comprehensive theory (Davis, 1972).

Notes

1. For elaboration of this point, see Davis (1972).
2. For a detailed critical analysis of these works that demonstrates their methodological problems, see Ward (1971) and Hagan (1972).

References

Akman, Dogan and A. Normandeau. 1968. "Towards the measurement of criminality in Canada: A replication study." Acta Criminological 1:135–260.
Becker, Howard S. 1963. Outsiders: Studies in the Sociology of Deviance. Glencoe, Illinois: Free Press.
Bedau, Hugo. 1964. The Death Penalty in America. Chicago: Aldine.

Black, Donald and A. Reiss. 1970. "Police control of juveniles." American Sociological Review 35:63–77.

Blalock, Hubert. 1972. Social Statistics. New York: McGraw-Hill.

Cicourel, Aaron. 1968. The Social Organization of Juvenile Justice. New York: John Wiley.

Clark, John and Eugene Wenninger. 1962. "Socio-economic class and area as correlates of illegal behavior among juveniles." American Sociological Review 27:826–834.

Davis, Nanette J. 1972. "Labeling theory in deviance research: A critique and reconsideration." Sociological Quarterly 13:447–474.

DeBoeck, A. and G. Houschou. 1968. "Prodegomenes a une statistique criminelle congolaise." Cahiers Economiques et Society 6.

Ferdinand, Theodore and Elmer Luchterhand. 1970. "Inner city youth, the police, the juvenile court and justice." Social Problems 18:510–527.

Figlio, Robert. 1972. The Seriousness of Offenses: An evaluation by Offenders and Nonoffenders, Ph.D. Dissertation, University of Pennsylvania.

Gibbs, Jack. 1966. "Conceptions of deviant behavior: The old and the new." Pacific Sociological Review 9:9–14; 1972. "Issues in defining deviant behavior," in Theoretical Perspectives on Deviance (ed.) R. Scott and J. Douglas. New York: Basic Books.

Goldman, Nathan. 1963. The Differential Selection of Juvenile Offenders for Court Appearance. National Council on Crime and Delinquency.

Hagan, John L. 1972. "The labelling perspective, the delinquent, and the police." Canadian Journal of Criminology and Corrections 14:150–165.

Hoebel, E. A. 1954. The Law of Primitive Man. Cambridge: Harvard University Press.

Hohenstein, William. 1969. "Factors influencing the police disposition of juvenile offenders," in Delinquency: Selected Studies (ed.) M. Wolfgang and T. Sellin. New York: John Wiley.

Hood, Roger and Richard Sparks. 1970. Key Issues in Criminology. London: Weidenfield and Nicolson.

Hsu, Marlene. 1969. "A study of the differential response to the Sellin-Wolfgang index of delinquency." Sociological Commentator Spring: 41–50.

Lemert, Edwin. 1972. Human Deviance, Social Problems and Social Control (2nd Edition). Englewood Cliffs: Prentice-Hall.

Linton, Ralph. 1952. "Universal ethical principles: An anthropological view," in Moral Principles of Action (ed.) R. Anshen. New York: Harper and Bros.

Lofland, John. 1969. Deviance and Identity. Englewood Cliffs: Prentice-Hall.

Matza, David. 1964. Delinquency and Drift. New York: John Wiley.

Merton, Robert. 1949. "Discrimination and the American Creed," in Discrimination and National Welfare (ed.) R. MacIver. New York: Institute for Religious and Social Studies.

Piliavin, Irving and Scott Briar. 1964. "Police encounters with juveniles." American Journal of Sociology 70:206–214.

Quinney, Richard. 1970. Social Reality of Crime. Boston: Little, Brown.

Quinney, Richard. 1973. "Crime control in capitalist society: A critical philosophy of legal order." Issues in Criminology 8:75–99.

Schrag, Clarence. 1971. Crime and Justice: American Style. Washington, D.C.: G.P.O.

Schur, Edwin. 1969. Our Criminal Society. Englewood Cliffs: Prentice-Hall.

Schur, Edwin. 1971. Labeling Deviant Behavior. Englewood Cliffs: Prentice-Hall.

Schwartz, Richard and Jerome Skolnick. 1964. "Two studies of legal stigma," in The Other Side (ed.) H. Becker. Glencoe, Illinois: Free Press.

Sellin Thorsten and Marvin Wolfgang. 1964. The Measurement of Delinquency. New York: John Wiley.

Tannenbaum, Frank. 1938. Crime and the Community. Boston: Ginn.

Terry, Robert. 1967. "Discrimination in the handling of juvenile offenders by social control agencies." Journal of Research in Crime and Delinquency 4:218–230.

Thornberry, Terrence. 1973. "Race, socio-economic status and sentencing in the juvenile justice system." Journal of Criminal Law and Criminology 64:90–98.

Turk, Austin. 1969. Criminality and the Legal Order. New York: Rand McNally.

Valez-Diaz, A. and Edward Megargee. 1971. "An investigation of differences in value judgments between youthful offenders and nonoffenders in Puerto Rico." Journal of Criminal Law, Criminology and Police Science 61:549–556.

Ward, Richard. 1971. "The labelling theory: A critical analysis." Criminology 9:268–290.

Warner, Lyle and Melvin DeFleur. 1969. "Attitude as an interactional concept: Social constraint and social distance as intervening variables between attitudes and actions." American Sociological Review 34:153–169.

Williams, Jay and Martin Gold. 1972. "From delinquent behavior to official delinquency." Social Problems 20:209–227.

Wolfgang, Marvin and Thorsten Sellin. 1964. The Measurement of Delinquency. Glencoe, Illinois: Free Press.

Wolfgang, Marvin, Robert Figlio, and Thorsten Sellin. 1972. Delinquency in a Birth Cohort. Chicago: University of Chicago Press.

PART 4

BECOMING CRIMINAL

While selections in this part touch upon existing laws (part one) and the reasons why individuals violate them (part three), the focus is on how people, through various types of associations and contacts, learn criminal activities, values, and traditions. The readings range from an introduction to the basic learning processes that occur in the early stages of criminal careers, to descriptions of selected types of crimes, to an assessment of the impact that involvement in crime may have on an individual's personal and public identity.

LEARNING CRIME

In "The Process of Becoming a Prostitute: A Comparison between Lower-Class and Middle-Class Girls," Tanice G. Foltz offers some observations based on existing research and her own recent study of an "escort service" and middle-class prostitutes in Southwestern City, a metropolitan community with a population of around 1,300,000. Foltz found that the process of becoming a prostitute was much the same for both middle-class and lower-class women. She discusses why women enter prostitution and how, through contact with insiders, the novice learns to rationalize her involvement. Learning such "techniques of neutralization," Foltz maintains, often increases the probability that a girl will become a prostitute. Foltz's description of the "occupational ideology" of prostitution, including the view that prostitutes provide services that benefit society (e.g., by functioning as sex therapists), is especially insightful.

The Foltz research corroborates the oft-repeated observation that becoming a successful criminal or professional involves a complicated set of concerns. Not only must one gain entry and exposure and thereafter learn the appropriate techniques, but one must frequently learn how to protect one's identity and self-image. The successful aspirant must also become familiar with and act in accordance with a prescribed *behavior system*. This is a main concern of Neal Shover's "The Social Organization of Burglary." Shover analyzes the burglary profession in terms of its *internal* and *external* social organization. The internal organization refers to the makeup of burglary "crews" and their mode of operation, while the external organization refers to the symbiotic relationships existing between the burglar and outsiders—tipsters, fences, attorneys, and bondsmen. Using a combination of data (interviews with imprisoned men, autobiographies of thieves, questionnaire data from inmates), Shover illustrates just how the burglary profession works.

As shown by the preceding materials, criminal activities, careers, and patterns vary. This is especially evident in Shover's discussion of factors that produce a "good" burglar. Obviously, not all who aspire to a lucrative or successful career in crime will succeed—there are frequently identity and structural barriers to be overcome. The readings in this section offer further insight into how criminal behavior may evolve. They also describe other types of crime. Throughout one can see how *situational determinants* give rise to a criminal act.

SITUATIONAL-PERSONAL CRIME

David F. Luckenbill, in "Criminal Homicide as a Situated Transaction," contends that though criminal homicide is often thought of as a one-sided event with the victim taking a passive role, this is frequently not the case. Rather, such acts of violence are often the result of situational factors and conditions. To support this claim, Luckenbill reconstructs actual incidents of homicide that occurred over a ten-year period, using police and witness reports, offender interviews, and the like. He concludes that murder is "the outcome of a dynamic interchange between an offender, victim, and, in many cases, bystanders" and that certain patterns seem to hold relatively independent of age, sex, race, time and place, use of alcohol, and proffered motive. The next three selections further illustrate how situational factors can serve as precursors to violence.

In "Women Who Kill," Alan Blum and Gary Fisher enumerate several popular stereotypes of female murderers and some of the "sexist explanations" that have been advanced to explain such murderers. The authors point out that such explanations presuppose "individual pathology." Such a model, they contend, is limited most notably by its failure to take into account such factors as race and class. Blum and Fisher then present some recent data about women who kill. They note, for example, that women are more likely than men to murder another family member and that the event is most likely to occur in a domestic setting. Blum and Fisher's observations of the importance of situational determinants aptly complement the Luckenbill research.

Fritz A. Henn, in "The Aggressive Sexual Offender," reviews various studies of rape. Once again, popular stereotypes, as well as presumed causative factors, are explored. The author then offers recent evidence on aggressive sexual offenders. He concludes, in part, that the characteristics of the typical rapist are similar in many respects to those of felons who commit crimes against persons and property.

"Violence in the Children's Room," by Wayne Sage, paints a grim scenario of the nature and extent of child abuse in the United States. The author, like others in this section, deals with some popular conceptions about abuse. He notes that, although reported cases of child abuse tend to be concentrated among the poor, it is a criminal act that permeates all echelons of society. The middle and upper classes, however, are often in a better position to hide such acts. The ability to escape detection, according to Sage, presents many problems to researchers and practitioners alike—problems that directly affect our knowledge about the volume of abuse and its causes, as well as our ability to help the abuser.

STREET CRIME

"Street," or "ordinary," crimes refer to such illegal activities as hustling, mugging, pimping, purse snatching, and auto theft. In "Auto Theft: Offender and Offense Characteristics," Charles H. McCaghy et al. analyze the traits of auto thieves, particularly their race and social class. After noting some commonly held assumptions concerning auto theft (e.g., that it is a favored-group delinquency or that most offenders are only joyriders), the researchers offer data which challenge many of these notions. For example, analysis of studies conducted in Toledo and Virginia indicates that even though the "favored group" (i.e., whites from "better" neighborhoods) accounts for a substantial portion of car thefts, this group is not responsible for the majority of juvenile auto thefts. The research also suggests that joyriding and stealing for profit are not the only motives for stealing cars. The investigators use data from law enforcement personnel as a basis for developing a five-fold typology of auto theft.

ORGANIZED CRIME

Although public and scholarly attention have traditionally focused on crimes of individuals, these cannot begin to compete with organized or corporate crime in terms of the sums of money involved. There are many reasons why the crimes of organizations have received less notice. One is the difficulties of gaining access to organizations and their records. Another is that even if indictments are levied against a corporation or underworld figure, the indicted party can usually afford to retain the very best legal counsel; this often means that court cases, as the result of the appeal procedure, may drag on for years.

In "Organized Crime and Labor Racketeering," August Bequai presents an overview of how organized crime has infiltrated the labor sphere. Bequai describes the forms of labor corruption and illustrates them with specific cases. He notes that attempts by the Justice Department to control these illegal practices have met with little success, one reason being the small number of investigators assigned to labor racketeering. In fact, Bequai points out, the Labor Department recently attempted to cut back its number of investigators from thirty to fifteen. Government laxity and idleness, Bequai contends, paved the road for infiltration of powerful unions by criminal syndicates. Other reasons include the relative inaccessibility to records, as well as the complex set of interlocking ties that frequently exist among the involved parties.

Francis A. J. Ianni provides a closer look at organized crime in "The New Mafia." Ianni contends that organized crime is in a state of transition, as Italian domination gradually gives way to increasing control by blacks and Hispanics. He explains how people become involved in organized crime, focusing on two distinct groups of factors. First are *causal relationships*, which introduce people into criminal pursuits. Included among these are childhood and prison relationships. Second are *criminal relationships*, which develop out of shared criminal activities. Examples are boss-employee and buyer-seller linkages. Ianni also comments on how the black and Hispanic code of rules that governs relationships differs from the Italian code. Ianni's data provide a graphic portrayal of how criminal careers arise and are perpetuated.

CORPORATE CRIME

Assessing the nature and extent of business crime is hampered by a lack of access to records and operations. In addition, people seem to be more accepting of corporate or white-collar crime; many people view such crimes as illegal but not criminal. The tendency toward tolerance or leniency also carries over into the courts. Thus corporate crime is viewed from a different frame of reference, even though it often exacts greater personal and financial tolls, such as through exposure to nuclear radiation or unsafe products and increased cost of products as a result of monopolies or price fixing.

In "Illegal Corporate Payments," Marshall B. Clinard et al. describe how corporations have used illegal payments to gain advantages over their competitors, to avoid harassment, and to influence political parties. Clinard et al. point out that even though wide publicity has been given to foreign payoffs, one must recognize that an extensive system of kickbacks also operates within the United States. They cite several such cases of bribery in support of this observation. The authors then move to an analysis of foreign payoffs, corporate payoffs, illegal political contributions, and the role of the accounting professions. Most disturbing to the researchers is the finding that top management often possesses knowledge of illegal practices.

GOVERNMENT CRIME

The Watergate scandal helped to sensitize people to the fact that, like corporations and their executives, governments and their representatives also commit crimes. The crimes attributed to governmental agents have ranged from illegal break-ins and wiretaps, smear campaigns against individuals, and opening up mail, to conducting experiments on naive subjects and political assassinations. "How Agnew Bartered His Office to Keep from Going to Prison," by James N. Naughton et al., offers a glimpse of a criminal career in the highest reaches of government. They document those illegal practices that former Vice President Spiro T. Agnew engaged in over a period of years (e.g., accepting groceries, accepting cash payments for official favors, and using funds to stock his wine cellar). The authors then describe the events that resulted in Agnew's resignation. Of interest, too, is the way in which Agnew attempted to use his office, power, and resources to discredit his denouncers. Ultimately, however, the discrediting tactics not only failed, but Agnew, in an effort to keep from going to prison, became involved in intense "plea bargaining." The authors' description of Agnew's career and its gradual demise provides insight into how powerful office-holders may feel that they are "above the law." The reading also offers further substance to the statements by Graham (part one) and Spitzer (part three), particularly their analysis of how the powerful frequently attempt to influence prevailing definitions of crime and the criminal.

EFFECTS OF INVOLVEMENT

As noted previously, involvement in activities viewed or defined as criminal is frequently not without its personal and social costs. The sex offender and the street hustler, for example, are committing crimes which, if detected, can lead to institutional processing and sentencing. Thus criminals must manage their behavior and mannerisms so as to avoid detection by social control agents. They must also try to protect their self-image. The last selection in part four deals with this problem.

Carl B. Klockars, in "The Fence and Society: Vincent's *Apologia Pro Vita Sua,*" not only introduces another type of criminal—the professional fence—but focuses on the "techniques of neutralization" (Sykes and Matza, part three, and Foltz, this part) that are used by Vincent (a fence), to rationalize his involvement in illegal activities. Klockars stresses that many of the rationalizations are nothing more than extensions of statements used by all of us. "If I don't buy it, somebody else will" and "Sure, I've done some bad things in my life, who hasn't?" are examples.

19. The Process of Becoming a Prostitute: A Comparison between Lower-Class and Middle-Class Girls

TANICE G. FOLTZ

The basis for the present research was information gathered from middle-class prostitutes. But earlier sociological studies focus on lower-class prostitution and provide interesting comparisons and similarities for understanding the newer sex-for-money scenes and those who participate in them.

Most studies of lower-class prostitution have implicitly if not explicitly posited that a low socioeconomic status brings with it many other factors that might predispose a girl to enter prostitution as a vocation (Davis, 1937; Lemert, 1951; Davis, 1971). Early sexuality is listed as a major factor. Studies show that the prostitute from a lower-class background is likely to have her first sexual experience in her very early teens, and then enter prostitution three or four years later (Lemert, 1951; Davis, 1971). In her study of thirty "common prostitutes," Davis (1971: 301–2) found several social preconditions which lead to early sexuality. These were (1) high levels of family permissiveness, (2) little familial control, (3) peer group norms, and (4) sexuality was associated with freedom (from family) or security (certainty of male companionship).

> The promiscuous pattern which developed for most girls . . . seems to reflect associates' expectations, the desire to attract males, and an opportunity structure which facilitated the behavior.

Peer group norms seem to be an exceptionally important influence, especially during adolescence. Shaw and McKay's (1942) theory of "cultural transmission" lends support to this. They would assert that a "criminal tradition" or value system has developed in certain urban neighborhoods and this value system is transmitted from one generation to the next. Thomas (1923:42) elaborates on this as a "definition of the situation":

> But the child is always born into a group of people among whom all the general types of situation which may arise have already been defined and corresponding rules of conduct developed and where he has not the slight-

est chance of making his definitions and following his wishes without interference.

In other words, promiscuity at an early age seems to be a preponderant subcultural value in lower-class areas.

Lemert (1951) and Merton (1938) indicate that lower-class prostitution may be partially due to lack of education and other occupational resources, in combination with middle-class material aspirations. Lemert (1951:247) expounds on this:

> The press of situational factors making for prostitution falls more heavily upon some women than upon others. It has already been indicated that prostitutes tend to come from families with low socioeconomic status. Their general education and their occupational resources may have been more restricted than is true of women in higher social classes. Nevertheless, they tend to develop the same standards of material aspiration as other women, through a common exposure to mass advertising and other sources of commercial propaganda. Within this general situational impasse and frustration, there are those girls who are more affected than others.

This "differential opportunity structure" perspective is commonly employed to explain deviance in the lower classes.

A similar subcultural orientation views the lower-class culture as a generating milieu of deviant behavior. The concept "milieu" is described by Miller (1972:138):

> The dominant component of motivation underlying these acts consists in a directed attempt by the actor to adhere to forms of behavior, and to achieve standards of value, as they are defined within that community. It takes as a premise that the motivation of behavior in this situation can be approached most productively by attempting to understand the nature of cultural forces impinging on the acting individual as they are perceived and evaluated from the reference position of another cultural system. . . . the cultural system which exerts the most direct influence on behavior is that of the lower-class community itself—a long-established, distinctively patterned tradition with an integrity of its own. . . .

In sum, the prevalent research on deviance in the lower classes is valid also for the vocation of prostitution. Briefly, we find the subculture (or milieu) itself as creating and transmitting values which differ from those of the middle class. In addition to values of promiscuity, there is also peer group pressure towards early sexuality. Since there are few legitimate opportunities to attain material aspirations seemingly shared by all classes, the vocation of prostitution becomes a logical and realistic possibility.

From an examination of the lower-class subcultural view, it may be surmised that identity of self as prostitute is not a problem to the lower-class girl. Davis (1971:316), however, proposes that even "common prostitutes" go through two stages previous to considering themselves a "prostitute" per se. She cites promiscuity as the first stage, and the second stage is characterized by a "drift" toward prostitution, involving occasional sex-for-money exchanges. It is only upon reaching the stage of "professionalization" that the girl's self-conception revolves around sex as a vocation.

An overview of the recent studies of prostitution indicates that the actual process of becoming a prostitute is similar across lower- and middle-class backgrounds (Davis, 1971; Douglas, 1977; Friedman, 1974; Geis, 1972; Hirschi, 1962; James, 1977; Rasmussen, 1979; Rosenblum, 1975; Saulutin, 1971; Stein, 1974; Velarde, 1975; and Winick and Kinsie, 1971). This is probably due to the fact that middle-class values and morality predominate in American society.

Prostitution has been labeled and stigmatized as "shameful," and traditionally only the very poor or very immoral women made a career of it. If a conventional family were to hear that their daughter had become a "fallen woman," surely the most common reaction to this news would be to "disown" her or "cast her out" of the family. The women interviewed for this research all indicated that they could not tell their parents of their occupation because "it would ruin them," "they just wouldn't understand," and "they would be so ashamed." These responses are illustrative of the strength of middle-class morality, even today, in an age of supposed "sexual liberation" (Douglas, 1977). Given the pervasive character of middle-class values, why would women from middle-class backgrounds choose a career in prostitution when they have skills and access to conventional, nondeviant occupations?

REASONS FOR ENTERING PROSTITUTION

A multitude of studies has been conducted on women in all levels of prostitution, and some basic explanations appear across the prostitution hierarchy. The prevailing research indicates that women in "the life" put a high value on money and the power and control it affords them in terms of the sexual transaction and with regard to their purchasing power. Additionally, the exposure to clientele of higher socioeconomic status elevates their own status, and the "fast" "adventuresome" lifestyle, combined with a greater degree of freedom and independence than most jobs can offer, seem to be the pertinent issues in the choice of prostitution. In the present study, the women confirmed all of these factors as influencing their career decision. It is important to note that these women complained they were "bored with" or "tired of" their previously respectable, sex-role defined, low-paying and service-oriented occupations which included mothering, waitressing, clerking, secretarial work, social work, and nursing.

In a recent study, James (1977) posits "prostitution is an institution-alized occupation choice," due to the sexual socialization process and the prevailing inequalities in the economic structure. She and Rosenblum (1975) claim that a woman's personal value is not separable from her value as a sex object, and prostitution is merely an extension of woman's sex role in "a cut and dried form." Rosenblum submits that the high social value placed on desirability influences women to expect a "payoff" for their desirability, even though they have limit-ed expectations regarding their own sexual fulfillment. Since women play out this role in everyday life, it is but a small step to adapt this role to full-fledged prostitution, which provides "benefits that out-weigh the privileges and limitations of socially respectable women's roles" (Rosenblum, 1975:395).

RATIONALIZATIONS, OR TECHNIQUES OF NEUTRALIZATION

From a sociology of deviance perspective, it is claimed that "tech-niques of neutralization" are necessary for the nondeviant's entrance into a deviant world (Sykes and Matza, 1957). For women coming from middle-class background, rationalizations or justifications in fa-vor of exchanging sex for money are an integral element in the pro-cess of becoming a prostitute (Douglas, 1977; Friedman, 1974; Hong and Duff, 1977; James, 1977; Rasmussen, 1979; Rosenblum, 1975; and Velarde, 1975).

Due to the prevailing atmosphere of sexual liberation which has become the norm for middle-class women, it is not difficult for them to perceive their various sexual-dating activities as a medium of ex-change for dinner, a night on the town, a weekend out of the city, et-cetera (Douglas, 1977; James, 1977; Rosenblum, 1975). Somewhere along the line women decide they can receive more adequate com-pensation for their sexual services—and acquire the freedom to use the money as they desire—by engaging in some form of prostitution. It is at this point when they seek out a friend as a sounding board to talk about the advantages and possibilities of prostitution as a voca-tional reality.

Douglas (1977:66) explains the beginning stages of this process with reference to middle- and upper-middle-class masseuses:

> They do not just fall into this by situational chance. They think about it and generally talk about it with similar friends—testing out the idea and its fateful shame implications. They are all intellectually convinced that sex-ual freedom and so on are good ideas, but their bodies at this stage are still saying something different—almost a dread of being shamefully ostracized from society, that is, stigmatized.

"INSIDER" CONTACT AND OCCUPATIONAL IDEOLOGY

Though the pre-prostitute may have her own rationalizations for desiring to enter the profession, there is little likelihood of desire becoming reality unless contact is established with an "insider." In fact, access to an experienced prostitute is an essential part of the process (Becker, 1963; Douglas, 1977; Gray, 1973; Greenwald, 1958; Hirschi, 1962; James, 1977; and Rosenblum, 1975, to name a few supporting sources).

Douglas (1977:67) continues:

This connection with the insider is often crucial. The person who is already inside has already overcome most of the fear of shame and may feel pride by now. They provide evidence that shame can be overcome or avoided, or . . . they act as if there is no such thing. . . .

If she continues at it, she is apt to either find and adopt or else to create a subculture ethos which gives her a sense of pride in the work, or at least rejects the ostracizers, the stigmatizing shamers.

The experienced prostitute has upgraded her profession by redefining and emphasizing its beneficial implications, both for society and for herself (Gebhard, 1969; Geis, 1972; Hirschi, 1962; Hong & Duff, 1977; James, 1977; Saulutin, 1971; and Stein, 1974). The sum of these positive aspects of the profession (along with the negative views of "straight" values) comprises the "vocational ethos" or "occupational ideology." This ideology is a justification for and normalization of the prostitution profession based on premises shared by most members of the larger society (Scott and Lyman, 1970). It serves to socialize the newcomer into the profession as well as to de-shame and destigmatize the occupation and the moral selves of those who practice it (Becker, 1963; Douglas, 1977; Goffman, 1963).

Once the pre-prostitute has taken the step of seeking out an "insider," she is receptive to the vocational ethos and the encouragement to "try it, just once." Equipped with these and her personal rationalizations, the woman is ready to enter the profession as a neophyte—of course, on a temporary basis (Douglas, 1977; Gebhard, 1969; Geis, 1972; Rasmussen, 1979; and Velarde and Warlick, 1973).

SHAME AND DUAL WORLDS

Most studies on prostitution have found that middle-class women enter it on a tenuous basis; that is, they are frightened to "jump in all the way" and so insist that they are "just trying it out." This insistence

on letting others know their involvement is only temporary is a response to the prostitute label—a stigmatized label with shameful
moral implications (Douglas, 1977; Kelly, 1979; Rasmussen, 1979). In
essence they take on the role of prostitute without defining themselves as such. The neophytes may "compartmentalize" or "dualize"
their lives, such that they have a working-world identity and also a
private-world identity. Jackman (1972) describes this phenomenon:

> ... They have seemingly dichotomized their world successfully by deper-
> sonalizing their prostitute roles and living almost entirely in the dominant
> world of American middle-class values. ... All of the respondents reported
> a certain amount of dissociation in their initial commercial experience.

The girls are careful to keep their friends and relatives "in the
dark" about their occupation, and may even lie outright about it. It
bothers them to be "forced to lie," yet they know their loved ones
"wouldn't understand." A little-spoken-about terror is that their relatives, mates or friends might find out about them through an associate who was one of their clients (Rasmussen, 1979).

At the beginning of their employment, the girls tend to disconnect
their "substantial selves" from their work. As more time is spent in
the occupation, they begin to "normalize" the sexual aspects of the
job, and also become less ashamed of it. Eventually they may become
proud of their proficiency at the game. With this gradual change in
attitude also comes an "opening up" or sharing of their occupational
secret with close friends and even mates. Douglas (1977:65) explains
the de-shaming process in more detail:

> This is actually a common finding with people who are not deviants, are
> just becoming deviant and have been deviant for a long time; they start
> out feeling paralyzed by the fear of being shamed, or mortified by shame
> at the thought of it, so they don't do it; they progress to doing it with situa-
> tionally intermittent feelings of fear of shame and sometimes actual self-
> shame; and shame becomes pride and confidence if they continue to get
> away with it—go unshamed.

Thus, the girl acquires an occupational ideology of her profession as
her middle-class values are neutralized. Hirschi (1962:47) defines occupational ideology as:

> ... a peculiar set of beliefs, rationalizations and what have you, that serve
> to justify the existence of profession both to those within and those with-
> out.

He also noted that most occupational ideologies have a "functionalist" orientation, and this is of primary importance in the ideology of
prostitution (this view is supported by all prostitution sources in the
"references" section). The reports of informants in this study strongly
supported and illustrated this suggestion. All of the women seem to

take pride in their profession; they claim to be a benefit to society rather than a detriment. Some of the most common elements of the prostitute's "occupational ideology" include the following:

(1) They provide a "no-strings-attached" sexual service, perhaps saving marriages;

(2) They are paid to satisfy their customers' sexual desires, no matter how "perverted" or unconventional they might be, thus possibly thwarting sexual assault attempts on innocent victims, including clients' wives or lovers;

(3) They service physically handicapped or deformed and socially awkward men who might not otherwise be able to obtain sexual release with a willing partner;

(4) They pride themselves as being "sexual therapists," since they boost clients' egos by putting on "grand performances" and also lend a sympathetic ear to clients' private troubles; and

(5) They tend to view themselves as "morally superior" to their "nondeviant" counterparts, that is, they feel they are honest about what they do, while hypocritical people seek out their services and then condemn them for it. Also, they consider women who are not "in the life" to be throwing away woman's major source of power and control, while they as prostitutes are using it to their own advantage as well as for the benefit of society at large.

This ideology tends to sustain them and keeps them working in the profession much longer than they had originally intended. It appears that the money, the acceptance of a deviant identity, and the independent and adventuresome lifestyle afforded by middle-class prostitution make it very difficult for prostitutes to leave the profession for a more conventional occupation.

References

Becker, Howard S. 1963. *Outsiders*, Glencoe, Illinois: Free Press.

Davis, Kingsley. 1937. "The sociology of prostitution." *American Sociological Review*, 2:744–755; 1961. "Prostitution." Pp. 262–288 in R. Merton and R. Nisbet (eds.), *Contemporary Social Problems*. New York: Harcourt, Brace and World.

Davis, Nanette, 1971. "The prostitutes: Developing a deviant identity." Pp. 297–322 in J. Henslin (ed.), *Studies in the Sociology of Sex*. New York: Appleton-Century-Crofts.

Douglas, Jack D. 1977. "Shame and deceit in creative deviance." Pp. 59–86 in E. Sagarin (ed.), *Deviance and Social Change*. Beverly Hills: Sage Publications, Inc.

Friedman, N. 1974. "Cookies and contests: Notes on ordinary occupational deviance and its neutralization." *Sociological Symposium*, 11:1–9.

Gebhard, Paul H. 1969. "Misconceptions about female prostitutes." *Medical Aspects of Human Sexuality*, July: 28–30.

Geis Gilbert. 1972. "Prostitution." Pp. 195–221 in G. Geis, *Not the Law's Business?* Rockville, Md.: National Institute of Mental Health.

Goffman, Erving. 1963. *Stigma.* Englewood Cliffs, N.J.: Prentice-Hall.

Gray, Diana. 1973. "Turning-out: A Study of teenage prostitution." *Urban Life and Culture*, 1:401–425.

Greenwald, Harold. 1958. *The Call Girl.* New York: Ballantine Books.

Hirschi, Travis, 1962. "The professional prostitute." *Berkeley Journal of Sociology*, 7:33–49.

Hong, Lawrence and Robert Duff. 1977. "Becoming a taxi-dancer: The significance of neutralization in a semi-deviant occupation." *Sociology of Work and Occupations*, 4:327–343.

Jackman, Norman K., R. O'Toole and G. Geis. 1972. "The self-image of the prostitute." Pp. 314–326 in C. D. Bryant (ed.), *The Social Dimensions of Work.* Englewood Cliffs, N.J.: Prentice-Hall.

James, Jennifer. 1977. "Prostitutes and prostitution." Pp. 368–428 in E. Sagarin and F. Montanino (eds.), *Deviants: Voluntary Actors in a Hostile World.* Morristown, N.J.: General Learning Press.

Kelly, Delos H. 1979. "The structuring and maintenance of a deviant identity: An analysis of lesbian activity." Pp. 592–603 in D. H. Kelly (ed.), *Deviant Behavior.* New York: St. Martin's Press, Inc.

Lemert, Edwin. 1951. *Social Pathology.* New York: McGraw-Hill.

Merton, Robert K. 1938. "Social structure and anomie." *American Sociological Review.* 3:672–682.

Miller, Walter B. 1972. "Lower-class culture as a generating milieu of gang delinquency." Pp. 137–150 in R. Gialilombardo (ed.), *Juvenile Delinquency.* New York: John Wiley.

Rasmussen, Paul K. 1979. "Massage parlor prostitution." Unpublished Ph.D. dissertation.

Rosenblum, Karen E. 1975. "Female deviance and the female sex role: A preliminary investigation." *British Journal of Sociology*, Vol. 26:169–185.

Saulutin, M. 1971. "Stripper morality." *Trans-Action*, 9:12–27.

Scott, Marvin B. and S. Lyman. 1970. "Accounts." Pp. 111–144 in M.B. Scott and S. Lyman (eds.), *A Sociology of the Absurd.* New York: Appleton-Century-Crofts.

Shaw, Clifford R. and H. D. McKay. 1942. *Juvenile Delinquency and Urban Areas.* Chicago: University of Chicago Press.

Stein, Martha. 1974. *Lovers, Friends and Slaves: The Nine Male Sexual Types, Their Psycho-Sexual Transactions with Call Girls.* New York: Berkley Publishing Corporation.

Sykes, Gresham M. and D. Matza. 1957. "Techniques of neutralization: A theory of delinquency." *American Journal of Sociology*, 22:664–670.

Thomas, William I. 1923. *The Unadjusted Girl.* New York: Harper & Row.

Velarde, Albert J. 1975. "Becoming prostituted." *British Journal of Criminology*, 15:251–263.

Velarde, A. and M. Warlick. 1973. "Massage parlours: The sensuality business." *Society*, 11:63–74.

Winick, Charles and P. Kinsie. 1971. *The Lively Commerce: Prostitution in the United States.* New York: Quadrangle Books.

20. The Social Organization of Burglary

NEAL SHOVER

INTERNAL SOCIAL ORGANIZATION

Skilled burglary by necessity is a social enterprise. Successful good burglars rarely work alone. The problems simply of managing the act requires at least two persons, frequently more. The work is often physically demanding, very time consuming, and must be performed under the apprehension of potential discovery, injury, or arrest. All of these problems must be dealt with, typically by task specialization among members of the burglary crew or "gang." The membership of these crews is in a nearly constant state of flux, as some thieves are arrested, drop out of crime, or are discarded by their crime partners for one reason or another. Although disparate crews may know one another, may hang out in the same joints, and may be linked together to some extent by occasionally overlapping memberships, it is the individual crew which forms the basic unit of social organization among working burglars. These crews are formed from the pool of available manpower which frequents the bars and lounges where thieves hang out, or they may be formed as a result of the assistance of tipsters and fences, who often will introduce burglars to one another.[1]

The key to understanding the social world of the good burglar is found in the recognition that he and his associates form a *category* of individuals, not a society or organization. As Goffman (1963:23–24) defines it,

> The term category is perfectly abstract and can be applied to any aggregate, in this case, persons with a particular stigma. A good portion of those who fall within a given stigma category may well refer to the total membership by the term "group" or to an equivalent, such as "we" or "our people." Those outside the category may similarly designate those within it in group terms. However, often in such cases the full membership will not be part of a single group, in the strictest sense; they will neither have a capacity for collective action, nor a stable and embracing pattern of mutual interaction. What one does find is that the members of a particular stigma category will have a tendency to come together into small social groups whose members all derive from the category, these groups themselves being subject to overarching organization to varying degrees. And one also

finds that when one member of a category happens to come into contact with another, both may be disposed to modify their treatment of each other by virtue of believing that they each belong to the same "group." Further, in being a member of the category, an individual may have an increased probability of coming into contact with any other member, and even forming a relationship with him as a result. A category, then, can function to dispose its members to group-formation and relations, but its total membership does not thereby constitute a group.

Two men, occasionally three, are usually the largest number of men who will remain together in burglary activities over a relatively long period of time. They tend to confine their burglaries with this same "partner," crew or gang. Whenever the problems expected on some particular score necessitate additional manpower, a not uncommon occurrence, someone who is known to them will be "filled in" for the job. The person who is filled in will be selected on the basis of his trustworthiness, specialized competence, and availability at the time the score is being planned. If he performs well on the job, he may be asked in on other jobs where a person with his qualifications is needed.

. . . The locus of much of the contact between members of the category of thief or burglar is the hangout, usually a bar, lounge, or restaurant. Gould et al. (1968) have similarly called attention to these hangouts as the places where thieves may recruit partners. In these hangouts thieves spend much of their free time in drinking and socializing. Here they exchange technical information, gossip about one another, talk about "old scores," and plan future ones. The significance of the hangout can be seen in the following remarks, which also tell a great deal about the process by which crews are formed and the loosely knit relationships between working crews.

Q: What are the determinants of whether or not a person gets taken in, or rather taken along, with a good group?
A: Generally you have to know somebody on the crew. Like when I came out of the joint in Iowa I came back to Chicago and I was going out with one guy, a guy I grew up in the neighborhood with. We were going into this joint where the thieves hang out and we made some nice jewelry scores. . . . And when we went into this joint I got in touch with a couple of fences through the guy that had [owned] this joint. . . . One particular night this one crew was in there and I got introduced and he more or less told them that I was alright, good people, a good thief and making it. I had a good score that I had looked at so I ran it down to them. So we went over and looked at it and everybody liked it. We all went together and made the score. Owing me something, a couple of weeks later they went out and scored a wholesale house and they called me for a fill in.
For awhile then I didn't work with that crew. But I got filled in with

another crew because they needed someone on the radio. One of the guys was in the hospital so I filled in with the crew on a couple of scores. Then I went back to work with the first crew on another score. And [then] this guy that owned the joint, he more or less started working with one guy from this crew and one guy from another crew. They filled me in and we had our own crew. And we started operating as a crew—but then we also worked intermittently too with the other crews (Prison interview, May 1, 1970).

As a consequence of these networks of relationships, even though the actual span of social organization is extremely limited, working thieves in even large cities often will know one another, although they may never have worked together.

> It's like everybody that is stealing—when you have several crews in a certain area—they generally know each other . . . even though it's no big organization thing—20 or 30 burglars and we all have some kind of conspiracy—it's just close-knit groups and we all know each other. If you don't know them all, you know two or three here and there, or one of your partners knows two or three, or a couple dudes you don't know. It's hard to explain. Over the years you get to know everybody (Prison interview, May 1, 1970).

Burglary crews, when working, usually function on a partnership basis (cf. Einstadter, 1969). Such differentiation of authority as does exist is usually grounded in marked internal differences in age, criminal experience, or skill. Rarely, however, is there a formally designated leader (cf. DeBaun, 1950). Tasks during scores are allocated on the basis of personal strengths and weaknesses, or personal preferences. An easy informally arrived at consensus seems to be the rule here. It is not uncommon for crews to contain at least one man whose mechanical prowess is quite high as evidenced, among other things, by his ability to open safes. Nor is it uncommon to find at least one man who seems to have a particularly good "eye for money" (i.e., who excels at locating potentially lucrative scores). Although each partner might keep his eyes open for "something that looked good," one of them would be more talented along these lines.

Potential scores are located through tips or direct personal selection. The burglar's various "connections" or *occupational contacts* (cf. Katz, 1958) are the most important source of tips. Burglars themselves often locate potential scores in a number of different ways. During their free time, for example, they will often go on automobile trips for hundreds of miles into nearby cities and towns looking over a variety of places. On "scouting trips" of this nature they will be especially alert for places similar to those they have made in the past (since chain stores, for example, will frequently purchase the same type of money safes for all of their stores).

Having once located a potential score, one or more of the crew will visit the place to make some preliminary observations. This can range from driving past a few times in an automobile to possibly walking around the place or even climbing to inspect the roof during non-business hours. During these early observations the location of the safe is of upmost importance. If it is located near a front window where there is no cover for anyone who would be trying to open it, and if it is also anchored to the floor, it represents a formidable challenge, one which will under most circumstances simply be passed up. On the other hand, if the safe is located in an area of the place which affords cover, the burglars will investigate further. In addition to providing cover from outsiders, the location of the place itself is extremely important. It should, ideally, provide privacy and more than one "out" or avenue of escape. If the place is "bugged," the burglars must determine what type of "bug" it is and the points of vulnerability. If it is a "safe score," they must determine, as precisely as possible, what type of safe it is. If it is a "merchandise score," they will need to know precisely what is to be taken and its location.

To get to and from the score, plans must be made for some kind of transportation. A "work car" is used for this purpose. A stolen car or a used car, commonly purchased for cash under an assumed name, is kept hidden away until needed. A truck might be obtained and used in a similar manner. Occasionally, when the risks and stakes dictate, more than one car or truck will be used during a score; one vehicle might be a legitimate one—valid title and license plates—while one or more others are stolen.

The score itself, as I have emphasized, is planned so that each participant knows exactly what he is expected to do. Three or four men are the most typical size of a crew who take off a score; but here again there is variation, depending upon unique circumstances and conditions. One man is usually left "on point" as a lookout.[2] He can be stationed anywhere that provides good visual coverage of the immediate area, either inside or outside of the place. Depending upon the distance of his station from the building, he might use a walkie-talkie to provide instant warning. Another man will "sit on the calls," listening to police calls on a portable radio, again so that instant warnings of detection can be provided. Another confederate might drive a "pick-up car." Occasionally both the "radio man" and the "point man" will be one and the same person. Most commonly, one or two others will actually make the entry and do the necessary work. This can involve opening a safe and/or preparing merchandise to be hauled away.

Preparations are frequently made in advance for the means and route of escape. The destination is fixed, especially if the burglary involves merchandise. Generally, in such a case, the first stop will be a "drop" where the fence or one of his agents will inspect the proceeds and arrange for it to be cut up and moved on. If multiple vehicles are used in leaving the score, a legitimate car may be used as a "crash car." The driver of this car will follow the vehicle containing the merchandise and see to it that no one overtakes it from the rear. In the event of failure, and one or more of the participants are arrested, those who escaped are ready and expected immediately to post bail for them.

Members of the crew usually share equally in the proceeds of a score (even "ends"). Any expenses incurred during the planning and carrying out of the score are also shared equally. (And it should be noted that the tools required are sometimes quite expensive.) If there is a "tipster" involved, he will receive an agreed-upon percentage of the gross proceeds, frequently a flat ten percent.

EXTERNAL SOCIAL ORGANIZATION

The most important of the social relationships which the good burglar maintains with persons outside his group are closely related to the problems he faces in this work. Collectively these social relationships are known as one's "connections"; the person who is "well connected" has been fortunate in establishing and maintaining a particularly profitable set of such relationships. Systematic burglars face several problems in their work; and their connections are particularly important in helping them to cope with these problems.

First, the good burglar must know before burglarizing a place that it would be worth his while to do so. He wants, above all, to avoid unnecessary exposure to the "bitch of chance" (Braly, 1967:233); so he tries, if possible, to assure himself in advance that a score will be rewarding. Second, if he steals a quantity of merchandise—or anything else that he cannot sell directly—he must have a safe outlet for it; he must be able to sell it without risk to himself of detection. And third, in the event of his arrest, he must be able to so thwart the criminal justice system, so that he either goes free or else receives an extremely light sentence for his crime(s). The first of these problems, the informational one, is handled by connections with "tipsters"; the second problem, the merchandising problem, is handled by relationships with the "fence"; the third is handled by attorneys, bondsmen, and occasionally the "fix."[3]

The Tipster

A tipster (also known as a "spotter" or "fingerman") is a person who conveys information to a burglar about some premises or its occupants which is intended to aid in burglarizing those premises. Among even moderately successful burglars, tipsters represent an important connection and source of information.

> Your professional burglars depend on information. Any time you read about a darn good burglary, they didn't just happen to be walking along the street and say, Here's a good-looking house, let's go in there. They depend upon information from strictly legitimate fellas (Martin, 1953:68).

Tipsters are of several types. Many of them (perhaps the majority) are fences who convey tips to thieves as a way of controlling their inventory. Another type is the ex-thief who holds legitimate employment but still maintains friendships with his old associates. A third type is the active thief who learns about some potentially lucrative score but cannot make it himself because the finger of suspicion would immediately be pointed at him. And finally, another type of tipster is what Hapgood (1903:262) referred to as the "sure thing grafter." This is a person, usually an older thief, who has become extremely selective in his scores. Whenever he hears about a score but does not want to make it himself, he may pass on the tip to some other thief of his acquaintance.

Tipsters of all four types are aware of the value of good information to the burglar; and should they ever receive such information, they are ready to pass it along to someone who can use it. Besides receiving tips from such individuals, the good burglar will, however, occasionally receive information from persons who are not so well informed on burglary and the role of the tipster. This may involve purchasing information from a person who is known to have it; while at other times it may involve the utilization of the knowledge of a personal friend—who may be employed on the premises or may have learned about it some other way.

> ... in all walks of life you've got people who are morally dishonest. They won't go and steal something themselves. But they'll buy something stolen if they get the right price and they'll give you a little information too. As long as they don't get hurt. Those people are usually legitimate businessmen. They're in a position to give you a lot of information that you couldn't get otherwise. About the protection of different places. About the assets of different places. And the different security measures of different business houses (Martin, 1953:65).

Or the burglar may take a more active part in the search for information.

> ... This particular place was here in town. I knew a girl that knew a girl that worked there. So I approached this girl and said, "Hey I'd like some information about this place. Why don't you ask her and see what she says 'cause I'll pay her for it?" ... So this girl came back and said, "Yeah, the 15th and 31st there's money there 'cause they cash company payroll checks. . . ." Then I sent back for some specific information, what kind of

safe it was and how the alarm was tied in . . . We got the place and then I gave this other girl $500 and I never heard anymore about it (Free world interview, March 30, 1971).

Having briefly considered the activities of the tipster, we might now inquire as to just who he is; what kinds of legitimate occupational roles do tipsters occupy? It must be emphasized at the outset that tipsters are not confined to any particular social strata. They are found at all levels of the social structure. As one thief has remarked: "There are some amazing people who come to you with information—people you just wouldn't believe could do such things" (Crookston, 1967:127). The following specific examples of the legitimate occupations of tipsters are mentioned in the autobiographical literature: night watchman (Genet, 1964:58), window cleaner (Page, not dated:76–77), prostitute (Wilson, 1964:57), attorney (Black, 1926:141; Crookston, 1967:128; Jackson, 1969:121–122), coal deliveryman (Martin, 1953:65), catering service employee (Malcolm X, 1964:140), jeweler, gambler, detective, and used car dealer (Barnes, 1971:51–68). . . .

There is reason to believe that the success of a burglar is directly related to the size of the geographical area over which he maintains connections such as relationships with tipsters (and fences). Some men scarcely know anyone outside of their own city, while others can count on receiving information and assistance from persons in widely separated parts of the United States—or even nearby countries such as Canada and Mexico. The following is a typical account of how these far-flung connections are established:

Q: How did you get connected as well as you were?
A: Well, first I was thrown in jail with a man who was pretty well respected throughout the country. I made three or four trips across the country with him, meeting friends of his. And then it just more or less snowballed. It developed that a person in one city [would] say, "If you're going to Miami stop and see so-and-so, tell him I sent you. [There] may be something laying around you can pick up." . . . (Free world interview, May 27, 1971).

The value of connections such as these can be appreciated.

Q: You've seen a lot of men, then, who never really amounted to anything stealing. Why was it that they never progressed or became more proficient?
A: Well, one reason is lack of intelligence. [Others are] a lack of connections, a lack of integrity—nobody would trust them—and possibly just no ambition.
Q: You mentioned connections. Do you think they're important?
A: Highly important—well, it depends. Some people are born, raised, steal, and die in the same town. They never get out of the state. They might get out of the city to go to the county jail or penitentiary, then

back home. Every policeman in the city knows who they are after they've fallen a couple of times on petty stuff. . . . They don't travel far and fast enough.

Q: In what way were connections important to you?

A: They're what I just said in an indirect manner. Because if you're far enough away and fast enough away—through connections—then the local heat don't even bother you. If somebody robbed a safe for $50,000 on westhill today, who would get the blame for it? Where would they start sweeping? All the known safecrackers in this area. Certainly no farther away than Toledo. But suppose someone flew in here from Los Angeles and flew out. He's just about as safe as he can be. Because nobody knows he was here, he don't know anybody in the town except the man who sent for him [tipster]. So he does his little piece of work and goes. The cops are running around picking up everybody in town. But they're not bothering him. You couldn't do that without connections (Free World interview, June 9, 1971).

The Fence

A fence is a person who buys stolen merchandise, or some other type of commodities (e.g., a coin collection), generally for purposes of resale, which he knows or strongly suspects are stolen. As in the case of tipsters, fences are stratified such that some are better able than others to dispose of a more diversified line of products, a larger quantity of products, and to handle more frequent purchases of products. Additionally, fences can be ordered hierarchically on the basis of how deeply and heavily involved they are in the purchase of stolen goods (cf. Hall, 1952:155–64; 218–9). The lowest level of fence would be the "square john," who purchases an occasional item from a thief for his own use; the highest level fence would be the person who is able to dispose of nearly any type and quantity of merchandise on the shortest of notices. If it were not for the existence of fences, thieves would have great difficulty disposing of the merchandise they steal. Indeed, systematic theft would be a quite different sort of enterprise without them.

Fences, as already suggested, are one of the most common sources of tips for good burglars. The reason for this is related to the fence's need to exercise some control over the nature and quantity of his inventory. "Giving up scores" (tips) to burglars is one tested and proven technique for doing so. Evidence indicates that this is a very common practice on the part of fences (cf. Malcolm X, 1964:144). In fact, it is this practice which seems to be largely responsible for the fence's having a ready buyer for his products before the thief even "takes off" the score. Giving up scores works, then, to the advantage of both the burglar and the fence. The latter must be seen as occupying a dual role in the behavior system of theft; he purchases stolen goods and simultaneously gathers information about future scores to which the good burglar can be tipped off. By searching out the kinds of merchandise he wants, and then giving the score to burglars, he is able to control his inventory.

But leaving aside the fence's role as a buyer of stolen merchandise, we find that sometimes their relationship with burglars is considerably more complex. Frequently, for example, the fence will be in a position to provide the burglar with several social services (cf. Martin, 1953:98–99). For example:

> I had . . . this one fence I was doing a lot of business with and he was giving me scores, too. . . . He wasn't a juice man [loan shark] but if you needed $500 and you did a lot of business with him, if you sold to him regularly, there was no problem. . . . If you had any problem and you needed money quick, say to go out of town to look at something, or if you got sort of short, he could come up with a G-note (Prison interview, March 13, 1970).

Moreover, because of their business contacts, fences occasionally learn about legitimate businessmen or business employees who have gotten themselves into some potentially embarrassing problem. For many of them, this is the kind of problem which could be solved by a contracted "burglary" (cf. Crookston, 1967:143–144). The fence can put the businessman in touch with a burglar; and the two of them can reach an agreement which works to the benefit of each. Still another service which the fence can provide for the burglar is the introduction of solitary burglars to established crews or gangs, thus helping to link together disparate elements in the thief category.

With few exceptions fences maintain some sort of role in the legitimate business world. Most of them do appear, in fact, to be businessmen of one kind or another. According to burglars, there are primarily three reasons for this. First, it is usually only the businessman who has on hand at any given time the ready cash required in dealings with thieves. Second, businessmen can utilize the contacts and knowledge acquired in their legitimate business activities to evaluate and dispose of illicit merchandise (cf. Hall, 1952:156–57). And third, the fence can use his legitimate business transactions to mask his illicit dealings, thereby making it more difficult for law enforcement officials to build a case against him (cf. Yoder, 1954). . . .

Bondsmen and Attorneys

Bondsmen and attorneys occupy positions in legitimate society which carry with them the socially sanctioned approval to associate, at least to some extent, with persons who are known to be criminals. That some of them are corrupted in the process is common knowledge (cf. Goldfarb, 1965); of much more fundamental consequence, however, for the stability and perpetuation of the activities of professional criminals—and this includes the good burglar—are the routinized working relationships and understandings which have emerged out of this socially sanctioned link between the underworld and quasi-representatives of the criminal justice system.

For both the attorney and the bondsman there are two extremely important consequences of prolonged contact with members of the underworld. The first of these is a knowledge of the differences in personal integrity which exist among some of the criminal offenders with whom they have contact. The second is a recognition that there are constraints which operate so as to reduce the risks which are run by anyone who, in doing business with thieves, crosses the line of unethical or illegal behavior. Both the attorney and the bondsman learn rather quickly that some members of the underworld are more trustworthy than others. One result of this is recognition that they need not fear the consequences of unethical or illegal transactions so long as they are selective in the types of clients with whom they have potentially embarrassing dealings. Moreover, they learn that members of the underworld usually cannot divulge their guilty knowledge anyway because they themselves would stand to lose much by doing so. They would be sufficiently stigmatized by such disclosures as to make it difficult to acquire competent legal counsel and the services of bondsman on any subsequent criminal charges. This sets the stage for the emergence and flowering of a number of quasi-ethical practices and working relationships.

It must be noted that these practices are further stimulated, and possibly even generated, by certain characteristics of the problems faced by criminal lawyers and bondsmen generally in their work. The former, for example, unlike his corporate counterpart, routinely deals with clients who have little ready cash with which to compensate him for his services.

> Now a criminal lawyer has to give credit, and the main reason for this is that burglars and armed robbers, if they had any money, they wouldn't be out stealing, they'd be partying. It's as simple as that. If they have money, they're partying, and when they're broke, they start to stealing again. If they get caught while they're stealing, they're broke (Jackson, 1969: 136).

One result of this is likely to be the attempt by his clients to obtain his services by offering other types of consideration (Carlin, 1966). Among these other kinds of consideration are such things as the sexual favors of wives or girl-friends, and property, both real and personal, some of which is almost certainly stolen. The good thief's ability to manipulate the criminal justice system cannot be comprehended unless it is recognized that he differs greatly from the petty thief and first-time offender in his knowledge of the workings of the system. Unlike them, he has had a great deal of contact with the various actors which comprise it.

When the good burglar is arrested—as he frequently is—he can count upon receiving the services of both a bondsman and an attorney, even if he has virtually no ready cash. In lieu of a cash down payment the thief will be able to gain his release from confinement, and also preliminary legal representation, on the basis of his reputation and a promise to deliver the needed cash at a later date. He will then search for one or more suitable burglaries (or some other type of crime) which holds out the promise of a quick and substantial reward—so that he can pay his attorney and bondsman. On occasion he will resort to high interest loan sharks ("juice loans") in order to quickly acquire the sums of cash which his attorney and bondsman demand for their services. This period of time when the thief is trying to acquire the cash which he so desperately needs is a particularly stressful one for him. Often he will resort to high-risk scores which he would under normal circumstances have passed up. One consequence of this high-risk stealing is likely to be another arrest, sometimes in a distant jurisdiction, thus only intensifying his problems.

The principal strategy which the good thief's attorneys use appears to be delay, in the hope that some kind of unforeseen contingency will arise which permits him to gain his client's release or, failing that, to strike a particularly favorable bargain. The fix, which once was relatively common in many American jurisdictions (cf. Byrnes, 1969), has become a much less predictable and available option for the good thief.[4] Admittedly, however, this is an area in which there has never been any thorough research. Nevertheless, if it is true that the fix has become less available for the good thief—as some have contended (cf. Gould et al., 1968)—this could account in part for the alleged decline in the ethical standards of thieves in their dealings with one another (cf. Gould et al., 1968); in a situation in which the probability of serving some time in prison has increased, it would be expected that the willingness of thieves to "cooperate" would similarly increase. And this could lead to a number of working relationships between thieves and the police (cf. Chambliss and Seidman, 1971:486–8). This also is an area in which more empirical research is needed.

Notes

1. Braly (1967:233–34) refers to the underworld as a "loosely cohesive and always shifting sub-world which include[s] a small manpower pool, fed by a trickle of youngsters outgrowing the teen gangs, and another trickle of men out on parole."

2. Cf. Einstadter (1969) for an excellent discussion of the social roles involved in heists. Einstadter, it should be noted, was only concerned with the *internal* social organization of armed robbery.

3. In many cities gamblers and loan-sharks are also important sources of support for working thieves. Because of their contacts in diverse social circles they are often instrumental in the integration of criminal networks, and in the integration of criminals with quasi-legitimate business and professional men.

4. Space precludes a discussion of the fix as it exists today; however, there is no doubt that the fix is still used in criminal cases. But there is real doubt about how often it is available to the *burglar*. My own views on the contemporary availability of the fix are quite similar to those expressed by Gould *et al.* (1968) and Jackson (1969).

References

Barnes, Robert Earl. 1971. Are You Safe from Burglars? Garden City, N.Y.: Doubleday.

Black, Jack. 1926. You Can't Win. New York: A. L. Burt.

Braly, Malcolm. 1967. On the Yard. Boston: Little, Brown.

Byrnes, Thomas. 1969. Professional Criminals of America. New York: Chelsea House.

Carlin, Jerome. 1966. Lawyer's Ethics. New York: Russell Sage Foundation.

Chambliss, Wm. and Robert B. Seidman. 1971. Law, Order, and Power. Reading, Mass.: Addison-Wesley.

Crookston, Peter. 1967. Villain. London: Jonathan Cape.

DeBaun, Everett. 1950. "The heist: The theory and practice of armed robbery." Harper's (February):69–77.

Einstadter, Werner J. 1969. "The social organization of armed robbery." Social Problems 17 (Summer): 64–82.

Genet, Jean. 1964. The Thief's Journal (trans. by Bernard Frechtman). New York: Grove Press.

Goffman, Erving. 1963. Stigma. Englewood Cliffs, N.J.: Prentice-Hall.

Goldfarb, Ronald. 1965. Ransom. New York: Harper and Row.

Gould, Leroy, Egon Bittner, Sol Chaneles, Sheldon Messinger, Kriss Novak, and Fred Powledge. 1968. Crime as a Profession. Washington, D.C.: U.S. Department of Justice, Office of Law Enforcement Assistance.

Hall, Jerome. 1952. Theft, Law and Society (revised edition). Indianapolis: Bobbs-Merrill.

Hapgood, Hutchins. 1903. Autobiography of a Thief. New York: Fox, Duffield.

Jackson, Bruce. 1969. A Thief's Primer. New York: Macmillan.

Katz, Fred E. 1958. "Occupational contact networks." Social Forces 37(October): 52–55.

Malcolm X (with the assistance of Alex Haley). 1964. The Autobiography of Malcolm X. New York: Grove Press.

Martin, John Bartlow. 1953. My Life in Crime. New York: Signet Books.

Page, Sir Leo. n.d. The Young Lag. London: Faber and Faber.

Wilson, Brian. 1964. Nor Iron Bars a Cage. London: Wm. Kimber and Co.

Yoder, Robert M. 1954. "The best friend a thief ever had." Saturday Evening Post 227 (December 25): 18–19; 72–73.

21. Criminal Homicide as a Situated Transaction

DAVID F. LUCKENBILL

By definition, criminal homicide is a collective transaction. An offender, victim, and possibly an audience engage in an interchange which leaves the victim dead. Furthermore, these transactions are typically situated, for participants interact in a common physical territory (Wolfgang, 1958: 203–205; Wallace, 1965). As with other situated transactions, it is expected that the participants develop particular roles, each shaped by the others and instrumental in some way to the fatal outcome (cf. Shibutani, 1961: 32–37, 64–93; Blumer, 1969: 16–18). However, research, with few exceptions, has failed critically to examine the situated transaction eventuating in murder (Banitt *et al.*, 1970; Shoham *et al.*, 1973). At most, studies have shown that many victims either directly precipitate their destruction, by throwing the first punch or firing the first shot, or contribute to the escalation of some conflict which concludes in their demise (Wolfgang, 1958: 245–265; Schafer, 1968: 79–83; Goode, 1969: 965; Toch, 1969; Moran, 1972). But how transactions of murder are organized and how they develop remain puzzles. What are the typical roles developed by the offender, victim, and possible bystanders? In what ways do these roles intersect to produce the fatal outcome? Are there certain regularities of interaction which characterize all transactions of murder, or do patterns of interaction vary among transactions in a haphazard fashion? Making the situated transaction the unit of investigation, this paper will address these questions by examining the character of the transaction in full.

METHOD

Criminal homicide is presently defined as the unlawful taking of a person's life, with the expressed intention of killing or rendering bodily injury resulting in death, and not in the course of some other criminal activity. This conceptualization excludes such forms of unnatural death as negligent homicide and vehicular manslaughter.

This investigation will examine all forms of criminal homicide but felony murder, where death occurs in the commission of other felony crimes, and contract murder, where the offender conspires with another to kill in his behalf for payment.

The present data were drawn from all cases of criminal homicide over a ten-year period, 1963–1972, in one medium-sized (350,000) California county. Sampling was of a multistage nature. Because criminal homicide may be mitigated through charging or plea negotiation to various types of manslaughter, it was necessary to gather all cases, for the years 1963–1972, found in the four charge categories of first and second degree murder, voluntary and involuntary manslaughter. In this way, ninety-four cases were gathered. Taking all cases of unnatural death except suicide documented in coroner's reports, those twenty-three cases not fitting the present conception of criminal homicide were eliminated. These consisted of fourteen vehicular manslaughters, eight felony murders, and one negligent homicide. The remainder, seventy-one deaths or seventy transactions (one double murder), were examined.

All official documents pertaining to these cases were secured. The character of the larger occasion as well as the organization and development of the fateful transaction were reconstructed from the content analysis of police, probation, psychiatric, and witness reports, offender interviews, victim statements, and grand jury and court testimony. These materials included information on the major and minor participants; who said and did what to whom; the chronology of dialogue and action; and the physical comportment of the participants. Material relating to matters of law and legal processing were not examined.

In reconstructing the transaction, I first scrutinized each individual document for material relating only to the step-by-step development of the transaction. I then used the information to prepare separate accounts of the transaction. When all the individual documents for each case were exhausted, one summary account was constructed, using the individual accounts as resources. In the process of case reconstruction, I found that the various parties to the transaction often related somewhat different accounts of the event. Discrepancies centered, in large part, in their accounts of the specific dialogue of the participants. Their accounts were usually consistent with respect to the basic structure and development of the event.[1] In managing discrepancies, I relied on interparticipant consistency in accounts.

This methodological strategy should provide a fairly strong measure of reliability in case reconstruction. By using several independent resources bearing on the same focal point, particular biases could be reasonably controlled. In other words, possible biases in singular archival documents could be corrected by relying on a multitude of independently produced reports bearing on the transaction. For example, the offender's account could be compared with witnesses' accounts and with reports on physical evidence.

THE SOCIAL OCCASION OF CRIMINAL HOMICIDE

Criminal homicide is the culmination of an intense interchange between an offender and victim. Transactions resulting in murder involved the joint contribution of the offender and victim to the escalation of a "character contest," a confrontation in which at least one, but usually both, attempt to establish or save face at the other's expense by standing steady in the face of adversity (Goffman, 1967: 218–219, 238–257). Such transactions additionally involved a consensus among participants that violence was a suitable if not required means for settling the contest.

Before examining the dynamics of these transactions, it is useful to consider the larger context in which they were imbedded. A "situated transaction" refers to a chain of interaction between two or more individuals that lasts the time they find themselves in one another's immediate physical presence (Goffman, 1963: 167). A "social occasion," in contrast, refers to a wider social affair within which many situated transactions may form, dissolve, and re-form (Goffman, 1963: 18). And, as Goffman aptly demonstrates, social occasions carry boundaries of sorts which establish what kinds of transactions are appropriate and inappropriate.

Social occasions which encompassed transactions ending in murder shared several features. First, all such transactions occurred in occasions of non-work or leisure-time (cf. Bullock, 1955; Wolfgang, 1958: 121–128; Wallace, 1965). The majority of murders occurred between the leisure hours of six p.m. and two a.m. and especially on weekends. More important, they were always found in leisure settings: almost half the cases occurred while members engaged in leisure activities at home; 15 percent occurred while members frequented a favorite tavern; another 15 percent occurred while members habituated a streetcorner or "turf"; little over 12 percent occurred while the offender and victim drove or "cruised" about the city, highway, or country roads; the few remaining cases occurred while members engaged in activities in some other public place such as a hotel room.

Second, occasions of murder were "loose" informal affairs permitting a wide range of activities definable by members as appropriate (cf. Goffman, 1963: 198–215). In contrast to work and such tighter occasions of leisure as weddings and funerals, where members are bound by rather strict sets of expectations, occasions of murder were permissive environs allowing the performance of various respectable and non-respectable activities. An "evening at home," the most prominent occasion in the cases, finds people engaging in many activities deemed suitable under the aegis of the private residence yet judged inappropriate for more formal affairs (cf. Cavan, 1963). Similarly, "an evening at the corner tavern," hanging out on street-corner," or "cruising about town" have long been recognized as permissive settings providing access and opportunity to drink, take drugs, sell and purchase sex, or gamble without fear of censure by colleagues.

In the sample, members engaged in a variety of activities within such loosely structured occasions. In about 75 percent of the cases, the offender and victim were engaged in pleasurable pursuits. They sought to drop serious or work roles and pursue such enjoyable activities as drinking alcoholic beverages, dancing, partying, watching television, or cruising main street. In the remainder of the cases, members were engaged in reasonably serious concerns. Here, conversations of marital or relational futures, sexual prowess, beauty, trustworthiness, and integrity were central themes about which members organized.

A third feature of such occasions was their population by intimates. In over 60 percent of the cases, the offender and victim were related by marriage, kinship, or friendship. In the remaining cases, while the offender and victim were enemies, mere acquaintances, or complete strangers, at least one but often both, were in the company of their family, friends, lovers, or co-workers.

DYNAMICS OF THE SITUATED PERFORMANCE

These are the occasions in which situated transactions resulted in violent death. But examination of the development of these situated interchanges is not to argue that such transactions have no historical roots. In almost half the cases there had previously occurred what might be termed rehearsals between the offender and victim. These involved transactions which included the escalation of hostilities and, sometimes, physical violence. In 26 percent of these cases, the offender and, sometimes, victim entered the present occasion on the assumption that another hostile confrontation would transpire.

Whether or not murderous episodes had such rehearsals, an examination of all cases brings to light a conception of the transaction resembling what Lyman and Scott (1970: 37–43) term a "face game." The offender and victim, at times with the assistance of bystanders, make "moves" on the basis of the other's moves and the position of their audience (cf. Goffman, 1967: 239–258; 1969: 107–812). While these moves are not always of the same precise content or degree, it was possible to derive a set of time-ordered stages of which each shares certain basic properties. Let me first say that the "offender" and "victim" are heuristic labels for the statuses that either emerge in the transaction or are an artifact of the battle. In 71 percent of the cases, the statuses of offender and victim are determined by one's statement of intent to kill or injure the other. Hence, in 63 percent of the cases, the victim initiates the transaction, the offender states his intention to kill or injure the victim, and the offender follows through by killing him. In 8 percent of the cases, the offender initiates the transaction, later states his intention to kill or injure the victim, and follows through by killing him. But in 29 percent of the cases, the statuses of offender and victim are determined by the results of the battle. Here, the initially cast victim initiates the transaction while the initially cast offender states his intention to kill or injure the victim. Due to strength or resources, the initially cast victim kills the initially cast offender in the course of battle. In discussing the first five stages, the labels of offender and victim will be used to refer to the statuses that emerge in the course of interaction and not the statuses resulting from the battle. Furthermore, the labels will be employed in a manner consistent with the pattern characteristic of the majority of the cases. Consequently, in 36 percent of the cases (those where the initially cast victim kills the initially cast offender and those where the offender initiates the transaction, later states his intention to kill or injure, and follows through), the adversary labeled "victim" kills while the adversary labeled "offender" is killed. In the discussion of the sixth stage the labels of offender and victim will be used to refer to the statuses resulting from the battle.

Stage I. The opening move in the transaction was an event performed by the victim and subsequently defined by the offender as an offense to "face," that image of self a person claims during a particular occasion or social contact (Goffman, 1967:5). What constitutes the real or actual beginning of this or any other type of transaction is often quite problematic for the researcher.[2] The victim's activity, however, appeared as a pivotal event which separated the previous occasioned activity of the offender and victim from their subsequent violent confrontation. Such a disparaging and interactionally disrupting event constitutes the initial move.

While the form and content of the victim's move varied, three basic types of events cover all cases. In the first, found in over 41 percent of the cases, the victim made some direct verbal expression which the offender subsequently interpreted as offensive. This class of events was obviously quite broad. Included were everything from insults levied at some particular attribute of the offender's self, family, or friends to verbal tirades which disparaged the overall character of the offender:

> *Case 34* The offender, victim, and two friends were driving toward the country where they could consume their wine. En route, the victim turned to the offender, both of whom were located in the back seat, and stated: "You know, you really got some good parents. You know, you're really a son-of-a-bitch. You're a leech. The whole time you were out of a job, you were living with them, and weren't even paying. The car you have should be your father's. He's the one who made the payments. Any time your dad goes to the store, you're the first in line to sponge off him. Why don't you grow up and stop being a leech?" The offender swore at him, and told him to shut up. But the victim continued, "Someone ought to come along and really fuck you up."

A second type, found in 34 percent of the cases, involved the victim's refusal to cooperate or comply with the requests of the offender. The offender subsequently interpreted the victim's action as a denial of his ability or right to command obedience. This was illustrated in transactions where parents murdered their children. When the parent's request that the child eat dinner, stop screaming, or take a bath went unheeded, the parent subsequently interpreted the child's activity as a challenge to rightful authority. In other cases, the violent escalation came about after the victim refused to conciliate a failing or dead relationship. In yet other cases, the victim failed to heed the offender's demand that he not enter some "off limits" territory, such as the "turf" of a juvenile gang.

The third type of event, found in 25 percent of the cases, involved some physical or nonverbal gesture which the offender subsequently defined as personally offensive. Often this gesture entailed an insult to the offender's sexual prowess, and took the form of affairs or flirtation:

> *Case 10* When the victim finally came home, the offender told her to sit down; they had to talk. He asked her if she was "fooling around" with other men. She stated that she had, and her boyfriends pleased her more than the offender. The offender later stated that "this was like a hot iron in my gut." He ripped her clothes off and examined her body, finding scars and bruises. She said that her boyfriends liked to beat her. His anger magnified.

Of course, the victim's activity was not always performed on the murderous occasion. In 15 percent of the cases, the event was performed on some previous occasion when the offender was not present. Nevertheless, it was on the murderous occasion that the event was made known to the offender by the victim or bystanders and so was symbolically re-enacted.

Although the content and the initial production of these events varied, each served to disrupt the social order of the occasion. Each marked the opening of a transformation process in which pre-homicide transactions of pleasurable, or serious yet tranquil, order came to be transactions involving an argumentative "character contest."

Stage II. In all cases ending in murder the offender interpreted the victim's previous move as personally offensive. In some cases the victim was intentionally offensive. But it is plausible that in other cases the victim was unwitting. In case 43, for instance, the victim, a five-week-old boy, started crying early in the morning. The offender, the boy's father, ordered the victim to stop crying. The victim's crying, however, only heightened in intensity. The victim was too young to understand the offender's verbal order, and persistent crying may have been oriented not toward challenging his father's authority, but toward acquiring food or a change of diapers. Whatever the motive for crying, the child's father defined it as purposive and offensive. What the victim intends may be inconsequential. What the offender interprets as intentional, however, may have consequences for the organization of subsequent activity.

In 60 percent of the cases, the offender learned the meaning of the victim's move from inquiries made of the victim or audience. In reply, the offender received statements suggesting the victim's action was insulting and intentional. In 39 percent of the cases, the offender ascertained the meaning of the impropriety directly from the victim:

Case 28 As the offender entered the back door of the house his wife said to her lover, the victim, "There's _____." The victim jumped to his feet and started dressing hurriedly. The offender, having called to his wife without avail, entered the bedroom. He found his wife nude and the victim clad in underwear. The startled offender asked the victim, "Why?" The victim replied, "Haven't you ever been in love? We love each other." The offender later stated, "If they were drunk or something, I could see it. I mean, I've done it myself. But when he said they loved each other, well that did it."

In another 21 percent of the cases, however, the offender made his assessment from statements of interested bystanders:

Case 20 The offender and his friend were sitting in a booth at a tavern drinking beer. The offender's friend told him that the offender's girlfriend was "playing" with another man (victim) at the other end of the bar. The offender looked at them and asked his friend if he thought something was going on. The friend responded, "I wouldn't let that guy fool around with

[her] if she was mine." The offender agreed, and suggested to his friend that his girlfriend and the victim be shot for their actions. His friend said that only the victim should be shot, not the girlfriend.

In the remaining 40 percent of the cases the offender imputed meaning to the event on the basis of rehearsals in which the victim had engaged a similar role. The incessant screaming of the infant, the unremitting aggressions of a drunken spouse, and the never-ending flirtation by the lover or spouse were activities which offenders had previously encountered and assessed as pointed and deliberate aspersions:

> *Case 35* During a family quarrel the victim had broken the stereo and several other household goods. At one point, the victim cut her husband, the offender, on the arm. He demanded that she sit down and watch television so that he could attend to his wound in peace. On returning from the bathroom he sat down and watched television. Shortly after, the victim rose from her chair, grabbed an ashtray, and shouted, "You bastard, I'm going to kill you." As she came toward him, the offender reached into the drawer of the end table, secured a pistol, and shot her. On arrest, the offender told police officers, "You know how she gets when she's drunk? I had to stop her, or she would have killed me. She's tried it before, that's how I got all these scars," pointing to several areas on his back.

Such previous activities and their consequences served the offender as an interpretive scheme for immediately making sense of the present event.

Stage III. The apparent affront could have evoked different responses. The offender could have excused the violation because the victim was judged to be drunk, crazy, or joking. He could have fled the scene and avoided further interaction with the victim by moving into interaction with other occasioned participants or dealt with the impropriety through a retaliatory move aimed at restoring face and demonstrating strong character. The latter move was utilized in all cases.

In countering the impropriety, the offender attempted to restore the occasioned order and reaffirm face by standing his or her ground. To have used another alternative was to confirm questions of face and self raised by the victim. The offender's plight, then, was "problematic" and "consequential" (Goffman, 1967: 214–239). He could have chosen from several options, each of which had important consequences both to the face he situationally claimed and to his general reputation. Thus, the offender was faced with a dilemma: either deal with the impropriety by demonstrating strength of character, or verify questions of face by demonstrating weakness (Goffman, 1969: 168–169).

In retaliating, the offender issued an expression of anger and contempt which signified his opinion of the victim as an unworthy person. Two basic patterns of retaliation were found. In 86 percent of the cases, the offender issued a verbal or physical challenge to the victim. In the remaining cases, the offender physically retaliated, killing the victim.

For the latter pattern, this third move marked the battle ending the victim's life:

> *Case 12* The offender, victim, and group of bystanders were observing a fight between a barroom bouncer and a drunk patron on the street outside the tavern. The offender was cheering for the bouncer, and the victim was cheering for the patron, who was losing the battle. The victim, angered by the offender's disposition toward the fight, turned to the offender and said, "You'd really like to see the little guy have the shit kicked out of him, wouldn't you, big man?" The offender turned toward the victim and asked, "What did you say? You want the same thing, punk?" The victim moved toward the offender and reared back. The offender responded, "OK, buddy." He struck the victim with a single right cross. The victim crashed to the pavement, and died a week later.

Such cases seem to suggest that the event is a one-sided affair, with the unwitting victim engaging a passive, non-contributory role. But in these cases the third stage was preceded by the victim's impropriety, the offender's inquiry of the victim or audience, and a response affirming the victim's intent to be censorious. On assessing the event as one of insult and challenge, the offender elicited a statement indicating to participants, including himself, his intended line of action, secured a weapon, positioned it, and dropped the victim in a single motion.

While ten cases witness the victim's demise during this stage, the typical case consists of various verbal and physically nonlethal moves. The most common type of retaliation was a verbal challenge, occurring in 43 percent of the cases. These took the form of an ultimatum: either apologize, flee the situation, or discontinue the inappropriate conduct, or face physical harm or death:

> *Case 54* The offender, victim, and two neighbors were sitting in the living room drinking wine. The victim started calling the offender, his wife, abusive names. The offender told him to "shut up." Nevertheless, he continued. Finally, she shouted, "I said shut up. If you don't shut up and stop it, I'm going to kill you and I mean it."

In about 22 percent of the cases, the offender's retaliation took the form of physical violence short of real damage or incapacitation.

> *Case 4* The offender, victim, and three friends were driving in the country drinking beer and wine. At one point, the victim started laughing at the

offender's car which he, the victim, scratched a week earlier. The offender asked the victim why he was laughing. The victim responded that the offender's car looked like junk. The offender stopped the car and all got out. The offender asked the victim to repeat his statement. When the victim reiterated his characterization of the car, the offender struck the victim, knocking him to the ground.

In another 10 percent, retaliation came by way of countering the victim's impropriety with similar insults or degrading gestures. This response entailed a name-calling, action-matching set of expressions resembling that which would be found between boys in the midst of a playground argument or "playing the dozens" (cf. Berdie, 1947).

The remaining cases, some 11 percent of the sample, were evenly divided. On the one hand, offenders issued specific commands, tinged with hostility and backed with an aggressive posture, calling for their victims to back down. On the other hand, offenders "called out" or invited their victims to fight physically.

This third stage is the offender's opening move in salvaging face and honor. In retaliating by verbal and physically nonlethal means, the offender appeared to suggest to the victim a definition of the situation as one in which violence was suitable in settling questions of face and reputation.

Stage IV. Except for cases in which the victim has been eliminated, the offender's preceding move placed the victim in a problematic and consequential position: either stand up to the challenge and demonstrate strength of character, or apologize, discontinue the inappropriate conduct, or flee the situation and thus withdraw questions of the offender's face while placing one's own in jeopardy. Just as the offender could have dismissed the impropriety, fled the scene, or avoided further contact with the victim, so too did the victim have similar alternatives. Rather than break the escalation in a manner demonstrating weakness, all victims in the remaining sample came into a "working" agreement with the proffered definition of the situation as one suited for violence. In the majority of cases, the victim's move appeared as an agreement that violence was suitable to the transaction. In some cases, though, the offender interpreted, sometimes incorrectly, the victim's move as implicit agreement to violence. A working agreement was struck in several ways.

The most prominent response, found in 41 percent of the cases, involved noncompliance with the offender's challenge or command, and the continued performance of activities deemed offensive:

Case 54 The victim continued ridiculing the offender before friends. The offender finally shouted, "I said shut up. If you don't shut up and stop it, I'm going to kill you and I mean it." The victim continued his abusive line of conduct. The offender proceeded to the kitchen, secured a knife, and returned to the living room. She repeated her warning. The victim rose from his chair, swore at the offender's stupidity, and continued laughing at her. She thrust the knife deep into his chest.

Similarly, a spouse or lover's refusal, under the threat of violence, to conciliate a failing marriage or relationship served as tacit acceptance that violence was suitable to the present transaction.

Whether the victim's noncompliance was intentional or not, the offender *interpreted* the move as intentional. Take, for example, the killing of children at the hands of parents. In an earlier illustration, the first move found the parent demanding obedience and backed by a hostile, combative stance. In several of these cases, the child was too young to understand what the parent demanded and the specific consequences for noncompliance. Nevertheless, the child's failure to eat dinner or stop screaming was interpreted by the parent as a voluntary protest, an intentional challenge to authority. Consequently, the unwitting activities of victims may contribute to what offenders define as very real character contests demanding very real lines of opposition.

A second response, occurring in 30 percent of the cases, found victims physically retaliating against their offenders by hitting, kicking, and pushing—responses short of mortal injury:

> *Case 42* The offender and a friend were passing by a local tavern and noticed the victim, a co-worker at a food-processing plant, sitting at the bar. The offender entered the tavern and asked the victim to repay a loan. The victim was angered by the request and refused to pay. The offender then pushed the victim from his stool. Before the victim could react, the bartender asked them to take their fight outside. The victim followed the offender out the door and, from behind, hit the offender with a brick he grabbed from a trash can immediately outside the door. The offender turned and warned the victim that he would beat the victim if he wouldn't pay up and continued his aggressions. The victim then struck the offender in the mouth, knocking out a tooth.

In the remaining cases, victims issued counter-challenges, moves made when offenders' previous moves involved threats and challenges. In some cases, this move came in the form of calling the offender's bluff. In other cases, the counter came in the form of a direct challenge or threat to the offender, a move no different from the ultimatum given victims by offenders.

Unlike simple noncompliance, physical retaliation against offenders and issuance of counter-challenges signify an explicit acceptance of violence as a suitable means for demonstrating character and maintaining or salvaging face.

Just as the victim contributed to the escalation toward violence, so too did the audience to the transaction. Seventy percent of all cases were performed before an audience. In these cases, onlookers generally engaged one or two roles. In 57 percent of these cases, interested members of the audience intervened in the transaction, and actively encouraged the use of violence by means of indicating to opponents the initial improprieties, cheering them toward violent action, blocking the encounter from outside interference, or providing lethal weapons:

> *Case 23* The offender's wife moved toward the victim, and hit him in the back of the head with an empty beer bottle stating, "That'll teach you to [molest] my boy. I ought to cut your balls off, you motherfucker." She went over to the bar to get another bottle. The victim pushed himself from the table and rose. He then reached into his pocket to secure something which some bystanders thought was a weapon. One of the bystanders gave the offender an axe handle and suggested that he stop the victim before the victim attacked his wife. The offender moved toward the victim.

In the remaining cases, onlookers were neutral. They were neither encouraging nor discouraging. While neutrality may have been due to fear, civil inattention, or whatever reason, the point is that inaction within a strategic interchange can be interpreted by the opponents as a move favoring the use of violence (cf. Goffman, 1967: 115).[3] Consider the statement of the offender in the following case:

> *Case 48* Police Officer: Don't you think it was wrong to beat [your daughter] when her hands were tied behind her back? [Her hands and feet were bound to keep her from scratching.]
> Offender: Well, I guess so. But I really didn't think so then, or [my wife] would have said something to stop me.

Stage V. On forging a working agreement, the offender and, in many cases, victim appeared committed to battle. They contributed to and invested in the development of a fateful transaction, one which was problematic and consequential to their face and wider reputation. They placed their character on the line, and alternative methods for assessing character focused on a working agreement that violence was appropriate. Because opponents appeared to fear displaying weakness in character and consequent loss of face, and because resolution of the contest was situationally bound, demanding an immediacy of response, they appeared committed to following through with expressed or implied intentions.

Commitment to battle was additionally enhanced by the availability of weapons to support verbal threats and challenges. Prior to victory, the offender often sought out and secured weapons capable of overcoming the victim. In about 36 percent of the cases, offenders carried hand guns or knives into the setting. In only 13 percent of these cases did offenders bring hand guns or knives into the situation on the assumption that they might be needed if the victims were confronted. In the remainder of these cases such weapons were brought in as a matter of everyday routine. In either event, to inflict the fatal blow required the mere mobilization of the weapon for action. In 64 percent of the cases, the offender either left the situation temporarily to secure a hand gun, rifle, or knife, or transformed the status of some existing situational prop, such as a pillow, telephone cord, kitchen knife, beer mug, or baseball bat into a lethal weapon. The possession of weapons makes battle possible and, in situations defined as calling for violence, probable.

The particular dynamics of the physical interchange are quite varied. In many cases, the battle was brief and precise. In approximately 54 percent of the cases, the offender secured the weapon and dropped the victim in a single shot, stab, or rally of blows. In the remaining cases, the battle was two-sided. One or both secured a weapon and exchanged a series of blows, with one falling in defeat.

Stage VI. Once the victim had fallen, the offender made one of three moves which marked the termination of the transaction. In over 58 percent of the cases, the offender fled the scene. In about 32 percent of the cases, the offender voluntarily remained on the scene for the police. In the remaining cases, the offender was involuntarily held for the police by members of the audience.

These alternatives seemed prompted by two lines of influence: the relationship of the offender and victim and the position of the audience vis-à-vis the offense. When there is no audience, the offender appeared to act on the basis of his relationship to the victim. When the offender and victim were intimately related, the offender typically remained on the scene and notified the police. Sometimes these offenders waited for minutes or hours before reporting the event, stating they needed time to think, check the victim's condition, and make arrangements on financial matters, the children, and work before arrest. In contrast, when victims were acquaintances or enemies, offenders typically fled the scene. Moreover, these offenders often attempted to dispose of their victims and incriminating evidence.

Seventy percent of the cases, however, occurred before an audience, and offenders' moves seemed related to audience reactions to the offense. Bystanders seemed to replace the victim as the primary interactant, serving the offender as the pivotal reference for his exiting orientations. The audience assumed one of three roles: hostile, neutral, or supportive. In the hostile role, accounting for nearly 35 percent of the cases, bystanders moved to apprehend the offender, assist the victim, and immediately notify police. Such audiences were generally comprised of persons who either supported the victim or were neutral during the pre-battle escalation. In several of these cases, bystanders suggested, without use of force, that the offender assist the victim, call the police, and so forth. These audiences were comprised of the offender's intimates, and he followed their advice without question. In either case, hostile bystanders forced or suggested the offender's compliance in remaining at the scene for police.

In almost 17 percent of the cases, the audience was neutral. These people appeared as shocked bystanders. Having witnessed the killing, they stood numb as the offender escaped and the victim expired.

In the remainder of the cases, the audience was supportive of the offender. These audiences were usually comprised of persons who encouraged the offender during the pre-battle stages. Supportive bystanders rendered assistance to the offender in his escape, destroyed incriminating evidence, and maintained ignorance of the event when questioned by the police, breaking down only in later stages of interrogation. Thus, while a hostile audience directs the offender to remain at the scene, the supportive audience permits or directs his flight.

CONCLUSION

On the basis of this research, criminal homicide does not appear as a one-sided event with an unwitting victim assuming a passive, noncontributory role. Rather, murder is the outcome of a dynamic interchange between an offender, victim, and, in many cases, bystanders. The offender and victim develop lines of action shaped in part by the actions of the other and focused toward saving or maintaining face and reputation and demonstrating character. Participants develop a working agreement, sometimes implicit, often explicit, that violence is a useful tool for resolving questions of face and character. In some settings where very small children are murdered, the extent of their participation cannot be great. But generally these patterns characterized all cases irrespective of such variables as age, sex, race, time and place, use of alcohol, and proffered motive.

Notes

1. Whenever detectives encountered discrepancies in accounts of the structure and development of the transaction, they would routinely attend to such discrepancies and repair them through their subsequent investigation.

2. The offender's location of the pivotal event may be self-serving. That is, the offender may select as an event leading to his violence one which places the brunt of responsibility for the murder on the victim. Whether or not the offender's location of the pivotal event is accurate is moot, for the victim may not be able to report his opinion. In this discussion I accept the offender's

contention that a particular activity performed by the victim was pivotal to the organization of his action.

3. When the audience voices its dissatisfaction over the escalation of a character contest, it typically deteriorates. Of the thirty-two rehearsals found in the histories of the cases, about half did not result in death because of the intervention of a dissenting bystander. Discouragement usually took the form of redefining the victim's impropriety as unintentional, or suggesting that backing down at the outset of the escalation is appropriate given the occasion as one for fun and pleasure. While bystanders can be either encouraging or neutral in situations of murder, Wallace (1965) found that in 20 percent of the cases with an audience, some bystanders sought to discourage a violent confrontation, and would themselves often end [up] in the hospital or city morgue. It cannot be determined if my findings are inconsistent with Wallace. He does not specify at what point in the development of the transaction discouraging bystanders intervene. While I found that bystanders were not discouraging in the escalation toward battle, I did find that several cases involved bystanders trying to discourage violence once opponents were committed to or initiated it. It was common in these cases for the bystander to suffer physical injury.

References

Banitt, Rivka, Shoshana Katznelson, and Shlomit Streit. 1970. "The situational aspects of violence: A research model." Pp. 241–258 in Israel Studies in Criminology, edited by Shlomo Shoham. Tel-Aviv: Gomeh.

Berdie, Ralph. 1947. "Playing the dozens." Journal of Abnormal and Social Psychology 42 (January): 102–121.

Blumer, Herbert. 1969. Symbolic Interactionism: Perspective and Method. Englewood Cliffs, N.J.: Prentice-Hall.

Bullock, Henry A. 1955. "Urban homicide in theory and fact." Journal of Criminal Law, Criminology and Police Science 45 (January–February): 565–575.

Cavan, Sherri. 1963. "Interaction in home territories." Berkeley Journal of Sociology 8: 17–32.

Goffman, Erving. 1963. Behavior in Public Places: Notes on the Social Organization of Gatherings. Glencoe: Free Press; 1967. Interaction Ritual: Essays on Face-to-Face Behavior. Garden City, N.Y.: Doubleday; 1969. Strategic Interaction. New York: Ballantine.

Goode, William J. 1969. "Violence among intimates." Pp. 941–977 in Crimes of Violence, prepared by Donald J. Mulvihill and Melvin M. Tumin. Washington: U.S. Government Printing Office.

Lyman, Sanford M. and Marvin B. Scott. 1970. A Sociology of the Absurd. New York: Meredith.

Moran, Alvin. 1971. "Criminal homicide: External restraint and subculture of violence." Criminology 8 (February): 357–374.

Shibutani, Tamotsu. 1961. Society and Personality: An Interactionist Approach to Social Psychology. Englewood Cliffs, N.J.: Prentice-Hall.

Shoham, Shlomo, Sara Ben-David, Rivka Vadmani, Joseph Atar, and Suzanne Fleming. 1973. "The cycles of interaction in violence." Pp. 69–87 in Israel Studies in Criminology, edited by Shlomo Shoham. Jerusalem: Jerusalem Academic Press.

Schafer, Stephan. 1968. The Victim and His Criminal. New York: Random House.

Toch, Hans. 1969. Violent Men: An Inquiry into the Psychology of Violence. Chicago: Aldine.

Wallace, Samuel E. 1965. "Patterns of violence in San Juan." Pp. 43–48 in Interdisciplinary Problems in Criminology: Papers of the American Society of Criminology, 1964, edited by Walter C. Reckless and Charles L. Newman. Columbus: Ohio State University Press.

Wolfgang, Marvin E. 1958. Patterns of Criminal Homicide. Philadelphia: University of Pennsylvania Press.

22. Women Who Kill

ALAN BLUM
GARY FISHER

Historically, simplistic explanations of women who murder—explanations reflecting stereotyped views of women—have been put forth.
Only in very recent years, with feminism having its effect on the social sciences, has the oversimplified, sexist portrayal of the woman
murderer been questioned and a more penetrating analysis, which
eventually may do justice to the multitude of issues involved, been
undertaken. In the past the field was dominated by popularized
"true" accounts of female criminals (the case history approach).
Reflecting and reinforcing our culture's conception of the murderess
as fascinating and mysterious, these accounts have focused on the
more heinous, bizarre crimes of women, replete with sensationalism.
The biased, sensational, moralistic, stereotypical, sexist flavor of these
accounts is pervasive: "Moreover, women who murder are apt to
have the motivation of sex at the time when the flame is burning so
brightly that passion rides high in command" (Sparrow, 1970, p. 156).
"The characteristics one may expect to find in criminal women are
vanity; dishonesty; craftiness; sensuality; a violent temper; contradictory religious tendencies; a capacity to lead a double life; and the tendency to place themselves in torturous situations" (Huggett and
Berry, 1956, p. 43). "Among the insects, the female of certain species
is more deadly than the male; among human beings, her poison is of
but equal potency, but when she chooses to use it, the victim is
caught unaware, for her sting is well concealed" (deRham, 1969, p.
337). The sexism is endemic and calls for closer examination. The pre-
suppositions so blatant in these accounts are characteristic of much of
the literature on women murderers, though they are usually expressed more subtly outside the genre of case histories.

There are primarily two interrelated aspects to the sexist portrayal
of women murderers. First, sexuality is seen as the root of female behavior, female murder in particular; and references to a particular
woman murderer's "hypersexuality," "overexcitability," "virginity,"
or "excessive masculinity," as the case may be, are common. The obvious social, economic, and situational factors involved in a specific

murder often are overlooked or given secondary importance, to be overshadowed by sexual causes. References to woman's supposed inherent deceitfulness (regarding the hiding of our murders) also are common. *The Criminality of Women* (Pollak, 1950), a classic in the field, utilizes this argument. Though this book is more sophisticated than the case histories quoted from and does provide factual information, Pollak's excessive concern with the "hidden nature of female crime" leads him to make some curious causative explanations for woman's deceitfulness based on the nature of her sexuality: "Man must achieve an erection in order to perform the sex act and will not be able to hide his failure. His lack of positive emotion in the sexual sphere must become overt to the partner, and pretense of sexual response is impossible for him, if it is lacking. Woman's body, however, permits such pretense to a certain degree and lack of orgasm does not prevent her ability to participate in the sex act" (p. 10).

The second and more basic aspect of the sexism that underlies much of the literature is the dichotomy of women in general into "good" versus "bad": our cultural polarization of women as either "mothers" or "whores," "the gentler sex" or "the more deadly species." According to this schema, those who conform to the idealized attributes of "femininity"—gentleness, purity, passivity, maternity— would never murder someone. Murderesses are, by definition, deviant and bad, since they have abandoned their "natural feminine roles." These women, then, have not merely killed another human being; more significantly, they have "betrayed their womanhood": "The criminal woman is . . . a monster. Her normal sister is kept in the paths of virtue by many causes, such as maternity, piety, weakness, and when these counter influences fail, and a woman commits a crime, we may conclude that her wickedness must have been enormous before it could triumph over so many obstacles" (Lombroso and Ferrero, 1897, p. 152).

Burkhart (1973) insightfully shows how this dichotomy directly affects women who have committed a crime. At first it apparently prejudices police, judges, and juries in favor of leniency toward women. Considered less dangerous and somehow "sacred" (the "good"), they are less likely to be arrested or convicted (and less often given capital punishment). However, a woman who has stepped far enough out of line to be convicted (the "bad") is no longer protected. Women who are caught and sentenced are often subject to additional disdain and abuse, often scorned as "tramps," "toughies," "loose," basically as "anti-mothers." The notion of "anti-mother" is probably at the root of the moral self-righteousness and vindictiveness with which some writers speak of women murderers. Shakespeare provides us with some enlightenment on the subject in his portrayal of Lady Macbeth—one of the rare classic murderesses:

I have given suck, and know
How tender 'tis to love the babe that milks me:
I would, while it was smiling in my face,
Have plucked my nipple from his boneless gums
And dashed the brains out

A devastating image indeed, for all of us who have (had) mothers.

The sexist explanations for female murders also possess another inadequacy: they generally presuppose an "individual-pathology" approach to violence. That is, they postulate a "pathology" (particularly in the sexual realm) in the individual to account for the murder. Although murder admittedly is uncommon, those who overemphasize its deviant character and view it apart from its social context present us with a very limited view. It is undoubtedly comforting for non-murderers to see murder as an isolated, perverse act; however, this view is not only limited but actually quite unhelpful. What is neglected is the fact that physical violence is a regular and standard feature of American society (and others, of course) and is inculcated and quite prevalent in the family setting (Gelles, 1974). In fact, murder by women is most common in the family setting. Violence is patterned and regular, not a series of isolated incidents. Murder is an extreme form of violence and must be understood in this context. Furthermore, there are "subcultures of violence" (Wolfgang and Ferracuti, 1967) within a country. In these subcultures violence, including murder, is much more common; the socialization process, the value system, and the interpersonal relationships of the individuals in the subculture are fraught with violence. Lower-class, twenty-year-old American males are a case in point.

The individual-pathology model ignores race and class issues; its use in this field has produced writings that might be said to have a racist flavor. Focusing on the sexuality and psychopathology of the individual murderess makes one lose sight of the fact that most of these women are poor and Third World women, living in very specific socioeconomic situations, exposed to very specific frustrations and specific options (Klein, 1973). Burkhart (1973) is the one author whose case histories show an awareness of socioeconomic and racial issues. Her "cases" read true; these murderesses (and other criminals) sound like real people who were involved in very real and often very difficult situations, responding in a way that "makes sense" given the context. Hartman (1977) is the only other author whose case histories seem real; but her focus is on "respectable," upper-middle-class Victorian murderesses. While her focus gets us away from racial and poverty issues, it does provide a context for understanding these Victorian ladies—seeing them not primarily as perverse, pathological deviants but as women responding to various social pressures and contradictions in a changing society.

Now that we have been sufficiently critical of the literature, it is time to present the facts that are known about women murderers. First, it is clear that men substantially outnumber women in the arena of murder. In 1970 in the United States, only 15.4 percent of all persons arrested for murder or manslaughter were women (Hoffman-Bustamente, 1973). While the rates vary from country to country, in every reported case men are significantly overrepresented. Pollak (1950), however, challenges these figures, pointing to what he considers the "masked nature of female crime." That is, he proposes that women "get away with murder" more often than men do. Women have traditionally utilized poison more frequently than men have, and poison is a more concealed approach; women also are overrepresented in terms of killing their own infants, another type of murder that perhaps may be more concealable. However, Pollak's argument is not very convincing here. Perhaps the actual number of murders by women is somewhat higher than reported (relative to men), but it seems evident that women have not murdered as frequently as men. An explanation for this is not hard to come by. Females are socialized to be less aggressive, are more closely supervised, and are more strictly taught to conform to rigid standards, whereas males are rewarded for aggressive behaviors. Role models for aggressive behavior abound for men; cowboys, football players, policemen, as well as television and movie figures, portray violent behavior, including murder, in certain contexts in a positive light. Such role models are lacking for women; in our literary tradition, comparatively few women murderers come to mind. Finally, women are also generally more restricted in the sphere of activities open to them and (until recently) in the types of encounters they have.

That this cultural explanation is reasonable can be seen from supportive evidence. First of all, the female crime rate (and murder rate) shows a tendency to approach closer to the male in countries where females have the greatest freedom and equality, such as Western Europe and the United States, and to vary most from the male rate in countries where females are most closely supervised (Hoffman-Bustamente, 1973; Sutherland and Cressey, 1974). In Algiers, for example, the male crime rate is 2,744 times that of the females. Second, the sex ratio appears to vary with the social position of the sexes in different groups within a nation. In the United States, for example, the sex ratio for crimes is less extreme among blacks than whites (Pollak, 1950;

Sutherland and Cressey, 1974), possibly because black males and females more closely resemble each other in social standing than do white males and females. Finally, the sex ratio for crimes also appears to vary with time. Today, with an increasing variety of roles opening to women, with greater equality and fewer restrictions, their criminal violence might be expected to increase. Police reports in the United States indeed indicate that violent crime by women is definitely increasing at a faster rate than that for men (Hoffman-Bustamente, 1973; Sutherland and Cressey, 1974). In addition, in war years, when women take over the occupations of men and in other ways approach social equality with men, the female crime rate increases substantially (Pollak, 1950; Sutherland and Cressey, 1974).

The second striking fact about female murders is their intrafamily setting. While murder in general is a very personalized crime, in the vast majority of cases taking place between people who know each other, female murder appears to be an especially intimate act. That is, women are more likely than men to murder another family member—particularly a husband or child; outside of husbands and children, the only other significant choice for women appears to be a lover. In his study of homicide in Philadelphia, Wolfgang (1958) found that women had killed their husbands in 45 percent of the cases (of women offenders), whereas men had killed their wives in 12 percent of male offender cases. Rosenblatt and Greenland's (1974) study in Ontario, Canada, showed that less than half of the victims of the men were family members, while almost all of the women's victims were family members. This family quality is understandable; since women have tended to spend a great deal of their time at home, their interactions have been confined largely to family members. Women are less likely to be involved in barroom brawls, for instance, since they are less likely to be in such bars. Economic motivation for violence and murder (leading to less intimate victims) has also been less likely for women, who until recently have been discouraged from actively participating in "breadwinning" roles.

The third point of information regards the setting and type of weapon. In accord with the last finding, it is not surprising that a domestic setting is paramount for female violence, while male murders are more commonly street occurrences (Lester, 1973). But even confining ourselves to domestic killings, we find differences between men and women. Women are most likely to kill their mates in the kitchen with a knife; men are most likely to kill their mates in the bedroom by a variety of methods (shootings, knifings, beatings) (Lester, 1973; Wolfgang, 1958).

As far as age is concerned, women apparently become murderers at a somewhat older age than men typically do (Pollak, 1950; Rosenblatt and Greenland, 1974). Although the precise statistics vary from country to country, a consistent trend can be seen: a pronounced delay in the rise, the peak incidence, and the decline of the crime rate for women relative to men. A probable explanation for this finding centers on the greater protection, supervision, and restriction of girls in our culture—with maturity bringing to women some broadening of autonomy, sphere of activities, opportunities, and temptations.

Finally, we come to a most interesting and controversial "fact" about women murderers: they tend to be seen—by prison psychiatrists and wardens and others—as more disturbed than their male counterparts (Eysenck and Eysenck, 1973), as well as more difficult to handle. There appears to be much "evidence" in support of this notion. Eysenck and Eysenck (1973) compared male and female prisoners and found that the females had higher scores for psychoticism (P scores); in contrast, male controls had higher P scores than female controls. Psychoticism on the Eysencks' scale appears to be related to psychopathy, including criminality. The Eysencks concluded that female prisoners are psychiatrically ill to a more marked degree than male prisoners—perhaps because "crime is so unusual an activity for women that only the most unusually high P scorers overcome the social barriers involved" (p. 695). Panton (1974), using Minnesota Multiphasic Personality Inventory (MMPI) profiles of male and female prisoners, reached similar conclusions. Finding high psychopathy (Pd) scores for all—with males higher on hysteria (Hs) and depression (D) and females higher on social introversion (Si) and paranoia (Pa)—he concluded that male prisoners are more antisocial and sociopathic, with some neurotic overlays, and that females are more asocial and have greater emotional disturbance; that is, he saw the men as more "criminal" and the women as more "mentally ill." Studies of parents who have killed one of their children are also supportive. In reviewing the literature on filicide, Resnick (1969) found that mothers who had killed a child were most frequently diagnosed as schizophrenic, whereas fathers were most often judged "nonpsychotic." Similarly, in his study of filicide, Myers (1970) found that fathers were typically judged sane and sent to prison, whereas a majority of mothers were judged to be psychotic.

All "scientific evidence," however, raises more questions than it answers. A study by McGlynn, Megas, and Benson (1976) is illuminating. College students were read a summary of a case of a violent murder in which an insanity plea was entered, with the sex of the hypothetical defendant varying. Interestingly enough, the subjects saw the female accused of a violent crime as more "sick" than an equivalent male; that is, women were more often seen as "insane," even though the murder and the background information were the same.

Thus, are women murderers really more "disturbed," more "insane," or are they judged to be so by others? It is impossible to sort it all out at this point. Clearly, there are different standards of mental health for women versus men. McGlynn and his colleagues point to previous studies that support this view; that is, where traits such as dominance and aggression were considered (by mental health professionals and college students) healthy for males, whereas the opposite traits of passivity and submission were considered healthy for females. Chesler (1972) has much to offer on this subject. Her thesis is rather complex but essentially speaks to the contradictions and complexities of the issue at hand. Not only are there differing standards of mental health for the two sexes, but each sex is encouraged into differing patterns of deviance. Women who are socialized "too well"—who incorporate the cultural ideals of femininity too completely, displaying much passivity, helplessness, feelings of inferiority, seductiveness, and so forth—end up being considered "neurotic" (most often "hysterical" or "depressed"). Men who display "masculinity" "too well"—who flaunt their strength and aggressivity—often end up incarcerated as "criminals" or "sociopaths." "The kinds of behaviors that are considered 'criminal' or 'mentally ill' are sex-typed and each sex is conditioned accordingly" (p. 57). Women are, in a sense, socialized into the help-seeking role of psychiatric patient, into thinking of themselves as "mad" or "neurotic," and are often judged by the psychiatric profession (which is very much dominated by males) as "mentally ill." Men, in contrast, are more often judged to be "criminals" or "sociopaths" and are less inclined to participate in the help-seeking role of psychiatric patient and less likely to see themselves as "mentally ill."

Women who murder are clearly deviating more from the "norm" than their male counterparts and are thus judged to be more "disturbed." They may also feel more disturbed, since they have less social validation for their action, but current evaluations of mental disturbance seem to confound the issue. The writings and studies reported are replete with biases that go unquestioned. Fathers who kill their children are seen as enraged as a result of provocation—as engaged in responsible albeit criminal action. Mothers are "invalidated"—their acts seen as a product of "mental illness." Adolescent delinquent girls are seen as oversensitive, resentful, and inferior, while delinquent boys are said to be demonstrating a need to be independent. Perhaps women who murder *are* more "disturbed"; but a much more sophisticated analysis, sorting out the multitude of preconceptions and controversies, is in order before this conclusion can be reached.

Having presented much of the information known about women murderers in general, we turn to some more specific information about a subcategory of murderesses: women who kill their own children. This area deserves attention, since it is evidently more common than might ordinarily be suspected. In 1966 one out of twenty-two murder victims in the United States was a child killed by his own parent (Resnick, 1969). Resnick distinguishes two types of child killing: the killing of a neonate within the first few hours of life (neonaticide) and the murder of a child who is more than a day old (filicide).

Filicide is committed twice as frequently by mothers as by fathers (Resnick, 1969). Fathers tend to use more active methods, such as striking, squeezing, or stabbing, whereas mothers more often drown, suffocate, or gas their victims. A large number of the victims are killed during the first six months of life, presumably as a result of maternal postpartum psychoses. The motivation for this type of murder is an important factor distinguishing it from other homicides. Almost half of the filicides involve an explicit altruistic motive; that is, they are performed to prevent the child from suffering. The suffering may not always be real (the mother may be delusional, for example) and occasionally may be anticipated (for example, after the mother's intended suicide). In contrast, neonaticide is an almost exclusively maternal act; nearly all the neonaticidal murderers are mothers (Resnick, 1970). As a group, these mothers tend to be significantly younger than the filicidal group. Comparison of the diagnoses of the two groups suggests that neonaticide and filicide are committed by two different psychiatric populations. Depression, psychosis, and suicide are much less common in neonaticidal mothers. The murder of a neonate is much less often seen as a product of mental illness; its most common motive appears to be that the child was unwanted, either illegitimate or the result of an extramarital affair. The neonaticidal mothers are typically seen as passive and immature—the murder being a desperate attempt to deal with a situation they had made no plans for. The pregnancy is often denied and hidden until too late; typically, no effort is made to obtain an abortion (Resnick, 1970).

The subject of abortion raises a number of relevant issues. In recent years the idea of abortion as murder has received attention. Whether or not it is seen as murder depends on one's values and frame of reference. As we saw the relativism regarding the standards of mental health and forms of deviance, we can see it here regarding the very definition of murder. Furthermore, the judgments placed on women who have had abortions have also changed relative to the times. Years ago, abortion was taboo: an antifamily action for a married woman, and revealing of sinful (sexual) behavior for an unmarried woman—thus, probably the product of "mental illness." At present, with the roles of women changing, as well as our ideas about the family, it is unlikely that the mental health profession would consider it an act of illness. On the contrary, the neonaticidal mother is now depreciated (seen as immature and passive) for not considering abortion.

So far, we have been critical and questioning of the findings about women murderers. We have been particularly attentive to the sexism and the drawbacks of a psychopathological model. The tendencies to overemphasize the woman murderer's deviance and pathology have been explored in numerous areas. The difficulties and biases of psychiatric diagnoses have also been touched on. Bearing all this in mind, we can now end with a psychodynamic study of "women who kill." While it certainly has many of the limitations discussed throughout . . . , it also is a significant contribution to the field. It is an attempt to explore the personality styles of murderesses—trying to find some common psychodynamic patterns that lead to the act of murder by women.

Cole, Fisher, and Cole (1968) did psychiatric evaluations of female homicide cases in California, developing a categorization based on personality style. They found six distinct groups of murderesses. The "masochistic" woman is described as stable, well controlled, and productive, though tending to choose an abusive, unstable mate. After years of abuse, she suddenly commits violent murder—often while being beaten or while fearful of being killed herself, using a weapon handy at the time (not premeditated). The "overtly hostile" woman is emotionally unstable, aggressive, and impulsive, with a history of violence and antagonism to authority. She characteristically attacks her victim with the intent to hurt but not kill. The "covertly hostile" murderess is usually not violent in general but murders violently. She fears the expression of hostility but tends to choose abusive mates. Her general functioning is usually poor, and she often kills her children. The "psychotic" woman killer murders while disturbed. She has a history of psychosis. She often does not recall the offense and expresses no remorse. The "amoral" woman kills deliberately for economic gain or to remove an interfering person. She has a history of antisocial behavior. Her intellectual level and level of functioning are generally high, but she shows a marked disregard for the feelings of others. The "inadequate" woman has little coping ability and depends upon a dominant male to take care of her. She typically kills in response to being ordered to do so by her partner. "It is, of course, clear that women of totally diverse personality style do commit murder" (p. 7).

We conclude . . . by noting that a dynamic process is occurring. As the role of women in society is changing, our understanding of women—including our understanding of female murderers—is also changing. With the rise of feminism, stereotyped, one-dimensional views of women are being questioned, and a more searching examination of the complexities of what it is to be a woman (and woman-murderer) is being undertaken. In addition, the rise of feminism has led to an increased participation of women in professional roles; their increased involvement as social scientists will inevitably broaden and deepen the understanding of women. Interestingly, the most recent and enlightening studies of women murderers have been done almost exclusively by women (see, for example, Hartman, 1977; Hoffman-Bustamente, 1973; Klein, 1973). Questions are being raised; and the exotic, sexist, oversimplified views of murderesses are being challenged. The result can only be a more penetrating understanding of the complexities of the subject.

References

Burkhart, K. *Women in Prison.* New York: Doubleday, 1973.

Chesler, P. *Women and Madness.* New York: Doubleday, 1972.

Cole, K., Fisher, G., and Cole, S. "Women Who Kill." *Archives of General Psychiatry,* 1968, *19,* 1–8.

deRham, E. *How Could She Do It?* New York: Potter, 1969.

Eysenck, S., and Eysenck, H. "The Personality of Female Prisoners." *British Journal of Psychiatry,* 1973, *122,* 693–698.

Gelles, R.J. *The Violent Home.* Beverly Hills, CA: Sage, 1974.

Hartman, M. *Victorian Murderesses.* New York: Schocken Books, 1977.

Hoffman-Bustamente, D. "The Nature of Female Criminality." *Issues in Criminology,* 1973, *8,* 117–136.

Huggett, R., and Berry, P. *Daughters of Cain.* London: Allen & Unwin, 1956.

Klein, D. "The Etiology of Female Crime." *Issues in Criminology,* 1973, *8,* 3–30.

Lester, D. "Murder: A Review." *Corrective and Social Psychiatry and Journal of Applied Behavior Therapy,* 1973, *19,* 40–50.

Lombroso, C., and Ferrero, G. *The Female Offender.* New York: Appleton-Century-Crofts, 1897.

McGlynn, R., Megas, J., and Benson, D. "Sex and Race as Factors Affecting the Attribution of Insanity in a Murder Trial." *Journal of Psychology,* 1976, *93,* 93–99.

Myers, S. "Maternal Filicide." *American Journal of Disabilities of Children,* 1970, *120,* 534–536.

Panton, J. "Personality Differences between Male and Female Prison Inmates Measured by the MMPI." *Criminal Justice and Behavior,* 1974, *1,* 332–340.

Pollak, O. *The Criminality of Women.* Philadelphia, PA: University of Pennsylvania Press, 1950.

Resnick, P.J. "Child Murder by Parents: A Psychiatric Review of Filicide." *American Journal of Psychiatry,* 1969, *126,* 325–334.

———. "Murder of the Newborn: A Psychiatric Review of Neonaticide." *American Journal of Psychiatry,* 1970, *126,* 1414–1420.

Rosenblatt, E., and Greenland, C. "Female Crimes of Violence." *Canadian Journal of Criminology and Corrections,* 1974, *16,* 173–180.

Sparrow, G. *Women Who Murder.* London: Abelard-Schuman, 1970.

Sutherland, E.H., and Cressey, D. *Criminology.* Philadelphia, PA: Lippincott, 1974.

Wolfgang, M.E. *Patterns in Criminal Homicide.* Philadelphia, PA: University of Pennsylvania Press, 1958.

Wolfgang, M.E., and Ferracuti, F. *The Subculture of Violence.* London: Tavistock, 1967.

23. The Aggressive Sexual Offender

FRITZ A. HENN

... Of those [sexual] offenses normally considered as significant crimes, only sodomy and rape consistently involve physical coercion and violence. Sodomy is so broadly and variously defined in different jurisdictions that the term has little meaning. That leaves rape as the only aggressive sexual offense which is well defined and involves violence. The study of rape and rapists has been sparse. The older literature, for the most part, dealt with psychological theories of motivation and involved few empirical studies. Within the last decade a number of studies have examined the characteristics of rapists in a controlled and systematic fashion. A compilation of these studies allows the formulation of a general profile of rapists. A comparison among studies also points to areas in need of further definition.

Even including the popular literature, only three widely read books on the topic of rape (Amir, 1971; Brownmiller, 1975; MacDonald, 1971) are to be found. In the earlier psychiatric literature, only a relatively small number of psychodynamically oriented studies of sexual offenders were devoted to rape. As Stürup (1968, pp. 9–10) has pointed out, "Those forms of sexual behavior which are considered the most deviant from a strictly psychiatric point of view [are] indecency toward children and exhibitionism. ... It is important, however, to distinguish between what may be deviant from a psychiatric point of view and what is most serious in its social consequences; these are by no means identical." The older psychiatric studies were more concerned with offenses that were clearly manifestations of a lasting personality defect and as such were ripe for dynamic speculation. Pedophilia and exhibitionism, for example, have exceptionally high rates of recidivism, and both of these deviant behavioral responses often continue through a major portion of the adult lives of the offenders. Therefore, they were of particular interest to psychiatrists. On the other hand, rape is a crime of violent young men and does not, except in rare instances, form a pattern of behavior which is repeated throughout adult life. Thus, it was not considered to be as interesting a psychiatric problem.

Before examining the offenders, let us examine the offense. The legal definition of rape involves the act of intercourse with a female against her will, with the stated exception of a man's wife in England and in the United States. This exception, as Brownmiller (1975) points out, no longer applies in Scandinavian countries and the countries of Eastern Europe. This difference provides a clue to the nature of rape. The exclusion of one's wife as a potential victim of rape is derived, in Anglo-American law, from the ancient notion of a wife as a possession. This concept, while no longer widely held, still forms the basis of current laws and suggests that rape, as a crime, has an element akin to a property offense. Rape can also be considered as a crime of violence or a crime of sexual lust. Rape as a pure crime of property does not occur frequently in our society, though rape in conjunction with burglary has an element of a property offense. Other cultures report more frequent occurrences of mixed sexual lust and property offense. For example, a documented outbreak of rape among the Gusii tribes of Kenya in 1937 apparently occurred because the price of a bride rose beyond the means of the Gusii young men (LeVine, 1959). Rape during war is an example of a crime mainly of violence.

In the United States rape, as an offense, is increasing faster than other assaultive crimes. From 1969 to 1975 rape increased by 41 percent. To what extent this is a reflection of better reporting, the initiation of special rape squads in major cities, or a real increase in the number of offenses committed is hard to say; however, according to the National Center for the Prevention and Control of Rape, the increase is, at least in part, real. In St. Louis, where our studies were carried out, arrests for rape in the decade 1964–1973 increased steadily until 1970, when they actually decreased for three years. In St. Louis, as in the nation, the most common violent crime was assault, followed by robbery, rape, and homicide. To give an example of the relative frequency of these crimes, the number of arrests in St. Louis in 1973 for homicide were 201; for rape, 253; for robbery, 1,179; and for assault, 1,442. One problem with figures such as these is that rape is the most underreported crime in police statistics. As an example, in 1967 interviewers at the National Opinion Research Center of the University of Chicago surveyed 10,000 households and established a rate of forcible rape over 3.5 times that reported in the U.S. Department of Justice's *Uniform Crime Reports* for 1967. Even despite the high rate for unreported rapes, the rate for reported rapes or rape attempts in the United States runs between forty and fifty per hundred thousand women. In contrast, rates in Northern Europe invariably are under ten per hundred thousand women. Since Northern European countries, on the whole, also have better reporting systems than the United States, the differences might be even larger between the two cultures. Similar low rates are found in the Mideast and Asia. This propensity for the commission of rape, as well as homicide, in the United States seems inexplicably high.

Rape is usually thought of as an individual crime. While this is generally the case, recent studies suggest that it is by no means an exclusive pattern. In six studies on this issue—involving rape in Philadelphia (Amir, 1971), Denver (MacDonald, 1971), Washington, D.C. (Hayman, 1971), Toronto (Mohr, 1965), Denmark (Svalastoga, 1962), and Finland (Antilla, 1968)—37 percent of the cases involved two or more rapists. Over one-third of all rapes involved two or more men assaulting a single woman. This certainly creates a more terrifying situation for the victim and one in which the rapists are assured of dominance. Group rape was noted by Amir (1971) in his study of rape in Philadelphia. This study of 646 cases of rape was the first large-scale examination of rape and rapists. In it Amir examined the records of 1,292 offenders involved in these rapes and found that only 57 percent of these cases involved rape by a single assailant. In 105 cases the rape was the result of two men, while in 171 cases the rape was a group event. MacDonald (1971) found this same phenomenon in Denver—particularly in low-income, minority neighborhoods. He found that black and Spanish-American offenders were overrepresented among rape offenders in the Denver area, but they were even more overrepresented when group rape was considered; the offender rate for group rape was six times higher for blacks and fifteen times higher for Spanish-American than for the white offenders. For the most part, group offenses are committed against victims with the same ethnic and social background as the offender and often evolve out of a gathering where drugs and/or alcohol is used. In general, a picture emerges of an offense committed by a group or gang who physically dominate and often end by degrading their victim. The act may be spontaneous, following a party situation in which alcohol and drugs are used, and it usually involves group pressure on reluctant members to maintain their group solidarity and participate in an act of violent machismo.

Understanding the nature of rape requires defining the role of individual deviance as compared to social pressure in the genesis of the offense. It also requires an examination of the sexual versus aggressive features of the crime. Perhaps the most likely avenue for understanding rape is to examine the perpetrator. Although rape has been neglected in both the psychiatric and the sociological literature, recently a number of large studies of rapists from a variety of urban centers have been reported (Amir, 1971; Henn, Herjanic, and Vanderpearl, 1976; MacDonald, 1971; McCaldon, 1967; Rada, 1975). In these studies sufficient demographic information was collected to describe the profile of rapists. The remarkably uniform picture that emerges is corroborated by the U.S. Department of Justice's *Uniform Crime Reports* (compiled by the Federal Bureau of Investigation). The age distribution of the rapist parallels the age distribution of other violent criminals. In most crimes young men dominate; in our study (Henn, Herjanic, and Vanderpearl, 1976) as in MacDonald's (1971), 75 percent of rape offenders were under 30; in Amir's study (1971) this figure was even higher, 82 percent. In marked contrast, the ages of child molesters (Henn, Herjanic, and Vanderpearl, 1976) and exhibitionists (Mohr, Turner, and Jerry, 1964) are distributed more evenly over the adult age range.

A racial breakdown of rapists consistently reveals an overrepresentation of minority groups. Amir found that 82 percent of the Philadelphia rapists were black; MacDonald found that 30 percent were black—at a time when the black population was under 7 percent in the Denver area; and 61 percent of the St. Louis offenders whom we studied were black. MacDonald also found that 34 percent of the Denver rapists were Spanish-American while this group constituted about 9 percent of the population. In the Amir and MacDonald studies, the victims of rape were predominantly of the same ethnic and socioeconomic background as the offenders. In our St. Louis study, rape also appeared to be predominantly intraracial. In the early 1960s interracial rape made up only about 9 percent of all rape cases. Unfortunately, these figures are not available for the 1970s. Two studies, however, do analyze the racial breakdown of offenders and victims in rape cases in the 1970s. Brown (1974), in a study of Memphis police files, reports that black offenders and white victims consituted 16 percent of the cases; and Hayman (1971) found black on white rape steadily rising in Washington, D.C., and reaching 21 percent of all reported rapes during 1965–1971. This suggests an increasing trend for black-white rapes, which were found under 5 percent in the 1950s, about double that in the 1960s, and again doubled to over 20 percent of cases in the 1970s. The reverse situation, of a white rapist with a black victim, appears to be decreasing; 4 percent of rapes in the 1950s and 1960s in St. Louis and Philadelphia were white on black, and roughly .5 percent of the rapes in Memphis and Washington, D.C., were of this type. These comparisons are made from statistics in different cities and therefore are tentative at best.

The suggestion of an eightfold decrease of white on black rape concurrent with an eightfold increase in black on white rape does point to an area meriting further investigation. This change occurred in spite of widespread awareness of discriminatory penalties being given to the black offender who chooses a white victim. The explanation for these trends is difficult, but Hayman (1971) feels that the interracial crimes represent a combination of hostility toward women and a racial hostility. This is clearly the attitude Eldridge Cleaver reveals in his 1967 autobiography, *Soul on Ice:* "It delights me that I was defying and trampling upon the white man's law, upon his system of values, and that I was defiling his women." Even with these changing trends, it must be remembered that the vast majority of rapes are intraracial, and black on black crime still remains the dominant form of sexual assault. This racial discrepancy may simply reflect the socioeconomic distribution of rapists. For they, like most felons, come from the poorest socially disorganized urban areas. A correlation between race and socioeconomic distribution of rapists was found in the previously reported studies of Denver, Philadelphia, and St. Louis and in most European studies as well. Thus, although blacks are overrepresented as offenders in all violent crimes on the basis of population, they may be proportionally represented with respect to the distribution of the population economically. There is admittedly a need for more data on this point, but the evidence suggesting such an explanation was supported by the President's Commission on Law Enforcement and Administration of Justice when it examined the question in 1967.

A typical rapist is likely to be young and poor. He may or may not be married. (Given the youth of the offenders, many of them are married—approximately 40 percent in most studies.) He is also likely to have had previous arrests. One of the most revealing statistics concerning rape in the United States is the high occurrence of previous criminal records among rape offenders. Amir (1971) noted that a majority of his offenders had previous criminal records, and MacDonald reported that 85 percent of his imprisoned cohorts had a previous record. The staff report on crimes of violence to the National Commission on the Causes and Prevention of Violence (1969) found that more than 70 percent of the rapists had previous records. In our study we compared the rates of violent criminal charges for rapists as opposed to other sexual offenders and found that rapists had nearly six times as many violent criminal charges as other sexual offenders. This tendency toward a history of violent offenses was also found in a Danish study (Svalastoga, 1962), where it was reported that 77 percent of the rapists had prior criminal records. These statistics strongly suggest that individuals involved in rape are predominantly antisocial, hostile, and violent—as opposed to having a specific, powerful, and uncontrolled sexual urge, as is suggested by some. Further support for this idea comes from Amir's finding that nearly three-quarters of all rapes are planned and that between a quarter and a half of all rapes involve two or more men.

Of special concern in our investigation was the role of psychiatric illness, particularly psychosis, in rape. We therefore made a study of all rapists referred from the court for a psychiatric evaluation in the city of St. Louis. A previous study of felons imprisoned from the St. Louis courts had revealed an extremely low incidence of psychosis among imprisoned felons, suggesting that psychiatrically ill offenders were screened out prior to imprisonment (Guze, 1976). This finding suggested to us that the sixty-seven rapists sent for psychiatric evaluations would include most, if not all, of the seriously ill defendants charged with rape in St. Louis. Over a twenty-one-year period, we found ten offenders who might have been psychotic. Since complete police records and psychiatric histories were available in the St. Louis area for the period between 1961 and 1973, these years were used in our investigation of the rate of schizophrenia and affective disorder among rapists. We found that eight of 2,657 rapists (.3 percent) had a diagnosis of schizophrenia or schizo-affective disorder, while no affective disorder, either depression or mania, was seen in any of the defendants charged with rape. This finding is consistent with MacDonald's impression that major psychiatric illness is rare in cases of rape and with the estimate of Gebhard, Gagnon, and Pomeroy (1965) that fewer than 1 percent of rapists have psychotic illnesses. These figures suggest that insanity (used in a legal sense) plays almost no role in rape. In contrast, nearly 70 percent of the rapists in our St. Louis study suffered from personality disorders; the vast majority (half of the total sample) had antisocial personalities. Similarly, in his study of convicted rapists in Canada, McCaldon (1967) found that half of his subjects had antisocial personalities.

Although objective studies are limited, alcohol use by the rapist also apparently plays a significant role in rape. Rada (1975) reviewed the role of alcohol in seventy-seven rapists involved in a special treatment program. He found that fully 35 percent were alcoholic and had been drinking heavily at the time of the crime. An additional 15 percent had been drinking prior to commission of their crimes. Rada's finding is consistent with the finding that alcohol is one of the principal factors in criminal recidivism (Guze, 1976) and that rape has a high rate of recidivism, over 35 percent in a California study (Frisbie and Dondis, 1965).

In summary, the profile of the rapist is similar to that of a felon involved in crimes against persons or property. He is a young, poor male; probably belongs to an ethnic minority; and is likely to have used alcohol or drugs just prior to his crime. He has a history of previous criminal activity and may well merit the diagnostic label of antisocial personality, but he is unlikely to suffer from a psychotic disorder. He is distinct from other sex offenders—especially pedophiliacs, exhibitionists, and voyeurs—primarily because of his violent tendencies.

When the average rapist is compared with other offenders charged with crimes against people, some useful comparisons emerge. The work of Lynn Curtis, as reported in the staff report to the National Commission on the Causes and Prevention of Violence (1969), has shown that in statistical profile the rapist falls between the defendant for aggravated assault and the defendant for robbery. The "median" rapist falls between the "median" robber and the "median" assailant. The average robber is older and less violent, uses and abuses few chemicals, operates further from his home, and has fewer psychiatric problems than the average rapist. Conversely, the defendant charged with assault is younger and more violent, is more likely to abuse drugs and alcohol, operates closer to his home, and is more likely to have psychiatric problems than an average rapist. The rapist is less likely to know his victim than is someone involved in assault, but more likely than a robber. He also has a greater likelihood of being involved in interracial crime than someone charged with assault, but the opposite is true in cases of robbery. Rape as an act can be seen as comprising some of the same elements as assault and robbery. Assault is a crime directed solely against a person; it is a hostile, violent act aimed at causing physical damage and humiliation in the victim. Robbery is basically a crime against property; violence may be an accessory in this act, but the principal motivation is acquisition (to get something). Rape contains both of these elements, violence and physical domination, along with a desire "to have" the woman. Brownmiller (1975, p. 201) also espouses this idea when she suggests that the rapist sees his victim as "both a hated person and desired property. Hostility against her and possession of her may be simultaneous motivations. . . . In one violent crime, rape is an act against person and property."

Studies of the victim are far less complete than analyses of the offenders. However, several issues have been raised and deserve comment. These, in general, fall under the heading of *precipitants.* The general attitude toward rape varies from the feminist point of view (Brownmiller, 1975, p. 5) that rape is "a conscious process of intimidation by which *all men* keep *all women* in a state of fear" to the attitude of Wisconsin judge Archie Simonson, who, while giving a young rapist a sentence of one year at home under court supervision, suggested that the boy was only reacting "normally" to the sexually permissive environment of Madison, Wisconsin, in the spring of 1977. These divergent views suggest that attitudes toward the victims also differ widely, from total sympathy to disbelief and a feeling that "she asked for it." This disparity in viewpoint and the level of emotions involved point toward the need for objective investigations in the area. Two detailed studies of the victims of rape concluded that rape frequently (that is, in approximately half of the cases studied) occurs among acquaintances. The act of rape usually involves a victim with the same ethnic and socioeconomic background as the rapist. Single women predominate among victims, and the women in general are young. For example, MacDonald (1971) found that 65 percent of the 200 rape victims studied in Denver were twenty-four or under. On the average, the victims were younger than the offender—although 7 percent of the victims in MacDonald's study were women over fifty. The study by Amir (1971) revealed that nearly one-fifth of the victims had an arrest record and that over half of these women had been previously charged with sexual offenses. This finding led to Amir's concept of "victim-precipitated rape"—that is, cases where the offender felt that a sexual invitation was issued but later retracted. These assaults often involved women with previous "bad reputations," alcohol use by both parties, and situations where the women had been picked up in a tavern or at a party. Again, little objective evidence has been collected on the question of alcohol or drug usage by the victim. More such studies are needed. Also needed are studies that examine the rapist's awareness of his victim's past history and criminal activity, as well as studies that examine the differences between women whose complaint of rape is unfounded, according to police, and victims who have a legitimate case. . . .

References

Amir, M. *Patterns in Forcible Rape.* Chicago: University of Chicago Press, 1971.

Antilla, I. *Kriminologinen Tutkimuslaitos.* Helsinki: 1968.

Brown, B.A. "Crime against Women Alone." Memphis, TN: Memphis Police Department, 1974. (Mimeograph)

Brownmiller, S. *Against Our Will: Men, Women and Rape.* New York: Simon & Schuster, 1975.

Cleaver, E. *Soul on Ice.* New York: McGraw-Hill, 1967.

Frisbie, L.V., and Dondis, E.H. *Recidivism among Treated Sex Offenders.* Research Monograph 5. Sacramento, CA: California Department of Mental Hygiene, 1965.

Gebhard, P.H., Gagnon, J.H., and Pomeroy, W.B. *Sex Offenders: An Analysis of Types.* New York: Harper & Row, 1965.

Guze, S.B. *Criminality and Psychiatric Disorders.* New York: Oxford University Press, 1976.

Hayman, C.R. "In Contrast to Amir." *Sexual Behavior,* 1971, *1,* 33.

Henn, F.A., Herjanic, M., and Vanderpearl, R.H. "Forensic Psychiatry: Profiles of Two Types of Sex Offenders." *American Journal of Psychiatry,* 1976, *133,* 694–696.

LeVine, R.A. "Gusii Sex Offenses: A Study in Social Control." *American Anthropologist,* 1959, *61,* 965–990.

MacDonald, J.H. *Rape: Offenders and Their Victims.* Springfield, IL: Thomas, 1971.

McCaldon, R.J. "Rape." *Canadian Journal of Corrections*, 1967, *9*, 37–43.

Mohr, J.W. *Rape and Attempted Rape*. Toronto, Canada: Toronto Hospital, 1965. (Mimeograph)

Mohr. J.W., Turner, R.E., and Jerry, M.B. *Pedophilia and Exhibitionism*. Toronto, Canada: University of Toronto Press, 1964.

National Commission on the Causes and Prevention of Violence. Staff Report, *Crimes of Violence*. Washington, D.C.: U.S. Government Printing Office, 1969.

Rada, R.T. "Alcoholism and Forcible Rape." *American Journal of Psychiatry*, 1975, *132*, 444–446.

Stürup, G.K. "Treatment of Sexual Offenders in Herstedvester, Denmark." *Acta Psychiatrica Scandinavia*, 1968, 44, Supplement 204.

Svalastoga, K. "Rape and Social Structure." *Pacific Sociological Review*, 1962, *5*, 48–65.

U.S. Department of Justice. *Uniform Crime Reports*. Washington, D.C.: U.S. Government Printing Office.

24. Violence in the Children's Room

WAYNE SAGE

At the recent hearings on child abuse before the California Senate Select Committee on Children and Youth, the deputy coroner of Los
Angeles described each case of child abuse that had passed through
the coroner's office during the past three years.

There were the children—a two-year-old baby strangled to death
by her mother who forced black pepper down the girl's throat and
into her windpipe: an eleven-year-old girl starved to a weight of thir-
ty-one pounds, deformed and retarded since age five from beatings
by her parents; other children less than three years old beaten,
burned, and suffocated.

And there were the parents—a fifteen-year-old girl who so feared
her parents would learn she had a baby that she threw the infant into
a trash can, and then, horrified by what she had done, retrieved it
and ran with it to the hospital, arriving too late to save it; a thirteen-
year-old girl who told the police she had the baby and then, to keep
her parents from finding out, wrapped the child in a pair of pajamas
and threw it out the window.

The deputy coroner described the parents involved as "not a very
truthful group of human beings," and their problems as "not something that any physician with any experience would be able to treat."

Asked chairperson Mervyn Dymally, if these parents had had social
services and aid programs available to help them, could the deaths of
their children have been prevented?

Responded the deputy coroner: "I don't believe the individuals involved have sufficient humanity at the present time—I could be mis-
taken—to deal with remorse. They would either use the facilities to
cop out or they would not show up."

Although the cases described were intended to represent only a
deviant minority of all child abusers, such has been the view of all
child abuse in the past—that it is a rare atrocity committed by a
handful of lower-class, psychopathic, sociopathic individuals beyond
help. Now, at last, society seems ready to face the fact that it is neither so uncommon, so limited to aberrant social situations, nor so
hopeless as was believed.

The current wave of interest in child abuse dates back to the 1950s,

311

when it was "discovered" by the press. The media dredged up stories of small children locked in closets for years, dunked alive in boiling water, raked against radiators, and otherwise maimed and tortured in ways more horrifying than anyone would have believed. For all their sensationalism, such accounts at least forced the public to accept the fact that child abuse has become a common and concrete nightmare of our supposedly enlightened age. Most experts admit they cannot explain it, but most agree that the problem is deeply rooted on both the personal and social levels and has become increasingly difficult to ignore.

"Child abuse is about as close to apple pie and motherhood as you can get," says UCLA psychiatrist Morris Paulson. "It's a symptom of the breakdown of the family, and this is why so many [people] are getting very concerned. My own personal bias is that the whole tension system within our culture is making child abuse happen more often. The whole country is much more mobile in identifying their needs. With the breakdown of the family unit, lack of communication between mothers and dads, absence of responsibility toward making the marriage work—that sort of cavalier attitude does not preserve a healthy environment and makes for more child abuse."

The number of reported cases of child abuse has indeed risen astronomically over the past decade. Whether it has always been with us in such high numbers or whether we have just become better at discovering it, no one knows. In 1962, the American Humane Association began following up the newspaper accounts in local communities around the country. Over a period of nine months, they learned of 662 such incidents. In search of those that had not made the headlines, pediatrician C. Henry Kempe, along with colleagues at the University of Colorado School of Medicine, surveyed 71 hospitals across the nation. Every institution contacted reported back such cases. As mandatory reporting laws began to come into force during the 1960s, requiring physicians to report such incidents to police and social agencies, more of the child-abuse iceberg began to surface.

In 1967 and 1968, the U.S. Children's Bureau enlisted the aid of Brandeis University professor of social work David Gil in an effort to study all incidents of child abuse reported through legal channels. Gil reported back a total of 13,000 cases. According to Paulson, the best current estimate based on reported cases is around 60,000 a year. But even as the numbers have continued to rise, many, probably most, cases go unreported. According to the testimony of one former child abuser before the U.S. Senate: "I identified myself ten times [to various social agencies], and I am not on the statistics. I can't understand what the criteria are for listing a case of child abuse."

Usually, the criterion for a reported case is that the child be injured so badly that he or she shows up in the emergency room of a hospital. But even there, battering parents are notoriously difficult to recognize, and even when the medical evidence is strong, physicians are reluctant to believe that parents would inflict such injuries on their children and they shy away from the legal entanglements of such an accusation. Comments Margo Fritz, director of training at Parents Anonymous (PA), a national self-help organization of parents with child-abuse problems:

> The statistics they use are based on reportable instances of inflicted trauma. That is such a miniscule fraction of the amount of abuse that actually occurs that it's almost laughable. There's all kinds of inflicted trauma going on or abuse that doesn't require medical treatment and doesn't turn up as a statistic, but it's abuse nonetheless. And we have those parents in our chapters.
>
> Most people are conditioned to think of abuse in the terms in which the media have presented it for years—burned babies, critically abused children whose life hangs by a thread, malnourished infants—that's the reportable statistic again and that is just a fragment. There is a whole range of abuse that has never been dealt with that the public doesn't even acknowledge as being part of the problem at this point. When a parent is hitting a child and is out of control of himself, when he is dumping his own rage on his child even if that child does not require treatment for inflicted trauma, that child has been abused and that parent is abusing. You let that go on long enough and the child will require treatment for inflicted trauma.

But even ignoring the number of cases that go unseen or unrecognized by medical personnel, even by conservative estimates, more children under the age of five die at the hands of their own parents than are killed by tuberculosis, whooping cough, polio, measles, diabetes, rheumatic fever and hepatitis combined.

There have always been abused children. In earlier centuries, they were crippled and mutilated to make them more pathetic and, therefore, more profitable beggars. Until the 1800s, dead or abandoned infants were almost commonplace on city streets. As late as 1892, 200 foundlings and 100 dead infants were found on the streets of New York City alone.

Until very recently, children have had little legal protection of any sort. The first child-battering case ever brought to the courts in this country was tried under regulations prohibiting cruelty to animals. The New York Society for the Prevention of Cruelty to Animals argued that a child named Mary Ellen, starved and kept in chains, was "a human animal" and therefore could not be so treated. There were no laws to prohibit mistreating children. The situation had changed little until 1963 when New York passed the first law requiring physicians to report cases of child abuse to police and social agencies while providing doctors immunity from lawsuits for making such reports. Today, all fifty states have such laws, in varying forms. The result has been the criminalization of child abuse and, in some cases, the battering by the legal system of abusive parents, who actually need even more help than do their children.

Understandably, until very recently, parents with abuse problems have been afraid to identify themselves, principally because any such parent who asked society for a helping hand got the long arm of the law. "Four years ago, before Parents Anonymous was started, you couldn't walk into a clinic or call a therapist and say, 'I have an abuse problem; I want help,' because what you anticipated was that you were going to have your kids taken away from you, and you probably would," says Fritz. Much of the difficulty in getting such parents to seek help has been the failure of those in authority to realize that even the most abusive parents often need and sometimes deeply love their children. "The parents in most cases don't like what they're doing," notes psychiatrist James Kent of Children's Hospital in Los Angeles, who has seen hundreds of abusive parents. "They are horribly ashamed and humiliated by what they are doing. It's very difficult for them to sort out some of their feelings as to why the abuse occurred. Most are chronic losers and the child abuse is just the latest instance of their losing."

Jolly K, the founder of Parents Anonymous, remarks on her own experience with social agencies that seemed able to offer her only two alternatives—placement of her child in a foster home or adoption, saying, "I wanted to keep my child. I wanted to get rid of my problem."

If the media have shown us the gruesome reality we did not want to see, they have also fomented a hysteria that has made the problem even more difficult to deal with. "Dead babies sell newspapers, and that's where they're coming from, man," comments Fritz of Parents Anonymous. "They [the media] are so hell bent on exploiting [us] to the extent that they can, the anxiety level around the problem of abuse is so damned high that most people can't deal with it at all. And if they do they get so upset that they just can't think rationally. We need to get out of that dead-baby bag so that people can deal with the problem in a rational way instead of with this intense anxiety-fear reaction."

Apparently in agreement, professionals are searching for the reasons that child abuse occurs and the ways to stop it.

In the accounts of the Los Angeles deputy coroner, the parents were described as evil people beyond redemption. Yet in the view of psychologist Patricia Keith-Spiegel of California State University at Northridge, such cases only underline the fact that child abuse is a tragedy for the parent as well. In the majority of the cases she described, the attacker was a woman. Often she was young, unmarried and acting alone to destroy her child during the first weeks of life, as though trying to carry out a belated abortion.

Keith-Spiegel believes the oppression of women and the mistreatment of children are intimately linked. She points to psychoanalytic reports of child abusers that have documented cases in which women attacked their children apparently because of their hatred of men. The women felt caged, according to the researchers. The jailers, their husbands, were unassailable, Their cagemates, their children, became the scapegoats. "Perhaps, for at least some frustrated and unhappy women, the only males in the environment who are less powerful than they are, and who can serve as close enough substitutes upon which to unleash impulses, are their own sons," says Keith-Spiegel.

Women's rage may be a factor in child abuse, but the roots of the problem run much deeper, on both the personal and social levels, and no single explanation is in sight. Women who react in the opposite way may find themselves in abusive situations as well. Says Dr. Kent: "You sometimes see the passive, masochistic woman very much needing support from the outside, who's willing to tolerate a boyfriend mistreating her children because she needs that person, that support. The guy drops in and the kid's up and around and crying too much and gets beaten up for it." Fathers abuse children as often as do mothers, and girls are assaulted as often as are boys, the data show. Probably, the reasons why and the specific dynamics in any two cases are never the same.

Reported cases of child abuse tend to concentrate in the lower socioeconomic levels of society, where the weight of poverty, ignorance, powerlessness and most other social ills are felt most strongly. Yet child abuse occurs in all echelons of society, and the bias toward the poor may be largely due to the rich being better able to hide such acts from suspicious social workers and hospital personnel. "I know in the years when my kids were small that at my peer level comfortably middle-class, well-educated, professional people were abusing their kids," says Fritz, "and I mean not just emotional and verbal abuse. I mean physical abuse. But the middle-class population for the most part does not end up as a reported statistic. But the more you open up this whole can of worms, the more aware and sensitive you can make people to the problem."

"We see those cases [middle-class abuse]," agrees Dr. Kent of Children's Hospital in Los Angeles. "They are handled differently because the parents have the means of avoiding and evading judicial review of the case. I think it probably happens less often, more often than is reported, but it happens less often [in the middle class] primarily because I think one of the major determinants is socioeconomic distress. When they live in impoverished, degrading living conditions, situations where people are isolated from neighbors with no means of escaping from the home and no respite care, no money for a baby sitter, those things increase the likelihood of abuse."

For the lower class, what Kent calls our "crazy system" for child welfare plays its role in abuse. The state of California, for example, is willing to pay $240 a month to keep a child under foster care. An adequate system of day-care centers would be much cheaper and would go a long way in relieving the strain on such parents. If the child is returned to the mother, she gets an increased allotment of $25 to take care of her own child.

Child-support payments for nonworking mothers, predicated on the vicious assumption that women are predisposed to have children to increase the size of their welfare checks, operates on a schedule of decreasing payments for each additional child. Thus the increased allotment for the last child may be only $20 or $25 a month. Not surprisingly, the last-born child is the most likely one to show up in hospital emergency rooms suffering from severe neglect. "Usually there is a better defined psychopathology for the upper class," Kent notes. "In the lower class, you usually see a parent who has just been worn down."

For what is probably a small minority of child abusers, psychologist Logan Wright of the University of Oklahoma seems to have documented the "sick but slick theory," which holds that child abusers sometimes are deeply disturbed but extremely adept at masking their pathology. Wright matched thirteen parents convicted of battering their children with thirteen nonbattering parents of similar age, sex, race, number of children, and marital and educational status and income. Both groups were subjected to a battery of psychological tests. On those tests (such as the *Rorschach*) where the subject is able to judge the social desirability of his response, the battering parents were actually able to appear significantly healthier than the control group. They seemed highly conforming and "very middle class," Logan reports. Yet on tests (such as the *MMPI*) where the socially desirable response is ambiguous, the batterers showed a near-classic profile for psychopathic deviance. "When they had a chance, they could fake it and look even healthier than the nonbattering parents. Where they couldn't fake their way through, their psychopathic deviances came out," says Logan. He warns colleagues "not to be lulled or conned into underestimating the potential of certain reasonable-appearing adults for disturbance and violence."

The ability of child abusers to escape detection has been documented by many professionals, and their ability to hide their deeds has led to the beguiling of medical personnel and sometimes the death of their children. A two-year-old boy died under surgery at a Los Angeles hospital following an all-out assault by his mother. At the time of his death, his broken left arm was still in a cast put there ten days earlier by the same staff. The medical records showed a series of such injuries beginning soon after his birth and increasing in severity until the time of his death.

Often the problem is not so much the physician's inability to discern what is happening as his reluctance to believe it. A string of articles in professional journals has sketched the warning signs of the "battered child syndrome" and exhorted doctors in particular to be on the lookout. Burns, broken bones, bruises, and slashes often simply could not have occurred as parents explain them. For children who are not yet walking, for example, the claim that a child caught his leg in the slats of the crib and broke it would be suspect. A baby's body does not generate enough torque while turning to break its own bones. Scald marks caused by a hot liquid accidentally splashed onto the child are not symmetrical, as are those that result when the fluid is poured directly and intentionally onto the child's skin. Bruises in the shape of a hand or belt buckle are obvious giveaways. Especially condemning are radiological examinations. "To the informed physician, the bones tell a story the child is too young and too frightened to tell," says Colorado pediatrician C. Henry Kempe. Even when the major injuries are confined to the skull, spine, or ribs, the "handles" for such assaults—the child's arms and legs—bear signs of separations and shearings in the surface of the bones that occur as the tiny body is grasped, swung, and twisted. Skeletal injuries and the way they heal can provide almost conclusive evidence that the traumas were inflicted. Yet, says Kempe, "many physicians find it hard to believe that such an attack could have occurred and they attempt to obliterate such suspicions from their minds, even in the face of obvious circumstantial evidence."

Even when the doctors accept the fact of the assault, they may be reluctant to acknowledge or report it. The child is often under three years old and, therefore, cannot take the stand to testify. As one Cincinnati doctor tells his staff, "If you're going to accuse someone of child abuse, you'd better have seen it happen and even then I hope you've got witnesses." Typically, there are no witnesses, and the number of such cases that are successfully prosecuted is minuscule. "Law is not the answer," insists Catherine Bone of the Children's Division of the American Humane Association. "We've had laws on the books for many years. We see the answer as building better families in the first place. And this is the responsibility of society as a whole.

Building more responsible people and offering more services when they realize that they have a problem."

Clinical observations of battering parents show remarkably consistent characteristics. They are generally emotionally immature, poorly prepared for parenthood, and unrealistic in their expectations, the experts report. For example, a Los Angeles physician currently has under his care a six-month-old infant who weighs eight pounds. The child's father refuses to give the boy milk. He spoons out food from the table, smashes it up with his hand and stuffs it into the child's mouth. He refuses to accept free milk for the child, insisting that the child should be able to eat what he eats.

Such mothers and fathers seem to see their child as existing to fulfill the parent's own emotional needs and expect them to provide the unconditional love the parents need. When the child proves helpless and demanding, too, they feel inadequate and rejected. Rage is the result. "I have never felt really loved all my life," confessed one young woman. "When the baby was born, I thought he would love me; but when he cried all the time, it meant he didn't love me, so I hit him." At age three weeks, her son was hospitalized for the damage his mother's blows had done to his skull and spine.

The most consistent of all such characteristics is that abusive parents almost invariably were themselves abused as children. Comments Fritz:

> You can make a case for the fact that abusers have themselves been abused, but what about that possible population of people who were abused but do not become abusers? Also, how I experience something is not necessarily how you experience the same thing. I may have felt abused as a child whereas you under similar conditions did not. What accounts for the difference in our perceptions of how we were raised? And is it what actually happened or is it the individual's perception of what happened? If your family structure was such that when Daddy came home from work, Mommy reported whatever you had done and then Daddy gave you the belt, and yet you grew up feeling good about yourself, good about your parents, and comfortable in your parenting relationship with your child, how do you explain you who experienced that and some other kid who felt abused in that same kind of situation? There is so damned much we don't know.

Nonetheless, the theory that violence against children begets violent adults is the mainspring on which some theorists hang the syndrome. According to Gil of Brandeis University, it is the fact that we allow children to be beaten at all that makes abuse possible. The weaknesses and problems of parents as well as the contributing irritants of poverty and ignorance find violent expression in such acts because our culture tolerates the physical punishment of children with no well-defined limits, Gil believes. When pressures on the parents increase, the beating of their children is available to them as an outlet and grows worse as their frustration mounts.

Toward eliminating tolerance or such punishment, campaigns are being waged to end all institutional corporal punishment. (Corporal punishment is still allowed in schools in forty-seven of the fifty states.) The movement is being led by End Violence Against the Next Generation (EVAN-G), half of whom are psychologists. Many of the others in its ranks are "people still mad about the way they were treated in school," according to EVAN-G director Adah Maurer. "The belief that hitting children is the way to raise them is pervasive in our culture," says Maurer. "Eliminate it in the public sector and this would be a way to turn down the fire."

Such thinking draws heavily on social learning theories of aggression, which hold that children learn aggression by witnessing adults use aggression, in this case on children. "People look to authority," says Maurer. "A person who doesn't get too far through school and has been spanked and slapped there may not have learned how to read very well, but he definitely has learned how to handle children. Later, when his own kid cries too much or messes his pants, he has no skills. The stresses mount. These become the battering parents who commit infanticide or brain-damage their kids. Get corporal punishment out of the schools, and people would temper their own violence."

If cultural acceptance of childrearing practices that include physical punishment is to blame, however, its elimination hardly can be expected to end child abuse in all its forms. As long as there are frustrated, troubled parents there will be abused children. Comments psychiatrist James Kent:

> Even if there were strong cultural prohibitions against physically aggressing against children, I don't think that it would diminish the other kinds of abuse that are significant. Psychological abuse would be one. One of the things that tends to happen when you first convince the parents to stop hitting the child is that the level of criticism escalates. What they seem to want to see is acknowledgment from the child that he did wrong, that he hurt the parent. If you spank him and he cries, that's one type of acknowledgment. He's sorry. He's crying. The business is finished. When that's blocked, what seems to happen with some of the parents is that they then displace it to a kind of belittling, critical, nagging, destructive kind of psychological abuse that doesn't get back that kind of response. So it continues indefinitely. This may be more difficult for the youngster to cope with in the long run than bruises and bones that are broken. They may heal. The effects of the verbal abuse, which is just as destructive, won't.

Other types of abuse that are absolutely taboo in our culture apparently are even more common than is child battering. The number of reported cases of sexual molestation of children is more than double that for those who are physically assaulted. Contrary to the stereo-type of the child molester as a pervert lurking in the bushes at the schoolyard, the problem is primarily a matter of incest. The most typical situation is that of a natural father (not a foster parent or step-father) sexually abusing his children with the mother's complicity. It seems to be common in middle- and upper-income families as well as among the poor.

Interestingly, mothers whose children are sexually abused run a rate of having been molested themselves that is three times greater than the rate for those of neglected or battered children. "I've seen it encouraged explicitly and justified by a mother who said, 'I wanted my daughter to learn about sex right—with my husband under con-trolled, supervised circumstances,' " says Dr. Kent. "It happens more covertly where the mother has been told or the daughter hints at it, but still the mother manages to leave her alone with the father or boyfriend time after time."

With both parents conspiring, when does it ever end? "Usually when the youngster blows the whistle in a way that nobody can deny," says Kent. Therefore, even at a rate of 50,000 to 100,000 such reported cases a year, the data probably represent a small fraction of the number of children being sexually abused. In one recent study, parents of such children often described their daughters as "difficult to discipline." Perhaps the kids who show up in the reported cases are simply those more likely to rebel against the way they are being treated. How many thousands are too frightened or passive to tell outsiders what is happening no one knows.

Even the legal system and the psychiatric establishment acting in concert have often proved ineffective. A former officer in the Los An-geles Police Department's Child Abuse Unit makes this observation. "I handled many, many cases where the mothers were undergoing psychiatric attention or counseling. They would disappear within a month and be gone. When we placed the children in protective cus-tody in foster homes, the mothers would often go to the foster home, take the children from there and disappear in the night."

Far more noteworthy than the efforts of professionals to under-stand child abusers has been the parents' ability to understand and help themselves. Four years ago, Jolly K, Parents Anonymous founder, sought help from ten different social agencies for her abuse problem, could not find it, and refused "to be pushed into one of the convenient psychological cubbyholes that people wanted to put her in," in the words of one of her friends. She banged her fist on a social worker's desk and exclaimed, "If something happens to my child, you're as responsible as I am."

Along with a young psychiatric social worker who heard of the incident, Jolly K founded Parents Anonymous, which since that time has grown to include more than 4,000 parents who have been involved in such chapters across the country. The members are mothers and fathers with abuse problems. Using a sort of self-help combination of behavioral and reality therapy, they first concentrate on stopping the abuse. A new member is told how to handle mounting rage by going into a room alone and then screaming, pounding the wall, kicking the furniture or otherwise getting out the aggressive impulses without hurting the children. Members then share their difficulties and work through them at the regular meetings. They also maintain a network of telephone numbers so they can call one another for help and support when a crisis moment is developing.

Says Fritz:

> I think if parents have not sought help, it's because help has not been available to them in a form that they could accept. They are terribly threatened by having to sit down and fill out forms and be evaluated. This is one of the great attractions of PA. They don't fill out any forms. Nobody is going to ask them any questions. They are simply told that a chapter meets at such and such a place on such and such a night, please come. When they get there, they recognize that everybody in that room shares the same problem. That doesn't mean that everybody in that room is the same by any manner or means. Child abuse is a multifaceted problem. And the specific dynamics of it are not going to be the same for any two people and the reasons why are not going to be the same for any two people.

Now that the media have made child abuse a hot topic, professionals and social agencies are beginning to develop programs as well, most of which are aimed not at taking the child from his parents but at aiding the troubled family, to strengthen it against the ravages of the modern age.

Jolly K, in an effort to gain federal support for abuse-prevention programs, testified before the Senate:

> By ignoring the problem, by not getting these funds in, in effect it [society] is telling me, "Make your case a top priority. Kill your kids or come close to it. Then we will pay attention. Unless you do something drastic and dramatic we don't care. We don't want to hear about you. We will keep you under the rug until you have made so much blood and gore we can no longer ignore you in society. Then we will spend money on you. We will spend thousands of dollars to keep you in jail. We will spend thousands of dollars to keep your kid in a foster home. When your kid starts acting out we will spend thousands of dollars on him in juvenile hall." It is cheaper to rehabilitate our family as a family so we can raise healthy children by direct example of healthy parents.

With the passage of the Mondale Bill (The Child Abuse Prevention Act), such funds have begun to flow, and state governments and private foundations have joined in as well. Research underway under the auspices of the National Institute of Mental Health; the Office of Child Development of the Department of Health, Education and Welfare; and the American Humane Association is exploring virtually every aspect of the problem. Among the most noteworthy programs developed by professionals is Parent Effectiveness Training Associates in Pasadena, California, which concentrates on developing good communication between parents and their children, on the theory that abuse often occurs because parents do not understand or know how to react to their children's expressions of need and affection. Other programs are attempting to teach ghetto mothers to spare the rod by using behavior mod. The assumption here is that if you are going to take physical punishment from parents with disciplinary problem children, you have to give them alternatives. Parents are trained in operant conditioning techniques that rely heavily on positive rewards. The idea is to catch the child being good, provide a reward, and then continue or withdraw the rewards as they are responded to. Hotlines, such as Los Angeles' Child Abuse Listening Line (CALL) are available twenty-four hours to parents who need counseling.

As evidenced by data collected by Dr. Kent, abused children often are described by their parents as "difficult to discipline," "irritable," and "active." Those suffering severe neglect often are described by their parents as having a poor appetite. Thus the problem may often result from the parents' inability to deal with a hyperactive or otherwise difficult child. Parent surrogate programs and other educational services offer training in child rearing as an aid to abuse problems.

Perhaps most comprehensive of all such programs is one underway at Johns Hopkins University that is attempting to prevent the abuse from developing in the first place. Under the direction of obstetrician-gynecologist David Youngs, a group of high-risk mothers—black, low-socioeconomic class, adolescent—were sought out while pregnant. The women are counseled and may choose to have abortions. Those who elect to have their child are given education in child rearing, nutrition, the use of drugs and are assisted in planning their futures and learning to use community services that are available to them when needed.

Such programs may bring help to many mothers who need it. But the growing awareness of the reality of child abuse in our society is also bringing fundamental changes in our thinking about children and their care. One of the most important of these is the idea that children have rights. Certainly no adult could be assaulted, cussed, or slandered as children commonly are without legal protection, and only parents and perhaps prison guards and drill sergeants have the control over another human being that would permit the sort of psychological abuse parents can inflict on their kids. "We as a society have never really looked closely at that idea [children's rights]" says psychologist Kerby T. Alvy of the Center for the Improvement of Child Caring in Venice, California. "That they are human beings with rights and not chattels or property to be used the way owners of property want to act. Children are children of humanity and not just children of their parents."

Such notions would logically realize themselves in an increasingly heavy public hand to help rock the cradle. "The notion of not taking public responsibility for the upbringing of kids pays off negatively in the long run," says Alvy. "If a kid is physically abused, he ends up striking back at the institutions of authority for our society. The fact that he develops this way results mainly from the way he is treated in the home, but the whole society pays for it."

Indeed, that seems to be the case, and the reality is dawning that child abuse is not just a personal problem of a minority of sick or ill-fated adults, but a social tragedy none of us can ignore. Policewoman Jackie Howells of the Los Angeles Police Department's Child Abuse Unit went back eighteen years to follow the fates of kids then rescued by police from abusive parents. Generally, she had to look no further than the criminal identification files in Sacramento. Over half the children whom the police had first seen when they rescued them from abusive parents later appeared in the criminal records on juveniles and even more showed up there years afterwards as adults. Since the primary mode of dealing with the problem by the courts had been to place the children in foster homes, Howell's search could well show the ultimate risk of prolonged foster care.

Seen in this light, the issue of child abuse broadens. In a social sense, any child who grows up in poverty, a string of foster homes that thwart basic emotional needs, is denied opportunities because of racial oppression or is otherwise mistreated by adults either individually or collectively is being abused, and we will all pay for ignoring such acts.

25. Auto Theft:
Offender and Offense Characteristics

CHARLES H. McCAGHY
PEGGY C. GIORDANO
TRUDY KNICELY HENSON

Sociological literature has generally downplayed auto thievery except for joyriding and occasional references to professional theft. An
investigator claimed that persons often steal cars for very practical
reasons: for example, youngsters caught in a rainstorm in a business
area take a car rather than wait for a bus; or an individual steals a car,
repaints it, and intends to keep it for several months. Neither of these
cases fits into the joyrider or profit-motivated offense categories; yet,
they deserve consideration since they may represent a substantial
proportion of the motivations behind auto theft.

DATA SOURCES

Data for this study were collected from three sources. The first involved the auto theft investigation unit and the juvenile bureau of
the Toledo, Ohio, police force. Between October 1, 1975, and May
31, 1976, officers in these units filled out a special form for the researchers each time an individual was apprehended for stealing a motor vehicle. This form contained questions concerning demographic
information about the subject, previous arrest record, description of
the auto, and circumstances surrounding the offense, including apparent reason for taking the car(s). A total of 103 of these cases were
obtained by these means.

The second source of data was the file of stolen automobile reports
located in the auto theft investigation unit of the Toledo Police Department. By a systematic random sampling process, 231 cases of recovered autos were selected from the period of January 1, 1975, to
April 30, 1976. This second source of data provides a more comprehensive perspective on the nature of auto theft since it represents
cases of all cars reported stolen and recovered, regardless of whether
an arrest was made. The following were obtained from these records:

address from which the car was stolen, address of recovery point, type of car, and condition of recovered car.

The third source was data collected for earlier study by Charles W. Thomas.[1] This involved a sample of 14,815 juveniles who had come before juvenile court in a Virginia SMSA (Norfolk, Chesapeake, Portsmouth, and Virginia Beach) between January 1, 1966, and July 31, 1973. This source was used because it allowed a comparison of auto thieves' demographic characteristics with those of juveniles apprehended for offenses other than auto theft. A similar control sample was impossible to obtain from the Toledo data.

RACE, SOCIAL CLASS, AND AUTO THEFT

The Toledo data on apprehended car thieves produce no major surprises regarding race of offenders: 55.9 percent were white and 42.2 percent were black with a few "other." As in the national statistics from the *Uniform Crime Reports*, arrested auto thieves are generally white. However, blacks are disproportionately represented since only 13.8 percent of the total Toledo population is black. Among offenders under eighteen years of age, the pattern is similar: 60.0 percent white and 36.7 percent black.

While race statistics are consistent with the favored-group hypothesis, the census tracts of residences of these auto thieves provide contradictory evidence. . . . 66.7 percent of all thieves and 67.8 percent of juveniles reside in tracts with a median income under $10,000 (the median income of Toledo is $10,500). In short, the Wattenberg-Balistrieri [1952] claim that adolescent car thieves primarily come from better neighborhoods does not hold true for Toledo.

When controlling for the race of juvenile offenders, we find that of those residing in the lower-income tracts, blacks comprise 36.2 percent and whites comprise 27.6 percent of all juveniles arrested. Those of the favored group—whites from the upper-income tracts—comprise only another 27.6 percent. Yet of *all* Toledo residents, 44.0 percent are whites residing in these upper-income tracts. Thus, in this city, favored-group juveniles did *not* contribute disproportionately to arrests for auto theft.

It appears, then, that the Toledo police appraisal of the situation was partially correct; lower classes evidently account for more theft than the sociological literature leads us to believe. But what of the police estimate that *blacks* account for *most* theft? It is obviously difficult to test the validity of this claim directly since it would require obtaining information of offenders not arrested. But there is an indirect way of estimating offenders' characteristics.

The assumption can be made that unless the thief disposes of the car through resale, chances are strong that he will abandon it close to his own residence. This would seem particularly true for young joy-riders who presumably lack other cars for returning home. To test the assumption, the sample of arrested offenders was examined. We wished to determine the extent to which blacks abandon stolen cars in areas with an above average percentage of blacks, and whites in predominantly white areas. We found that in 61.0 percent of the cases, cars taken by black offenders were recovered in tracts with 25.0 percent or more black population. By contrast, 9.6 percent of the white offenders had abandoned their cars in the same areas. Therefore, we assumed that the majority of cars recovered in these areas were stolen by blacks.

Examining the sample of stolen-car reports, we find [that] . . . of all cars recovered, 43 percent are found in tracts that are 25 percent and above black compared with 36.7 percent in tracts of less than 25 percent. Allowing for the 20.4 percent of cars found outside of town, it appears that investigators searching for cars within the city limits have better than an even chance of locating them in areas with high-er densities of blacks. Since, as indicated above, blacks often leave stolen cars in solid white areas as well as black areas, while whites rarely abandon cars in above average black areas, the distribution . . . suggests that arrest statistics may be underestimating blacks' partici-pation in the offense.

The data from the Virginia study also tend to undermine the fa-vored-group hypothesis. Of the 1,239 juveniles ever charged with an auto-theft offense, 46.2 percent were black and 53.7 percent were white; but of the 13,184 youths charged with any other offenses ex-cept auto theft, 48.6 percent were black and 51.3 percent were white. In short, auto theft by juveniles does not appear to be uniquely white-dominated in Virginia either.

The Toledo study relied on census tract characteristics (median in-come) for ascertaining the social class of sample members—a practice not without its limitations. The Virginia data contain information on fathers' occupations both for juveniles charged with an auto theft and for those with any other offense. However, caution must be taken when interpreting [these data]: no report on fathers' occupation was found for 47.9 percent of the auto thieves and 62.3 percent of the controls. The importance of these missing data is of course unknown.

The similarities of fathers' occupations between auto thieves and controls are striking. For example, among auto thieves, 21.5 percent were professional-managerial, compared with 20.1 percent among controls. When controlling for race, again juvenile auto thieves ap-pear to be in no way exceptional when compared with other juve-niles reaching court.

It is apparent from both the Toledo and Virginia data that a sizable proportion of cars are stolen by juveniles who can be described as a favored group. They are white, they come from "better" neighborhoods and families of higher occupational status. But it is also apparent that this group does not account for the majority of juvenile auto thieves. In the Toledo data, white juveniles from two upper-median income tracts account for 27.6 percent of all juvenile auto thieves. In the Virginia data, white juveniles whose fathers were white collar and professional-managerial account for 35.6 percent of all auto thieves. But white juveniles from the same occupational background also account for 34.9 percent of non-auto theft offenders reaching court. These data suggest that juvenile auto theft should not be conceived as a favored-group delinquency.

TOWARD A TYPOLOGY OF AUTO THEFT

The criminological literature on auto thieves has concentrated almost exclusively on juvenile joyriders. While some authors have made passing reference to the existence of several types of auto thieves (Gibbens, 1958; Gibbons, 1977; Glaser, 1975), the general implicit impression in the literature is that car thieves can be simply dichotomized into the white middle-class, nonpredatory "joyrider" and the predatory "professional" of uncertain characteristics (cf. Hall, 1952; Clinard and Quinney, 1973).

Law enforcement officials, on the other hand, claim that car thieves are a more complex lot if only because of the multitude of reasons why cars are stolen. Drawing upon the impressions of Toledo auto-theft squad members and of other law-enforcement personnel, we suggest the following tentative typology of auto theft.[2]

Joyriding

Writers have assigned a wide variety of motivations to joyriding. They include: simply "to have a good time" (Schepses, 1961), "general problems of adolescence" including "striving for status and recognition" (Short and Strodtbeck, 1965), "to prove his masculinity" (Gibbens, 1958), and oral deprivation (Noshpitz, 1975). The automobile's symbolism to Americans certainly cannot be overlooked as contributing to auto theft. For many individuals wishing emphatically to tell friends and the public what kind of persons they are, no means is as effective as the cars they drive. The car frequently embodies and projects for its occupant degrees of status, power, aggressiveness, and sex as no other bit of property can. The very acts of obtaining a driver's license and buying one's first car are rites of passage into adulthood in a society where such rites are scarce indeed (Bloch and Niederhoffer, 1958).

Whatever the specific motivations—entertainment, power, recognition, sex—of the individuals involved, the term joyriding in this typology denotes essentially recreational, nonutilitarian, short-term use of cars. This is not to say that the car may not be of real practical value to the individual in terms of bolstering self-esteem or status. But it can be considered nonutilitarian to the extent that the thief's goal is not strictly limited to obtaining a mode of transportation or a means of obtaining funds. The automobile symbolism is predominant: the car is stolen not for what it does, but for what it means.

Short-term Transportation

Like joyriding, this type of theft involves only short-term use of the car. But it is used primarily as a means of transportation directly from one location to another. There is no information in the literature concerning this type, but our informants claim it constitutes a large proportion of car theft by juveniles, perhaps equaling that of joyriding.

Generally, short-term transportation theft involves going from one place in the city to another. In other, more serious cases, the thief may drive to another city or state and steal yet another car to continue his journey; he often leaves a trail of incidents in which he purchases gasoline and leaves the station without paying.

It is tempting to speculate that some proportion of these types undergo a process of closure similar to that which Lemert (1953) describes concerning naive check forgers. The check forger defines himself as being in an urgent situation and with limited alternatives. In this context, the passing of a forged check is seen as a simple solution. Similarly, an individual might experience situational pressures in which rapid geographical mobility is seen as necessary: e.g., an intolerable family situation. Due to a perceived lack of alternatives, he decides that stealing a car provides the simplest means of escape.

Long-term Transportation

In these instances, as the label suggests, the thieves intend to retain the cars for personal use. Auto-theft investigators state that many times these thieves would be from outside the city, since keeping the car in Detroit, Toledo suburbs, or other areas outside Toledo would minimize chances of detection. To further minimize risk, the cars frequently are repainted by the new possessors. The only characteristics which can be conjectured for these types are that they are from the lower socioeconomic levels and are adults—inquisitive parents would likely deter most juveniles from possessing an unexplained car.

Profit

By necessity, this type includes a wide variety of individuals of differing sophistication who steal cars for the purpose of reselling the parts or the cars as a whole. At one extreme are the highly organized professionals who resell expensive cars domestically or overseas with altered vehicle identification numbers and falsified registration papers, or who cut up cars into parts for resale. They concentrate particularly on the hood, fenders, bumpers, and grills; chassis, engines, and transmissions are usually destroyed since they are too readily identifiable (Hellman, 1971; Smith, 1975). At the other extreme are the "amateur" strippers who primarily steal the batteries, tires, wheel covers, generators and whatever else is readily taken. In some cases, these amateurs may reequip their own cars with some parts. The theft by either professionals or amateurs is based on the automobile as a valuable piece of property, not as a symbol or a form of transportation. Consequently, one would anticipate individuals of this type to be similar in characteristics to property offenders generally.

Commission of Another Crime

Examples here are cases in which cars are stolen especially for use in robberies, burglaries, other larcenies, as well as rapes and other abductions. Although undoubtedly representing only a small proportion of all car theft, this is another offense type in which the motivation is utilitarian. Mobility and anonymity are often critical to successful crime, and the stolen automobile is perfect for those purposes. The characteristics of the offenders probably are not unique from characteristics of offenders associated with the primary crimes.

To acquire some empirical data on these various types, the researchers' form completed by Toledo police contained a check list of apparent reasons for the theft. . . . Obviously, the findings must be approached with caution because the motive imputed by police to offenders may be in error in instances.

As anticipated, joyriders have the lowest mean age, steal relatively early model cars because they lack anti-theft devices, rely heavily on opportunities provided by careless car owners who leave keys or the ignition unlocked, and many have companions during the theft.

Short-term transportation theft displays many characteristics similar to joyriders except offenders are somewhat older, less likely to damage or steal from the car, and fewer have companions. These attributes are consistent with the notion that short-termers are interested in taking a car primarily for transportation.

One interesting contrast between joyriders and short-termers concerns the tract of residence. As is the case for all types, the majority live in the two lowest median income tracts. However, short-termers are more likely to be from "better" neighborhoods than are joyriders. The evidence is too shaky to claim that the favored-group delinquents are short-termers rather than joyriders, but it does suggest that middle-class car thieves may be more utilitarian than sociologists suspect.

The long-term transportation type is older than either joyriders or short-termers and, as expected, has the largest proportion of offenders from out of town. Some of the offense characteristics are particularly interesting for this type. The car is rarely damaged; in four instances the owner received the car in better condition than when it was stolen. Also, this type displays more technical sophistication than joyriders or short-termers: about one-third started the cars without benefit of keys left in the cars or the ignitions being left unlocked, as compared to 18.2 percent for the joyriders and 18.8 percent for the short-termers.

Only six subjects were classified by police as profit motivated, but the data are consistent with expectations. The offenders are the oldest of all types and come primarily from low-income tracts. This type concentrates on newer cars, as indicated by the cars' median model year, 1973. The profit type is more likely than any other to "hot wire" or punch out the ignition rather than rely on opportunities, as do joyriders and short-termers. Most of the subjects were "strippers"; thus, a high percentage of the cars were damaged.

The commission of another crime was attributed to only three cases, too few for any conclusions except that the type is of little consequence for the auto-theft picture.

Two final aspects. . .are noteworthy. First, race shows little variation from one type to another. This appears to confirm our contention that race has minimal explanatory value in describing the various motivations for this crime. Second, auto theft appears to be a group crime regardless of the reason for stealing.

CONCLUSIONS

Findings from three data sources, buttressed by interviews with police, compromise two sociological assumptions about auto theft: first, that it is a favored-group delinquency, and second, that offenders are either joyriders out for a good time or professionals out for a profit. While a portion of auto thieves are white juveniles from better neighborhoods and socioeconomic backgrounds, they do not account for a disproportionate number of juvenile car thieves, as the Wattenberg-Balistrieri findings indicate. Furthermore, there is evidence that the proportion of white, middle-class juveniles among those who steal cars is no greater than the proportion involved in delinquencies other than auto theft.

Our findings also indicate that joyriding and stealing for profit are only part of the range of motivations for stealing cars. A broader typology also includes short-term transportation, long-term transportation, and commission of another crime. These types vary according to age of offenders, degree of sophistication in stealing cars, extent of damage inflicted, and model year of cars stolen.

Notes

1. This aspect of the research was supported by the National Institute of Law Enforcement and Criminal Justice of the Law Enforcement Assistance Administration, grants #73-NI-03-0002 and #75-NI-99-0031. Financial support from NILECJ does not necessarily indicate the concurrence of the Institute in any of the statements or conclusions in this article.

2. The typology is derived from a mixture of sources. The most influential were comments of Don Masztak of the Toledo Police Department and a lecture by Glen A. Shifflett of the National Automobile Theft Bureau, Eastern Division, given before the Institute on Motor Vehicle Theft at Case Western Reserve University, April 2, 1969. Other items of influence were by Smith (1975), Hellman (1971), and Gibbens (1958).

References

BLOCH, H. A. and A. NIEDERHOFFER (1958) The Gang: A Study in Adolescent Behavior. New York: Philosophical Library.

CLINARD, M. B. and R. QUINNEY (1973) Criminal Behavior Systems. New York: Holt, Rinehart & Winston.

GIBBENS, T.C.N. (1958) "Car thieves." British J. of Delinquency 8: 257–265.

GIBBONS, D.C. (1977) Society, Crime and Criminal Careers. Englewood Cliffs, NJ: Prentice-Hall.

GLASER, D. (1975) Strategic Criminal Justice Planning. Washington, DC: National Institute of Mental Health.

HALL, J. (1952) Theft, Law and Society. Indianapolis: Bobbs-Merrill.

HELLMAN, P. (1971) "Stealing cars is a growth industry." New York Times Magazine (June 20): 7, 41–45.

LEMERT, E. M. (1953) "An isolation and closure theory of naive check forgery." J. of Criminal Law, Criminology and Police Science 44 (September-October): 296–307.

NOSHPITZ, J. D. (1975) "The meaning of the car," pp. 204–209 in R. Slovenko (ed.) Sexual Behavior and the Law. Springfield, IL: Charles C Thomas.

SCHEPSES, E. (1961) "Boys who steal cars." Federal Probation (March): 56–62.

SHORT, J. F., Jr. and F. L. STRODTBECK (1965) Group Process and Gang Delinquency. Chicago: University of Chicago.

SMITH, W. D. (1975) "Car strippers prowl streets of the city." New York Times (October 12, Section 11):5.

26. Organized Crime and Labor Racketeering

AUGUST BEQUAI

In a lonely street in one of Chicago's suburbs a key government witness was recently gunned down by syndicate hit men. He was to testify in a federal case involving a $1.4 million loan from a labor union pension fund to a New Mexico firm with organized crime links. In Cleveland the secretary-treasurer of a union local was killed when a bomb was set off by remote control. He had been involved in a power struggle for control of union locals by organized crime members.[1]

In New York dissident Teamsters called for a federal investigation of New York Teamsters funds.[2] The group alleged that more than $500,000 from local Teamster funds had made its way into organized crime-controlled businesses. A six-month investigation into labor racketeering in Queens County resulted in the indictment of two union leaders.[3] One of the defendants was alleged to have had ties to organized crime. The defendants were charged with threatening bodily harm against the employees of a firm they were trying to unionize. In Washington, D.C., a high U.S. Labor Department official was charged with operating a fraudulent scheme.[4]

These are examples of labor racketeering, what has come to be called an American tragedy. The United States may be unique in Western society in its corruption of labor. Powerful labor unions, with millions of members and billions of dollars in treasuries, are presently manipulated by criminal syndicates. Union welfare and pension funds are open to looting, and federal and state governments have done little to stop it. Labor racketeering provides criminal cartels with large amounts of interest-free capital to invest in business ventures and powerful voting blocks that give them leverage with national and local political figures. It is a serious and growing problem. It threatens not only the labor movement and the world of business but also our very democratic fiber. . . .

CATEGORIES OF LABOR CORRUPTION

Corrupt practices within the labor movement can take four major forms: rivalries for leadership, abuses involving the union-employer relationship, collusion between labor and organized crime, and frauds involving union welfare and pension funds. Labor racketeering may take any of these forms. Members of criminal syndicates are often involved in these corrupt practices. Labor is not always an unwilling victim. In great part labor racketeering is the result of corruption among labor leaders and lax enforcement of federal and state laws.

The Central States Pension Fund is said to have assets of more than $1 billion and investments in Las Vegas casinos, Florida hotels, and large restaurant chains.[5] Union welfare and pension funds are estimated to amount to more than $100 billion and to be growing by billions of dollars annually.[6] The leadership of the labor movement presently bears little relationship to the labor organizers of the late nineteenth century. The presidency of a union is highly prized; it provides a large salary and numerous fringe benefits, as well as political power. It is so highly prized that rivalries for the presidency sometimes culminate in violence. The United Mine Workers provide an example of such violence. In 1974 the president of this large and once powerful labor union was convicted of the murder of his rival.[7] On December 31, 1969, Joseph (Jack) Yablonski, his wife, and his daughter were shot to death while they lay asleep in their Pennsylvania home. Three UMW members later confessed to the murder and implicated the president of their union. The conspiracy was hatched in a Kentucky motel in November 1969.[8]

In Howell, Michigan, the candidate for the presidency of a local union, influential in Michigan labor and political circles, was found slumped over his car's steering wheel; he had been shot to death.[9] In 1967 James R. Hoffa, president of the Teamsters, one of the largest labor unions in the United States, entered federal prison, leaving his hand-picked successor to run the union. On July 30, 1975, Hoffa disappeared when he attempted to regain his presidency.[10] High union offices are highly prized. Labor leaders have access to large fortunes and numerous positions that they can fill with their allies and relatives. "Dirty tricks"—even murder—have been employed to discredit and defeat opponents. Rivalries for union leadership have allied some factions with criminal syndicates. Hoffa, it is said, first formed his alliance with organized crime when in search of support of his bid for power. However, these rivalries have sometimes had a serious impact on the rest of society. The United Mine Workers, disillusioned with their leadership and highly fragmented, brought this country to a standstill with a national strike that crippled America's energy needs for more than ninety days. The victim in this instance was not only the union but also the public.

In 1954 the United States Court of Appeals for the Eighth Circuit upheld the conviction of a labor leader who had obtained property from corporate employers through fear and the threat of violence.[11] The defendant had been charged with violating Section 1951 of Title 18 of the United States Code. The statute provides as follows:

> Whoever in any way or degree obstructs, delays or affects commerce or the movement of any article or commodity in commerce, by . . . extortion or attempts to conspire so to do . . . shall be fined not more than $10,000 or imprisoned not more than twenty years, or both.

At an ammunition plant in the Midwest, corrupt unions bilked their employer of more than $10 million in cost overruns.[12] Abuses involving the "union-employer relationship" are numerous. In many instances they are the outcome of a mutual understanding. Some employers give in for fear of labor strife. One employer told a state investigating commission the following:

> Q. Before you joined the union, did an accident occur with regard to your premises, Mr. B?
> A. Oh, my windows were broken.
> Q. All of them?
> A. All of them, yes.

Employers have been known to retain racketeers as labor consultants. Some firms have paid an average of $15,000 annually for their services. The consultant ensures labor peace through his contacts within the union. Some union officials receive kickbacks from those consultants. In other situations the payoffs take a more direct route. Federal investigators have uncovered a national practice of payoffs, ranging up to $50,000, at most posts.[13] Payoffs to corrupt union officials have become so common in these ports that employers pass them off as a cost of doing business and include them in their shipping rates. In New York a key official of the International Longshoreman's Association was indicted by a grand jury for accepting more than $50,000 in cash payments from a multinational corporation.[14] In return, prosecutors allege, the employer was promised labor peace.

Employers are not always the victims of those union-employer abuses. The vice-president of a national chain store was indicted for soliciting the aid of organized crime to persuade unions to meet his company's demands. Many employers willingly enter into sweetheart contracts with corrupt labor officials. Under these agreements union members settle for lower wages and fewer benefits, while their leaders pocket cash payoffs and other benefits from the employers. Some corrupt union officials, with the aid of criminal syndicates, establish dummy locals and through this vehicle negotiate payoffs with employers. Phony welfare plans are used to elicit payoffs from employers. These schemes are so common and so lucrative that some racketeers specialize in setting up dummy union locals. Corrupt members of management may also receive kickbacks from these union shells. Although the corrupt practices take many forms, the losers are always the union members and the stockholders of the firm. One corporate officer described the union-employer relationship to government investigators as follows:

> *Q.* Actually you don't negotiate anything. They just bring a piece of paper to you which is a form and actually it is a Xerox copy, something like that. They fill in the names and sign it. Isn't that about the way it happened?
>
> *A.* . . . yes.

Although the Taft-Hartley Act makes it illegal for employers to pay labor leaders, the practice continues and by all indications has increased dramatically. In some instances the employer is an unwilling participant; in others, a willing contributor. For a fixed fee many employers hope to avoid labor strife and thus gain an edge over their competitors. One prosecutor noted that if employers came forth, these practices would not continue.

The McClellan investigation disclosed that Anthony "Tony Ducks" Corallo, a known Mafia leader, was in control of several Teamster locals. Mr. Corallo was also alleged to have been a key figure in the narcotics trade. When Hoffa was asked whether he had taken any steps against Corallo and other racketeers who had penetrated Teamster locals, his answer was "as of now, no." In 1972 Lloyd Hicks announced his candidacy for president of Teamster Local 390 in Miami.[15] Two days later he was gunned down. In New Jersey the sixty-year-old secretary-treasurer of a powerful local union was reindicted on kickback-conspiracy charges.[16] The defendant is alleged to have strong links to organized crime and is under investigation on charges that he may have taken part in the murder of a well-known gangland figure in upstate New York in 1961. The working relations between organized crime and unions go back to the early part of this century. Many of these relationships have become institutionalized. One investigator remarked, "It's difficult to tell a labor leader from a member of organized crime."

In the early history of the labor movement employers hired gangs of thugs to intimidate workers or break strikes. The rising unions, in turn, employed gangs to assist them against their employers. Violence was met with violence. In the 1930s gangsters began to infiltrate the labor movement. By the 1940s their foothold was well established. In some industries racketeering and labor went hand in hand. Albert Anastasia, a leader in New York's underworld, selected his brother to head the Brooklyn longshoremen's union. The balkanized nature of the longshoremen's unions and other fragmented labor groups further facilitated the rise of organized crime within the labor movement. Corruption on New York's docks became so common that the Waterfront Commission was finally established in 1953 to clean it up. Numerous union officials have been convicted of racketeering activities. For example, a head of the New York longshoremen's union was indicted on fifty-one counts of misusing union funds.[17] But the payoffs, kickbacks, and thefts, continue.

In 1956 James R. Hoffa, in an attempt to gain control of the Teamsters, enlisted the assistance of organized crime. In 1975 these allies played a key role in his demise. His union fell, in large part, to their control. Through the Teamsters, these criminal syndicates were able to exert pressure even on the White House. With their pension funds and large membership, the Teamsters became tools of criminal cartels. In 1969 these criminal elements conceived a union insurance scheme that bilked Teamster locals of large sums of money. Under this scheme employers paid $40 per week to buy individual insurance policies for their employees; employers who refused to go along suffered the union's wrath. These funds were eventually drained away by organized crime in the form of large commissions and administration fees.[18]

For organized crime the labor movement represents a powerful political tool as well as a vehicle for monetary gains. Control over labor groups gives organized crime a powerful political voice and enables criminal elements to hire themselves out to employers as labor consultants who ensure labor peace in return for payoffs. In 1968 a grand jury indicted the president of a multibillion-dollar corporation on charges of perjury.[19] The defendant had lied about his attempts to enlist several members of the Mafia as labor consultants.

In late March 1978 Salvatore Briguglio, a syndicate-connected union leader, was shot to death by two hired assassins in New York.[20] During this time an official high in the Labor Department was reassuring an audience of concerned citizens that the federal government's crackdown on labor racketeering had proven a success. In Las Vegas federal sources were expressing concern that a key Mafia leader had made an attempt to gain control of some local unions.[21] Other government sources were expressing concern that one of the nation's largest labor unions might soon elect an ex-felon as its president.[22] The individual involved is alleged to have strong links with organized crime, has been under investigation by federal authorities for more than a dozen years, was once convicted for obstruction of justice, and served a brief prison term. His second-in-command also has a history of criminal involvement and has been indicted three times by federal prosecutors.[23]

A Florida federal grand jury has been looking into kickbacks involving labor officials. Federal investigators have been looking into a $3 million union fund loan to several businessmen. One union official was said to have received a $100,000 kickback.[24] The administrator of a union welfare fund testified before a U.S. Senate subcommittee that the fund was under the total control of a known "mobster."[25] He also noted that the Labor Department had been dragging its feet. A multinational firm with organized crime ties is said to have obtained a $13 million loan from a union fund.[26]

Frauds involving union pension and welfare funds have become a serious problem. Many of these funds have been depleted by loans to anyone willing to give a kickback to corrupt union officials; organized crime-owned businesses have received loans under these terms. Funds have also been invested in elaborate securities schemes. Union funds have been used to hire racketeers as consultants at exorbitant salaries, as well as pay for boats, airplanes, and even private homes for corrupt labor officials. In 1974, under increasing criticism, the federal government established the little-known Pension Benefit Guaranty Corporation (PBGC). The program is financed by insurance premiums assessed against employers who operate private pension funds. The latter fall into two categories: single-employer funds, where one firm pays into the funds, and multiemployer funds, in which a number of employers pay into the same fund. The obligations of these private pension funds are now about $350 billion, while their assets are about $200 billion. About 12 percent of these private funds are experiencing serious difficulties. If they went broke, the PBGC would find it difficult to insure them all adequately, and many union members would go without compensation. The impact on the overall economy could be staggering.

In 1977 one pension fund lost about $7 million as a result of an insurance fraud that involved two hundred thousand of its members.[27] A police pension fund may have been defrauded of more than $500,000, and a pension fund in New Jersey went bankrupt as a result of possible fraud. Millions of dollars of union members' pension and welfare funds are invested in fraudulent schemes. Corrupt union officials, in conjunction with criminal syndicates, are bilking their members. Many of these investments vanish in the air. Although corrupt union officials receive large kickbacks, their members stand to lose all their benefits. For example, corrupt officials of one union decided without consulting their members to make a multimillion-dollar loan to a firm owned by organized crime. The meeting went as follows:

Mr. W.: I so move, Mr. Chairman.

Mr. S.: Second the motion.

Chairman: You have heard the motion and seconded. Are you ready for the question? ... The motion was put to a vote and carried without dissent. ... It is so ordered.[28]

This brief discussion awarded an organized crime agent more than $100 million, over a ten-year period, in union pension funds. Unless the federal government acts decisively, union welfare and pension funds will continue to be pillaged. The PBGC is far from adequate for dealing with criminal syndicates and corrupt labor leaders bent on bankrupting union treasuries.

THE REGULATORS

A high Justice Department official recently told the U.S. Senate Judiciary Committee that efforts to get the Labor Department to take an aggressive posture toward labor racketeering, "including the infiltration of labor unions" by organized crime, had not proven successful.[29] The Labor Department has conceded that it has committed only thirty investigators to labor racketeering. Plans to reduce that force to fifteen investigators were cancelled when the Congress and Justice Department voiced their opposition. More than three hundred local unions, belonging to five international unions, are presently under federal investigation.[30]

The Labor Department, charged with administering and policing the federal labor laws,[31] was created by act of Congress in 1913. It assumed the role first played by the Bureau of Labor, which had been created in 1884 and had been incorporated within the Interior Department. In 1903 the bureau was placed under the Department of Commerce. The creation of a ninth executive department was convincing proof of the growing role and power of organized labor in this country. The chief officer of the Department of Labor is the secretary, who is assisted by a number of deputy undersecretaries and a staff of executive assistants. The department has its home offices in Washington, D.C., and has ten regional offices, each headed by a regional director. The department has no direct criminal jurisdiction. All criminal cases are referred to the Justice Department for prosecution. The Labor Department has only direct civil jurisdiction; it can only go to court and ask for an injunction. An injunction hardly suffices to deter organized criminal activity in the labor movement.

Under growing criticism, the Labor Department has taken some civil action against several unions. In Ohio the department obtained a court order removing the administrator and trustees of a union health and welfare fund. The department charged that the administrator had been paid "far in excess of reasonable compensation."[32] The department also announced plans to sue a number of former trustees of a $1 billion pension fund.[33] The former trustees have been accused of corrupt practices and mismanagement of the fund. The department initiated its investigation some fifteen years after the frauds began, and then only under congressional pressure. Other federal agencies had been urging the department for several years to act. Some charge it has acted too late.[34]

The Labor Department also supervises various public service jobs, including the Compehensive Education and Training Act (CETA). The program covers more than seven hundred thousand public service jobs and is funded by more than $11 billion. CETA is one of many programs established by Congress to help employ the unemployable, the poor, and minority groups. The program has come under attack, and there are now more than a hundred allegations of mismanagement and fraud. Critics charge that perhaps as much as $1 billion in CETA funds may have been misused and that the new programs have only opened new opportunities for criminal groups.

The department is undermanned. Its entire investigative team consists of only two hundred individuals, a number barely sufficient to meet the present needs of the department let alone investigate new areas of fraud. Without proper supervision the infusion of federal funds into the labor market and union area will only create additional opportunities for organized crime. Programs similar to CETA can easily fall prey to criminal attack as the many antipoverty programs have.

The real target of labor racketeers is no longer the traditional arena; these criminal elements, allied with corrupt union and government officials, are now focusing their attention on white-collar crime. Employers have been found to lease machinery from firms connected or associated with corrupt labor leaders or their relatives. For example, one union leader, with a criminal record dating back to 1925, was renting machinery to employers dealing with his union.[35] On the open market the machinery sells for about $50,000; renting it from the union boss costs about $45,000 a year. These new forms of union corruption, or sweetheart agreements, are the wave of the future.[36] Whether the Labor Department has the expertise and the will to commit resources in this arena remains to be seen.

DETECTING LABOR CORRUPTION

A number of indicators could assist both the public and law enforcement in detecting labor racketeering. For example, where wages of workers in one union are much lower than those of other unions doing similar work, the difference could be due to union-employer abuses, employment of organized crime figures as labor consultants, or both. The employment of labor consultants known to have links to organized crime is also an indication of corrupt labor practices. For example, a company retains the services of the ABC, Inc., consulting firm to advise it on labor problems; the fee paid is extremely high, and Mr. X, president of the consulting company, is known to have links with criminal syndicates.

Buying from certain suppliers, even though the same products might be cheaper if purchased from other sources, is also an indicator of labor-related fraud. For example, Mr. X sells company YT machinery for $100,000; the same equipment is available from another source at $60,000. In addition, Mr. X is a relative of the president of the local union whose members are employed by YT. Another common practice is for union officials to openly ask for gratuities or for certain individuals to be hired over others. Work slowdown, wildcat strikes, sabotage, and other forms of violence against an employer are also indications of corrupt labor practices. Intimidation of a firm's clients or patrons may also indicate labor racketeering. A tolerance by employers of gambling and loansharking operations on their premises is also an indicator of some understanding between the employer and the union leadership or those who control it.

If a firm is under no pressure to unionize while other employers have been forced to do so, the employer and organized crime figures may have some agreement, or the firm itself may be controlled or owned by organized crime. Pressures on management to contribute to union affairs may also be an indication of some corrupt agreement between labor and management. For example, employers commonly contribute large sums of money to charities sponsored by unions known to have organized crime connections. Whether the funds ever reach the charity is dubious: the charity may be a funnel for illegal payments to union leaders. In addition, unions with officers known to have criminal records or criminal ties may also indicate corrupt practices within that union.

In 1977 a major national television network disclosed that federal investigators had evidence of a $250,000 illegal payment to the Nixon White House by the heads of one of the nation's largest unions in order to release their former president.[37] Soon after, he was paroled. Control of an airport local union in a large eastern city has given organized crime access to valuable freight.[38] These are but a few examples of the problems posed by labor racketeering. The labor movement, born in violence, has found itself the target of gangster elements. Through collusion with some dishonest employers and corrupt union officials, criminal syndicates have infiltrated a number of powerful national unions. The federal government has sat idle for too long; that laxity has in large part facilitated the infiltration of organized crime into every aspect and level of the American labor system.

Notes

1. The deceased, John Anardi, had been involved in Teamster affairs for many years and had an extensive history of criminal involvement in labor matters ("The Frank Fitzsimmons Invitational Golf Tournament," *Overdrive*, April 1975, p. 54).

2. "Teamster Group Asks for Probe of New York Fund," *Burlington Free Press*, August 25, 1977, p. 5A.

3. "Indictment Names Three of Teamsters in Case Involving Tiger Unit," *Wall Street Journal*, December 23, 1977, p. 3.

4. "U.S. Labor Deputy Charged in Fraud," *New York Times*, December 1, 1977, p. 63.

5. Jack Anderson and Les Whitten, "Sources Say Mob Eliminated Hoffa," *Washington Post*, August 21, 1975, p. F-21; see also Donald R. Cressey, *Theft of the Nation* (New York: Harper & Row, 1969), pp. 95–99.

6. U.S. Chamber of Commerce, *Deskbook on Organized Crime*, p. 35.

7. "Boyle Set to Appeal Second Conviction in Yablonski Deaths," *Wall Street Journal*, February 21, 1978, p. 12.

8. "Ex-Aide Testifies Boyle Delayed, Then Ordered Yablonski Slaying," *Miami Herald*, February 3, 1978, p. 22-A.

9. "Teamster Leader Shot," *Washington Post*, December 14, 1977, p. A-6.

10. Jack Anderson and Les Whitten, "Chile Resorts to Book Burning," *Washington Post*, August 30, 1975, p. E-21.

11. Hulahan v. United States, 214 F 2d 441 (1954).

12. U.S. Chamber of Commerce, *Deskbook on Organized Crime*, p. 36.

13. Nicholas Gage, "Dock Payoffs Reported Found in Undercover Inquiry by FBI," *New York Times*, September 1, 1977, p. A-1.

14. Kramer, "Accuse a Top Banana in ILA of 100 G Bribes," p. 7.

15. Lester Velie, "The Mafia Tightens Its Grip on the Teamsters," *Readers Digest*, August 1974, p. 99.

16. "Provenzano Reindicted," *Washington Post*, December 20, 1977, p. A-3.

17. "On the Waterfront, Then and Now," *New York*, August 15, 1977, p. 42.

18. Velie, "The Mafia Tightens Its Grip on the Teamsters," pp. 100–102.

19. Cressey, *Theft of the Nation*, p. 98.

20. "N.J. Teamster Official Killed by Two Gunmen," *Washington Post*, March 23, 1978, p. A-8.

21. "Police Discredit Story of Possible Gang War," *Las Vegas Sun*, October 25, 1974, p. 6.

22. Jim Drinkhall, "Teamsters Chief May Soon Depart," *Washington Post*, October 29, 1977, p. A-3.

23. Jim Drinkhall, "Witness in Protective Custody Alleged Role in Kickback to Teamster Official," *Wall Street Journal*, August 18, 1977, p. 4.

24. Ibid., p. 4.

25. "Teamster Fund Controlled by Mobster, Official Says," *New York Times*, November 1, 1977, p. 23.

26. "Central States Pension Fund Loans Help Tell Tale of Teamsters Officials, Organized Crime and the Attorney General of the United States," *Overdrive*, June 1974, p. 46; see also "Meet 'Mr. Manipulator'—The Criminal Lawyer through Whose Fingers Has Poured 200 Million Teamster Dollars, Morris Shenker," *Overdrive*, January 1975, pp. 58–66.

27. Jim Drinkhall, "The Teamsters Accuse an Insurance Promoter of Defrauding Them," *Wall Street Journal*, October 24, 1977, pp. 1, 27; see also "Avalanche of Indictments Hit Organized Crime's Web of Pension Fraud," *Overdrive*, April 1974, pp. 48–50.

28. "The Intricate Financial Web of Allen Dorfman," *Overdrive*, February 1974, p. 55.

29. "Civiletti Chides Labor Department on Strike Force Cooperation," *Washington Post*, March 3, 1978, p. A-29.

30. J. Thomas, "Labor Agency, in Shifts, May Widen Crime Inquiries," *New York Times*, April 10, 1978, p. A-21.

31. 5 U.S.C. 611.

32. "Court Orders Teamsters Fund in Ohio to Remove Its Administrator, Trustees," *Wall Street Journal*, January 4, 1978, p. 8.

33. "Labor Department Seen Prepared to Sue Ex-Trustees of Teamsters' Pension Fund," *Wall Street Journal*, February 1, 1978, p. 7.

34. "Labor Agency Demands Detailed Records of Dorfman's Pact with Teamsters Fund," *Wall Street Journal*, July 26, 1977, p. 7.

35. "On the Waterfront, Then and Now," *New York*, August 15, 1977, p. 42.

36. Dang Ireland, "New York's Mr. Lucky," *New York*, August 15, 1977, pp. 40–43.

37. "Hoffa Prison Release Subject of New Probe," *Washington Post*, July 30, 1977, p. A-2.

38. Velie, "The Mafia Tightens Its Grip on the Teamsters," p. 99; see also Public Citizens Staff Report, *White Collar Crime* (Washington, D.C.: Congress Watch, 1974), pp. 18–19.

27. The New Mafia

FRANCIS A. J. IANNI

Organized crime is more than just a criminal way of life; it is an American way of life. It is a viable and persistent institution within American society with its own symbols, its own beliefs, its own logic, and its own means of transmitting these systematically from one generation to the next. As an integral part of economic life in the United States it can be viewed as falling on a continuum which has the legitimate business world at one end and what we have come to call organized crime at the other. Viewed in this way, organized crime is a functional part of the American social system and, while successive waves of immigrants and migrants have found it an available means of economic and social mobility, it persists and transcends the involvement of any particular group and even changing definitions of legality and illegality in social behavior.

At present organized crime is in a period of transition. Italian domination has begun to give way to that of a new group: the blacks and Hispanics. During the next decade we will see the presently scattered and loosely organized pattern of their emerging control develop into a new Mafia. This black and Hispanic involvement can be examined as part of the process of ethnic succession. They, like other minorities before them, are inheriting a major instrument to social and economic mobility.

How does this new group differ from its predecessors? What is common and what is different in these groups in comparison to the Italians who preceded them? To answer these questions it is necessary to examine the networks of criminal operation in order to determine the types of relationships which bring people together, foster some kind of criminal partnership, then lead to the formation of organized criminal networks.

To research the nature of crime in America a major study using anthropological field-work techniques was undertaken. All of the classifications, descriptions, and antecdotes which follow are drawn from field work. Information was received either from members of networks or from those familiar with criminal networks. Although we focused on the patterns of black and Hispanic crime activists, previous research on Italian-American patterns was utilized for comparison.

ORGANIZATION OF CRIME NETWORKS

The first step in determining the pattern or patterns of organization in the networks we observed was to ask the questions: What brings and holds people together in these networks? How are relationships of mutual dependence and responsibility established among people who will engage in organized crime? From our analyses of the networks we found two distinct types of linkages: *causal relationships*, which serve to introduce individuals to each other and into joint criminal ventures; and *criminal relationships*, which are based on a common core of activity in crime. We identified six sets of causal relationships in our networks. All are marked by a sense of mutual trust in the personal characters of those within the relationship.

Childhood

While childhood gangs are an obvious place to look for such friendships, the childhood friendship does not require a gang to establish a potentially criminal relationship. Reggie Martin and Jimmie Brown were childhood friends on 143rd Street, and later, when both were grown and successful in their individual criminal ventures, they joined together to "launder" some of their illicit profits through a joint enterprise in boutiques. The long-term relationship which grows out of childhood friendships is not, of course, restricted to crime circles and is also found in legitimate social relationships. It seems particularly potent in organized crime networks, however. In every case of childhood friendship which grew into an adult criminal partnership, the individuals involved were of the same ethnic or racial grouping and usually of approximately the same age. Obviously, this is not the result of any innate criminality in any of the ethnic groups but rather results from the fact that street society, where kids meet, is based on residential patterns which tend to follow racial and ethnic lines as well as socioeconomic ones. Reggie Martin and Jimmie Brown could just as easily have been meeting in the Grill Room of the Yale Club and discussing the formation of a joint stock venture if their childhood circumstances had been different. But youngsters growing up in the ghetto have a different set of experiences, a different set of role models, and so a different pattern of life chances. One of our interviewees in Central Harlem makes just this point:

> Again I stress the point of making the right kind of friends, from the time you're a little kid, then building up the right kind of respect among your

associates, and carrying yourself so that those people who have always known you can continue to depend on you, to think that you are okay. For every friend you have, you have that much more chance to get in on deals, to make it in crime. You are able to be in touch; people will give you their address, their telephone number. Otherwise you are outside looking in— you are nobody. It's a thing in New York that people just don't take you in unless you know somebody. It's a city thing, a poverty thing.

The Recruits

A second type of linkage develops when an experienced criminal in the neighborhood sees a young boy or gang of young boys with talent and recruits them into organized criminal ventures. This is the most common mode of entry into organized crime and represents the first step in criminal apprenticeship. The War Dragons, a young gang, were recruited in this way following a successful whiskey theft. Recruitment was also the means by which Rolando Solis was brought into the lower echelons of the Cuban Connection (a drug ring) as the first step up the ladder of criminal success. Thus recruitment may involve either individuals, as in the case of Rolando, or groups, as with the War Dragons. Like all social relationships, however, this causal link between younger and older crime activists is two-sided; not only does the older criminal seek out the younger, the youngsters also seek to be recruited and to emulate their elders in crime. It is this role-modeling which gives generational continuity to organized crime and accounts, in part, for its persistence in society.

There were numerous examples throughout the observations and interviews of both blacks and Puerto Ricans which document this apprenticeship system. The process is described by a black from Paterson, New Jersey:

> You can know who is connected and who is involved but you can't go to them and say, "Hey, man, I want to be one of you!" You can know for certain that Joe Blow is the biggest man in Paterson. He knows me and I know him but I can't approach that man about it. If I ask him something about that directly he might cuss me out. This is the way it happens. If he has been watching me and he likes what he sees and he wants to give me a little play, he might tell me one day to go see Joe. He won't ever turn around and commit himself to me the first time. You just take this for granted that you don't approach these guys at that level. . . .

Finally, there is the simple, but telling observation by one of our field assistants about the lack of positive influences and legitimate role models for ghetto youngsters:

> The ones you see are the ones that interest you. If it had been doctors and lawyers who drove up and parked in front of the bars in their catylacks, I'd

be a doctor today. But it wasn't, it was the men who were into things, the pimps, the hustlers and the numbers guys.

Prison Acquaintanceship

Incarceration can provide very strong and durable links among men who have already been involved in crime and who in the prison atmosphere come to feel themselves segregated from society and find natural linkages among themselves. The chances of these prison links leading to later joint criminal activity and forming the basis for organized crime networks seem to be quite high. Moreover, a multiplier effect is at work here since sometimes being a friend of a friend is enough to establish a link among ex-convicts. The role of prison experience bringing blacks and Puerto Ricans together in crime networks is also an important difference between these groups and the Italians who preceded them. Prison experience, often beginning early in the crime activist's experience, is found very commonly among the blacks and Puerto Ricans in the networks which we have described but seems to have been absent to any sizable degree among Italian-Americans. The strength of kinship and family which binds Italian syndicates together is not found among blacks and is less pronounced among Puerto Ricans that it is among Italians. Thus, the linkages among Italian-Americans are formed early enough so that apprehension and consequent incarceration seem to be less common among Italians than among blacks and Puerto Ricans.

Throughout the networks we found numerous examples of the importance of prison experience in bringing crime activists into contact with each other.

> When if I do need him outside [prison], I go to his neighborhood. Everybody is leery of telling me where I can find him or even telling me they know him. But the minute I mention that I did time with him and where, then immediately they come around. They get less scared I may be a cop. When I get to my friend he can take me around so all the people know I'm OK because we did time together.

Prison experience also fosters the strong relationship between a man and "the man who watches my back." The mutual loyalty has been forged during periods of trouble in prison. One inmate protects another. This is one of the strongest links found in black and Puerto Rican crime networks and rivals childhood friendship as a bond.

> It sounds strange, but you make your best friends in prison. I could remember a time when something would go down like a strike or something like that. It is like going to a shooting gallery. Someone's waiting to put a

shiv in your ribs. But you got friends. The guy in front of me, I'd watch his back; the guy in the back of me watches mine and down the line.

Wives and Lovers

A fourth type of linkage is the infrequent but potent causal type of relationship which seems to exist between individuals in black and, to a lesser extent, Puerto Rican organized crime networks and their wives or lovers. Black and Puerto Rican members of organized crime networks involve women, particularly their lovers, in their criminal activity. Women may be involved in theft rings or in numbers operations. Sometimes they attain fairly high positions within an organization. Here there is a distinctive difference between the emerging black and Puerto Rican organized crime networks and those found traditionally among Italian-Americans. Once again it may represent the strength of family and kinship among Italian-Americans but it may also be a result of the less highly organized and consequently less professionalized relationships among blacks and Puerto Ricans. It is interesting to note that in our field experience we have found that Cubans, who are much more highly organized than either Puerto Ricans or blacks, do not use women in their crime groups. The usual reason given for this by the informants was that the Cubans are "more like the Italians."

> Among the blacks there have always been women involved in numbers and dope. You find the same thing in the Puerto Rican race sometimes where they are runners in the numbers; they don't actually "run" numbers from place to place but they do have people come to their house and you leave your number and your money there. Where you don't find any women is with the Cubans. If a Cuban woman gets into drugs or into hustling her ass, she is dead in the Cuban sections, and she better get out as fast as she can.

Kin

Although family is less important than among the Italian-Americans, kinship ties will sometimes foster a criminal linkage among blacks and Puerto Ricans. Our experience indicates that there is some greater reliance upon kinship among Puerto Ricans than among blacks and that once again, the Cubans seem more like the Italians in that among them, kinship is an important element. One interesting point is that all the kinship ties in our study were between brothers; none were between a father and a son. This could be a function of the limited size of our sample but it could also be a function of the relatively short period of time in which organized crime networks such as those we have described have been in existence in black and Puerto Rican societies. However, the importance of kinship ties, even among blacks, was commented on by a number of informants:

There is a great deal to the observation that trust is given more easily to a boy if he has a relative—a father, uncle, brother, an aunt—involved in crime. Many times, people want to know who a guy is, that is, they want to know his pedigree. A guy is accepted more easily if he has a "crime-heritage."

Partners

The sixth and most common causal type of linkage is the meeting of two men, either through intermediaries or casually, who happen to be in complementary business positions, and consequently form a linkage for common profit. A feeling of mutual trust is established. These kinds of relationships, premised on business, can lead to a great deal of criminal activity. Characteristically, some of the activities are legitimate and some are illegal, but the activity tends to move from one form of organized crime operation to another. Some partnerships are episodic as when a particularly good opportunity arises and two or more individuals along with their associates will join together briefly for a common venture. In other cases the relationship grows over a period of time as expertise and special skills are required for the continuation of certain types of activities. In either case, the rules of good business practice are as true here as in the world of legitimate business:

I find that in order for people to put the right kind of opportunities in your path on the streets there must be respect given to the people in positions in crime. They, in turn, must respect your ability as a person or a hustler, or whatever. In this way—through a system of mutual respect—there is the chance that you will be given the opportunity for profit-making in crime. Drug addicts, for instance, are never really successful because they are not respected—they are hooked on dope and cannot be trusted.

CRIMINAL LINKS IN CRIME NETWORKS

In addition to these causal types of linkages in the networks, there are also a number of substantive "criminal relationships," links which develop out of joint criminal operations within a network. Here it is the activity rather than the people which fosters the relationship.

Employer-Employee Relationship

This is the most common by far, just as it is in the legitimate business world. The employer hires the employee for a salary to do certain things that the employer requires of him. In nearly every one of the networks we find many such relationships. Our study revealed men such as Thomas Irwin who employed a group of thieves, and George the Fence and his employees in the whorehouse, Roberto Mateo and the neighborhood women who worked for him, and Jimmie Mitchell who employed a group of pushers.

Joint Venture

A second type of substantive criminal relationship is provided in the partnership and joint-venture type of linkage in criminal networks. The partners or associates share equally in the risks, responsibilities and profits. This relationship differs from the employer-employee relationship in that the two individuals involved are in association without a dominant-submissive relationship; there are no fixed leaders or followers. In some cases, however, one partner does seem to have greater authority and perhaps more influence than the others. The childhood gang often operates in this fashion and it appears that older groups do also.

Buyers and Sellers

A third type of relationship is that which occurs between the buyer and seller of goods. This type of relationship is, of course, very important in the narcotics, boosting, and stolen-car trades. However, we have found in most of our networks that this type of relationship exists in a number of the activities of networks. In some cases, it is a well-established pattern such as those where illegally acquired goods such as guns or cars are sold either through a middleman or directly as part of the network. In others it tends to be episodic, as when an individual or group learns that someone has some "hot" goods to sell.

Related to the buyer and seller of goods relationship is the buyer and seller of services relationship. In all networks this involves chiefly a specialized criminal skill, such as locksmithing. Other skills such as prostitution or numbers running are less specialized but still important in the networks which include these activities. In the buyer and seller of services relationship, there is usually an established pattern so that the same locksmith, for example, is used repeatedly.

Leaders and Followers

There is also a complex linkage that exists between a leader of an informal gang and his followers. The most significant examples of this appear in prison life, although it does appear in other networks in some form. This relationship seems to be too informal to maintain a stable operation except in prisons where incarceration keeps inmates in close, continuous association. Here our data are too thin on hierarchical placement, dominance, submission, and other organizational features to allow us to do more than speculate that these informal relationships represent first stages in the formalization of leadership in organized crime networks.

Esprit de Corps

Another type of linkage is that which exists among and between fellow employees, or among and between followers in a gang. Although this type of relationship seldom brings a criminal venture into existence, it is often on this type of relationship that the success of a venture rests. Poor coordination of effort and a lack of cohesion in the group seem to have doomed some of the criminal efforts described in our networks. For example, Luis Santos was a leader of a gang whose downfall was caused by this lack of cohesion. In a traditional legitimate business relationship this would be described as morale, or esprit de corps, within the company.

There are also a few relationships which are somewhat less common than the foregoing but they do emerge with some frequency and seem important to a number of criminal operations. The first of these is that which obtains *between a granter and a grantee of a privilege*, as when, in the Paterson network, Bro Squires inherited his brother's business and his connections and followers as well. In effect this relationship defines property and territorial rights in much the same way as in Italian-American organized crime circles. Another type of relationship which seems to be present in our networks is that which is engendered by bribes and favors; that between *the giver and the recipient of the bribe or favor*. Here the basis of the relationship is the exchange of goods and services based upon mutual needs and the assumption that the exchange is in some fashion mutually beneficial. This is not an uncommon activity even outside of organized crime, but the relationship is an important one for keeping the networks in operation and protected:

> Even to survive with the law you have to be connected. The cops will not take money from just anyone. They are in the business of being a cop for money and they are interested in pulling in bribes, but they want it in a safe way. The safety comes in knowing the guy from whom they take money. The cop takes the money from a successful man and grants him his protection so that the man can carry out his numbers or dope thing which allows the money to keep flowing to the cop.

Finally, there is a substantive relationship which is not as frequent but should be noted. This is *the relationship engendered by a simple, direct assault.* For example, one of our informants described a police-man in Central Harlem who shakes down addicts to obtain narcotics for resale on the street. We do not have a great deal of data on the use of violence and assault as techniques for compelling behavior in organized crime. Our informants reported repeatedly that violence does occur but is not an important factor since it is the certainty of re-lationships and the mutual profit among members of the network which keeps it in operation. It is important, however, to remember that criminal business is not always tidy, and consequently violence certainly does occur.

Identification of the causal links which lead to the formation of net-works and the criminal links which sustain them helps to clarify the nature of criminal networks and the functional bases on which they are organized. There seem to be two forms of behavioral organiza-tion into which all networks can be divided. One type is character-ized by the term *associational networks.* These are networks held together by close personal relationships where strong emphasis is placed on mutual trust, and causal links are the usual agents of their formation. We found two forms of associational networks in our field experience.

The first of these is the childhood gang as a beginning criminal partnership. In these associational networks, black or Puerto Rican youngsters growing up in the same neighborhood were involved in criminal activities and then through the process of recruitment be-came involved in organized crime as a group. The friendships and ties among these youngsters were such that they continued into adulthood. It is important to point out, however, that youthful gangs as such should not be included under organized crime networks be-cause although they might occasionally participate in organized criminal activites, they are not organized entirely for participation in such activities. Rather their importance is as a beginning step and as a source of recruitment into organized crime.

It is this partnership of old neighborhood friends which is most characterized by the sharing of risks and profits, by unclear lines of authority, by expressed concern over many aspects of the personal-ities of the members, and by the youthfulness of the partnership's members. This type of network seldom lasts beyond early adulthood, but individual relationships may be maintained long after.

The importance of these childhood relationships in building a "rep" and in forming crime networks is obvious in this excerpt from an interview:

You've got to be forceful and be willing to do things like putting your life out on the line because somebody just took $10,000 from you. You also have to always be thinking about your business and what you're going to do with it. What happens to it depends on who comes along. Everything works on the basis that you are liked, either because you have qualities that are likeable or because you have qualities that are recognized, such as being a nice guy but still being a regular guy, somebody that is good to be with or a bright kid. These things lead to your being discovered. These are the things that oldtimers look for. It is a tradition.

The second major type of associational network which we found was the prison court, where individuals within prison band together along very strict racial lines and form strong bonds with each other. In addition to racial segregation these prison courts are characterized by strong leadership and a sensitivity to being together under a coercive and authoritarian system. As is true of childhood associations the relationships which are formed tend to be highly personalized and consequently tend to be very lasting. They have the character of partnerships since they do depend on mutual trust and responsibility as well as compatibility of the individuals.

While the chief purposes of the prison court do not include the commission of crime, there is impressive evidence in our data that prison activities are linked to external criminal activities and that base recruitment and basic relationships which serve to structure organized crime networks in the post-release period are often first formed in prison courts. These prison courts are characterized (1) by a single strong leader and his followers, (2) by strict racial segregation, and (3) by extreme sensitivity to the closed environment of prison life. It is within these courts that the exchange of favors—the concept of mutual rights and obligations—seems to become well established. The possession or lack of material advantages is an important factor in the adjustment of relations within the prison court. Thus, the individual who is able to provide goods or services is able to achieve a leadership position with the group. The relationships thus established become binding in the sense that there are expectations built up on both sides of each interpersonal relationship.

The second type of behavioral organization is the *entrepreneurial network*. This seems to be a more advanced form among blacks and Puerto Ricans than the associational types. It is the model of the small businessman, the individual entrepreneur, whose illegal activities are carried out through a network of individuals related to him in that activity. In many respects, these crime networks are similar or identical to the kind of network that would coalesce around an individual who establishes his own small legitimate business. The pattern of this type of structure is quite familiar throughout our research and is found in networks ranging from Thomas Irwin's gang of thieves to the gypsy cab industry. Its characteristics seem always the same. One man is basically in charge of the activity by virtue of the fact that he pays the salaries or commissions of the other men. There is not a great deal of hierarchical arrangement among the employees. Most employees seem to have some direct contact with the boss and they identify with him more than they do with other members of the network except in those specific cases where we have seen direct partnerships or long standing relationships among the employee-members. The boss or center of the network is in most cases the only one in the net who has accumulated any risk capital. In fact, if an employee does accumulate risk capital he is likely to try to go off and set up some enterprise of his own. Again it seems that the salaried or commissioned employees, even when they are out on the street, are likely to view their activities as little different from "a job." Similarly, the boss, if the business of the network is successful, is likely to have many of the traits of any good small businessman—economy, prudence, firmness, a sensitivity to when he is being cheated or lied to, and status as a businessman in his neighborhood. It is this relationship between the illegal business set and the community which is most significant as we review the data in the various networks. There are probably no more secrets or confidences within the group of employees in these networks than there would be within any comparable group of employees in legitimate small business. What is different is that despite the illegal nature of the activities, many co-ethnics and neighborhood associates of these networks view them as legitimate.

THE CODE

Like any legitimate organization, criminal networks require a code of rules which regulates relationships between the network and the outside world. It is the code which keeps the network functioning, defines relationships within it, and establishes who is inside and who is outside the net. Control systems of this sort begin with values which define what is "good" and what is "bad." Ultimately, however, human behavior, whether in organized crime or in legitimate enterprises, is guided by specific rules which attempt to operationalize these values and apply them to everyday situations. Thus, while values give us some general sense of what is expected, it is the rule which states what actions will be approved and which forbidden. Rules do not stand alone but are usually grouped into codes or sets of rules which cover specified classes of behavior and the sanctions to be applied when the rule is broken. The rules which govern behavior in organized criminal networks follow just as surely all of these characteristics and direct behavior just as forcefully as do more legitimate codes.

Like so much in the study of organized crime, descriptions of codes for organized criminals have usually been derived by analogy—that is, rather than looking directly at the behavior of criminal syndicate members and extrapolating a code from their words and actions, investigators have tried to apply codes drawn from observations of other groups. One favorite source of analogies for rules of conduct in American criminal syndicates is the "Code of the Mafia," which originated in Sicily. The Task Force on Organized Crime set up in the Johnson Administration, for example, points out that since "there is great similarity between the structure of the Italian-Sicilian Mafia and the structure of the American confederation of criminals, it should not be surprising to find great similarity in the values, norms, and other behavior patterns of the two organizations."

The reason, suggests the report, is that organized crime in America is an off-shoot of the Mafia. As the report freely admits, however, the Mafia code itself is also quite similar to those which govern any secret societies such as Mau Mau, or even to those of secret organizations who, like the Irish Republican Army, seek to overthrow the authority in power.

Both Ralph Salerno and Donald Cressey, two leading experts on organized crime in America, further compare these rules of behavior to the Prisoners' Code, an unwritten by widely accepted set of rules which operates among inmates in American prisons. This similarity may be credited to the need of any underground organization for secrecy and control.

Deriving rules of behavior by analogy, however, can only be a valid technique if the values of the organization or group being studied are similar to those of the organization or group from which the analogy is borrowed. There is no certainty that present-day organized crime groups share the values of the Mafia in Sicily in 1900 or, for that matter, of prisoners and thieves. In my recent study of the Lupollo "family," rules were derived from observed behavior rather than by analogy. Our method was to observe and record social action within the Lupollo family and then to seek regularities in behavior which have enough frequency to suggest that the behavior results from the pressures of the shared social system rather than from idiosyncratic behavior. We also asked family members and others about rules, usually by asking why some member of the family behaved in a particular way. Thus, reconstruction of rules of conduct came both from our own observations and from the explanations of observed behavior by the people living under those rules.

In analyzing the data we found three basic rules which organize behavior in the Lupollo family: (1) primary loyalty is vested in the family rather than in the individual lineages or families which make up the overall organization; (2) each member of the family must act like a man and do nothing which brings disgrace on the family; (3) family business is privileged matter and must not be reported or discussed outside the group. These three rules were the basics for maintaining membership within the group but there were a number of informal rules under each which explain why some members are more successful at playing the game than others.

In studying black and Hispanic organized crime networks, we again tried to extract rules from observed behavior rather than by analogy. A similar but functionally different code of rules exists for each of the two forms of organization we found in our networks.

In associational networks—prison and youthful partnerships—rules seem more likely to speak to intimate personal characteristics:

1. *Don't be a coward.* This rule, which is found in both the prison court and in the youthful networks, enjoins the individual to be a man but has a more physical connotation than we found to be true among the Italian-Americans. Essentially, it indicates that the individual is always willing to fight for his own rights and safety and to a lesser extent for those of his colleagues in the network.

2. *Don't be disloyal.* Here again, the injunction is less positive in terms of its relationship to the group than we found among the Lupollos. What is called for here is a feeling of membership in a group and a basic loyalty rather than the intensely socialized family membership code among the Italian-Americans. Loyalty in this context means acceptance of membership in a group with the consequent requirements that ousiders be rejected.

3. *Don't be a creep.* Here, the rule calls for a normalizing of behavioral relationships among members in the network. What this rule does is to exclude from membership aberrant individuals—those who are somewhat deficient or who cannot for some reason enjoy full membership—and consequently establishes rules of behavior.

These rules are of course not written and they are usually expressed in terms of punitive or critical actions toward any behavior which violates them. No one says "Be loyal," but when an act by a member of the network is perceived as disloyal by his fellows, he will be subject to verbal and sometimes physical abuse as well. Neither are these rules normally taught in any formal manner; they are learned by experience and taught by example. In effect, these are expected norms of behavior which are socialized into individual network members as a result of their membership in the network in day-to-day experiences.

In prison perhaps more than in the youthful partnerships (and for obvious reasons) shrewdness and the capacity to keep calm seem to be required. Thus, in the prison network we found greater emphasis upon a fourth rule: "Be smart," which enjoins the individual to learn to acquiesce to some regulations which cannot be ignored but at the same time to determine ways to beat the system. This rule, which we found only in the prison networks, is also a rule in what we have earlier called the code of American prisoners. Prisoner-to-prisoner injunctions such as "don't whine . . . don't cop out . . . be tough . . . play it cool and do your own time . . ." are responses to the imposed authoritarian environment which is found in prisons but not in the youthful gangs.

In the entrepreneurial networks, rules speak much more to the impersonal requirements of the activities of the network than to the personal qualities we have described in the prison and youthful gang networks. In these business-related networks we found three major rules:

1. *Don't tell the police.* This rule also includes the caution against telling anyone who is likely to tell the police either through malice or weakness. While the rule is strongest within the networks themselves, we found that it reaches beyond the networks into the community and that (just as we found among the Italian-Americans) there is a great reluctance on the part of the community to inform on organized crime activities. To some extent this is the result of fear but it also results from an antagonism toward the criminal justice system and a stronger identification on the part of the community members with their co-ethnics in the networks than with the criminal justice system.

2. *Don't cheat your partner or other people in the network.* This rule places a highly "moral" standard on interpersonal behavior within the network but does not carry outside that group. Thus an individual is expected not to cheat with money inside the network but is not enjoined against doing it externally.

3. *Don't be incompetent in your job.* This rule sets standards of excellence within the network and again it establishes confidence among its members. What this rule suggests is that an individual— thief, numbers runner, prostitute, pimp, locksmith, dealer of stolen goods, narcotics pusher, or hijacker—should do his job well.

These rules seem far less related to personal characteristics than they are to business relationships, because the relationships are more situational or episodic than is true in the prison court or in the youthful gangs. Individuals come together in these entrepreneurial models largely for mutual profit and their dependence upon each other is related entirely to advancing that profit. In the prison court or youthful gang model, however, personal relationships develop out of long-term, intense interaction and are designed to build trust.

While the rules which govern associational networks emphasize personal characteristics and those of entrepreneurial networks emphasize conduct, there is an important relationship between them. The more highly personalized rules take place within networks which might be considered training and testing grounds for the more profitable but also more demanding entrepreneurial networks. Thus recruitment of blacks and Puerto Ricans into sophisticated organized crime networks usually seems to come as a result of prior experience either in a youthful gang or in prison where they are identified as promising individuals. Unfortunately, our data about youth gangs and prison experience among Cubans is quite sparse and we cannot support similar observations there. We do know from our informants that Cubans must go through a preliminary street experience before they are accepted into more important positions. Among blacks and Puerto Ricans, however, enough information is available to codify this process by adding a fifth rule, to be used as a general guide for the entrepreneur type of network which we described earlier: In order to join the "organization" one must have passed through some kind of accredited criminal training course in which it can be assumed that the personal qualities valued in organized crime were duly tested.

Among youthful criminal partnerships, lines of authority seem in general to be poorly drawn—there is little sense of who is obliged to follow whose orders except in particular circumstances. On the other hand, in prison and in the small criminal businesses, certain lines of authority seem to be clearly drawn. In prison, one man in each court is the leader, based on personal qualities and criminal expertise, and all of the others are his followers. In the entrepreneurial network the authority pattern is simple: whoever pays the salaries gives the orders.

Comparing the code of rules for the black and Hispanic network structures with the code of the Lupollo family, there are some obvious similarities and some important differences as well. Both the Italian and the black and Hispanic codes establish who is inside the net and who is an outsider. Those rules demanding loyalty and secrecy serve to establish the boundaries of the network or family and set up behavioral standards as well. It is, of course, not surprising that an organization or network which is engaged in illegal activity should require of its members that they show their loyalty to the group by respecting its confidences and maintaining secrecy. Secret societies of any sort, whether criminal, fraternal, or revolutionary could not long survive without requiring both loyalty to the organization and some degree of secrecy. Thus the similarity in the two codes results from the generic nature of organized crime as joint clandestine activity. The other similarity between the two codes also derives from the nature of organized criminal activity. These injunctions, which are described in terms such as "be a stand-up guy," "be competent in what you do," or "don't be a coward" are rules which reinforce the feeling of trust among the members of the network or family.

There are also some important differences between the sets of codes. While each of the major rules found among the Lupollos is also found in black and Hispanic networks, these rules do not seem to operate with the same degree of force within the black and Puerto Rican organized crime networks. While the Italian code subordinates the individual and stresses protection of the family—usually a larger organization than a typical black or Puerto-Rican network, the latter codes tend to emphasize the individual and secondarily stress loyalty to the network. This may be because of the relatively recent development of networks in comparison to the long history of the Italian crime family.

28. Illegal Corporate Payments

MARSHALL B. CLINARD
with
PETER C. YEAGER
JEANNE BRISSETTE
DAVID PETRASHEK
ELIZABETH HARRIES

Nothing has so tarnished the image of corporations within recent years as has the public revelation of the widespread violations of law in the form of corporate illegal payments to attain certain corporate objectives. For the most part, these exposures developed from the Watergate investigations of the 1970s. The federal government's SEC disclosure drive on questionable domestic and foreign payments revealed that up until 1978 at least $1 billion had been paid illegally by many of the *Fortune* 500 largest industrial corporations (*The Wall Street Journal*, June 28, 1978). These payments have included kickbacks, foreign payoffs, and illegal political contributions. Kickbacks and foreign payoffs have had a long history in a wide variety of fields; corporate contributions to political figures have been a long-established practice, but only recently have certain contributions become illegal. All of them are practiced for the purpose of influencing corporate objectives: to obtain advantages over competitors, to avoid harassment, and either to influence or support a political party in this country or abroad.

Examined together, these payments are forms of bribery, either for the purpose of selling a commodity or influencing decisions. Foreign payoffs, for example, represent another form of kickbacks; they are paid to government officials to influence certain decisions, usually by these same officials, to purchase a specific corporation's commodity rather than that of a competitor. This is similar to domestic kickbacks, but here the purchasing agents of the business concern, generally private, make decisions for the corporation. Political contributions to a specific party serve similar purposes.

These improper payments first came under close government scrutiny beginning about 1973 following the disclosures of political contributions by the Special Watergate Prosecutor when the Securities and Exchange Commission (SEC) ruled that any use of a corporation's funds for illegal and undisclosed purposes are of significance to shareholders. In 1974, then, the SEC began to look into the manner in which federal securities laws might have been violated. In their investigation they discovered that a large number of corporate financial records had been falsified in order to hide the source of corporate funds, along with the disbursement of "slush funds" not handled in the normal financial accountability system (Kugel and Gruenberg, 1977: 45). These practices reflected on the honesty and reliability of corporate accounting and thus represented threats to the system of full disclosure of information which the securities laws were designed to insure in order to protect public investors. The primary interest of such disclosure is to guarantee that investors and stockholders receive accurate information on which to make informed investment decisions, to assess the effectiveness of management, and to make sure that certain corrective measures are taken by management to curb any improper practices.

The most disturbing disclosure about illegal payments was that in a large number of cases "corporate management had knowledge of, approval of, or participated in the questionable and illegal activities" (Securities and Exchange Commission, 1976: 41). A tally was made from SEC data, where the information was available, on the involvement of management in fifty-eight corporations. Top management of twenty-six corporations had knowledge of the illegal activities; in seventeen they appeared to have had no knowledge, and it was not clear in fifteen if top management was involved or not. Of the twenty-six reporting involvement, all or some of the board of directors of eight corporations had knowledge about the illegal payments.

DOMESTIC KICKBACKS

Much of the wide publicity given foreign payoffs has failed to recognize fully the similarities between them and kickbacks as a form of doing business in the United States. "Domestic bribes and kickbacks paid by one American company to another, although long recognized as a serious problem, are coming under new scrutiny as a result of disclosures of similar payoffs overseas" (Jensen, 1976: 1). Domestic kickbacks are extensive according to a *New York Times* survey of businessmen, lawyers, investigators, and accountants; they occur in a wide range of industries at retail, wholesale, and manufacturing levels (*The New York Times*, March 16, 1976: 1).

The common corporate and general business practice is to give kickbacks in the form of money to a purchaser in order to make the sale. This bribery is illegal in certain areas as, for example, in the sale of alcohol products; it is also generally illegal because it is concealed from stockholders or illegally deducted from income tax reports. *Bona fide* discounts are properly recorded; kickbacks are concealed from government agencies through false invoices, bills of lading, and accounting entries. They may constitute fraud under the IRS code, unfair competition as defined by FTC, restraint of trade as defined by the Sherman Antitrust Act, and, if not disclosed, violations of the SEC regulations since true income and expenses are concealed from the stockholder or stock purchaser.

Bribes range as high as $100,000, and a large number of kickbacks appear to fall in the $25,000-to-$50,000 range. Payments take several forms, such as contributing money to a recipient's favorite charity, to the surreptitious deposits of thousands of dollars in a secret bank account or a phony consulting company set up solely to receive them. Individuals are more likely to be prosecuted for these offenses than corporations.

FOREIGN PAYOFFS

Another form of bribery is the system of paying off foreign officials and governments, a question that involves a number of ethical issues in regard to its propriety. One example is the effect it has on American foreign relations, a serious and far-reaching consequence. For example, Lockheed's payment of $90,000 to Japanese Prime Minister Tanaka and a much larger sum (probably $1 million) to Prince Bernhard of the Netherlands resulted in the criminal prosecution of the former and nearly brought down the royal house of Orange in the latter country. Foreign payoffs have been illegal since 1976 when the Foreign Corrupt Practices Act was passed. Prior to its becoming illegal, it had been illegal not to disclose such payments properly in financial reports submitted to the SEC and IRS. Although they had been the general practice for many years, corporate bribery to obtain business was made illegal in 1977, with jail terms up to five years (compared to three years for antitrust violations), and a fine up to $10,000.

By August 1976, 136 of *Fortune's* 500 largest corporations had made disclosure of millions of dollars of domestic and illegal payments overseas. Of them, 32 had made foreign payments of over $1 million each, and 4 corporations as high as $20 million or more. Lockheed made the largest overseas contributions, $250,750,000, with Exxon second, $77,761,000. The revelations continued to come in years later. For example, the SEC in 1979 accused McDonnell Douglas of $15.6 million in payoffs to various foreign officials. Some large corporations were "clean"; IBM, for example, whose sales total in the billions, was able to discover improper payments of only $53,000 over a seven-year period, and there appears to have been relatively little involvement of General Electric and Kodak.

International payoffs are made directly or indirectly (Kugel and Gruenberg, 1977: 16–19). The direct method is simple; it involves direct payoffs of bribes to an influential person, but the risk of discovery is great. Indirect clandestine payments are more common; they involve banks, subsidiaries, dummy corporations, and sales agents.

The most common method of channelling foreign payoffs is through the sales agent. Many multinational corporations find it too expensive as well as unnecessary to establish an office in each country in which they operate; they use instead sales agents who often are well established in a particular country. These sales agents are able to facilitate marketing arrangements which are maintained with provisions for special favors; they also know channels through which payoffs can flow. Grumman Corporation, for example, used sales agents to negotiate its deals in Iran. One Grumman executive, according to internal company correspondence, described one agent as a "bagman," and his partner described himself to Grumman officials simply as an "errand boy" for military higher-ups in Tehran. These two sales agents were paid $2.9 million in 1975 by Grumman, after the Shah's air force had ordered eighty Grumman F14 Tomcat fighter planes (Landauer, 1978).

> In one four-year period, Iran signed orders for U. S. arms costing $10 billion, incentive enough to generate bribes disguised as sales commissions. During that period, Textron's Bell Helicopter division and at least six other U.S. suppliers funnelled fees to Air Taxi Company, the Tehran sales agency that was owned in part by the late General Khatemi. The Air Taxi manager, A. H. Zanganeh, handled commissions from American companies as if he hadn't heard of the Shah's anticorruption campaign (Landauer, 1978).

"In payment for the sale of aircraft, Rockwell International on one occasion had deposited $574,612 to Air Taxi's account at First National Bank and Trust Company in Oklahoma City; from that account Mr. Zanganeh had drawn a check for $260,000 payable to General Khatemi" (Landauer, 1978).

Payoffs are often made through a dummy corporation. This method was used by Northrop Corporation in Switzerland to pay some $30 million in commissions and to bribe government officials and agents in the Netherlands, Iran, France, the Federal German Republic, Saudi Arabia, Brazil, Malaysia, and Taiwan. Through such means commissions were channelled to influential foreigners who then helped the corporation sell airplanes. The parent corporation pays the dummy corporation the sales commissions, and the latter then passes it on to independent agents. With this arrangement the corporation can claim it does not know to whom the payments are made and thus cannot be directly linked to them.

CORPORATE PAYOFFS AND THE MARKET SITUATION

An economist has contended that corporate bribery is neither an aberration nor a special problem of morality, or even of business ethics.

> Rather, it is a manifestation of two more general and interrelated problems: the concentrated market and political power of large corporations in the context of a democratic society and the conflicts posed by large numbers of significant transnational actors in a world of nation states (Kobrin 1976: 106).

The internal organization of a corporation may reflect the wish to facilitate low-level corruption, with executives delegating responsibilities and thus avoiding close monitoring, thus creating a general atmosphere in which corruption can exist or even flourish (Rose-Ackerman, 1978: 191). Of the thirty-two industries that spent more than $1 billion in improper overseas payments, half were in aircraft, oil, food, and drugs. Seven were in drugs, which was the most common. From one study of this concentration it was concluded that it was due in part to varying market conditions (Kugel and Gruenberg, 1977: 47–48). In the aircraft industry the lack of their own sales forces within the host country generally necessitates the employment of foreign sales agents by the multinational corporations; and since these sales agents are independent contractors who operate for the most part outside the control of the corporations, their large sales commissions, warranted by the multimillion-dollar purchase price for aircraft, is likewise outside of their control (Kugel and Gruenberg, 1977: 62). Special problems exist in such extractive industries like oil in the maintenance of a profitable relationship with the host country. Particularly in the developing countries the multinational corporation has the initial bargaining power on its side, as it is being wooed to invest tremendous sums of capital within the country. As the installations are completed, however, a shift results in the bargaining power. The frequent foreign payoffs in the drug industry involve two situations. It is not unusual for drug companies to deal with government officials in arranging purchases of their products, in view of the general world-wide programs for marketing that most drug companies have, along with the fact the governments in most of the developing countries and some of the West European countries are in control of most of the country's health activities.

EVALUATION OF IMPROPER FOREIGN PAYMENTS

The arguments against multinational corporation payoffs are that they conceal an accurate financial picture of the corporation, endanger the credibility of the corporation, endanger foreign relations and the American image, jeopardize the internal operations of the corporation, and do not necessarily improve the national economic picture.

(1) The prospective investor or stockholder, as well as the government, does not have an accurate financial picture of the corporation.

(2) These practices can be concealed only through various devious means or through improper accounting procedures, both of which endanger the credibility of corporations.

(3) Through the bribery of foreign officials such payoffs endanger the relations with other governments and the American image among the general population.

(4) They endanger the internal operations of the corporation itself. As explained by Gabriel (1977: 50):

> In abiding or abetting corruption of public officials, a company gradually corrupts itself. No organization can remain for long in a state of moral schizophrenia, violating legal or ethical norms abroad while seeking to maintain its institutional integrity at home. In time, the lower standards accepted as the way of life abroad will corrupt standards of corporate life at home.

(5) Sorensen (1976: 729) maintains that there

> ... was no gain to our country's balance of payments or economy when U.S. companies paid bribes to win a contract that would otherwise have gone to another U.S. company. On the contrary, the added cost of these improper contracts to the host country further weakened the market for other U.S. exporters. The fact that some American companies have succeeded in these countries without the payment of bribes is an indication that U.S. exports will not suffer all that severely from an end to such payments. Those governments desirous of obtaining U.S. technology and quality will unquestionably learn to buy our goods without any special inducement.

ILLEGAL POLITICAL CONTRIBUTIONS

Since 1972 corporations have been prohibited from making direct contributions to candidates seeking election to federal offices. Corporate campaign contributions have generally been given for economic reasons: to secure bureaucratic favors and to influence policy decisions that will result in increases in corporate profits. They are also given to prevent certain legislation from being passed on decisions that might result in a decrease in corporate profits.

The Watergate investigations revealed extensive illegal contributions to the Nixon campaign fund by U.S. corporations. More than 300 corporations were eventually involved, some of them having contributed illegally large sums of money as late as 1976. Seventeen corporations pleaded guilty and were fined (generally $5,000 or less), as were some eighteen officials of different corporations (fined $2,000 or less). Although many corporations and executives were convicted during the two years following, there should obviously have been far more prosecutions. Jaworski has pointed out that this was difficult since the statute (18 U.S.C. 610) requires that the recipient either knew of the corporate source of political contribution or received such money in "reckless disregard" of whether the source was a corporation or not.

> The experience of our investigations demonstrated the virtual impossibility of proving such knowledge by the recipient. The corporate officials making the contribution, not surprisingly, did not tell the recipient that the money was corporate. Customarily, the contributions were delivered "from your friends at X Co." (Jaworski, 1977: 314).

As contrasted with foreign payoffs, there is no question about the issues and consequences of corporate political contributions. Many illegal campaign contributions have involved a great deal of deception; for example, Swiss bank accounts have been used, or money has been taken from overseas subsidiaries in sealed envelopes carried by special messengers and brought into the country illegally. In order to avoid the possibility that the public will learn about the contributions, transfer pricing was used, resulting in what has been characterized as "money-laundering through foreign subsidiaries and Swiss bank accounts . . . a lesson in corporate wheeling and dealing" (*Newsweek*, November 26, 1978: 34). Gulf Oil Corporation "laundered" millions of dollars in illegal contributions through a subsidiary in the Bahamas (*The Wall Street Journal*, November 14, 1977). This money had been brought in illegally and distributed to various candidates, primarily President Nixon.

CORPORATE ILLEGALITIES AND THE ACCOUNTING PROFESSION

Public corporations are required by the federal securities laws to report accurate financial information. These reports have often been revealed to have been falsified so that illegal domestic and foreign payments, frauds, price-fixing, and other violations have been concealed from the public and the government. In its 1976 special report to the Senate on questionable illegal and foreign payments and practices, the Securities and Exchange Commission stated:

> The almost universal characteristic of the cases reviewed to date by the Commission has been the apparent frustration of our system of corporate accountability which has been designed to assure that there is a proper accounting of the use of corporate funds and that documents filed with the Commission and circulated to shareholders do not omit or misrepresent material facts. Millions of dollars of funds have been inaccurately recorded in corporate books and records to facilitate the making of questionable payments. Such falsification of records has been known to corporate employees and often to top management, but often has been concealed from outside auditors and counsel and outside directors (Securities and Exchange Commission, 1976).

Many cases of improper or illegal foreign payments that have been examined by the SEC have involved both inadequate and improper corporate books and records that have concealed questionable payments from independent auditors as well as from some or all of the top management and the board of directors. The maintenance of funds outside the normal accountability system was also involved in some cases for similar purposes. Falsifications or inadequate records were found to be deliberate in some cases, representing careful attempts of some corporate executive or members of boards of directors to hide their activities from other company officers, members of the board, and the auditors. Such defects in the corporate accountability system had in many instances been instituted at lower levels of the corporate hierarchy.

It is the responsibility, in the maintenance of all records, of the independent accountant to certify that the corporate financial statements have been presented according to generally accepted accounting principles.

> Accountants are not free to close their eyes to facts that come to their attention, and in order properly to satisfy their obligations, they must be reasonably sure that corporate books and records are free from defects that might compromise the validity of these statements (Securities and Exchange Commission, 1976: 49).

As one example, the Commission specifically noted the manner in which Lockheed's illegal payments had been concealed:

> Among other things, it was alleged that the defendants disguised these secret payments on Lockheed's books and records by utilizing, or causing to be utilized, false accounting entries, cash and "bearer" drafts payable directly to foreign government officials, nominees and conduits for payments

to government officials and other artifices and schemes. As a result of their activities, at least $750,000 was not expended for the purpose indicated on the books and records of Lockheed and its subsidiaries and was deposited instead in a secret Swiss bank account, and an additional $25 million was expended in secret payments to foreign officials. In addition, the Commission alleged that over $200 million was disbursed to consultants and commission agents without adequate records and controls to insure that the services were actually rendered. The practices were alleged to have resulted in the filing of inaccurate financial statements with the Commission with respect to the income, cost and expenses of the company (Securities and Exchange Commission, 1976: B-23).

Until quite recently there has been little emphasis on the responsibility of the auditor other than for detecting accounting errors and irregularities; most have felt they were not responsible for detecting the illegal acts committed by corporate clients. The traditional position of the American Institute of Certified Public Accountants (AICPA) has been that "the normal audit arrangement is not designed to detect fraud and cannot be relied upon to do so" (Baron et al., 1977: 56). Normally the audit is assumed to be conducted in an atmosphere of honesty and complete integrity. In making any examination, however, an independent auditor is not always aware that there may have been fraud and that if the fraud is sufficiently material it might affect his opinion of the financial statements (SAS, No. 1, Section 110.05).

Difficulties remain, however, in the auditor's ability to determine the legality or the illegality of an act. Several limitations are typically cited by the profession: (1) The scope of professional competence is limited; the determination of legality is the function of an attorney, not an auditor. (2) The illegal act may have arisen from a situation not associated with the financial aspects of the organization being audited and thus difficult if not impossible for the auditor to determine, as for example, in the realm of occupational, health, and safety regulations and truth-in-lending rules. (3) Some acts may be borderline cases in which legality is questionable, as for example, when a client pays fees to a foreign official to act as a sales agent without knowing if this official is sharing the fee illegally with others (Solomon, 1977: 53). (4) The client might possibly have covered up all traces of an illegal act so that an auditor will not discover it in the course of a normal routine examination.

In the past five years much publicity has been given to the role of accountants and auditors in the concealment of corporate crime. As a result, the accounting profession has been re-examining its standards and its codes of conduct in relation to corporate violations. In 1979 the AICPA proposed that in quarterly financial reports of publicly-held corporations, the corporation counsel, rather than the auditor, would indicate if he were "aware of any material modifications" that should be made in the interim financial data to conform with generally accepted accounting principles (*The Wall Street Journal,* January 2, 1979). There has even been some demand for federal legislation to ensure that the accounting profession adequately carries out its obligations to the financial community and to the public.

References

Baron, C. David, Douglas A. Johnson, D. Gerald Searfoss, and Charles H. Smith. 1977. "Uncovering corporate irregularities: Are we closing the expectation gap?" *Journal of Accountancy* (October).

Gabriel, Peter P. 1977. "A case for honesty in world business." *Fortune* (December): 49–50.

Jaworski, Leon. 1977. *The Right and the Power.* New York: Pocket Books.

Jensen, Michael C. 1976. "Companies' payoffs in U.S. come under new scrutiny." *The New York Times* (March 16), p. 1.

Kobrin, Stephen J. 1976. "Morality, political power and illegal payments by multinational corporations." *Columbia Journal of World Business* 11 (Winter): 105–110.

Kugel, Yerachmiel, and Gladys W. Gruenberg. 1977. *International Payoffs: Dilemma for Business.* Lexington, Mass.: Lexington Books.

Landauer, Jerry. 1978. "Documents at Grumman raise questions about role of Shah's aides in plane sales." *The Wall Street Journal* (November 28), p. 40.

Rose-Ackerman, Susan. 1978. *Corruption: A Study of Political Economy.* New York: Academic Press.

Securities and Exchange Commission. 1976. *Report of the Securities and Exchange Commission on Questionable and Illegal Corporate Payments and Practices.* Submitted to the Senate Committee on Banking, Housing and Urban Affairs, U.S. Senate, 94th Congress. Washington, D.C.: U.S. Government Printing Office.

Solomon, Kenneth I. and Hyman Muller. 1977. "Illegal payments: Where the auditor stands." *Journal of Accountancy* 143 (January): 51–57.

Sorensen, Theodore C. 1976. "Improper payments abroad: Perspectives and proposals." *Foreign Affairs* 54 (July): 719–733.

29. How Agnew Bartered His Office to Keep from Going to Prison

JAMES M. NAUGHTON
JOHN CREWDSON
BEN A. FRANKLIN
CHRISTOPHER LYDON
AGIS SALPUKAS

THE INVESTIGATION

It started with a casual remark, over lunch in Baltimore, late in the fall of 1972.

Robert Brown, director of the local Internal Revenue Service intelligence unit, mentioned a curious matter to George Beall, the United States Attorney. The intelligence unit had been poking into the income tax returns of Maryland officials and some of them "don't jibe," said Mr. Brown.

With equal nonchalance, Mr. Beall replied that he had heard rumors of local officials taking kickbacks from government contractors. Perhaps, the two men agreed, it was time to seek a connection between the tax returns and the rumors.

The investigation centered in suburban Baltimore County, where a Democrat, N. Dale Anderson, succeeded Mr. Agnew as the county executive in 1967. On December 4, Mr. Beall had United States District Judge C. Stanley Blair—who had been Vice President Agnew's chief of staff until his appointment to the bench in 1971—impanel a federal grand jury.

The objectives were modest. Maybe they would catch "a couple of building inspectors" on the take, Mr. Beall thought. He assigned the case to three young assistants—Barnet D. Skolnik, Russell T. Baker, Jr., and Ronald S. Liebman.

Agnew Heard Rumors

In January, they subpoenaed truckloads of official records from Baltimore County. By February, the county seat, Towson, was alive with speculation about the inquiry, and rumors of it reached Mr. Agnew.

He was startled, but outwardly unconcerned. He had done nothing wrong in his tenure there, he confided to friends.

Then the prosecutors traced the suspicious pattern of payoffs to two contractors who had long been associates of Mr. Agnew: Jerome B. Wolff, who had served as a public works staff man to County Executive Agnew, state roads commissioner under Governor Agnew, and science adviser to Vice President Agnew; and Lester Matz, a partner in a consulting firm that had had many dealings with Mr. Agnew's county and state administrations.

The two contractors were alarmed. They warned Mr. Agnew that his name would be dragged into the investigation if it were not cut short.

One account, from an Agnew associate, is that the two men approached the vice president directly last spring, but Mr. Agnew told them he had nothing to fear and would not intervene.

Agnew Reassurance

Another version—which the prosecutors in Baltimore were exploring as the basis for a possible obstruction of justice charge against Mr. Agnew—was more involved. It was that Mr. Matz and Mr. Wolff had sent their message through I. H. Hammerman, a wealthy Maryland mortgage banker who had begun an Agnew-for-President movement for his close friend with "Spiro of '76" bumper stickers. Mr. Agnew was said to have sent back a rejoinder, paraphrased by one prosecutor:

"Don't worry. It's going to be stopped. You'll be indicted, but what's an indictment? You can beat it. The prosecutors will be kicked upstairs and it will end."

Whichever version was more correct, Mr. Agnew decided in April that he had to have legal advice. He got in touch with Charles W. Colson, the former White House special counsel. It was a curious choice. Mr. Colson was himself coming under investigation by the Senate Watergate committee for his activities on behalf of President Nixon and had gone so far as to take a lie detector test to demonstrate that he was not involved in the Watergate burglary on June 17, 1972.

Mr. Colson met a number of times with Mr. Agnew. He also is known to have discussed the situation with the president. He asked his law partner, Judah Best, to get in touch with United States Attorney Beall.

Just before Easter, on April 19, Mr. Best went to Baltimore to declare that Mr. Agnew was concerned that "people were putting pressure on him to stop the investigation," and he wanted Mr. Beall to know that the last thing the vice president "wanted to do in the middle of Watergate was to cover up."

As he later recalled it:

"I explained to Beall that I represented the vice president, that the vice president had heard these stories that he'd better stop the investigation or they'd make charges about him, and also that we'd heard about the dubious loyalties and lack of discretion of people on his (Beall's) staff."

Skolnik Pursued It

The last remark was a reference to Mr. Skolnik, the most expert of the three assistant prosecutors on corruption cases—"I have an instinct for going after public officials who take cash in envelopes," he later boasted—but a liberal Democrat who had taken a leave from the prosecutor's office to work in the unsuccessful 1972 presidential campaign of Senator Edmund S. Muskie, Democrat of Maine.

It was Mr. Skolnik who pursued the investigation until it touched on Mr. Agnew, a point that later would lead one of the vice president's strategists to complain that Mr. Beall, a Republican whose father had been and brother was a United States senator, had "lost control" of the inquiry.

In April, though, Mr. Agnew had yet to be implicated. Mr. Beall told the vice president's lawyer that there was nothing to warrant any suggestion that Mr. Agnew was involved, said that he understood the delicacy of the situation, and agreed to keep Mr. Best advised of the progress of the case.

Through June, Mr. Best kept telephoning Mr. Beall every ten days or so and getting the same report: don't worry.

They didn't. Mr. Agnew discussed with his staff the prospect of another trip abroad on behalf of the White House. He submitted to a series of interviews in which he was able to note that he alone, among the officials closest to the president, had escaped any hint of involvement in the burgeoning Watergate scandal.

Three Were Pressing

But Mr. Skolnik and his two colleagues were pressing hard with the tactic that prosecutors employ to get lesser figures to implicate higher-ups.

"The train is at the station," they would warn a potential criminal defendant. "Lots of people are getting on. Room is running out. Time is also running out. The train may leave at any moment."

On June 4, the Baltimore County administrator, William E. For-noff, succumbed to the tactic and gave the prosecutors detailed allegations that led to a subsequent grand jury indictment of Dale Anderson. Unknown to the vice president, however, Fornoff gave no information involving him.

But Fornoff's actions apparently threatened Mr. Wolff and Mr. Matz. On June 11, almost simultaneously, they reached the prosecutors and started talking. By the end of June, the case against Vice President Agnew had begun to take shape.

NO MORE SMILES

The routine call from Judah Best to George Beall, in early July, did not elicit the routine assurance. Instead, the United States attorney told Mr. Agnew's lawyer, "It would be beneficial if we didn't talk again."

To Mr. Best, the implication was clear. "All smiles ended in early July."

It was universal, among those involved. On July 3, Mr. Beall and his three assistants came to Washington to alert Attorney General Elliot L. Richardson to the important new turn in the case.

"Boy, do we have bad news for you," one of them said as they entered the office of the nation's top law enforcement official.

Richardson's Concern

They outlined the charges: For a decade, up to last December, Mr. Agnew had accepted, perhaps even solicited, cash payments from contractors in return for official favors.

Mr. Richardson listened, leaned back in his chair when the prosecutors had finished, and lit up a cigar. It was the eve of Independence Day. The attorney general immediately cast the situation in its most broad and serious context. What was at stake, he remarked, was "the continuing capacity of the nation to govern itself."

All during the previous week, John W. Dean 3d, the former White House legal counsel, had been testifying to the Senate Watergate committee that President Nixon was an active participant in the Watergate cover-up.

Beyond that, Mr. Richardson voiced concern—which he would repeat many times over the next three months—that Mr. Agnew was one step away from becoming president of the United States.

"The president's plane could go down tomorrow," the attorney general kept saying. "There could be an assassin's bullet. He could die tomorrow. Here we have a vice president under a cloud."

He told the Baltimore prosecutors to proceed. They expected, as one of them later put it, "some midnight phone calls" to order that they direct the investigation away from the vice president. The calls never came.

Much later, after Mr. Agnew had resigned, an associate attributed Mr. Agnew's denouement to the turmoil that Watergate had stirred in the Nixon administration.

"If it hadn't been for Watergate," he said, "this whole thing would have been manageable. We wouldn't have had Richardson in the Justice Department, for one thing. I sure as hell would rather have dealt with Kleindienst"—former Attorney General Richard G. Kleindienst.

The point was not that Mr. Kleindienst might have been induced to cover up the case. It was that he might have understood better than Mr. Richardson—a Boston Brahmin whose politics had never depended upon others' wealth—how Mr. Agnew could rationalize a political life-style in which secret gifts from others were considered necessary for survival.

From the outset of the case against him through his televised explanation of his resignation last Monday, Mr. Agnew insisted that he was innocent of any wrongdoing, that he had never violated a public trust in return for political contributions.

For Mr. Agnew, it was all essential to survival, a basic platform from which he could continue to pursue higher office. Having entered big-time politics without benefit of wealth, he felt constant pressure to live up to the standards of his wealthier peers.

He accepted groceries from a supermarket executive. His restaurant tabs were picked up by Mr. Hammerman. He used funds given to him when he was governor to stock a wine cellar. When he traveled as vice president to Palm Springs, California, everything was paid for him there by Frank Sinatra or Bob Hope. Early this year he moved into a $190,000 home with a $160,000 mortgage—and could not afford new draperies.

As one of his closest associates stated it, Mr. Agnew felt that "you can't go to (political) rallies if you don't have shoes, and gasoline in the car."

But as the Agnew supporters suspected, Attorney General Richardson took the view—as did the prosecutors in Maryland—that what the vice president was accused of was illegal and immoral.

"How can he stay in office?" Mr. Richardson asked colleagues in one Justice Department meeting. "I couldn't do it."

FROM X TO Y TO Z

On the last day of July, George Beall telephoned Judah Best and asked him to come to Baltimore. Mr. Best asked if he could do so in a few days, but the United States attorney said, "You'd better make it tomorrow."

When Mr. Best entered Mr. Beall's office the next day, August 1, the three other prosecutors already were there. Mr. Beall asked, "Do you want to sit with your back to the wall?"

"If it's all the same to you," Mr. Best answered, "I'd rather sit by the window."

Mr. Beall handed him a letter advising Mr. Best that the vice president was under investigation for possible violations of the federal criminal code and internal revenue statutes. Mr. Best read it, folded it up, and without a word, left the office.

He drove back to Washington and made arrangements through Mr. Colson to see the vice president, who was then in New York, the next day. Then another partner, David I. Shapiro, telephoned to the New York law firm of Paul, Weiss, Rifkind, Garrison & Wharton to ask Jay H. Topkis, a specialist in tax fraud cases, to join in the defense.

"We've got a very high government official we'd like you to defend," Mr. Shapiro said.

There was a pause at his end of the telephone conversation and then he told Mr. Topkis, "Well, no, not quite *the* highest."

Mr. Topkis agreed and added Martin London of the New York firm to the defense team. From that point on, in many telephone conversations about defense strategy, the lawyers referred to the vice president only as "the client" and spoke in what they later described as a "highly elliptical" manner. They suspected that the government would tap their phones.

The three principal defense lawyers—Messrs. Best, Topkis, and London—had their first meeting with Mr. Agnew on the morning of August 6, in the vice president's suite in the Executive Office Building.

The meeting lasted all day. In the afternoon, Mr. Agnew's telephone rang. He picked it up, then announced: "It's Richardson. He's coming over."

The attorney general joined them and recited the case as it then stood. It consisted of allegations by Mr. Matz and Mr. Wolff and by Allen Green, the principal in a large engineering company, that they had funneled thousands of dollars to Mr. Agnew on a regular basis in exchange for favors.

PURGATORY

The messages had been coming with some regularity from Mr. Hammerman. Mr. Agnew would answer the phone and an intermediary would say, "We may be in trouble."

Then came the day in August when there was a final, shocking message: "You may be in big trouble."

There were no more cryptic calls after that, and the vice president knew what that meant: even Mr. Hammerman had turned on him. But he set out to win vindication. The process was complicated by the suddenness with which the case against him had become an open fight, in full view of the public. Before it would end, he would describe it as a "purgatory."

The same day that Mr. Richardson outlined to Mr. Agnew the government's evidence against him, the vice president learned that someone had already outlined part of it to Jerry Landaur of *The Wall Street Journal.*

With the aid of the lawyers, he prepared a brief statement acknowledging that he was being investigated and proclaiming innocence of any violations of law.

On August 8, Mr. Agnew conducted a news conference at which he called the charges against him "damned lies," pledged cooperation with the prosecutors, and said he had "absolutely nothing to hide."

It was the first step in an intricate campaign to place pressure on the president and, through him, on the Department of Justice.

As one official knowledgeable about Mr. Agnew's strategy deliberations characterized it, the news conference was intended to draw a sharp contrast between a cooperative vice president and a president who was withholding Watergate tapes from the Senate and government investigators. Second, it was intended to "use the press, in the classic sense, to counter the other side's use of the press" through leaks of evidence against the vice president. Finally, it was meant to be a warning to the president: "We're going to fight; we're not going to be pushed around."

Mr. Nixon and Mr. Agnew never became close personally.

When the two senior officials of the United States government met in private they were uncomfortable with one another. Cordial, yes. Respectful, always, but never fully candid. When the Agnew scandal became a public property, it was doubly so. Mr. Nixon at first gave periodic and seemingly begrudged expressions of public confidence in Mr. Agnew. Later he began volunteering the statement that no improprieties had been cited—while Mr. Agnew was vice president—a qualification that later proved to be erroneous.

The White House kept insisting, after each of a series of private meetings between the president and vice president, that no requests had been made by Mr. Nixon for the resignation of the man he twice had picked for his heir apparent. Most Washington skeptics automatically disbelieved it. Curiously enough, it was true, strictly speaking.

NO DEAL

The president discussed the criminal case with the vice president on September 1. He reportedly wanted Mr. Agnew to resign, but recoiled from the task of making a direct appeal.

Instead, he sent an agent to see the vice president some time during the first few days of September. An Agnew associate said that it was Bryce N. Harlow, a gentle but politically streetwise counselor to the president who had developed a close relationship with Mr. Agnew during the 1970 campaign but was closest of all to Mr. Nixon.

Mr. Harlow described the severity of the charges against Mr. Agnew. He suggested that a resignation might be best, "for the good of the country." And he alluded to an understanding in the White House that the consequences for Mr. Agnew should be made minimal in return for an act of patriotism.

From the outset, Mr. Agnew expressed interest in the proposal but would stand and fight if any such proposal involved the risk of imprisonment. It was, said one of the half-dozen people with whom he consulted about the overture, "very, very important to him, the most important thing of all, that he not go to prison." He continued to profess his innocence, but he understood that resignation would be taken as a token of guilt and a presumption of guilt might well be a prelude to conviction and jail.

On September 14, Mr. Agnew asked his closest confidant in the Senate, Barry Goldwater of Arizona, to meet with him. He told the senator, whose support for him had rallied other American conservatives, that he was seriously weighing a presidential request for his resignation.

Mr. Goldwater told the vice president that was fine if he were guilty. If not—as Mr. Agnew assured him—then he should fight it to the end.

Later that morning, Senator Goldwater telephoned Mr. Harlow and was harshly critical of the request and the pressure it presented. The senator then flew to his home in Phoenix.

To the senator's surprise, Mr. Harlow arrived by jet in Phoenix not long afterwards, accompanied by J. Fred Buzhardt, Jr., the president's special counsel on Watergate. The purpose of their journey was to dissuade the senator from continuing to support Mr. Agnew.

Resented Publicity

For an hour, the two presidential assistants outlined the evidence, but Mr. Goldwater told them it contained nothing he had not already seen in the newspapers, a fact he resented nearly as much as Mr. Agnew for its prejudicial impact on the vice president's defense. In his customary blunt style, Mr. Goldwater said that he did not care if Mr. Agnew was "as guilty as John Dillinger"—what mattered was that he was not getting fair treatment from the Department of Justice.

But Mr. Agnew was already secretly beginning to try to make a satisfactory bargain with Justice. Each side withheld from the opposite a private fear that prosecution could be disastrous: the government lawyers because they thought it inevitable that one or more jurors would shrink from convicting a vice president, Mr. Agnew's attorneys because they were uncertain that jurors would accept a contention that their client had abided by a code of ethics, however questionable, that was standard in Maryland politics.

Buzhardt Was Broker

Each side had a fundamental demand that was to imperil the negotiations. Mr. Agnew would not go to prison; the Baltimore prosecutors insisted that he should. The government had to be able to avoid cover-up charges by publishing the core of its evidence; Mr. Agnew's lawyers wanted some opportunity to insist on his innocence and thus salvage some dignity.

Mr. Buzhardt played the role of broker to get the two sides to the bargaining table. Who instructed him to do so remains unclear, but to Assistant Attorney General Petersen, "it was clear where he was from. It was clear that the quicker it could be resolved the better the president would like it." But Mr. Buzhardt made no suggestions. He didn't have to. When the two sets of lawyers met the first time on September 13, Judah Best made a startling proposal.

"My line was," he later reminisced, "I want an end of this, an end of the investigation. And his resignation is part of it. Let's cut a deal.

A nolo plea (nolo contendere, or no contest, the legal equivalent of a plea of guilt without the admission) to a one-count information. No jail term. And he'll resign. And I want to save this man's honor to the extent I can."

Henry Petersen was "dumfounded." He had encountered nothing like it in twenty-five years of the Justice Department. "When a guy comes in and wants to plead before indictment, you've got him whipped," he said. "That's extraordinary in itself."

But the senior law enforcement officials wrangled for five days over whether to accept. The arguments were ferocious. Mr. Richardson sat at the head of a large conference table with five aides and the four Baltimore prosecutors shouting at one another. Mr. Skolnik in particular demanded stern retribution, a prison term. Others argued about the impact of a deal on the public image of a Justice Department already soiled by Watergate. Everyone worried about the political implications, the effect on legal institutions from a vice president copping a plea vs. the damage to the nation and the Republican party from a bitter and long public prosecution.

The attorney general refereed for the most part, but periodically he would chime in with the same insistent theme: Mr. Agnew must not become president. Mr. Nixon had been hospitalized with viral pneumonia in July. And, a colleague of Mr. Richardson's said, the attorney general "was very worried about Nixon—he might be impeached, assassinated, he was not in the best psychological condition."

On Wednesday, September 22, it leaked into print that plea bargaining was under way. Mr. Best denied it; Justice waffled. And Mr. Agnew called it off.

"No," he told his lawyers, "it's impossible. We're negotiating in a posture where I'm plea bargaining. I'm innocent, and the public perception must be that I'm innocent."

PRESSURE

On September 23, the vice president set up a legal defense fund. On September 25, he urged the House of Representatives to conduct a full public inquiry that would give him an opportunity to vindicate himself. On September 26, House Speaker Carl Albert shelved the request. On September 27, the Baltimore prosecutors began presenting evidence against Mr. Agnew to the grand jury. On September 28, Mr. Agnew's lawyers filed suit in the federal courts to block the grand jury action, contending that the constitution forbade the indictment of a vice president and that news leaks had irreparably damaged the prospect of a fair trial.

Pressure Tactics

On September 29, the vice president vowed in a Los Angeles speech not to resign even if indicted and accused the Justice Department of trying to "destroy" his career. On October 3, Judge Hoffman granted Mr. Agnew unparalleled authority to subpoena prosecutors and journalists to find the sources of news leaks. On October 5, the Justice Department asserted in a legal memorandum that a president could not be indicted but a vice president could.

It occurred with such breathtaking rapidity and mounting intensity that the nation seemed confronted with not merely another but a whole series of new legal, constitutional, and political crises. The cascade of developments was, in fact, the public product of a strategy to strengthen Mr. Agnew's hand at the secret bargaining table or, failing there, to build a foundation for a long-drawn-out effort in the courts.

The bid for a House inquiry—an open invitation to impeachment— was the most excruciating of the pressure tactics. It was designed to pose a risk to a besieged president that the derelict constitutional machinery of impeachment would be overhauled for an Agnew case and, oiled, humming, and ready to perform, be available for use against Mr. Nixon himself.

The legal argument that Mr. Agnew could not be indicted in office contained a threat of a Supreme Court ruling that might also set a precedent for the presidency.

The legal and oratorical charges that the Justice Department was systematically leaking damning accusations against Mr. Agnew were meant to generate public support for his role as an underdog and thus put more heat on the prosecutors.

An admirer once credited Mr. Agnew with an uncanny ability to compartmentalize his activities, erecting watertight barriers that kept some of his closest associates from knowledge of what equally close aides were doing on his behalf.

Only three other persons were aware of Mr. Agnew's strategy of escalating pressure. They were Arthur J. Sohmer, the vice president's administrative assistant; Major General John M. Dunn, his military aide; and Mary Ellen Warner, Mr. Agnew's confidential secretary.

The message, later summarized by a marveling admirer of the strategy, was basic: "We need help. Wanted help. Demanded help." The White House got the message.

THE BARGAIN

Within days of Mr. Agnew's September 29 attack in Los Angeles against the Justice Department and his vow to stand and fight, a channel of communication that none of the participants would specify but one called "bizarre" fed a response to Mr. Agnew from the White House: resume the bargaining and this time it will work.

J. Marsh Thomson, the vice president's spokesman, was advising newsmen that Mr. Agnew would deliver another stern rebuke to the prosecutors on October 4 at a Republican party banquet in Chicago. But a day earlier, Mr. Thomson was suddenly ordered to make himself totally unavailable to news outlets. The speech turned out to be unfettered praise of the president, with only a cryptic reference to the Baltimore investigation.

"A candle is only so long and eventually it goes out," the vice president told a mystified Chicago audience.

The next day, Mr. Agnew told Mr. Best, "I think they're ready to negotiate."

Once again the broker was Mr. Buzhardt and it was implicit for whom he was acting. As Mr. Petersen stated it, "The president would be a blithering idiot if he weren't trying to exert some role in this thing. It's his administration! He had both a political interest and a constitutional interest in getting a resolution of the situation."

Settled on Wording

Late on Friday, October 5, Mr. Best caught a plane to Miami to meet with Mr. Buzhardt, who was at nearby Key Biscayne with the president's entourage. From midnight until 3 A.M. Saturday, in Mr. Best's room at the Marriott Hotel, they settled on the wording of a statement in which Mr. Agnew would acknowledge evading income taxes in 1967, and they reached an "ironclad agreement" that the vice president could see the summary of the evidence against him before it was published.

"The key," Mr. Best said, "was Agnew's capacity to deny it."

But the question of punishment still had to be settled, and that would mean involving a federal judge in the private negotiations.

On Columbus Day, October 8, Judge Hoffman met from 5 to 7 P.M. in the Old Colony Motel, across the Potomac River from the capital in Alexandria, Va., with three representatives from each side: Messrs. Petersen, Beall, and Skolnik for the government and Messrs. Topkis, London, and Best for the vice president. The tentative agreement was outlined, but Mr. Agnew's lawyers wanted a decision on the sentence they could expect, and Judge Hoffman refused to make any commitment without a recommendation from the attorney general's office.

Couldn't Agree on Penalty

Mr. Petersen said he could not give a recommendation, and the meeting broke up with resolution still eluding the negotiators.

The government could not agree on the punishment it wished to exact. The argument broke out again and it became apparent, in the words of one source, that they would have to "trample on Skolnik" to get his support for a recommendation of leniency.

At 8:45 that night, Mr. Petersen was driving home from the office. On his car radio he heard part of a speech by Secretary of State Kissinger to Pacem in Terris, a conference on the search for world peace.

"A presumed monopoly on truth obstructs negotiation and accommodation," Mr. Kissinger was saying. "Good results may be given up in the quest for ever-elusive ideal solutions." Policy makers, he said moments later, must understand "the crucial importance of timing. Opportunities cannot be hoarded; once past, they are usually irretrievable."

The next morning, Mr. Petersen had his secretary type copies of two pertinent pages from Mr. Kissinger's text. The assistant attorney general gave them to the Baltimore prosecutors and told Mr. Skolnik, "We can bring him (Mr. Agnew) to his knees. There's no doubt about that. The question is, should we?"

Disgrace, he said, would be sufficient without sending the vice president to prison.

Later that day, October 9, the negotiations resumed before Judge Hoffman. This time, however, they were at the Justice Department. Attorney General Richardson was present and he was prepared to recommend against a prison sentence.

"It is my understanding," Mr. Richardson told the judge, "that for you to give a guarantee you need an affirmative recommendation from me. Judge, if it's a must, you've got it."

"If I've got it, okay, I will commit myself," Judge Hoffman replied. It was a bargain.

30. The Fence and Society: Vincent's *Apologia Pro Vita Sua*

CARL B. KLOCKARS

DENIAL OF RESPONSIBILITY

The way I look at it, I'm a businessman. Sure I buy hot stuff, but I never stole nothin' in my life. Some driver brings me a couple a cartons, though, I ain't gonna turn him away. If I don't buy it, somebody else will. So what's the difference? I might as well make money with him instead of somebody else.

In the above statement Vincent (1) denies that he ever stole anything in his life. He then asserts either directly or by implication (2) that there is an important distinction between stealing and receiving stolen goods; (3) that the criminal act of receiving would take place even if he were not the one to do it; and (4) that he does not cause the goods to be stolen. Let us consider each of these defenses separately.

He Never Stole Anything in His Life

In two rigorous senses Vincent has stolen. First, in a number of anecdotes about his childhood ... Vincent has described his juvenile industry at theft. He dismisses those events as irrelevant to the above statement, explaining that although he says "never in my life," his childhood does not count. This is illogical in a strict sense of the words used. However, biographical claims are often intended more as moral advertisements than historical descriptions. When such is the intention, it is quite acceptable social form to exclude from public reflections on "true character" those moments of one's life when one was not in full control of one's self. Consider such statements as "All my life I've followed the Golden Rule." (From age two? seven? ten? twenty-one?) Or, "He really is a gentle man, but watch out when he's drunk."

Second, according to a strict legal interpretation of his adult behavior, Vincent does steal. He does, as the common-law definition of theft provides, "take the goods of another, without permission, with the intent to permanently deprive that person of his rightful property." However, the law makes distinctions between theft and receiving (often attaching a lower penalty to receiving), and I suspect that few readers are troubled by Vincent's simultaneous claim both that he has never stolen anything and that he does buy stolen property. It is, for most of us, an understandable social distinction. What Vincent means is that he is not a thief.

There Is an Important Distinction between Stealing and Receiving

Vincent claims not to be a thief, and we understand what he means. For Vincent himself, there are differences not only between thieves and receivers, but also between thieves and drivers.

> See, Carl, what you gotta understand is when I say "driver" I don't mean "thief." I don't consider a driver a thief. To me, a thief is somebody who goes into a house an' takes a TV set and the wife's jewelry an' maybe ends up killin' somebody before he's through. An' for what? So some nothin' fence will steal the second-hand shit he takes? To me that kind a guy is the scum of the earth.
>
> Now a driver, he's different. A driver's a workin' man. He gets an overload now an' then or maybe he clips a carton or two. He brings it to me. He makes a few bucks so he can go out on a Friday night or maybe buy his wife a new coat. To me, a thief an' a driver is two entirely different things.

Those things which distinguish the driver and the thief in Vincent's estimation may point to distinctions that the larger society makes between receiving stolen goods and actually stealing them. The fence, like the driver, does not enter homes or stores to remove property; there is no danger of violence in his presence. A thief, on the other hand, could do anything: he may well be a drug addict, rapist, robber, burglar, or assaulter, or, if the situation arose, a murderer. Society has no clear expectations about the limits of criminality involved.

On the other hand, a fence, Vincent claims, is a businessman who buys and sells stolen property. Like the driver, the fence commits his crime in the course of behavior which differs only minutely from that of legitimate members of his trade. And like the driver, the fence has a relatively stable social identity: the driver will presumably be at work again tomorrow; Vincent is in his store every day of the week. Vincent buys and sells things, waits on customers, and walks public streets openly. Truck drivers perform public tasks as well. Thieves are shadowy figures, sneaking around behind the scenes and even hiding their right names behind aliases.[1]

In sum, when Vincent begins his apologia by saying "I never stole nothin' in my life," he magnifies a common distinction between a receiver and a thief. He means, first, that he does not actually take merchandise from its owners. But second, and more importantly, he means that the fear, disgust, and distaste which "thief" connotes to some people should not and do not properly apply to him. The law, his customers, his friends, and his neighbors know there are differences between thieves and receivers, and so does Vincent.

Receiving Would Take Place Even without Him

By saying "If I don't buy it, somebody else will," Vincent attempts to minimize his responsibility by pointing to the presumed consequences of his private refusal to buy. They are, he asserts, nil; therefore his responsibility is nil. This is a patently attractive moral position, and one which is echoed frequently. Let us first examine the accuracy of the assertion before evaluating the moral position which Vincent derives from it.

Would someone else buy the merchandise if Vincent refused? I think they probably would. Although Vincent is able to dispose of some merchandise which other fences might have great difficulty selling (e.g., dental supplies), the vast majority of merchandise in which Vincent trades could be handled by many other fences. The related question, of course, is whether or not the particular thief or driver who approached Vincent with stolen property would be able to locate another fence to sell to if Vincent refused. This is problematic. In my estimation, many would find another outlet almost immediately, some would find one after a bit of looking and asking, and a very few might not be able to find another buyer. Depending on the character both of the merchandise and of his friends and neighbors, the thief or driver might well be able to sell stolen merchandise to them at a better price than he could get from Vincent.

If the accuracy of Vincent's statement is conceded, its moral implications remain to be considered. Certainly one can find examples of the same form of rationalization being offered in quite disparate social situations. The physician on trial for performing a criminal abortion claims that he performed the requested operation rather than have the woman find another, possibly less competent, conspirator. The arms manufacturer claims that he cannot be held responsible for a war because if he had not sold weapons to the participants they would have bought them elsewhere. Likewise, the conscripted soldier who opposes war but fights anyway may take comfort in the knowledge that his participation will not affect the waging of a given war or its outcome.

The moral position upon which such arguments rest is that a person's culpability for participation in an immoral or illegal act disappears or is mitigated if the act is likely to occur even if he does not participate in it. Such a position can be extended to cover situations even less pleasant that those listed above. For example, it removes responsibility in almost all incidents of mob violence. Is no one in a lynch mob responsible because others are also willing to string the victim up? Is looting at a riot scene excusable because others are looting too? Is vandalism blameless when it is a group affair? To push the position harder still, one could envision a small team of paid professional killers who always shoot their victims simultaneously so that no one gunman feels guilty. Even firing squads, so legend has it, reject such nonsense by actually loading one gun with blanks.

Responsibility for action is responsibility for action. Whether or not an act is likely to occur without one is simply irrelevant to the evaluation of one's own conduct. To surrender that elementary premise of simple moral philosophy is to abandon the responsibility to refuse to participate when one believes that others are doing wrong. Middle-class mothers everywhere, sensitive always to the seductions of the world, have correctly admonished their children who "went along with the crowd": "Just because everybody else jumps off a cliff doesn't mean you have to." It is an admonition of considerable rhetorical sophistication which has absolutely nothing to do with jumping off of cliffs, but gets instantly to the heart of patently attractive denials of responsibility like "If I don't buy it somebody else will."

He Does Not Cause the Goods to Be Stolen

With this statement Vincent suggests his relationship to drivers (and, by extension, thieves) who supply him with stolen merchandise. In Vincent's consideration he is merely a commercial respondent to theft whereas it is thieves and drivers who must bear responsibility for it.

For Vincent, the etiology of theft is a considerably less difficult problem than it is for criminologists: people steal because they want money. Why else should anyone steal? In general, why they want money is their own business, but Vincent, like most small businessmen, is close enough to those he works with to reflect on their motives. For most thieves, Vincent finds that drugs, gambling, and "high living" (Cadillacs for blacks is Vincent's most frequent example) are the main incentives for illegal earnings. Drivers, on the other hand, often use the proceeds from what they sell to add "a little extra" to the family income. To Vincent, it is preposterous to suggest that it is he, rather than the factors which thieves and drivers themselves cite, that is responsible for theft. . . .

DENIAL OF VICTIMS

The first line of defense in Vincent's apologia is his denial of responsibility for theft and his argument that for him to refrain from buying stolen goods would be inconsequential. His second line of argument is to deny that his activities have any meaningful victims or inflict any significant injury. To appreciate Vincent's second defense one must consider some of the experiences from which he reasons.

More than most people, Vincent witnesses extensive violations of the law against receiving. He sees respectable society, including police and judicial officials, coming to him for bargains that they know are suspect. Because of his reputation, he is often solicited by otherwise legitimate businessmen interested in buying something that they deal in should he come across it. He also encounters respectable types who find something romantic about his being a fence. For example:

> I got to know my doctor real good when I was in for my last operation. Somebody told him about me, I guess. Well, I started tellin' him about stuff, you know, buyin', sellin', thieves, boosters. He just couldn't get over it. He wanted me to get him some hot suits. You know, have him pick out the suits and send some boosters in to get 'em. He really wanted to do it. You shoulda seen how excited he was talkin' about swag. Imagine a guy like that, a big doctor an' all, gettin' so excited about hot stuff.

This widespread trafficking with him, and occasional fascination for his work, have consequences for the way Vincent sees his own behavior. First of all, he is conscious of a certain hypocrisy in society's attitude toward dealing in stolen property. He is aware of the legal prohibition against receiving, yet sees frequent evidence of willful, guilt-free violation of it by those who ought to know better. Vincent's recall of occasions when highly respectable citizens bought stolen goods or what they thought were stolen goods is extremely acute. Legitimate citizens of high status are truly "significant others" for Vincent.

Indeed, Vincent sees the patronage of such legitimate citizens as a reflection of his own worth. Their buying from him and maintaining friendly relations with him are considered by Vincent to constitute an important vindication of the possibly shady character of what he does. It is true that Vincent is an attractive and enjoyable person; but even if his friendly acquaintances seek him out only for this social aspect of his personality, Vincent finds it easy to perceive that they are not sufficiently offended by his receiving to limit their association with him.[2]

Given the highly supportive character of Vincent's immediate environment he is able to think of his victim and the injury he receives as someone or something "out there," removed from him physically and normatively, and separated by the intervening actions and responsibility of the thief or driver. Only very rarely does Vincent ever confront the victim of a theft. The latter is likely to direct his rage at the thief, his employee's carelessness, or his faulty security system rather than at the fence who eventually buys what was stolen from him.

From this detached perspective, Vincent contemplates the extent of his victims' losses:

> Did you see the paper yesterday? You figure it out. Last year I musta had $25,000 worth a merchandise from Sears. In this city last year they could'a called it Sears, Roebuck, and Swaggi. Just yesterday in the paper I read where Sears just had the biggest year in history, made more money than ever before. Now if I had that much of Sears's stuff can you imagine how much they musta lost all told? Millions, must be millions. And they still had their biggest year ever.

Vincent reads Sears's declaration of success as evidence of the inconsequential character of his receiving their stolen merchandise. Hence, he considers any possible claim on their part that he or hundreds of others like him are substantially harming business as at least greedy if not absurd. The logic of such an analysis is the same, on a larger scale, as the "Ma Bell can afford it" reasoning invoked by the pay-phone patron who receives a windfall from a malfunctioning unit. Vincent does not stop there in his consideration of Sears's success, however.

> You think they end up losing when they get clipped? Don't you believe it. They're no different from anybody else. If they don't get it back by takin' it off their taxes, they get it back from insurance. Who knowns, maybe they do both.
>
> Carl, if I told you how many businessmen I know have a robbery every now an' then to cover expenses you wouldn't believe it. What does it take? You get some trusted employee, and you send him out with an empty truck. He parks it somewhere an' calls in an' says he was robbed. That's it. The insurance company's gotta pay up. The driver makes a couple a hundred bucks and it's an open-an'-shut case. You can't do it every year but once in a while it's a sure thing.
>
> Oh, there's millions a ways to do it. You come in in the mornin' an break your window. Call the cops, mess some stuff up. Bang! You got a few thousand from the insurance company. I'm tellin' ya, it happens all the time.

Thus Vincent denies significant injury to Sears not only because of their net profits but because they can be seen as recovering most of their loss from insurance payments or through tax write-offs.[3] The reality for Vincent, in sum, is the comparatively trivial effect of theft on the insured victim. Inconvenient, perhaps; devastating, no! Hence: no real injury, no real victim.

The problem remaining is the general effect on pricing that theft produces. As a businessman, Vincent is in agreement with his counterparts that theft and shrinkage result in higher mark-ups and higher prices. But Vincent again falls back on the question of the ultimate consequences of his particular refusal to buy. Assuming his thieves and drivers could not find anyone else to sell to, the entire result of Vincent's private refusal to buy might amount to a penny a person for the entire year, if it were distributed over the total population of the city. And on the other side of the ledger, Vincent reckons that some of his other services to the general welfare of the community more than balance what he takes out.

The questions of the moral responsibility involved in buying stolen goods, and of the consequences of such an act for any putative victims, would be even less problematic for Vincent's customers than for Vincent were they to confront them. Given that a particular item is on Vincent's shelf and is known to be stolen, a particular purchase will not affect Vincent's survival as a fence. I do not believe that a rational economic argument can be made against an individual decision to buy stolen goods. The claim that theft costs everyone as reflected in high costs and insurance rates is inadequate. It costs everyone surely, but those who buy stolen goods manage to offset these higher costs and rates. In fact, were it simply a question of a personal economic strategy, one might argue that the only way to beat the consequences of the thieves' market is to patronize it. The only argument left seems to be to appeal to a responsibility to the general welfare of others.

To legalize receiving stolen goods would legitimize an institution which is intolerable. It would encourage theft and have a pernicious effect on society. Clearly it is an absurd suggestion. But the conflict is still real. The department-store sweater costs $15.99. Vincent is selling it for $10.00. In this particular case it is a question of saving $5.99 or making an economic gesture to the general welfare. All day long Vincent sees the general welfare lose out to bargains. . . .

THE METAPHOR OF THE LEDGER

Sure I've done some bad things in my life. Who hasn't? Everybody's got a skeleton in his closet somewhere. But you gotta take into account all the good things I done too. You take all the things I done in my life and put 'em together, no doubt about it, I gotta come out on the good side.

As a businessman, Vincent is familiar with the use of a ledger for evaluating the success or failure of enterprise. He knows that there are different ways of setting up and managing accounts. Some entries are puffed a bit more than they deserve; other profits don't show up in the counting. Occasionally, one shows a loss so as to make things look normal or to prevent having to pay too much in the end. Business accounts, properly managed by able accountants, set things in order for the businessman and those who are interested in judging what he has accomplished. When all is said and done, the ledger tells whether or not one comes up in the red or in the black.

A metaphorical ledger is equally useful in evaluating life histories: good in the credit column is balanced against evil in the debit column. Thus, acts of charity and benevolence offset entries of greed or selfishness. It is an attractive metaphor. From the scales of justice to the Great Book of St. Peter, the notion of a balancing between good and evil has proven to be a persuasive one for the common comprehension and consideration of penance, indulgence, grace, judgment, atonement, salvation, and contrition.[4]

To Vincent, a businessman all his life, the metaphor of the ledger comes easily. In accounting for his conduct, Vincent considers his criminality and his exemplary behavior on the same balance sheet.

> When it comes to fences I consider myself in a class by myself. I don't consider your street-corner fences, buyin' an' sellin' secondhand stuff, to be anything like me at all. For one thing they're all no good. They're all cheap, greedy bastards who'd sell their mother if they had a chance. I figure I have a certain class, ya know, a certain way of doin' things. To me them guys are nothin'. They're stupid, ignorant people. I can't even stand bein' around 'em.

Thieves and Drivers

In reckoning credits for his self-evaluation, Vincent points to those good things he has done for people which his role did not require him to do. For example:

> Take what I done for Artie, for instance. Now there's a guy, he's been a thief for years, an' nothin' to show for it. That year alone I musta given him $25,000. One day I'd give 'em a hundred bucks, the next day he'd be back askin' for a loan. So I had a talk with him. I told him, "Look, you're makin' good money. Why don't you put it toward a house?" So we set up a little deal where I'd keep a little each time we had a deal; then when he had enough we'd put it toward a house.
> Well it took about three months an' he had about $1,500 with me. So I

got a real-estate agent I knew to get him a place, nothin' fancy but a pretty good neighborhood. It was colored but clean. Well, you know what happened? His wife came down with his kids an' she couldn't thank me enough. They had been livin' in one of those welfare high rises and she hated it. Every now an' then she comes by to tell me how things are goin'.

Don't get me wrong. I made a lot of money off of Artie, but I set him straight too.

What places Vincent's efforts in Artie's behalf on the credit side of the ledger is the fact that Artie and his wife appreciated Vincent's assistance and that Vincent did not have to give it. Vincent has repeated similar anecdotes to me frequently.

I am good to children. You know "Eyeball," right? All the trouble I had with him? His wife came in at Christmastime last year. When she left she had at least a hundred dollars worth of clothes and toys for her kids. I knew Eyeball was in jail an' she didn't have nothin'. Carl, if you knew how much stuff I gave to people, outright gifts, you wouldn't believe it.

Would you believe it if I told you that I got a thief who calls me "his white father"? It's true. I been good to him. Posted bail for him a couple of times. He tells everybody, "Vincent Swaggi, he's my white father."

The matter of the posted bail in the second anecdote raises a number of complications in the matter of crediting Vincent's generosity. One could interpret Vincent's bailing out the thief as self-serving, since Vincent knew that once back on the street, the thief would resume bringing him merchandise. The extent to which such actions should be seen as impelled by generosity becomes even more problematic in those cases where Vincent benefits more than does the recipient. Many people turn to Vincent for "help" when they are in a jam and don't know what to do. Providing alibis, referrals to persuasive lawyers, loans at high interest, and the kind of encouragement a man occasionally needs to get back to his work are all well appreciated. Just a little bit of help sometimes pays off handsomely.

I had this guy bringin' me radios. Nice little clock radios, sold for $34.95. He worked in the warehouse. Two a day he'd bring me, an' I'd give him fifteen for the both of 'em. Well, after a while he told me his boss was gettin' suspicious "cause inventory showed a big shortage. So I asked him how he was gettin' the radios out. He says he puts 'em in his locker at lunch an' takes 'em to me after work. So I ask him if anybody else is takin' much stuff. He says a couple of guys do. I tell him to lay off for a while an' the next time he sees one of the other guys take somethin' to tip off the boss. They'll fire the guy an' clear up the shortage. Well he did it an' you know what happened? They made my man assistant shipper. Now once a month I get a carton delivered right to my store with my name on it. Clock radios, percolators, waffle irons, anything I want, fifty off wholesale.

Though Vincent is reluctant to place such profitable assistance in his credit column, one must consider the matter from the perspective of the newly appointed shipper: Vincent advised him well. He saved him from his suspicious boss, cleared his reputation, got him promoted, probably with a raise, and made it possible for him not only to increase his earnings from theft but to steal with greater security as well. For Vincent, on the other hand, such an incident cancels itself out; it was good advice which paid off. Yet, although such events cannot, because they paid off so well, be offered individually as evidences of virtue, in the aggregate they enhance Vincent's professional self-conception. However, they leave a residual magnanimity which surfaces in statements such as the following:

> I treat the people I deal with right. If they're in a jam an' I can help 'em out, I'll do it. And I don't mean just your high-class types either. I mean thieves, drivers, police, customers, anybody. I'm known for helpin' people out when I can.
>
> You don't have to be a bastard to be in this business, you know. You can treat people decent. Some guys, like my brother, never learn that. They think a black man comes into the store, you can push 'm around, call him "colored" or "boy"; you just can't do that no more. Times have changed.

Notes

1. The matter of "potential for deviance," by which I mean people's estimations of the probability that one type of deviance implies the capacity for other types, merits systematic criminological examination. As an example, our treatment of the insane by incarceration seems to presume that relatively mild violations of social propriety suggest a capacity for more serious and perhaps violent deviance. Similarly, before the time when long hair was co-opted by an economic establishment willing to capitalize on it, long hair seemed to be regarded by many as a certain sign of the willingness of the wearer to engage in other, non-tonsorial forms of deviance. Likewise, society may well assume that, all other things being equal, a thief has a greater "potential for deviance" than a fence.

2. The idea of *innocence by association* raises important questions for researchers in the sociology of deviance. Simply by associating with deviants the field researcher gives tacit reinforcement to them. My association with Vincent was interpreted by him as quite complimentary, and the vast majority of thieves I have interviewed have felt similarly flattered. My generally nonjudgmental attitude was uniformly construed as approval. Likewise, I find that a text like my own is easy to interpret as being supportive of deviant careers in spite of my protestations that it is primarily descriptive and analytical, in the way sociology must be. A similar case can be made regarding the degree of attention paid to militant blacks in the liberal press. (See Nathan Glazer and Daniel P. Moynihan. *Beyond the Melting Pot*, 2d ed., rev. [Cambridge: M.I.T. Press, 1970], p. lxxxvii).

3. Months after Vincent told me about his views on Sears's profits in spite of their losses from theft, I ran across the following obscure news item (John Manning, ed., "No Money Down" [Philadelphia: Publication of the Model Cities Consumer Protection Program, vol. 1, no. 3], p. 3). It is rather perverse to print it here but I cannot resist the irony.

SEARS FASTBUCK: Second Income News relates how Richard W. Sears, founder of Sears, Roebuck, got started in business. Sears was a railroad telegrapher with a sideline business of selling watches. His gimmick was to buy watches at $2 apiece, affix $20 price-tags, and mail them to fictitious locations across the country. When the packages came back "undeliverable," Sears would open them in presence of fellow employees and palm the watches off as "bargains"—at $10 apiece.

4. Reference to a Book of Life wherein all of man's deeds are recorded is found throughout Scripture. For example, Rev. 20: 11–15 states:

[11] Then I saw a great white throne and him who sat upon it; from his presence earth and sky fled away, and no place was found for them. [12] And I saw the dead, great and small, standing before the throne, and books were opened. Also another book was opened, which is the book of life. And the dead were judged by what was written in the books, by what they had done. [13] And the sea gave up the dead in it, Death and Hades gave up the dead in them, and all were judged by what they had done. [14] Then Death and Hades were thrown into the fire; [15] And if any one's name was not found written in the book of life, he was thrown into the lake of fire.

PART 5

CONTROLLING CRIME AND THE CRIMINAL

In part four we looked at interactional processes and conditions that may lead to criminal activities and ultimately a criminal career. We also saw how involvement in crime affects an actor's view of self and carries with it the risk of criminal processing—and of being officially labeled as a criminal.

The selections in this part explore how social control agents attempt to regulate crime and the criminal. First, we examine methods used to identify clients for processing as criminals. Then the processing and sentencing procedures themselves are described. These readings provide insight not only into how the "organizational paradigm" (described in the general introduction) operates but also into how social control agents—the police, the courts, and others—actually produce crime data. The part concludes by offering an assessment of how the accused person and the agents who deal with him or her perceive and respond to criminal processing.

FINDING CRIMINALS

As was pointed out in part two, little systematic attention has been given to how crime rates are arrived at, despite a consensus that they often present an inaccurate picture of crime and the criminal. If one is to make statements and generalizations about causation, distribution, prevention, and needed treatment and control strategies, one needs to analyze how crime data are organizationally generated; this requires, to begin with, an analysis of how institutional personnel go about identifying people for processing.

In "Clearance Rates" Jerome H. Skolnick points out that to detectives the most important measure of accomplishment is the clearance rate, or the percentage of crimes *known* to the police that are "solved." To illustrate the importance of the clearance process, Skolnick compares how the police designate offenses in two cities, Westville and Eastville. In Westville, for example, "suspicious circumstances" are treated as *reported* offenses, while in Eastville they are recorded as *actual* offenses; this produces a much higher clearance rate for Westville and, consequently, feelings of resentment among Eastville detectives. Skolnick goes on to show how the manipulation of clearance rates may *reverse the hierarchy of penalties* associated with the law. For example, a detective may try to "clear" crimes by persuading a burglar to confess to several prior offenses in exchange for reduced charges or a light sentence. In one case, such inducements led a suspect to provide the police with over four hundred clearances. Thus criminality becomes a "commodity" for exchange. The stress on efficiency, the author points out, is not unique to the police profession but a central feature of most organizations.

Obviously, other control agents play an important role in identifying criminals. Suzanne Weaver, in "The Antitrust Division: Finding Cases," describes how lawyers go about discovering cases. Her observations are based on approximately one hundred interviews conducted in 1971 and 1974. She looks at how the Antitrust Division uses its *discretionary powers* to bring cases to court. Weaver points out that when staff lawyers receive information on possible antitrust violations, they have three main options: they can ask for a preliminary investigation, call for a full investigation, or recommend prosecution. She then illustrates how selected categories of cases are handled. Throughout Weaver's description one can obtain an excellent feel for the role that institutional and individual discretion plays in decision making.

PROCESSING CRIMINALS

Once criminal cases have been identified, they may become subject to prosecution. The decision to prosecute, however, is not necessarily based on standardized criteria or procedures. In deciding to prosecute, the attorney must consider several factors and options. George F. Cole, in "The Decision to Prosecute," documents some of these considerations.

Cole contends that the prosecuting attorney's office must be viewed as a component in an *exchange system*. Such a model assumes that an organization not only interacts with many clients but is dependent on them for certain resources. The prosecuting attorney's office, for example, is required to work with the police and the courts; it must also be attuned to prevailing community sentiments and norms. The cases presented by the police, the decisions handed down by the courts, and the pressures exerted by the public all affect—and are affected by—prosecutorial behavior. The resulting exchange relationships are characterized by a system of checks and balances, many of which have a direct bearing on the disposition of cases. Cole concludes that even though the prosecuting attorneys are allowed to exercise their discretionary power, it must be done within the network of exchange relationships.

Another factor that influences the disposition of cases is to be found in the personal attributes—race and demeanor, for example—of the defendant. Steven Barnet Boris deals with this issue in "Stereotypes and Dispositions for Criminal Homicide." Boris describes how criminal homicide cases are disposed of at the preliminary hearing. Some interesting findings emerge concerning the effects of the occupational status of the offender and victim, the age of the offender, and race. He observes, for example, that unemployed offenders are more likely than the employed to have their cases prosecuted further. Young offenders also run a higher risk than older suspects. On the other hand, the race of neither victim nor offender appears to affect disposition.

Jeffrey H. Reiman's work, "The Rich Get Richer and the Poor Get Prison: Convictions and Sentencing," discusses the final outcome of court processing: the official adjudication of a person as guilty or innocent and sentencing. His major contention is that the poor often lack the resources needed to post bail or retain legal counsel; as a result, many remain in prison until their trial and have public defenders assigned to their cases. These lawyers, according to Reiman, do not generally devote the time and resources necessary for the defense of their clients. Reiman concludes by giving examples of the relatively light sentences meted out to affluent defendants and the heavier ones given to the poor.

EFFECTS OF CRIMINAL PROCESSING

The effect of criminal processing on a suspect's self-image is described by Abraham S. Blumberg in "The Moral Career of an Accused Person." During the processing the accused's public and private identity is subjected to attack by various institutions and their agents, who often perceive and respond to the person as a criminal. This, in turn, may mean that the accused is pressured into accepting criminal status. Blumberg notes that although the poor and powerless are most likely to succumb to the pressures, even an individual with considerable personal and economic resources has great difficulty resisting them. A redefinition of self as guilty may alleviate an identity crisis for the accused; it also enables the police and the courts to process a case with the greatest possible dispatch.

31. Clearance Rates

JEROME H. SKOLNICK

For detectives, the most important measure of accomplishment has come to be the "clearance rate."[1] Indeed, Griffin states that the clearance rate is the most important indication of the efficiency of the police force as a whole.[2] The clearance rate is also strongly endorsed as a control measure by the leading authority on police management and professionalization, O. W. Wilson. Wilson does not see detectives as dedicated plyers of their trade, much less as heroes; instead, his basic assumption is that investigators, unless checked on, drift into inactivity. At the same time, he is not unduly concerned by this problem, because the control mechanisms are, in his opinion, clear and effective. He says:

> In no branch of police service may the accomplishment of the unit and of its individual members be so accurately evaluated as in the detective division. Rates of clearances by arrest, of property recovered, and of convictions, serve as measures of the level of performance. Current accomplishments in the same class of crime may reveal significant variations between the accomplishment of the incumbent and his predecessor, or between the present and past performance of the same detective. Similar comparisons may be made between local accomplishments and the accomplishments in comparable communities. Chance may cause an unfavorable comparison during a short period, but when the failure in performance extends over six months or a year, a conclusion of diminished effectiveness seems justified.
>
> A detective division built of members retained on this selective basis is most likely to contain the best investigators on the force.[3]

Wilson and Griffin are by no means isolated spokesmen in their high estimation of clearance rates as a measure of police efficiency. The Federal Bureau of Investigation also compiles national statistics of clearance rates, published in an *Annual Bulletin* for the year following the date of clearance. These data are collected from 3,441 cities (population, 101,285,000) in the United States. Thus, the clearance rate has evidently been adopted by most police departments in the United States as a primary means to evaluate detectives.

What is the clearance rate? This is a simple question demanding a complicated answer. Briefly stated, it is the percentage of crimes known to the police which the police believe have been "solved." It is important to note that the clearance rate is based upon *offenses known to the police.* Thus, there can be no clearance rate for crimes without citizen complainants. Although there are difficulties in counting such crimes as homicide, robbery, and burglary, they can be counted. It is impossible, however, to count crimes without complainants. As a result, such offenses as bookmaking, the illegal use of narcotics, and prostitution cannot be analyzed by clearance rates.

In the materials that follow, I should like, mainly from observations of burglary enforcement, to illustrate two processes: (1) how the employment of these quantitative criteria—clearance rates—leads to practices that in turn attenuate the validity of the criteria themselves as measures of quality control; and (2) how emphasis on these criteria has consequences for the administration of justice that may interfere with the legality and the stated aims of law enforcement. It should be emphasized that these analytically distinct processes are closely related to each other empirically. What the policeman does in order to amplify clearance rates may have the consequence of both weakening the validity of clearance rates and interfering with legality and aims of law enforcement. Empirically, however, these processes are not separated.

CATEGORIES OF "CLEARANCE"

... The designation "cleared" [is] a police organizational term bearing no *direct* relation to the administration of criminal law. That is, no set of statistics describing the processes of criminal law—statistics on arrest and prosecution—gives rise to a similar or even a consistently related set of clearance figures. For example, of the 29 percent of burglaries "cleared" by the Westville police, less than one-quarter (6 percent) were "cleared" by arrest and prosecution for that offense, while almost two-fifths (11 percent), were "cleared" through prosecution for another offense. Furthermore, the percentage for any category will vary from year to year. Thus, the designation "cleared" merely means that the police believe they know who committed the offense, *if* they believe an offense has been committed. It does not indicate, however, *how* the crime was cleared. ... of the 3,719 burglary offenses reported to the Westville police, 3,578 were considered *actual* offenses. The "actual offense" figure, which provides the denominator for computing the clearance rate, is derived by subtracting the "unfounded" reports from the reported offenses and adding the "suspicious circumstances—changed to burglary" figure to the difference.[4]

The possibility of "unfounding" (to coin an inelegant verb) suggests the first move of the detective—to determine whether in fact an offense has been committed. This procedure requires the detective to assess the motives of the complainant. In investigating a robbery, for instance, there are certain situations which indicate quite clearly to the detective that the complainant is not a victim. For instance, if a man reports that he was robbed at 11 P.M. on 7th and State, and a policeman says he saw him in another part of town at the same hour, the suspicion is that the man did something with his paycheck which he would rather his wife did not know about, and has reported a crime to police to "take off the heat from his old lady."

Seen the other way round, the complainant must be able to justify himself or herself as a victim. The situation here is a familiar one, existing in any context where a claim of victimization is made to a higher authority. To do this, the victim must be able to produce symbols of victimization to the higher authority, symbols appropriate to the victimization context. In a tennis game, for instance, chalk marks on a ball would be appropriate to show that a player's baseline shot had fallen in bounds. Thus, when called out, the player would be "victimized." In other social situations, the rules of the game are not quite so clear—the jilted suitor may consequently have more or less difficulty sustaining an impression of himself as a victim, depending on whose sympathy he is trying to get. In the criminal law context, the rules of the game are less clear than tennis rules, more clear than those between lovers.

An incident may also be recorded as a "suspicious circumstance" in Westville. The more or less official definition of a suspicious circumstance is that a crime appears to have been committed, but that one of its elements is missing. For example, the major element of the crime of burglary is "the burglarious intent, the intent to commit either grand or petit theft or any felony after the entry has been effected. This requisite intent must exist at the time of the entry."[5] There must also be entry into a building (or one of the other places listed in the statute). If some men happened to be shooting craps in the rear of a store, and entered ostensibly for that purpose, there was no burglary. The patrolman, however, may suspect that the real reason for the entry was to steal, not merely to throw dice. If so, his offense report would list a suspected burglary. Or perhaps a householder reports the theft of a watch, but the patrolman cannot find a point of entry. In such an instance, the patrolman will report a "suspicious circumstance," and an investigation will follow. Thus, complaints are typically screened by patrolmen before being presented to the detectives for further investigation.

In addition to deciding whether an offense has been committed, the patrolman must decide what the offense was, if any. The citizen often makes a general noise—which is partly why citizen complaints are referred to in many police departments as "squeals." A woman may call the police and complain that she has been raped, when in fact she has also been robbed. Because the robbery may appear easier to prove than the rape—for example, if corroborating evidence has been found on the person of the defendant—the patrolman reports a robbery and includes the surrounding circumstances.

Even when it is clear that an offense has occurred, the patrolman (usually with the advice of his sergeant, if the offense appears serious) may decide not to write up an offense report. The following notes illustrate:

> It was a very quiet evening for crime. Only one interesting happening—a call that an assault had been committed. After some time trying to find the house—in one of the courtyards of a city project—Sergeant L. and I arrived on the scene after one of the "beat" patrolmen. (The sergeant is in charge, by the way, of about nine men who cover six beats, and whenever one of them has a special problem the sergeant will likely arrive.) We walked into a poorly furnished house. A large, rather handsome black man was seated on a couch daubing at his ear with a towel and being aided by a five- or six-year-old boy.
>
> The man looked dazed and the sergeant inquired brusquely as to what had happened. (He knew already; before we entered the patrolman told us the man had been cut in the ear by his wife, and also that the man didn't want to file a complaint.)
>
> "She cut me," the man mumbled.
>
> The sergeant flashed his light on the man's ear. It had been slashed a good half inch through right above the lobe. The beam of the flashlight revealed fingernail marks on the man's neck.
>
> The sergeant continued to ask the man what had happened. Answers were mumbled and incoherent. In essence, they amounted to: "Nothing really happened, she just came at me with the knife; I was drinking, she came at me with the knife."
>
> There was discussion of whether the man wanted an ambulance. Arrangements were made with a neighboring relative to drive the man to the county hospital.
>
> Before leaving, the sergeant made sure the man didn't want to file a complaint. We left the house with the sergeant admonishing him to have the ear taken care of. The patrolman remarked, "As they say, she done stuck."

No offense report is made out for such an incident. It is a family squabble with no complainant. (That the man is black is also relevant. If the family were white, the police would take the offense more seriously. A stabbing by a white woman of her husband suggests a potential homicide to police, while a similar black cutting can be written off as a "North Westville battery."[6]) Instead, an *assignment report* recording the incident suffices. Incidents described on assignment reports are not tabulated and are not sent for further investigation to the detective division. An incident may be unfounded only when reported as an offense or as a suspected offense.

In Westville, a large proportion (20 to 25 percent) of burglary complaints processed by patrolmen are recorded as suspected offenses ("suspicious circumstances") for follow-up investigation by a detective. The detective is allowed wide discretion in the filing of burglary complaints as "suspicious circumstances." Not only does he record a complaint as a suspected offense when one or more of the elements of the alleged crime appears to be missing, but he also may list a complaint as a suspected offense when he believes—even in the absence of hard evidence to support his suspicion—that the complaint is unfounded. For instance, a black delivery boy claims to have been robbed of the money he was supposed to deposit for his employer. He shows a lump on his head and holds to his story, but the detective does not believe him. Such a complaint is filed as a suspicious circumstance, and as such does not fall into the category of "offenses reported." When a complaint is filed as a "suspicious circumstance," it is "cleared" for practical purposes. Usually the detective concentrates on "actual" offenses and ignores further investigation of "suspicious circumstances." In effect, therefore, every time a complaint is filed as a "suspicious circumstance" instead of as a reported offense, the clearance rate rises (since it is based on the ratio of "cleared" to "actual" offenses).[7]

In Eastville, on the other hand, virtually every complaint is recorded as an actual offense. This reporting system was introduced in Eastville as a strong means of control. As form follows function, so may tight controls follow corruption. For example, during the period of my observations in Eastville, a known prostitute reported she had been assaulted and raped. A desk sergeant recorded her complaint as rape, and Eastville's crime rate was thereby heightened. In Westville, a similar complaint would have been recorded as "suspicious circumstance—rape" on grounds that a person practicing criminality is not a reliable complainant. The complaint would therefore not appear in Westville's crime statistics as an offense known to the police.

Many of the Eastville detectives resent the requirement that every complaint be recorded as an actual offense. They feel that, as several noted to me, "It makes us look bad." I questioned one of the supervisory policemen regarding the practice of recording, and he said:

> Well, we're an honest police department. All these other departments
> that have these fancy clearance rates—we know damned well they're

stacking the cards. It's easy to show a low crime rate when you have a category like suspicious circumstance to use as a wastebasket. Here, at least we know what's going on—everything is reported. Sure the prostitute could have been lying, and probably was. But the fact is that a prostitute can be raped, and prostitutes sometimes are. After all, a prostitute has a right not to go to bed with somebody if she doesn't want to.

It is certainly possible that the number of reported offenses in many police departments may be manipulated in order to exaggerate the efficiency of the burglary division. Since approximately 20 percent of the original reports never find their way into the crime statistics and assignment reports are not included in crime reports (thereby greatly reducing the visibility of police discretion), any small statistical changes—on the order of, say, 2 or 3 percent per year—should be given little significance in the evaluation of a department's performance. Yet this is the order of magnitude frequently suggested—in staff meetings, conferences, to outsiders—as evidence of a department's competence. Thus, in general, 22 percent is regarded as a low burglary clearance rate, 35 percent is seen as a high one (the national average for 1962 was 28 percent). A burglary clearance rate which has risen from 27 to 31 percent, for example, is presented as an indicator of significant change.

CLEARANCE RATES AND THE ADMINISTRATION OF JUSTICE

From the above analysis, it is evident that clearance rates are a somewhat suspect method of judging the competence of an individual policeman, a division of a department, or a department as a whole, assuming for the moment that the qualities clearance rates purport to measure are appropriate indicators of police proficiency. If statistical manipulation were the only unanticipated consequence of this control mechanism, the problems created might be relatively inconsequential. To be sure, the clearance rate might not mirror "real" differences in individual ability from one year to the next, as it purports to, nor might it accurately reflect differences in the proficiency of police departments when these are compared. The implications of these errors might appear serious to individual policemen or to individual police departments when invidious conclusions are drawn about their competence. When it can be shown that under certain conditions the attention paid by working detectives to clearance rates may *reverse the hierarchy of penalties* associated with substantive criminal law, the resulting issues are of greater theoretical and practical importance.

To understand the process of reversal, it is useful to ask how the burglary detective goes about obtaining clearances. The simplest answer is that he persuades a burglar to admit having committed several prior offenses. That is, the exchange principle again operates: in order to gain such admissions, the police must provide the burglar with either rewards or penalties to motivate self-incrimination. In the "professional" Westville Police Department, one sees relatively little evidence of the "stick" and much of the "carrot." In what follows, I should like to describe two cases from Westville, one a routine case, the other a "big" case, to illustrate the strategies and rewards used by burglary detectives to obtain clearances, and to analyze how these strategies may undermine legislative and judicial aims regarding law enforcement.

The first case is the routine "good pinch." Arthur C. was arrested as an auto thief and cooperated with the police by confessing to the commission of two additional thefts of autos and five "classy" burglaries. In return for this cooperation, Arthur received several assets. First, the police agreed to drop the two counts of auto theft and to charge Arthur with only one count of burglary. Secondly, Arthur's formal confession as given to the court showed that he had committed only one burglary. As the sergeant handling his case said:

> We had him cop out to only one charge because we don't really want it made public that he committed the other burglaries. If it were made public, then the question might be raised as to why we didn't charge him with the other burglaries, and the public doesn't understand these things.

What the sergeant intended to indicate is that the public typically does not understand that the sentence would not be different if the defendant had confessed to one burglary or to five—and the severity of the sentence is the most important consideration to all of the active participants in the system, the judge and the attorneys as well as the defendant and the police. None is especially impressed by the "rehabilitative" capacities of the penal system. Thus, the sergeant added, when asked by the writer if the court did not realize that perhaps other offenses had been committed:

> Of course the courts know. In fact we tell the judge that the defendant committed other burglaries, but we don't want it put on the record. So we take the confession in such a way as to implicate the guy with only one burglary, and then that's what he gets sentenced for.

Of course, from the parole board's point of view, it might be of some significance that the defendant had actually committed five burglaries instead of one. Since an extensive burglary record could conceivably reduce the convicted defendant's chances for parole, a confession showing him to have committed only one burglary is to his advantage.

In addition to possibly receiving a reduction of charges and counts, and a recorded minimization of his appearance of criminality, the defendant who "cops out" and clears burglaries is also said to "clean" himself. The term "cleaning" in this context means that the defendant is afforded virtual immunity for future arrests on past burglaries. Thus, if the police have cleared ten burglaries with the defendant's help, he is no longer liable to be arrested for having committed them (even though the statute of limitations might permit prosecution). As a result, when the defendant completes his sentence, he need not fear apprehension for any of the crimes he committed before.

These, then, are the three basic "commodities" which the detective exchanges in return for the defendant's cooperation in admitting to prior offenses: reduction of charges and counts, concealment of actual criminality, and freedom from further investigation of prior offenses. Since it is in the interest of both the defendant and the policeman that the defendant "clear" crimes, the defendant typically cooperates with the policeman once a deal has been set in motion. Indeed, the defendant may occasionally become "too" cooperative by confessing to crimes he never committed, since liability does not increase as a result of admissions made for the purpose of clearing crimes.

It is impossible to know how often defendants claim to have committed the crimes of others. When such claims occur, however, they necessarily undermine the aims of law enforcement by presenting the police with "false positives"—"solved cases" for which synthetic solutions are reached. On the other hand, the policeman's ability to determine the truth of defendants' assertions might minimize error of this sort. Nevertheless, the pressures in the situation are clearly in the direction of overlooking or not inquiring too carefully into the defendant's representations.

CRIMINALITY AS COMMODITY FOR EXCHANGE

There is a more serious problem about clearance rates as a control mechanism. If clearances are valued, then criminality becomes a commodity for exchange. Thus, it is possible that in some cases defendants who confess to large numbers of crimes will tend to be shown more leniency in prosecution than those who are in fact less culpable. This is not to suggest that an inverse correlation actually exists between the number of offenses which a person admits having committed and the severity of the penalty which he receives. (To test the truth of any such generalization would be difficult since it would be necessary to have an accurate accounting of the crimes for which defendants actually were responsible. Because the maintenance of such records would in itself threaten to upset the operation of the system for maximizing clearance rates, an observer would need at least to see the processing of the cases themselves.) Rather, the situation in which detectives are expected to demonstrate proficiency is structured so as to invite the policeman to undermine the hierarchy of penalties found in substantive criminal law. The following case is presented to illustrate more fully the process of undermining. This case, a "big one," is not statistically "representative," but does, I believe, fairly represent pressures inherent in the situation. It was not especially selected, but simply occurred during the period of observation.

Essentially, the undermining process in the "big" case is more conspicuous because the police "get" more and have to "give" more in exchange. The process by which the police obtain clearance in a "big" case is therefore merely an exaggerated instance of the process in the routine case. In this case (the Moore case), approximately thirty-five thousand dollars worth of jewels, furs, and other valuable objects had been stolen from a leading citizen. Partly as a result of the citizen's status, and partly because of the value of the stolen goods, the police looked upon the case as an unusually important one to "break." "Breaking it" would and did lead to praise from the general community, including the press and television. I was able to work on the case with the sergeant to whom it had been assigned, and followed him on the laborious and time-consuming round of checking out false leads, questioning neighbors and witnesses, and interviewing informants and potential informants. The description of the development of such a case would make interesting popular nonfiction. I intend to describe only that part of it relating to the analytical point of how emphasis on clearance rates as a measure of the competence of detectives can interfere with stated aims of law enforcement by creating an informal hierarchy of penalties. That part of the case follows:

After considerable investigation, two of the four suspects were "picked up on a roust," that is, they were arrested on minor charges in order to give the police an opportunity to interrogate them. After they had been placed in custody in Jonesville, an all-points bulletin was sent out which came to the attention of the Westville detectives assigned to the Moore case. The Westville detectives were given permission to interrogate the suspects by the Jonesville Police Department and especially, as a matter of courtesy, through the Jonesville detective who arranged the "roust."

In the meantime, the Westville detectives had independently gath-

ered information which, added to the considerable information held
by the Jonesville detective, pointed to the culpability of these suspects in the Moore case. The information regarding the recent activities of one of the suspects, who will be called Jerome, was especially
comprehensive. As the sergeant put it in describing the interrogation
to me:

> We know enough to make him feel that we got him by the balls. We
> have enough information so that we can almost tell him where he took a
> piss twenty-four hours a day for the last few days. Actually, we don't know
> what is what so far as real evidence is concerned, but we know so much
> about his general activities, that he thinks we know a lot more than we ac-
> tually do.[8]
>
> After six hours he finally says he wants to make a deal. It turns out that
> he's got a charge hanging over him in another state and says he'll make a
> deal if we don't send him back. Then he copped out and told us how he did
> the Moore job and who he did it with.
>
> He agreed to work for us and so we turned him loose and told him we
> wanted the fence. The first thing he did was to set up Rich [another mem-
> ber of the burglary team; the third was James, and there was also a fence].
> Then James, who's in jail in Smithville, calls us up and says he wants to
> help us out, and with his help and Jerome's help we got the fence all wired
> up tight. [There was an additional reason for "helping" here. Jerome and
> James both mistrusted—indeed hated—the fence, since in their opinion he
> had cheated them by pretending to have gotten less for the stolen articles
> than he actually had.]

Over a period of about ten days after the arrest, burglary police
from neighboring cities frequently visited the Westville jail, since, between the two of them, Jerome and James could account for more
than five hundred burglaries. James himself provided the police with
more than four hundred clearances. I witnessed several interroga-
tions of James regarding burglaries he had presumably committed
and, in my opinion, it was relatively simple for him to "fake" clearances. One need not have been exceptionally shrewd—and James
was—to sense the detectives' pleasure at writing off old cases. This is
not to say that the detectives who interviewed him were easily deceived. But from the detail with which he recalled burglaries he had
committed in the past year, the policemen could tell that James had
committed numerous burglaries. When he expressed vagueness of
memory as to those two or three years old, he thereby created a situation in which the police would have either to be extremely scrupu-
lous, and thus forego potential clearances, or "feed" him information
to refresh his recollection (which, to this observer, appeared to be
rather easily renewed).

Rich and the fence each received substantial prison sentences. Jerome and James were charged as misdemeanants. Jerome spent four months in custody, while James was permitted to finish out sentence on another charge, for which he was already serving time, and was released after thirty days. In part, Jerome and James were given a liberal reduction in charges because they had served as informants and also because they had agreed to appear as State's witnesses. These services were an important aspect of their "cooperation" with law enforcement.

At the same time, however, the two burglars had also given the police numerous clearances. While it would be virtually impossible to separate out the effect of their "cooperation" as informants and State's witnesses as against their "cooperation" in giving clearances, it would be unrealistic to discount the importance of their providing "clearances" in accounting for their lenient treatment. James, who had certainly committed numerous burglaries and had admitted having participated in more than four hundred, received what he regarded as no sentence at all. Jerome, James, the sergeant, and I spent almost five hours reconstructing the events of the case, the backgrounds of Jerome and James, and the morality of the outcome. All agreed that "it wasn't right" that the penalties should have been distributed as they were, although the defendants felt that rough justice had been served since they claimed to have been mistreated by law enforcement authorities in the past. The sergeant, also a shrewd observer, sensed that there was something decidedly wrong with the process. From his point of view, which was largely shared by other detectives interviewed, the society would be better served

... if we didn't have this clearance business hanging over our heads. We get guys like this and they hand us clearance after clearance and on FBI books we look terrific. But the fact is that large numbers of burglaries are committed by a relatively small group and when we get one of them we have to give him a good break in order to make ourselves look good. It's a ridiculous system, but that's the way they run things upstairs.

The reader may raise the question as to how the police arranged these low charges with the district attorneys of several jurisdictions. It was not always easy. In one jurisdiction, the district attorney insisted upon heavy prosecution despite the fact that a promise of leniency had already been made to one of the suspects. Eventually, the police view prevailed, on the grounds that unless the district attorney agreed to "back up" the discretionary actions of the police, they would, in future burglary investigations, be seriously impaired. It is unlikely that police discretion can, as one writer has suggested,[9] be exercised without the cooperation of the district attorney. Since the district attorney depends largely upon the policeman for evidence, the policeman has a good deal of influence over the district attorney's exercise of discretionary authority. It is not that the policeman interferes with the work of the district attorney when his work is in the traditional legal domain; rather, the policeman, by gaining the cooperation of the district attorney, usurps the prerogatives of the prosecutor to control the policeman's activities.

SUMMARY AND CONCLUSIONS

This [paper] has described and analyzed the processes by which clearance rates are constructed, as part of the broader issue of how the ambiguous institutional character of police influences the actual administration of criminal law. Thus, the [paper] concentrated on the issue of how clearance rates—so important to internal control processes—may affect the penalty structure associated with substantive criminal law.

The behavior of the detectives involved should not be seen as an instance of corruption or even of inefficiency. On the contrary, their actions are to be interpreted as an unanticipated consequence of their superiors' development of a method of controlling their efficiency. The response of the detective to the clearance rate is easily understandable. It stems from a sociological tendency manifesting itself in all work organizations: the worker always tries to perform *according to his most concrete and specific understanding of the control system*. That is, in general, workers try to please those supervising *routine* activities. Thus, in prisons (or at least in the one studied by Sykes), the guard is judged according to how successfully he maintains a smoothly running cell block. Prison authorities overlook infractions in minor rules and judge the guard's competence by the composure of his cell block. As a consequence, guards permit minor rules to be broken in order to comply with their immediate superiors' over-all aim of keeping the prison under physical control.[10] (How such arrangements react upon the still more general aims of incarceration, such as building up respect for law, is a question beyond the scope of the present study, but surely significant for sanctioning policy.)

Actually, police practices about clearance rates are more strictly comparable to the practices of foremen and production line workers rather than to those of prison guards and inmates. There are numerous examples and allusions in sociological literature of "positive deviance" on the production line—of reshaping, reinterpreting, or ignoring formal rules in order to make the best possible appearance in terms of the most current and pressing demands.[11] A most dramatic recent one is contained in Bensman and Gerver's[12] description of the use of the "tap" in a wartime airplane plant. The tap is a hard steel screw used to bring nuts and bolts into a new but not true alignment on airplane wings, and its use is described as being both "the most serious crime of workmanship conceivable" and "imperative to the functioning of the production organization." The pressure, for these workers, is to show a high production rate. The *ultimate* goal may be ignored under the more immediate pressures to produce. When means are found to raise production, rules are circumvented—not with impunity, however, but only under the strain of production quotas.

Similarly, the detective is inclined to engage in those activities improving *his* appearance as a competent worker. One cannot say that the detective is unconcerned about his work, but rather that he typically engages in practices—such as, for instance, "saving" clearances from month to month—that put the best possible light on his competence and dependability when his record is examined by superiors. Thus, the perceived necessity of measures of departmental efficiency results in the development of techniques by detectives to enlarge the magnitude of the criteria for measuring their performance. One of these techniques is to exchange the prerogative of charging crime for "clearances," with the result that in major cases criminality may inadvertently be rewarded. Thus, the statistical control system, intended to prevent detectives from drifting into inactivity, may tend to reverse the hierarchy of criminal penalties established by the legislature.[13]

These consequences do not, however, stem from the personal deficiencies either of working policemen or those men who might be termed police "efficiency experts"—men like O. W. Wilson or the personally dedicated and honest head of the Westville Police Department, who are attempting to develop methods for running a "modern and efficient" police department. Instead, the problem stems from the well-motivated attempts of such experts to develop measurable standards of efficiency. Unfortunately, meeting these standards tends to become an end in itself, a transformation found in many organizations. In this process, Blau and Scott interpret the organization's relation to its environment as a crucial factor. They write, "As long as its very survival is threatened by a hostile environment, its officers will seek to strengthen the organization by building up its administrative machinery and searching for external sources of support."[14] As an organization, the police provide a clear example of this development. Requiring a "set of books" to demonstrate competence of performance, the "clearance rate" has been developed as a measure of the effectiveness of the police department, especially the detective branch. This concern with efficiency, however, may also have the unanticipated consequence of developing detective initiative to the point of reversing the hierarchy of penalties associated with the substantive criminal law. Thus, the standard of efficiency employed in police departments may not only undermine due process of law, but also the basic standard of justice—that those equally culpable shall be given equal punishment.[15]

Notes

1. Among educators, for instance, there are similar questions of what the goals of the profession are. Some emphasize the development of measurable skills, while others maintain a broader conception of the aims of education. One sociologist of education has suggested that the popularity of such devices as teaching machines may in part be attributed to the facilitation of evaluative and control functions. (See Martin Trow, "American Education and the New Modes of Instruction," mimeographed paper.) Thus, whatever may be said for or against "programmed" teaching and its ultimate effect not only upon knowledge and skill, but also upon creativity, it does permit the administrator to rate attainment more easily.

2. John Griffin, *Statistics Essential for Police Efficiency* (Springfield: Charles C Thomas, 1958), p. 69.

3. O. W. Wilson, *Police Planning* (Springfield: Charles C Thomas, 1962), p. 112. The Chicago Crime Commission recently lauded Wilson's work as head of the Chicago police force by stating that the improvement in police efficiency measured by the percentage of offenses cleared by arrest was "tremendous." *(New York Times,* July 19, 1964).

4. It is highly difficult to track down the number of instances in which a complaint was first recorded as a suspected crime other than burglary and then changed to burglary. Generally, the Westville police consider the difference between "offenses reported" and "actual offenses" to be "unfounded" reports.

5. C. W. Fricke, *California Criminal Law* (Los Angeles: Legal Book Store, 1956), p. 310.

6. For a similar illustration, see Wayne R. LaFave, "The Police and Nonenforcement of the Law—Part II," *Wisconsin Law Review* (March, 1962), 207–210.

7. Eight hundred and five suspicious-circumstance burglaries were reported by patrolmen in Westville in 1962. Of these, 286 remained as such after detective investigation and never found their way into the crime reports. Of the remaining 517, an unknown number were called actual offenses and became part of the crime report; the remainder were unfounded and never entered the crime report.

8. This is a typical ploy detectives use during interrogation. By indicating to the suspect that they know more than they actually do, they frequently are able to bluff the suspect into believing that they have "hard" evidence.

9. Joseph Goldstein, "Police Discretion Not to Invoke the Criminal Process: Low Visibility Decisions in the Administration of Justice," *Yale Law Journal,* 69 (March, 1960) 568–569.

10. Gresham M. Sykes, "The Corruption of Authority and Rehabilitation," *Social Forces,* 34 (March, 1956), 257–267.

11. Probably the best-known illustration is found in George C. Homans'

The Human Group (New York: Harcourt, Brace and Company, 1950), pp. 48–80.

12. Joseph Bensman and Israel Gerver, "Crime and Punishment in the Factory: The Function of Deviancy in Maintaining the Social System," *American Sociological Review, 28* (1963), 588–598.

13. On the problems created by statistical records in a similar setting, see Peter M. Blau, *The Dynamics of Bureaucracy* (Chicago: University of Chicago Press, 1955), pp. 36–67.

14. Peter M. Blau and W. Richard Scott, *Formal Organizations: A Comparative Approach* (San Francisco: Chandler Publishing Company, 1962), p. 231.

15. It is worth noting that the findings of this [paper] also strongly support the idea that rates of deviant behavior are as dependent on the actions of officials, as on the conduct of so-called deviants. For a brief and cogent development of this position see John I. Kitsuse and Aaron V. Cicourel, "A Note on the Uses of Official Statistics," *Social Problems, 11* (Fall, 1963), 131–139.

32. The Antitrust Division: Finding Cases

SUZANNE WEAVER

Somewhere between 80 and 90 percent of the matters that come across an antitrust lawyer's desk are, according to those interviewed, given no more than a few days' investigating time, and even of those matters to which the lawyers say they have devoted more than a minimal amount of time, fewer than half are recommended for prosecution.[1] As far as one can tell from these interviews, three reasons account for the vast majority of all these negative decisions. Either something is by no stretch of the imagination an antitrust violation, or the lawyer sees no hope of finding evidence to prove it in court, or there is no possible relief to be gained from prosecution. Decisions made for these reasons, in most cases, are highly consensual; they are agreed upon by the lawyer making the decision, by his colleagues, and by superiors. The lawyer does not think he is exercising any discretion in turning down such cases; he turns them down because he sees no chance of making or winning them. He is almost never exercising any purely personal preference for "going easy" on any particular industry or type of violation, whether from some competing theoretical considerations or for more idiosyncratic reasons. He builds his cases where he can; the chief constraint he feels is the scarcity of information from which to construct them.

FINDING A CASE

This picture of the lawyers' operating procedures argues that the lawyers are particularistic in their decisions, judging each piece of information according to whether it contributes to a successful prosecution; that most of the work is a process of turning down cases for prosecution; and that one could hardly do better in describing the reasons for these rejections than to describe antitrust case law, federal rules of evidence, and the facts available in the particular case at hand.

This picture is, however, incomplete. First of all, it suggests a subservience to "the law" in its current state that contradicts our previous picture of the staff attorney as an aggressive prosecutor, trying to

412

maximize his prosecutorial reach. But more important, it ignores two obvious facts. The first is that in many areas the antitrust law is ambiguous. Even where the law as interpreted by the courts clearly prohibits certain categories of conduct, it may not be clear whether the conduct at hand falls into the proscribed category. Or there may be a special exemption for the group in question that makes it unclear whether the law can be applied.[2] And sometimes the law is in dispute with regard to even more fundamental questions.

Moreover, the interpretation of the antitrust laws has changed in major ways since their passage—and many of these changes have occurred as a direct result of new arguments that the division has made before the courts. It is not merely that staff lawyers value aggressive prosecution; it is that they actually behave as aggressive prosecutors, in ways that significantly affect antitrust doctrine. Staff lawyers explicitly claim that most changes in antitrust laws emerged from the minds of government trial attorneys. "Every new idea around here," as one of them puts it, "has been discussed up and down these corridors for years."

So if most staff lawyers spend the bulk of their time discarding matters they see as unambiguously beyond the reach of the antitrust laws and of the division, this does not mean that they consider themselves absolutely bound by the law as it stands. On the contrary, part of the division's prevailing definition of a good prosecutor entails precisely the ability to bring into prosecutorial reach situations that on first inspection would seem to be beyond that reach. And this definition has consequences for the way the staff deals with situations that are ambiguous.

One factor in particular is crucial to understanding how the lawyers treat a doubtful situation—the length and complexity of antitrust investigations. The length of these investigations, if they are not very quickly disposed of, is commonly measured not in weeks but in months or years. One lawyer noted that his section chief did not even begin to ask seriously how an investigation was going until four months after it had begun. Another staffer complained that these investigations took much too long; more of them, he said, could be done quickly and still be done well, as had happened on an important case of his in which special time pressures had forced the division to move with unusual speed. When asked how long this "quick" investigation had gone on, he answered, "Ten months."

The reason for this extreme length is a matter of dispute. Some lawyers claim that the division itself, both front office and staff, is simply slower than it need be, particularly when a case is not especially exciting or when there is no special need—such as that provided by the pending consummation of a merger—to move quickly. One young lawyer told how, when he had first arrived in the division, "We worked all the time on the ⎯⎯⎯⎯ case. I didn't even go home for Thanksgiving. I loved it. But I wouldn't do that for any of the cases I'm working on now." But it is also pointed out that when the division does have some special reason to move quickly—for instance, when it does want to stop a merger from being consummated so that it can avoid the problems posed by divestiture—it can prepare its motions for preliminary injunctions with some speed.

There is another probable reason for the extreme length. When dealing with "structural" violations, the division lawyers claim that they would be perfectly happy to bring cases on the basis of less evidence than they currently present, with more exclusive reliance on what they call "objective" economic data and less attention to company history, practices, and motives. But, they say, federal judges would simply not be persuaded by such "bare bones" arguments. The judges are not social scientists, the lawyers observe; even when dealing with a statute such as the Clayton Act, which does not require the presence of any anticompetitive motives in order for the court to bar a company's action, the courts persist in seeking out such motives, or their absence, in a wealth of detail concerning the particular firms at issue.

It is not clear how much credence should be given to this explanation. Other staff lawyers discount their colleagues' opinion that the courts contribute to the length of investigations. District court judges, they think, would be only too happy to have shorter antitrust briefs and trials to deal with. The staff lawyers, they say, fill their briefs, arguments, and investigative time with a wealth of detail because *they* are not persuaded by exclusively economic arguments, even where these might be thought to suffice.

Still other lawyers point to an additional reason for the length of the investigations. Defense counsel, they say, often obstruct the division's efforts to gather information. The staff admits that defense counsel tend to delay partly because they know that there is often no particular time pressure on the division lawyers, but the staff also claims that their opponents' major motive is simply their interest in extending the time available for merger plans to be completed, for the facts of a general situation to change, or for prosecution witnesses to grow dim in their recollection of past events. Some members of the private antitrust bar said that this was true, at least in the case of mergers. One of them explained that he was happy to see his current merger litigation with the division go on as long as possible: "These things are harder to break up once the eggs are scrambled." And another ex-defense attorney joked about his past career, "Ah, yes, I remember the room where we let the government lawyers examine our documents—the one with the cigar smoke piped in." A division lawyer pointed out that in the field of banking, where a special statute automatically bars any merger beginning at the time the division announces its intention to challenge it until the case is concluded, the gathering of facts proceeds much more quickly and without so much delay by the defense.

The division keeps no statistics on the length of its investigations. But a rough estimate from these interviews is that in even the relatively quick banking investigations, the usual duration is six months or more. So one must conclude that important reasons for this length lie in the nature of the investigative process itself and in the lawyers' expectations of these investigations.

In the first place, making most antitrust cases simply requires large amounts of information, much of which is difficult to collect, digest, and interpret. Monopolization cases provide the most extreme example. Division lawyers must have, in effect, a complete history of the firm under investigation—its organization, its practices and pricing policies, its internal growth and acquisitions, its relations with customers, competitors, and suppliers, its record of patents and of research and innovation in general—as well as information on industry structure, technical knowledge of the firm's products, and histories of the firm's competitors. One such recently active investigation file, lawyers report, contained well over one hundred thousand documents, outside of information from publications and from interviews conducted by the lawyers themselves or by the FBI. Indeed, older lawyers in the division are convinced that one reason the division did not make more effort until recently to affect industry structure through monopolization prosecutions is that their younger colleagues, eager to expand their experience by participating in a series of cases and proceedings, were not so eager to undertake investigations of the length that a monopolization case requires.

Even a "simple" merger case may entail, as did a recent investigation that one lawyer described, an examination of over fifty thousand documents, and criminal price-fixing cases may also require a detailed examination of industry structure and history and of pricing patterns. Obviously, the lawyers develop special skill and judgment in deciding which documents and pieces of information merit careful scrutiny. Still, the lawyers uniformly and persuasively point out that the work is inherently time-consuming and filled with drudgery. As one much-respected division lawyer said, "Ninety-five percent of my work is just digging up those facts."

As a result of the large amount of time required to develop anything that has substantial promise of becoming a case, the staff lawyers have considerable personal interest in seeing the matter grow into a prosecution. And because the work involved means that not very many case possibilities will be open to a lawyer at one time, the attorneys want to see to it that what they work on for so long finally bears fruit.

The lawyers themselves certainly say that this is true. "Once you've spent so much time on one of these damn things," one of them remarked, "you tend to get pretty attached to it." And to a surprisingly large extent, the staff feels supported in this attitude by the section chiefs and even the front office. This is not to say that the higher levels of the organization are no more critical of the lawyers' work than the lawyers themselves are. But the section chiefs, as well as the lawyers directly involved, are reluctant to close a substantial investigation. The prevailing attitude was expressed in virtually the same words by both a staff lawyer and a section chief: "If something goes on long enough," the lawyer said, "you *know* there's got to be something there." And his section chief said, "If you press hard enough, *something* will come out." A frequently heard comment among the staff lawyers was the observation that "it's twice as hard to get permission to close an investigation around here as it is to open one." So not only does the length of the investigation dispose the lawyers to continue each one until some case emerges, there also seems to be a lack of pressure from superiors to counter this disposition.

This impulse to find a case where one has investigated expresses itself in several ways. In the first place, the staff lawyers are overwhelmingly likely to resolve their own doubts about the worth and probable success of a case in favor of prosecution. This point will be discussed more extensively later on; here it need only be said that in at least 80 percent of the cases that the lawyers themselves mentioned as being "hard" for them to decide about, they finally recommended that the division prosecute. One lawyer in the section that handles banking matters, a field especially plagued with problems of theory and evidence, was asked about the cases in which he had recommended against prosecution. He answered, "I can't think of a case where the staff *didn't* want to sue. . . . If we don't act, it's because we have absolutely no cause."

The second way this impulse to prosecute is expressed is in the lawyer's attempts to extend the reach of the antitrust laws. These attempts occur, with slight variations, both in the cases where the lawyers feel the state of the law to be fairly clear on what constitutes a prohibited action and in those cases where the law is not so clear.

When they are dealing with types of offenses already clearly prohibited, the lawyers tend to exercise their ingenuity on matters of proof and jurisdiction. They admit freely that even when they are fairly sure of the offense they are going to allege and the arguments by which they are going to try to prove it, they examine much more factual material than is likely to be directly relevant. They simply do not want to stop sifting through their material until they have culled every piece of evidence for their argument. Even if they already think they have a strong case, they want it to be stronger. "We're all looking," one lawyer laughed, "for the magic document in the last box." Thus their desire to make a case out of each investigation is not only an effect of the long investigations but a cause of them as well.

Just as important, the lawyers take some pride in their ability to solve practical problems of evidence in new ways. Some of these discoveries involve ingenious proofs. During grand jury proceedings concerning an alleged price-fixing, one attorney had been temporarily frustrated by the defendant companies' claims that their prices *appeared* to change simultaneously, but in fact did so only because each company, in preparing its catalogs and price lists, responded to price changes revealed in its rivals' most recent new catalogs. "But I looked at those catalogs," the lawyer remembered, "and I noticed that they were very thick. I figured it must take quite a while to print them. So I checked with the printing companies, and I found out that the last printing order had come in *before* the first catalog had come out."

The lawyers also try to extend their reach by applying existing antitrust law to lines of commerce or geographical areas where it has never been applied before. One attorney claimed as noteworthy a relatively small and clear case that had been brought in an American protectorate where the antitrust law had never been previously applied.

Another staff attorney described as novel a case in which the "new" feature was the line of commerce. It involved a regulated industry that because of economic and technical requirements held a series of legal local monopolies over the service it provided. The industry practice was to agree to supply this service only to privately owned distributors, while refusing to deal with distributors owned by municipalities. The lawyer described his argument: "The _____ companies say they don't have to provide this service to the municipalities. But we say they're a bottleneck. . . . Yes, I suppose that *is* just a replay of the old AP [Associated Press] case. But it's a different thing to apply it, to prove it in *this* area."

Finally, the lawyers often have to solve new jurisdictional problems in order to extend substantively clear antitrust law into new lines of commerce. The lawyer quoted above went on to give one of the reasons why his case represented an advance for the reach of the antitrust laws and the reach of the division. "Unlike the AP case,"[3] he explained, "we have to deal with some new jurisdictional problems.

We have to prove that the _____ [agency] doesn't have primary jurisdiction over this particular practice."

In cases such as these, where the law is relatively clear, two further tendencies may be seen in the staff lawyers' exercise of their inventive energies. The first is related to the structure of available opportunity. At present, the regulated industries present the largest lines of commerce previously untapped by the division and thus the greatest opportunities for new prosecutions under established antitrust principles. So, many of the problems that the lawyers mention as new and exciting deal with attempts to reach a certain line of regulated commerce by limiting the jurisdiction that its regulatory agency can exercise.

Second, several lawyers mentioned that certain types of offenses, offenses they found especially heinous, would move them to make particularly vigorous efforts at investigation and argument. Most of these lawyers said they held a special animus against boycotts; if a pattern of action even vaguely suggested one, they would try very hard to prove that it *was* one. And one lawyer, somewhat more idiosyncratically, began his own list of odious offenses by saying, "Tie-ins. I'll always 'reach' on a tie-in."

So far, these examples of innovation on the lawyers' part seem relatively trivial. The law is clear; the question is one of proof or jurisdiction; the invention that takes place is of a relatively low order; aside from a special attention to particularly predatory offenses, these exercises in ingenuity are ad hoc, determined largely by accidental difficulty or opportunity. The lawyers are perfectly aware of this. The reason, they say, is that in the area where inventions of this type occur, in the area of "conduct" violations, they are fairly well satisfied with the current state of the law. "Sure, there are always things to be done," one of them remarked, "patents, for instance. But with most of these violations, we already have good case law. Now you take merger law—*that's* where the action is."

It is undoubtedly merger law where the division lawyers think "the action is" and where individual lawyers think themselves the most theoretically creative. It has already been suggested that lawyers begin with a "list" of possible anticompetitive effects when they study a merger, that they will refuse to investigate a merger seriously only where it is very clear that none of them exist, and that they usually recommend against prosecution only where they have managed to find none. The converse, though, is also true: They will investigate wherever there is even the possibility of some anticompetitive effect. And it is not surprising that once such an investigation has begun, they will be reluctant to end it without "finding something there."

Therefore the first effect of the desire to find a merger case—as with conduct cases—is to lengthen investigations. The investigations in merger cases lengthen because, as the lawyers themselves say, they look for more kinds of anticompetitive effects than they can possibly hope to find. They begin investigations with a "feeling," as some of them say, that a particular merger is "a bad merger." This feeling (the attorneys tend to speak of it as ineffable intuition, the fruit of years of experience, as against mere calculation of probabilities) may amount to nothing more than a discovery of the obvious, as when a clearly illegal feature is almost certain to be present in a merger. One lawyer explained, talking about his decision to pursue a certain transportation merger, "[Company X] ran from [Point A] to [Point B], but they didn't carry any traffic from [Point B] to [Point C]. But if they bought [Company Y], which already has a lot of the [Point B–Point C] traffic, it was obvious that there was likely to be a foreclosure problem."

On the other hand, this "feeling" that a merger is "bad" may not have such obvious justification; indeed, it may have very little to do with the antitrust laws at all. One lawyer spoke of a merger that had on its face seemed relatively uninteresting:

> They don't really compete directly; all their products are patented, anyway. But both these firms are now doing research in the _____ area, which I consider crucial to the future of mankind, and if they merge their research facilities, that development is going to slow down. I figured that's where the case was going to be.

Another lawyer told about a series of mergers between American companies in an industry and their counterparts in a foreign country, mergers that had come to his attention through public sources: "They looked okay. But what worried me about them was what if _____, _____, and _____ start using these foreign companies to produce all their component parts and take jobs away from American labor? The problem is that I don't know how to get *at* these things; I haven't found an argument to use." This particular lawyer evidently did manage to find an argument; a month after this statement, he was busily at work on an investigation to provide evidence for it.

So in these cases, investigation begins on the basis of suspicions rather than full-fledged theory. Sometimes the suspicion is only indirectly based on antitrust offenses per se; in that case, a lawyer must investigate various possibilities until he finds evidence that *does* bear on some category of antitrust violation. But even where a lawyer has an initial hypothesis about what is legally or economically wrong with a merger, he will not stop investigating if his search fails to bear out his original theory.

Thus investigations lengthen as lawyers try out a whole series of theories on a particular merger. Several lawyers talked about this process. One attorney spoke of mergers in the international field:

> I'll look for direct competition first, of course—though there won't be any. I could try potential competition—but I suspect that's going to be a little hard, since there are *lots* of potential competitors of that type. I don't know. Maybe I can show that the companies were competitors in *other* parts of the world and could start allocating markets there to increase their profits. . . .

The last strategy he mentioned entailed a considerable increase in the information he would require.

Another young attorney told of a bank merger case in which the original staff inclination had been to challenge the merger exclusively on the theory that it removed an important potential independent competitor from the market. "But then," he remembered,

> it appeared that there might be vertical foreclosure, too. It dealt with correspondent banking services that the [big city] banks perform for smaller ones. The small banks "pay" for this by keeping more money on deposit with the [big] banks than they need to. So we investigated the excess deposits—they're kept in a separate account—as a proxy measure of this business in correspondent services. Unfortunately, we only came up with 1 percent foreclosure. . . .

Not only will the lawyers try out a whole series of arguments on a particular merger, they are not put off if the arguments seem at first glance to be internally inconsistent. This is not to say that they are always unable to reconcile these inconsistencies, but they are hardly what one would call fully self-critical in their deliberations. One lawyer was asked about seeming inconsistencies in the argument he was using in a certain case and about whether these presented an intellectual problem for him. "Intellectual problems?" he answered. "I may have trouble working this out, but I don't have any *intellectual* problems. A lot of this is mostly personal competitiveness. . . ." This was an advocate speaking, not a judge.

Attorneys gave other examples of how, during the course of investigations, they brought seemingly incompatible arguments "into line." One lawyer was describing a vertical merger he had investigated, in which a producer had bought one of the several firms that were supplying it with a particular component:

> When we started, the foreclosure argument was very strong: We thought that _____ was foreclosed as a purchaser of _____, thus making it harder for anyone else to enter the supplier's business. But then it appeared that the customer itself might be a potential independent competitor in the

supplier's business. Of course the potential competition argument isn't so strong, and it's still unclear. And there was a bigger problem: The arguments cut across each other. How can a company be both a potential purchaser and a potential independent competitor? But we did figure out a way to do both.

Another example of the same process occurred when an attorney was investigating a merger that appeared not to be anticompetitive—and appeared so because, according to the market definition the division was already using in another ongoing case, this staff lawyer's two companies were simply not in the same line of commerce: "So I started looking at both lines of commerce, to see if they could really be one line. . . . Of course defense counsel in both cases were communicating with each other and accusing us of using inconsistent theories. But . . . [we] worked it out." So the desire to make a case from each investigation leads to a very marked determination to "work out" theoretical inconsistencies.

But the same impulse, the impulse to find a merger case, has yet a third important effect: It encourages lawyers to improvise, to innovate, and to extend the law. Whether all these innovations are what an outsider would call substantial, and whether they represent sufficient progress in the direction that some observers want the antitrust laws to take, is quite another matter, though one on which the examples below may shed some light. But many of the attorneys who had worked on merger investigations could point to what they thought were genuinely new arguments developed in the course of their work.

It may be remembered, for instance, that a lawyer quoted above had argued that there could be "sublines" of commerce within a single line. The invention and acceptance of this argument were important, he said, because they increased the number of mergers the division could prosecute in related lines of commerce.

Another attorney said that he had invented a whole new category of anticompetitive effects under similar circumstances. He was convinced that a certain merger in a regulated industry was anticompetitive, and the division intervened in the regulatory agency proceeding that was to judge the merger. The lawyer's problem was that the two companies in question did not compete directly and could not be assumed to be capable of doing so in the foreseeable future. His response was a new argument to the agency about the circumstances under which companies could be said to be competing: "We're saying that even if they're in *different* territories they're competitive because they compete to have industries locate in their areas. And even newer than that, we're saying that there's 'yardstick competition'—different prices in *another* area can raise a public stink. . . ."

Even more extreme was the recounting by another lawyer who had responded to a particular problem of his by proposing—albeit unsuccessfully—a major reinterpretation of the Sherman Act. The lawyer's problem was a merger between two large firms, but in a market of such large absolute size (and without any significant trend toward concentration) that "substantially lessened competition" under the Clayton Act would be extremely difficult to argue. He found the answer to his problem, he reported, by rereading the first "trust-busting" cases brought under the Sherman Act. The law, as he read it, could apply to single mergers in a manner much broader than had been generally assumed since the passage of the Clayton Act. And by attacking the merger under the Sherman Act, he said, he would be free of the necessity to deal with the merging firms' relatively small market shares.

Thus an important effect of the lawyers' desire to make cases is a certain tendency to try to stretch the law to cover what it did not quite fit before. As with "conduct" cases, one may then ask another question: Are there any patterns to be found in this activity, any types of cases where the lawyers are particularly likely to make special efforts? It may be remembered that one such uniformity in conduct cases had to do with the type of violation suspected: Offenses that attorneys found personally objectionable moved them to special efforts. The analogous consideration in mergers is size. Just as there are some mergers that are prima facie "too small" for the lawyers to investigate, so too are there mergers among companies so large that their acquisitions are automatically investigated and seriously challenged no matter how innocent they seem on their face.

The exact effect of the lawyers' animus against bigness is hard to measure. The division is by no means engaged in a single-minded attack on the nation's largest firms. In part this dispersion of energies can be explained by the nature of the information the division receives and by the staff's desire to bring the cases it *can* bring: Most of the time, the complaint or notice at hand does not concern Exxon, IBM, or AT&T. But it is true that when a case involving a very large firm comes to the division's attention, the lawyers' suspicion will spur them to shape principles that will reach these cases.

So what is "big"? There is no single standard the lawyers say they apply. Other things being equal, an acquisition by a firm with fifty million dollars in annual sales and a clear 50 percent of its market will be of more interest as a potential case than an acquisition by a seventy-five-million-dollar firm with a 10 percent market share. To be sure, a lawyer may take special interest in a merger for reasons other than size or market share alone. But in the above examples of "new" arguments, the lawyer was dealing either with a local market monopolized by one firm or with a company in the Fortune 500.

The lawyers' evaluations of the importance of absolute size vary. But the following statement by one lawyer is a fair summary of prevailing staff attitudes:

> Usually, we look at market concentration more than at absolute size. For instance, in the _____ merger I was telling you about, [Firm A] was the number-two firm in a market where the top two firms had 85 percent. And [Firm B] was third in the market. But I would say we *are* more' concerned about larger firms. For instance in banking, we won't look at acquisitions under ten million dollars, though we'll lower it some if the market is very small and localized. But with smaller firms, you always have to pay attention to the size of the market. Not with the bigger companies so much. For instance, you take the conglomerates. Absolute size is why we've been so innovative there. . . . If I had to name an absolute level where I'm *really* going to go all out to get them, I'd say that the Fortune 500 is the trigger.

Thus when dealing with an acquisition by a relatively small firm, the lawyers profess themselves more willing to accept concentration levels, market definitions, and the possible range of anticompetitive effects as given. A large firm will encourage them to find new definitions of concentration levels and markets and new varieties of anticompetitive effects.

But the impact of the lawyers' views on bigness or other such factors is limited by the ad hoc nature of their inventions. In the absence of a particular case, they seem not to spend time thinking about where the law should be going or where the economy needs more competition. There are exceptions; a few lawyers in the division do think along these lines. One of them defined his list of future antitrust targets in this way: ". . . lawyers' fee-fixing, the NAB code—there are thousands of these things. Some are legitimate—but for instance, what about the TV advertising boycotts on contraceptives and hard liquor? And the rule that they can't disparage each other's products?" And not just individuals but some special sections of the division—the patents unit, for instance—have a comparably clear notion of how they would change antitrust law in their areas.

But a more typical lawyer, when asked for his own antitrust agenda, sighed and said, "You just don't have time to sit around and think about busting up GM."

Notes

1. A few staff lawyers do report higher proportions of positive recommendations.

2. For instance, various kinds of exemptions exist for regulated industries,

for export associations, for agricultural cooperatives, for concerted action in dealing with governmental bodies, for labor unions, for patented products. See A.D. Neale, *The Antitrust Laws of the U.S.A.* (Cambridge: Cambridge University Press, 1970), for an introduction.

3. *Associated Press v. United States* (S.C. 1945), in which it was decided that the Associated Press, by denying its near-unique services to its members' competitors, was engaging in illegal restraint of trade.

33. The Decision to Prosecute

GEORGE F. COLE

This paper is based on an exploratory study of the Office of Prosecuting Attorney, King County (Seattle), Washington. The lack of social scientific knowledge about the prosecutor dictated the choice of this approach. An open-ended interview was administered to one-third of the former deputy prosecutors who had worked in the office during the ten-year period 1955–1965. In addition, interviews were conducted with court employees, members of the bench, law-enforcement officials, and others having reputations for participation in legal decision making. Over fifty respondents were contacted during this phase. A final portion of the research placed the author in the role of observer in the prosecutor's office. This experience allowed for direct observation of all phases of the decision to prosecute so that the informal processes of the office could be noted. Discussions with the prosecutor's staff, judges, defendant's attorneys, and the police were held so that the interview data could be placed within an organizational context.

The primary goal of this investigation was to examine the role of the prosecuting attorney as an officer of the legal process within the context of the local political system. The analysis is therefore based on two assumptions. First, that the legal process is best understood as a subsystem of the larger political system. Because of this choice, emphasis is placed upon the interaction and goals of the individuals involved in decision making. Second, and closely related to the first point, it is assumed that broadly conceived political considerations explained to a large extent "who gets or does not get—in what amount—and how, the good (justice) that is hopefully produced by the legal system."[1] By focusing upon the political and social linkages between these systems, it is expected that decision making in the prosecutor's office will be viewed as a principal ingredient in the authoritative allocation of values.

425

THE PROSECUTOR'S OFFICE IN AN EXCHANGE SYSTEM

While observing the interrelated activities of the organizations in the legal process, one might ask, "Why do these agencies cooperate?" If the police refuse to transfer information to the prosecutor concerning the commission of a crime, what are the rewards or sanctions that might be brought against them? Is it possible that organizations maintain a form of "bureaucratic accounting" that, in a sense, keeps track of the resources allocated to an agency and the support returned? How are cues transmitted from one agency to another to influence decision making? These are some of the questions that must be asked when decisions are viewed as an output of an exchange system.

The major findings of this study are placed within the context of an exchange system.[2] This serves the heuristic purpose of focusing attention upon the linkages found between actors in the decision-making process. In place of the traditional assumptions that the agency is supported solely by statutory authority, this view recognizes that an organization has many clients with which it interacts and upon whom it is dependent for certain resources. As interdependent subunits of a system, then, the organization and its clients are engaged in a set of exchanges across their boundaries. These will involve a transfer of resources between the organizations that will affect the mutual achievement of goals.

The legal system may be viewed as a set of interorganizational exchange relationships analogous to what Long has called a community game.[3] The participants in the legal system (game) share a common territorial field and collaborate for different and particular ends. They interact on a continuing basis as their responsibilities demand contact with other participants in the process. Thus, the need for the cooperation of other participants can have a bearing on the decision to prosecute. A decision not to prosecute a narcotics offender may be a move to pressure the United States' Attorney's Office to cooperate on another case. It is obvious that bargaining occurs not only between the major actors in a case—the prosecutor and the defense attorney—but also between the clientele groups that are influential in structuring the actions of the prosecuting attorney.

Exchanges do not simply "sail" from one system to another, but take place in an institutionalized setting that may be compared to a market. In the market, decisions are made between individuals who occupy boundary-spanning roles, and who set the conditions under which the exchange will occur. In the legal system, this may merely mean that a representative of the parole board agrees to forward a recommendation to the prosecutor, or it could mean that there is extended bargaining between a deputy prosecutor and a defense attorney. In the study of the King County Prosecutor's Office, it was found that most decisions resulted from some type of exchange relationship. The deputies interacted almost constantly with the police and criminal lawyers; the prosecutor was more closely linked to exchange relations with the courts, community leaders, and the county commissioners.

THE PROSECUTOR'S CLIENTELE

In an exchange system, power is largely dependent upon the ability of an organization to create clientele relationships that will support and enhance the needs of the agency. For, although interdependence is characteristic of the legal system, competition with other public agencies for support also exists. Because organizations operate in an economy of scarcity, the organization must exist in a favorable

Superior court
(Bound over)   774

Plead guilty	510
Plead innocent	240
Dismissed	24
Found guilty	216
Found innocent	24

Justice court
(Cases filed)

Felonies	2471
Gross misdemeanors	629
Misdemeanors	574
Traffic violations	20
Game violations	6
	3700

Justice court

(Reduced to
misdemeanor)	1697
Plead guilty	1595
Plead innocent	4
Dismissed	98
Found guilty	3
Found innocent	1

Figure 1.   Disposition of Felony Cases—King County, 1964.

power position in relation to its clientele. Reciprocal and unique claims are made by the organization and its clients. Thus, rather than being oriented toward only one public, an organization is beholden to several publics, some visible and others seen clearly only from the pinnacle of leadership. As Gore notes, when these claims are "firmly anchored inside the organization and the lines drawn taut, the tensions between conflicting claims form a net serving as the institutional base for the organization."[4]

An indication of the stresses within the judicial system may be obtained by analyzing its outputs. It has been suggested that the administration of justice is a selective process in which only those cases that do not create strains in the organization will ultimately reach the courtroom.[5] As noted in Figure 1, the system operates so that only a small number of cases arrive for trial, the rest being disposed of through reduced charges, *nolle pros.*, and guilty pleas.[6] Not indicated are those cases removed by the police and prosecutor prior to the filing of charges. As the focal organization in an exchange system, the office of prosecuting attorney makes decisions that reflect the influence of its clientele. Because of the scarcity of resources, marketlike relationships, and the organizational needs of the system, prosecutorial decision making emphasizes the accommodations made to the needs of participants in the process.

Police

Although the prosecuting attorney has discretionary power to determine the disposition of cases, this power is limited by the fact that usually he is dependent upon the police for inputs to the system of cases and evidence. The prosecutor does not have the investigative resources necessary to exercise the kind of affirmative control over the types of cases that are brought to him. In this relationship, the prosecutor is not without countervailing power. His main check on the police is his ability to return cases to them for further investigation and to refuse to approve arrest warrants. By maintaining cordial relations with the press, a prosecutor is often able to focus attention on the police when the public becomes aroused by incidents of crime. As the King County prosecutor emphasized, "That [investigation] is the job for the sheriff and police. It's their job to bring me the charges." As noted by many respondents, the police, in turn, are dependent upon the prosecutor to accept the output of their system; rejection of too many cases can have serious repercussions affecting the morale, discipline, and workload of the force.

A request for prosecution may be rejected for a number of reasons relating to questions of evidence. Not only must the prosecutor believe that the evidence will secure a conviction, but he must also be aware of community norms relating to the type of acts that should be prosecuted. King County deputy prosecutors noted that charges were never filed when a case involved attempted suicide or fornication. In other actions, the heinous nature of the crime, together with the expected public reaction, may force both the police and prosecutor to press for conviction when evidence is less than satisfactory. As one deputy noted, "In that case [murder and molestation of a six-year-old girl] there was nothing that we could do. As you know the press was on our back and every parent was concerned. Politically, the prosecutor had to seek information."

Factors other than those relating to evidence may require that the prosecutor refuse to accept a case from the police. First, the prosecuting attorney serves as a regulator of case loads not only for his own office, but for the rest of the legal system. Constitutional and statutory time limits prevent him and the courts from building a backlog of untried cases. In King County, when the system reached the "overload point," there was a tendency to be more selective in choosing the cases to be accepted. A second reason for rejecting prosecution requests may stem from the fact that the prosecutor is thinking of his public exposure in the courtroom. He does not want to take forward cases that will place him in an embarrassing position. Finally, the prosecutor may return cases to check the quality of police work. As a former chief criminal deputy said, "You have to keep them on their toes, otherwise they get lazy. If they aren't doing their job, send the case back and then leak the situation to the newspapers." Rather than spend the resources necessary to find additional evidence, the police may dispose of a case by sending it back to the prosecutor on a lesser charge, implement the "copping out" machinery leading to a guilty plea, drop the case, or in some instances send it to the city prosecutor for action in municipal court.

In most instances, a deputy prosecutor and the police officer assigned to the case occupy the boundary-spanning roles in this exchange relationship. Prosecutors reported that after repeated contacts they got to know the policemen whom they could trust. As one female deputy commented, "There are some you can trust, others you have to watch because they are trying to get rid of cases on you." Deputies may be influenced by the police officer's attitude on a case. One officer noted to a prosecutor that he knew he had a weak case, but mumbled, "I didn't want to bring it up here, but that's what they [his superiors] wanted." As might be expected, the deputy turned down prosecution.

Sometimes the police perform the ritual of "shopping around," seeking to find a deputy prosecutor who, on the basis of past experience, is liable to be sympathetic to their view on a case. At one time, deputies were given complete authority to make the crucial decisions without coordinating their activities with other staff members. In this way the arresting officer would search the prosecutor's office to find a deputy he thought would be sympathetic to the police attitude. As a former deputy noted, "This meant that there were no departmental policies concerning the treatment to be accorded various types of cases. It pretty much depended upon the police and their luck in finding the deputy they wanted." Prosecutors are now instructed to ascertain from the police officer if he has seen another deputy on the case. Even under this more centralized system, it is still possible for the police to request a specific deputy or delay presentation of the case until the "correct" prosecutor is available. Often a prosecutor will gain a reputation for specializing in one type of case. This may mean that the police will assume he will get the case anyway, so they skirt the formal procedure and bring it to him directly.

An exchange relationship between a deputy prosecutor and a police officer may be influenced by the type of crime committed by the defendant. The prototype of a criminal is one who violates person and property. However, a large number of cases involve "crimes without victims." This term refers to those crimes generally involving violations of moral codes, where the general public is theoretically the complainant. In violations of laws against bookmaking, prostitution, and narcotics, neither actor in the transaction is interested in having an arrest made. Hence, vice control men must drum up their own business. Without a civilian complainant, victimless crimes give the police and prosecutor greater leeway in determining the charges to be filed.

One area of exchange involving a victimless crime is that of narcotics control. As Skolnick notes, "The major organizational requirement of narcotics policing is the presence of an informational system."[7] Without a network of informers, it is impossible to capture addicts and peddlers with evidence that can bring about convictions. One source of informers is among those arrested for narcotics violations. Through promises to reduce charges or even to *nolle pros.*, arrangements can be made so that the accused will return to the narcotics community and gather information for the police. Bargaining observed between the head of the narcotics squad of the Seattle police and the deputy prosecutor who specialized in drug cases involved the question of charges, promises, and the release of an arrested narcotics pusher.

In the course of postarrest questioning by the police, a well-known drug peddler intimated that he could provide evidence against a pharmacist suspected by the police of illegally selling narcotics. Not only did the police representative want to transfer the case to the

friendlier hands of this deputy, but he also wanted to arrange for a reduction of charges and bail. The police officer believed that it was important that the accused be let out in such a way that the narcotics
community would not realize that he had become an informer. He
also wanted to be sure that the reduced charges would be processed
so that the informer could be kept on the string, thus allowing the
narcotics squad to maintain control over him. The deputy prosecutor,
on the other hand, said that he wanted to make sure that procedures
were followed so that the action would not bring discredit on his office. He also suggested that the narcotics squad "work a little harder"
on a pending case as a means of returning the favor.

Courts

The ways used by the court to dispose of cases is a vital influence in
the system. The court's actions affect pressures upon the prison, the
conviction rate of the prosecutor, and the work of probation agencies. The judge's decisions act as clues to other parts of the system, indicating the type of action likely to be taken in future cases. As noted
by a King County judge, "When the number of prisoners gets to the
'riot point,' the warden puts pressure on us to slow down the flow.
This often means that men are let out on parole and the number of
people given probation and suspended sentences increases." Under
such conditions, it would be expected that the prosecutor would respond to the judge's actions by reducing the inputs to the court either
by not preferring charges or by increasing the pressure for guilty
pleas through bargaining. The adjustments of other parts of the system could be expected to follow. For instance, the police might sense
the lack of interest of the prosecutor in accepting charges, hence
they will send only airtight cases to him for indictment.

The influence of the court on the decision to prosecute is very real.
The sentencing history of each judge gives the prosecutor, as well as
other law-enforcement officials, an indication of the treatment a case
may receive in a courtroom. The prosecutor's expectation as to
whether the court will convict may limit his discretion over the decisions on whether to prosecute. "There is great concern as to whose
court a case will be assigned. After Judge _____ threw out three
cases in a row in which entrapment was involved, the police did not
want us to take any cases to him." Since the prosecutor depends upon
the plea-bargaining machinery to maintain the flow of cases from his
office, the sentencing actions of judges must be predictable. If the defendant and his lawyer are to be influenced to accept a lesser charge
or the promise of a lighter sentence in exchange for a plea of guilty,
there must be some basis for belief that the judge will fulfill his part
of the arrangement. Because judges are unable formally to announce

their agreement with the details of the bargain, their past performance acts as a guide.

Within the limits imposed by law and the demands of the system, the prosecutor is able to regulate the flow of cases to the court. He may control the length of time between accusation and trial; hence he may hold cases until he has the evidence that will convict. Alternatively, he may seek repeated adjournment and continuances until the public's interest dies; problems such as witnesses becoming unavailable and similar difficulties make his request for dismissal of prosecution more justifiable. Further, he may determine the type of court to receive the case and the judge who will hear it. Many misdemeanors covered by state law are also violations of a city ordinance. It is a common practice for the prosecutor to send a misdemeanor case to the city prosecutor for processing in the municipal court when it is believed that a conviction may not be secured in justice court. As a deputy said, "If there is no case—send it over to the city court. Things are speedier, less formal, over there."

In the state of Washington, a person arrested on a felony charge must be given a preliminary hearing in a justice court within ten days. For the prosecutor, the preliminary hearing is an opportunity to evaluate the testimony of witnesses, assess the strength of the evidence, and try to predict the outcome of the case if it is sent to trial. On the basis of this evaluation, the prosecutor has several options: he may bind over the case for trial in superior court; he may reduce the charges to those of a misdemeanor for trial in justice court; or he may conclude that he has no case and drop the charges. The President Judge of the Justice Courts of King County estimated that about 70 percent of the felonies are reduced to misdemeanors after the preliminary hearing.

Besides having some leeway in determining the type of court in which to file a case, the prosecutor also has some flexibility in selecting the judge to receive the case. Until recently the prosecutor could file a case with a specific judge. "The trouble was that Judge _____ was erratic and independent, [so] no one would file with him. The other judges objected that they were handling the entire workload, so a central filing system was devised." Under this procedure cases are assigned to the judges in rotation. However, as the chief criminal deputy noted, "the prosecutor can hold a case until the 'correct' judge comes up."

Defense Attorneys

With the increased specialization and institutionalization of the bar, it would seem that those individuals engaged in the practice of criminal law have been relegated, both by their profession and by the community, to a low status. The urban bar appears to be divided into three parts. First, there is an inner circle, which handles the work of banks, utilities, and commercial concerns; second, another circle includes plaintiff's lawyers representing interests opposed to those of the inner circle; and finally, an outer group scrapes out an existence by "haunting the courts in hope of picking up crumbs from the judicial table."[8] With the exception of a few highly proficient lawyers who have made a reputation by winning acquittal for their clients in difficult, highly publicized cases, most of the lawyers dealing with the King County Prosecutor's Office belong to this outer ring.

In this study, respondents were asked to identify those attorneys considered to be specialists in criminal law. Of the nearly sixteen hundred lawyers practicing in King County only eight can be placed in this category. Of this group, six were reported to enjoy the respect of the legal community, while the others were accused by many respondents of being involved in shady deals. A larger group of King County attorneys will accept criminal cases, but these lawyers do not consider themselves specialists. Several respondents noted that many lawyers, because of inexperience or age, were required to hang around the courthouse searching for clients. One Seattle attorney described the quality of legal talent available for criminal cases as "a few good criminal lawyers and a lot of young kids and old men. The good lawyers I can count on my fingers."

In a legal system where bargaining is a primary method of decision making, it is not surprising that criminal lawyers find it essential to maintain close personal ties with the prosecutor and his staff. Respondents were quite open in revealing their dependence upon this close relationship to pursue their careers successfully. The nature of the criminal lawyer's work is such that his saleable product or service appears to be influence rather than technical proficiency in the law. Respondents hold the belief that clients are attracted partially on the basis of the attorney's reputation as a fixer, or as a shrewd bargainer.

There is a tendency for ex-deputy prosecutors in King County to enter the practice of criminal law. Because of his inside knowledge of the prosecutor's office and friendships made with court officials, the former deputy feels that he has an advantage over other criminal law practitioners. All of the former deputies interviewed said that they took criminal cases. Of the eight criminal law specialists, seven previously served as deputy prosecutors in King County and the other was once prosecuting attorney in a rural county.

Because of the financial problems of the criminal lawyer's practice, it is necessary that he handle cases on an assembly-line basis, hoping to make a living from a large number of small fees. Referring to a fellow lawyer, one attorney said, "You should see _____. He goes up there to Carroll's office with a whole fistful of cases. He trades on some, bargains on others and never goes to court. It's amazing but it's the way he makes his living." There are incentives, therefore, to bargain with the prosecutor and other decision makers. The primary aim of the attorney in such circumstances is to reach an accommodation so that the time-consuming formal proceedings need not be implemented. As a Seattle attorney noted, "I can't make money if I spend my time in a courtroom. I make mine on the telephone or in the prosecutor's office." One of the disturbing results of this arrangement is that instances were reported in which a bargain was reached between the attorney and deputy prosecutor on a "package deal." In this situation, an attorney's clients are treated as a group; the outcome of the bargaining is often an agreement whereby reduced charges will be achieved for some, in exchange for the unspoken assent by the lawyer that the prosecutor may proceed as he desires with the other cases. One member of the King County Bar has developed this practice to such a fine art that a deputy prosecutor said, "When you saw him coming into the office, you knew that he would be pleading guilty." At one time this situation was so widespread that the "prisoners up in the jail had a rating list which graded the attorneys as either 'good guys' or 'sell outs.' "

The exchange relationship between the defense attorney and the prosecutor is based on their need for cooperation in the discharge of their responsibilities. Most criminal lawyers are interested primarily in the speedy solution of cases because of their precarious financial situation. Because they must protect their professional reputations with their colleagues, judicial personnel, and potential clientele, however, they are not completely free to bargain solely with this objective. As one attorney noted, "You can't afford to let it get out that you are selling out your cases."

The prosecutor is also interested in the speedy processing of cases. This can only be achieved if the formal processes are not implemented. Not only does the pressure of his caseload influence bargaining, but also the legal process, with its potential for delay and appeal, creates a degree of uncertainty that is not present in an exchange relationship with an attorney with whom you have dealt for a number of years. As the Presiding Judge of the Seattle District Court said, "Lawyers are helpful to the system. They are able to pull things together, work out a deal, keep the system moving."

Community Influentials

As part of the political system, the judicial process responds to the community environment. The King County study indicated that there are differential levels of influence within the community and that some people had a greater interest in the politics of prosecution than others. First, the general public is able to have its values translated into policies followed by law-enforcement officers. The public's influence is particularly acute in those gray areas of the law where full enforcement is not expected. Statutes may be enacted by legislatures defining the outer limits of criminal conduct, but they do not necessarily mean that laws are to be fully enforced to these limits. There are some laws defining behavior that the community no longer considers criminal. It can be expected that a prosecutor's charging policies will reflect this attitude. He may not prosecute violations of laws regulating some forms of gambling, certain sexual practices, or violations of Sunday Blue Laws.

Because the general public is a potential threat to the prosecutor, staff members take measures to protect him from criticism. Respondents agreed that decision making occurs with the public in mind— "will a course of action arouse antipathy toward the prosecutor rather than the accused?" Several deputies mentioned what they called the "aggravation level" of a crime. This is a recognition that the commission of certain crimes, within a specific context, will bring about a vocal public reaction. "If a little girl, walking home from the grocery store, is pulled into the bushes and indecent liberties taken, this is more disturbing to the public's conscience than a case where the father of the girl takes indecent liberties with her at home." The office of King County Prosecuting Attorney has a policy requiring that deputies file all cases involving sexual molestation in which the police believe the girl's story is credible. The office also prefers charges in all negligent homicide cases where there is the least possibility of guilt. In such types of cases the public may respond to the emotional context of the case and demand prosecution. To cover the prosecutor from criticism, it is believed that the safest measure is to prosecute.

The bail system is also used to protect the prosecutor from criticism. Thus it is the policy to set bail at a high level with the expectation that the court will reduce the amount. "This looks good for Prosecutor Carroll. Takes the heat off of him, especially in morals cases. If the accused doesn't appear in court the prosecutor can't be blamed. The public gets upset when they know these types are out free." This is an example of exchange where one actor is shifting the responsibility and potential onus onto another. In turn, the court is under pressure from county jail officials to keep the prison population down.

A second community group having contact with the prosecutor is composed of those leaders who have a continuing or potential interest in the politics of prosecution. This group, analogous to the players in one of Long's community games, are linked to the prosecutor because his actions affect their success in playing another game. Hence community boosters want either a crackdown or a hands-off policy toward gambling, political leaders want the prosecutor to remember the interests of the party, and business leaders want policies that will not interfere with their own game.

Community leaders may receive special treatment by the prosecutor if they run afoul of the law. A policy of the King County Office requires that cases involving prominent members of the community be referred immediately to the chief criminal deputy and the prosecutor for their disposition. As one deputy noted, "These cases can be pretty touchy. It's important that the boss knows immediately about this type of case so that he is not caught 'flat footed' when asked about it by the press."

Pressure by an interest group was evidenced during a strike by drugstore employees in 1964. The striking unions urged Prosecutor Carroll to invoke a state law which requires the presence of a licensed pharmacist if the drugstore is open. Not only did union representatives meet with Carroll, but picket lines were set up outside the courthouse protesting his refusal to act. The prosecutor resisted the union's pressure tactics.

In recent years, the prosecutor's tolerance policy toward minor forms of gambling led to a number of conflicts with Seattle's mayor, the sheriff, and church organizations. After a decision was made to prohibit all forms of public gaming, the prosecutor was criticized by groups representing the tourist industry and such affected groups as the bartender's union which thought the decision would have an adverse economic effect. As Prosecutor Carroll said, "I am always getting pressures from different interests—business, the Chamber of Commerce, and labor. I have to try and maintain a balance between them." In exchange for these considerations, the prosecutor may gain prestige, political support, and admission into the leadership groups of the community.

SUMMARY

By viewing the King County Office of Prosecuting Attorney as the focal organization in an exchange system, data from this exploratory study suggest the marketlike relationships that exist between actors in the system. Because prosecution operates in an environment of scarce resources and because the decisions have potential political ramifications, a variety of officials influence the allocation of justice. The decision to prosecute is not made at one point, but rather the prosecuting attorney has a number of options he may employ during various stages of the proceedings. But the prosecutor is able to exercise his discretionary powers only within the network of exchange relationships. The police, court congestion, organizational strains, and community pressures are among the factors that influence prosecutorial behavior.

Notes

1. James R. Klonoski and Robert I. Mendelsohn, "The Allocation of Justice: A Political Analysis," *Journal of Public Law* 14 (May 1965): 323–342.

2. William M. Evan, "Towards a Theory of Inter-Organizational Relations," *Management Science* 11 (August 1965): 218–230.

3. Norton Long, *The Polity* (Chicago: Rand McNally, 1962), p. 142.

4. William J. Gore, *Administrative Decision-Making* (New York: John Wiley, 1964), p. 23.

5. William J. Chambliss, *Crime and the Legal Process* (New York: McGraw-Hill, 1969), p. 84.

6. The lack of reliable criminal statistics is well known. These data were gathered from a number of sources including: King County, "Annual Report of the Prosecuting Attorney," State of Washington, 1964.

7. Jerome L. Skolnick, *Justice without Trial* (New York: John Wiley, 1966), p. 120.

8. Jack Ladinsky, "The Impact of Social Backgrounds of Lawyers on Law Practice and the Law," *Journal of Legal Education* 16 (1963): 128.

34. Stereotypes and Dispositions for Criminal Homicide

STEVEN BARNET BORIS

INTRODUCTION AND PRIOR LITERATURE

This is a study of the differential treatment of offenders arrested for criminal homicide and the dispositional decision made at their preliminary hearing. Differential treatment of persons is a popular, as well as controversial, topic in criminology. The process by which persons come to have criminal status conferred upon them has been a central concern of writers in this field. A guiding theme of the literature on police, attorney, and judicial behavior has been the question of whether the reactions of these social control agents vary with the social attributes of the alleged deviant or criminal.

Within the literature on police and attorney behavior, some consensus that not all persons are reacted to equally has been reached. The classic findings of Pilivan and Briar (1964) and Bittner (1967) have not been successfully challenged. Essentially, these writers argue that there does exist differential reaction to persons the police encounter during their patrol activities. The development of differential reactions is seen as resulting from a reliance upon preconceived rules about who is potentially dangerous or criminal. These rules, in part, are derived from behavioral cues and social attributes, such as demeanor or race, and are crucial in the definition and maintenance of criminal labels.

Whether social reaction covaries with the social and situational attributes of accused offenders is the subject of Sudnow's (1965) study. Sudnow analyzes the processing activities of public defenders and concludes that organizationally defined rules govern the mass processing of accused offenders into typical categories, i.e., "normal crimes." A decade later, Rosett and Cressey (1976) investigated both defense attorneys' and prosecutors' activities and argue, among other things, that organizational imperatives (resources and relationships) mandate "normal" plea bargaining in the criminal justice system, for persons who cannot afford more justice.

The alleged differential treatment of adjudicated offenders has been intensely studied, the theme being that working-class and black defendants are more severely sanctioned than their middle-class and white counterparts. Bullock (1961) has shown that while black defendants receive harsher prison sentences for burglary, they receive shorter sentences for criminal homicide. Green (1964) concludes that blacks are sanctioned in a harsher manner than whites, but that sanction is mediated by the seriousness of the offense. Nagel (1969) investigated sentencing discrepancies, concluding that for the indigent prison sentences were both more frequent and longer than for the nonindigent. Hagan (1974), however, recomputed these statistics and concludes that Nagel's findings are spurious due to the effects of prior record on prison sentence. More recently, Thomas and Cage (1977) emphasized the salience of the relationship between prior record and adjudication in their review of discrimination within the juvenile court.

Chiricos and Waldo argue in their study of sentencing practices in the South that "socioeconomic status of convicted criminal offenders is unrelated to the severity of the state's official sanction" (1975:766). Swigert and Farrell (1976) conclude the opposite in their study of criminal homicide offenders in one northeastern jurisdiction. Finally, Burke and Turk (1975) found limited support for the notion that class-linked behavior of criminal justice decision makers accounts for the differences in the outcomes of cases for a variety of felonies, misdemeanors, and traffic offenses.

A review of these studies, then, leads one to conclude that there is no consensus as to whether or not differential treatment of social groups exists at the level of judicial decision making. Further, the dependent variable, in the vast majority of these studies, is sentence. With the possible exception of Burke and Turk (1975), the decisions and discretions which occur prior to sentencing are either ignored or tenuously held constant through statistical manipulation. These prior decisions must be examined before meaningful statements about case dispositions can be discussed (Bernstein et al., 1977). It is important to view these prior decisions in the context of the criminal justice system—that is, antecedent conditions bear influence on later decisions.

THE PRESENT STUDY

Some of the weaknesses outlined above are addressed in this study. First, in response to Bernstein et al. (1977), a prior decision point in the criminal justice system is addressed: the decision made at the preliminary hearing. It is at this crucial stage that the decision to prosecute or to dismiss a case is made. Second, only one form of criminal behavior is discussed here, criminal homicide. This, in effect, controls for severity of the crime. Homicide is probably the least hidden of deviance. Its rate of detection (clearance rates by the police) indicates, in Swigert and Farrell's words, "that individuals charged with murder are characteristic of persons who actually commit murder" (1976:5–6). This is not the case for less serious offenses. Swigert and Farrell are supported by the fact that results of victimization surveys do not even address the issue of disparity between known offenses of homicide and any "dark figures" as they do for larceny, for one example. Third, as is the case for the studies discussed above, socioeconomic variables comprise the major independent variables. In addition, however, prior criminal record is also a predictor of whether a case is, or is not, dismissed. Using multiple regression, the combined and individual effects of all of the independent variables on the decision to prosecute or dismiss is possible.

Lastly, this study also incorporates the characteristics of the victims of criminal homicide into the analysis. Within a symbolic interactionist framework, it is argued that the demographic and criminal biographies of homicide victims and offenders will help explain the differences in legal treatment of the offenders.

THEORETICAL ISSUES

American society is stratified. The social distance produced between classes and races determines the nature and amount of knowledge which groups have of one another. In addition, the basis of social interaction is the sharing of symbols and meanings (Mead, 1934). When these are minimally shared, as in a stratified society, interaction can only be based on what is brought into the current situation from past experiences—stereotypes. Swigert and Farrell concur:

> Where interaction is incomplete or results from impersonal contacts, definitions and meanings attributed to others tend to develop along stereotypic lines [1976:22].

Further, intrapsychic social control rests on the taking of the roles of significant others (Mead, 1934). Significant others differ between strata. Members in differing strata, thus, will view the social world in different ways—the ways of their particular reference group. This process has been explicated by Goffman (1963) and empirically tested by Scheff (1966) and other theorists who ground their work in symbolic interactionism. These theorists conclude that persons who, in the popular mind, should be deviant are treated as such.

Casting the above into a political perspective, the shared meanings of the upper-level stratum of society are the meanings which become institutionalized. It is at this level where the beliefs of the powerful are codified into laws, and the actions of those persons without power are labeled deviant (Turk, 1969; Chambliss and Siedman, 1971; Black, 1976). This perspective, then, regards the social structure as criminogenic and victimogenic. The legal system represents and protects the values of the powerful (of interest groups) and evaluates the behavior of those without political power.

Given the above perspective, the decision to invoke sanctions, the amount of sanction or to dismiss charges depends not so much on the deviant act committed but rather on determining the extent to which individuals conform to the stereotype "criminal." In the case of criminal homicide, then, harsher sentences imposed on the young, the poor, and the black may be not only cases of outright racism or classism but also responses and reactions to the belief that the young, the poor, and the black are criminal.

Research conducted by Swigert and Farrell (1976) supports the notion of stereotypic reaction to criminal homicide offenders. These authors develop the thesis that the successful application of a stereotype, designated the "Normal Primitive," results in the award of official deviance. Swigert and Farrell (1976) conclude that conformity to the criminal stereotype—especially in terms of social class (working) and race (black)—has significant consequences for the assignment of public counsel, denial of bail, and a plea of guilt before the judge. This lack of access to legal resources, in turn, produces more severe convictions and harsher sentences.

The present study expands the work of Swigert and Farrell (1976) in three ways. First, as noted earlier, the dependent variable is the decision to prosecute or dismiss a case. Swigert and Farrell's analysis jumps from arrest to assignment of bail. This study looks in between these processes.

Second, the sociodemographic and criminal biographies of both the victim and the offender are used to predict whether a case is dismissed or prosecuted. If the theoretical concept of stereotypic reactions to criminals is valid, then it may be valid for the victims of criminal homicide because the roles of victim and offender are often interchangeable (Hentig, 1948; Schaffer, 1968: Avison, 1974). Barber (1974) has argued that the perceived "moral" characters of rape victims are important determinants of the severity of sentences imposed on their rapists. A similar view might hold for reactions to homicide because these two violent crimes, in terms of the community outrage they cause, are similar.

The third, and final, way in which this study expands upon Swigert and Farrell's is that two distinct forms of criminal homicide are investigated. Homicides are either categorized as "social conflict" or "crime specific" (Wilt, 1974). The former are those homicides committed during everyday social interaction, such as during a domestic dispute. The latter are those homicides which occur as a result of the commission of another crime. This second form is similar to the criminal homicides governed by the felony murder rule.

Wilt's contribution lies in the discovery that significant differences exist between the victims and the perpetrators of social conflict and crime specific homicides in terms of relationships, motives, and other factors. The legal categories offenders were placed in (first degree murder vs. second degree vs. nonnegligent manslaughter, and so on) were found to be of less importance in explaining this form of violence than were the sociological categories. Wilt concludes that the differences between social conflict and crime specific homicides are of greater import than are any variations within the two types.

METHODOLOGY

Sample

The data were collected by Wilt (1974) for all criminal homicides which occurred in a large northern industrial city in 1972. Excluding missing data, analysis is performed on 383 cases. Of these 383 cases, 258 are classified as social conflict homicides and 125 are classified as crime specific homicides.

Variables

The dependent variable is the disposition of the case at the preliminary hearing. This variable is operationalized as either "dismissed" or "prosecuted." Including cases in which either sociodemographic or criminal history variables are missing,[1] the differences between social conflict and crime specific dispositions are interesting to note. More than 67 percent of all cases were dismissed and 60 percent of these were social conflict homicides. Also, and statistically significant, the difference between the two types of homicides is reflected in terms of the proportions of dismissal: 76.2 percent of crime specific cases were dismissed compared with 62.7 percent for social conflict cases.[2] These distributions lend evidence to the dichotomization of criminal homicide into two distinct forms.

The following variables represent the attributes of the stereotype criminal. For both the offender and the victim, sociodemographic and criminal history variables were collected. Demographic variables include occupational status, race, age, and education.

Criminal history (record) of both offender and victim are operationalized as four variables: number of felony property convictions, number of felony property arrests, number of aggravated assault convictions, and number of aggravated assault arrests.

Analysis

Bivariate analysis is performed first to assess any relationships between each independent variable and the dependent variable. Following this method, multiple regression is employed for the remainder of the study. This method allows for the assessment of the relative impact of each independent variable working alone and in combination with all of the other independent variables on the dependent variable. Nominal level variables are dichotomized so that they can be treated as "scores" in the regression equation (Kerlinger and Pedhazur, 1973; Nie et al., 1975).

HYPOTHESES

The explanation of whether a case of criminal homicide will be dismissed or prosecuted resides, in part, in the sociodemographic and criminal biographies of both the offender and the victim. This postulate generates two hypotheses: (1) The sociodemographic and criminal biographies of the offender and the victim will explain more variance in the disposition in cases of crime specific homicide than they will for cases of social conflict homicide. (2) The greater the conformity to the institutionalized stereotype criminal by the offender and the less conformity to this stereotype by the victim, the harsher the disposition of a case.

FINDINGS

To test Hypothesis 1—that dispositions within crime specific homicide will be explained to a greater extent than within social conflict homicide—the Pearson product-moment (r) correlations for the relationships between each sociodemographic and criminal biography variable and the disposition of the case were computed. Table 1 presents these correlations within social conflict homicide.

Table 1 indicates that the prediction power of every independent variable, except the number of felony property arrests of the victim, is severely limited. An explanation of this finding is offered below, after a discussion of the crime specific correlations.

Table 2 presents the product-moment correlations between the dependent variables and disposition for crime specific homicides, offering a number of interesting findings. Statistically significant relationships exist between the dependent variable of disposition and race of both offender and victim, occupation of both offender and victim, education of victim (an unreliable correlation because of missing data), and age of both offender and victim.

Looking first at the relationship between race and disposition, black offenders have cases prosecuted to a greater extent than do their white counterparts. Conversely, when the victim is white, the dispositional decision will be in the direction of prosecution.

Looking next at the relationship between occupation and disposition, the variance is again related. The unemployed offenders have their cases prosecuted to a significantly greater extent than do higher-status—employed—offenders. Likewise, when the victim is employed—high status—the chance of prosecution increases.

Education of the offender is not shown to be related to disposition, while education of victim is shown to be related to disposition. However, because of missing data, these results are not reliable.

Finally, age is significantly related to disposition. The older offend-

Table 1. Pearson (r) Correlations between Disposition of Case and All Independent Variables for Social Conflict Homicides

Independent Variables	r Correlation
Race of offender	+.033
Race of victim	+.0003
Occupation of offender	−.050
Occupation of victim	+.059
Education of offender	−.060
Education of victim	−.062
Age of offender	−.060
Age of victim	+.012
Number of felony property convictions of offender	−.030
Number of felony property convictions of victim	−.053
Number of felony property arrests of offender	−.009
Number of felony property arrests of victim	−.135**
Number of aggravated assault convictions of offender	+.053
Number of aggravated assault convictions of victim	−.093
Number of aggravated assault arrests of offender	−.081
Number of aggravated assault arrests of victim	−.069

**p less than .01.

Table 2. Pearson (r) Correlations between Disposition of Case and All Independent Variables for Crime Specific Homicides

Independent Variables	r Correlation
Race of offender	+.267**
Race of victim	−.140*
Occupation of offender	+.473***
Occupation of victim	−.260**
Education of offender	+.062
Education of victim	−.479[a]
Age of offender	−.300***
Age of victim	+.267**
Number of felony property convictions of offender	+.092
Number of felony property convictions of victim	−.260**
Number of felony property arrests of offender	+.037
Number of felony property arrests of victim	−.230**
Number of aggravated assault convictions of offender	+.202**
Number of aggravated assault convictions of victim	+.076
Number of aggravated assault arrests of offender	−.062
Number of aggravated assault arrests of victim	+.025

*p less than .05.
**p less than .01.
***p less than .001.
[a]This correlation is unreliable due to missing data.

ers have their cases dismissed to a greater extent than do younger offenders. Conversely, offenders who have allegedly murdered older victims have their cases prosecuted significantly more often than offenders who have younger victims.

Within crime specific homicide, three of the criminal record variables are significantly related to the disposition of the preliminary hearing. The fewer the number of felony property convictions a victim has, the greater the chance of prosecution. The fewer the number of felony property arrests, the greater the odds of prosecution. Finally, the greater the number of aggravated assault convictions of the offender, the harsher is the disposition.

For crime specific homicide, then, seven of a possible eight sociodemographic predictors are related to disposition. Three of a possible eight criminal record variables are related to disposition also. The finding that more "property" variables covary with disposition than do "assault" variables is explained by assuming that property offenses are as valid a measure of criminality as are assaultive offenses. The type of criminality, in this study, is not at issue. General conformity to the stereotype criminal is the crucial issue.

Especially with respect to the sociodemographic predictors, the above results support the notion that having certain social attributes (young, black, unemployed, and possibly undereducated) affects whether a case is dismissed or prosecuted at the preliminary hearing for crime specific homicides. Limited support, then, is found for Hypothesis 2—that the greater conformity to the stereotype criminal by the offender and the less conformity by the victim, the harsher the disposition.

Returning to Hypothesis 1, the explanatory power of the independent variables within crime specific homicide is related to disposition to a greater extent than within social conflict homicide. The explication of this finding may lie in the differences between the homicide participants in each type. Persons involved in social conflict homicides, which many times evolve from less violent interpersonal disputes, are often intimates, friends, or neighbors. These disputants are, in effect, sociologically similar (Wilt, 1974; Wolfgang, 1967; Block, 1977). Therefore, those persons who conform to stereotypic expectations about who a criminal should be, should tend to interact with more frequency and with greater intensity with similar types of persons. If we assume that disputants in crime specific homicides tend to be more different from one another than are the disputants in social conflict homicides, then the victim in a crime specific homicide will generally not conform to the stereotype of criminal. This argument may not hold true for all crime specific cases, but may for the majority in which robbery was the offender's original motive. In the sample under discussion, robbery constituted the original crime in 73 percent of the crime specific cases.[3]

An alternative, but not contradictory, explanation of why the attributes of the participants in social conflict homicide are not as powerful in predicting disposition as are the attributes of persons involved in crime specific homicide is victim precipitation. Victim precipitation is probably more common in social conflict than in crime specific homicide. If this is the case, self-defense pleas will mitigate against a case proceeding beyond the preliminary hearing. The result is that in order to meaningfully investigate the relationship between criminality and case disposition, the effects of victim precipitation must be controlled. This was not done for the present study and, therefore, social conflict homicide will be dropped from further analysis. For the modest purposes of this paper, Hypothesis 1 is confirmed and the argument that homicide is two distinct forms of violence is supported (Wilt, 1974).

Multiple Regression

The conclusion that the sociodemographic and criminal histories of homicide participants are related to disposition may be misleading.

The effects of any one independent variable on the dependent variable may be, in fact, spurious because other independent variables may have introduced confounding effects in the correlations. For this reason, multiple regression was performed, resulting in the control of any possible confounding effects. The strength of this method is that it allows the assessment of the relative impact of each independent variable working alone (controlling all others) and in combination with other predictor variables working on the dependent variable.

Two regressions are performed. The first includes the effects of race of offender and victim, occupational status of offender and victim, age of both, and the three significant criminal history variables— felony property convictions of the victim, felony property arrests of the victim, and aggravated assault convictions of the offender.

The second regression on the dependent variable is one in which scales have been constructed from two of the sociodemographic variables for both offender (Scale SESO) and victim (Scale SESV). The scores each offender and victim received on race and occupation have been reversed and combined in an additive fashion. Thus, a score of "0" for SESO means the offender is black and unemployed. A score of "2" means that the offender, or victim, is white and employed. A score of "1" signifies an unemployed white or an employed black. By using these scores, the offenders and victims are placed on their respective scales depending on the number of criminal attributes they possess. It is predicted that these offender and victim scales will account for more variance in the dependent variable than will either race or occupational status alone.

Table 3 presents the results of the first regression analysis: 42.6 per-

Table 3. Standardized Regression Coefficients (Beta) between Disposition of Case and Selected Independent Variables for Crime Specific Homicides

Independent Variables	Beta
Race of offender	+.125
Race of victim	−.045
Occupation of offender	+.410**
Occupation of victim	−.193**
Age of offender	−.142**
Age of victim	+.042
Number of felony property arrests of victim	−.131
Number of felony property convictions of victim	−.049
Number of aggravated assault convictions of offender	+.149**

**p less than .01.
R^2 = 42.6, F = 7.182 for all variables. p less than .01.
R^2 = 33.7, F = 23.946 for Occupation of offender and Occupation of victim together. p less than .01.

cent of the variance in case disposition is explained by the combined effects of race, occupation, age, and the three criminal record variables of both the offender and the victim. These results are substantial and imply that extralegal factors are determinants of whether a case is dismissed or prosecuted.

As noted earlier, multiple regression is also a means for the examination of the contribution of each of the independent variables while controlling the effects of all other independent variables. Since four different measuring units are employed for the variables (race as black or white; occupation as level of employment status; age as years; and criminal record as number of offenses), standardized regression coefficients (Betas) are analyzed.

The two occupation variables account for most of the variance. All other things being equal, the unemployed offenders have their cases prosecuted to a significantly greater degree than do the employed offenders. Conversely, when the victim is employed, offenders have their cases prosecuted to a greater degree than if the victims had been unemployed. Working in combination, the occupational status of the offender and the victim accounts for 79 percent of the total explained variance of 42.6 percent, or, $R^2 = 33.7$ percent for these two variables.

The third most influential independent variable is the age of the offender. The younger offender, then, runs a greater risk of further adjudication. There is no corresponding relationship between the age of the victim and the disposition. This can be accounted for by the fact that a victim's age is not related in a linear fashion to disposition. That is, violent crimes committed against the very young and the very old are probably reacted to as more heinous by the court than are violent crimes committed against able-bodied adults who can protect themselves to some degree. If this is true, the severity of disposition is harshest against those who have very young or very old victims. This is a curvilinear relationship—a relationship not picked up by the methodology employed in this study.

Looking next at race, the most interesting results, in light of the original correlation coefficients, are noted. The race of neither the offender nor the victim is related to disposition. The explanation for this may lie in the fact that race and occupation are highly correlated. That is, the race of both victims and offenders is confounded with occupational status. Blacks, on the whole, have less occupational status than whites. The effects of race in the Pearson correlations are spurious due to this confounding effect. With the occupation of victim and offender statistically controlled, race loses most of its power of explanation.

With respect to the effects of criminal record on disposition, the number of aggravated assault convictions is significantly related to dispositional decision. Thus, the greater the number of assault convictions, the harsher the decision, or the greater the chance that the case will be further prosecuted.

In sum, the first regression analysis supports the hypothesis that conformity to the stereotype criminal by the offender, or not by the victim, does lead to harsher dispositions for crime specific homicide. However, only one sociodemographic characteristic of the victim, occupational status, contributed to this finding. The effects of the offender's biography are, it seems, of prime importance in understanding why a case is prosecuted or dismissed.

A second multiple regression analysis was performed in which the race and occupation of offenders and victims were combined into scales SESO and SESV. The underlying assumption of this analysis is that race and occupation are so highly correlated that the creation of the new variables SESO and SESV will be a more powerful predictor than either race or occupation working individually. The combination of race and occupation does explain more variance, but it is negligible.[4] However, inspection of the new regression coefficients enables one to notice that both of the newly created variables are more strongly related to disposition than were their component parts in the first regression. The magnitude of SESO increased to Beta = −.476 from +.410 for occupation of offender and +.125 for race of offender. The magnitude of SESV increased to Beta = +.352 from −.193 for occupation of victim and −.045 for race of victim. Thus, the direct effects of the new variables on disposition are stronger than the direct effects of occupation and race in their original form. If employment status and race can be taken as a measure of class, these results are compatible with the predictions of Chambliss and Siedman (1971) and Turk (1969).

The results of this study may have implications for an integrated theory of law if viewed within the perspective that law, as a quantifiable variable, varies with its social environment (Black, 1976). Specifically, Black (1976) argues that law varies with vertical and horizontal stratification, culture, organization, and social control. Because the amount of law varies with each of these factors, the greater seriousness of a crime by a lower-status person against a higher-status person, compared with the opposite situation, is seen in terms of the behavior of law (Black, 1976: 31), rather than with regard to the motivation of the individual, as is the case in much labeling, deprivation and subcultural theory (compare Matza, 1964; Henry and Short, 1954; Miller, 1958).

The results that the attributes of both victim and offenders impact criminal homicide dispositions is compatible with this perspective.

But more important, seemingly unrelated deviant phenomena may be theoretically linked. For example, we could predict that the higher the social rank of a thief, the less the sanction. Further, we could also predict that the social distance (both horizontal and vertical) between the thief and the victim results in different amounts of law. Within this framework, meaningful analysis of white-collar crime could be made (see Cressey, 1953) as well as of mental illness (see Hollingshead and Redlich, 1958).

Returning to homicide, dispositional decisions for criminal homicide, then, are just one phenomenon of a class of phenomena understood in terms of the distance between the participants. A truly complete analysis of the data in this study would, then, not only look at the relationship between the homicide victim and offender but also would trace the same offender from arrest through sentencing, examining the same stratification and decision-making factors at each juncture in the process. That task is, however, beyond the scope of this paper.

CONCLUSIONS

The partial explanation of one decision in the criminal justice system about one form of criminal behavior in one city during one year has been explored in this paper. The results may be applicable to other crimes, times, or locales within a theory of the behavior of law. Yet, at a minimum, the results lend credence to the position that extralegal factors are important determinants of who is labeled as criminal. The occupation (or lack of it), age, and criminal record of the offender and the occupational status of the victim were found to influence post-arrest reactions to criminal homicide offenders. The results that the social attributes of the offender, while controlling for crime and criminal record, influence the legal outcomes of these cases supports the work of Swigert and Farrell (1976). The result that one of these social attributes of the victim also influences legal outcomes expands Swigert and Farrell's work. Further, these results complement the theory that law varies with its social environment (Black, 1976). Within this view, a process analysis of legal decision making is called for.

Notes

1. Sociodemographic data are missing from more cases than are dispositional data. The missing data do not, however, significantly alter the distribution of cases.

2. $X^2 = 9.248$, p $< .01$.

3. See Block (1977) for a discussion of criminal homicide as an outcome of robbery.

4. The amount of explained variance increased from $R^2 = 33.7$ for race and occupation in the first regression to $R^2 = 34.8$ in the second regression.

References

AVISON, N. H. (1974) "Victims of homicide." Int. J. of Criminology and Penology 2: 225–237.

BARBER, R. (1974) "Judge and jury attitudes toward rape." Australian and New Zealand J. of Criminology 7: 157–172.

BERNSTEIN, I. N., W. R. KELLY, and P. A. DOYLE (1977) "Societal reaction to deviants: The case of criminal defendants." Amer. Soc. Rev. 42: 743–755.

BITTNER, E. (1967) "The police on skid-row: A study of peace keeping." Amer. Soc. Rev. 32: 699–715.

BLACK, D. (1976) The Behavior of Law. New York: Academic Press.

BLOCK, R. (1977) Violent Crime, Environment, Interaction and Death. Lexington, MA: D. C. Heath.

BULLOCK, H. (1961) "Significance of the racial factor in length of sentencing." J. of Criminal Law, Criminology and Police Sci. 52: 411–417.

BURKE, P. J. and A. T. TURK (1975) "Factors affecting post-arrest dispositions: A model for analysis." Social Problems 22: 313–332.

CHAMBLISS, W. J. and R. B. SIEDMAN (1971) Law, Order and Power. Reading, MA: Addison-Wesley.

CHIRICOS, T. G. and G. P. WALDO (1975) "Socioeconomic status and criminal sentencing: An empirical assessment of a conflict proposition." Amer. Soc. Rev. 40: 753–772.

CRESSEY, D. R. (1953) Other People's Money: A Study in the Social Psychology of Embezzlement. New York: Macmillan.

GOFFMAN, E. (1963) Stigma. Englewood Cliffs, NJ: Prentice-Hall.

GREEN, E. (1964) "Inter- and intra-racial crime relative to sentencing." J. of Criminal Law, Criminology and Police Sci. 55: 348–358.

HAGAN, J. (1974) "Extra-legal attributes and criminal sentencing: An assessment of a sociological viewpoint." Law and Society Rev. 8:357–383.

HENRY, A. F. and J. F. SHORT (1954) Suicide and Homicide: Some Economic, Sociological and Psychological Aspects of Aggression. New York: Macmillan.

HENTIG, H. von (1948) The Criminal and His Victim: Studies in the Sociobiology of Crime. New Haven, CT: Yale Univ. Press.

HOLLINGSHEAD, A. B. and F. C. REDLICH (1958) Social Class and Mental Illness: A Community Study. New York: John Wiley.

KERLINGER, F. N. and E. J. PEDHAZUR (1973) Multiple Regression in Behavioral Research. New York: Holt, Rinehart and Winston.

MATZA, D. (1964) Delinquency and Drift. New York: John Wiley.

MILLER, W. B. (1958) "Lower-class culture as a generating milieu of gang delinquency." J. of Social Issues 14(3): 5–13.

MEAD, G. H. (1934) Mind, Self and Society. Chicago: Univ. of Chicago Press.

NAGEL, S. (1969) The Legal Process from a Behavioral Perspective. Homewood, IL: Dorsey.

NIE, H. N., C. H. HULL, J. G. JENKINS, K. STEINBRENNER, and D. H. BENT (1975) Statistical Package for the Social Sciences. New York: McGraw-Hill.

PILIVAN, I. and S. BRIAR (1964) "Police encounters with juveniles." Amer. J. of Sociology 70: 206–214.

ROSETT, A. and D. R. CRESSEY (1976) Justice by Consent. Philadelphia: Lippincott.

SCHAFFER, S. (1968) The Victim and His Criminal. New York: Random House.

SCHEFF, T. (1966) Being Mentally Ill: A Sociological Theory. Chicago: Aldine.

SUDNOW, D. (1965) "Normal crimes: Sociological features of the penal code in a public defender office." Social Problems 12: 255–276.

SWIGERT, V. L. and R. A. FARRELL (1976) Murder, Inequality and the Law. Lexington, MA: D. C. Heath.

THOMAS, C. W. and R. J. CAGE (1977) "The effects of social characteristics on juvenile court dispositions." Soc. Q. 18: 237–252.

TURK, A. T. (1969) Criminality and Legal Order. Chicago: Rand McNally.

WILT, G. M. (1974) Towards an Understanding of the Social Realities of Participants in Homicides. Ann Arbor, MI: University Microfilms.

WOLFGANG, M. E. (1967) Patterns in Criminal Homicide. New York: John Wiley.

35. The Rich Get Richer and the Poor Get Prison: Convictions and Sentencing

JEFFREY H. REIMAN

CONVICTIONS

Between arrest and imprisonment lies the crucial process that determines guilt or innocence. Studies of individuals accused of similar offenses and with similar prior records show that the poor defendant is more likely to be adjudicated guilty than is the wealthier defendant.[1] In the adjudication process the only thing that *should* count is whether the accused is guilty and whether the prosecution can prove it beyond a reasonable doubt. Unfortunately, at least two other factors that are irrelevant to the question of guilt or innocence significantly affect the outcome: one is the ability of the accused to be free on bail prior to trial, and the second is access to legal counsel able to devote adequate time and energy to the case. Since both bail and high-quality legal counsel cost money, it should come as no surprise that there as elsewhere the poor do poorly. "A defendant in a criminal court," writes Abraham Blumberg, "is really beaten by the deprivations and limitations imposed by his social class, race, and ethnicity. These in turn preclude such services as bail, legal counsel, psychiatric services, expert witnesses, and investigatory assistance. In essence the concomitants of poverty are responsible for the fact that due process sometimes produces greatly disparate results in an ill-matched struggle."[2]

Being released on bail is important in several respects. First and foremost, of course, is the fact that those who are not released on bail are kept in jail like individuals who have been found guilty. They are thus punished while they are still legally innocent. In 1972, 51,000 (out of a total of 142,000) inmates of local jails were confined while awaiting trial. Their average pretrial or presentence confinement was three months, and 60 percent of the nation's jails do not separate pretrial defendants from convicted offenders. Beyond the obvious ugliness of punishing people before they are found guilty, confined

453

defendants suffer from other disabilities. Specifically, they cannot actively aid in their own defense by seeking out witnesses and evidence. Several studies have shown that among defendants accused of the same offenses, those who make bail are more likely to be acquitted than those who do not.[3]

Furthermore, since the time spent in jail prior to adjudication of guilt may count as part of the sentence if one is found guilty, the accused are often placed in a ticklish position. Let us say the accused believes that he or she is innocent or at least that the state cannot prove guilt, and let us say also that he or she has been in the slammer for two months awaiting trial. Along comes the prosecutor to offer a deal: If you plead guilty to such-and-such (usually a lesser offense than has been charged, e.g., possession of burglar's tools instead of burglary), the prosecutor promises to ask the judge to sentence you to two months. In other words, plead guilty and walk out of jail today— or maintain your innocence, stay in jail until trial, and then be tried for the full charge instead of the lesser offense! Plea bargaining is an everyday occurrence in the criminal justice system. Contrary to the Perry Mason image, the vast majority of criminal convictions in the United States are reached without a trial. It is estimated that between 70 and 95 percent of convictions are the result of a negotiated plea,[4] that is, a bargain in which the accused agrees to plead guilty (usually to a lesser offense than he or she is charged with or to one offense out of many he or she is charged with) in return for an informal promise of leniency from the prosecutor with the tacit consent of the judge. If you were the jailed defendant offered a deal like this, how would you choose? Suppose you were a poor black man not likely to be able to retain F. Lee Bailey or Edward Bennett Williams for your defense?

The advantages of access to adequate legal counsel during the adjudicative process are obvious but still worthy of mention. In 1963, the U.S. Supreme Court handed down the landmark *Gideon* v. *Wainwright* decision, holding that the states must provide legal counsel to the indigent in all felony cases. As a result, no person accused of a serious crime need face their accusers without a lawyer. However, the Supreme Court has not held that the Constitution requires that individuals are entitled to lawyers able to devote equal time and resources to their cases. Even though *Gideon* represents significant progress in making good on the Constitutional promise of equal treatment before the law, we still are left with two transmission belts of justice: one for the poor and one for the affluent. There is, to be sure, an emerging body of case law on the right to effective assistance of counsel;[5] however, this is yet to have any serious impact on the assembly-line legal aid handed out to the poor.

Indigent defendants, those who cannot afford to retain their own lawyers, will be defended either by a public defender or by a private attorney assigned by the court. Since the public defender is a salaried attorney with a case load much larger than that of a private criminal lawyer,[6] and since court-assigned private attorneys are paid a fixed fee that is much lower than they charge their regular clients, neither is able or motivated to devote much time to the indigent defendant's defense. Both are strongly motivated to bring their cases to a close quickly by negotiating a plea of guilty. Since the public defender works in day-to-day contact with the prosecutor and the judge, the pressures on him or her to negotiate a plea as quickly as possible, instead of rocking the boat by threatening to go to trial,[7] are even greater than those that work on court-assigned counsel. In an essay, aptly entitled "Did You Have a Lawyer When You Went to Court? No, I Had a Public Defender," Jonathan Casper reports the perceptions of this process from the standpoint of the defendants:

> Most of the men spent very little time with their public defender. In the court in which they eventually plead guilty, they typically reported spending on the order of five to ten minutes with their public defender. These conversations usually took place in the bull-pen of the courthouse or in the hallway.
>
> The brief conversations usually did not involve much discussion of the details surrounding the alleged crime, mitigating circumstances, or the defendants' motives or background. Instead, they focused on the deal, the offer the prosecution was likely to make or had made in return for a cop out. Often the defendants reported that the first words the public defender spoke (or at least the first words the defendants recalled) were, "I can get you . . . , if you plead guilty."[8]

Abraham S. Blumberg studied 724 male felony defendants who pleaded guilty in a large metropolitan court. He found that in the majority of cases it was the defense counsel who first suggested a guilty plea and who most influenced the defendant's decision to plead guilty. More striking still, however, was the finding that public defenders and court-assigned lawyers suggested the plea of guilty *earlier* than privately retained attorneys. On this, Blumberg comments, "Legal-aid and assigned counsel are apparently more likely to suggest the plea in the initial interview, perhaps as a response to pressures of time and, in the case of the assigned counsel, the strong possibility that there is no fee involved."[9] Privately retained counsel suggested the plea in the initial meeting in 35 percent of their cases, public defenders in 49 percent, and assigned counsel in 60 percent.[10] It should be noted that Blumberg concludes that these differences have little impact on the eventual outcome. Other findings point to a different conclusion.

As might be expected, with less time and resources to devote to the case, public defenders and assigned lawyers cannot devote as much time and research to preparing the crucial pretrial motions that can often lead to dismissal of charges against the accused. One study shows that public defenders got dismissals in 8 percent of their cases, assigned lawyers in 6 percent, and privately retained counsel in *29 percent of their cases.*[11] And, as also might be expected, the overall acquittal rate for privately retained counsel is considerably better than that for public defenders and assigned counsel. The same study shows that public defenders achieved either dismissal of charges or a finding of not guilty in 17 percent of the indictments they handled, assigned counsel did the same in 18 percent, and privately retained counsel got their clients off the hook in *36 percent of their indictments.* The picture that emerges from the federal courts is not much different.[12]

Needless to say, the distinct legal advantages that money can buy become even more salient when we enter the realm of corporate and other white-collar crime. Indeed, it is often precisely the time and cost involved in bringing to court a large corporation with its army of legal eagles that is offered as an excuse for the less formal and more genteel treatment accorded to corporate crooks. This excuse is, of course, not equitably distributed to all economic classes, any more than quality legal service is. What this means in simple terms is that regardless of actual innocence or guilt, one's chances of beating the rap increase as one's income increases. Regardless of what fraction of crimes are committed by the poor, the criminal justice system is distorted so that an even greater fraction of those convicted will be poor. And with conviction comes sentencing.

SENTENCING

He had a businessman's suit and a businessman's tan, but Jack L. Clark no longer had a business. His nursing home construction company had collapsed in a gigantic stock fraud, leaving shareholders out $200 million and leaving Clark in a federal courthouse, awaiting sentence for stock manipulation. Ten million of the swindled dollars had allegedly gone for Clark's personal use, and prosecutors accused him of stashing away 4 million unrecovered dollars in a retirement nest egg. Out of an original indictment of sixty-five counts, Clark had pleaded guilty to one charge. He faced a maximum penalty of a $10,000 fine and five years in prison. But the judge, before passing sentence, remembered the "marked improvement" in care for the elderly that Clark's nursing homes had provided. . . . He considered that Clark was a forty-six-year-old family man who coached little kids in baseball and football. Then he passed sentence. No fine. One year in prison. Eligible for parole after four months.

In another federal courtroom stood Matthew Corelli (not his real name), a forty-five-year-old, $125-a-week laborer who lived with his wife and kids in a $126-a-month apartment. Along with three other men, Corelli had been convicted of possessing $5,000 of stolen drugstore goods that government prosecutors identified as part of a $63,000 shipment. The judge considered Corelli's impoverished circumstances, his number of dependents, the nature of his crime, and then passed sentence: four years in prison. Or in other words, four times the punishment Clark received for a fraction of the crime.[13]

Jack Greenberg took $15 from a post office; last May in Federal Court in Manhattan he drew six months of jail. Howard Lazell "misapplied" $150,000 from a bank; in the same month in the same courthouse he drew probation.[14]

The first quotation is the opening passage of a magazine article on white-collar crime, aptly titled "America's Most Coddled Criminals." The second quotation is the opening paragraph of a *New York Times* article, more prosaically titled "Wide Disparities Mark Sentences Here." Both, however, are testimony to the fact that the criminal justice system reserves it harshest penalties for its lower-class clients and puts on kid gloves when confronted with a better class of crook.

The system is doubly biased against the poor. First, there is the class bias *between* crimes that we have just seen. The crimes that poor people are likely to commit carry harsher sentences than the "crimes in the suites" committed by well-to-do people. Second, for *all* crimes, the poor receive less probation and more years of confinement than better-heeled defendants *convicted of the same offense,* assuring us once again that the vast majority of those who are put behind bars are from the lowest social and economic classes in the nation.

The *New York Times* article referred to above reported the results of a study done by the *New York Times* on sentencing in state and federal courts. The *Times* reports that "crimes that tend to be committed by the poor get tougher sentences than those committed by the well-to-do," that federal "defendants who could not afford private counsel were sentenced nearly twice as severely as defendants with private or no counsel," and that a "study by the Vera Institute of Justice of courts in the Bronx indicates a similar pattern in the state courts."[15]

Looking at federal and state courts, Stuart Nagel concludes that

not only are the indigent found guilty more often, but they are much less likely to be recommended for probation by the probation officer, or to be granted probation or suspended sentences by the judge.

And, further, that

the federal data show that this is true also of those with *no* prior record: 27 percent of the indigent with no prior record were *not* recommended for probation against 16 percent of the non-indigent; 23 percent indigent did *not* receive suspended sentences or probation against 15 percent non-indigent. Among those of both groups with "some" prior record the spread is even greater.[16]

Eugene Doleschal and Nora Klapmuts report as "typical of American studies," Thornberry's analysis of "3,475 Philadelphia delinquents that found that blacks and members of lower socioeconomic groups were likely to receive more severe dispositions than whites and the more affluent even when the appropriate legal variables [i.e., offense, prior record, etc.] were held constant."[17]

As usual, data on racial discrimination in sentencing exist in much greater abundance than data on class discrimination, but they tell the same story of the treatment of those who cannot afford the going price of justice. Most striking perhaps is the fact that over 40 percent of the inmates of all correctional facilities in the United States—state and federal prisons as well as local jails—are black, while blacks account for a little over one-quarter of all arrests in the nation. Even when we compare the percentage of blacks arrested for serious (i.e., FBI Index) crimes with the percentage of blacks in federal and state prisons (where presumably those convicted of such offenses would be sent), blacks still make up over 40 percent of the inmates but only about 36 percent of the arrestees, which is still a considerable disparity. Furthermore, when we look at federal prisons, where there is reason to believe racial and economic discrimination is less prevalent than in state institutions, we find that the average sentence for a white inmate in 1972 was 45.4 months, as compared to 59.1 months (over a year more!) for nonwhite inmates. The nonwhite inmate serves, on the average, 3 more months than a white inmate for burglary, 21 more months for a drug law violation, and more than twice as long for income tax evasion![18]

Studies have confirmed that black burglars received longer sentences than do white burglars. And blacks who plead guilty receive harsher sentences than whites who do, although by an act of dubious mercy of which Americans ought hardly be proud, blacks often receive lighter sentences for murder and rape than whites as long as the victim was black as well.[19] Mary Owen Cameron studied the sentencing practices of judges in the Chicago Women's Court during a three-year period. Her findings were as follows:

> Judges found 16 percent of the white women brought before them on charges of shoplifting to be "not guilty," but only 4 percent of the black women were found innocent. In addition, 22 percent of the black women as compared to 4 percent of the white women were sent to jail. Finally, of the twenty-one white women sentenced to jail, only two (10 percent) were to be jailed for thirty days or more; of the seventy-six black women sen-

tenced to jail, twenty (26 percent) were to be jailed for thirty days or more.[20]

Many studies have shown that blacks convicted of murder or of rape—where rape is a capital offense—are much more likely to be sentenced to death than are whites, except where the victim is black.[21] Another study has shown that among blacks and whites on death row, whites are more likely to have their sentences commuted. And blacks or whites who have private counsel are more likely to have their execution commuted than condemned persons defended by court-appointed attorneys.[22]

As I have already pointed out, justice is increasingly tempered with mercy as we deal with a better class of crime. The Sherman Antitrust Act is a criminal law. It was passed in recognition of the fact that one virtue of a free enterprise economy is that competition tends to drive consumer prices down, so agreements by competing firms to refrain from price competition is the equivalent of stealing money from the consumer's pocket. Nevertheless, although such conspiracies cost consumers far more than lower-class theft, price-fixing was a misdemeanor until 1974.[23] In practice, few conspirators end up in prison, and when they do, the sentence is a mere token, well below the maximum provided in the law. Thus, based on the government's track record, there is little reason to expect things to change significantly now that price-fixing is a felony.

In the historic *Electrical Equipment* cases in the early 1960s, executives of several major firms secretly met to fix prices on electrical equipment to a degree that is estimated to have cost the buying public well over a billion dollars. The executives involved knew they were violating the law. They used plain envelopes for their communications, called their meetings "choir practice," and referred to the list of executives in attendance as the "Christmas card list." This case is rare and famous because it was one in which the criminal sanction was actually imposed. Seven executives received and served jail sentences. But in light of the amount of money they had stolen from the American public, their sentences were more an indictment of the government than of themselves: *thirty days in jail!*

The President's Crime Commission reports "that since that case no antitrust defendant has been imprisoned. In seven cases since then, involving forty-five individual defendants, prison sentences were imposed, but in each case the sentence was suspended." In any event, the commission reports that "the Antitrust Division does not feel that lengthy prison sentences are ordinarily called for. It 'rarely recommends jail sentences greater than six months—recommendations of thirty-day imprisonment are most frequent.' "[24]

Table 1.   Sentences for Different Classes of Crime

	Average Sentence (in months)	Average Time until Parole (in months)
Crimes of the poor		
Robbery	133.3	51.2
Burglary	58.7	30.2
Larceny/theft	32.8	18.7
Crimes of the affluent		
Embezzlement	21.1	13.2
Fraud	27.2	14.3
Income tax evasion	12.8	9.7

Source. Federal Bureau of Prisons—Statistical Report, Fiscal Year 1973.

In general the crimes of the poor receive stiffer sentences than the crimes of the well-to-do. For instance, Marvin Frankel points out, in his book *Criminal Sentences: Law without Order*, that "of 502 defendants convicted for income tax fraud 95, or 19 percent, received prison terms, the average being three months. Of 3,791 defendants sentenced for auto theft, 2,373, or 63 percent, went to prison, the average term being 7.6 months."[25] More recent figures fit this pattern. A statistical report of the Federal Bureau of Prisons yields information about the average sentences received by inmates of federal institutions and the average time served until parole (see Table 1). Keep in mind while looking at these figures that *each* of the "crimes of the affluent" costs the public more than *all* of the "crimes of the poor" put together.

A study of sentencing practices in the Southern District of New York, optimistically entitled *Justice in Sentencing*, found

> plain indications that white-collar defendants, predominantly white, receive more lenient treatment as a general rule, while defendants charged with common crimes, largely committed by the unemployed and undereducated, a group which embraces large numbers of blacks in today's society, are more likely to be sent to prison. If these indications are correct, then one may conclude that poor persons receive harsher treatment in the federal courts than do well-to-do defendants charged with more sophisticated crimes.

Specifically, the study reports that "during the six-month period covered by the Southern District of New York sentencing study, *defendants convicted of white-collar crimes stood a 36 percent chance of*

This isn't the Chamber of Commerce list of brightest young businessmen, and it's not the ten best-dressed list. It's a list of ten very respectable criminals. . . .

Criminal	Crime	Sentence
Jack L. Clark	President and chairman of Four Seasons Nursing Centers, Clark finagled financial reports and earnings projections to inflate his stock artificially. Shareholders lost $200 million.	One year in prison.
John Peter Galanis	As portfolio manager of two mutual funds, Galanis bilked investors out of nearly $10 million.	Six months in prison and five years probation.
Virgil A. McGowen	As manager of the Bank of America branch in San Francisco, McGowen siphoned off $591,921 in clandestine loans to friends. Almost none of the money was recovered.	Six months in prison, five years probation and a $3,600 fine.
Valdemar H. Madis	A wealthy drug manufacturer, Madis diluted an antidote for poisoned children with a worthless, look-alike substance.	One year probation and a $10,000 fine.
John Morgan	President of Jet Craft Ltd, John Morgan illegally sold about $2 million in unregistered securities.	One year in prison and a $10,000 fine.
Irving Projansky	The former chairman of the First National Bank of Lincolnwood, Ill., Projansky raised stock prices artificially and then dumped the shares, costing the public an estimated $4 million.	One year in prison and two years probation.
David Ratliff	Ratliff spent his 21 years as a Texas state senator embezzling state funds.	Ten years probation.
Walter J. Rauscher	An executive vice-president of American Airlines, Rauscher accepted about $200,000 in kickbacks from businessmen bidding for contracts.	Six months in prison and two years probation.
Frank W. Sharp	The multimillion-dollar swindles of Sharp, a Houston banker, shook the Texas state government and forced the resignation of the head of the Criminal Division of the Justice Dept.	Three years probation and a $5,000 fine.
Seymour R. Thaler	Soon after election to the N.Y. State Supreme Court, Thaler was convicted of receiving and transporting $800,000 in stolen U.S. Treasury bills.	One year in prison and a fine of $10,000.

Source. Blake Fleetwood and Arthur Lubow, "America's Most Coddled Criminals," *New Times Magazine*, September 19, 1975.

going to prison; defendants convicted of nonviolent common crimes stood a 53 percent chance of going to prison; and defendants convicted of violent crimes stood an 80 percent chance of going to prison."[26] Several things are worthy of note here. First, the study carries forth the distorted conventional wisdom about crime by distinguishing between "white-collar" and "common" crime, when, as we have found, there is every reason to believe that white-collar crime is just as common as the so-called common crimes of the poor. Second, the disparities reported refer only to likelihood of imprisonment *for any length of time,* and so they really understate the disparities in treatment, since the so-called common crimes also receive *longer* prison sentences than the white-collar crimes. But third, and most importantly, the disparities cannot be explained by the greater danger of lower-class criminals because even the perpetrators of *nonviolent common crimes* stand a 50 percent greater chance of going to prison than do white-collar crooks.

A graphic illustration of the way the criminal justice system treats the wealthy is provided by Fleetwood and Lubow in their article "America's Most Coddled Criminals." They put together their pick of ten convicted white-collar criminals, comparing their sentences with the crimes they committed. The chart speaks for itself (see Table 2).

Equally eloquent testimony to the merciful face that the criminal justice system turns toward upper-class crooks is to be found in a *New York Times* report on the fate of twenty-one business executives found guilty of making illegal campaign contributions during the Watergate scandal:

> Most of the twenty-one business executives who admitted their guilt to the Watergate Special Prosecutor in 1973 and 1974—especially those from large corporations—are still presiding over their companies. . . .
> Only two went to jail. They served a few months and were freed. . . .
> Furthermore, the fines of $1,000 or $2,000 that most of the contributors of illegal funds had to pay have not made much of a dent in their style of living. . . .
> An investigation into the whereabouts and financial status of the twenty-one executives involved in illegal contributions leads to a conclusion that the higher the position the more cushioned the fall—if indeed there was a fall.[27]

Notes

1. See, for example, Theodore G. Chiricos, Phillip D. Jackson, and Gordon P. Waldo, "Inequality in the Imposition of a Criminal Label," *Social Problems,* 19, No. 4 (Spring, 1972), pp. 553–572.

2. Abraham S. Blumberg, *Criminal Justice* (Chicago: Quadrangle, 1967), p. 33. Even for a middle-class defendant, the state with its greater financial,

investigatory, and legal personnel resources holds the advantage over the accused—so the poor person is doubly disadvantaged. Cf. Abraham S. Goldstein, "The State and the Accused: Balance of Advantage in Criminal Procedure," in *Crime, Law and Society*, eds., Abraham Goldstein and Joseph Goldstein, New York: Free Press, 1971, pp. 173–206.

3. See, for example, C. E. Ares, A. Rankin, and J. H. Sturz, "The Manhattan Bail Project: An Interim Report on the Use of Pre-Trial Parole," *NYU Law Review*, 38 (1963), p. 67; C. Foote, "Compelling Appearances in Court-Administration of Bail in Philadelphia," *University of Pennsylvania Law Review*, 102 (1954), pp. 1031–79; and C. Foote, "A Study of the Administration of Bail in New York City," *University of Pennsylvania Law Review*, 106 (1958), p. 693. For statistics on persons held in jail awaiting trial, see *Black Population in the U.S.*, p. 171; and U.S.L.E.A.A., *Survey of Inmates of Local Jails 1972—Advance Report* (Washington, D.C.: U.S. Government Printing Office, 1974), pp. 5 and 8.

4. Blumberg, *Criminal Justice*, pp. 28–29; *The Challenge of Crime in a Free Society* (Washington: U.S. Government Printing Office, 1967), p. 134; and Donald J. Newman, *Conviction: The Determination of Guilt or Innocence Without Trial* (Boston: Little, Brown, 1966), p. 3.

5. A good summary of these developments can be found in Joel Jay Finer, "Ineffective Assistance of Counsel," *Cornell Law Review*, 58, No. 6 (July, 1973), pp. 1077–1120.

6. See, for example, Dallin H. Oaks and Warren Lehman, "Lawyers for the Poor," in *Law and Order: The Scales of Justice*, ed., A. Blumberg (Chicago: Aldine, 1970), pp. 92–93; also Jerome H. Skolnick, "Social Control in the Adversary System," in *Criminal Justice: Law and Politics*, ed., Cole (Belmont, California: Duxbury, 1972), p. 266. "The National Legal Aid and Defender Association has suggested that experienced attorneys handle no more than 150 felony cases per year, rather than . . . the case load of over 500 felony cases per attorney with which some public defender offices in major cities are burdened." Finer, "Ineffective Assistance of Counsel." (p. 1120)

7. In several essays, Abraham S. Blumberg has described the role of the public defender as an officer of the court bureaucracy rather than as a defender of the accused. See his "Lawyers with Convictions," in *Law and Order: The Scales of Justice*, pp. 51–67; "The Practice of Law as Confidence Game: Organizational Cooptation of a Profession," in *Criminal Law in Action*, ed., William J. Chambliss (Santa Barbara, California: Hamilton Publishing Co., 1975), pp. 262–275; and his book *Criminal Justice* (Chicago: Quadrangle, 1967), esp. pp. 13–115.

8. Jonathan D. Casper, "Did You Have a Lawyer When You Went to Court? No, I Had a Public Defender," in *Criminal Justice: Law and Politics*, ed., Cole, pp. 239–240.

9. Blumberg, "Lawyers with Convictions," pp. 62–65; and his *Criminal Justice*, pp. 92–93.

10. Ibid.; percentages are rounded to nearest whole number.

11. Oaks and Lehman, "Lawyers for the Poor," p. 95.

12. Of those defendants who were *convicted* in U.S. District Courts in 1971, 46 percent had assigned lawyers (including public defenders); of those *acquitted*, 37.5 percent had assigned counsel; and of those *dismissed*, only 33.3 percent had assigned counsel. *Sourcebook of Criminal Statistics—1974* (Washington: U.S. Government Printing Office, 1975), p. 388.

13. Blake Fleetwood and Arthur Lubow, "America's Most Coddled Crimi-

nals," *New Times* (September 19, 1975), pp. 26–29. *New Times Magazine,* copyright © 1975. Reprinted by permission of *New Times Magazine.*

14. Lesley Oelsner, "Wide Disparities Mark Sentences Here," *New York Times,* September 27, 1972, p. 1. Stuart Nagel writes, "The reasons for the economic class sentencing disparities, holding crime and prior record constant, are due possibly to the quality of legal representation that the indigent receive and probably to the appearance that an indigent defendant presents before a middle-class judge or probation officer." "Disparities in Sentencing Procedure," *UCLA Law Review,* 14 (August, 1967), p. 1283.

15. Oelsner, p. 1.

16. Stuart Nagel, "The Tipped Scales of American Justice," in *Law and Order: The Scales of Justice,* ed., A. Blumberg (Chicago: Aldine, 1970), p. 39.

17. Eugene Doleschal and Nora Klapmuts, "Toward a New Criminology," *Crime and Delinquency Literature,* 5 (December, 1973), p. 613; reporting the findings of Terence Patrick Thornberry, *Punishment and Crime: The Effect of Legal Dispositions on Subsequent Criminal Behavior* (Ann Arbor, Michigan: University Microfilms, 1972).

18. *Sourcebook,* pp. 333, 463, 443.

19. Henry Allen Bullock, "Significance of the Racial Factor in the Length of Prison Sentences," in *Crime and Justice in Society,* ed., R. Quinney (Boston: Little, Brown, 1969), p. 425.

20. William J. Chambliss and Robert B. Seidman, "Sentencing and Sentences," in *Criminal Law in Action,* ed., Chambliss, p. 339; reporting the findings of Mary Owen Cameron, *The Booster and the Snitch: Department Store Shoplifting* (New York: Free Press, 1964).

21. Marvin E. Wolfgang and Marc Riedel, "Race, Judicial Discretion and the Death Penalty," in *Criminal Law in Action,* ed., Chambliss, p. 375.

22. Marvin E. Wolfgang, Arlene Kelly, and Hans C. Nolde, "Comparison of the Executed and the Commuted among Admissions to Death Row," in *Crime and Justice in Society,* ed., Quinney, pp. 508, 513.

23. "Antitrust: Kauper's Last Stand," *Newsweek,* June 21, 1976, p. 70. On December 21, 1974, the "Antitrust Procedures and Penalty Act" was passed, striking out the language of the Sherman Antitrust Act, which made price-fixing a misdemeanor punishable by a maximum sentence of one year in prison. According to the new law, price-fixing is a felony punishable by up to three years in prison. Since prison sentences were a rarity under the old law and usually involved only 30 days in jail when actually imposed, there is little reason to believe that the new law will strike fear in the hearts of corporate crooks.

24. *Task Force Report: Crime and Its Impact,* pp. 105, 106.

25. Marvin E. Frankel, *Criminal Sentences: Law without Order* (New York: Hill and Wang, 1972), p. 24, footnote.

26. *Justice in Sentencing: Papers and Proceedings of the Sentencing Institute for the First and Second U.S. Judicial Circuits,* eds., Leonard Orland and Harold R. Tyler, Jr. (Mineola, New York: Foundation Press, 1974), pp. 159–160. (Emphasis added.)

27. Michael C. Jensen, "Watergate Donors Still Riding High," *The New York Times,* August 24, 1975, sec. 3, pp. 1, 7. Copyright © 1975 by The New York Times Company. Reprinted by permission.

36. The Moral Career of an Accused Person

ABRAHAM S. BLUMBERG

We have described the journey of an accused person through the sifting process of the court system as a "career." Sociologists use the term not necessarily to describe conventional notions of occupational careers but to delineate the social-psychological steps in transition from one status to another.[1] Erving Goffman speaks of "the moral aspects of career—that is, the regular sequence of changes that career entails in the person's self and in his framework of imagery for judging himself and others."[2] Goffman elaborates:

> The moral career of a person of a given social category involves a standard sequence of changes in his way of conceiving of selves, including, importantly, his own[self]. . . . Each moral career, and behind this, each self, occurs within the confines of an institutional system, whether a social establishment such as a mental hospital or a complex of personal and professional relationships. The self, then, can be seen as something that resides in the arrangements prevailing in a social system for its members. The self in this sense is not a property of the person to whom it is attributed, but dwells rather in the pattern of social control that is exerted in connection with the person by himself and those around him. This special kind of institutional arrangement does not so much support the self as constitute it.[3]

One can apply Goffman's analysis to the case of the accused person who moves from civilian to criminal, or is convicted. We begin with a complainant, who may be a private individual, a policeman, the district attorney, or an administrative agency. If the gravamen of his complaint is sustained in a lower criminal court of first instance, the individual complained of has become an accused person. Henceforth the accused will be dealt with and processed by a variety of mediators and agencies who will relay him along. But already he has marked the first milestone in his career—he has become an accused person.

He may now face an assistant district attorney who will point to the multiple counts of an indictment and ask whether the accused would rather go to trial than plead to some proposed lesser offense. Even the most obtuse accused will understand the full import of this.

To police administrations, a plea of guilty is a welcome addition to the statistical evidence of their effectiveness, for they correlate a favorable public image and a high conviction rate. Equally important is the fact that valuable police time that would be spent in trial testimony is freed for other activities.

Most police work at every level—federal, state, and local—is conducted on the basis of information furnished by informers and paid agents. Because of the nature of this mode of operation, which encroaches on dearly held ethical values, police work and negotiation with other agencies is best carried on in relative secrecy. Thus the kind of informal negotiations which are conducted by police, district attorney, defense counsel, and judge in connection with a negotiated plea are best performed in virtual secrecy. In bargaining with an accused, the police use the possibility of a negotiated plea as leverage, usually to get further information. Of course, at times they are completely out of bounds in their zeal, making offers of immunity or threats of punishment wholly beyond their authority or function.

The vested interest of the district attorney and the police, and their role as agents, is readily perceived and understood by an accused person. He will have sensed certain negative attitudes toward police and will have internalized them long before he has ever been arrested. The agent-mediator roles of judges, lawyers, probation officers, psychiatrists, and members of his own family are not so easily understood. The accused could reasonably define them as allies.

But some of the same reasons which serve as the basis for the district attorney's actions apply also to the judge. According to the ideology of the law, the judge is required to be not only impartial but active in seeking out and preserving the rights of all offenders. Nevertheless, he also has a vested interest in a high rate of negotiated pleas. He shares the prosecutor's earnest desire to avoid the time-consuming, expensive, unpredictable snares and pitfalls of an adversary trial. He sees an impossible backlog of cases, with their mounting delays, as possible public evidence of his "inefficiency" and failure. The defendant's plea of guilty enables the judge to engage in a social-psychological fantasy—the accused becomes an already repentant individual who has "learned his lesson" and deserves lenient treatment. Indeed, as previously indicated, many judges give a less severe sentence to a defendant who has negotiated a plea than to one who has been convicted of the same offense after a trial.[4]

The lawyer, whether a public defender or a privately retained defense counsel, is subject to pressures peculiar to his role and organizational obligations. But ultimately he is also concerned with strategies leading to a plea. Again, impersonal elements prevail—the economics of time, labor, expense, and the commitment of the defense counsel to the rationalistic values of the court organization; the accused who expects a personal, affective relationship with his lawyer is likely to be disappointed. The lawyer regulars of Metropolitan Court are frequently former staff members of the prosecutor's office. They utilize the charisma, "know-how," and contacts of their former affiliation as part of their stock in trade. An accused and his kin, as well as others outside the court community, are unable to comprehend the nature and dimensions of the close relations between the lawyer "regular" and his former colleagues in the prosecutor's office. Their continuing colleagueship is based on real professional and organizational needs of a quid pro quo, which goes beyond the limits of an accommodation one might ordinarily expect in a seemingly adversary relationship. Indeed, adversary features are for the most part muted and exist in their attenuated form largely for external consumption. The principals—lawyer and assistant district attorney—rely upon each other's cooperation for their continued professional existence, and so the bargaining between them usually is "reasonable" rather than fierce.

In his relations with his counsel, the accused begins to experience his first sense of "betrayal." He had already sensed or known that police and district attorneys were adversaries, and perhaps even a judge might be cast in such a role, but he is wholly unprepared for his counsel's performance as an agent or mediator.

It is even less likely to occur to an accused that members of his own family may become agents of the court system. Upon the urging of other agents or mediators, relatives may believe they are really helping an accused negotiate the best possible arrangement under the circumstances. Usually the lawyer will activate next of kin in this role, his ostensible motive being to arrange for his fee. But soon counsel will suggest that they appeal to the accused to "help himself" by pleading. *Gemeinschaft* sentiments are to this extent exploited by a defense lawyer (or even at times by a district attorney) to achieve specific secular ends, to conclude the matter with all possible dispatch.

Sooner or later the probation officer becomes an agent in an accused's processing, depending upon when his services are invoked by judicial requisition. In his role as an agent-mediator there is a fundamental theme—the professional self-conception of a "case worker in an authoritative setting." Probation officers and psychiatrists in the court must, according to established procedures, accept as a "given" the facts of a defendant's case as they are presented by the police and the district attorney. This has specific consequences in their relations with an accused. In other words, they view important aspects of a defendant's social biography in terms and meanings defined for them by agents hostile to the accused. Thus they see him, whether before or after he has pleaded, as already "in treatment."

The accused is usually unable to understand that he does not enjoy the worker-client or doctor-patient relationship with these functionaries. On the contrary, their professional services are preempted by the court organization, and they tend to impute primacy to the organization for the content and meaning of their roles. Usually, a defendant speaks much more freely and reveals a good deal more about himself to psychiatrists and probation officers than he would to other agent-mediators. But he can also reveal too much; he overlooks the lack of real confidentiality present in his relationship with them, and this too has consequences in terms of his ultimate disposition. The court organization may rely heavily on probation and psychiatric reports, especially in those cases where there are no other firm compelling legal, political, personal, or other criteria to use as a basis for disposing of a case. Bear in mind that the justifications and rationales employed by these agents are grounded in a stock of knowledge about the accused that is precast by police and prosecutor, whose objectivity may be problematic. So, to a large extent, probation and psychiatric reports reaffirm and recirculate the same knowledge about the accused originally furnished by police and prosecutor—refurbished in the patois and argot of social work and psychiatry.

The probation officer has an important function as an agent-mediator, especially after the accused has pleaded and has begun to have second thoughts about the matter. This function may be best described as "cooling the mark out." The phrase was originally used to describe that part of a confidence game in which the operatives leave one of their number behind to discourage the victim from going to the police and to help him accept his new social situation. The victim of, let us say, a swindle must be furnished with a set of apologia or rationales so that he can redefine himself in suitable and defensible terms, instead of going to the police to complain. His embarrassment and defeat are assuaged by the operative who is "cooling him." In similar fashion, on other social matrices, losers and defeated persons must be somehow "cooled out" in order to avoid some sort of social explosion. Erving Goffman furnishes an illustration in which one spouse "decourts" another by maneuvering the marital partner into a divorce without incurring undue hostility. Or in the case of a dying person, the cooling role is assumed by a doctor or priest.[5] Helping an accused person to accept defeat is another aspect of the agent-mediator role which is thus of great significance. The lawyer, probation officer, psychiatrist, and next of kin perform important "cooling out" functions. Even the police, prosecutor, and judge may occasionally find it necessary to perform such a function as an accused is processed toward a reconceptualization of self, in the course of changing his initial plea of "not guilty" to one attesting guilt.

We have previously noted that the short-term jail which houses defendants awaiting disposition is frequently crowded to double the intended capacity. Although this is a state of affairs not deliberately created, the discomforts occasioned thereby are employed as a weapon against the accused by the prosecutor and judge. A recalcitrant accused can be socialized relatively quickly by an extended sojourn in the remand jail, including setting bail at a level high enough so that he cannot meet it. The common refrain heard in the remand jail, from those who have been there for an extended period, is a desire to plead quickly and get sentenced, so that they can be moved to a more commodious prison. The greatly crowded conditions, while unintended and unforeseen, are used as part of the process of reducing an accused's resistance to the various agent-mediators.

While it is true that efforts have been made to simplify and develop less onerous bail procedures,[6] most defendants are still subject to the usual difficulties connected therewith. The bail-or-jail feature of the system is not the crucial one in terms of an accused's defeat; it is only one feature in the total array of structure and personnel in the prosecutor's arsenal of weapons.

Although many accused persons are never confronted with the problem, their alleged wrongdoing being unsung in the press, there are instances in which the news media serve in an agent-mediator role. Obviously this is not their intention, for they desire to serve publics and ends of their own. But it is virtually impossible for an accused to receive a fair trial by an "impartial jury," should he elect to do so, because an "impartial jury" could never be constituted if the press, radio, and television have established for weeks in advance of his "trial" that a defendant is guilty.

In summary, the accused is confronted by definitions of himself which reflect the various worlds of the agent-mediators—yet are consistent for the most part in their negative evaluation of him. The agent-mediators have seized upon a wholly unflattering aspect of his biography to reinterpret his entire personality and justify their present attitude and conduct toward him. Even an individual with considerable personal and economic resources has great difficulty resisting pressures to redefine himself under these circumstances. For the ordinary accused of modest personal, economic, and social resources, the group pressures and definitions of himself are simply too much to bear. He willingly complies with the demands of agent-mediators, who in turn will help "cool him out."

Figure 1 . . . does not spell out the interrelationships of the various

Figure 1. The Accused vis-à-vis His Agent-Mediators.

agent-mediators, but it depicts the accused's ultimate situation. Of course, he does not initially assume that all these pressures are allied against him.

One of the major requisites of due process is a "public trial," but justice by negotiation avoids public scrutiny. Technically, it may meet the minimum requirements of due process (the defendant having waived jury trial), but whether it meets the ideological and historical criteria of due process is at least an open question.

The court, unlike most other formal organizations, functions as a genuinely "closed community" in that it successfully conceals the true nature of its routine operations from the view of outsiders—and sometimes even from some of the participants themselves. It socializes its members and participants toward compliance with specific objectives which are not part of the official goals of justice and due process.

But the usual organizational use of ideological goals and internal discipline are inadequate in the court situation. They must be augmented and implemented. In dealing with this problem the court is unique in a number of respects, and organizational solutions that have been elaborated are calculated to overcome not only the resistance of the accused but the possible reluctance and work alienation of his accusers.

Notes

1. Erving Goffman, *Asylums* (New York: Doubleday, 1961), pp. 127–169. See also a most recent example of the use of the "career" concept by a sociologist whose basic focus is the tuberculosis patient, but who also employs it

in an analysis of prisoners, airline pilots, and business executives. Julius A. Roth, *Timetables: Structuring the Passage of Time in Hospital Treatment and Other Careers* (New York, 1963).

2. Ibid., p. 128.

3. Ibid., p. 168.

4. Lloyd E. Ohlin and Frank J. Remington, "Sentencing Structure: Its Effects upon Systems for the Administration of Criminal Justice," *Law and Contemporary Problems* 23 (Summer 1958): 495–507.

5. Erving Goffman, "On Cooling the Mark Out: Some Aspects of Adaptation to Failure," in Arnold M. Rose, ed., *Human Behavior and Social Processes* (Boston, 1962), pp. 482–505.

6. See, for example, one major effort in this direction which is summarized in Charles E. Ares, Anne Rankin, and Herbert Sturz, "The Manhattan Bail Project: An Interim Report on the Use of Pre-Trial Parole," *New York University Law Review* (January 1963): 67–95.

PART 6

CHANGING CRIME
AND THE CRIMINAL

The idea that the subject of crime can be viewed most productively from an *interactional-organizational* frame of analysis, that is, through an examination of how individual traits articulate with organizational components and processes to produce crime, has been stressed throughout this volume. Hence many of the readings have focused on the way in which criminal careers and identities are *structured* and *maintained.*

In this final part we turn to the manner by which various factors may operate to alter the nature and extent of crime—alterations that have implications for other criminological concerns, such as the efforts to define and explain crime. We also look at the *transformation* of criminal identities. The selections include a discussion of some of the important theoretical issues in the area of crime correction, a comprehensive review of the effectiveness of correctional programs and strategies, an account of how inmates cope with interracial conflict in prison, and, finally, a presentation of specific tactics to change the definition of crime.

ISSUES IN CORRECTIONS

It has been shown repeatedly how individuals may not only be tagged as criminals, but may come to view themselves as criminals. People respond differently to labeling, however; some may accept or reject a criminal label, while others may attempt to ignore it. Predicting the response of actors is, therefore, frequently difficult.

In "Theoretical Justifications for Prison: Retribution, Deterrence, and Isolation," Leonard Orland provides substance to this contention. Orland argues that the three justifications named in the title are at the core of any policy of criminal justice. Two of them—deterrence and isolation—purport to reduce crime: the first, by causing people to abstain from crime because of the threat of punishment; the second, by keeping wrongdoers "off the street." The trouble, Orland says, is that both theories suffer from a lack of empirical evidence. It is difficult to demonstrate that more people would commit crimes if they thought they would go unpunished, and studies have shown that even the experts cannot accurately predict which criminals will commit further crimes. Punishment, then, may or may not be an effective way to deal with criminals. Nevertheless, Orland argues, the fact remains that punishment, and not rehabilitation, is the guiding principle of our justice system.

Some of the same concerns are echoed by David F. Greenberg and Drew Humphries in "The Cooptation of Fixed Sentencing Reform." The authors note that the philosophy and goals of American penal reformers have moved away from the "rehabilitative ideal" to the "justice model," which is based in part on the advancement of prisoners' rights and interests and the promotion of radical social change. Drawing heavily from the book *Struggle for Justice*, Greenberg and Humphries cite several reasons for this shift. One is that both rehabilitation programs and attempts to predict criminality and recidivism have been largely unsuccessful. In addition, the rehabilitative ideal (or myth) takes a clinical, or individualistic, approach to crime and tends to produce and legitimate discriminatory practices against the disadvantaged. Such weaknesses, according to the authors, gave rise to a set of proposals to reform the sentencing of criminals. One aim of the proposals would be to sanction crime in proportion to its social harmfulness, a principle that would direct law enforcement toward crimes of corporations and the state. After describing the increasing conservatism of the reform agenda, Greenberg and Humphries review legislation passed by various states. Although ostensibly based on the justice model, these laws have done little to decriminalize lesser offenses, criminalize serious offenses committed by government or business, or restrict the discretionary powers of the courts; and the length of sentences has actually been increased. The failure to obtain significant reform is attributed in part to the inability of liberals and the oppressed to lead the attack.

In spite of the models advanced, or the strategies developed to control the criminal, it is obvious that prediction remains an imprecise science. Ted Bartell and L. Thomas Winfree, Jr., underscore this point in "Recidivist Impacts of Differential Sentencing Practices for Burglary Offenders." They examine how burglars having specific biographical traits respond to sentencing. Some interesting patterns emerge from these data. For example, the probability of subsequent conviction for a crime (recidivism) is less for offenders put on probation than for those given any other type of sentence (e.g., incarceration). Age, prior imprisonment, and type of sentence evolve as the strongest predictors of recidivism. Other factors, such as length of sentence and number of prior arrests, appear to have a minimal impact on subsequent convictions.

Despite the failures of treatment programs and strategies, efforts continue to be made to develop new ways of "rehabilitating" criminals. It must be recognized, however, that even if a person does decide to try to shed his or her criminal identity and become a law-abiding citizen, the person will in most cases be confronted with numerous barriers, both *psychological* (e.g., feelings of inferiority or a low conception of self) and *structural* (e.g., the lack of job opportunities or discrimination). The "structures," or those conditions that may have given rise to law-violating behavior, remain intact. Thus the major thrust of virtually all correction programs is placed on the individual, even though the evidence indicates that societal conditions, as well as inequities in identifying and processing criminals, guarantee the continued production of offenders.

Another barrier standing in the way of successful correction programs is that although the imposition of a criminal label is often a systematic and efficient institutional process, the reverse process of *institutional delabeling* is anything but systematic and efficient. There are, so to speak, no rites of passage whereby the criminal label and its associated—and enduring—stigma are deliberately removed. Of course, the labeling process does not affect everyone equally. People like Agnew and corporation executives who accept illegal payments have an eminently greater chance of avoiding stigmatization than a burglar or a street hustler. Their power and resources virtually guarantee success.

For all these reasons, any model of change that concentrates on the individual and ignores structural factors is almost certainly doomed to fail. And understanding structures requires that we carefully analyze how the powerful define, relate to, and process the powerless. We must also consider how the powerless perceive and respond to the powerful. In other words, conceptions of crime and the criminal are tied inherently to the political process.

John Irwin, in "The Contemporary Prison," provides an overview of how prisons have changed since the 1960s. He notes the hatred between blacks and whites and finds that inmates show an increasing tendency to join groupings that share their interests (e.g., in terms of criminal orientation or preprison experiences). Irwin points out that racial hatred and inmate divisions extend to guards and administrators. Probably the most noticeable and significant change in the last two decades is the increase in prison violence. According to Irwin, a major reason behind the increased incidence of robbery, attack, and retaliation among inmates can be attributed to the fact that many powerful gangs (e.g., the Mexican Mafia and the Black Guerilla Family) have emerged; this is especially so in California and Texas.

Robert Martinson, in "What Works? Questions and Answers about Prison Reform," reviews the effectiveness of a range of efforts to rehabilitate offenders. He begins his analysis by offering a summary of his findings: "With few and isolated exceptions, the rehabilitative efforts that have been reported so far have had no appreciable effect on recidivism." He then assesses the weight of empirical evidence reported in studies covering such traditional strategies as educational and vocational programs in prisons, individual and group counseling, medical treatment, differential sentencing, and decarceration. Perhaps, Martinson suggests, the programs are not good enough or therapy is not skillfully administered. But a more radical flaw in the programs is that they seem to be based on a "disease" theory of crime—a theory that overlooks the normality of crime in society and the personal normality of many offenders. He concludes by noting that attention might be more fruitfully turned to strategies that *deter* crime.

REDEFINING CRIME

Not only have correctional programs ignored societal conditions or situational determinants that may lead to crime, but they have paid scant attention to the nature of crime itself, particularly its definitional components and presumed causative factors. If, however, crime is a matter of public definition, then changing definitions (or laws) must produce changes in the picture of crime. And if negative experiences and "failure" labels, both within socializing and social control institutions, can give rise to adult criminal careers, then some changes are called for in schools and other institutions. Similarly, if blocked opportunity leads either directly or indirectly to criminal activities, then manipulation of opportunity structures will affect the overall volume of crime. The point is that any serious effort to alter the picture of crime must deal not only with individual criminals but also with the total range of criminological concerns explored in this volume. Many of the needed changes are outlined in the final two selections.

Norval Morris and Gordon Hawkins, in "The Overreach of the Criminal Law," argue that any effort to deal with crime in America must deal with the "overreach" of the criminal law. According to the authors, the application of criminal sanctions to such activities as gambling and drug usage actually contributes in many ways to the crime problem. For example, police efforts to enforce statutes pertaining to such behaviors deplete needed resources for dealing with crimes of violence and theft. Morris and Hawkins review the laws relating to drunkenness, narcotics and drug abuse, gambling, disorderly conduct and vagrancy, and sexual behavior, citing the extent to which the laws are violated and recommending changes in the penal code.

Several selections in this book have explored the topic of corporate or business crime. One of the messages offered has been that even though the cost of corporate crime is many times greater than that of street and ordinary crime, relatively little direct empirical attention has been given to the subject. Obviously, if corporate crime becomes more tightly regulated (e.g., through the passage of laws and more stringent enforcement policies), then the nature and extent of crime will exhibit different patterns. The last selection, by Marshall B. Clinard et al., "Controlling Corporate Crime," outlines specific measures that could be used to regulate corporate crime and hence affect the crime statistics generated. They argue that such crime can be combated from three different angles: (1) by changing corporate attitudes or structures; (2) by deterring or punishing crimes through the use of legal measures; and (3) by making effective use of consumer and public pressures. The authors outline various steps that could be taken under each approach. For example, in their call for more severe penalties, they list eight possibilities, including much larger fines and greater prosecution of corporate officials.

37. Theoretical Justifications for Prison: Retribution, Deterrence, and Isolation

LEONARD ORLAND

RETRIBUTION

The ancient justification for punishment was moral and retributive. The function of criminal law was to exact vengeance on one who deserved vengeance. The Old Testament called for an eye for an eye. The infliction of terrible punishment on the wrongdoer was seen as a moral good. "Who does evil will have evil done to him" *(Qui malum fecit, malum ferat)* is an early theological theme.

The doctrine of retribution justice, however, is not merely a relic of theological antiquity. Kant, in the eighteenth century, took a similar approach: "Juridical Punishment can never be administered merely as a means for promoting another Good either with regard to the Criminal himself or to Civil Society, but must in all cases be imposed only because the individual on whom it is inflicted *has committed a Crime.*" According to Kant, only the law of retribution *(lex talionis)* can determine exactly the kind and degree of punishment.[1]

Pope Pius XII, in 1954, addressed himself to the continuing viability of this doctrine. The man who commits a criminal act, Pius declared, "rejects" and "refuses to obey" the demand to be good and rather "accepts the evil." Criminal acts are directed not just against a thing or a person, but also against higher authority, and "therefore in the end always against the authority of God." Since "every criminal act is an opposition to God Himself," the "author of the [criminal] act becomes deserving of punishment *(reatus poenae).*" Punishment "accomplishes its purpose . . . inasfar as it compels the criminal, because of the act performed, to suffer, that is it deprives him of good and imposes upon him an evil."[2]

It is significant, as Nigel Walker reminds us, that the genuine retributive penologist believes that "the enforcement of atonement is a proper aim of penal systems whether or not his enforcement reduces the incidence of the offenses in question, and whether or not it protects the offender against unofficial retaliation." Indeed, the retributivist must be prepared to argue that "the penal system should enforce atonement even if by so doing it increases the frequency of the offense in question (as imprisoning some homosexuals is said to do), and even if it renders the offender more exposed to unofficial retaliation (as the pillory did)."³

This seemingly strange viewpoint was defended by the Victorian jurist Sir James Stephen, who, in a classic statement, concluded that the legal infliction of punishment gives expression and ratification to the hatred excited by the commission of crime. The criminal law proceeds on the principle "that it is morally right to hate criminals," and justifies that sentiment by inflicting punishment on criminals. Moreover, it is "desirable that criminals should be hated," and that punishment continue to be inflicted in order to give expression to and justify hatred of criminals.⁴

While Stephen's language is unusually blunt, Herbert Packer observes that it does not express a pure revenge theory. Rather, it proceeds on the closely related but distinguishable notion that "punishment is justifiable because it provides an orderly outlet for emotions that, denied it, would express themselves in socially less acceptable ways."⁵ That idea was classically expressed by Émile Durkheim and restated by Jackson Toby. Toby tells us that for Durkheim, punishment was not "mere vindictiveness." Durkheim felt that unpunished deviance would tend to demoralize the conformist, the "upright people," while punishment would "heal the wounds made upon the collective sentiments of upright people."⁶

The rationale for punishment, according to Durkheim's disciples, is not that it deters and not that punishment of the evildoer is a good in itself; rather, punishment of the criminal reinforces the collective sentiments of the majority that crime is bad, and that he who commits a criminal act should be punished.

DETERRENCE

A familiar justification for punishment is that it deters crime. The problem with general deterrence theory is that its validity depends on our knowing what might have happened in the absence of the deterrent. How does one go about empirically demonstrating that a given punishment is effective in deterring crimes on the part of people who would otherwise commit them? Do people forego criminal opportunities because of the mere *threat* of sanction? Shall we remove that threat and find out?

Despite these difficulties, the theory of general deterrence, popular in the eighteenth century, appears to be enjoying a rebirth. The original notion stems from the eighteenth-century utilitarianism of

Bentham and Beccaria. Deterrence theory is derived directly from the hedonistic calculus of Bentham, who believed that the potential criminal would be prevented from performing a criminal act if the pain of punishment exceeded the pleasure expected from the act. To Bentham, "everyone, even the madman, calculates pleasures versus pain."[7] The same approach is evident in the works of Cesare Beccaria.[8] The purpose of punishment is not to torment the criminal nor to undo a crime already committed, but rather "to prevent the criminal from inflicting new injuries on . . . citizens and to deter others from similar acts." Accordingly, "for a punishment to attain its end, the evil which it inflicts has only to exceed the advantage derivative from the crime." In this excess of evil, Beccaria included the certainty of punishment and the loss of the good which the crime might have produced. Moreover, he felt that punishment would be more just and useful if it closely followed the commission of a crime.

The most forceful contemporary restatement of classical deterrence theory comes from Andenaes.[9] He refers to "general prevention," which he defines as the restraints which emanate from criminal law. This differs from simple deterrence in that it also includes the "moral or socio-pedagogical" influence of punishment (and is therefore closer to Durkheim's concept of punishment). To Andenaes, general prevention may depend on the deterrent effects of punishment, but it also involves the ability of criminal law to evoke other inhibitions in the public. The idea is that punishment "helps to form and strengthen the public moral code and thereby create both conscious and unconscious inhibitions against the commission of crimes." According to Andenaes, punishment serves a threefold function: to deter, to strengthen moral inhibitions, and to stimulate habitual law-abiding conduct. Andenaes readily acknowledges that the problem with his theory is that it cannot be validated, simply because the deterrent effects of punishment cannot be measured.

This lack of empirical validation for deterrence theory is but part of the larger problem—the lack of empirical validation for *any* theory of punishment. A recent evaluation of punishment literature by Bailey and Smith observes that deterrence research has typically been quite limited in scope, concerned for the most part with one offense, homicide, and one punishment, capital punishment.[10] These studies tell us little, if anything, about deterring noncapital crimes. Moreover, deterrence studies are sharply limited in that they fail to validate empirically the theoretical assumption that maximum deterrence is achieved if punishment is severe and certain.

Deterrence, Nigel Walker observes, "has become a dirty word in penological discussion, partly because it has so often been the battle-cry of those who support capital or corporal punishment," partly because it is more "fashionable," "enlightened" and "scientific to talk about rehabilitation."[11] The shortcoming of deterrence theory, as Packer has noted, is that deterrence, to the extent it is effective, deters those who are subject to socializing influences. But deterrence cannot threaten those beyond the point of hope. It cannot improve the morality of those whose value system is closed. And, even if deterrence is possible, it may work only at too great a price—by cruel and rigorous enforcement and by widespread suppression of individual freedom.

ISOLATION

The theory of general deterrence is closely related to another theoretical justification for punishment: isolation, or "keeping them off the streets."

Isolation is a fairly straightforward notion: for as long as a man is locked up in a cell, he is unable to commit another crime. This appears, at first blush, to be a self-evidently sound basis for the punishment of offenders. But the problem is again one of prediction. Isolation theory assumes that it is possible to predict that the person actually isolated for a specific crime is likely to commit other crimes. Does the incarcerated criminal in fact have a tendency to commit other crimes? In order words, will he recidivate?

Unfortunately, our knowledge is not advanced to the point where we can predict human behavior with any degree of confidence, let alone predict that a convicted burglar will, if released, commit another burglary. The logic of isolation theory is that it permits criminals to be locked up for a long period of time even though there is no basis for reliably predicting that they will recidivate. Pushed to its logical extreme, it permits imprisonment for life for relatively minor offenses if the offender is perceived to be a recidivist.

Our profound inability to predict recidivism is underscored by three recent efforts to appraise our capacity to predict violence. In 1972, a sophisticated California social science group headed by Dr. Ernst A. Wenk attempted to identify felons who upon release would commit further violent acts. The results are dramatic evidence of our inability to predict: 86 percent of those identified by the research group as dangerous did not commit a violent act on parole.[12]

Similar failures were reported by a group headed by Dr. Harry L. Kozol. Employing all the diagnostic tools currently available, including independent examinations by two psychiatrists and a social worker, Kozol attempted to predict dangerousness among high-risk prison offenders in Massachusetts. The Kozol group compared the behavior of patients released on its recommendation with the behavior of those who were released against its advice. The results: thirty-two of the forty-nine inmates released against the advice of the psychiatric team did not commit any serious unsolved crimes in the five years following their release.[13]

A third key study was that reported by Dr. Henry Steadman, based on observation of patients held as criminally insane at New York's Dannemora and Matteawan institutions. In 1966, the United States Supreme Court had ruled that it was unconstitutional for the New York institutions to confine such patients beyond the maximum of their original criminal sentence without new proceedings that met constitutional guarantees of due process.[14] As a result of the decision, 967 patients were either released or transferred to civil mental hospitals. Dr. Steadman's four-year follow-up of these patients concludes: "Between 1966 and 1970, barely 21 of the 967 Baxstrom patients returned to Matteawan or Dannemora. All the findings seriously question the legal and psychiatric structures that retained these 967 people an average of thirteen years in institutions for the criminally insane."[15]

The implications of these data are direct and inescapable: neither the best trained of psychiatrists or social scientists nor the best intentioned of judges or parole boards is capable of accurately predicting violent recidivism.

The theories of retribution, deterrence, and isolation—often conflicting rationalizations for punishment—are at the core of any policy of criminal justice. We would be better served by facing the existence of these core theories, with all their inadequacies, than by continuing to deceive ourselves with the pious—and unrealistic—rhetoric of rehabilitation.

Notes

1. Kant, *The Philosophy of Law* (1887, Hastie, tr.), pp. 194–201.
2. Pope Pius XII, "Crime and Punishment," *Catholic Lawyer* 92 (1960) 6.
3. Walker, *Sentencing in a Rational Society* (1969), p. 5.
4. Stephen, II *History of Criminal Law* (1883), p. 8.
5. Packer, *The Limits of the Criminal Sanction* (1968), p. 37.
6. Toby, "Is Punishment Necessary?" JOURNAL OF CRIMINAL LAW, CRIMINOLOGY AND POLICE SCIENCE 332 (1964) 55.
7. Bentham, *Principles of Penal Law* (1843), p. 396.
8. Beccaria, *On Crimes and Punishments* (1963), pp. 42–44.
9. Andenaes, "The General Preventive Effects of Punishment," 114 U. PA. L. REV. (1966) 949. See also Andenaes, *Punishment and Deterrence* (1974).
10. Bailey and Smith, "Punishment: Its Severity and Certainty," JOURNAL

OF CRIMINAL LAW, CRIMINOLOGY AND POLICE SCIENCE (1972) 63. See also Zimring and Hawkins, *Deterrence: The Legal Threat in Crime Control* (1973).

11. Walker, *supra*, p. 56, n. 3.

12. Wenk, Robison, and Smith, "Can Violence Be Predicted?" 18 CRIME AND DELINQUENCY (1972), p. 393.

13. Kozol, Boucher and Garofalo, "The Diagnosis and Treatment of Dangerousness," CRIME AND DELINQUENCY 371 (1972), 18.

14. Baxstrom *v.* Herold, 383 U.S. 107 (1966).

15. Steadman and Keveles, "The Community Adjustment and Criminal Activity of the Baxstrom Patients: 1966–70," AMERICAN JOURNAL OF PSYCHIATRY 304 (1972) 129.

38. The Cooptation of Fixed Sentencing Reform

DAVID F. GREENBERG
DREW HUMPHRIES

The correctional philosophy and programmatic goals of American penal reforms have recently shifted away from the "rehabilitative ideal" or "treatment model" toward what is coming to be known as the "justice model" of correction. Although the early advocates of justice model principles saw themselves as advancing prisoners' interests and contributing to a broader process of radical social change, the model has taken on an increasingly conservative cast in the past few years. This essay documents the ideological transformation of the justice model [and] examines the consequences of this transformation for the administration of justice and social change more generally. . . .

THE ESSENCE OF THE TREATMENT MODEL

The treatment model of correction originated in the period following the Civil War, when reformers criticized judicially imposed sentences of fixed duration as retributive and too mechanical to reform prisoners effectively. In place of fixed sentences they advocated a sentencing scheme that would enlist the prisoner's will in the cause of reformation by providing an incentive in the form of early release from incarceration, and that would at the same time permit the extended imprisonment of incorrigibles. Thus, prison sentences were to be indefinite in extent (e.g., five to ten years, or five years to life), with decisions concerning release to be made on the basis of rehabilitative criteria.

Implementation, though slow at first and always partial, made major strides during the Progressive era. By the early decades of the twentieth century, the federal government and almost all state legislatures had established parole boards authorized to release prisoners administratively at any time within legislatively or judicially determined minimum and maximum limits.

Though isolated features of the system had received sporadic criticism over the years,[1] the treatment model continued to enjoy extremely wide support. It was embraced in such popular works as Karl Menninger's *The Crime of Punishment*[2] and Ramsey Clark's *Crime in America*,[3] as well as in the report of the President's Crime Commission.[4] In interviews carried out as recently as 1973, the "correctional elites" of several states overwhelmingly said that they regarded the rehabilitation of offenders to be a goal of the highest priority.[5]

THE ATTACK ON THE TREATMENT MODEL

The long-held consensus about the goals of penal reform began to fall apart around 1970. One of the first and most far-reaching criticisms of the accepted wisdom appeared in a report prepared by a Working Party of the American Friends Service Committee (AFSC) published under the title *Struggle for Justice.*[6]

The AFSC Working Party pointed out that criminal justice practitioners had never developed the technical capabilities required to implement the model. Evaluations of rehabilitation programs had consistently failed to find persuasive evidence for the success of treatment; after fifty years of research on the prediction of criminality, postrelease recidivism still could not be predicted accurately. The prospects of major improvement in these areas were questioned on theoretical grounds: If crime is not the product of an individual pathology, then it cannot be "cured." However, even if these programs did become effective, it was argued, they were limited in the effect they could have on the crime problem because such a small proportion of the population of law violators were actually subjected to imprisonment and exposed to "treatment."

Going beyond this technical criticism, the Working Party rejected coerced therapy as undignified and potentially repressive, and attacked individualization in sentencing as a violation of fundamental norms of distributive justice and proportionality. These violations were placed in the political context of a dual system of justice which ignores or provides minimal punishment for immensely destructive actions of corporations and the state, while reserving the full weight of repressive enforcement for the poor and members of racial, political, and cultural minorities whose infractions are frequently minor or harmless.

This inequality of treatment, it was argued, is not solely a reflection of the substantive provisions of the criminal code. Although these provisions do reflect inequalities of wealth and power, in both the offenses included and those excluded, the Working Party pointed to differential enforcement of the law, itself a product of institutionalized arrangements that contribute to or encourage discretionary decision making, as another important mechanism by which social inequality is translated into legal inequality. Where decisions are unstructured by law, regulation, or even meaningful guidelines and are for the most part unreviewed and unchecked, decisions supposedly to be made on the basis of criteria related to rehabilitation can be and sometimes are made on the basis of other criteria that are legally irrelevant and discriminatory in their impact, such as race, class, sex, life style, and political affiliations. Disproportionate representation of the poor and minorities in prison was attributed not to their greater criminality, but to the covert use of these criteria in decision making.

Seen in this light, rehabilitation was not merely a laudable goal that scientific research had unfortunately failed thus far to achieve, but something far more insidious—an ideology that explained crime in highly individualistic terms and legitimated the expansion of administrative powers used in practice to discriminate against disadvantaged groups and to achieve covert organizational goals (such as alleviating court backlogs and repressing political opposition).

This analysis provided the foundation for a set of proposals to reform criminal sentencing. These proposals had two aspects. One involved the prosecution and sanctioning of crime according to its social harmfulness. This principle would direct law enforcement toward the crimes of the corporation and the state, reduce penalties for crimes commonly committed by the lower classes, and, in the case of "victimless" crimes and some of the lesser offenses against property and public order, lead to decriminalization.

The second aspect of the proposed restructuring concerned the justification of punishment and the related question of the principles of sentencing. On technical, moral, and political grounds, the Working Party called for the exclusion of mandatory treatment programs and the termination of preventive confinement on a predictive basis. Deterrence of the general public to procure conformity to some minimal set of essential prohibitions was to constitute the sole ground for punishment, and the administration of this punishment was to be constrained by norms of distributive justice. Discretionary decision making, lacking any rationale under these principles, was to be reduced or eliminated wherever possible, and replaced by sentences of fixed length that were much shorter than those presently imposed.

To the authors of *Struggle for Justice*, a nondiscretionary system of justice was expected to have implications not only for the elimination of discrimination in sentencing but also for the reform of the substantive law. In a discretionary system, Robert Kennedy's son can be given probation for possession of marijuana while a white hippie or black ghetto youth is sent to prison. In a nondiscretionary system, everyone—or no one—must go to prison. Faced with the prospect of sending Robert Kennedy's son to prison, it was argued, legislators would repeal the marijuana laws and other nonessential prohibitions. Thus, it was hoped that the adoption of formal rules of sentencing would help to bring about substantive reform of the criminal law.

This analysis did not come out of the blue. The attention paid to the discriminatory aspects of criminal justice administration reflected the impact of a decade of civil rights activity and growing black militancy. One of the targets of the civil rights movement was the unequal and sometimes brutal treatment of blacks at the hands of law enforcement officials. The understanding that the criminal justice system is sometimes used for political repression came at the end of a decade in which Southern sheriffs clubbed, hosed, cattle prodded, and jailed civil rights activists; demonstrators clashed with police on campuses and in the streets; and the FBI and local law enforcement agencies tapped telephones, burglarized apartments and offices, opened mail, and used infiltrators and provocateurs to disrupt and destroy radical organizations and programs. Liberal assumptions about the benevolence of the state could no longer be sustained. The Working Party itself was formed because traditional AFSC involvement in criminal justice reform no longer made sense in light of these events.

The AFSC analysis was further shaped by the imprisonment of civil rights activists and war resisters, and by the dissemination of writings (such as *The Autobiography of Malcolm X* and Eldridge Cleaver's *Soul on Ice*) by articulate black prisoners or exprisoners, many of them radicalized by developments occurring in and out of prison. The public image of the prisoner was humanized and politicized. Instead of being seen as public enemies or defectives in need of "correction," defendants and prisoners became victims of discrimination in the society at large, who were further victimized by the criminal justice system.

The political delegitimation of the state in connection with the war in Vietnam further eroded the legitimacy of correction as a criminal justice goal. The concept of correction implies that those who administer it know what is "correct." Once that confidence is lost, correction comes to be seen as a means of procuring conformity to an oppressive social system rather than a way to help unfortunates.

Finally, prisoners themselves began to reject important elements of the treatment model. In California, where indeterminate sentencing had been implemented more extensively than anywhere else in the country, prisoners placed the indeterminate sentence high on their list of grievances.[7] The prisoners who seized D Yard in Attica considered themselves political prisoners and called not for rehabilitation but for release. It was in the context of these developments that brief published summaries of the as yet unpublished findings of Douglas Lipton, Robert Martinson, and Judith Wilks concerning the failure of rehabilitation[8] were interpreted as demonstrating the bankruptcy of a system organized around treatment goals, rather than as the occasion for a call to redouble research efforts.

In contrast with most proposals for criminal justice reform, *Struggle for Justice* was not addressed to official policy makers; as beneficiaries or representatives of the beneficiaries of the present system, they could hardly have been expected to take the initiative in changing it. Instead, those whom the system oppressed were to be the central actors.

> Central to our framework for action is the concept of *empowerment*. As a basis for social change, start with the people who suffer most grievously under the present system. Actions that shift power relationships, that place power in the hands of the heretofore powerless, have the potential for creating basic change. Such actions place people in new relationships to institutions. . . .
>
> The concept of empowerment leads to the organization of oppressed peoples and abused groups for self-determination.[9]

The proposals were therefore addressed to the insurgent groups that were politically active at the end of the 1960s: prisoners, blacks, and Hispanics, as well as liberal whites who could ally with these groups.

The substantive content of the AFSC proposals was based on this political perspective. Whereas previous proposals for penal reform had been premised on purely technical criticism or were suffused by paternalism and in practice tended to heighten the powerlessness of prisoners, the AFSC proposals were intended to shift power to defendants and prisoners, enabling them to set their own priorities.[10]

The Working Party was politically diverse and consequently never achieved a full consensus concerning the precise nature of the relationship between its proposals and movements to achieve broader social change.[11] However, the report established a clear link between criminal justice reform and efforts to bring about a more egalitarian society: "The construction of a just system of criminal justice in an unjust society is a contradiction in terms." There must be "fundamental reallocations of power and resources . . . a radical change in our values and a drastic restructuring of our social and economic institutions."[12] Clearly, the proposals for criminal justice reform were to be part of a wider struggle to bring about change in a number of different areas of American life. These struggles were conceived as being grassroots in character, rather than as originating at the top governmental and organizational levels.

For at least one of the members of the Working Party,[13] the AFSC proposals fit logically into a program for building a socialist movement in the United States because of the difficulty of implementing the proposals within the existing institutional framework of American society.

In a judicial system that manages to avoid paralysis by securing 90 to 95 percent of its convictions through guilty pleas often obtained through plea bargaining, the elimination of the prosecutorial and judicial discretion that makes these bargains possible cannot be accomplished solely by freeing resources through the repeal of victimless crime laws. Given the volume of crime in the United States, it would be necessary to stop prosecuting crimes of medium seriousness (e.g., burglary) as well, and this is not politically possible. The proposed reforms, then, are in fact feasible only in the context of a society that generates less crime than occurs in the United States, or is willing to allocate more resources to controlling crime.

Although subject to flagrant violations in practice in low-visibility proceedings, concepts like "equal treatment under the law," "due process," and "right to trial by jury" are important elements of the American political system and enjoy wide support. Even those who do not particularly value economic equality are nevertheless likely to believe that at least in court everyone should be treated equally. The contradiction between the norm of equality under law and the routine violation of the norm necessitated by the high crime rate generated by a deteriorating capitalist social system seemed to hold out the possibility for building a mass movement to reform the criminal justice system that would be likely to take a socialist direction as it encountered the limitations imposed on the implementation of these ideals by the exigencies of a capitalist economy.[14]

The structural basis for carrying out such a strategy had been created by the very social developments that led to the AFSC proposals. The civil rights movement and the war had partially destroyed the legitimacy of official authority for a substantial portion of the population and nurtured widespread skepticism about the benevolence of the state. Within the prisons, striking and rebellious prisoners posed new problems for management of the institutions. The publicity given to the brutal and sometimes lethal repression of prisoners' protests and to the grossly disproportionate representation of minorities and poor people in prisons was creating a legitimacy crisis for the criminal justice system. Opinion polls showed widespread sympathy for rebelling prisoners; and the judiciary responded to revelations of mistreatment and brutality in lawsuits brought by prisoners with intervention of unprecedented scope on behalf of prisoners' rights. Entire prisons were declared to be violating inmates' constitutional rights and were ordered closed. Some wondered whether the prison could function much longer as an institution:

> I am persuaded that the institution of prison probably must end. In many respects it is as intolerable within the United States as was the institution of slavery, equally brutalizing to all involved, equally toxic to the social system, equally subversive of the brotherhood of man, even more costly by some standards, and probably less rational.[15]

In addition, the system's seeming ineffectiveness in curbing rapidly rising crime rates evoked widespread attention and concern, at first primarily among conservative politicians and the white, blue-collar workers, then more broadly across the political spectrum exclusive of the Left. These developments made it seem plausible that the restructuring of prosecution and sentencing was an issue that could potentially be placed on the political agenda through mass organizing.

TRANSFORMATION OF THE REFORM AGENDA

Although the analysis presented in *Struggle for Justice* can be faulted on a number of counts,[16] we want to focus here not on its analytical weaknesses, but on the reception the book has received, the transformation of its proposals in the past few years, and the political implications of these changes.

In many respects *Struggle for Justice* has been remarkably influential. Its criticism of mandatory treatment programs and preventive confinement on the basis of predictions of future criminality has been widely accepted by penologists. According to Edith Flynn,

> As early as 1971 the American Friends' Service Committee called for the abolition of the indeterminate sentence and for return to short flat sentences for most offenders as the only way for achieving justice. They were quickly joined in their proposal by such groups as prisoners' rights organizations, legislators, politicians, states' attorneys, as well as by many disillusioned liberal reformers. The uniting element for these ideologically disparate groups is the appalling state of today's sentencing practices.[17]

Virtually all recent commission reports and many books and articles concerned with criminal justice policy either accept or build on, elaborate or qualify its ideas.[18] Michael Serrill notes, "Today it is difficult to find a prominent member of the academic, prison reform or liberal political community who does not favor a drastic reduction in the amount of discretion exercised within the criminal justice system."[19] According to Marvin Zalman, "Virtually all academic writing on sentencing since 1972 has favored a turn toward definite sentencing and recent legislation has also moved toward definite sentencing."[20]

This speedy adoption of a new conceptual framework for penological thought and criminal justice practice has by no means constituted a victory for the radical political perspective of *Struggle for Justice;* on the contrary, the proposals outlined in that book have been narrowed and modified so drastically that their adoption amounts to a serious political defeat. It is to these developments that we now turn.

Conceptual Elaboration of the Justice Model

Following the publication of *Struggle for Justice,* several philosophical treatments of punishment have given great emphasis to the place of the "just deserts" concept in a sentencing scheme. The kernel of this approach is that law violators should be punished according to what they deserve based on what they have done. Its advocates interpret this principle to mean that sentencing should be influenced by only a limited amount of information about an offender, primarily his or her past illegal behavior. This represents a more radical break with utilitarianism than is found in *Struggle for Justice* and arguably provides a logically more coherent rationale for the principles of distributive justice and proportionality of penalty to offense. The report of the Committee for the Study of Incarceration (CSI)[21] represents the most significant contribution to this development. We will focus our comments on this work because it is more rigorous in its analysis than other works in the same vein.

At least potentially, the principle that offenders should be punished according to what they deserve has a critical edge. By any conceivable standard of deserts, most persons now in prison in the United States receive punishment that is grossly in excess of what they deserve on the basis of the harm they have done or intended to do. At the same time, corporate and government executives responsible for actions that jeopardize the lives and health of thousands and damage the material interests of millions receive sanctions of unmerited leniency in the few cases in which they are punished at all. The justice model provides a conceptual framework for criticizing these gross departures from the principle of proportionality.

On the other hand, it is a direct consequence of the class distribution of power in a capitalist society that the state will not itself take the initiative in revising the distribution of legal sanctions it imposes to reflect the class distribution of culpability for socially injurious acts. Proposals to impose even modest penalties for corporate offenses are vigorously resisted by those who would be liable, as the history of recent environmental and occupational safety legislation illustrates. As Dean Clarke notes, the picture of "Presidents, Congressmen and corporate bosses on long-term prison sentences for tax frauds, illegal profiteering, and war-mongering, while petty thieves freely wander the streets attending occasional, and voluntary, therapy classes . . . is as absurd as it is meaningless."²² Only rarely have changes in the direction required by a justice model been achieved, and then only as the result of organized working-class or populist campaigns, or when the state's legitimacy needs required the sacrifice of the interests of individual members of the capitalist class.

It follows that the critical potential of the just deserts philosophy will be realized in practice only if politically organized opposition groups make an issue of the discrepancy between moral culpability and existing sentencing patterns and bring concerted pressure to bear on the state to revise its sentencing structure—or if they capture the state and create a new social order that does not require the judicial sacrifice of mass interests.

In the absence of such efforts, the state will simply employ the *vocabulary* of just deserts to legitimate its traditional sentencing patterns. It will continue to ignore upper-class criminals and overpunish lower-class criminals. Instead of imprisoning the latter to cure them (and then ignoring the mandate to cure), as in the past, it will imprison them for the same long periods to deter crime or because severe punishment is required by considerations of just deserts. In the early 1970s, when the rhetoric of rehabilitation had been exposed as an obfuscation covering up repressive social control, criminal justice functionaries found the jargon of the justice model especially appealing. It supplied exactly what they needed—a new ideology to use in placating critics.

It is commonplace in textbook discussions of sentencing to refer to the four classic "functions" of punishment: retribution, deterrence, rehabilitation, and restraint of the dangerous. However, the social consequences of adopting a particular sentencing philosophy are not restricted to these functions. Viewed as ideology, a sentencing philosophy has profound ideological implications for the society as a whole. In the case of the justice model, they can be profoundly conservative.

For one thing, a just deserts philosophy focuses attention on the individual perpetrator alone. If I lose my job because the economy is in a state of contraction and then steal to support myself and my family—or if I am a juvenile and steal because the state has passed child labor legislation—or if I strike out in rage because the color of my skin subjects me to discrimination that reduces my opportunities—the just deserts model simply indicates that I should be punished for my wrongful act, though perhaps not as severely as I would be at present. One need not deny individual responsibility altogether in such cases to see that, in placing my culpability and the punishment I should receive at the center of attention, other topics are pushed to the periphery: the dynamics of the capitalist economy; the manner in which it allocates benefits and injuries among classes, races, and sexes—and in so doing generates the structural conditions to which members of the society respond when they violate the law; and the way class interests are represented in or excluded from the law. All these are neglected in favor of an abstract moral preoccupation with the conduct of the individual offender. But it is on precisely these excluded issues that a movement for radical political change must focus. The just deserts model interferes with this task, not merely by giving unduly abstract answers to the questions it asks (answers that neglect the social situation of the criminal actor), but even more by choosing to ask the questions it does.[23]

To the extent that the reporting of state-imposed punishment in the mass media contributes to the shaping of popular conceptions of criminality and moral worth, the language of the justice model, when employed in the context of a system that selects individuals for prosecution on a basis that is sharply class biased, continues to reinforce ideas about crime and morality favorable to the powerful.

The text of *Doing Justice*, like other justice model literature, displays no awareness of these difficulties. In focusing almost entirely on a consideration of the classic "functions" of sentencing, their justification, and their implications for a sentencing scheme, and for the most part ignoring the question of the kind of society in which the punishment system is to function, it was not led to these issues. Since none of the members of the CSI appears to have shared the goal of abolishing capitalism and establishing a socialist society, or considered the question of sentencing in the light of this goal, this neglect is not surprising.[24]

The political distance between the CSI report and the report of the AFSC Working Party is maintained even in the final chapter of the former, "Just Deserts in an Unjust Society." Here, where the larger social setting is finally brought into the picture, the author notes that, in the preceding sixteen chapters, "We have scarcely mentioned poverty and social class."[25] By contrast, poverty and class are kept in the forefront throughout the text of *Struggle for Justice*. In this final chapter, von Hirsch grapples with the difficulty raised for the justice model by the existence of pronounced social inequality and injustice. For many offense categories, social disadvantages would have to be regarded as ground for reduced culpability. Yet under the system of formal equality which has been derived from the just deserts principle, those who are disadvantaged are to be punished as severely as those whose biography justifies no such mitigation.

We are persuaded, as was the CSI, that the implementation of the justice model would represent a distinct gain for those who are now socially disadvantaged even though formally equal sentences might in particular cases be substantively unequal and therefore unjust. As both the AFSC and the CSI reports note, a socially disadvantaged background is more likely to constitute grounds for aggravation of sentence than for mitigation in a utilitarian, treatment-based discretionary system.

Nevertheless, the contradiction remains. To a radical, the limitations to the implementation of a system of equal treatment under law posed by a stratified class system become grounds, along with many others, for attacking and abolishing the class system. For the CSI, this limitation is simply the occasion for feeling uneasy about a "morally flawed" system of punishment.[26]

It is revealing that two of the members of the CSI comment in an introduction to *Doing Justice* that

> ... we are not happy. Our solution is one of despair, not hope. We recognize that, in giving up the rehabilitative model, we abandon not just our innocence but perhaps more. The concept of deserts is intellectual and moralistic; in its devotion to principle, it turns back on such compromising considerations as generosity and charity, compassion and love. It emphasizes justice, not mercy, and while it need not rule out tempering justice with mercy, by shifting the emphasis from concern for the individual to devotion to the moral right, it could lead to an abandonment of the former altogether. ...
>
> Perhaps it is not the most compelling advertisement for one's committee to conclude that the principles we advocate here will do less mischief and perpetuate less inequity than the system with which we now live. But if we can deflate the rhetoric and limit the reach of programs that now pretend to do good, then our time and energy has been well spent.[27]

This *cri de coeur* represents the anguish of the modern liberal intellectual faced with the contradiction between liberal ideals and a capitalist society which stands in the way of achieving liberal ideals—and which the liberal cannot conceive of replacing.

In the three decades following 1940, the treatment model made a certain amount of sense. Unemployment remained fairly low, so that there seemed to be a place in the economy for those who wanted it—with the exception of blacks, whose exclusion was attributed to individual prejudice and was thus not regarded as systemic. Following the Second World War through the 1960s, treatment specialists of all kinds entered the prison in ever-increasing numbers, with solid support from liberal intellectuals. The deterioration of the economy in the 1970s, with its seemingly intractably high levels of inflation and unemployment, had destroyed the material base for the rehabilitative ideal (at the same time that prisoner politicization and rebellion destroyed its organizational basis). The hope that all who want a job can have one if they can be given appropriate training or resolve their psychological conflicts is no longer even remotely believable.

With no plausible solution to the problem of crime or racial oppression (much of the liberal intellectual community has abandoned its earlier commitment to integration in the face of Northern white opposition to school busing, the white flight to the suburbs, and affirmative action programs), the most liberals can offer is a system of punishment that promises to do a little less damage. This intellectual collapse has been one factor in the legislative developments we discuss below.

Modification of Programmatic Goal

A second line of development has been the modification of important features of the *Struggle for Justice* proposals to help enable implementation. Our concern with this lies not with the minor modifications that are inevitably required to realize abstract principles, but with those that are sufficiently drastic to jeopardize the initial goal of eliminating discrimination and unjustified disparities in sentencing. Thus, Richard McGee, Norval Morris, and David Fogel all advocate an end to indefinite sentences and propose sentencing to fixed terms (with allowance for good behavior),[28] but none of them favors an end to plea bargaining even though it is widely conceded that this practice is a major source of disparity in sentencing.[29]

If one is concerned with the immediate implementation of the proposals, this flexibility is understandable, even astute. As noted above, an end to plea bargaining would probably require decriminalization on a scale that is politically inconceivable or a growth in the magnitude of resources allocated to enforcement that is fiscally inconceivable. Even if these apparently insurmountable obstacles could somehow be overcome, the elimination of plea bargaining would still pose grave problems of implementation.

There may, of course, be some benefits for defendants or prisoners even in a highly restricted version of the justice model. The elimination of uncertainty concerning the date of release from prison is a positive step, and the small number of prisoners who serve unusually long sentences for reasons unrelated to offense are likely to get out sooner. But these benefits will affect only a fairly limited number of prisoners and will at best make a modest contribution to the elimination of class-based and racial disparities in sentencing. Even less will they help to build a larger radical movement.

Legislative Implementation

Within the past three years, several states have restructured their sentencing provisions, ostensibly along justice model lines and with the encouragement and support of justice model advocates. Arizona, California, Illinois, Indiana, Maine, and Minnesota have all passed new sentencing bills, and legislation to restructure sentencing or eliminate parole is under consideration or has recently been considered in at least a dozen states. A bill to reform federal sentencing[30] was introduced into the United States Senate by Senators Kennedy and McClellan with the support of the Carter administration and was passed early in 1978.

In one way or another all the bills seek to restrict the range of sentences permitted for a given offense by proportioning the penalty to the severity of the offense, at least roughly, and by creating mechanisms for specifying the aggravating and mitigating circumstances that can increase or decrease the sentence within a permitted range.[31] (This last feature is present in only some of the new legislation.)

From the point of view articulated in *Struggle for Justice*, a number of features of the new sentencing bills are disappointing. First, the substantive features of the criminal codes remain unchanged. Neither substantial decriminalization of lesser offenses nor criminalization of serious capitalist offenses or of government repression has taken place. Indeed, the federal Criminal Code Reform Act of 1977 has drawn wide criticism for its expansion of government powers of political repression. Thus the substantive class, political, and cultural biases of existing law have not been reduced.

Second, some of the bills retain rehabilitative and predictive criteria. In Maine, a prisoner given a fixed sentence can be resentenced at the request of the Department of Corrections on the basis of his or her progress toward a noncriminal way of life. California's S.B. 42 rewards participation in rehabilitation programs, though it limits the reduction in sentence to one month for every eight served. Where judicial discretion is comparatively unconstrained, as in Indiana or Maine, where aggravating and mitigating factors are not legislatively prescribed, nothing is to prevent judges from considering predictive criteria.

Third, prosecutors and judges retain substantial discretion under most of the new laws. No attempt has been made in any of the recent legislation to constrain the discretion of the prosecutor in charging the defendant, or to eliminate plea bargaining. In Maine, the elimination of the parole board enhanced judicial discretion in sentencing. Under S.B. 42 in California, the guidelines provided for the judge's decision to grant or withhold probation are extremely vague and are unlikely to reduce disparities in the granting of probation to a significant extent. The bill left judges with the option of imposing consecutive or concurrent sentences at their discretion, as well as to enhance or not to enhance the sentence because of other circumstances (prior prison terms, possession of a deadly weapon). Nevertheless, California prosecutors initiated a campaign to widen this discretion on the ground that when sentences are restricted too narrowly by law, prosecutors cannot offer defendants a sufficient incentive to coerce a guilty plea. Joined by criminal justice functionaries, they have succeeded in having S.B. 42 amended in ways that further enhance prosecutorial and judicial discretion.[32] Additional amending legislation, adopted in 1978 (S.B. 709), extends these discretionary powers even farther.

Fourth, the new legislation will increase rather than reduce sentence lengths. Although a definite prediction about how sentence lengths in California will change cannot yet be made because of uncertainty as to how prosecutors and judges will make use of their discretionary powers, preliminary projections based on S.B. 42 suggest that the average time spent in prison might increase somewhat.[33] Sheldon Messinger and Phillip Johnson concluded that the first piece of amending legislation, A.B. 476, would substantially increase sentence lengths,[34] while S.B. 709 raised the maximum penalties permitted in forty major crime categories and established provisions requiring multiple sentences to be served consecutively rather than concurrently. These amendments will increase average time spent in prison.

Trends toward increased sentence lengths have not been restricted to California. Indiana has established extremely high maximum sentences (e.g., forty years for noncapital murder, plus twenty years for aggravation or less ten in mitigation; thirty years for a serious narcotics offense, plus twenty or minus ten), with an additional thirty years possible for multiple offenders. Time served is up in Maine, and legislation recently introduced in the Ohio legislature will increase sentence lengths. In Colorado, a new sentencing act was vetoed by the governor on the grounds that the sentences it provided were too short. Following a gubernatorial veto in Minnesota on similar grounds, new legislation was adopted in which sentencing guidelines are to be determined by an appointed commission. In Illinois, Governor Thompson successfully insisted that legislation to abolish parole release and reform sentencing incorporate high minimum sentences for specified offenses.

In the federal system, parole guidelines adopted administratively have been advertised as based on existing sentencing practices. Janet Schmidt, however, finds that the guidelines actually set sentences higher than previous parole board practice.[35] Then, in 1976, the Federal Parole Commission issued new guidelines extending the time to be served in prison in nine offense categories on the grounds that "the public welfare would best be protected by increased periods of incarceration for certain prisoners." It also increased the severity with which several offense types were to be regarded (though the severity classification of marijuana offenses was reduced).[36] In New York City, sentence lengths have also increased in the absence of legislation. According to William Gallagher, director of administration for the city's court system, "The average time for a person convicted of a felony in the city has doubled, if not tripled, in the last few years," in response to public pressure and administrative measures that enhance prosecutorial power.[37]

On a number of key issues, then, legislative and administrative reform has veered sharply away from the program outlined by justice model advocates. The substance of the criminal code has not been revised; coerced rehabilitation and sentencing on the basis of predictive criteria have not been eliminated; substantial discretion in sentencing remains; and sentence lengths have been increased, not reduced. The changes that have occurred bear only a superficial resemblance to the principles they purport to embody. While some of these changes may bring limited benefits to some defendants or prisoners, these benefits must be weighed against other provisions that are profoundly detrimental to the interests of prisoners.

Notes

1. Frances A. Allen, *The Borderland of Criminal Justice* (Chicago: University of Chicago Press, 1964); Norval Morris and Colin Howard, *Studies in Criminal Law* (Oxford, England: Clarendon Press, 1964); and C. S. Lewis, "The Humanitarian Theory of Punishment," in *God in the Dock: Essays on Theology and Ethics*, Walter Hooper, ed. (Grand Rapids, Mich.: Eerdmans, 1970).

2. Karl Menninger, *The Crime of Punishment* (New York: Viking, 1968).

3. Ramsey Clark, *Crime in America: Observations on its Nature, Causes, Prevention and Control* (New York: Simon & Schuster, 1970).

4. President's Commission on Law Enforcement and Administration of Justice, *The Challenge of Crime in a Free Society* (Washington, D.C.: Govt. Printing Office, 1967).

5. Richard A. Berk and Peter H. Rossi, *Prison Reform and State Elites* (Cambridge, Mass.: Ballinger, 1977).

6. AFSC Working Party, *Struggle for Justice: A Report on Crime and Punishment in America* (New York: Hill and Wang, 1971).

7. Jessica Mitford, *Kind and Usual Punishment: The Prison Business* (New York: Knopf, 1973), pp. 86–87; and Robert J. Minton, Jr., *Inside: Prison American Style* (New York: Random House, 1971), pp. 209–325.

8. Douglas Lipton, Robert Martinson, and Judith Wilks, *The Effectiveness of Correctional Treatment: A Survey of Treatment Evaluation Studies* (New York: Praeger, 1975).

9. AFSC Working Party, *Struggle for Justice*, pp. 158–59.

10. The contrast between earlier penal reform efforts and the AFSC ap-

proach is exemplified by the composition of the AFSC Working Party: Few if any official commissions on criminal justice include former prisoners; the AFSC Working Party contained several.

11. AFSC Working Party, *Struggle for Justice*, pp. 157–58.

12. Ibid., pp. 9, 12–13, 16.

13. The first-named author of this paper.

14. One can see in this perspective the influence of Andre Gorz, *Strategy for Labor: A Radical Proposal* (Boston: Beacon, 1969), whose ideas about how to revitalize the European Left were influential within the American New Left and among several members of the AFSC Working Party.

15. Federal Judge James Doyle, Western District of Wisconsin, in Morales v. Schmidt, 340 F. Supp. 544 (W.D. Wis. 1972).

16. The analysis can be criticized for imprecision concerning the class nature of American society, oversimplification of historical materials, vagueness as to the characteristics of the more egalitarian and pluralistic society held out as an ideal, and possible overstatement of the extent to which racial and class differences in sentencing outcomes are the product of discrimination on the part of individual decision makers against individuals within offense categories. These limitations in part reflect the intellectual limitations of the New Left during the period when the book was written, and in part the political diversity of the Working Party itself, which stood in the way of agreement on some of these questions. Thus, Dean Clarke, "Marxism, Justice and the Justice Model," *Contemporary Crises*, January 1978, pp. 27–62, is quite accurate in characterizing the criticism in *Struggle for Justice* as moral and empirical rather than analytical.

17. Edith Flynn, "Turning Judges into Robots," *Trial Magazine*, March 1976. The influence of *Struggle for Justice* on more recent work in this field has also been noted by Tony Platt and Paul Takagi, "Intellectuals for Law and Order: A Critique of the New 'Realists,' " *Crime and Social Justice*, Fall–Winter, 1977, p. 7.

18. These include Mitford, *Kind and Usual Punishment;* Richard A. McGee, "A New Look at Sentencing: Part II," *Federal Probation*, September 1974, p. 3; Norval Morris, *The Future of Imprisonment* (Chicago: University of Chicago Press, 1974); Ramsey Clark and David Rudenstine, *Prison without Walls: Report on New York Parole* (New York: Praeger, 1975); David Fogel, *". . . We Are the Living Proof . . . ": The Justice Model of Corrections* (Cincinnati: Anderson, 1975); John P. Conrad, "We Should Never Have Promised a Hospital," *Federal Probation*, December 1975, pp. 3–8; David Stanley, *Prisoners among Us: The Problem of Parole* (Washington, D.C.: Brookings Institution, 1976); Twentieth Century Fund Task Froce, *Fair and Certain Punishment* (New York: McGraw-Hill, 1976); and Andrew von Hirsch, *Doing Justice: The Choice of Punishments* (New York: Hill and Wang, 1976).

19. Michael S. Serrill, "Determinate Sentencing: History, Theory, Debate," *Corrections Magazine*, September 1977, p. 11.

20. Marvin Zalman, "The Rise and Fall of the Indeterminate Sentence, Part III," *Wayne Law Review*, March 1978, p. 857. These developments cannot be attributed to the influence of *Struggle for Justice* alone. Judge Marvin Frankel, *Criminal Sentences* (New York: Hill and Wang, 1972), independently criticized unfettered discretion in sentencing; the Kafkaesque operation of an ostensibly therapeutic institution for defective delinquents operating under an indeterminate sentencing law was documented by E. Barrett Prettyman, Jr., "The Indeterminate Sentence and the Right to Treatment,"

American Criminal Law Review, 1972, p. 7; and, as noted by April Kestell Cassou and Brian Taugher, "Determinate Sentencing in California: The New Numbers Game," *Pacific Law Journal,* January 1978, p. 5, beginning in 1972 the California Supreme Court began to impose limited elements of procedural due process on parole decision making and to fashion a doctrine of proportionality in sentencing. Within the last two years, however, a few dissenting voices from within the academy have been raised, among them Franklin Zimring, "Making the Punishment Fit the Crime," *Hastings Center Report,* December 1976, pp. 13–17; Benedict S. Alper and Joseph W. Weiss, "The Mandatory Sentence: Recipe for Retribution," *Federal Probation,* December 1977, pp. 15–20; Donald R. Cressey, "Criminological Theory, Social Science, and the Repression of Crime," *Criminology,* August 1978, pp. 171–92; and Daniel Glaser, "The Counterproductivity of Conservative Thinking about Crime," *Criminology,* August 1978, pp. 209–24.

21. von Hirsch, *Doing Justice.*

22. Clarke, "Marxism, Justice and the Justice Model," p. 53.

23. The individualistic and moralistic focus of a "justice model" even has conservative implications when used to analyze the crimes of the capitalist class: It focuses on the failings of particular individuals rather than on the dynamics of the social system. It seems to imply that the injuries caused by corporate action are to be remedied by replacing corrupt or greedy executives with others who are honest, altruistic, or socially conscious, rather than the abolition of corporate capitalism. Its attention to legally defined crimes of the capitalist class seems to suggest that, if capitalists conformed to their own rules, if they were "good capitalists," all would be well; in other words, it is not the normal functioning of capitalism that causes trouble, but its abnormal functioning.

24. As a member of the staff of the Committee for the Study of Incarceration, the first-named author was present at all of its meetings. The assertion in the text is based on first-hand observation.

25. von Hirsch, *Doing Justice,* p. 143.

26. Ibid., p. 149. This difference is revealed in the titles of the two books. The title of the AFSC report indicates that justice is to be achieved through "struggle," while the title of the CSI report suggests that justice is simply something to be "done"—presumably by the prosecutors and judges who run the present system. It is conceived as a purely administrative matter, not involving social conflict. Implementation is not seen as the outcome of pressure from below that proponents help to organize, but is to be achieved by persuading legislators and other influential persons of the merits of the approach. Several of the CSI members and its executive director have been active in high-level lobbying and drafting of legislation to implement sentencing reform.

27. Willard Gaylin and David Rothman, in von Hirsch, *Doing Justice,* pp. xxxix-xl.

28. McGee, "A New Look at Sentencing"; Morris, *The Future of Imprisonment;* and Fogel, *". . . We Are the Living Proof . . . ".*

29. Current reform proposals are criticized on precisely these grounds by Albert Alschuler, "Sentencing Reform and Prosecutorial Power," in Proceedings of the Special Conference on Determinate Sentencing, *Determinate Sentencing: Reform or Regression?* (Washington, D.C.: Govt. Printing Office, 1978), pp. 59–88; and Caleb Foote, "Deceptive Determinate Sentencing," in Proceedings, *Determinate Sentencing: Reform or Regression?*

30. The Criminal Code Reform Act of 1977, S. 1437.

31. Useful reviews of the provisions of these acts and proposals can be found in Cassou and Taugher, "Determinate Sentencing in California"; Zalman, "The Rise and Fall of the Indeterminate Sentence"; and Stephen Gettinger, "Three States Adopt Flat Time: Others Wary," *Corrections Magazine*, September 1977, pp. 16–42.

32. Prisoner's Union, "Senate Bill 42, Where Are You?" *The Outlaw*, January-February 1977.

33. Sheldon L. Messinger and Phillip D. Johnson, "California's Determinate Sentence Statute: History and Issues," in Proceedings, *Determinate Sentencing: Reform or Regression?*

34. Ibid.

35. Janet Schmidt, *Demystifying Parole* (Lexington, Mass.: Lexington Books, 1977), p. 52.

36. Ibid., p. 142.

37. Selwyn Raab, "New York City's Judges Give More Criminals More Prison Time," *New York Times*, July 17, 1978, pp. B1, B4.

39. Recidivist Impacts of Differential Sentencing Practices for Burglary Offenders

TED BARTELL
L. THOMAS WINFREE, JR.

Few issues currently confronting social scientists elicit a wider range of responses than does the question of the effects of official sanctions, especially those sentences rendered by courts of law. Glaser (1964), for example, indicates that in most follow-up studies of persons placed on probation, 70 percent to 90 percent of the probationers exhibit a lack of further misdemeanor or felony activities for as long a period as five years. Glaser also reviewed eight major studies of inmates released from prisons in the United States. After follow-up periods ranging from six months to ten years, the rate of return to prison varied from a low of 20 to a high of 44 percent. While these data are not directly comparable, they would tend to lend support to the contention that the label of convict, or minimally the prison experience, has a negative impact on chances of post-sanction survival.

Other studies that have more directly compared released incarcerees and probationers have similarly indicated that releasees have higher rates of subsequent arrest and commitment than probationers (Uniform Crime Reports, 1968; Levin, 1971). However, Tittle (1975) questions the validity of any conclusions drawn from comparisons of the recidivism rates of released incarcerees and probationers.

Tittle (1975) does not believe that the nature of the evidence warrants the total support of the labeling argument that incarcerees fail as a result of the successful attachment of a label. Rather, the differences in recidivism rates are more likely a result of a selection process prior to sentencing. He contends, drawing support from Wilkins (1969), that only the best risks are placed on probation and therefore have lower rates of recidivism. Finally, Tittle notes that while the existing data are more consistent with sanctions as deterrents, sanctions are probably a two-edged sword. At times sanctions actually deter persons from further crime. At other times sanctions label the offender and probably produce increased recidivism as a consequence for certain types of offenders. And not infrequently they do neither.

The question for the researcher to probe is an obvious but difficult one: What makes the difference? Or in the case at hand, what difference does the type of sentence make on the recidivism of any particular offender? This question is doubly critical when one considers not only the widely recognized financial costs of imprisonment but also the social and personal costs, if the supporters of labeling are correct. If, as Neil (1974) contends, a large portion of those offenders sent to prison would make good candidates for probation and if prisons have little or no deterrent effect on their former charges, then reconsideration of current sentencing practices is in order.

The current research represents an attempt to explore this question. Using the specific case of the burglary offender, there was an attempt to discover what makes the difference in post-sanction survival. The answer to this question, while it will not resolve the deterrence/labeling controversy, should nevertheless provide us with a better understanding of the differential effects of sentencing on the criminal offender at various stages of a deviant career. As will be demonstrated, it makes a difference (a) to whom the sanction is applied; and (b) at what stage in the deviant career alternative sanctions are utilized.

RESEARCH DESIGN

Burglary offenders sentenced in Albuquerque in 1971 were chosen for this study of the effects of sentencing for several reasons. First, burglary offenders constitute the highest number of commitments and releases in the New Mexico State Penitentiary in any given year, and thus provide a population from which to draw an adequate sample for intensive analysis. Second, while the normal sentence for convicted burglars is two to ten years, first-time offenders usually average about one year in prison. It was felt that choosing a group of offenders convicted for burglary in 1971 would thus allow ample time for possible recidivism. Third, it was known from other sources that burglary convictions in the Second Judicial District result in roughly equal numbers of offenders being placed on probation and being sent to prison. This latter characteristic was extremely beneficial since we were mainly interested in comparing the long-term effects of these two types of sentences on offenders.

The data collection effort began at the District Attorney's Office where all burglary cases presented in 1971 were examined for case number, offense charged, offender's name, and date of birth. Next, rap sheets for each offender were reviewed at the Albuquerque Police Department and Bernalillo County Sheriff's Department to obtain background information on prior arrests and dispositions, as well as information on any arrests and convictions that may have occurred subsequent to the 1971 burglary conviction. Information on any subsequent imprisonment was then obtained for all persons in the study at the State Department of Corrections. Names, aliases, and dates of birth were cross-checked on each offender to assure reliable data. Once the data forms were completed and keypunched, all identifiers were removed so as to protect confidentiality of information and anonymity of subjects during the computer analysis.

Information was gathered on a total of 149 burglary cases. Of this number, 45 cases were dropped from analysis because they resulted in either acquittals or dismissals. Of the remaining 104 cases, 4 could not be tracked through the files due to insufficient identifying information.

Of the 100 cases included in the analysis, 45 resulted in probation, 34 offenders were imprisoned, and 21 offenders were given some other sentence (such as fines, restitution, drug and alcohol rehabilitation, community service, suspended or deferred sentences). Persons receiving split sentences were combined with probationers for purposes of analysis. Of all offenders, 47 percent were in the age group eighteen to twenty-one. Of the subjects, 97 percent were male, and 75 percent had pleaded guilty to the charge; 72 percent had at least one prior misdemeanor arrest in 1971, and 54 percent had at least one prior felony arrest. However, only 35 percent had ever been previously arrested for burglary, and only one-fourth of these had prior burglary convictions.

Multiple regression analyses indicated that offenders were more likely to get incarcerated sentences if (a) they had a higher number of previous arrests, and (b) they were older. This relationship held true, controlling for the possible effects of such alternative explanations as the types of burglary committed (whether residential or commercial), the arresting agency, plea, number of prior burglary arrests or convictions, number of prior convictions or incarcerations for any crime, and number of prior burglary incarcerations.

ARRESTS

In order to determine the effects of alternate sentencing types for burglary offenses in 1971, four distinct types of recidivism were analyzed: subsequent arrests for any felony, subsequent arrests for burglary, subsequent convictions for any crime, and subsequent convictions for burglary.

The single best predictor of subsequent arrest for a felony was age.

Younger persons were significantly more likely than older offenders to be arrested on a felony charge. Interestingly enough, compared to those receiving "other" sentences, *both* probationers and incarcerated offenders were less likely to be arrested subsequently on a felony count. The effects of imprisonment were somewhat stronger statistically than probation, indicating either a deterrent effect due to experience with incarceration, or the relatively shorter time the incarcerated group had been back on the streets and consequently a lower chance of being arrested.

These relationships held, controlling for number of prior arrests for burglary or all crimes, number of prior convictions for burglary or all crimes, number of prior incarcerations for burglary or all crimes, number of months imprisoned on the 1971 convictions, and manner of release from prison on the 1971 convictions (whether paroled, discharged, or maxed-out).

The two best predictors of subsequent arrest for burglary were the number of prior arrests for burglary and age. The larger the number of prior burglary arrests, the greater the probability that the offender would subsequently be arrested for burglary. Also, the younger the offender, the higher the likelihood of some subsequent burglary arrest. Type of sentence (whether probation, incarceration, or other) appeared to have no significant effect on the probability of later arrest. These relationships held, controlling for the possible effects not only of sentence type, but also of number of all prior arrests, number of prior convictions for burglary or all crimes, number of prior incarcerations for burglary or all crimes, number of months imprisoned on the 1971 conviction, and manner of release from prison.

Subsequent arrest by law enforcement authorities can be and oftentimes is simply a function of the labeling process whereby convicted felons are the first suspects in any new case. Our own inclination is to regard convictions as a somewhat "harder" measure of recidivism.

CONVICTIONS

The best predictor of subsequent conviction for any crime (including both felonies and misdemeanors) was age, with younger offenders more often being convicted of a subsequent offense. Two other variables that were related to subsequent conviction were previous incarceration for burglary and a probationary sentence. Persons with prior incarceration for burglary were less apt to be convicted of a later crime. Also, offenders who were placed on probation were less likely to be convicted subsequently of another crime. The same set of control variables was utilized in these regressions as for the equations predicting arrest.

Additional cross-tabular analyses indicated that (a) the lowest risk groups appeared to be offenders aged twenty-eight and over, regardless of sentence type (with the one exception being incarcerated persons aged twenty-eight to thirty-four who had somewhat higher recidivism rates); (b) probationers consistently did better than persons given other sentences, particularly those under twenty-two years of age; and (c) the highest risk groups were offenders aged eighteen to twenty-one who were given non-probationary sentences.

When felony convictions were isolated for further analysis, it was found that the relationships described for all convictions (felonies and misdemeanors combined) were obtained. However, one important difference was evident. The strongest predictor of lack of subsequent conviction for a felony became probation rather than age. Probationers were substantially less likely to be convicted of a subsequent felony, controlling for previous arrest record and the like.

The most important predictor of subsequent burglary convictions was the number of previous incarcerations for any crime. Persons with higher numbers of previous incarcerations were more likely to be convicted subsequently of burglary. Persons incarcerated for the 1971 conviction were also more likely to be convicted of burglary, a fact that reinforces the general observation that prisons are breeding grounds for crime. These observed relationships held, controlling for other possible influencing effects.

Age was once again found to be significantly related to convictions, with younger persons more often experiencing subsequent burglary convictions. A precipitous drop in burglary arrests around the age of thirty has been observed previously by other researchers (Glaser, 1964). Law enforcement and correctional officials also frequently remark about a recurrent "burn-out" of burglary offenders in this age group.

The variance explained by each of the several regression equations predicting the likelihood of subsequent arrest or conviction ranged from 22 percent to 30 percent.

SUMMARY AND CONCLUSION

The findings of this study, though based on small numbers of cases, seem to suggest that for persons sentenced for burglary the likelihood of subsequent conviction for a felony or for any crime is less for offenders placed on probation than for any other sentence type. Length of sentence, type of release, and number of previous arrests are essentially unrelated to subsequent rates of recidivism.

The strongest predictors of recidivism (defined as subsequent convictions for a crime) were tentatively identified as age, previous incarceration experience, and sentence type. Age was inversely related to recidivism, with younger offenders consistently experiencing relatively higher rates of subsequent conviction.

The findings for previous incarceration were mixed. Whereas previous incarceration *for a burglary* seemed to depress recidivism rates for felonies and other offenses, prior incarceration *for any crime* appeared to have the reverse effect on subsequent burglary convictions. In the latter case, both the number of previous incarcerations for any crime and incarceration for the specific burglary conviction in 1971 appeared to increase rates of subsequent burglary conviction.

One interpretation of these findings has to do with the normal progression through criminal careers. Young offenders who first get arrested and imprisoned for other crimes acquire the techniques and motivation for burglary while in prison. Upon release they are more likely to commit a burglary. If apprehended and incarcerated for this burglary conviction, they are more likely to be convicted subsequently of another burglary but less likely to be convicted of any other crime.

The findings for sentence type are clear and unequivocal. Persons placed on probation consistently had lower rates of subsequent conviction than offenders given incarceration and other sentences. This was true despite the fact that persons on probation had more time to recidivate than incarcerated offenders, since they were on the streets the full four years. The beneficial effect of probation was most pronounced among younger offenders.

These findings raise serious questions about the efficacy of current sentencing practices. Burglary offenders, it appears, are more likely to receive incarcerated sentences if they are older and have a large number of previous arrests. However, the number of prior arrests is unrelated to subsequent conviction, and older offenders are less likely to recidivate, regardless of sentence type. In fact, the one exception to this generalization for older offenders was the group aged twenty-eight to thirty-four who actually were *more* likely to recidivate following incarceration.

When one additionally estimates the economic costs of such practices—in terms of custodial costs for large numbers of inmates who if not incarcerated would put society at no greater risk, and in terms of the increased likelihood of subsequent burglary due to the social learnings acquired in prison—consideration of alternative public policies would seem to be warranted. The findings of this preliminary study suggest the desirability of extending the present research effort to (a) other crime types; (b) larger samples of cases for each type of conviction investigated; (c) multi-state tracking of sample cases to eliminate any bias due to possible differential mobility and reporting on the subsequent recidivism of offenders of varying sentence type.

References

GLASER, D. (1964) The Effectiveness of a Prison and Parole System. Indianapolis: Bobbs-Merrill.

LEVIN, M. A. (1971) "Policy evaluation and recidivism." Law and Society Rev. 6 (August): 17–46.

NEIL, T. C. (1974) "Who should go and who stay: a study of prison commitments." Criminology 12 (May): 107–113.

TITTLE, C. R. (1975) "Deterrents or labeling." Social Forces 53 (March): 399–410.

Uniform Crime Reports (1968) Crime in the United States, 1967. Washington, D.C.: Government Printing Office.

WILKINS L. T. (1969) Evaluation of Penal Measures. New York: Random House.

40. The Contemporary Prison

JOHN IRWIN

The reverberations from the 1960s left most men's prisons fragmented, tense, and often extremely violent. The old social order, with its cohesion and monotonous tranquility, did not and perhaps will never reappear. The prisoners are divided by extreme differences, distrust, and hatred. Nonwhites, especially blacks, Chicanos, and Puerto Ricans, have risen in numbers and prominence. A multitude of criminal types—dope fiends, pimps, bikers, street gang members, and very few old-time thieves—assert themselves and compete for power and respect.

Nevertheless, chaos and a complete war of all against all have not resulted. They never do. When human social organizations splinter and friction between the parts increases, people still struggle to maintain old or create new collective structures that supply them with basic social needs, particularly protection from threats of violence. Complex social forms and a high degree of order still exist among prisoners, even in the most violent and fragmented prisons, like San Quentin, but it is a "segmented order" similar to that which Gerald Suttles discovered in the Addams slum area of Chicago.[1]

This particular slum had features like many contemporary prisons. Several different, relatively poor, working-class and lower-class segments—Italians, Mexicans, Puerto Ricans, and blacks—shared the neighborhood and were generally prejudiced and hostile toward each other. In addition, this slum, like most slums, contained many persons who lacked the commitment to public morality that ordinarily promotes a high degree of safety among strangers. In this situation of distrust, people living in the Addams area employed two main strategies for increasing their safety, voluntary segregation and personalized relationships. In Suttles's words:

> First, social relations can be restricted to permit only the safest. Families can withdraw to their households where they see only close relatives. Age grading along with sex and ethnic segregation are maneuvers that will avoid at least the most unfair and likely forms of conflict and exploitation. Remaining in close proximity to the household cuts down on the range of anonymity and reduces the number of social relations.

Second, slum residents can assuage at least some of their apprehensions by a close inquiry into each other's personal character and past history. Communication, then, should be of an intimate character and aimed toward producing "personal" rather than formal relations. In turn, social relations will represent a sort of private "compact" where particularistic loyalties replace impersonal standards of worth.[2]

So it is in prison today. Races, particularly black and white, are divided and hate each other. In general, prisoners distrust most other prisoners whom they do not know well. The strategies for coping with this are similar to those employed in the Addams area. There are virtually no sex strata[3] and much less age stratification in the prison, but increasingly prisoners restrict their interaction to small friendship groups and other small social units (gangs, for example) formed with members of their own race. Other than race, prisoners retreat into small orbits based on social characteristics such as (1) criminal orientation, (2) shared preprison experiences (coming from the same town or neighborhood or having been in other prisons together), (3) shared prison interests, and (4) forced proximity in cell assignment or work.

RACIAL DIVISIONS

The hate and distrust between white and black prisoners constitute the most powerful source of divisions. After being forestalled by the moves toward unity during the prison movement, [previous] conditions and trends . . . were reestablished. Black prisoners continued to increase in numbers and assertiveness. Whites, led by the more prejudiced and violent, increasingly reacted. Hate, tension, and hostilities between the two races escalated. An Illinois black prisoner describes the posture of black prisoners toward whites.

> In the prison, the black dudes have a little masculinity game they play. It has no name, really, but I call it whup or fuck a white boy—especially the white gangsters or syndicate men, the bad juice boys, the hit men, etc. The black dudes go out of their way to make faggots out of them. And to lose a fight to a white dude is one of the worst things that can happen to a black dude. And I know that, by and far, the white cats are faggots. They will drop their pants and bend over and touch their toes and get had before they will fight. So, knowing this, what kind of men did this make us? They told us where, how, when to shit, eat, sleep.[4]

White prisoners, whether or not they were racially hostile before prison, tend to become so after experiencing prison racial frictions. Edward Bunker, who served several terms in California prisons and writes insightfully about contemporary prison processes and relationships, described a middle-class white prisoner's entrance into racial hatred:

> After 10:30, the noise dropped a decibel or two, and from the morass of sound Ron began to recognize certain voices by timbre and catch snatches of conversation. Above him, perhaps on the second tier, he picked up a gumboed black voice saying he'd like to kill all white babies, while his listener agreed it was the best way to handle the beasts—before they grew up. A year earlier, Ron would have felt compassion for anyone so consumed by hate, and whenever whites casually used "nigger" he was irked. Now he felt tentacles of hate spreading through himself—and half an hour later, he smiled when a batch of voices began chanting: "Sieg Heil! Sieg Heil! Sieg Heil!"[5]

Whites hate and, when they are not organized to resist, fear black prisoners. Carroll quoted a white prisoner in the Rhode Island prison that he studied:

> They think they're superior and they push us around all the time. Like in the dining hall. If I was late and trying to catch up with a buddy and cut in front of one of them, I'd probably get piped. But they cut in front of white men all the time and nothing happens. . . . It's the same in the wings. The tier I'm on used to be all white. Now it's 50–50 and it ain't safe for a white to walk along it. If he does, he better walk quick and keep his eyes open.[6]

The divisions and hatreds extend into the guard force and even into the administrations. Leo Carroll and Erik Olin Wright documented bias against black prisoners in administrative decisions, particularly disciplinary proceedings.[7] Black prisoners have consistently testified that white guards verbally and physically abuse them and discriminate against them.[8] Some radical commentators have suggested that guards and administrators have political motivations in their expression of racial hatred. This may be true, in some very indirect fashion. But the discrimination against blacks by white staff has a more immediate source: hatred for black prisoners. In expressing their hate, they sometimes give license to racist prisoners. Edward Bunker describes the situation in San Quentin:

> But he knew that some of the license given tough white and Chicano convicts by certain other guards was because of the racial conflict. Blacks had killed several guards in the three tough prisons during the past two years and guards who had once been mild bigots were now outright racists. Certain of them would frisk a white or Chicano convict, feel a shiv and pass the man by. It was an unholy alliance, alien to all of Earl's values.[9]

White and black prisoners do not mix in informal prisoner groups, and many form groups for the purpose of expressing racial hatred and protecting their friends from the other race. A wife of a San Quentin prisoner described her husband's drift toward organized racial hatred: "He didn't used to be prejudiced but now he hates blacks. He and some other white friends formed an American National Socialists group which I guess is a nazi group because they hate blacks so much."[10]

Like the Addams area, the public spaces are divided by the different racial groups, particularly white and black prisoners. . . . Edward Bunker described the patterns in San Quentin:

> The blacks, however, congregated along the north cellhouse wall, an area nicknamed "Nairobi." A decade of race wars had made it impossible to relax without a territorial imperative.
>
> . . . Blacks turned into one row, while whites and Chicanos turned into another. When their row filled before that of the blacks, they started another. Official segregation had ended a decade earlier; the regulations now said that convicts could enter any of three rows but nobody crossed lines and nobody wanted to. Racism was a mass obsession that infected everyone and there was continual race war. So, the mess hall had a row of blacks, followed by two or three rows of whites and Chicanos, then another row of blacks.[11]

Other minority groups, such as Chicanos, Puerto Ricans, Chinese, American Indians, and French Canadians, relate to whites and blacks in a more complex fashion. For instance, Chicanos in California prisons are more hostile toward black than toward white prisoners. White prisoners generally fear, distrust, and dislike Chicanos, because Chicanos speak Spanish or Calo and are believed to have a tendency to attack other prisoners with relatively less provocation than members of other groups. However, most white prisoners respect them for their toughness and do not threaten or derogate other white prisoners who befriend, hang around, or identify with Chicanos. Many white and Chicano prisoners have associated with each other in the "streets" and other joints and still maintain close friendship ties, even in the racially divided prison milieu. Puerto Rican, American Indian, French Canadian, and other racial or ethnic minorities have similar ambivalent positions in the complex racial matrix.

VIOLENT CLIQUES AND GANGS

In many men's prisons today, groups of prisoners regularly rob and attack other prisoners and retaliate when members of their clique or gang have been threatened or attacked. This has intensified the fear and widened the gap between prisoners, particularly between prisoners of different races. Presently these groups—which range from racially hostile cliques of reform school graduates, friends from the streets, biker club members, or tough convicts to large, relatively organized gangs—dominate several prisons.

Prisons have always contained violence-prone individuals, who were kept in check by the elders and the code enforced by the elders. In the 1950s and 1960s, small cliques of young hoodlums, such as the lowriders described earlier, hung around the yard and other public places together, talked shit (loudly bragged), played the prison dozens, occasionally insulted, threatened, attacked, and robbed unprotected weaker prisoners, and squabbled with other lowrider groups, particularly those of other races. Billy "Hands" Robinson, a prison writer, characterized a group of these youngsters in an Illinois prison:

> There were four other dudes in the hole cell they put him in when he first got there, all of them young, what Tank called gang-bangers. He didn't like or understand the youngsters but the joint was full of them now and he couldn't avoid them. They were like a herd of animals, he thought. They wolf-packed people and were nothing as individuals.[12]

Most of these early lowriders were young juvenile prison graduates and fuck-ups (unskilled, lower- and working-class criminals) who had low respect among older, "solid" criminals and regular convicts. But they were a constant threat to the other prisoners who were trying to maintain peace. For most of the 1950s and 1960s, other prisoners disparaged, ignored, and avoided the lowriders, whose activities were kept in check by the general consensus against them and the belief (accepted by the lowriders and most other prisoners) that if the lowriders went too far, the older prison regulars would use force, including assassination, to control them.[13]

Lowriders steadily increased in numbers. In the states with large cities whose ghettos bulged during the 1950s and 1960s and whose youth prison systems expanded to accommodate the increase in youth crime, the adult prisons began to receive growing numbers of tough youth prison graduates and criminally unskilled, more openly aggressive young urban toughs. They could no longer be controlled. They entered the growing racial melee and stepped up their attacks and robberies on other prisoners. When there were no successful countermoves against them, they took over the convict world and particularly one of its most important activities: the sub rosa economic enterprises.[14]

In different states the young hoodlums arrived at the adult prisons with different backgrounds and consequently formed different types of groups in the prison. In California the takeover began in 1967 in

San Quentin when a tightly knit clique of young Chicanos, who had known each other on the streets of Los Angeles and in other prisons, began to take drugs forcefully from other prisoners (mostly Chicano). The clique gained a reputation for toughness and the label of "the Mexican Mafia." Other aspiring young Chicano hoodlums became interested in affiliating with the Mafia, and, according to rumor, the Mafia members insisted that initiates murder another prisoner. This rumor and the actual attacks aroused and consolidated a large number of "independent" Chicanos, who planned to eliminate the Mafia members. On the planned day, the other Chicanos pursued known Mafia members through San Quentin, attempting to assassinate them. Several dozen prisoners were seriously wounded and one was killed in this day-long battle, but the Mafia held its ground, won many of the knife fights, and was not eliminated. After this unsuccessful attempt, some of the formerly independent Chicanos, particularly from Texas and the small towns in California, who had been in conflict with Los Angeles Chicanos for decades, formed a countergroup: La Nuestra Familia. In the ensuing years, the conflict between the two Chicano gangs increased and spread to other prisons and even to the outside, where the gangs have tried to penetrate outside drug trafficking.[15] The attacks and counterattacks between members of the two gangs became so frequent that the prison administrators attempted to segregate the gangs, designating two prisons, San Quentin and Folsom, for the Mafia and two, Soledad and Tracy, for La Nuestra Familia. When Chicanos enter the California prison system, they are asked their gang affiliation; if they are to be sent to any of those four prisons (which are the medium- to maximum-security prisons), they are sent to one dominated by their gang.

The Chicano gangs' escalation of robbery, assault, and murder also consolidated and expanded black and white lowrider groups, some of which had already been involved in similar violent and rapacious activities, but on a smaller scale. Two gangs, the Aryan Brotherhood and the Black Guerilla Family, rose in prominence and violent activities. Eventually, the Aryan Brotherhood formed an alliance with the Mafia and the Black Guerilla Family with La Nuestra Familia, and a very hostile and tentative stalemate prevailed. However, peace has not returned. Other racist cliques among the black and white prisoners occasionally attack other prisoners; the Chicano gangs still fight each other; and there seem to be factions within the Chicano gangs themselves. Although the California prisons have passed their peak of violence, the violence and fear are still intense.

Notes

1. Gerald Suttles, *The Social Order of the Slum* (Chicago: University of Chicago Press, 1968).

2. Ibid., p. 8.

3. The prison-identified homosexuals—the queens, punks, and kids—do constitute a very small, separate stratum.

4. Billy "Hands" Robinson, "Love: A Hard Legged Triangle," *Black Scholar*, September 1971, p. 29.

5. *Animal Factory* (New York: Viking Press, 1977), p. 92. This novel, in which Bunker employs his extensive direct experience and excellent sociological imagination, is used here as a source of data for San Quentin.

6. Leo Carroll, *Hacks, Blacks, and Cons* (Lexington, Mass.: Lexington Books, 1974), p. 147.

7. Ibid., chap. 6; Erik Olin Wright, *The Politics of Punishment* (New York: Harper & Row, 1973), p. 114.

8. *Attica: The Official Report of the New York State Special Commission on Attica* (New York: Praeger, 1972) has the most convincing reports on such testimony.

9. *Animal Factory*, p. 42.

10. Interview, San Francisco, January 1978.

11. *Animal Factory*, p. 20.

12. "Love: A Hard Legged Triangle," p. 39.

13. This was usually the case, but Richard McCleery reported that a group of young reform school graduates, allied with older, violent prisoners, took over the prison in Hawaii during a period of disorganization by a changeover in administration and the introduction of rehabilitation ("The Governmental Process and Informal Social Control," in Donald Cressey, ed., *The Prison* [New York: Holt, Rinehart and Winston, 1961], p. 177).

14. Virgil Williams and Mary Fish use this label in the best study to appear on prisoner economic systems: *Convicts, Codes and Contraband* (Cambridge: Ballinger Publishing, 1974).

15. The policy agencies in California have argued and produced some evidence that activities of the prison gangs have splashed out of the prisons. The gangs are believed to struggle with each other, with factions within the gangs, and against other drug dealers. Many outside assassinations have been blamed on the gangs. "Pierce [a police lieutenant] said authorities believe a feud between two gangs, the Mexican Mafia and La Nuestra Familia, to be responsible for a recent chain of crimes in the area" (*San Francisco Chronicle*, March 7, 1977, p. 20).

41. What Works? Questions and Answers about Prison Reform

ROBERT MARTINSON

In the past several years, American prisons have gone through one of their recurrent periods of strikes, riots, and other disturbances. Simultaneously, and in consequence, the articulate public has entered another one of its sporadic fits of attentiveness to the condition of our prisons and to the perennial questions they pose about the nature of crime and the uses of punishment. The result has been a widespread call for "prison reform," i.e., for "reformed" prisons which will produce "reformed" convicts. Such calls are a familiar feature of American prison history. American prisons, perhaps more than those of any other country, have stood or fallen in public esteem according to their ability to fulfill their promise of rehabilitation.

One of the problems in the constant debate over "prison reform" is that we have been able to draw very little on any systematic empirical knowledge about the success or failure that we have met when we *have* tried to rehabilitate offenders, with various treatments and in various institutional and noninstitutional settings. The field of penology has produced a voluminous research literature on this subject, but until recently there has been no comprehensive review of this literature and no attempt to bring its findings to bear, in a useful way, on the general question of "What works?" My purpose in this essay is to sketch an answer to that question.

THE TRAVAILS OF A STUDY

In 1966, the New York State Governor's Special Committee on Criminal Offenders recognized their need for such an answer. The committee was organized on the premise that prisons could rehabilitate, that the prisons of New York were not in fact making a serious effort at rehabilitation, and that New York's prisons should be converted from their existing custodial basis to a new rehabilitative one. The problem for the committee was that there was no available guidance on the question of what had been shown to be the most effective means of rehabilitation. My colleagues and I were hired by the committee to remedy this defect in our knowledge; our job was to undertake a comprehensive survey of what was known about rehabilitation.

In 1968, in order to qualify for federal funds under the Omnibus Crime Control and Safe Streets Act, the state established a planning organization, which acquired from the Governor's Committee the responsibility for our report. But by 1970, when the project was formally completed, the state had changed its mind about the worth and proper use of the information we had gathered. The Governor's Committee had begun by thinking that such information was a necessary basis for any reforms that might be undertaken; the state planning agency ended by viewing the study as a document whose disturbing conclusions posed a serious threat to the programs which, in the meantime, they had determined to carry forward. By the spring of 1972—fully a year after I had re-edited the study for final publication—the state had not only failed to publish it, but had also refused to give me permission to publish it on my own. The document itself would still not be available to me or to the public today had not Joseph Alan Kaplon, an attorney, subpoenaed it from the state for use as evidence in a case before the Bronx Supreme Court.[1]

During the time of my efforts to get the study released, reports of it began to be widely circulated, and it acquired something of an underground reputation. But this article is the first published account, albeit a brief one, of the findings contained in that 1,400-page manuscript.

What we set out to do in this study was fairly simple, though it turned into a massive task. First we undertook a six-month search of the literature for any available reports published in the English language on attempts at rehabilitation that had been made in our corrections systems and those of other countries from 1945 through 1967. We then picked from that literature all those studies whose findings were interpretable—that is, whose design and execution met the conventional standards of social science research. Our criteria were rigorous but hardly esoteric: A study had to be an evaluation of a treatment method, it had to employ an independent measure of the improvement secured by that method, and it had to use some control group, some untreated individuals with whom the treated ones could be compared. We excluded studies only for methodological reasons: They presented insufficient data, they were only preliminary, they presented only a summary of findings and did not allow a reader to evaluate those findings, their results were confounded by extraneous factors, they used unreliable measures, one could not understand their descriptions of the treatment in question, they drew spurious conclusions from their data, their samples were undescribed or too small or provided no true comparability between treated and untreated groups, or they had used inappropriate statistical tests and did not provide enough information for the reader to recompute the data. Using these standards, we drew from the total number of studies 231 acceptable ones, which we not only analyzed ourselves but summarized in detail so that a reader of our analysis would be able to compare it with his independent conclusions.

These treatment studies use various measures of offender improvement: recidivism rates (that is, the rates at which offenders return to crime), adjustment to prison life, vocational success, educational achievement, personality and attitude change, and general adjustment to the outside community. We included all of these in our study; but in these pages I will deal only with the effects of rehabilitative treatment on recidivism, the phenomenon which reflects most directly how well our present treatment programs are performing the task of rehabilitation. The use of even this one measure brings with it enough methodological complications to make a clear reporting of the findings most difficult. The groups that are studied, for instance, are exceedingly disparate, so that it is hard to tell whether what "works" for one kind of offender also works for others. In addition, there has been little attempt to replicate studies; therefore one cannot be certain how stable and reliable the various findings are. Just as important, when the various studies use the term "recidivism rate," they may in fact be talking about somewhat different measures of offender behavior—i.e., "failure" measures such as arrest rates or parole violation rates, or "success" measures such as favorable discharge from parole or probation. And not all of these measures correlate very highly with one another. These difficulties will become apparent again and again in the course of this discussion.

With these caveats, it is possible to give a rather bald summary of our findings: *With few and isolated exceptions, the rehabilitative efforts that have been reported so far have had no appreciable effect on recidivism.* Studies that have been done since our survey was completed do not present any major grounds for altering that original conclusion. What follows is an attempt to answer the questions and challenges that might be posed to such an unqualified statement.

EDUCATION AND VOCATIONAL TRAINING

1. *Isn't it true that a correctional facility running a truly rehabilitative program—one that prepares inmates for life on the outside through education and vocational training—will turn out more suc-*

cessful individuals than will a prison which merely leaves its inmates to rot?

If this *is* true, the fact remains that there is very little empirical evidence to support it. Skill development and education programs are in fact quite common in correctional facilities, and one might begin by examining their effects on young males, those who might be thought most amenable to such efforts. A study by New York State (1964) found that for young males as a whole, the degree of success achieved in the regular prison academic education program, as measured by changes in grade achievement levels, made no significant difference in recidivism rates. The only exception was the relative improvement, compared with the sample as a whole: greater progress was made in the top 7 percent of the participating population—those who had high I.Q.'s, had made good records in previous schooling, and who also made good records of academic progress in the institution. And a study by Glaser (1964) found that while it was true that, when one controlled for sentence length, more attendance in regular prison academic programs slightly decreased the subsequent chances of parole violation, this improvement was not large enough to outweigh the associated disadvantage for the "long-attenders": Those who attended prison school the longest also turned out to be those who were in prison the longest. Presumably, those getting the most education were also the worst parole risks in the first place.[2]

Studies of special education programs aimed at vocational or social skill development, as opposed to conventional academic education programs, report similarly discouraging results and reveal additional problems in the field of correctional research. Jacobson (1965) studied a program of "skill re-education" for institutionalized young males, consisting of ten weeks of daily discussions aimed at developing problem-solving skills. The discussions were led by an adult who was thought capable of serving as a role model for the boys, and they were encouraged to follow the example that he set. Jacobson found that overall, the program produced no improvement in recidivism rates. There was only one special subgroup which provided an exception to this pessimistic finding: If boys in the experimental program decided afterwards to go on to take three or more regular prison courses, they did better upon release than "control" boys who had done the same. (Of course, it also seems likely that experimental boys who did *not* take these extra courses did *worse* than their controls.)

Zivan (1966) also reported negative results from a much more ambitious vocational training program at the Children's Village in Dobbs Ferry, New York. Boys in his special program were prepared for their return to the community in a wide variety of ways. First of all, they were given, in sequence, three types of vocational guidance:

"assessment counseling," "development counseling," and "preplacement counseling." In addition, they participated in an "occupational orientation," consisting of role-playing, presentations via audio-visual aids, field trips, and talks by practitioners in various fields of work. Furthermore, the boys were prepared for work by participating in the Auxiliary Maintenance Corps, which performed various chores in the institution; a boy might be promoted from the Corps to the Work Activity Program, which "hired" him, for a small fee, to perform various artisans' tasks. And finally, after release from Children's Village, a boy in the special program received supportive after-care and job placement aid.

None of this made any difference in recidivism rates. Nevertheless, one must add that it is impossible to tell whether this failure lay in the program itself or in the conditions under which it was administered. For one thing, the education department of the institution itself was hostile to the program; they believed instead in the efficacy of academic education. This staff therefore tended to place in the pool from which experimental subjects were randomly selected mainly "multi-problem" boys. This by itself would not have invalidated the experiment as a test of vocational training for this particular type of youth, but staff hostility did not end there; it exerted subtle pressures of disapproval throughout the life of the program. Moreover, the program's "after-care" phase also ran into difficulties; boys who were sent back to school before getting a job often received advice that conflicted with the program's counseling, and boys actually looking for jobs met with the frustrating fact that the program's personnel, despite concerted efforts, simply could not get businesses to hire the boys.

We do not know whether these constraints, so often found in penal institutions, were responsible for the program's failure; it might have failed anyway. All one can say is that this research failed to show the effectiveness of special vocational training for young males.

The only clearly positive report in this area comes from a study by Sullivan (1967) of a program that combined academic education with special training in the use of IBM equipment. Recidivism rates after one year were only 48 percent for experimentals, as compared with 66 percent for controls. But when one examines the data, it appears that this difference emerged only between the controls and those who had successfully *completed* the training. When one compares the control group with all those who had been *enrolled* in the program, the difference disappears. Moreover, during this study the random assignment procedure between experimental and control groups seems to have broken down, so that towards the end, better risks had a greater chance of being assigned to the special program.

In sum, many of these studies of young males are extremely hard to interpret because of flaws in research design. But it can safely be said that they provide us with no clear evidence that education or skill development programs have been successful.

TRAINING ADULT INMATES

When one turns to adult male inmates, as opposed to young ones, the results are even more discouraging. There have been six studies of this type; three of them report that their programs, which ranged from academic to prison work experience, produced no significant differences in recidivism rates, and one—by Glaser (1964)—is almost impossible to interpret because of the risk differentials of the prisoners participating in the various programs.

Two studies—by Schnur (1948) and by Saden (1962)—*do* report a positive difference from skill development programs. In one of them, the Saden study, it is questionable whether the experimental and control groups were truly comparable. But what is more interesting is that both these "positive" studies dealt with inmates incarcerated prior to or during World War II. Perhaps the rise in our educational standards as a whole since then has lessened the differences that prison education or training can make. The only other interesting possibility emerges from a study by Gearhart (1967). His study was one of those that reported vocational education to be nonsignificant in affecting recidivism rates. He did note, however, that when a trainee succeeded in finding a job related to his area of training, he had a slightly higher chance of becoming a successful parolee. It is possible, then, that skill development programs fail because what they teach bears so little relationship to an offender's subsequent life outside the prison.

One other study of adults, this one with fairly clear implications, has been performed with women rather than men. An experimental group of institutionalized women in Milwaukee was given an extremely comprehensive special education program, accompanied by group counseling. Their training was both academic and practical; it included reading, writing, spelling, business filing, child care, and grooming. Kettering (1965) found that the program made no difference in the women's rates of recidivism.

Two things should be noted about these studies. One is the difficulty of interpreting them as a whole. The disparity in the programs that were tried, in the populations that were affected, and in the institutional settings that surrounded these projects makes it hard to be sure that one is observing the same category of treatment in each case.

But the second point is that despite this difficulty, one can be reasonably sure that, so far, educational and vocational programs have not worked. We don't know why they have failed. We don't know whether the programs themselves are flawed, or whether they are incapable of overcoming the effects of prison life in general. The difficulty may be that they lack applicability to the world the inmate will face outside of prison. Or perhaps the type of educational and skill improvement they produce simply doesn't have very much to do with an individual's propensity to commit a crime. What we do know is that, to date, education and skill development have not reduced recidivism by rehabilitating criminals.

THE EFFECTS OF INDIVIDUAL COUNSELING

2. *But when we speak of a rehabilitative prison, aren't we referring to more than education and skill development alone? Isn't what's needed some way of counseling inmates, or helping them with the deeper problems that have caused their maladjustment?*

This, too, is a reasonable hypothesis; but when one examines the programs of this type that have been tried, it's hard to find any more grounds for enthusiasm than we found with skill development and education. One method that's been tried—though so far, there have been acceptable reports only of its application to young offenders—has been individual psychotherapy. For young males, we found seven such reported studies. One study, by Guttman (1963) at the Nelles School, found such treatment to be ineffective in reducing recidivism rates; another, by Rudoff (1960), found it unrelated to *institutional* violation rates, which were themselves related to parole success. It must be pointed out that Rudoff used only this indirect measure of association, and the study therefore cannot rule out the possibility of a treatment effect. A third, also by Guttman (1963) but at another institution, found that such treatment was actually related to a slightly *higher* parole violation rate; and a study by Adams (1959b and 1961b) also found a lack of improvement in parole revocation and first suspension rates.

There were two studies at variance with this pattern. One by Persons (1967) said that if a boy was judged to be "successfully" treated—as opposed to simply being subjected to the treatment experience—he did tend to do better. And there was one finding both hopeful and cautionary: At the Deuel School (Adams, 1961a), the experimental boys were first divided into two groups, those rated as "amenable" to treatment and those rated "nonamenable." Amenable boys who got the treatment did better than nontreated boys. On the other hand, "nonamenable" boys who were treated actually did *worse* than they would have done if they had received no treatment at all. It must be pointed out that Guttman (1963), dealing with younger boys in his Nelles School study, did not find such an "amenability" effect, either to the detriment of the nonamenables who were treated *or* to the benefit of the amenables who were treated. But the Deuel School study (Adams, 1961a) suggests both that there is something to be hoped for in treating properly selected amenable subjects and that if these subjects are *not* properly selected, one may not only wind up doing no good but may actually produce harm.

There have been two studies of the effects of individual psychotherapy on young incarcerated *female* offenders, and both of them (Adams 1959a, Adams 1961b) report no significant effects from the therapy. But one of the Adams studies (1959a) does contain a suggestive, although not clearly interpretable, finding: If this individual therapy was administered by a psychiatrist or a psychologist, the resulting parole suspension rate was almost two-and-a-half times *higher* than if it was administered by a social worker without this specialized training.

There has also been a much smaller number of studies of two other types of individual therapy: counseling, which is directed towards a prisoner's gaining new insight into his own problems, and casework, which aims at helping a prisoner cope with his more pragmatic immediate needs. These types of therapy both rely heavily on the empathetic relationship that is to be developed between the professional and the client. It was noted above that the Adams study (1961b) of therapy administered to girls, referred to in the discussion of individual psychotherapy, found that social workers seemed better at the job than psychologists or psychiatrists. This difference seems to suggest a favorable outlook for these alternative forms of individual therapy. But other studies of such therapy have produced ambiguous results. Bernsten (1961) reported a Danish experiment that showed that socio-psychological counseling combined with comprehensive welfare measures—job and residence placement, clothing, union and health insurance membership, and financial aid—produced an improvement among some short-term male offenders, though not those in either the highest-risk or the lowest-risk categories. On the other hand, Hood, in Britain (1966), reported generally nonsignificant results with a program of counseling for young males. (Interestingly enough, this experiment *did* point to a mechanism capable of changing recidivism rates. When boys were released from institutional care and entered the army directly, "poor risk" boys among both experimentals *and* controls did better than expected. "Good risks" did worse.)

So these foreign data are sparse and not in agreement; the American data are just as sparse. The only American study which provides a direct measure of the effects of individual counseling—a study of California's Intensive Treatment Program (California, 1958a), which was "psychodynamically" oriented—found no improvement in recidivism rates.

It was this finding of the failure of the Intensive Treatment Program which contributed to the decision in California to deemphasize individual counseling in its penal system in favor of group methods. And indeed one might suspect that the preceding reports reveal not the inadequacy of counseling as a whole but only the failure of one *type* of counseling, the individual type. *Group* counseling methods, in which offenders are permitted to aid and compare experiences with one another, might be thought to have a better chance of success. So it is important to ask what results these alternative methods have actually produced.

GROUP COUNSELING

Group counseling has indeed been tried in correctional institutions, both with and without a specifically psychotherapeutic orientation. There has been one study of "pragmatic," problem-oriented counseling on *young* institutionalized males, by Seckel (1965). This type of counseling had no significant effect. For adult males, there have been three such studies of the "pragmatic" and "insight" methods. Two (Kassebaum, 1971; Harrison, 1964) report no long-lasting significant effects. (One of these two did report a real but short-term effect that wore off as the program became institutionalized and as offenders were at liberty longer.) The third study of adults, by Shelley (1961), dealt with a "pragmatic" casework program, directed towards the educational and vocational needs of institutionalized young adult males in a Michigan prison camp. The treatment lasted for six months, and at the end of that time Shelley found an improvement in attitudes; the possession of "good" attitudes was independently found by Shelley to correlate with parole success. Unfortunately, though, Shelley was not able to measure the *direct* impact of the counseling on recidivism rates. His two separate correlations are suggestive, but they fall short of being able to tell us that it really is the counseling that has a direct effect on recidivism.

With regard to more professional group *psychotherapy*, the reports are also conflicting. We have two studies of group psychotherapy on young males. One, by Persons (1966), says that this treatment did in fact reduce recidivism. The improved recidivism rate stems from the improved performance only of those who were clinically judged to have been "successfully" treated; still, the overall result of the treatment was to improve recidivism rates for the experimental group as a whole. On the other hand, a study by Craft (1964) of young males designated "psychopaths," comparing "self-government" group psychotherapy with "authoritarian" individual counseling, found that the "group therapy" boys afterwards committed *twice* as many new offenses as the individually treated ones. Perhaps some forms of group psychotherapy work for some types of offenders but not others; a reader must draw his own conclusions, on the basis of sparse evidence.

With regard to young females, the results are just as equivocal. Adams, in his study of females (1959a), found that there was no improvement to be gained from treating girls by group rather than individual methods. A study by Taylor of borstal (reformatory) girls in New Zealand (1967) found a similar lack of any great improvement for group therapy as opposed to individual therapy or even to no therapy at all. But the Taylor study does offer one real, positive finding: When the "group therapy" girls *did* commit new offenses, these offenses were less serious than the ones for which they had originally been incarcerated.

There is a third study that does report an overall positive finding as opposed to a partial one. Truax (1966) found that girls subjected to group psychotherapy and then released were likely to spend less time reincarcerated in the future. But what is most interesting about this improvement is the very special and important circumstance under which it occurred. The therapists chosen for this program did not merely have to have the proper analytic training; they were specially chosen for their "empathy" and "nonpossessive warmth." In other words, it may well have been the therapists' special personal gifts rather than the fact of treatment itself which produced the favorable result. This possibility will emerge again when we examine the effects of other types of rehabilitative treatment later in this article.

As with the question of skill development, it is hard to summarize these results. The programs administered were various; the groups to which they were administered varied not only by sex but by age as well; there were also variations in the length of time for which the programs were carried on, the frequency of contact during that time, and the period for which the subjects were followed up. Still, one must say that the burden of the evidence is not encouraging. These programs seem to work best when they are new, when their subjects are amenable to treatment in the first place, and when the counselors are not only trained people but "good" people as well. Such findings, which would not be much of a surprise to a student of organization or personality, are hardly encouraging for a policy planner, who must adopt measures that are generally applicable, that are capable of being successfully institutionalized, and that must rely for personnel on something other than the exceptional individual.

TRANSFORMING THE INSTITUTIONAL ENVIRONMENT

3. *But maybe the reason these counseling programs don't seem to work is not that they are ineffective* per se, *but that the institutional environment outside the program is unwholesome enough to undo any good work that the counseling does. Isn't a truly successful rehabilitative institution the one where the inmate's whole environment is directed towards true correction rather than towards custody or punishment?*

This argument has not only been made, it has been embodied in several institutional programs that go by the name of "milieu therapy." They are designed to make every element of the inmate's environment a part of his treatment, to reduce the distinctions between the custodial staff and the treatment staff, to create a supportive, nonauthoritarian, and nonregimented atmosphere, and to enlist peer influence in the formation of constructive values. These programs are especially hard to summarize because of their variety; they differ, for example, in how "supportive" or "permissive" they are designed to be; in the extent to which they are combined with other treatment methods such as individual therapy, group counseling, or skill development; and in how completely the program is able to control all the relevant aspects of the institutional environment.

One might well begin with two studies that have been done of institutionalized adults, in regular prisons, who have been subjected to such treatment; this is the category whose results are the most clearly discouraging. One study of such a program, by Robison (1967), found that the therapy did seem to reduce recidivism after one year. After two years, however, this effect disappeared, and the treated convicts did no better than the untreated. Another study by Kassebaum, Ward, and Wilner (1971), dealt with a program which had been able to effect an exceptionally extensive and experimentally rigorous transformation of the institutional environment. This sophisticated study had a follow-up period of thirty-six months, and it found that the program had no significant effect on parole failure or success rates.

The results of the studies of youth are more equivocal. As for young females, one study by Adams (1966) of such a program found that it had no significant effect on recidivism; another study, by Goldberg and Adams (1964), found that such a program *did* have a positive effect. This effect declined when the program began to deal with girls who were judged beforehand to be worse risks.

As for young males, the studies may conveniently be divided into those dealing with juveniles (under sixteen) and those dealing with youths. There have been five studies of milieu therapy administered to juveniles. Two of them—by Lavlicht (1962) and by Jesness (1965)—report clearly that the program in question either had no significant effect or had a short-term effect that wore off with passing time. Jesness does report that when his experimental juveniles did commit new offenses, the offenses were less serious than those committed by controls. A third study of juveniles, by McCord (1953) at the Wiltwyck School, reports mixed results. Using two measures of performance, a "success" rate and a "failure" rate, McCord found that his experimental group achieved both less failure *and* less success than the controls did. There have been two positive reports on milieu therapy programs for male juveniles; both of them have come out of the Highfields program, the milieu therapy experiment which has become the most famous and widely quoted example of "success" via this method. A group of boys was confined for a relatively short time to the unrestrictive, supportive environment of Highfields; and at a follow-up of six months, Freeman (1956) found that the group did indeed show a lower recidivism rate (as measured by parole revocation) than a similar group spending a longer time in the regular reformatory. McCorkle (1958) also reported positive findings from Highfields. But in fact, the McCorkle data show, this improvement was not so clear: The Highfields boys had lower recidivism rates at twelve and thirty-six months in the follow-up period, but not at twenty-four and sixty months. The length of follow-up, these data remind us, may have large implications for a study's conclusions. But more important were other flaws in the Highfields experiment: The populations were not fully comparable (they differed according to risk level and time of admission); different organizations—the probation agency for the Highfields boys, the parole agency for the others—were making the revocation decisions for each group; more of the Highfields boys were discharged early from supervision, and thus removed from any risk of revocation. In short, not even from the celebrated Highfields case may we take clear assurance that milieu therapy works.

In the case of male youths, as opposed to male juveniles, the findings are just as equivocal, and hardly more encouraging. One such study by Empey (1966) in a residential context did not produce significant results. A study by Seckel (1967) described California's Fremont Program, in which institutionalized youths participated in a combination of therapy, work projects, field trips, and community meetings. Seckel found that the youths subjected to this treatment committed *more* violations of law than did their nontreated counterparts. This difference could have occurred by chance; still, there was certainly no evidence of relative improvement. Another study, by Levinson (1962–1964), also found a lack of improvement in recidivism rates—but Levinson noted the encouraging fact that the treated group spent somewhat more time in the community before recidivating, and committed less serious offenses. And a study by the State of California (1967) also shows a partially positive finding. This was a study of the Marshall Program, similar to California's Fremont Program but different in several ways. The Marshall Program was shorter and more tightly organized than its Fremont counterpart. In the Marshall Program, as opposed to the Fremont Program, a youth could be ejected from the group and sent back to regular institutions before the completion of the program. Also, the Marshall Program offered some additional benefits: the teaching of "social survival skills" (i.e., getting and holding a job), group counseling of parents, and an occasional opportunity for boys to visit home. When youthful offenders were released to the Marshall Program, either directly or after spending some time in a regular institution, they did no better than a comparable regularly institutionalized population, though both Marshall youth and youth in regular institutions did better than those who were directly released by the court and given no special treatment.

So the youth in these milieu therapy programs at least do no worse than their counterparts in regular institutions and the special programs may cost less. One may therefore be encouraged—not on grounds of rehabilitation but on grounds of cost-effectiveness.

WHAT ABOUT MEDICAL TREATMENT?

4. *Isn't there anything you can do in an institutional setting that will reduce recidivism, for instance, through strictly medical treatment?*

A number of studies deal with the results of efforts to change the behavior of offenders through drugs and surgery. As for surgery, the one experimental study of a plastic surgery program—by Mandell (1967)—had negative results. For nonaddicts who received plastic surgery, Mandell purported to find improvement in performance on parole; but when one reanalyzes his data, it appears that surgery alone did not in fact make a significant difference.

One type of surgery does seem to be highly successful in reducing recidivism. A twenty-year Danish study of sex offenders, by Stuerup (1960), found that while those who had been treated with hormones and therapy continued to commit both sex crimes (29.6 percent of them did so) and nonsex crimes (21.0 percent), those who had been castrated had rates of only 3.5 percent (not, interestingly enough, a rate of zero; where there's a will, apparently there's a way) and 9.2 percent. One hopes that the policy implications of this study will be found to be distinctly limited.

As for drugs, the major report on such a program—involving tranquilization—was made by Adams (1961b). The tranquilizers were administered to male and female institutionalized youths. With boys, there was only a slight improvement in their subsequent behavior; this improvement disappeared within a year. With girls, the tranquilization produced worse results than when the girls were given no treatment at all.

THE EFFECTS OF SENTENCING

5. *Well, at least it may be possible to manipulate certain gross features of the existing conventional prison system—such as length of sentence and degree of security—in order to affect these recidivism rates. Isn't this the case?*

At this point, it's still impossible to say that this is the case. As for the degree of security in an institution, Glaser's (1964) work reported that, for both youth and adults, a less restrictive "custody grading" in American federal prisons was related to success on parole; but this is hardly surprising, since those assigned to more restrictive custody are likely to be worse risks in the first place. More to the point, an American study by Fox (1950) discovered that for "older youths" who were deemed to be good risks for the future, a minimum-security institution produced better results than a maximum-security one. On the other hand, the data we have on youths under sixteen—from a study by McClintock (1961), done in Great Britain—indicate that so-called Borstals, in which boys are totally confined, are more effective than a less restrictive regime of partial physical custody. In short, we know very little about the recidivism effects of various degrees of security in existing institutions; and our problems in finding out will be compounded by the probability that these effects will vary widely according to the particular *type* of offender that we're dealing with.

The same problems of mixed results and lack of comparable populations have plagued attempts to study the effects of sentence length. A number of studies—by Narloch (1959), by Bernsten (1965), and by the State of California (1956)—suggest that those who are released earlier from institutions than their scheduled parole date, or those who serve short sentences of under three months rather than longer sentences of eight months or more, either do better on parole or at least do no worse.[3] The implication here is quite clear and important: Even if early releases and short sentences produce no improvement in recidivism rates, one could at least maintain the same rates while lowering the cost of maintaining the offender and lessening his own burden of imprisonment. Of course, this implication carries with it its concomitant danger: the danger that though shorter sentences cause no worsening of the recidivism rate, they may increase the total amount of crime in the community by increasing the absolute number of potential recidivists at large.

On the other hand, Glaser's (1964) data show not a consistent linear relationship between the shortness of the sentence and the rate of parole success, but a curvilinear one. Of his subjects, those who served less than a year had a 73 percent success rate, those who served up to two years were only 65 percent successful, and those who served up to three years fell to a rate of 56 percent. But among those who served sentences of *more* than three years, the success rate rose again—to 60 percent. These findings should be viewed with some caution since Glaser did not control for the preexisting degree of risk associated with each of his categories of offenders. But the data do suggest that the relationship between sentence length and recidivism may not be a simple linear one.

More important, the effect of sentence length seems to vary widely according to type of offender. In a British study (1963), for instance, Hammond found that for a group of "hard-core recidivists," shortening the sentence caused no improvement in the recidivism rate. In Denmark, Bernsten (1965) discovered a similar phenomenon: that the beneficial effect of three-month sentences as against eight-month ones disappeared in the case of these "hard-core recidivists." Garrity found another such distinction in his 1956 study. He divided his offenders into three categories: "pro-social," "anti-social," and "manipulative." "Pro-social" offenders he found to have low recidivism rates regardless of the length of their sentence; "anti-social" offenders did better with short sentences; the "manipulative" did better with long ones. Two studies from Britain made yet another division of the offender population, and found yet other variations. One (Great Britain, 1964) found that previous offenders—but not first offenders—did better with *longer* sentences, while the other (Cambridge, 1952) found the *reverse* to be true with juveniles.

To add to the problem of interpretation, these studies deal not only with different types and categorizations of offenders but with different types of institutions as well. No more than in the case of institution type can we say that length of sentence has a clear relationship to recidivism.

DECARCERATING THE CONVICT

6. *All of this seems to suggest that there's not much we know how to do to rehabilitate an offender when he's in an institution. Doesn't this lead to the clear possibility that the way to rehabilitate offenders is to deal with them outside an institutional setting?*

This is indeed an important possibility, and it is suggested by other pieces of information as well. For instance, Miner (1967) reported on a milieu therapy program in Massachusetts called Outward Bound. It took youths fifteen and a half and over; it was oriented toward the development of skills in the out-of-doors and conducted in a wilderness atmosphere very different from that of most existing institutions. The culmination of the twenty-six-day program was a final twenty-four hours in which each youth had to survive alone in the wilderness. And Miner found that the program did indeed work in reducing recidivism rates.

But by and large, when one takes the programs that have been administered in institutions and applies them in a noninstitutional setting, the results do not grow to encouraging proportions. With casework and individual counseling in the community, for instance, there have been three studies; they dealt with counseling methods from psycho-social and vocational counseling to "operant conditioning," in which an offender was rewarded first simply for coming to counseling sessions and then, gradually, for performing other types of approved acts. Two of them report that the community-counseled offenders did no better than their institutional controls, while the third notes that although community counseling produced fewer arrests per person, it did not ultimately reduce the offender's chance of returning to a reformatory.

The one study of a noninstitutional skill development program, by Kovacs (1967), described the New Start Program in Denver, in which offenders participated in vocational training, role playing, programmed instruction, group counseling, college class attendance, and trips to art galleries and museums. After all this, Kovacs found no significant improvement over incarceration.

There have also been studies of milieu therapy programs conducted with youthful male probationers not in actual physical custody. One of them found no significant improvement at all. One, by Empey (1966), did say that after a follow-up of six months, a boy who was judged to have "successfully" completed the milieu program was less likely to recidivate afterwards than was a "successful" regular probationer. Empey's "successes" came out of an extraordinary program in Provo, Utah, which aimed to rehabilitate by subjecting offenders to a nonsupportive milieu. The staff of this program operated on the principle that they were *not* to go out of their way to interact and be empathetic with the boys. Indeed, a boy who misbehaved was to be met with "role dispossession": He was to be excluded from meetings of his peer group, and he was not to be given answers to his questions as to why he had been excluded or what his ultimate fate might be. This peer group and its meetings were designed to be the major force for reform at Provo; they were intended to develop, and indeed did develop, strong and controlling norms for the behavior of individual members. For one thing, group members were not to associate with delinquent boys outside the program; for another, individuals were to submit to a group review of all their actions and problems; and they were to be completely honest and open with the group about their attitudes, their states of mind, their personal failings. The group was granted quite a few sanctions with which to enforce these norms: They could practice derision or temporary ostracism, or they could lock up an aberrant member for a weekend, refuse to release him from the program, or send him away to the regular reformatory.

One might be tempted to forgive these methods because of the success that Empey reports, except for one thing. If one judges the program not only by its "successful" boys but by all the boys who were subjected to it—those who succeeded and those who, not surprisingly, failed—the totals show *no* significant improvement in recidivism rates compared with boys on regular probation. Empey did find that both the Provo boys and those on regular probation did better than those in regular reformatories—in contradiction, it may be recalled, to the finding from the residential Marshall Program, in which the direct releases given no special treatment did *worse* than boys in regular institutions.

The third such study of nonresidential milieu therapy, by McCravey (1967), found not only that there was no significant improvement, but that the longer a boy participated in the treatment, the *worse* he was likely to do afterwards.

PSYCHOTHERAPY IN COMMUNITY SETTINGS

There is some indication that individual psychotherapy may "work" in a community setting. Massimo (1963) reported on one such program, using what might be termed a "pragmatic" psychotherapeutic approach, including "insight" therapy and a focus on vocational problems. The program was marked by its small size and by its use of therapists who were personally enthusiastic about the project; Massimo found that there was indeed a decline in recidivism rates. Adamson (1956), on the other hand, found no significant difference produced by another program of individual therapy (though he did note that arrest rates among the experimental boys declined with what he called "intensity of treatment"). And Schwitzgebel (1963, 1964), studying other, different kinds of therapy programs, found that the programs *did* produce improvements in the attitudes of his boys— but, unfortunately, not in their rates of recidivism.

And with *group* therapy administered in the community, we find yet another set of equivocal results. The results from studies of pragmatic group counseling are only mildly optimistic. Adams (1965) did report that a form of group therapy, "guided group interaction," when administered to juvenile gangs, did somewhat reduce the percentage that were to be found in custody six years later. On the other hand, in a study of juveniles, Adams (1964) found that while such a program did reduce the number of contacts that an experimental youth had with police, it made no ultimate difference in the detention rate. And the attitudes of the counseled youth showed no improvement. Finally, when O'Brien (1961) examined a community-based program of group psychotherapy, he found not only that the program produced no improvement in the recidivism rate, but that the experimental boys actually did worse than their controls on a series of psychological tests.

PROBATION OR PAROLE VERSUS PRISON

But by far the most extensive and important work that has been done on the effect of community-based treatments has been done in the areas of probation and parole. This work sets out to answer the question of whether it makes any difference how you supervise and treat an offender once he has been released from prison or has come under state surveillance in lieu of prison. This is the work that has provided the main basis to date for the claim that we do indeed have the means at our disposal for rehabilitating the offender or at least decarcerating him safely.

One group of these studies has compared the use of probation with other dispositions for offenders; these provide some slight evidence that, at least under some circumstances, probation may make an offender's future chances better than if he had been sent to prison. Or, at least, probation may not worsen those chances.[4] A British study, by Wilkins (1958), reported that when probation was granted more frequently, recidivism rates among probationers did not increase significantly. And another such study by the state of Michigan in 1963 reported that an expansion in the use of probation actually improved recidivism rates—though there are serious problems of comparability in the groups and systems that were studied.

One experiment—by Babst (1965)—compared a group of parolees, drawn from adult male felony offenders in Wisconsin, and excluding murderers and sex criminals, with a similar group that had been put on probation; it found that the probationers committed fewer violations if they had been first offenders, and did no worse if they were recidivists. The problem in interpreting this experiment, though, is that the behavior of those groups was being measured by separate organizations, by probation officers for the probationers, and by parole officers for the parolees; it is not clear that the definition of "violation" was the same in each case, or that other types of uniform standards were being applied. Also, it is not clear what the results would have been if subjects had been released directly to the parole organization without having experienced prison first. Another such study, done in Israel by Shoham (1964), must be interpreted cautiously because his experimental and control groups had slightly different characteristics. But Shoham found that when one compared a suspended sentence plus probation for first offenders with a one-year prison sentence, only first offenders under twenty years of age did better on probation; those from twenty-one to forty-five actually did *worse*. And Shoham's findings also differ from Babst's in another way. Babst had found that parole rather than prison brought no improvement for recidivists, but Shoham reported that for recidivists with four or more prior offenses, a suspended sentence was actually *better*— though the improvement was much less when the recidivist had committed a crime of violence.

But both the Babst and the Shoham studies, even while they suggest the possible value of suspended sentences, probation, or parole for some offenders (though they contradict each other in telling us *which* offenders), also indicate a pessimistic general conclusion concerning the limits of the effectiveness of treatment programs. For they found that the personal characteristics of offenders—first-offender status, or age, or type of offense—were more important than the form of treatment in determining future recidivism. An offender with a "favorable" prognosis will do better than one without, it seems, no matter how you distribute "good" or "bad," "enlightened" or "regressive" treatments among them.

Quite a large group of studies deals not with probation as compared to other dispositions, but instead with the type of treatment that an offender receives once he is *on* probation or parole. These are

the studies that have provided the most encouraging reports on rehabilitative treatment and that have also raised the most serious questions about the nature of the research that has been going on in the
corrections field.

Five of these studies have dealt with youthful probationers from
thirteen to eighteen who were assigned to probation officers with
small caseloads or provided with other ways of receiving more intensive supervision (Adams, 1966—two reports; Feistman, 1966; Kawaguchi, 1967; Pilnick, 1967). These studies report that, by and large,
intensive supervision does work—that the specially treated youngsters do better according to some measure of recidivism. Yet these
studies left some important questions unanswered. For instance, was
this improved performance a function merely of the number of contacts a youngster had with his probation officer? Did it also depend
on the length of time in treatment? Or was it the quality of supervision that was making the difference, rather than the quantity?

INTENSIVE SUPERVISION: THE WARREN STUDIES

The widely reported Warren studies (1966a, 1966b, 1967) in California constitute an extremely ambitious attempt to answer these questions. In this project, a control group of youths, drawn from a pool of
candidates ready for first admission to a California Youth Authority
institution, was assigned to regular detention, usually for eight to
nine months, and then released to regular supervision. The experimental group received considerably more elaborate treatment. They
were released directly to probation status and assigned to twelve-
man caseloads. To decide what special treatment was appropriate
within these caseloads, the youths were divided according to their
"interpersonal maturity level classification," by use of a scale developed by Grant and Grant. And each level dictated its own special
type of therapy. For instance, a youth might be judged to occupy the
lowest maturity level; this would be a youth, according to the scale,
primarily concerned with "demands that the world take care of
him. . . . He behaves impulsively, unaware of anything except the
grossest effects of his behavior on others." A youth like this would be
placed in a supportive environment such as a foster home; the goals
of his therapy would be to meet his dependency needs and help him
gain more accurate perceptions about his relationship to others. At
the other end of the three-tier classification, a youth might exhibit
high maturity. This would be a youth who had internalized "a set of
standards by which he judges his and others' behavior. . . . He shows

some ability to understand reasons for behavior, some ability to relate to people emotionally and on a long-term basis." These high-maturity youths could come in several varieties—a "neurotic acting out," for instance, a "neurotic anxious," a "situational emotional reactor," or a "cultural identifier." But the appropriate treatment for these youths was individual psychotherapy, or family or group therapy for the purpose of reducing internal conflicts and increasing the youths' awareness of personal and family dynamics.

"Success" in this experiment was defined as favorable discharge by the Youth Authority; "failure" was unfavorable discharge, revocation, or recommitment by a court. Warren reported an encouraging finding: Among all but one of the "subtypes," the experimentals had a significantly lower failure rate than the controls. The experiment did have certain problems: The experimentals might have been performing better because of the enthusiasm of the staff and the attention lavished on them; none of the controls had been *directly* released to their regular supervision programs instead of being detained first; and it was impossible to separate the effects of the experimentals' small caseloads from their specially designed treatments, since no experimental youths had been assigned to a small caseload with "inappropriate" treatment, or with no treatment at all. Still, none of these problems were serious enough to vitiate the encouraging prospect that this finding presented for successful treatment of probationers.

This encouraging finding was, however, accompanied by a rather more disturbing clue. As has been mentioned before, the experimental subjects, when measured, had a lower *failure* rate than the controls. But the experimentals also had a lower *success* rate. That is, fewer of the experimentals as compared with the controls had been judged to have successfully completed their program of supervision and to be suitable for favorable release. When my colleagues and I undertook a rather laborious reanalysis of the Warren data, it became clear why this discrepancy had appeared. It turned out that fewer experimentals were "successful" because the experimentals were actually committing more offenses than their controls. The reason that the experimentals' relatively large number of offenses was not being reflected in their failure rates was simply that the experimentals' probation officers were using a more lenient revocation policy. In other words, the controls had a higher failure rate because the controls were being revoked for less serious offenses.

So it seems that what Warren was reporting in her "failure" rates was not merely the treatment effect of her small caseloads and special programs. Instead, what Warren was finding was not so much a change in the behavior of the experimental youths as a change in the behavior of the experimental *probation officers*, who knew the "special" status of their charges and who had evidently decided to revoke probation status at a lower than normal rate. The experimentals continued to commit offenses; what was different was that when they committed these offenses, they were permitted to remain on probation.

The experimenters claimed that this low revocation policy, and the greater number of offenses committed by the special treatment youth, were *not* an indication that these youth were behaving specially badly and that policy makers were simply letting them get away with it. Instead, it was claimed, the higher reported offense rate was primarily an artifact of the more intense surveillance that the experimental youth received. But the data show that this is not a sufficient explanation of the low failure rate among experimental youth; the difference in "tolerance" of offenses between experimental officials and control officials was much greater than the difference in the rates at which these two systems detected youths committing new offenses. Needless to say, this reinterpretation of the data presents a much bleaker picture of the possibilities of intensive supervision with special treatment.

"TREATMENT EFFECTS" VERSUS "POLICY EFFECTS"

This same problem of experimenter bias may also be present in the predecessors of the Warren study, the ones which had also found positive results from intensive supervision on probation; indeed, this disturbing question can be raised about many of the previously discussed reports of positive "treatment effects."

This possibility of a "policy effect" rather than a "treatment effect" applies, for instance, to the previously discussed studies of the effects of intensive supervision on juvenile and youthful probationers. These were the studies, it will be recalled, which found lower recidivism rates for the intensively supervised.[5]

One opportunity to make a further check on the effects of this problem is provided, in a slightly different context, by Johnson (1962a). Johnson was measuring the effects of intensive supervision on youthful *parolees* (as distinct from probationers). There have been several such studies of the effects on youths of intensive parole supervision plus special counseling, and their findings are on the whole less encouraging than the probation studies; they are difficult to interpret because of experimental problems, but studies by Boston University in 1966, and by Van Couvering in 1966, report no significant effects and possibly some bad effects from such special programs. But Johnson's studies were unique for the chance they provide to measure both treatment effects and the effect of agency policy.

Johnson, like Warren, assigned experimental subjects to small caseloads, and his experiment had the virtue of being performed with two separate populations and at two different times. But in contrast with the Warren case, the Johnson experiment did not engage in a large continuing attempt to choose the experimental counselors specially, to train them specially, and to keep them informed about the progress and importance of the experiment. The first time the experiment was performed, the experimental youths had a slightly lower revocation rate than the controls at six months. But the second time, the experimentals did *not* do better than their controls; indeed, they did slightly worse. And with the experimentals from the first group—those who *had* shown an improvement after six months—this effect wore off at eighteen months. In the Johnson study, my colleagues and I found, "intensive" supervision did *not* increase the experimental youths' risk of detection. Instead, what was happening in the Johnson experiment was that the first time it had been performed—just as in the Warren study—the experimentals were simply revoked less often per number of offenses committed, and they were revoked for offenses more serious than those which prompted revocation among the controls. The second time around, this "policy" discrepancy disappeared; and when it did, the "improved" performance of the experimentals disappeared as well. The enthusiasm guiding the project had simply worn off in the absence of reinforcement.

One must conclude that the "benefits" of intensive supervision for youthful offenders may stem not so much from a "treatment" effect as from a "policy" effect—that such supervision, so far as we now know, results not in rehabilitation but in a decision to look the other way when an offense is committed. But there is one major modification to be added to this conclusion. Johnson performed a further measurement (1962b) in his parole experiment: He rated all the supervising agents according to the "adequacy" of the supervision they gave. And he found that an "adequate" agent, whether he was working in a small *or* a large caseload, produced a relative improvement in his charges. The converse was not true: An *in*adequate agent was more likely to produce youthful "failures" when he was given a *small* caseload to supervise. One can't much help a "good" agent, it seems, by reducing his caseload size; such reduction can only do further harm to those youths who fall into the hands of "bad" agents.

So with youthful offenders, Johnson found, intensive supervision does not seem to provide the rehabilitative benefits claimed for it;

the only such benefits may flow not from intensive supervision itself but from contact with one of the "good people" who are frequently in such short supply.

INTENSIVE SUPERVISION OF ADULTS

The results are similarly ambiguous when one applies this intensive supervision to adult offenders. There have been several studies of the effects of intensive supervision on adult parolees. Some of these are hard to interpret because of problems of comparability between experimental and control groups (general risk ratings, for instance, or distribution of narcotics offenders, or policy changes that took place between various phases of the experiments), but two of them (California, 1966; Stanton, 1964) do not seem to give evidence of the benefits of intensive supervision. By far the most extensive work, though, on the effects of intensive supervision of adult parolees has been a series of studies of California's Special Intensive Parole Unit (SIPU), a ten-year-long experiment designed to test the treatment possibilities of various special parole programs. Three of the four "phases" of this experiment produced "negative results." The first phase tested the effect of a reduced caseload size; no lasting effect was found. The second phase slightly increased the size of the small caseloads and provided for a longer time in treatment; again there was no evidence of a treatment effect. In the fourth phase, caseload sizes and time in treatment were again varied, and treatments were simultaneously varied in a sophisticated way according to personality characteristics of the parolees; once again, significant results did not appear.

The only phase of this experiment for which positive results were reported was Phase Three. Here, it was indeed found that a smaller caseload improved one's chances of parole success. There is, however, an important caveat that attaches to this finding: When my colleagues and I divided the whole population of subjects into two groups—those receiving supervision in the north of the state and those in the south—we found that the "improvement" of the experimentals' success rates was taking place primarily in the north. The north differed from the south in one important aspect: Its agents practiced a policy of returning both "experimental" and "control" violators to prison at relatively high rates. And it was the north that produced the higher success rate among its experimentals. So this improvement in experimentals' performance was taking place only when accompanied by a "realistic threat" of severe sanctions. It is interesting to compare this situation with that of the Warren studies. In the Warren studies, experimental subjects were being revoked at a relatively *low* rate. These experimentals "failed" less, but they also committed more new offenses than their controls. By contrast, in the northern region of the SIPU experiment, there was a policy of *high* rate of return to prison for experimentals; and here, the special program *did* seem to produce a real improvement in the behavior of offenders. What this suggests is that when intensive supervision *does* produce an improvement in offenders' behavior, it does so not through the mechanism of "treatment" or "rehabilitation," but instead through a mechanism that our studies have almost totally ignored—the mechanism of *deterrence*. And a similar mechanism is suggested by Lohman's study (1967) of intensive supervision of probationers. In this study intensive supervision led to higher total violation rates. But one also notes that intensive supervision combined the highest rate of technical violations with the lowest rate for *new* offenses.

THE EFFECTS OF COMMUNITY TREATMENT

In sum, even in the case of treatment programs administered outside penal institutions, we simply cannot say that this treatment in itself has an appreciable effect on offender behavior. On the other hand, there is one encouraging set of findings that emerges from these studies. For from many of them there flows the strong suggestion that even if we can't "treat" offenders so as to make them do better, a great many of the programs designed to rehabilitate them at least did not make them do *worse*. And if these programs did not show the advantages of actually rehabilitating, some of them did have the advantage of being less onerous to the offender himself without seeming to pose increased danger to the community. And some of these programs—especially those involving less restrictive custody, minimal supervision, and early release—simply cost fewer dollars to administer. The information on the dollar costs of these programs is just beginning to be developed but the implication is clear: *that if we can't do more for (and to) offenders, at least we can safely do less.*

There is, however, one important caveat even to this note of optimism: In order to calculate the true costs of these programs, one must in each case include not only their administrative cost but also the cost of maintaining in the community an offender population increased in size. This population might well not be committing new offenses at any greater rate; but the offender population might, under some of these plans, be larger in absolute *numbers*. So the total number of offenses committed might rise, and our chances of victimization might therefore rise too. We need to be able to make a judgment about the size and probable duration of this effect; as of now, we simply do not know.

DOES NOTHING WORK?

7. Do all of these studies lead us irrevocably to the conclusion that nothing works, that we haven't the faintest clue about how to rehabilitate offenders and reduce recidivism? And if so, what shall we do?

We tried to exclude from our survey those studies which were so poorly done that they simply could not be interpreted. But despite our efforts, a pattern has run through much of this discussion—of studies which "found" effects without making any truly rigorous attempt to exclude competing hypotheses, of extraneous factors permitted to intrude upon the measurements, of recidivism measures which are not all measuring the same thing, of "follow-up" periods which vary enormously and rarely extend beyond the period of legal supervision, of experiments never replicated, of "system effects" not taken into account, of categories drawn up without any theory to guide the enterprise. It is just possible that some of our treatment programs *are* working to some extent, but that our research is so bad that it is incapable of telling.

Having entered this very serious caveat, I am bound to say that these data, involving over two hundred studies and hundreds of thousands of individuals as they do, are the best available and give us very little reason to hope that we have in fact found a sure way of reducing recidivism through rehabilitation. This is not to say that we found no instances of success or partial success; it is only to say that these instances have been isolated, producing no clear pattern to indicate the efficacy of any particular method of treatment. And neither is this to say that factors *outside* the realm of rehabilitation may not be working to reduce recidivism—factors such as the tendency for recidivism to be lower in offenders over the age of thirty; it is only to say that such factors seem to have little connection with any of the treatment methods now at our disposal.

From this probability, one may draw any of several conclusions. It may be simply that our programs aren't yet good enough—that the education we provide to inmates is still poor education, that the therapy we administer is not administered skillfully enough, that our intensive supervision and counseling do not yet provide enough personal support for the offenders who are subjected to them. If one wishes to believe this, then what our correctional system needs is simply a more full-hearted commitment to the strategy of treatment.

It may be, on the other hand, that there is a more radical flaw in our present strategies—that education at its best, or that psychotherapy at its best, cannot overcome, or even appreciably reduce, the powerful tendency for offenders to continue in criminal behavior. Our present treatment programs are based on a theory of crime as a "disease"—that is to say, as something foreign and abnormal in the individual which can presumably be cured. This theory may well be flawed, in that it overlooks—indeed, denies—both the normality of crime in society and the personal normality of a very large proportion of offenders, criminals who are merely responding to the facts and conditions of our society.

This opposing theory of "crime as a social phenomenon" directs our attention away from a "rehabilitative" strategy, away from the notion that we may best insure public safety through a series of "treatments" to be imposed forcibly on convicted offenders. These treatments have on occasion become, and have the potential for becoming, so draconian as to offend the moral order of a democratic society; and the theory of crime as a social phenomenon suggests that such treatments may be not only offensive but ineffective as well. This theory points, instead, to decarceration for low-risk offenders— and, presumably, to keeping high-risk offenders in prisons which are nothing more (and aim to be nothing more) than custodial institutions.

But this approach has its own problems. To begin with, there is the moral dimension of crime and punishment. Many low-risk offenders have committed serious crimes (murder, sometimes), and even if one *is* reasonably sure they will never commit another crime, it violates our sense of justice that they should experience no significant retribution for their actions. A middle-class banker who kills his adulterous wife in a moment of passion is a "low-risk" criminal; a juvenile delinquent in the ghetto who commits armed robbery has, statistically, a much higher probability of committing another crime. Are we going to put the first on probation and sentence the latter to a long term in prison?

Besides, one cannot ignore the fact that the punishment of offenders is the major means we have for *deterring* incipient offenders. We know almost nothing about the "deterrent effect," largely because "treatment" theories have so dominated our research, and "deterrence" theories have been relegated to the status of a historical curiosity. Since we have almost no idea of the deterrent functions that our present system performs or that future strategies might be made to perform, it is possible that there is indeed something that works— that to some extent is working right now in front of our noses, and that might be made to work better—something that deters rather than cures, something that does not so much reform convicted offenders as prevent criminal behavior in the first place. But whether that is the case and, if it is, what strategies will be found to make our deterrence system work better than it does now, are questions we will not be able to answer with data until a new family of studies has been brought into existence. As we begin to learn the facts, we will be in a better position than we are now to judge to what degree the prison has become an anachronism and can be replaced by more effective means of social control.

Notes

1. Following this case, the state finally did give its permission to have the work published; it will appear in its complete form in a forthcoming book by Praeger.
2. The net result was that those who received *less* prison education—because their sentences were shorter or because they were probably better risks—ended up having better parole chances than those who received more prison education.
3. A similar phenomenon has been measured indirectly by studies that have dealt with the effect of various parole policies on recidivism rates. Where parole decisions have been liberalized so that an offender could be released with only the "reasonable assurance" of a job rather than with a definite job already developed by a parole officer (Stanton, 1963), this liberal release policy has produced no worsening of recidivism rates.
4. It will be recalled that Empey's report on the Provo program made such a finding.
5. But one of these reports, by Kawaguchi (1967), also found that an intensively supervised juvenile, by the time he finally "failed," had had more previous *detentions* while under supervision than a control juvenile had experienced.

References

Adams, Stuart. "Effectiveness of the Youth Authority Special Treatment Program: First Interim Report." Research Report No. 5. California Youth Authority, March 6, 1959. (Mimeographed.)

Adams, Stuart. "Assessment of the Psychiatric Treatment Program: Second Interim Report." Research Report No. 15. California Youth Authority, December 13, 1959. (Mimeographed.)

Adams, Stuart. "Effectiveness of Interview Therapy with Older Youth Authority Wards: An Interim Evaluation of the PICO Project." Research Report No. 20. California Youth Authority, January 20, 1961. (Mimeographed.)

Adams, Stuart. "Assessment of the Psychiatric Treatment Program, Phase I: Third Interim Report." Research Report No. 21. California Youth Authority, January 31, 1961. (Mimeographed.)

Adams, Stuart. "An Experimental Assessment of Group Counseling with Juvenile Probationers." Paper presented at the 18th Convention of the California State Psychological Association, Los Angeles, December 12, 1964. (Mimeographed.)

Adams, Stuart, Rice, Robert E., and Olive, Borden. "A Cost Analysis of the Effectiveness of the Group Guidance Program." Research Memorandum 65-3. Los Angeles County Probation Department, January 1965. (Mimeographed.)

Adams, Stuart. "Development of a Program Research Service in Probation." Research Report No. 27 (Final Report, NIMH Project MH007 18.) Los Angeles County Probation Department, January 1966. (Processed.)

Adamson, LeMay, and Dunham, H. Warren. "Clinical Treatment of Male Delinquents. A Case Study in Effort and Result," *American Sociological Review*, XXI, 3 (1956), 312–320.

Babst, Dean V., and Mannering, John W. "Probation versus Imprisonment for Similar Types of Offenders: A Comparison by Subsequent Violations," *Journal of Research in Crime and Delinquency*, II, 2 (1965), 60–71.

Bernsten, Karen, and Christiansen, Karl O. "A Resocialization Experiment with Short-term Offenders," *Scandinavian Studies in Criminology*, I (1965), 35–54.

California, Adult Authority, Division of Adult Paroles. "Special Intensive Parole Unit, Phase I: Fifteen-man Caseload Study." Prepared by Walter I. Stone. Sacramento, Calif., November 1956. (Mimeographed.)

California, Department of Corrections. "Intensive Treatment Program: Second Annual Report." Prepared by Harold B. Bradley and Jack D. Williams. Sacramento, Calif., December 1, 1958. (Mimeographed.)

California, Department of Corrections. "Special Intensive Parole Unit, Phase II: Thirty-man Caseload Study." Prepared by Ernest Reimer and Martin Warren. Sacramento, Calif., December 1958. (Mimeographed.)

California, Department of Corrections. "Parole Work Unit Program: An Evaluative Report." A memorandum to the California Joint Legislative Budget Committee, December 30, 1966. (Mimeographed.)

California, Department of the Youth Authority. "James Marshall Treatment Program: Progress Report." January 1967. (Processed.)

Cambridge University, Department of Criminal Science. *Detention in Remard Homes.* London: Macmillan, 1952.

Craft, Michael, Stephenson, Geoffrey, and Granger, Clive. "A Controlled Trial of Authoritarian and Self-Governing Regimes with Adolescent Psychopaths," *American Journal of Orthopsychiatry*, XXXIV, 3 (1964), 543–554.

Empey, LeMar T. "The Provo Experiment: A Brief Review." Los Angeles: Youth Studies Center, University of Southern California. 1966. (Processed.)

Feistman, Eugene G. "Comparative Analysis of the Willow-Brook-Harbor Intensive Services Program, March 1, 1965 through February 28, 1966." Research Report No. 28. Los Angeles County Probation Department, June 1966. (Processed.)

Forman, B. "The Effects of Differential Treatment on Attitudes, Personality Traits, and Behavior of Adult Parolees." Unpublished Ph.D. dissertation, University of Southern California, 1960.

Fox, Vernon. "Michigan's Experiment in Minimum Security Penology," *Journal of Criminal Law, Criminology, and Police Science*, XLI, 2 (1950), 150–166.

Freeman, Howard E., and Weeks, H. Ashley. "Analysis of a Program of Treatment of Delinquent Boys," *American Journal of Sociology*, LXII, 1 (1956), 56–61.

Garrity, Donald Lee, "The Effects of Length of Incarceration upon Parole Adjustment and Estimation of Optimum Sentence: Washington State Correctional Institutions." Unpublished Ph.D. dissertation, University of Washington, 1956.

Gearhart, J. Walter, Keith, Harold L., and Clemmons, Gloria. "An Analysis of the Vocational Training Program in the Washington State Adult Correctional Institutions." Research Review No. 23. State of Washington, Department of Institutions, May 1967. (Processed.)

Glaser, Daniel. *The Effectiveness of a Prison and Parole System.* New York: Bobbs-Merrill, 1964.

Goldberg, Lisbeth, and Adams, Stuart. "An Experimental Evaluation of the Lathrop Hall Program." Los Angeles County Probation Department, December 1964. (Summarized in: Adams, Stuart. "Development of a Program Research Service in Probation," pp. 19–22.)

Great Britain. Home Office. *The Sentence of the Court: A Handbook for Courts on the Treatment of Offenders.* London: Her Majesty's Stationery Office, 1964.

Guttman, Evelyn S. "Effects of Short-Term Psychiatric Treatment on Boys in Two California Youth Authority Institutions." Research Report No. 36. California Youth Authority, December 1963. (Processed.)

Hammond, W. H., and Chayen, E. *Persistent Criminals: A Home Office Research Unit Report.* London: Her Majesty's Stationery Office, 1963.

Harrison, Robert M., and Mueller, Paul F. C. "Clue Hunting about Group Counseling and Parole Outcome. " Research Report No. 11. California Department of Corrections, May 1964. (Mimeographed.)

Havel, Joan, and Sulka, Elaine. "Special Intensive Parole Unit: Phase Three." Research Report No. 3. California Department of Corrections, March 1962. (Processed.)

Havel, Joan. "A Synopsis of Research Report No. 10, SIPU Phase IV—The High Base Expectancy Study." Administrative Abstract No. 10. California Department of Corrections, June 1963. (Processed.)

Havel, Joan. "Special Intensive Parole Unit—Phase Four: 'The Parole Outcome Study.'" Research Report No. 13. California Department of Corrections, September, 1965. (Processed.)

Hood, Roger. *Homeless Borstal Boys: A Study of Their After-Care and After-Conduct.* Occasional Papers on Social Administration No. 18. London: G. Bell & Sons, 1966.

Jacobson, Frank, and McGee, Eugene. "Englewood Project: Re-education: A Radical Correction of Incarcerated Delinquents." Englewood, Colo.: July 1965. (Mimeographed.)

Jesness, Carl F. "The Fricot Ranch Study: Outcomes with Small versus Large Living Groups in the Rehabilitation of Delinquents." Research Report No. 47. California Youth Authority, October 1, 1965. (Processed.)

Johnson, Bertram. "Parole Performance of the First Year's Releases, Parole Research Project: Evaluation of Reduced Caseloads." Research Report No. 27. California Youth Authority, January 31, 1962. (Mimeographed.)

Johnson, Bertram. "An Analysis of Predictions of Parole Performance and of Judgments of Supervision in the Parole Research Project," Research Report No. 32. California Youth Authority, December 31, 1962. (Mimeographed.)

Kassebaum, Gene, Ward, David, and Wilnet, Daniel. *Prison Treatment and Parole Survival: An Empirical Assessment.* New York: Wiley, 1971.

Kawaguchi, Ray M., and Siff, Leon, M. "An Analysis of Intensive Probation Services—Phase II." Research Report No. 29. Los Angeles County Probation Department, April 1967. (Processed.)

Kettering, Marvin E. "Rehabilitation of Women in the Milwaukee County Jail: An Exploration Experiment." Unpublished Master's thesis, Colorado State College, 1965.

Kovacs, Frank W. "Evaluation and Final Report of the New Start Demonstration Project." Colorado Department of Employment, October 1967. (Processed.)

Lavlicht, Jerome, et al., in *Berkshire Farms Monographs*, I, 1 (1962), 11–48.

Levinson, Robert B., and Kitchenet, Howard L. "Demonstration Counseling Project." 2 vols. Washington, D.C.: National Training School for Boys, 1962–1964. (Mimeographed.)

Lohman, Joseph D., et al., "The Intensive Supervision Caseloads: A Preliminary Evaluation." The San Francisco Project: A Study of Federal Probation and Parole. Research Report No. 11. School of Criminology, University of California, March 1967. (Processed.)

McClintock, F. H. *Attendance Centres.* London: Macmillan, 1961.

McCord, William and Joan. "Two Approaches to the Cure of Delinquents," *Journal of Criminal Law, Criminology, and Police Science*, XLIV, 4 (1953), 442–467.

McCorkle, Lloyd W., Elias, Albert, and Bixby, F. Lovell. *The Highfields Story: An Experimental Treatment Project for Youthful Offenders.* New York: Holt, 1958.

McCravy, Newton, Jr., and Delehanty, Dolores S. "Community Rehabilitation of the Younger Delinquent Boy, Parkland Non-Residential Group Center." Final Report, Kentucky Child Welfare Research Foundation, Inc., September 1, 1967. (Mimeographed.)

Mandell, Wallace, *et al.* "Surgical and Social Rehabilitation of Adult Offenders." Final Report. Montefiore Hospital and Medical Center, with Staten Island Mental Health Society. New York City Department of Correction, 1967. (Processed.)

Massimo, Joseph L., and Shore, Milton F. "The Effectiveness of a Comprehensive Vocationally Oriented Psychotherapeutic Program for Adolescent Delinquent Boys," *American Journal of Orthopsychiatry*, XXXIII, 4 (1963), 634–642.

Minet, Joshua, III, Kelly, Francis J., and Hatch, M. Charles. "Outward Bound Inc.: Juvenile Delinquency Demonstration Project, Year End Report." Massachusetts Division of Youth Service, May 31, 1967.

Narloch, R. P., Adams, Stuart, and Jenkins, Kendall J. "Characteristics and Parole Performance of California Youth Authority Early Releases." Research Report No. 7. California Youth Authority, June 22, 1959. (Mimeographed.)

New York State, Division of Parole, Department of Correction. "Parole Adjustment and Prior Educational Achievement of Male Adolescent Offenders, June 1957–June 1961." September 1964. (Mimeographed.)

O'Brien, William J. "Personality Assessment as a Measure of Change Resulting from Group Psychotherapy with Male Juvenile Delinquents." The Institute for the Study of Crime and Delinquency, and the California Youth Authority, December 1961. (Processed.)

Persons, Roy W. "Psychological and Behavioral Change in Delinquents Following Psychotherapy," *Journal of Clinical Psychology*, XXII, 3 (1966), 337–340.

Persons, Roy W. "Relationship between Psychotherapy with Institutionalized Boys and Subsequent Community Adjustment," *Journal of Consulting Psychology*, XXXI, 2 (1967), 137–141.

Pilnick, Saul, *et al.* "Collegefields: From Delinquency to Freedom." A Report . . . on Collegefields Group Educational Center. Laboratory for Applied Behavioral Science, Newark State College, February 1967. (Processed.)

Robison, James, and Kevotkian, Marinette. "Intensive Treatment Project: Phase II. Parole Outcome: Interim Report." Research Report No. 27. California Department of Corrections, Youth and Adult Correctional Agency, January 1967. (Mimeographed.)

Rudoff, Alvin. "The Effect of Treatment on Incarcerated Young Adult Delinquents as Measured by Disciplinary History." Unpublished Master's thesis, University of Southern California, 1960.

Saden, S. J. "Correctional Research at Jackson Prison," *Journal of Correctional Education*, XV (October 1962), 22–26.

Schnur, Alfred C. "The Educational Treatment of Prisoners and Recidivism," *American Journal of Sociology*, LIV, 2 (1948), 142–147.

Schwitzgebel, Robert and Ralph. "Therapeutic Research: A Procedure for the Reduction of Adolescent Crime." Paper presented at meetings of the American Psychological Association, Philadelphia, Pa., August 1963.

Schwitzgebel, Robert, and Kolb, D. A. "Inducing Behavior Change in Adolescent Delinquents," *Behavior Research Therapy*, I (1964), 297–304.

Seckel, Joachim P. "Experiments in Group Counseling at Two Youth Authority Institutions." Research Report No. 46. California Youth Authority, September 1965. (Processed.)

Seckel, Joachim P. "The Fremont Experiment, Assessment of Residential Treatment at a Youth Authority Reception Center." Research Report No. 50. California Youth Authority, January 1967. (Mimeographed.)

Shelley, Ernest L. V., and Johnson, Walter F., Jr. "Evaluating an Organized Counseling Service for Youthful Offenders," *Journal of Counseling Psychology*, VIII, 4 (1961), 351–354.

Shoham, Shlomo, and Sandberg, Moshe. "Suspended Sentences in Israel: An Evaluation of the Preventive Efficacy of Prospective Imprisonment," *Crime and Delinquency*, X, 1 (1964), 74–83.

Stanton, John M. "Delinquencies and Types of Parole Programs to Which Inmates Are Released." New York State Division of Parole, May 15, 1963. (Mimeographed.)

Stanton, John M. "Board Directed Extensive Supervision." New York State Division of Parole, August 3, 1964. (Mimeographed.)

Stuerup, Georg K. "The Treatment of Sexual Offenders," *Bulletin de la societe internationale de criminologie* (1960), pp. 320–329.

Sullivan, Clyde E., and Mandell, Wallace, "Restoration of Youth through Training: A Final Report." Staten Island, New York: Wakoff Research Center, April 1967. (Processed.)

Taylor, A. J. W. "An Evaluation of Group Psychotherapy in a Girls' Borstal," *International Journal of Group Psychotherapy*, XVII, 2 (1967), 168–177.

Truax, Charles B., Wargo, Donald G., and Silber, Leon D. "Effects of Group Psychotherapy with High Adequate Empathy and Nonpossessive Warmth upon Female Institutionalized Delinquents," *Journal of Abnormal Psychology*, LXXI, 4 (1966), 267–274.

Warren, Marguerite. "The Community Treatment Project after Five Years." California Youth Authority, 1966. (Processed.)

Warren, Marguerite, *et al.* "Community Treatment Project, an Evaluation of Community Treatment for Delinquents: Fifth Progress Report." C.T.P. Research Report No. 7. California Youth Authority, August 1966. (Processed.)

Warren, Marguerite, *et al.* "Community Treatment Project, an Evaluation of Community Treatment for Delinquents: Sixth Progress Report." C.T.P. Research Report No. 8. California Youth Authority, September 1967. (Processed.)

Wilkins, Leslie T. "A Small Comparative Study of the Results of Probation," *British Journal of Criminology*, VIII, 3 (1958), 201–209.

Zivan, Morton. "Youth in Trouble: A Vocational Approach." Final Report of a Research and Demonstration Project, May 31, 1961–August 31, 1966. Dobbs Ferry, N.Y., Children's Village, 1966. (Processed.)

42. The Overreach of the Criminal Law

NORVAL MORRIS
GORDON HAWKINS

Most of our legislation concerning drunkenness, narcotics, gambling, and sexual behavior and a good deal of it concerning juvenile delinquency is wholly misguided. It is based on an exaggerated conception of the capacity of the criminal law to influence men. We incur enormous collateral disadvantage costs for that exaggeration, and we overload our criminal justice system to a degree which renders it grossly defective as a means of protection in the areas where we really need protection—from violence, incursions into our homes, and depredations of our property.

The present "overreach" of the criminal law contributes to the crime problem in the following ways, which will be more fully documented as we deal with particular areas of that overreach:

1. Where the supply of goods or services is concerned, such as narcotics, gambling, and prostitution, the criminal law operates as a "crime tariff" which makes the supply of such goods and services profitable for the criminal by driving up prices and at the same time discourages competition by those who might enter the market were it legal.

2. This leads to the development of large-scale organized criminal groups which, as in the field of legitimate business, tend to extend and diversify their operations, thus financing and promoting other criminal activity.

3. The high prices which criminal prohibition and law enforcement help to maintain have a secondary criminogenic effect in cases where demand is inelastic, as for narcotics, by causing persons to resort to crime in order to obtain the money to pay those prices.

4. The proscription of a particular form of behavior (e.g., homosexuality, prostitution, drug addiction) by the criminal law drives those who engage or participate in it into association with those engaged in other criminal activities and leads to the growth of an extensive criminal subculture which is subversive of social order generally. It also leads, in the case of drug addiction, to endowing that pathological condition with the romantic glamour of a rebellion against authority or of some sort of elitist enterprise.

5. The expenditure of police and criminal justice resources involved in attempting to enforce statutes in relation to sexual behavior, drug taking, gambling, and other matters of private morality seriously depletes the time, energy, and manpower available for dealing with the types of crime involving violence and stealing which are the primary concern of the criminal justice system. This diversion and overextension of resources results both in failure to deal adequately with current serious crime and, because of the increased chances of impunity, in encouraging further crime.

6. These crimes lack victims, in the sense of complainants asking for the protection of the criminal law. Where such complainants are absent it is particularly difficult for the police to enforce the law. Bribery tends to flourish; political corruption of the police is invited. It is peculiarly with reference to these victimless crimes that the police are led to employ illegal means of law enforcement.

It follows therefore that any plan to deal with crime in America must first of all face this problem of the overreach of the criminal law, state clearly the nature of its priorities in regard to the use of the criminal sanction, and indicate what kinds of immoral or antisocial conduct should be removed from the current calendar of crime.

DRUNKENNESS

One of every three arrests in America—over two million each year—is for the offense of public drunkenness; more than twice the number of arrests in the combined total for all of the seven serious crimes which the FBI takes as its index crimes (willful homicide, forcible rape, aggravated assault, robbery, burglary, theft of $50 or over, and motor vehicle theft). The cost of handling each drunkenness case involving police, court, and correctional time has been estimated at $50 per arrest. We thus reach a conservative national estimate of annual expenditure for the handling of drunkenness offenders (excluding expenditure for treatment or prevention) of $100 million. In addition, the great volume of these arrests places an enormous burden on the criminal justice system; it overloads the police, clogs the courts, and crowds the jails.

The extent to which drunkenness offenses interfere with other police activities varies from city to city, but in the majority of cities it involves a substantial diversion of resources from serious crime. Thus, in Washington, D.C., during a nine-month period, it was found that 44 percent of the arrests made by the special tactical police force unit used "to combat serious crime" was for drunkenness. A similar situation exists in relation to correctional systems. In one city it was reported that 95 percent of short-term prisoners were drunkenness offenders. One-half of the entire misdemeanant population consists of drunkenness offenders. Yet the criminal justice system is effective neither in deterring drunkenness nor in meeting the problems of the chronic offenders who form a large proportion of those arrested for drunkenness. All that the system appears to accomplish is the temporary removal from view of an unseemly public spectacle.

We think that the use of the police, the courts, and the prisons on this scale to handle unseemliness at a time when one-third of Americans are afraid to walk alone at night in their own neighborhoods is so ludicrously inept and disproportionate that we need no more than point it out to justify the removal of drunkenness from the criminal justice system. This is not to say that if a person while drunk causes damage to property, steals, or assaults another person, he should not be arrested under the appropriate statutes dealing with malicious damage, theft, or assault. But there should always be some specific kind of offensive conduct in addition to drunkenness before the criminal law is invoked.

It is sometimes argued that we have a choice between the criminal law model and the medical model in the treatment of drunkenness. And there is a considerable literature which deals with the dangers of medical authoritarianism. To us this is a false dichotomy; our choice need not be so narrowly restricted. A social welfare model may, in the present state of medical knowledge, be preferable to either the criminal law or the medical model.

For the police lockups, courts, and jails we would substitute community-owned overnight houses capable of bedding down insensible or exhausted drunks. For the police and the paddy wagons we would substitute minibuses, each with a woman driver and two men knowledgeable of the local community in which the minibus will move. A woman is preferred to a man as the driver-radio-operator because it is our experience that the presence of a woman has an ameliorative effect on the behavior of males, even drunken males.

The minibus would tour the skid row area, picking up the fallen drunks and offering to help the weaving, near-to-falling drunks. If there be a protest or resistance by a drunk, cowardice and withdrawal must control our team's actions; if there be assaults or other crimes, a police transceiver will call those who will attend to it; if there be unconsciousness or drunken consent, the minibus will deliver the body to the overnight house.

If there be talk by the drunk the next day of treatment for his social or alcoholic program, let him be referred, or preferably taken, to whatever social assistance and alcoholic treatment facilities are available. Indeed, let such assistance be offered if he fails to mention them; but let them never be coercively pressed.

The saving effected by abolishing the costly and pointless business of processing drunkenness cases through the criminal justice system would vastly exceed the cost of providing such facilities and treatment programs for those willing to accept them.

Such a system may be less effective than a medical detoxification model of the type now operating in New York and Saint Louis, but it is clearly cheaper and more humane than our present processes and does not distract the criminal justice system from its proper and important social functions.

NARCOTICS AND DRUG ABUSE

As in the case of drunkenness, so in regard to the use of other drugs, the invocation of the criminal process is wholly inappropriate. Yet at present, although drug addiction itself is not a crime in America, the practical effect of federal and state laws is to define the addict as a criminal. According to FBI arrest data, 162,177 arrests for violations of the narcotic drug laws were made in 1968. As the President's Crime Commission report puts it, ". . . the addict lives in almost perpetual violation of one or several criminal laws." Neither the acquisition nor the purchase nor the possession nor the use of drugs should be a criminal offense. This elimination of criminal prosecution provisions should apply to the narcotics (opiates, synthetic opiates, and cocaine), marihuana, hallucinogens, amphetamines, tranquilizers, barbiturates, and the volatile intoxicants.

Those who support the present laws and the traditional methods of enforcement commonly claim a causal connection between drug use and crime. Yet leaving aside crime to raise funds to support the inflated costs of purchasing legally proscribed drugs, the evidence of a causal connection between drug use and crime is slight and suspect.

As with alcohol, the fact that drugs not only release inhibition but also suppress functions is commonly ignored. They may well inhibit more crime than they facilitate; heroin for example has a calming depressant effect, and the "drug-crazed sex fiend" of popular journalism has no counterpart in reality although the myth dies hard. The prototypal headline "Addict Rapes Widow" is misleading—the truth would be "Addict Nods While Widow Burns."

There seems to be no doubt, however, that the policy of criminalization and the operations of criminal justice agencies in this field have in themselves been criminogenic without measurably diminishing the extent of the drug problem or reducing the supply of narcotics entering the country. There is substantial evidence that organized criminals engaged in drug traffic have made and continue to make high profits. There is evidence, too, that criminalization of the distribution of drugs has caused much collateral crime with drug addicts, "to support their habits," as the President's Crime Commission puts it, "stealing millions of dollars worth of property every year and contributing to the public's fear of robbery and burglary."

The one certain way totally to destroy the criminal organizations engaged in the narcotics trade and to abolish addict crime would be to remove the controls and make narcotics freely available to addicts. As Harvard economist Thomas C. Schelling puts it, "If narcotics were not illegal, there could be no black market and no monopoly profits, and the interest in 'pushing' it would probably be not much greater than the pharmaceutical interest in pills to reduce the symptoms of common colds."

We do not propose the abolition of all controls over the importation, manufacture, and distribution of drugs, nor the abolition of penalties against those unauthorized persons who trade in drugs for profit; but we are convinced that if addiction were treated as a medical matter this would undercut the illicit traffic and largely eliminate the profit incentive supporting that traffic. The British approach to this problem, which involves the maintenance of strict control over the supply of drugs but leaves the treatment of addicts (including maintenance doses to addicts) in the hands of the medical profession, has resulted in a situation where no serious drug problem exists.

Certain difficulties in the British approach have recently emerged. Heroin addiction has increased with immigration of groups having larger addict subcultures within them and for other reasons. But though the increase, stated as a percentage, seems great, it starts from a base so very much smaller than that in the United States that the figures showing increase misstate the problem. It remains a problem of little social significance. Further, the outlets for medical prescription and administration of drugs need to be better controlled to avoid the development of a black market. But these are details in a scheme of incomparably sounder structure than we have evolved in this country.

With regard to marihuana, it is necessary to say something further. At present marihuana is equated, in law, with the opiates, although its use does not lead to physical dependence nor does tolerance and the desired dose increase over time. Further, the risks of crime, accident, suicide, and physical or psychological illness are less than those associated with alcohol.

At the moment the law, by treating marihuana as equivalent to opiates, may well foster the belief that there is no difference between them. Yet as marihuana can be relatively easily obtained in most states and found not to have the dramatically deleterious effects advertised, graduation to the use of heroin, which *is* addictive and harmful, could be stimulated by this policy. Worse still, because mari-huana is bulky and detection is thereby facilitated, youthful experi-menters are encouraged to move to dangerous and addictive drugs which are more easily concealed. As with alcohol, controls relating to the sale or other disposition of the drug to minors are necessary, but that is all.

One of the principal advantages of the decriminalization and the pathologization of addiction is that the "image" of drug taking as an act of adventurous daring conferring status on the taker as a bold challenger of authority, convention, and the Establishment will be destroyed. With punitive laws and the brunt of law enforcement fall-ing heavily on the user and the addict rather than on traffickers, we have created a persecuted minority with its own self-sustaining myths and ideology. The alcoholic, on the other hand, is nowhere seen as a heroic figure in our culture but quite commonly as a person to be pitied and treated as sick. Consequently, no addict subculture with a morale-enhancing, self-justifying ideology and recruitment process has developed in this area.

GAMBLING

Gambling is the greatest source of revenue for organized crime. Esti-mates of the size of the criminal revenue from gambling in the Unit-ed States vary from $7 to $50 billion, which means that it is huge but nobody knows how huge. Because statutes in every state, except Ne-vada, prohibit various forms of gambling, criminals operate behind the protection of a crime tariff which guarantees the absence of le-gitimate competition. This has led to the development of a powerful and influential vested interest opposed to the legalization of gam-bling.

Despite sporadic prosecution, the laws prohibiting gambling are poorly enforced and there is widespread disregard for the law. We do not face a choice between abolishing or legalizing gambling; the choice is between leaving gambling and the vast profits which accrue from it in the hands of criminals or citizens taking it over and run-ning it for the benefit of society or, by licensing and taxation mea-sures, controlling it.

The position regarding betting on horse races is highly irrational. In many states those who attend races are allowed to bet on horses and a portion of the money wagered is paid as a tax to the state trea-sury. Yet it is illegal to accept off-track wagers. But as most people cannot find time to go to the track, such wagers are placed on a scale far exceeding the legitimate ones. The President's Crime Commission cites "estimates by experts" which state that the total involved in off-track betting "is at least two or three times as great" as the total of $5 billion involved in legal betting at race tracks. Yet of the sum of from $10 to $15 billion wagered off-track, nothing at all is forfeit to the state treasury.

It has proved impossible to enforce the laws against betting, and all attempts to make the laws effective have failed. In this situation a major step toward insuring rational and socially beneficial control of gambling would be the institution of state lotteries, such as operate in New Hampshire and New York. More than twenty-five governments, from the Kenyan, which makes $42,000 a year, to the Spanish, which makes $70 million, run national lotteries. Norway, Sweden, France, and Australia all have such lotteries with a substantial levy on gross revenue going to state treasuries.

In addition to the provision of state lotteries, off-track betting can be controlled by the establishment of state-run betting shops as in Australia. Insofar as gambling is harmful, the harm can at least be reduced by fixing limits to wagers and other measures of control. As for other forms of gambling, the Nevada solution whereby the state tax commission administers gambling by supervising a license system under which all applicants have to be cleared by the commission—and state, county, and city taxes and license fees represent a substantial revenue—has operated with success for many years. The infiltration of organized criminals has been blocked by screening all applicants for criminal records. The tax commission employs inspectors and has held hearings and revoked several licenses. The principal lesson to be learned from Nevada is that gambling can be kept clean and does not have to be run by criminals.

DISORDERLY CONDUCT AND VAGRANCY

According to the *Uniform Crime Reports*, there were nearly six hundred thousand arrests for disorderly conduct in 1968. This represents more arrests than for any other crime except drunkenness. Disorderly conduct statutes vary in their formulation, and the conduct dealt with as disorderly includes a wide variety of petty misbehavior including much that is harmless, although annoying, and not properly subject to criminal control.

Criminal codes and statutes should prohibit specific, carefully defined, serious misconduct so that the police can concentrate on enforcing the law in that context. Disorderly conduct statutes allow the police very wide discretion in deciding what conduct to treat as criminal and are conducive to inefficiency, open to abuse, and bad for police-public relations.

Similar considerations apply to vagrancy. It is a criminal offense in all states, with over ninety-nine thousand arrests in 1968. Here, however, it is not a question of more rigorously defining the type of behavior to be prohibited but rather of entirely abandoning the vagrancy concept. The commentary to the American Law Institute's Model Penal Code states: "If disorderly conduct statutes are troublesome because they require so little in the way of misbehavior, the vagrancy statutes offer the astounding spectacle of criminality with no misbehavior at all." And the fact is that those statutes, which frequently make it an offense for any person to wander about without being able to give a "good account of himself," burden defendants with a presumption of criminality and constitute a license for arbitrary arrest without a warrant.

Vagrancy laws are widely used to provide the police with justification for arresting, searching, questioning, and detaining persons whom they suspect may have committed or may commit a crime. They are also used, according to the President's Crime Commission task force report on the courts, "by the police to clean the streets of undesirables, to harass persons believed to be engaged in crime, and to investigate uncleared offenses." These laws often make possible the conviction of persons without proof of antisocial behavior or intention and in general confer unbounded discretion on the police.

In our view the police need authority to stop any person whom they reasonably suspect is committing, has committed, or is about to commit a crime and to demand his name, address, and an explanation of his behavior—to stop and frisk, now clearly constitutionally permissible. The police need such powers of inquiry to control crime and to protect themselves in dealing with persons encountered in suspicious circumstances, and they should have these powers without having to resort to the subterfuge of vagrancy arrest.

As for such behavior as begging, which is included in many vagrancy statutes, we agree with the American Law Institute's Model Penal Code commentary that "municipalities may properly regulate the use of sidewalks to safeguard against annoying and importunate mendicants and merchants; but such legislation does not belong in the penal code."

SEXUAL BEHAVIOR

With the possible exception of sixteenth-century Geneva under John Calvin, America has the most moralistic criminal law that the world has yet witnessed. One area in which this moralism is most extensively reflected is that of sexual behavior. In all states the criminal law is used in an egregiously wide-ranging and largely ineffectual attempt to regulate the sexual relationships and activities of citizens. Indeed, it is as if the sex offense laws were designed to provide an enormous legislative chastity belt encompassing the whole population and proscribing everything but solitary and joyless masturbation and "normal coitus" inside wedlock.

It is proper for the criminal law to seek to protect children from the sexual depradations of adults, and adults and childen from the use of force, the threat of force, and certain types of fraud in sexual relationships. Further, there is some justification for the use of the criminal law to suppress such kinds of public sexual activity or open sexual solicitation as are widely felt to constitute a nuisance or an affront to decency. But beyond this, in a post-Kinsey and post-Johnson and Masters age, we recognize that the criminal law is largely both unenforceable and ineffective, and we think that in some areas the law itself constitutes a public nuisance. We shall deal with some of the principal areas of conduct from which the criminal law should be withdrawn in whole or in part; types of behavior which although at present adjudged criminal are more properly regarded as matters of private morals.

Adultery, Fornication, and Illicit Cohabitation

Extramarital intercourse is punishable in the majority of states with penalties ranging from a $10 fine for fornication to five years' imprisonment and a $1,000 fine for adultery. Mercifully, prosecutions are rare. The vast disparity between the number of divorces on the ground of adultery and the minute number of prosecutions for that offense reveals that enforcement is deliberately kept at a microscopic level.

A situation of this kind constitutes a double threat to society. In the first place it provides opportunities for victimization and discriminatory enforcement often provoked by jealousies. In the second place the promulgation of a code of sexual behavior unrelated to actuality (according to Kinsey, 95 percent of the male population is criminal by statutory standards), and its enforcement on a derisory scale, and in arbitrary fashion, cannot but provoke contempt and resentment.

It is one thing to retain laws which, because of difficulty of detection, cannot be rigorously enforced, quite another to preserve those which are not seriously intended to be applied. At a time when it is of considerable importance that the law should mean what it says, anything likely to make citizens take it less than seriously can only be harmful. It is at least a reasonable assumption that anything which provokes cynicism, contempt, derision, indifference, resentment, and hostility toward the law and law enforcement agencies is likely to have undesirable repercussions on behavior. At this time it seems unwise to incur the risk of such costs and for no discernible gain.

Statutory Rape or Carnal Knowledge

Sexual intercourse with a willing female under the statutory age of consent is sometimes referred to as "carnal knowledge," sometimes as "statutory rape." It is usually a felony. The statutory age of consent varies from ten years of age (in Florida, South Dakota, and New Mexico) to eighteen years of age (in New York and thirteen other states) and, in Tennessee, twenty-one years of age. Such variations must confuse the divining rod of the natural lawyer! The maximum penalties range from death (in fifteen states) to ten years' imprisonment (in New York). In general these penalties are exceeded only by those for murder and equaled only by those for forcible rape and kidnapping. In North Carolina and Washington sexual intercourse between an adult female and a male under the age of consent is also statutory rape on the part of the female, but in general, as one textbook puts it, "the criminality of statutory rape seeks to protect the purity of young girls."

A great deal of statutory rape legislation is totally unrealistic in a number of respects. Most age limits were fixed at a time when physical maturity was attained later than it is now. Furthermore, nowadays teenage girls are far more knowledgeable and sophisticated than the law appears to recognize, and the assumption that in cases of consensual intercourse the male is necessarily the initiator and the female always plays a passive, bewildered role is unlikely to correspond closely to reality. Moreover, even if the male genuinely believes, on reasonable grounds, that the girl is over the age of consent, he has, except in California, no defense to a charge of statutory rape; it is thus clear that not only rationality but also justice is sacrificed in the pursuit of purity.

The offense of statutory rape should clearly be abolished and since in all such cases the girl has given her consent—otherwise it would be rape, viking rape not statutory rape—the man's offense should be that of intercourse with a minor. In our view, the function of the law in relation to sexual behavior of this nature should be restricted to providing protection for the immature in cases where there is significant disparity of age between the male and the female.

An abuse of a relation of trust or dependency should be regarded as an aggravating circumstance. This need would be adequately met if the age of consent were fixed at sixteen. The accused should be acquitted if he can establish that he reasonably believed the girl to be past her sixteenth birthday. It should be added that we are speaking of adult criminal liability here; that is, we are not talking about problems of sexual experimentation by youths and criminal liability within whatever is the juvenile court age in any jurisdiction.

Bigamy

Bigamy, the triumph of hope over experience, is contracting a second marriage during the existence of a prior marriage and is a statutory crime. It does not constitute a serious part of the crime problem. We mention it only as an interesting example of the legal stigmatization and punishment of conduct which may (as when both parties are aware of the previous marriage, which is the general situation) harm no one although it offends some religious and moral codes. It may be that a certain amount of wrath on the part of the Deity is engendered, but his appeasement is no longer regarded as a function of the criminal law. The bigamous marriage itself is legally a nullity.

In many cases the only antisocial consequences of bigamy are the falsification of state records and the waste of time of the celebrating officer. This problem would be better handled by penalties for false declarations in relation to ceremonies of marriage. Sanctions are to be found in all criminal codes for giving false information in relation to official processes, and deceiving the woman would be an aggravating circumstance relevant to sentencing. If necessary, the maximum punishment for such false declarations could be statutorily increased.

The great value of such a low-key approach to a practical problem is that it avoids the trails of ecclesiastical glory that accompany the crime of bigamy at present. Commonly all that is involved in bigamy is, as Glanville Williams puts it, "a pathetic attempt to give a veneer of respectability to what is in law an adulterous association," and prosecution serves no purpose and achieves no object other than increasing the sum of human misery.

One Australian judge, impressed with this analysis, in sentencing a convicted bigamist upbraided him thus: "Wretched man! Not only have you and this young lady deceived your friends. Worse, you have thrown Her Majesty's records into confusion."

Incest

Incest is sexual intercourse between persons related within prohibited degrees which vary widely. In some societies the interpretation of incest is so broad as to exclude half the available population. In America, a number of states prohibit the marriage of first cousins and few if any permit the marriage of those more closely related than that.

Incest is an ecclesiastical offense. In England it did not become a criminal offense until 1908. In America it has also generally been made a crime by statute and usually includes affinity (i.e., relationship by marriage) as well as consanguinity.

The statutory prohibition of marrying one's deceased brother's wife was designed to reduce fratricide, suggesting a somewhat cynical estimate of the nature of brotherly love. By contrast, marrying one's deceased sister's husband is generally not proscribed, revealing the law's gallant misjudgment of female determination. In some gentler societies it is thought admirable and is sometimes obligatory to assume matrimonial responsibilities for one's brother's widow and children.

Although incest figures prominently in the literature of psychoanalysts, all available evidence indicates that it is rare, and certainly prosecutions for it are exceptional. We mention it here merely as an example of the law trying to enforce morality, for where both parties are adult and commit incest with full consent, no other purpose is served. Insofar as children need protection from adults, or force or the threat of force is involved, protection is already provided by other statutes. Incest between consenting adults in private is not a proper subject for the criminal law.

Sodomy and Crimes against Nature

Statutes concerning sodomy and crimes against nature include within their scope such sexual behavior as bestiality, both homosexual and heterosexual, anal and oral copulation, and mutual masturbation. These laws receive only capricious and sporadic enforcement, usually, although not exclusively, in regard to such relations outside marriage. Obviously laws of this kind are peculiarly liable to abuse because of the wide discretion involved.

No social interests whatsoever are protected by desultory attempts to impose upon persons adherence to patterns of sexual behavior arbitrarily selected from the great variety which forms our mammalian heritage. Bestiality would be more properly dealt with under statutes relating to cruelty to animals where any cruelty is involved; otherwise, there is no reason to include it within the criminal law.

Homosexual Acts

Homosexual offenses are treated under such titles as sodomy, buggery, perverse or unnatural acts, and crimes against nature; homosexual practices are condemned as criminal in all states but Illinois, usually as a felony. Penalties vary enormously. A consensual homosexual act which is legal in Illinois is a misdemeanor in New York and can be punished as a felony by life imprisonment in some states. The Kinsey report states: "There appears to be no other major culture in the world in which public opinion and the statute law so severely penalize homosexual relationships as they do in the United States today."

Our primacy in this field is purchased at a considerable price. Although the Kinsey report maintains that "perhaps the major portion of the male population, has at least some homosexual experience between adolescence and old age," only a small minority are ever prosecuted and convicted. Yet the law in this area, while not significantly controlling the incidence of the proscribed behavior, not only increases unhappiness by humiliating and demoralizing an arbitrarily selected sample of persons every year and threatening numberless others, but at the same time encourages corruption of both the police and others who discover such relationships by providing opportunities for blackmail and extortion.

As far as the police are concerned, a great deal has been written both about corruption in this area and the degrading use of entrapment and decoy methods employed in order to enforce the law. It seems to us that the employment of tight-panted police officers to invite homosexual advances or to spy upon public toilets in the hope of detecting deviant behavior, at a time when police solutions of serious crimes are steadily declining and, to cite one example, less than one-third of robbery crimes are cleared by arrest, is a perversion of public policy both maleficent in itself and calculated to inspire contempt and ridicule.

In brief, our attitude to the function of the law in regard to homosexual behavior is the same as in regard to heterosexual behavior. Apart from providing protection for the young and immature; protection against violence, the threat of violence, and fraud; and protection against affronts to public order and decency, the criminal law should not trespass in this area. If all the law enforcement agents involved in ineffectual efforts to control buggery were to be diverted to an attempt to improve the current 20 percent clearance rate for burglary, it is unlikely that there would be an immediate fall in the burglary rate. But it is utterly unlikely that there would be an increase in buggery; for people's sexual proclivities and patterns are among the least labile of their responses, as the almost total failure of "cures" and treatment programs for homosexuals should have taught us. And in the long run such a strategic redeployment of resources could not but be beneficial to society.

Prostitution

According to Kinsey almost 70 percent of the total white male population of the United States has some experience with prostitutes. But many of them have never had more than a single experience, and relations with female prostitutes represent a very small part of the total sexual outlet of the male population. It would appear that the incidence and importance of prostitution in this country have been greatly exaggerated in the literature, much of which seems to be the product of a prurient interest in the subject. In fact, professional prostitution is said by some authorities to be declining as a result of increasing sexual permissiveness, which eliminates some of the need for such outlets. The *Uniform Crime Report* shows 42,338 arrests for "prostitution and commercialized vice" in 1968, but many arrests of prostitutes are included in the four hundred thousand yearly arrests for "disorderly conduct," so that the figures cannot be regarded as a meaningful index.

Prostitution is commonly statutorily defined as the indiscriminate offer by a female of her body for sexual intercourse or other lewdness for the purpose of gain and is a criminal offense in all states. The penalties most commonly imposed are fines or short prison sentences.

At one time it was widely believed that most prostitutes were unfortunate women who had been "driven" to a life of prostitution by poverty, bad upbringing, seduction at an early age, or broken marriages, but some research sponsored by the British Social Biology Council suggests that in the majority of cases this way of life is chosen because it offers greater ease, freedom, and profit than available alternatives. There is no evidence that the incidence of neurosis or psychological abnormality is greater among prostitutes than among housewives.

Prostitution is an ancient and enduring institution which has survived centuries of attack and condemnation, and there is no doubt that it fulfills a social function. It is often asserted that prostitution provides an outlet for sexual impulses which might otherwise be expressed in rape or other kinds of sexual crime. No research has been done in this area but the notion has a certain plausibility. It is undeniable, however, that prostitutes are sought out by some men who, because of a physical deformity, psychological inadequacy, or (in the case of foreigners and immigrants) unfamiliarity with the languages and customs, find great difficulty in obtaining sexual partners. The Kinsey report states that prostitutes provide a sexual outlet for many persons who without this "would become even more serious social problems than they already are."

The costs of attempting to enforce our prostitution laws have been admirably summarized by Professor Sanford Kadish:

> ... diversion of police resources; encouragе nent of use of illegal means of police control (which, in the case of prostitution, take the form of knowingly unlawful harassment arrests to remove suspected prostitutes from the streets; and various entrapment devices, usually the only means of obtain-

ing convictions); degradation of the image of law enforcement; discriminatory enforcement against the poor; and official corruption.

Once again it is our view that the use of law enforcement resources in this way, in a fruitless effort to promote moral virtue, is wasteful and socially injurious. Insofar as prostitution itself is responsible for social harms like the spread of venereal disease, regular compulsory medical inspection would provide better protection than our present haphazard enforcement policies. Moreover, all the evidence indicates that it is ordinary free promiscuity which is more largely responsible for the spread of venereal disease. Insofar as public solicitation constitutes an affront to some persons' susceptibilities, it would be perfectly possible (as has been done in some German cities) for municipal regulation to confine the activities of prostitutes to certain prescribed areas. As in many cases they are already largely confined in this way for purely commercial reasons, this would create few enforcement problems.

43. Controlling Corporate Crime

MARSHALL B. CLINARD
with
PETER C. YEAGER
JEANNE BRISSETTE
DAVID PETRASHEK
ELIZABETH HARRIES

The control of corporate crime can follow three approaches. It can be examined in terms of changing corporate attitudes or structures, it can be viewed as requiring the strong intervention of the political state through forced changes in corporate structure and effective legal measures to deter or punish, or it can be seen as needing effective consumer and public pressures. The first approach can imply the development of stronger business ethics and corporate organization reforms. Government control of corporations, on the other hand, can mean federal corporate chartering, deconcentration and divestiture, larger and more effective enforcement staffs, more severe penalties, the wider use of publicity as a sanction, and, as a last resort, nationalization. Third, consumer pressures can be exerted through selective buying, consumer boycotts, and the establishment of large consumer cooperatives. Along with all these possible measures there is the obvious need for improved information on corporate crime.

DEVELOPMENT OF STRONGER BUSINESS ETHICS

In any field ethics is a discipline that deals with what is good and bad, what is right and wrong, and the principles of what constitutes a moral duty or an obligation. Ethics in business stresses the evaluation of truth and justice in all spheres of business activities—advertising, public relations, the handling of communications, social responsibility, consumer relations, corporate behavior abroad, and even the question of the rightness of the power of corporate size (Walton, 1977: 6). Often only a small step separates an ethical from an unethical act and, similarly, an unethical tactic from an actual violation of law.

Many corporate practices formerly considered simply unethical have now become illegal and thus subject to punishment. They include such practices of tax evasion as false inventory values; unfair labor practices involving union rights, minimum wage regulations, specific working conditions, and overtime; violations of safety regulations related to occupational safety and health; the fixing of prices to stabilize them on the market and to eliminate competition; food and drug law violations; air and water pollution that violate government standards; violations of regulations established to conserve energy; submission of false information for the sale of securities; false advertising; and illegal rebates.

Many types of ethical violations exist today in business, all of them closely linked to corporate crime: misrepresentation in advertising; deceptive packaging; the lack of social responsibility in television programs and, particularly, commercials; the sale of harmful and unsafe products; the sale of virtually worthless products; restricting development and built-in obsolescence; polluting the environment; kickbacks and payoffs; unethical influences on government; unethical competitive practices; personal gain for management; unethical treatment of workers; and the victimization of local communities where plants are located for the benefit of the corporation.

Businesses, and particularly large corporations, commonly complain that most government regulations are largely unnecessary. One could agree readily with this complaint if assurances could be given that the basic ingredient of strong ethical principles guided the conduct of corporate business (Walton, 1977; and Silk and Vogel, 1976). It is inherently dangerous to believe that when certain corporate behavior is not prohibited by law it can be considered permissible, regardless of the consequences. Individuals are not supposed to operate on this basis, and it is even more dangerous to society when applied to corporations. In the past few years numerous laws against pollution have been passed due to great citizen pressures to protect society from businesses that pollute. But the question has been raised as to why the businesses failed to regulate themselves without government intervention when it was realized that it was wrong for businesses to pollute. Corporations should at least manifest enough concern about the effects their products might have on consumers that when illnesses or injuries do occur they will take corrective steps and at the same time notify government agencies of these possibilities rather than to deny them or to cover up the apparent risks. Recently the pressures of consumer and other citizen interests, as well as the government, have forced a rising concern for the ethics and social responsibility of their operations.

When policy decisions that involve ethical questions as well as their consequences within a corporation are raised, who should be involved? All of the directors? The executive committee? The audit committee of the board? The corporate general counsel? These persons are but a few of those within the organization who must decide the ethical questions for the corporation. Unfortunately, the interpretations of normative ambiguity have fallen on other professions, not management alone. Corporate lawyers increasingly interpret conduct to escape ethical considerations through noting and acting upon legal loopholes; accountants and auditors are often willing to close their professional eyes to an inaccurate financial disclosure. As corporations increasingly employ specialists like accountants and lawyers to advise corporate managers about how much they may get away with, this very specialization may contribute to law violations.

The conduct of corporate business engenders moral anxiety in the public mind. Distrust of corporations and a general antibusiness sentiment have developed from an aversion to big corporations generally, consumerism, environmentalism, and antagonism to excessive profits and monopolistic control, what has become known as the "big rip-off." Yet in the long run reliance cannot be placed exclusively on the development of government regulations, with its concomitant legal force, to straighten out unethical practices and the lack of social responsibility among large corporations. Both management itself and the schools of business administration must show more concern with the issue of ethical standards of business conduct.

The inculcation of ethical principles forms the very basis of all crime prevention and control, whether ordinary, white-collar, or corporate. Deterrence affects only the small proportion of those who rationally choose to avoid "pain" by not violating the law. Any attempt to reorganize corporate structures (or to institute a federal chartering for corporations) must inevitably rely upon a broad compliance with the law. Persons in the corporate realm, whether management or boards of directors, must recognize that the very nature of laws that regulate antitrust, pollution, unfair labor practices, product safety, occupational health and safety, taxes, and other areas represent a compelling force for compliance.

The development of stronger business ethics must come first from the individual corporation and second from corporate business codes and more effective trade associations and related organizations. Some degree of stigma and censure must be directed at the violators of business ethical codes. Schools of business administration could more effectively instill realistic business ethics in their graduates. The self-policing of corporate behavior must be the fundamental prop on which government regulation rests. A House of Representatives Select Committee on Crime observed that no government regulation can be as effective as the careful monitoring of its own sales by private enterprise. Manufacturers must also realize the dangerousness of their products when abused, and thus they "have a duty to the public to see that these products are put to their intended legitimate use" (quoted in Stone, 1975: 118).

CORPORATE ORGANIZATIONAL REFORM

Some experts in the area of corporate violations are skeptical of how successful legal means can be in achieving corporate compliance; the nature of the available legal means makes deterrence largely ineffective against the corporations. These experts feel that remedial actions such as monetary payments or fines do not seriously hurt a large corporation and that imprisonment, the traditional method of controlling human behavior, is impossible except for some corporation officers. The entire regulatory process is too complex to be successful.

If such a position is adopted, the major alternative appears to be some type of corporate organizational reform that would more effectively prevent violations. Corporations are run by a professional management appointed by a board of directors elected by the stockholders. Although in theory the stockholders exercise control over the corporation's affairs, in practice the board usually becomes a self-perpetuating body whose recommendations, including new board member nominations, are routinely ratified by the stockholders. Little can be expected of the shareholders as they are a largely anonymous body that must deal with a group of strangers in management and on the boards of directors.

If corporate reform is to succeed, it is essential to focus more directly on the processes of the corporate decision-making structure. It is unwise to rely on traditional legal strategies since they generally do not alter the internal institutional structure, without which "the corporation is not likely to 'go straight' in the future" (Stone, 1975: 120). A number of changes in corporate structure have been suggested, particularly by Stone, changes that hopefully would make law violations less likely (Stone, 1975; also see Stone, 1977). They include, primarily, a more effective role for the board of directors and the appointment of public directors by government. At present generally no clear functions of corporate boards of directors are specified; they have frequently been charged as being merely rubber stamps for management decisions and recommendations. Their functional relationship and responsibility to actual corporate operations must be clarified and established. If this is done the board of directors would be responsible not only for the corporate financial position and stockholder dividends but also for the public interest, which would include preventing illegal activities to increase profits. If this is to be accomplished, the interlocking of board memberships with other related corporations should obviously be prevented in order to assure that the board membership retains a personally disinterested financial position. Boards of directors should have independent staffs of their own to gather necessary information on corporate operations and to check on the claims of corporate executives and management generally.

Increasingly persons from outside the business world are being selected to represent the public, primarily as a result of outside pressures. At present, public directors generally hold token memberships on most boards. The selection of these public members by the board itself, however, is not likely to result in serious questioning of management's activities. In order to counteract this tendency it has been proposed that general public directors be nominated for the larger corporations by a Federal Corporation Commission. The appointment of public board members is not far removed from the growing practice of putting a union representative on the board. In the Federal German Republic, for example, large corporations are now required to have labor representatives on their boards, and for some time Sweden has had worker-directors for all companies that employ at least a hundred persons.

Stone has proposed that general public directors should consititute 10 percent of its directors for every billion dollars of sales or assets, whichever is greater (Stone, 1975: 158). Due to their knowledge of corporate operations, these members probably would be semiretired business executives or academics, but they could be chosen to represent various constituents such as the public at large or consumers, suppliers, or workers. Such public board members would represent the public and consumer concerns and ascertain that the corporation is complying with the law. They would assist and maintain corporate public responsibility through probing into and being generally vigilant about corporate operations. They would help monitor the internal management system to discover, for example, any faulty workmanship and report it to the board, conduct impartial studies of the effects, for example, of corporation-made detergents on the environment or of the safety of an auto, tire, or toy. As government employees themselves they would serve as a liaison with government agencies on needed legislation or to establish standards.

Finally, they might possibly serve as an ombudsman for plant employees. They would be paid, it has been recommended, at the highest level of the Civil Service scale; they would have a small staff and would maintain an office at the corporation's place of business, where they would be expected to spend at least half their time on the corporation's affairs.

FEDERAL CORPORATE CHARTERING

A somewhat related but still different approach is the requirement that all large corporations be federally chartered and consequently subject to the control provisions of such a charter. Corporations are chartered under the laws of the various states, not under federal law. Over the years most large corporations were incorporated in the small state of Delaware, where the laws were very permissive and the state lacked strong enforcement resources as well as the will to use them. By 1960 a third of the top 600 industrial corporations were chartered in Delaware, including one-half of the top 100 U.S. industrial corporations and one-third of all the corporations listed on the New York Stock Exchange.

Corporation chartering is a business. States like Delaware find attractive the income from the corporate fees and the corporate taxes that are levied. State chartering has many limitations in addition to the generally favorable management terms offered competitively. States create corporations which market products beyond state borders nationally and internationally. State governments largely fail to discover antisocial and illegal acts of corporation against stockholders and consumers. In fact, the revision of New Jersey's business code in 1968 stated that "it is clear that the major protections to investors, creditors, employees, customers, and the general public have come, and must continue to come, from federal legislation and not from state corporation acts" (Israels, 1969).

It is obvious that since the states cannot effectively accomplish this mandate against the large corporations, one alternative is for the federal government to take over the chartering.

> Some form of federal chartering should become law before the end of the decade. The present system of state chartering is simply too insulting to public-policy intelligence to remain inviolate. It is perhaps quaint but certainly foolish to assume that Delaware exerts any impact on the giant firms it charters, which market not statewide, not nationwide, but worldwide. Only the federal government has the authority (though not yet the conviction) to be able to hold our largest corporations accountable to more than the fiction of their state charters (Luthans and Hodgetts, 1976: 512).

Today the best-known specific proposals for federal chartering are those of Ralph Nader's Corporate Accountability Research Group

(Nader, Green, and Seligman, 1976; Nader, 1973: 85–90). Under these proposals federal chartering would be required of any industrial retailing or transportation corporation engaged in interstate commerce if annual domestic sales were $250 million or more, or if there were at least 10,000 employees. Specifically, federal chartering, it is maintained, would result in greater social responsibility, increased accountability, and wider disclosure. It would also make possible more effective regulation of corporations by various federal agencies, both in prevention and enforcement.

To support all of these provisions there would be graduated penalties for violations, depending upon their nature and frequency. Penalties could range from absolute fines to fines as a percentage of sales, management reorganization and executive suspensions, public trusteeship, or the dissolution of the corporate charter, the most severe penalty and perhaps somewhat unrealistic for most corporations.

Obviously corporate chartering alone would not in itself necessarily offer a solution to all corporate law violations; it would offer simply a better situation for accountability. The provisions of the charter would still have to be enforced by government agencies. Yet, the more uniform framework of a federal charter might offer greater coordination than is now provided by the SEC, the FTC, and other agencies that try independently to regulate illegal activities and secure disclosure, often without adequate legal weapons.

DECONCENTRATION AND DIVESTITURE

The extensive evidence that has been presented in this study should leave little doubt of the immensity and the corresponding power of the large corporations. Few of them operate exclusively in a single product line; rather, they have extended holdings and operations in diverse fields. In some areas so great is the concentration of a few corporations that they can virtually control prices, thus leading to frequent antitrust and other suits. Concentration is particularly evidenced in the areas of oil, iron and steel, motor vehicles, electrical machinery and equipment, computers, and communications. Many are multinationals that operate globally with substantial profits from foreign sales, the legality of which is difficult to supervise.

The size and the complex interrelationships of large corporations make it extremely onerous for government agencies to exercise any effective social control, or even to compete with them on an equal basis, as for example in investigations and litigation. Some government suits have involved millions of pages of testimony and documents, thousands of exhibits, and hundreds of witnesses. Conglomerates are able to maintain a high degree of corporate secrecy since their consolidated financial statements give overall data, and the data for the subsidiaries are only occasionally given in spite of a recent court decision that requires that these data be furnished to the FTC. This thwarts the shareholders' abilities to assess the performance of individual firms and thus makes extremely arduous any enforcement efforts of the government agencies. Consequently, a partial solution would be to break up the power of the large corporations by forcing them to deconcentrate and to divest themselves of certain product lines or subsidiaries.

On the grounds that large mergers are unproductive and that it is difficult to prosecute the violations of law, Senator Kennedy in 1979 introduced an anticonglomerate bill. Under its provisions, corporations with $2.5 billion in sales or $2 billion in assets would be prohibited from merging no matter how distant their lines of commerce. Corporations with $350 million in sales or $200 million in assets would have to prove that any proposed merger would yield increased efficiencies.

Legislation has been introduced to break up or divest major "integrated" oil corporations of their control over the entire oil market. Such legislation would prohibit producers of crude oil from owning refineries or transmission pipelines (Press Associates, Inc., 1976: 135). Likewise, a bill has been proposed to prohibit "horizontal" ownership by oil firms of other energy resources, a proposal that would forbid corporations which produce or refine oil or natural gas from "owning any interest in the coal, oil shale, uranium, nuclear reactor, geothermal steam (produced by natural hot springs under the ground), or solar energy business" (*Congressional Digest,* 1976: 135).

LARGER AND MORE EFFECTIVE ENFORCEMENT STAFFS

The evidence shows that regulatory agencies, either at the federal or state level, do not have adequate resources to deal with either white-collar or corporate crime. The detection, investigation, and prosecution of corporate crime is time-consuming; since it is organizational crime it cannot in any way be compared to ordinary crime. Evidence is secured only with great difficulty, and the scope of a corporate trial tests the skills of legal counsel on both sides. An individual antitrust case, as in the case of IBM and AT&T, for example, may take as much as ten years to carry through to completion. Government lawyers, either in administrative or legal plea bargaining or in actual trial, face tremendous defensive power, particularly in the number and caliber of corporate legal counsel, both in-house and outside counsel. In a given trial the annual salary of one corporate defense lawyer may exceed that of four or five government attorneys; the age and experience may be twice or more that of a government prosecutor.

Federal regulatory agencies and the Department of Justice, as well as departments at the state level, should have greatly increased enforcement budgets with which to employ additional investigators and lawyers. Also greatly needed are adequate specialized technical personnel such as accountants, engineers, and laboratory technicians to deal with the investigation of corporate crime. It will not be easy to secure sufficient additional personnel for the enforcement of corporate regulations. Powerful opposition will come from business and conservative members of Congress. In addition, the inflationary pressures of the late 1970s have resulted in taxpayer pressures for budget reductions and strong opposition to the expansion of government operations for any purpose.

MORE SEVERE PENALTIES

It has generally been conceded among knowledgeable persons that penalties for corporate offenses are far too lenient. . . . Administrative actions such as warnings and consent agreements are used too often. Civil and criminal actions are infrequently utilized, and monetary penalties, frequently because of statutory limitations, are often ludicrous in terms of the corporations' assets, sales, and profits. Although executive responsibility and consequent criminal prosecutions are increasing, the number prosecuted is still small and many of them are *nolle prossed*. In most cases of conviction, the offender is put on probation. Some persons, however, take the position that increased penalties are no solution because regardless of the size of the monetary penalties, they can be absorbed readily; also it is so hard to convict management that, on either score, there is little deterrence. Consequently, Stone proposes changes in corporate structure as an alternative (Stone, 1975). Others would link increased penalties to federal corporate chartering (Nader, 1973).

Assuming that penalties offer some deterrence if they are strong enough, what changes might be adopted? Among the possibilities that appear to be feasible are:

(1) Consent decrees should be strengthened so that they call for substantial remedial actions.

(2) With few exceptions, if the corporation has previously been involved in a similar offense, new cases of violation would involve ad-

ministrative monetary payment or the filing of civil or criminal litigation.

(3) Where fines are fixed by statute, they would be increased to a minimum of $100,000 and a maximum of $1 million, but even these large sums can be absorbed by big corporations. Preferable would be a fine assessed in terms of the nature of the violation and in proportion to the assets or annual sales of the corporation. The latter is something like the "day fine" that has been proposed for individuals in ordinary crime or instances in which the fine would be set according to their income.

(4) More adequate would be fines that are levied by the day, as in the case of the EPA criminal fine of $25,000 each day a corporation is in violation and $50,000 if there have been previous convictions.

(5) More extensive prosecution of corporate officials should take place. Criminal penalties against white-collar offenders and corporate executives should be more widely used because it appears that the higher the social scale, the greater the effect (Edelhertz, 1970: 59). If convicted, a mandatory sentence of four months, or possibly in particularly flagrant cases a minimum sentence of eighteen months, should be levied. Probation could not be given except for extreme circumstances. The use of community service instead of imprisonment would be prohibited by law except in unusual circumstances

(6) Indemnification of convicted corporate officers by their corporations would be prevented by federal legislation which would pre-empt state laws permitting it.

(7) Any management official who is convicted of criminally violating his corporate responsibilities would be deprived of assuming similar management positions within his corporation or exercising such duties in any other corporation for a period of three years.

(8) By legislation nearly all corporate civil or criminal convictions shall be publicized at the expense of the firm. Major administrative decisions, particularly in the area of false advertising, shall also be publicized by the corporation.

Rather than penalizing corporations, the federal government might well inaugurate a program for rewarding those corporations who had not been found in violation of the law. This might be accomplished through preference in government contracts, tax breaks, or by giving such corporations some recognition, such as a symbol of compliance which could be used in their advertising. Those executives of corporations with a record of nonviolation might be invited to a Washington conference where they could discuss what measures they used to achieve compliance.

PUBLICITY AS A SANCTION

Media publicity can be either informal or formal. Informal publicity is that ordinarily carried in the media as news items. In formal publicity the corporation is required as a part of an enforcement action to give the media an advertisement or other statement of acknowledgement of a violation and the corrective measures being taken. Conversations with numerous federal and state enforcement officials revealed that possible publicity about law violations in the mass media is probably the most feared consequence of sanctions imposed on corporations. In fact, on this assumption government agencies are frequently able to obtain an informal solution or a consent agreement or decree to a violation with little effort. This may involve remedial action, with either retroactive or future remedial provisions. Corporations generally do not wish to risk the publicity certain to arise from a prolonged court case or the imposition of a civil or criminal penalty that might, as a result of publicity, come to the attention of prominent segments of the public or to the public as a whole. Corporations usually feel it is better to make a deal because if the case goes to trial it will become more widely known to the public, as well as to competitors, and become embarrassing to the corporation image. Corporations who violate the law fear newspaper publicity or television coverage.

Publicity about sanctions has many advantages (Fisse, 1971). Presumably it increases the deterrent effects of the sanction. Second, it may be useful in warning prospective buyers of such things as deceptive advertising, defects in products, and of general consumer fraud practices. Third, publicity tends to inform the public about the actual operation of regulatory controls and enables the public to see more clearly the underlying purpose of the controls in the face of corporate defenses.

Studies have indicated that a relatively small number of violations, as well as enforcement actions that involve corporations, are publicized in the general media. If there is publicity, it is most likely to appear on the financial pages of the newspapers, that section of the paper that is seldom read by the general public. The paucity of media coverage of business crimes has been well illustrated by the press reaction to the well-known electrical equipment price-fixing case of 1961. One survey of newspapers that included 15 percent of the U.S. market found that only 16 percent of them gave first-page coverage to the story on the day after the indicted corporations admitted their guilt; in no paper was the story given more than a single column headline (*Yale Law Journal*, 1961: 288–289). The story was given less than a column of print on an inside page in another 11 percent; 43 percent gave less than half a column on an inside page; and another 30 percent had no reference of any kind to the story. After the corporations had been convicted and several corporate executives imprisoned, another survey was carried out of 300 newspapers, covering 20 percent of all papers sold throughout the country. Forty-five percent of them did not carry the story on the front page. Even with these unprecedented sentences of jail terms for a number of executives, the newspaper stories often failed to mention the guilt of the convicted corporations, although they usually mentioned the sentenced executives, the references to them being phrased in terms of crime and criminal convictions. More neutral terms such as "suits" and "penalties" were used to refer to the corporations, rather than "criminal conviction"; in this particular case press coverage would not seriously harm the corporation's public image, nor would it diminish corporation sales. The executives' convictions often served as convenient scapegoats.

Most of the numerous articles concerning corporate violations and enforcement actions that are reported in *The Wall Street Journal* rarely appear in the general news media, and if they do are more likely to be in the business or financial section of the newspaper or magazine. In converse fashion, *The Wall Street Journal* seldom covers cases of ordinary crime other than some reporting of organized crime: these cases generally are related to business. A study was made of *The Wall Street Journal*, using a thirteen-issue representative sample of the year 1977–1978 and 82 articles to measure news space devoted to the reporting of corporate illegalities. There were an estimated 1,066 articles involving corporations in which a legal action was instituted, a sanction imposed, a recall campaign begun, pending legal actions, investigations, dismissals and settlements, regulations, competitor antitrust suits, editorials and labor violations. Stockholder, competitor non-antitrust, and contract dispute suits were excluded. Of these 1,066 articles, 213 were related to those 582 parent corporations and 101 subsidiaries included in the sample used in this research.

Publicity can also constitute a formal action, a sanction in itself (Fisse, 1971). This is an effective and practical means of deterrence which is offered through the use of formal publicity methods, such as mass-media advertisements (e.g., corrective advertising), setting out the details of a corporation's illegal conduct, compulsory notification to the shareholders and to others by means of an annual report, and even a temporary ban on corporate advertising (see Thain, 1973; and

Pitofsky, 1977). The proposed new Federal Criminal Code (Sec. 2005) states that a court may order a convicted corporation to

> give notice and explanation to such corrections, in such form as the court may approve to the class of persons or to the section of the public affected or financially interested in the subject matter of the offense, by mail, by advertising in designated areas or through designated media or by other appropriate means.

Corrective advertising, which requires corporate offenders to inform the public of false past advertising, has been used particularly during the 1970s by the FTC, as well as by the FDA and other agencies. Such corrective advertisements forced the makers of products like STP Motor Oil and Listerine to run a series of nationwide advertisements admitting their transgressions.[1] Such negative publicity following sanctions might deter corporations from violating the law by more directly hurting their sales.

PUBLIC OWNERSHIP

Public ownership, or nationalization, is one alternative means of socially controlling certain large corporations, possibly the means of last resort. Galbraith points out that private stockholders have little say in management in any enterprise, as they are run by management. "This has come to be well understood in many countries with the consequence that public ownership has been reconciled with extensive operational autonomy and marked commercial success" (Galbraith, 1974: 14). Few persons recognize the fact that the federal government is one of the largest business concerns in the United States, controlling national forests, operating huge dams including the Hoover Dam, engaging in flood control, operating the TVA, one of the largest utilities in the country, and owning and operating buildings and such huge operations as NASA. The military forces are enormous establishments run and operated by the government. The American public fails to realize that nearly all utilities, electricity, and telephones are government-operated in every major country in the world except the United States, the Federal Republic of Germany, and Spain. Likewise, all foreign railroads and major airlines, except Swissair, are publicly owned, including one of the two main Canadian rail lines. The French government produces the Renault auto, and the Italian government owns the Alfa Romeo auto company and the Agip stations that sell most of the retail gasoline in the country. The Austrian steel industry is government-owned. With few exceptions in the large democracies, radio and television are publicly owned and administered by a board, much as is National Educational Television in the United States. Ultimately the Swiss watch industry depends for its efficiency on the largely publicly owned firm that manufactures the watch movements, an important component of any watch (Galbraith, 1974: 14).

These examples from foreign countries are only a few instances of government ownership in other democracies. As a viable alternative in the context of corporate crime control, public ownership or nationalization should be considered only for those large industries that have become oligopolies with little or no competition, and socially irresponsible both to national interests and those of the consumer. Henry Simons, a leading economist and advocate of the free enterprise system in the United States, has stated, for example, that government should directly own and operate those few industries where competition cannot be made to function effectively (Simons, 1948).

CONSUMER PRESSURES

There is an implicit assumption in the notion of social responsibility that the "good behavior" of corporations will be recognized by the consumer and rewarded in the marketplace; conversely it is implicit that irresponsibility and illegal behavior will result in decreased patronage, even consumer boycott. Were this the case consumer pressure, through the withdrawal of patronage, could be an effective tool in the control of illegal corporate behavior. Unfortunately, this relatively simple measure of social control appears not to be effective. In the first place, it assumes that persons who will withdraw patronage know that a corporation has been engaging in either irresponsible or illegal activities. If the consumer does not even know that a given corporation's product is injurious or unsafe, how could he or she be expected to know that the corporation is violating antitrust laws or polluting the environment? The news media, the press, the television, or the radio simply do not furnish the public the type of prominent display of information on corporate crime and ethics as they do on ordinary crime.

Second, the relation of social irresponsibility and illegality to a corporation is complicated by the existence of multiple component firms. Most persons do not know that Greyhound Corporation owns Armour meatpacking company.

Third, when cognizant of the reputation of the corporation and constantly pressured by favorable corporation advertising to purchase a product, the consumer is not likely to relate the personal failure to purchase a product to the possible control of the corporation.

Without some form of organized boycott, as the effective ones of the 1970s against Gallo Wine Company and Farah Corporation for anti-union activities, the consumer generally regards his or her individual withdrawal of a small amount of patronage as totally ineffective.

Consumer pressure might be expected through the increased development of large cooperatives. Large merchandising cooperatives are common in Canada and in Europe, particularly in Sweden and Switzerland. In fact in highly capitalist Switzerland, Migros, a cooperative which is the largest merchandising corporation in the country, controls an enormous part of retail trade. Cooperatives are associated with ethical responsibility of business. They also have an indirect influence in being able to dictate the quality standards of the products they purchase and sell. The cooperative movement offers an alternative method of controlling corporate crime; at the same time they make it possible to sell cheaper products of higher quality to the consumer. Cooperatives also offer a more active control by the consumer over management decisions than is provided the shareholders in large corporations.

Notes

1. For the FTC order on Listerine, see Warner-Lambert Company, 86 FTC 1398 (1975), Affirmed 562 F. 2d 749 (D.C. C/R 1977).

References

Edelhertz, Herbert. 1970. *The Nature, Impact and Prosecution of White-Collar Crime.* Washington, D.C.: U.S. Government Printing Office.

Fisse, Brent. 1971. "The use of publicity as a criminal sanction against business corporations." *Melbourne University Law Review* 8 (June): 107–150.

Galbraith, John K. 1974. "What comes after General Motors?" *The New Republic* (November 2): 13–14.

Israels, Carlos L. 1969. "The corporate triangle—some comparative aspects of the New Jersey, New York and Delaware statutes." *Rutgers Law Review* 23 (Summer): 615–631.

Luthans, Fred and Richard M. Hodgetts. 1976. *Social Issues in Business: A Text with Current Readings and Cases.* New York: Macmillan.

Nader, Ralph. 1973. "The case for federal chartering." Pages 67–93 in Ralph Nader and Mark J. Green (eds.), *Corporate Power in America.* New York: Grossman.

Nader, Ralph, Mark J. Green, and Joel Seligman. 1976. *Taming the Giant Corporation.* New York: W. W. Norton.

Pitofsky, Robert. 1977. "Beyond Nader: Consumer protection and the regulation of advertising." *Harvard Law Review* 90: 661.

Press Associates, Inc. 1976. "Proposals to break up major U.S. oil companies." *Congressional Digest* 55(May): 135; 1976. "Proposed 'horizontal divestiture' legislation pending in Congress." *Congressional Digest* 55(May): 135.

Silk, L. Howard and David Vogel. 1976. *Ethics and Profits: The Crisis of Confidence in American Business.* New York: Simon and Schuster.

Simons, Henry C. 1948. *Economic Policy for a Free Society.* Chicago: University of Chicago Press.

Stone, Christopher. 1975. *Where the Law Ends: The Social Control of Corporate Behavior.* New York: Harper & Row; 1977. "Controlling corporate misconduct." *Public Interest* 48 (Summer): 55–71.

Thain, Gerald. 1973. "Corrective advertising: Theory and cases." *New York Law Forum* 19(Summer): 1–34.

Walton, Clarence (ed.). 1977. *The Ethics of Corporate Conduct.* Englewood Cliffs, N.J.: Prentice-Hall.

Yale Law Journal. 1961. "Notes and comment: Corporate crime." 71(December): 280–306.

Acknowledgments (continued from p. iv)

Charles E. Silberman, "Race, Culture, and Crime." From *Criminal Violence, Criminal Justice*, by Charles E. Silberman. Copyright © 1978 by Charles E. Silberman. Reprinted by permission Random House, Inc.

Stephen A. Cernkovich & Peggy C. Giordano, "A Comparative Analysis of Male and Female Delinquency." Reprinted with permission from *The Sociological Quarterly*, Vol. 20, No. 1 (Winter 1979): 131–145.

Suzanne K. Steinmetz & Murray A. Straus, "The Family as Cradle of Violence." Published by permission of Transaction, Inc. from *Society*, Vol. 10, No. 6. Copyright © by Transaction, Inc.

Kenneth Polk, "Delinquency and Adult Criminal Careers." The original version of this article appeared under the title, "Schools and the Delinquency Experience," in *Criminal Justice and Behavior*, Vol. 2, No. 4 (Dec. 1975) pp. 315–338 and is excerpted and reprinted herewith by permission of the publisher, Sage Publications, Inc.

C. Ronald Huff, "Historical Explanations of Crime: From Demons to Politics." Reprinted with permission from James A. Inciardi and Kenneth C. Haas, eds., *Crime and the Criminal Justice Process*. Copyright © 1978 by Kendall/Hunt Publishing Company.

Steven Spitzer, "Toward a Marxian Theory of Deviance." Reprinted with the permission of the author and The Society for the Study of Social Problems from *Social Problems*, 22:5 (June 1975).

Howard S. Erlanger, "The Empirical Status of the Subculture of Violence Thesis." Excerpted and reprinted with the permission of the author and The Society for the Study of Social Problems from *Social Problems*, 22:4 (December 1974).

Richard A. Cloward & Lloyd E. Ohlin, "Differential Opportunity and Delinquent Subcultures." Reprinted with permission of Macmillan Publishing Co. Inc. from *Delinquency and Opportunity* by Richard A. Cloward and Lloyd E. Ohlin. © The Free Press, a Corporation, 1960.

Gresham M. Sykes & David Matza, "Techniques of Neutralization: A Theory of Delinquency." Reprinted with permission of The American Sociological Association from *American Sociological Review*, Vol. 22, 1957.

Travis Hirschi, "A Control Theory of Delinquency." Reprinted from *Causes of Delinquency* by Travis Hirschi. Copyright 1969 by The Regents of the University of California; reprinted by permission of the University of California Press.

Charles Wellford, "Labeling Theory and Criminology: An Assessment." Excerpted and reprinted with the permission of the author and The Society for the Study of Social Problems from *Social Problems*, 22:3 (February 1975).

Tanice G. Foltz, "The Process of Becoming a Prostitute: A Comparison Between Lower-Class and Middle-Class Girls." From Tanice G. Foltz, "Escort Services: An Emerging Middle Class Sex-for-Money Scene," *California Sociologist*, Vol. 2, No. 2 (Summer 1979) pp. 121–128 *only*. Reprinted by permission of the *California Sociologist*.

Neal Shover, "The Social Organization of Burglary." Excerpted and reprinted with the permission of the author and The Society for the Study of Social Problems from *Social Problems*, 20:4 (Spring 1973).

582 Acknowledgments

David F. Luckenbill, "Criminal Homicide as a Situated Transaction." Reprinted with permission of the author and The Society for the Study of Social Problems from *Social Problems*, 25:2 (December 1977).

Alan Blum & Gary Fisher, "Women Who Kill." Reprinted with permission from *Violence: Perspectives on Murder and Aggression*, edited by Irwin L. Kutash, Samuel B. Kutash, Louis B. Schlesinger, and associates. Copyright © 1978 Jossey-Bass Publishers.

Fritz A. Henn, "The Aggressive Sexual Offender." Reprinted with permission from *Violence: Perspectives on Murder and Aggression*, edited by Irwin L. Kutash, Samuel B. Kutash, Louis B. Schlesinger, and associates. Copyright © 1978 Jossey-Bass Publishers.

Wayne Sage, "Violence in the Children's Room." Copyright © 1975 *Human Behavior* Magazine. Reprinted by permission.

Charles H. McCaghy, Peggy C. Giordano, & Trudy Knicely Henson, "Auto Theft: Offender and Offense Characteristics." The original version of this article appeared under the same title in *Criminology*, Vol. 15, No. 3 (Nov. 1977) pp. 367–385 and is reprinted herewith by permission of the publisher, Sage Publications, Inc. Tables have been edited out.

August Bequai, "Organized Crime and Labor Racketeering." Reprinted by permission of the publisher, from August Bequai, *Organized Crime: The Fifth Estate* (Lexington, Mass.: Lexington Books, D.C. Heath and Company. Copyright 1979 D.C. Heath and Company).

Francis A. J. Ianni, "New Mafia." Published by permission of Transaction, Inc. from *Society*, Vol. 11, No. 3. Copyright © 1974 by Transaction, Inc.

Marshall B. Clinard et al., "Illegal Corporate Payments." Excerpted with permission from *Illegal Corporate Behavior* (Washington, D.C.: U.S. Department of Justice, 1979).

James M. Naughton et al., "How Agnew Bartered His Office to Keep from Going to Prison." © 1973 by The New York Times Company. Reprinted by permission.

Carl B. Klockars, "The Fence and Society: Vincent's *Apologia Pro Vita Sua*." Reprinted with permission of Macmillan Publishing Co., Inc., from *The Professional Fence* by Carl B. Klockars. Copyright © 1974 by Carl B. Klockars.

Jerome H. Skolnick, "Clearance Rates." From *Justice Without Trial*, second edition, by Jerome Skolnick. Copyright © 1975 John Wiley & Sons. Reprinted by permission of John Wiley & Sons.

Suzanne Weaver, "The Antitrust Division: Finding Cases." Reprinted from *Decision to Prosecute: Organization and Public Policy in the Antitrust Division* by Suzanne Weaver by permission of the MIT Press, Cambridge, Massachusetts. Copyright © 1977 by The Massachusetts Institute of Technology.

George F. Cole, "The Decision to Prosecute," Reprinted with permission from *Law & Society Review*, Vol. 4 (1970) pp. 331–343. Copyright © 1970 by the publisher, The Law and Society Association.

Steven Barnet Boris, "Stereotypes and Dispositions for Criminal Homicide." The original version of this article appeared under the same title in *Criminology*, Vol. 17, No. 2 (August 1979) pp. 139–158 and is reprinted herewith by permission of the publisher, Sage Publications, Inc.

Jeffrey H. Reiman, "The Rich Get Richer and the Poor Get Prison: Convictions and Sentencing." From *The Rich Get Richer and the Poor Get Prison* by Jeffrey H. Reiman. Copyright © 1979 John Wiley & Sons. Reprinted by permission of John Wiley & Sons.

Abraham S. Blumberg, "The Moral Career of an Accused Person." From *Criminal Justice* by Abraham S. Blumberg, copyright © 1967 by Abraham S. Blumberg. First New Viewpoints edition published 1974 by Franklin Watts, Inc. Used by permission of Franklin Watts, Inc.

Leonard Orland, "Theoretical Justifications for Prison: Retribution, Deterrence, and Isolation." Reprinted with permission of Macmillan Publishing Co., Inc. from *Prisons: Houses of Darkness* by Leonard Orland. Copyright © 1975 by The Free Press, a Division of Macmillan Publishing Co., Inc.

David F. Greenberg & Drew Humphries, "The Cooptation of Fixed Sentencing Reform." Reprinted with the authors' permission from *Crime & Delinquency*, April 1980, pp. 206–225.

Ted Bartell & L. Thomas Winfree, Jr., "Recidivist Impacts of Differential Sentencing Practices for Burglary Offenders." The original version of this article appeared under the same title in *Criminology*, Vol. 15, No. 3 (Nov. 1977) pp. 387–396 and is reprinted herewith by permission of the publisher, Sage Publications, Inc.

Robert Martinson, "What Works? Questions and Answers about Prison Reform." Reprinted with permission from *The Public Interest*, No. 35 (Spring 1974), pp. 22–24. © 1974 by National Affairs, Inc.

John Irwin, "The Contemporary Prison." From John Irwin, *Prisons in Turmoil*, pp. 181–191. Copyright © 1980 by John Irwin. Reprinted by permission of Little, Brown and Company.

Norval Morris & Gordon Hawkins, "The Overreach of the Criminal Law." Reprinted from *The Honest Politician's Guide to Crime Control* by Norval Morris and Gordon Hawkins by permission of the University of Chicago Press. © 1970 by The University of Chicago. All rights reserved. This material appeared in condensed form in *Midway*, Winter 1969, © 1969 by The University of Chicago.

Marshall B. Clinard et al., "Controlling Corporate Crime." Excerpted with permission from *Illegal Corporate Behavior* (Washington, D.C.: U.S. Department of Justice, 1979).